# 1984

# Medical and Health Annual

## Encyclopædia Britannica, Inc.

CHICAGO

AUCKLAND • GENEVA • LONDON • MANILA • PARIS • ROME • SEOUL • SYDNEY • TOKYO • TORONTO

# 1984 Medical and Health Annual

| | |
|---|---|
| Director of Yearbooks | Bruce L. Felknor |
| Editor | Ellen Bernstein |
| Associate Editor | Linda Tomchuck |
| Contributing Editor | Charles Cegielski |
| Medical Editor | Drummond Rennie, M.D. Chairman of Medicine, West Suburban Hospital, Oak Park; Professor of Medicine, Rush Medical College, Chicago; Senior Contributing Editor, *The Journal of the American Medical Association* |
| Art Director | Cynthia Peterson |
| Design Supervisor | Ron Villani |
| Picture Editors | Holly Harrington, *senior picture editor;* LaBravia J. Jenkins |
| Layout Artist | David Segev |
| Illustrators | John L. Draves, Richard A. Roiniotis |
| Art Staff | Patricia Henle, William Karpa, Lillian Simcox, Paul Rios |
| Director, Copy and Composition | J. Thomas Beatty |
| Manager, Copy Department | Anita Wolff |
| Senior Copy Editor | Barbara Whitney |
| Copy Staff | Marsha Check, Robert Curley, Stephen Isaacs, Elizabeth Laskey |
| Manager, Copy Control | Mary C. Srodon |
| Copy Control Staff | Marilyn Barton, Mayme Cussen |
| Manager, Composition Department | Dora Jeffers |
| Composition Staff | Duangnetra Debhavalya, Judith Kobylecky, John Krom, Jr., Thomas Mulligan, Van Smith |
| Director, Editorial Computer Systems | Melvin Stagner |
| Manager, Computer Operations | Ronald Laugeman |
| Computer Operators | Arnell Reed, Michael Schramm |
| Manager, Program Development | Walter Markovic, Jr. |
| Programmer | Mansur Abdullah |
| Manager, Index Department | Frances E. Latham |
| Assistant Manager | Rosa E. Casas |
| Index Staff | Drake A. Beadle, Edward Paul Moragne |
| Librarian | Terry Miller |
| Associate Librarian | Shantha Channabasappa |
| Administrative Secretary | Sheila G. Baumiller |

Editorial Administration

Philip W. Goetz, Editor-in-Chief
Margaret Sutton, Executive Editor
Robert Dehmer, Executive Director, Production
Verne Pore, Director of Budgets and Controller

Encyclopædia Britannica, Inc.

Robert P. Gwinn, Chairman of the Board
Charles E. Swanson, President

Library of Congress Catalog Card Number: 77-649875
International Standard Book Number: 0-85229-412-3
International Standard Serial Number: 0363-0366
Copyright © 1983 by Encyclopædia Britannica, Inc.
Printed in U.S.A.

# Foreword

**Maze.** A structure consisting of a network of winding and intercommunicating paths and passages arranged in bewildering complexity, so that without guidance it is difficult to find one's way in it.

*—Oxford English Dictionary*

The decade of the 1980s is seeing one of the most alarming infectious disease epidemics of the 20th century. Since the first cases of acquired immune deficiency syndrome—AIDS—were identified in a few homosexual men in the U.S. in 1980, the disease has assumed the proportions of a major health problem of great concern to the general public. The number of cases has more than doubled in each six-month period since 1981, so that by 1983 the term epidemic was both appropriate and accurate. AIDS, which is now known to strike many groups and has already killed about 40% of those afflicted, appears to be a new disease. But the key question—What is the cause?—remains unanswered.

A feature article in this volume focuses on the frightening AIDS problem. It was written as new developments were occurring at a dizzying pace. Author David Durack, chief of the Division of Infectious Diseases at Duke University and head of an AIDS clinic, sorts the facts from the fear-stimulated rumors and half-truths, and he defines the enormous task ahead for epidemiologists. We have titled the article "An Epidemiologic Maze" because at the present time medical scientists and the public are in a state of bewilderment as they attempt to thread their way through the devious paths and blind alleys that characterize AIDS. The exit will not be found easily; epidemiological investigation by its very nature involves slow, plodding work with a good many wrong turns before meaningful junctions are reached. The important thing is that there is a way out; with persistence and adequate financial support the right road will be found.

\* \* \*

In other feature articles:

• A Nobel laureate examines laboratory experimentation on animals to advance medical knowledge: What are the limits of decency? What are the responsibilities of scientists to prevent creature suffering?
• A neurologist presents fascinating data that are emerging about left-handers.
• An obstetrician-gynecologist offers some enlightened answers to nature-versus-nurture questions of human destiny — in particular, female destiny.
• A *New York Times* science correspondent who has been following genetic engineering since its beginnings reports that humans are already benefiting from the new science of cutting and splicing the stuff of life, DNA.
• A physician examines the baffling symptoms and the curious patterns that typify outbreaks of mass hysteria.
• NASA's medical services director describes the many challenges to aerospace medicine today.
• A layman turns to the world's great literature to see how physicians have fared. He acquaints us with a lively cast of characters that includes "good doctors," heroes, charlatans, and buffoons.

• A physiologist cites new findings that explain why dieters usually fail. There is now very strong evidence that exercise—not dieting—is the key to lasting weight loss.
• Physicists take us beyond the CAT scan into the revolution in diagnostic radiology that is opening new windows on the body.
• The official White House physician to three contemporary U.S. presidents provides an "inside" view of what is involved in caring for the man who assumes the awesome responsibilities of this high office.

\* \* \*

Also in this volume: an extensive, illustrated section we call The World of Medicine. Major developments in many medical specialties are described in sufficient detail to enable readers to grasp their importance. This section includes Special Reports on: the care of severely burned children; laughter and health; the eating disorder bulimia; hypnosis; prostaglandins; the ailments of musicians; suicide in children; and the costs of medical innovation.

\* \* \*

Instructive articles on such health-related concerns as physical fitness, medical procedures, caring for children, drugs, nutrition, and preventive medicine constitute the Health Education Unit section of the *Annual.* Two of the units in the present volume were prepared in part by Jory Graham (1925–83), a writer whose syndicated newspaper column, "A Time to Live," chronicled the author's own eight-year battle with cancer. In the last weeks of her life Ms. Graham completed articles for us on the topics of coping with cancer pain and the value of support groups. Like her column, these articles will be of enormous value to countless sick and suffering people for years to come. We deeply regret that Jory Graham did not live to see them in print.

\* \* \*

Finally, a First Aid Handbook prepared in conjunction with the American College of Emergency Physicians provides illustrated, up-to-date instructions for handling medical emergencies.

\* \* \*

All the articles in the many sections of the *Medical and Health Annual* have been prepared in the manner of *Encyclopædia Britannica*—by outstanding authorities in their respective fields. We hope their efforts will help readers keep pace with the exciting developments in medicine today.

*Ellen Bernstein* —Editor

# Contents

# On the Use of Animals in Research

## by Sir Peter Brian Medawar

The enormities of inhumanity that accompanied or preceded World War II led in the Western world to a great revolution of sensibility that gave rise to a new and deeper awareness of our moral responsibilities toward our fellow human beings and our fellow creatures generally. Among the passionate movements energized by this postwar revolution was one concerned with the welfare of animals—in particular, with the degree to which animal welfare is put at risk in medical and scientific research.

The degree of solicitude for animals varies greatly from culture to culture, ranging from the callous indifference to be found in some peasant cultures to the religious worship of animals that in the Western world are not normally thought intrinsically worthy of reverence; but so far as any generalization is possible amidst this diversity, it may be said that kindness shown for animals is most articulate and active in the advanced Western world—in the countries of northern Europe and in the United States. However, any self-satisfaction this apparent concern for creatures may give must be instantly qualified by the fact that it is in just these countries that people will not scruple to have pets destroyed when they become bored with them or, when departing for vacations, they find them a nuisance.

### The animal welfare issue

The great benefits accruing to human beings from the use of experimental animals are not now seriously in question. What is contentious is the morality

6

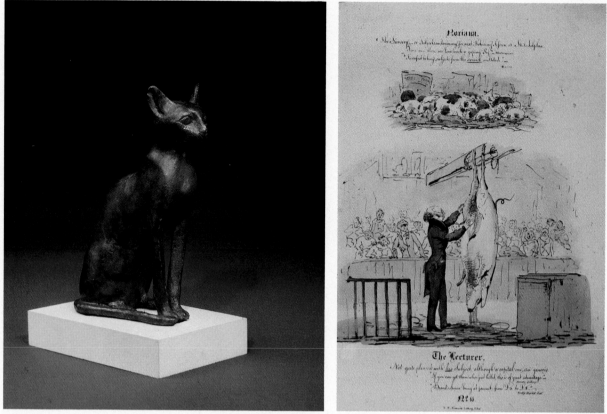

and efficacy of treating animals as if they were freely expendable and of exposing them to any treatment that common sense—always impatient of epistemological niceties—judges likely to cause pain. Perhaps in their feelings toward animals the general public is still in that unenlightened state lampooned by the novelist Thomas Love Peacock in *Headlong Hall* (1816). Says one of his characters, the Rev. Dr. Gaster:

"Nothing can be more obvious than that all animals are created solely and exclusively for the use of man."

"How do you prove it?" asks a companion.

"It requires no proof," says Dr. Gaster. "It is written, therefore it is so."

The number of animals used by the pharmaceutical industry in the assay and safety control of drugs and medicines for internal use or (as in the cosmetics industry) for external use can be assessed only in those countries that provide for the registration of experimenters and the reporting to a licensing authority of all experiments performed. Such a country is Great Britain, where the records of the licensing authority show that the number of animals involved is of the order of millions. Thus, it may be presumed that the number of animals used in medical research worldwide would be of the order of tens of millions.

Special kinds of animals are used for special purposes (as at one time ferrets were used in the investigation of influenza), but matters of supply and cost and ease of husbandry weigh most heavily in the choice of subjects for research, which ranges all the way from mice to primates, not excluding hu-

**Sir Peter Brian Medawar**
*is a member of the scientific staff of the Medical Research Council's Clinical Research Centre, Middlesex, England. In 1960 he received the Nobel Prize for Physiology or Medicine for pioneering work in the fields of immunology and tissue transplantation.*

*(Overleaf) Baby rhesus monkey undergoing preparation for soap toxicity testing in a laboratory; photograph, Susan McElhinney—Woodfin Camp & Associates*

8

man beings. Writing on smallpox in one of his witty *Lettres Philosophiques* from England, the 18th-century French writer Voltaire put it on record that the efficacy of variolation—a forerunner to vaccination—was tested with the connivance of king and court upon six condemned felons in Newgate Prison. The six were pardoned and did not get smallpox. It was a typically Anglo-Saxon madness, Voltaire remarked flippantly, to protect people from small-pox by giving it to them deliberately; but it would have been more in keeping with his reputation if he had reprobated the use of condemned criminals for such a purpose. Today the use of prison volunteers for surgical experiments much less risky than variolation is prohibited in all civilized communities.

Variolation, the procedure by which lasting immunity to smallpox is pro-cured by the deliberate infection of the subject by inoculation with matter from a pustule in a mild case of the disease, was in many respects a test case. The procedure had a long history of use in the Near East and Far East, and during the 18th century it was widely adopted in the Western world. It is sometimes used as evidence that very great medical advances can be made by purely clinical procedures that do not involve experimentation upon ani-mals, but this is a shortsighted view. Are not human beings animals too? Dis-regarding the condemned prisoners referred to above, variolation was clear-ly tried out experimentally on a large number of people; we have no records of the number of subjects who died or were not protected.

## The need for experimentation

Experiments *must* be done, for neither physicians nor their patients would countenance the fumbling empiricism of trial and error. The question of whether such experiments should be done on lower animals or on man lies at the very center of the moral debate between experimenters and abolitionists.

Vaccination, a later procedure for conferring immunity to smallpox, is a good example of a medical advance brought about by clinical reasoning and clinical experimentation without the use of laboratory animals. But here, too,

*Man's regard for animals has ranged from religious devotion to callous cruelty. The ancient Egyptians, for example, had the highest respect for the cat (opposite page, left); they worshiped cats in temples, formed religious "cat cults," and had a cat-headed goddess named Bast. Yet felines have also been among the most cruelly mistreated of animals and have long been the objects of a great many superstitions. It is well accepted that much can be learned from the study of animals. It is regrettable, however, that sometimes animals are treated as if they are freely expendable, as in the 19th-century lecture scene (opposite page, right).*

National Library of Medicine, Bethesda, Maryland

*The French microbiologist Louis Pasteur used animals in his laboratory in the 1800s to perfect techniques of immunization against anthrax, chicken cholera, and rabies—immunizations that are beneficial to both humans and animals. In the picture at left Pasteur directs an experiment on a chloroformed rabbit.*

Detroit Institute of Arts, Founders Society Purchase, Edsel B. Ford Fund and gift of Edsel B. Ford

*Evaluation of a new medical treatment is a complicated process. Generally, scientists conduct* in vitro *experiments (in test tubes) before they proceed to* in vivo *tests using living animals. Finally, the ultimate test is to try it on humans. Diego Rivera's painting "Vaccination" encompasses several of the stages in the development of the immunization that protected against the disease smallpox.*

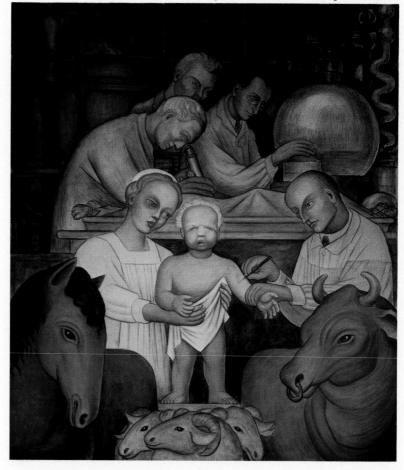

experiments were done, and their subjects were human beings. In 1980 the World Health Organization (WHO) announced the virtual disappearance of smallpox from the face of the Earth.

Vaccination against polio was, like variolation against smallpox, an important test case. With the wisdom of hindsight it is possible to invent a scenario in which experimental animals were not used to validate the clinical procedures actually used in making and administering the vaccine. This hindsight, however, takes no account of the existence of a great storehouse of immunologic and virologic knowhow accumulated through experiments on animals. It must be stressed that it was the prior existence of this knowledge, together with that additional knowledge accumulated for the purpose by Jonas Salk and his colleagues, that made the whole vaccination project in the 1950s a feasible one.

That the treatment of insulin-dependent diabetes by insulin was made possible through experimentation on animals is not now to be seriously disputed. Animals were used in establishing the causal connection between the pancreas and sugar metabolism and to demonstrate the curative powers of pancreatic extracts. Here, certainly, no amount of hindsight makes it possible to construct a scenario in which animals did not play principal parts.

10

*Many believe that there is a special case for exercising the greatest solicitude in experiments using primates—monkeys and apes—because they are so closely similar to human beings not only in structure but also in behavioral repertoire, presumably including "feelings."*

## Should all animals be treated equally?

The question of whether all animals deserve humane treatment has to be answered forthrightly: Yes. The case for restricting the use of animals in biomedical research would be morally crippled if solicitude for animals were confined to pets, cuddly creatures, and nursery familiars and withheld from pests and from other animals judged to be undesirable or unattractive—rats and other rodents, in particular.

It is sound evidence of the probity of spokesmen for the interests of animals that they do *not* distinguish between "deserving" and "undeserving" species. Nevertheless, the regulations in force in Great Britain tend to give the impression of special kindness for cats, dogs, and the Equidae (the horse and its relatives) while being somewhat more permissive toward experiments on animals of other kinds.

There is a case, moreover, for exercising the very greatest solicitude in experiments using monkeys and a *fortiori* anthropoid apes; it would be merely flippant to write this practice off as an exercise of nepotism on behalf of our closest living relatives in the animal kingdom. The case for special treatment is straightforwardly humanitarian; the great apes are so closely similar to human beings in structure, developmental pattern, and behavioral repertoire—including what have been described as rudiments of a faculty of speech—and so similar also in apparent emotional reactivity that it would be pure obstinacy or mere philosophic preciosity to deny them feelings and states of mind cognate with, even if simpler than, our own. It cannot be taken for granted then that apes and monkeys do not have emotions of fearful anticipation and anxious foreboding—the presumed absence of which in lower animals is sometimes thought to extenuate procedures that would certainly be judged inhumanly cruel if carried out upon human beings. Moreover, monkeys and apes easily become bored and lonely; they require the kind of

11

*The animal behaviorist Donald R. Griffin has shown that animals have nervous systems and pain receptors and indeed many behavioral characteristics that are similar to those of humans. This knowledge makes the argument of the huntsman, that it is the hunted animal's "nature" to enjoy the chase, a deplorable and inexcusable one.*

sensory stimulation that comes from companionship and play.

Nevertheless, it must also be said that illness in human beings is darkened by a penumbra of gloomy imaginings about what its outcome might be, by cares for relatives upon whom their illness may be an imposition, and by worries about the competence of medical treatment, job security, unfulfilled engagements, and so on. Animals, clearly, are spared these concerns and the distress they bring. They can live in and for the present as human beings cannot.

## Do animals have feelings?

Samuel Johnson abhorred cruelty to animals and experimentation upon them. In *The Idler* (essay No. 17) he wondered how medical students who carried out experiments on living animals "were yet suffered to erect their heads among human beings." From a moral standpoint very much turns upon the question of animal awareness, which is naturally of central importance in considering the moral justification for experimentation on animals. The problem of the degree to which animals have feelings and states of mind similar to our own, even if in lower key, cannot be solved. Many generations of philosophers of the persuasion known as Idealism have argued that we cannot have certain knowledge of these matters even in respect of our fellow human beings. (It should be made clear that the species of philosopher here referred to should be thought of not as an "ideal-ist" but rather as an "idea-list"—one who, like Bishop George Berkeley [1685–1753], believes that the world is known only as and can be known to exist only as ideas or representations in the mind of the beholder.) A philosophically minded student of animal behavior, Donald R. Griffin, has argued that animals such as mice have so much of the physical plant (*e.g.*, nervous systems and pain receptors) and so many behavioral characteristics that we associate with human beings that it would be cruelly unjust to deny dogmatically their possession of a rudimentary form of awareness and sensibility. While we cannot positively affirm it, of course, neither can we dogmatically deny it.

12

Peter B. Kaplan

*About 500,000 dogs are used annually in medical research. In many circumstances dogs provide accurate models of the human system. One of medicine's most famous experiments—the successful extraction of insulin from the pancreas of a mongrel—paved the way for the insulin treatment of human diabetics. The Animal Center of the National Institutes of Health in Poolesville, Maryland (left), breeds about 800 dogs a year, mostly for use in cardiovascular studies. But many animal rights activists and antivivisectionists protest vehemently against the use of man's best friend in any research (below) and especially against pound seizures—the practice of taking lost or strayed pets from animal shelters for laboratory research.*

Griffin's argument is based upon the notion of evolutionary continuity—in this context, the extreme unlikelihood that any complicated human behavioral repertoire could have sprung into being without evolutionary anticipations in lower animals. The reasonableness of this view is made apparent by considering an emotion such as mother love. Mice and rats and cats and dogs behave toward their offspring in just the way that, when it occurs in human beings, is the authority that entitles us confidently to declare that we ourselves feel mother love. If Griffin's conclusions are accepted, then medical scientists must learn to treat animals with a more respectful circumspection than ever before, and huntsmen must henceforward and forevermore abstain from the utterance of such familiar idiocies as that hunted animals enjoy the chase because it is in their nature to do so.

## The unending debate

The gravity and the difficulty of the problems raised by the practice of experimentation on animals makes it especially disagreeable to be obliged to admit that the disputation between medical experimentalists and those who urge prohibition of all experiments on animals is habitually conducted by the most fruitless of dialectic forms: the alternation of earnest affirmation with earnest denial, both parties safeguarding themselves against any charge of tepid advocacy by tending somewhat to exaggerate their respective cases. The militant abolitionists incline to believe their own propaganda and are incited by it to acts of cruelty and violence toward both human beings and animals. It may cause some surprise to include animals themselves among the victims of the militant abolitionists, but the case for doing so is twofold. First, experiments on animals have brought benefit to animals themselves; the control of distemper is one such benefaction, and the practical success of veterinary surgery is another. We may expect, too, that within a decade the animal illnesses rabies and foot-and-mouth disease will be conquered by medical science even in countries in which they are endemic. In the second place, anyone with even the most rudimentary knowledge of the savage exaction of mortality in natural populations of animals (one thinks of

Robert Holcepl

13

British biologist David Lack's revelations of the dismayingly high annual death rates suffered by small songbirds) would know that the liberation of caged laboratory animals or the supposedly magnanimous action of "giving a caged bird its freedom" are not acts of kindness but acts of folly of which the intended beneficiaries are the principal victims.

Needless to say, experimentation on animals can only very rarely lead to benefactions of the order of magnitude of vaccination against smallpox or polio or the control of puerperal sepsis by sulfanilamide. The advance of medicine is almost never a series of breakthroughs or a bounding from pinnacle to pinnacle of achievement; it is a gradual accumulation of knowledge about the causes and consequences of disease. As a generalization it can be said that the use of experiments on animals is essential. The point was made by one of the world's foremost pharmacologists, a pioneer in the devising of drugs to control hypertension: "Here is a simple test of the importance of animal work: open the British *Pharmacopoeia* at any point, and of the entries so found, ask, 'Could this have been developed without animal experiment?' Whenever I have tried it the answer has always been 'No.'"

The benefactions conferred upon mankind are the most important evidence for the favoring of carrying out experiments that make use of animals.

14

The case, then, rests upon acknowledging the overriding and unqualified priority of human welfare even though sometimes at the expense of our fellow living creatures. There can be no *ex cathedra* pronouncement of right or wrong, for we are here in that twilight zone in which judgments cannot be wholly ratiocinative in character. They must rest upon the consensus of judgment among folk of goodwill, which, though nowhere written down or spelled out in the form of imperatives, is based upon consensus and precedent growing out of repeated exercises of moral judgments combined with a certain sense of the fitness of things. The necessity for using living animals in medical research presents a judgment based upon the moral equivalent of the Common Law. This point is of some importance because in a strictly legal sense animals have no rights in Common Law, though, like children, they enjoy certain statutory safeguards that protect them from wanton cruelty or inhuman exploitation.

It is profitless to turn to the Bible for an overriding moral judgment on the usage of our fellow creatures, for the message of the Pentateuch is that animals were created to *serve* man and to nourish him. There is no specific enjoinder to treat beasts with charity or compassion, for it is not likely that any such enjoinder would carry weight among peoples who might not have thought domestic animals so very much worse off than themselves. Kindness and considerateness to animals in peasant cultures and among children does not come naturally, though of course it can be learned. The Greek pastoral poet Bion put it neatly thus: "Boys stone a frog in fun, but the frog dies in earnest."

## "Pure" research

Although the popular consensus allows it that benefit to mankind through the advancement of medicine justifies the use of experimental animals in medical research, it is by no means so obvious or so readily conceded that it is equally proper and justifiable to use animals for what is vaguely called "pure" research (*i.e.*, that carried out for the advancement of learning rather than for the solution of concrete medical problems), and scientists themselves are known to have had grave misgivings about the propriety of using animals merely to enlarge the understanding. No sharp line of demarcation can, of course, be drawn between "pure" and "applied" research, for what is pure in one generation may in the next turn out to be the theoretical foundation of a prosperous and enormously useful practical advance. The Salk vaccine, to take only one example, could not have been devised unless over many years immunologists using experimental animals had studied in great detail the formation of antibodies against viruses.

Although it is hardly possible to assay such a characteristic, most scientists will feel that what is important in the conduct of pure research is the performer's own attitude of mind. Research using animals that is done merely to gratify curiosity or to answer the most abjectly feeble question any scientist can put to himself ("What would happen if . . . ?") or, more generally, research carried out in the spirit of a pastime or intellectual game would hardly rank as a justification of experiments that threaten in any way an animal's welfare. However, the categorical dismissal of a research project as

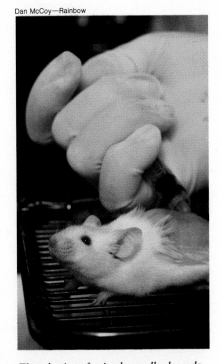

*The selection of animals usually depends on the kind of research being conducted. Availability and expense are also prime considerations. Among the most widely used experimental animals are rodents and rabbits. Recent estimates are that some 50 million mice, 20 million rats, and 2 million rabbits are used in laboratories annually. This great demand has led to the breeding of animals for specific research purposes. Rats, mice, and guinea pigs, for example, can be bred in isolation chambers free of bacteria and parasites so that they develop specific immunities only to microbes that are purposely introduced into a controlled environment. The picture on the opposite page, far left, shows a specially bred hairless mouse in a germ-free lab at the U.S. National Institutes of Health.*

15

having no practical relevance is hardly ever possible, and confident pronouncements are so often falsified that scientists of judgment are seldom guilty of them. It is useful to examine a number of particular situations involving the use of animals in research.

## Experiments on animals by schoolchildren

The United States is probably the only country in which experiments on animals by children are condoned. In grade school and high school science classes children may be encouraged, for example, to verify by direct experimentation that certain kinds of nutritional deprivation will inevitably lead to illness and death. They may be encouraged to execute quite radical surgical procedures upon animals, often and very likely with the piffling ambition of winning a prize in a science fair. Teachers may use experimental animals to impress their lessons vividly upon the minds of the young, though only at the cost of habituating children to the spectacle of distress and death in creatures whose life or death is at their command. As a consequence, the sensibilities of schoolchildren may become so dulled that nothing but actions of extreme and wanton cruelty would have the power to arouse their consciences. Children do not have a natural or instinctive compassion or even heightened concern for animals, but the habits of humane thinking can be learned if they are taught; accordingly they *should* be taught. The children themselves cannot be blamed, but their teachers certainly can be. There is very good reason to question, moreover, the didactic value of experimentation on animals; most of what a child can accept as true is accepted on the authority of his teachers. There is no reason why science should be an exception.

## Animals in cosmetics testing

There is a moral case for using experimental animals to devise, improve, or certify the safety of true medicines. But what about cosmetics, which are used primarily for vanity? Even if it is allowed that judicious use of cosmetics is psychologically beneficial to humankind and therefore the cosmetics in-

*Animal welfare activists have been especially vocal about animals in cosmetics testing. These New York City demonstrators are protesting the use of the Draize eye-irritancy test, which involves instilling drops of an unmarketed preparation into a rabbit's eye to see if the conjunctival blood vessels react. Protagonists of the Draize test claim that it can be skillfully carried out without causing undue suffering to the rabbits. Antagonists claim that the procedure inflicts great pain and sometimes blinds the test animals. A number of cosmetics companies are currently funding research to find suitable alternatives to the use of animals in testing the safety of commercial products.*

Mark Graham/*Discover* Magazine © 1981 Time Inc.

*"Remember the good old days when we only had to smoke a few cigarettes and eat saccharin?"*

dustries perform a socially useful function, the case is quite different from the one for drugs. Cosmetics producers are vulnerable because the market for their products is a population accustomed to the idea of utilizing legislation if cosmetics prove to be deleterious. The cosmetics manufacturer must take the utmost pains to ensure that his products are in no way noxious and must be able to prove, if necessary in a court of law, that those pains have been taken.

Soaps and salves, and indeed all preparations intended for external application, must not be toxic and must not give rise to "primary irritation," by which is meant an irritation due to the direct immediate physical action of the product such as would be produced by an agent that is too acid or too alkaline. For this purpose it is customary to instill a drop of the preparation into a rabbit's eye, the conjunctival blood vessels of which can be relied upon to react promptly and reliably to stinging or destructive agents. If such a test is quickly and skillfully carried out, preferably upon an animal that has not been used for the same purpose before, it need not be thought to cause greater distress than a human being might feel as a consequence of getting soap or shampoo into his eye. Moreover, the industry's knowhow is such that no preparation would be used if there existed a *prima facie* suspicion that the agent would be noxious or in any way offensive. The weakness of this test is that it can screen only for primary irritation and not for irritation that is secondary to the well-known tendency of cosmetic preparations to arouse allergies with certain characteristic cutaneous manifestations.

Testing for capacity to arouse a secondary irritation generally is not practical. Almost all substances applied to the skin may be allergenic to people with a high natural allergic reactivity, so it would be equally fruitless to test toxicity of a cosmetic product in an animal very susceptible or not especially susceptible to allergic reactivity, as the information from both sources could be seriously misleading.

The use of animals in cosmetics testing is clearly undesirable because of the element in it of exploitation. If it is true that the tests never cause more

17

(Top, left to right) E. Marshall Johnson, Daniel Baugh Institute of Anatomy, Thomas Jefferson University; (bottom, left) Smith Kline & French Laboratories; photograph, Burt Glinn—Magnum; (bottom, right) Dan McCoy—Rainbow

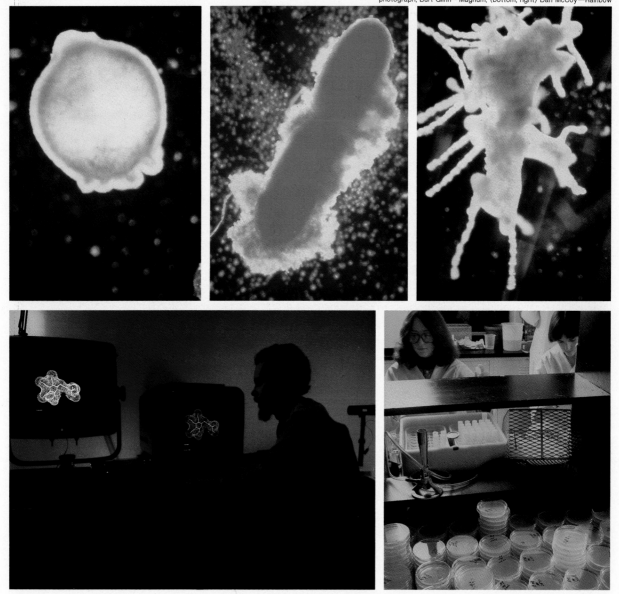

than the pain or discomfort that a human being would dismiss as merely annoying or trivial, then it is not clear why the tests are not carried out on human volunteers—from a company's own workforce, for example. However, it is most unlikely that any cosmetics manufacturer would willingly enter, however circumspectly, into such a legislative minefield.

## Safety testing of drugs

The safety testing and standardization of medications is an entirely different matter from the safety testing of cosmetics, for, as implied earlier, such tests *must* be carried out, if not on animals then on human beings in the course of clinical trial. What is at issue here, then, is the choice between the two. Unless human beings are to be deprived of the privileges of being what is after all "the top animal," the choice must be unhesitatingly in favor of the

18

use of animals. If for any reason it had not been possible for Howard Florey and his colleagues to try out the protective action of penicillin upon those now famous eight mice into which it was first injected, then it would have been used for the first time on human beings, so incurring the odium of carrying out experiments on man.

## Substitutes for laboratory animals

Except when it is essentially a whole-body performance that is being studied (for example, temperature regulation, osmotic and electrolyte control, or the mobilization of body defenses against the intrusion of nonself substances), no scientist would use a sentient living organism for an experiment—least of all to assay the potency or toxicity of a drug—if he could do otherwise. Most whole-body performances have no meaning in respect to the behavior of individual cells or isolated strips of tissue removed from the body, so there is no substitute for the organism as a whole. Very often the same applies to the assessment of toxicity, to which the behavior of isolated tissue cultures (that is, of isolated cells kept alive outside the body in nutrient media) may not be a reliable guide, and often not a guide of any kind to the behavior of a drug in the body. Thus, substances that are lethally toxic when administered *in vivo*—into a living body—(certain snake venoms among them) may be innocuous to cells in tissue culture. Likewise, some substances that are murderously toxic to isolated cells *in vitro*—outside a living body, *i.e.,* in an artificial environment—may be used in the lavage of wounds in the attempt to control wound infection. Proflavine sulphate is one such substance and the dye crystal violet another (the latter has been used externally in the treatment of burns).

In the estimation of the potency of drugs, the goal to be aimed for is, of course, chemical characterization followed by a chemical assay. For many biological substances this is too farfetched an ambition, but approximations to it are constantly being devised, often along lines that cannot be foreseen or predicted. There exists, for example, the procedure known as the radioimmunoassay (RIA) developed by Rosalyn Yalow and colleagues in the 1950s and '60s, which combines in itself the exquisite specificity, sensitivity, and resolving power of immunologic procedures, especially those making use of antibody formation, with the unparalleled power of radioactive labels to cause a chemical substance to make its presence manifest. It is no wonder that clinical scientists use such methods when they can, because they are intrinsically more discriminating and reliable than tests carried out upon organisms that may be physiologically fickle because of genetic variations from one to another or of physiologic variations depending upon the time of day, the stage in a sexual cycle, etc.

Because of their tendency to be taken in by their own propaganda, advocates of the abolition of animals in medical research disregard or underestimate the eager willingness of scientists to substitute *in vitro* methods for experimentation on living organisms. Many experimentalists look with amused wonder on those organizations that have sprung up to advocate and to urge upon medical scientists the use of *in vitro* substitutes for the use of whole organisms—earnest declarations that disregard totally the degree to which

*(Opposite page) The move to develop alternatives to traditional animal experimentation is aimed at replacing animals whenever possible, reducing the numbers of animals required, and refining techniques in order to minimize creature suffering—the three R's. The hydra represents such an alternative. This freshwater creature, which measures only a quarter of an inch yet has a complex tissue and organ system, can regenerate its entire body in a very short time. Thus it can be used instead of rodents and rabbits to test for birth defects caused by chemicals. The first photograph (top, left) shows an adult hydra displaying a full toxic response to a minimum dose of a chemical, which has caused significant clubbing of its tentacles; this hydra is then ground into individual cells. In the second photograph, a four-hour-old artificial embryo develops from an adult hydra cell. The next photograph (top, right) shows an almost fully formed new hydra less than four days old; researchers are able to observe the presence or absence of birth defects in the new adult hydra. Another approach (bottom, left) that may one day affect the number of animals used in drug development research involves creating blueprints for new drugs by means of computers. The computer can be used as a prelude to test-tube and animal investigations. Scientists can study exact molecular structure on a computer screen, which will facilitate the understanding of what effects a drug will have on living cells, thus enabling scientists to avoid experiments that would produce data of little value and to discard some agents that would not be effective or safe. The Ames test (bottom, right), which has been widely used since the 1970s, has spared many a lab animal. The highly accurate test uses specially bred bacteria to determine whether chemicals cause damage to the hereditary material in living cells—the DNA—thus predicting carcinogenic potential.*

Photographs, Alexander Tsiaras

*The rhesus monkey fetus at top was partially removed from the womb at 96 days to undergo surgery to remove an accumulation of fluid in the brain (hydrocephalus) and was later born normal. The child at right, a victim of hydrocephalus, also had an experimental procedure performed while still in his mother's womb. A shunt, which he will have to wear throughout his life, was implanted in his skull to drain fluid to the abdomen. The success of the monkey surgery suggests that human fetuses might be similarly treated. This would be a great medical achievement because hydrocephalus strikes one in 2,000 human fetuses and causes severe mental retardation.*

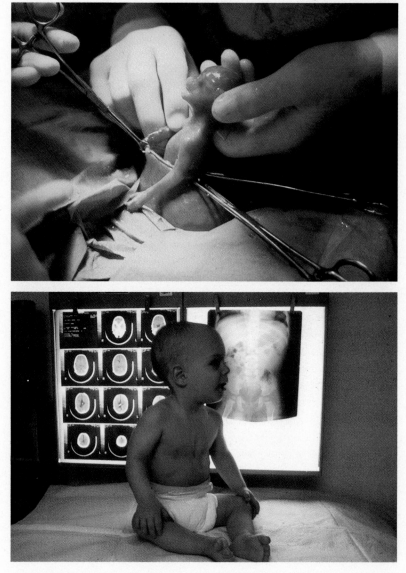

such ambitions are already entertained by scientists and are already being achieved.

## The law

Although the United Kingdom has no monopoly on righteousness, it was the pioneer in the introduction of legislation concerning experimentation upon living animals. The famous Cruelty to Animals Act of 1876 controlling experimentation on animals was a natural development of the humanitarian movement that in 1824 laid the foundation of the first society to promote the welfare of animals, the Society for the Prevention of Cruelty to Animals (SPCA), which soon was at the behest of royalty to become the RSPCA.

The British law unconditionally requires that those who carry out experiments on animals be qualified by their training to undertake them and perform them only on premises approved and registered for the purpose. The experiments must have a declared purpose approved by the body responsible for enforcement and be manifestly such as to improve medicine or surgery or to increase the likelihood of their improvement. The law calls for the recording and annual return of all experiments performed, and the use of anesthetics is insisted upon for all experiments causing or likely to cause distress.

The enforcement of the law is the task of a number of inspectors with medical or veterinary qualifications who make it their business wherever possible to meet licensees personally and to acquaint themselves directly with the progress of their work. Such officers vary in competence and knowhow, as is the case in other professions, but the best can be actively helpful in an advisory capacity that aids animals and experimenters alike. Such officers frequently make unannounced visits to laboratories licensed for the conduct of animal experiments and on these occasions satisfy themselves that the experiments have been duly recorded and that their subjects are not distressed. In the main, medical scientists welcome the regulations and regard them as a safeguard against malicious misrepresentation of what they do. No scientists who conduct their experiments rationally and humanely have anything to fear.

It would be wrong, though, to paint too rosy a picture of the workings of the Cruelty to Animals Act of 1876. Many of the decisions that must be made pose problems to which there would not normally be a straightforward, black-or-white answer. Decisions, then, will be based upon acts of judgment by no means immune to bias and error. Moreover, obligations upon inspectors are manifold and onerous, so that the bureaucratic machinery tends to be slow moving, with the effect that newly arrived staff members or guest workers may find themselves unable to get on with their work in the long period during which the bureaucratic procedures are carried out. Understandably, these delays have earned the law a degree of reprobation; nonethe-

*The chimpanzee pictured here was used in the testing of a vaccine that now protects humans against hepatitis B. According to the researchers, only one chimp of the 200 that were used died as a consequence of the hepatitis B studies. Chimpanzees are genetically so similar to humans that they have been extremely important in medical and psychological research. But they are an endangered species. Whether they should be regarded as sentient beings with rights similar to those of humans poses a difficult ethical dilemma.*

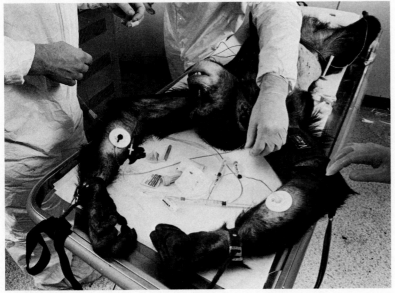

Joseph Kugielsky

*For the most part, the biomedical research community is deeply concerned about preventing animal suffering in the lab. The monkey pictured here is wearing a nylon net jacket specially designed to be comfortable and adjustable and to protect surgical wounds and limit irritation. It replaces constrictive devices that were once used. There are times when tests that do not involve living sentient beings are preferable. An example is the procedure known as radioimmunoassay, which measures with exquisite sensitivity chemical toxicity and drug potency. In another use, this miraculous assay measures hormones in the body, such as thyroid levels in newborns (below). There is no question that animal experimentation has been and will continue to be vital to the spectacular progress of medical research that has provided great benefits to man. The specially bred spontaneously hypertensive rat in a blood pressure measuring device (opposite page) is being used in current hypertension research—research that may one day benefit the many millions of people around the world who suffer from this "silent killer."*

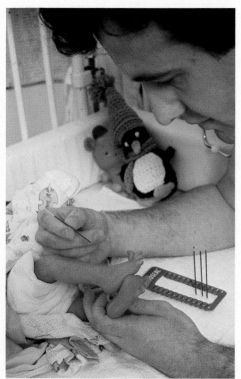

Dan McCoy—Rainbow

less, it would appear that the scientific community in Great Britain generally approves of legislation restricting animal experimentation and believes it is in the hands of those competent to carry it out.

In Europe legislation varies greatly from country to country in degree of permissiveness. Liechtenstein forbids animal experimentation altogether, so we shall not look to Liechtenstein for major advances of medical treatment or understanding. Scandinavian countries have realistic and effective legislation, and in Denmark animals may not be used whenever *in vitro* alternatives are feasible. West Germany's legislation is similar to Britain's, and in The Netherlands experiments may be carried out only upon animals bred and raised for the purpose; licenses are issued to establishments, not to individuals. Legislation in Belgium, France, and Italy is untidy and unduly permissive, but in Austria it is detailed and specific and especially insistent on the keeping of records of experiments that are open to official inspection at any time. Legislation in eastern Europe does not appear to be such as to prohibit the conduct of animal experiments merely to gratify curiosity. Owing to the widely divergent laws, a European committee acting for the European Economic Community in Strasbourg, France, is devising a European convention for the protection of laboratory animals.

An Animal Welfare Act in the United States was enacted in 1966 and has been twice revised. It differs in an important way from the corresponding legislation in England because it does not focus primarily on laboratory experiments on animals but on the care of animals in general, including housing and husbandry and the prevention of experimentation on animals procured by theft. There is no effective and enforceable legislation affecting the conduct of laboratory experiments. Thus, applying as it does principally to circuses, zoos, and dealers in pets, it is not to be wondered at that the Animal Welfare Act in the United States lacks a cutting edge. It falls far short of the cogency and effectiveness that animal welfare groups in the United States hope and press for.

In the United States some experiments have been done that would not

22

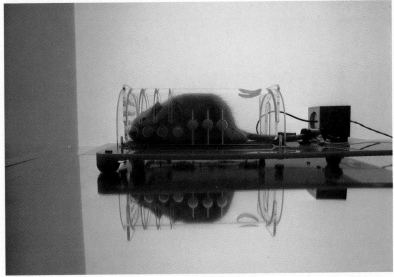

have been allowed in the United Kingdom, but the comparative ineffectiveness of U.S. legislation must on no account be taken to imply that cruelty to animals is the rule, for there is not the slightest reason to suppose that American men and women of science have coarser sensibilities than their European colleagues or have less concern for the common decencies as they affect the welfare of animals. But that the United States is backward in legislating for the welfare of animals is not to be denied. It should be remembered, however, that a factor that may militate against the U.S. adoption of controls as demanding and particular as those currently in force in the United Kingdom is a deep repugnance for the intrusion of government into everyday affairs—a mood confirmed and heightened by the Reagan administration.

## The three R's

Experimentation upon animals for the purpose of enlarging medical understanding and for improving medical treatment must be carried out. Such experimentation is likely to continue for many years to come unless human beings are to be put unreasonably at a disadvantage. Moreover, inanimate and physical and chemical systems cannot yet substitute for the use of living animals, though it should be our continuing ambition to bring about a state of affairs in which they can do so. All the problems connected with animal experimentation are grave and difficult, and no scientist may stand aside.

There may be no solution that is fair both to animals and to human beings. What is of overriding importance is that medical scientists should work toward the realization of the ambitions embodied in what W. M. S. Russell and R. L. Burch have described most felicitously as the three R's of humane experimental practice: (1) replacement of animals by nonsentient systems wherever possible; (2) refinement of experimental procedures; and (3) reduction of the number of animals used to the very minimum that will serve a useful purpose.

FOR ADDITIONAL READING:
Griffin, Donald R. *The Question of Animal Awareness.* New York: Rockefeller University Press, 1981.

Russell, W. S., and Burch, R. L. *The Principles of Humane Experimental Technique.* London: Methuen & Co., 1959.

Sperlinger, David (ed.). *Animals in Research: New Perspectives in Animal Experimentation.* New York: John Wiley & Sons, 1981.

# An Epidemiologic Maze
## by David T. Durack, M.D., D. Phil.

In 1980 physicians in New York City, San Francisco, and Los Angeles reported the deaths of several young homosexual men from a rare type of lung infection (pneumocystis pneumonia) or a rare tumor (Kaposi's sarcoma). Some patients had both. These cases were especially puzzling, as neither illness was recognized as one of the several sexually transmitted diseases common among homosexuals. These were the first documented U.S. cases of the extraordinary disease—initially dubbed the "gay plague"—that has since been named the acquired immune deficiency syndrome—AIDS. In the short span of three years since AIDS was first identified, new developments have occurred at a dizzying rate: the number of cases reported has increased rapidly, and the number of different infections and tumors found in AIDS patients has proliferated. Cases have been identified in at least 16 countries outside the United States, and the patient population now includes—in addition to homosexual and bisexual men—intravenous drug abusers, Haitian immigrants in the United States and Europe, hemophiliacs, and sex partners, infants, and young children of AIDS victims or persons at high risk for the disease. By 1983 the disease clearly had ceased to be a medical curiosity and had assumed the proportions of a major health problem. The sheer number of patients involved was impressive; this number was increasing; and the possibility that other groups might be affected clearly existed. The cause of AIDS, whatever it might be, was obviously of great importance—not only to homosexuals and other groups at risk but to medical science and the general public as well.

## Clinical features of AIDS

**David T. Durack, M.D., D. Phil.,** *is Professor of Medicine, Professor of Microbiology and Immunology, and Chief of the Division of Infectious Diseases at the Duke University Medical Center in Durham, North Carolina.*

*(Opposite) Poster for AIDS benefit, Gay Men's Health Crisis, Inc.*

AIDS is a condition that meets the medical criteria of a syndrome; *i.e.,* a disease with several clinical findings that "run together." The following notable features commonly appear—separately or together—in patients with AIDS:

1. severe weight loss, intermittent fever, fatigue, weakness, and malaise (general discomfort);
2. enlarged lymph glands—lymphadenopathy—in neck, armpits, or groin;
3. increased incidence of a variety of opportunistic infections;

24

Photographs, Centers for Disease Control, Atlanta

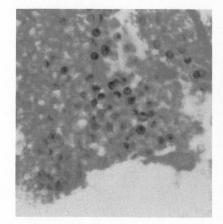 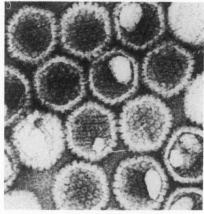

4. increased incidence of certain tumors;

5. abnormalities in the numbers and function of specialized cells, especially certain lymphocytes, responsible for normal immunity; and

6. high risk of death within one to two years of onset.

So-called opportunistic infections are caused by numerous organisms—bacteria, fungi, viruses, or various protozoans—that are harmless to most normal, healthy people; in individuals whose immune mechanisms are compromised, these infections can take advantage of failures in host defenses, causing serious disease. Such failures of immunity may be inborn or may be acquired later in life. Physicians have long been familiar with opportunistic in-

**Some important opportunistic infections and tumors that have occurred in AIDS**

| organism | diseases | comments |
|---|---|---|
| *Pneumocystis carinii* (protozoan) | pneumonia | rare except in immunosuppressed patients; leading cause of death in AIDS; treatable |
| *Candida albicans* (fungal) | thrush of mucous membranes (mouth, esophagus, gut) | often coexists with more serious infections; may be an early warning sign of AIDS; treatable |
| herpes simplex virus (viral) | facial, genital, or anal ulcers | can cause severe disease; treatable |
| cytomegalovirus (viral) | hepatitis, retinitis, pneumonitis | often causes low grade or asymptomatic infection; can cause blindness; virtually untreatable |
| tuberculosis (bacterial) | pulmonary or disseminated infection | more common in Haitians than in other AIDS patients; often disseminated |
| atypical tuberculosis (bacterial) | pulmonary or disseminated infection | disseminated atypical TB is rare in normal people |
| *Toxoplasma gondii* (protozoan) | brain infection; disseminated disease | can simulate brain tumor or encephalitis; often fatal |
| *Cryptosporidium* (protozoan) | cryptosporidiosis with severe diarrhea; enterocolitis | can cause severe weight loss and dehydration; difficult to cure |
| *Cryptococcus neoformans* (also called *Filobasidiella neoformans;* fungal) | pneumonia; meningitis; disseminated disease | usually found in immunosuppressed patients; treatable; high mortality in AIDS |
| unknown (bacterial?) | Whipple's disease of small intestine | rare disease caused by an unidentified bacterium |

| tumor | sites affected | comments |
|---|---|---|
| Kaposi's sarcoma | skin, lymph nodes, gastrointestinal tract, lungs | previously rare, occurring in the elderly and renal transplant recipients; more common in younger people in parts of equatorial Africa |
| undifferentiated non-Hodgkin lymphoma | lymph nodes, spleen, central nervous system | an aggressive tumor that usually relapses quickly after treatment; high mortality |
| primary lymphoma of brain | brain | very rare in normal people; several cases in AIDS |
| squamous cell carcinoma | anal canal | can also occur in homosexuals who do not have AIDS |

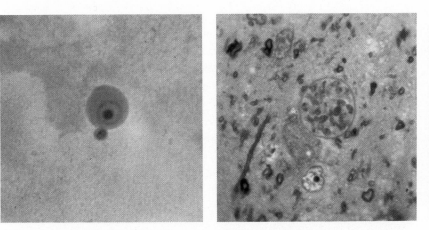
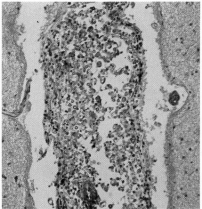

fections among patients with immune system depression caused by chronic, debilitating diseases or congenital immunodeficiencies and those receiving immunosuppressive drugs to treat cancers or to prevent rejection of organ transplants. Thus, the pattern of infections noted in AIDS patients was immediately recognized as similar to the pattern already observed in patients with known defects of the cellular immune system. A list of some of these infections appears in the table on page 26.

Before its appearance in AIDS victims, Kaposi's sarcoma (KS) was considered an extremely rare tumor. In the United States it occurred only in a few elderly male patients, usually of Mediterranean ancestry, and as an occasional complication of immunosuppressive drugs. Outside the United States Kaposi's sarcoma is also rare, with one exception: it has been recognized as a fairly common tumor among young people in certain parts of equatorial Africa, roughly in those regions where Burkitt's lymphoma, a tumor known to be associated with a specific virus—Epstein-Barr virus (EBV)—is also common. Among Americans of African descent—other than AIDS victims—Kaposi's sarcoma is extremely rare.

In elderly patients, Kaposi's sarcoma usually progresses so slowly that the patient is more likely to die of an unrelated cause than from the tumor itself. In renal transplant patients KS is sometimes more aggressive but will often regress if immunosuppressive drugs are discontinued. This observation indicates that Kaposi's sarcoma is an opportunistic tumor, advancing when host defenses are weakened and regressing if normal defenses recover.

Many homosexual males have developed lymphadenopathy and an imbalance of certain lymphocytes (white blood cells active in the immune response) often without any other obvious signs of illness. Only a few of these men have developed unequivocal AIDS. This group is now being closely studied to determine the significance of lymphadenopathy and abnormal lymphocyte ratios; researchers are investigating the possibility that this condition is a precursor, or prodrome, of the full-blown disease.

## Facts about the AIDS epidemic

**Incidence.** Between June 1981 and the late summer of 1983, about 2,000 cases of AIDS were reported to the U.S. Centers for Disease Control (CDC) in Atlanta, Georgia, and close to 800—or nearly 40%—of these patients had

*A variety of opportunistic infections are characteristic of AIDS. The above photomicrographs, from laboratory slides stained to enhance the visibility of the pathological organism, show (left to right)* Pneumocystis carinii *in the alveolar spaces of a human lung; herpes simplex virus (black and white); cytomegalovirus; toxoplasmosis of the brain; and cryptococcosis of the brain.*

27

*Kaposi's sarcoma, a malignant tumor formerly quite rare in the United States, is another manifestation of the AIDS syndrome. The typical skin discolorations, which usually appear on the extremities, are dark reddish-purple or bluish raised spots superficially resembling bruises; unlike bruises, however, Kaposi's lesions do not heal, nor do they disappear within two to three weeks.*

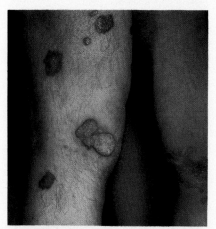

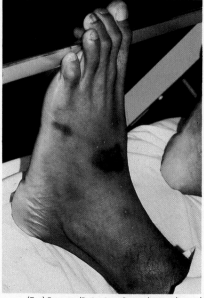

died of the disease. The number of reported cases has more than doubled in each six-month period since 1981; in one six-week period in midsummer of 1983, some 331 new cases were reported to the CDC.

In the United States alone the incidence of AIDS is already greater than the annual incidence of such other important but uncommon diseases as tetanus, diphtheria, brucellosis, tularemia, rabies, and plague combined. The term epidemic is justified. Furthermore, because the incidence of AIDS is concentrated in certain large U.S. cities (in order of magnitude: New York City; San Francisco; Los Angeles; Miami, Florida; Newark, New Jersey; Houston, Texas; and Chicago), the disease represents an even greater problem in these areas than the total number of cases suggests. On the other hand, in many other parts of the United States, including some large cities, AIDS is still rare.

Overall, male patients outnumber females by a ratio of about 14 to 1. Among drug addicts, however, the male-female ratio is about 3 to 1. The median age of patients is 35 years, but the age range is fairly wide. One infant developed AIDS after receiving multiple blood-product transfusions from several donors; one of the donors was identified as a homosexual who subsequently manifested the symptoms of AIDS and eventually died of the disease. Pediatricians in New York and New Jersey have identified an AIDS-like syndrome in about 15 infants and young children of high-risk families, including children of some drug addicts. Very few older children or teenagers with AIDS have been reported, and only a few cases of AIDS have been diagnosed in people over the age of 55.

**Persons at risk.** In early reports the first AIDS patients were almost exclusively male homosexuals. Later the backgrounds of the patient population broadened, although homosexuals remained a clear majority; at present, approximately three-quarters of all patients are homosexual or bisexual men. Few lesbians have developed AIDS, a fact compatible with the generally low incidence of other sexually transmitted diseases in this group.

Surveys have revealed a profile of the group at highest risk. They are sexually active homosexuals with many casual, often anonymous sexual contacts and an urban life-style with access to gay bars and bathhouses. Many are users of various recreational drugs, especially inhaled amyl nitrite ("poppers"). Many AIDS patients regularly travel to other cities to attend gay parties or take vacation cruises that cater to homosexuals, thus multiplying opportunities for dissemination of a possible infectious agent. Interestingly, many of the hundred or so patients diagnosed abroad are homosexuals who have visited the United States—and New York City, in particular—at least once in recent years.

The next largest group of patients consists of drug addicts. Most often the drugs taken by this group are intravenous narcotics—in contrast to the sexually stimulating inhaled drugs favored by the gay population—often administered with shared, *i.e.,* contaminated, needles.

A smaller subgroup of patients are Haitians, mostly recent immigrants to the United States, although some cases have been reported in France and in Haiti. Haitian patients are more likely than others with AIDS to suffer from toxoplasmosis of the brain or from tuberculosis. In the United States the

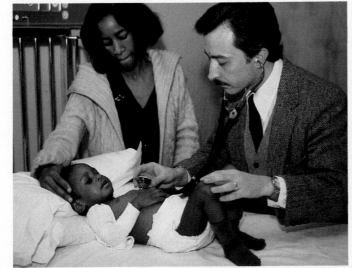

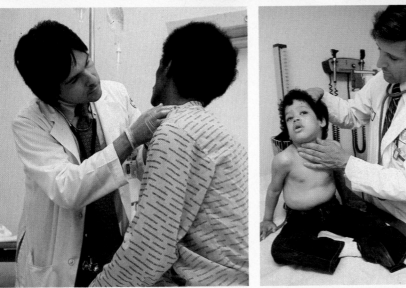

Haitian-born patients—who constitute about 5% of the total patient population—are an especially puzzling group. Most strongly deny previous history of homosexual contact or intravenous drug use, but reliable information about these practices is virtually impossible to obtain because of the stigma associated with these activities in Haitian culture. In addition, because of difficulties in diagnosis and other uncertain factors, there is growing controversy among local and national health authorities regarding the consideration of Haitian nationality as a risk factor. Some municipal health departments have removed Haitian-Americans from the list of groups at risk, although the Centers for Disease Control disputes this judgment.

According to some Haitian medical investigators, about 150 cases of AIDS have also been documented in Haiti among native black inhabitants, primarily residents of a poverty-ridden section of Port-au-Prince. Interestingly, most of these Haitian AIDS victims fall into two categories: male and female prostitutes who cater to a U.S. tourist clientele and poor people whose basic

*In addition to homosexual and bisexual men, persons at greatest risk for AIDS include intravenous drug users; hemophiliacs and other recipients of blood and blood products (the man pictured [top right] is a hemophiliac believed to have acquired AIDS from a contaminated dose of blood concentrate); and children of AIDS patients, as well as children of individuals in high-risk categories. A small percentage of cases have also been identified among Haitian immigrants; the inclusion of all Haitian-Americans in the high-risk group, however, has been challenged.*

*The extremely high mortality rate of AIDS victims, coupled with the fears and misconceptions about transmission of the disease, produces devastating psychosocial consequences—loss of jobs, dwindling financial resources, ostracism by peers and family, and, in some cases, refusal of services by hospital personnel. The continuing emotional support of friends and relatives has been cited by clinicians as an important factor in the long-term survival of AIDS patients.*

health care is provided by unlicensed physicians who routinely administer injections with unsterilized reusable needles.

Another small but critically important group of cases has been identified among hemophiliacs. Although to date there have been only 18 definite cases reported to the CDC, the fact that these nonhomosexual, non-drug-addicted individuals have received multiple transfusions of blood products provides a strong clue that AIDS may be caused by an infectious agent found and transmitted in human blood. Because the manufacture of the clotting factor taken by many hemophiliacs requires pooled plasma from several thousand donors—possibly as many as 20,000 to 30,000 individuals—some researchers have speculated that a breakdown of normal immune responses may be induced by the repeated infusion of foreign proteins in commercial blood products. Alternatively, some investigators theorize that blood from a single AIDS victim—any one of the thousands of donors—may transmit the disease. Whatever the source of infection, the mortality rate among hemophiliacs who have contracted AIDS has, thus far, exceeded 50%.

A few fascinating cases of multiple, severe opportunistic infections among previously healthy people in Zaire and other parts of equatorial Africa have recently been reported, and European physicians in Paris and Brussels have begun to identify AIDS in African patients there. These observations have caused physicians to ask: Do these individuals have AIDS itself or another similar kind of immune disorder? Is the African form of Kaposi's sarcoma actually due to AIDS? Thus far unsubstantiated is the speculation that central Africa is the origin of and reservoir for the infectious agent of AIDS.

Can the female sexual partner of an AIDS victim contract AIDS? Evidently so, although to date only about 130 women in all have been recognized as having the disease. A medical team in New York City examined seven female partners of male AIDS patients (primarily drug addicts); one had AIDS, one had lymphadenopathy, and four, who had no overt symptoms, displayed some abnormalities in laboratory tests of immune factors. Only one seemed to be completely normal. These findings raise justified fears that AIDS may be spread by sexual contact and could eventually affect larger segments of the general population.

**Mortality.** The death rate from AIDS is extremely high. By August 1983

30

about 40% of all patients reported to the CDC had already died. To put this figure in perspective, it must be noted that even the legendary epidemics of black plague and typhus fever carried a lower overall mortality than AIDS. Patients with Kaposi's sarcoma alone tend to survive longer than those who have multiple opportunistic infections; the death rate among patients with pneumocystis pneumonia is about 60%. The damage to host defenses is not only broad but apparently irreversible; thus when one opportunistic infection has been treated successfully, another may soon develop. Repeated attacks of these infections produce a cumulative mortality of about 60% after one year and about 80% by two years after diagnosis.

## The immune system in AIDS

Because the system of cellular defenses against infection seems to undergo almost total collapse in AIDS patients, changes in cellular immunity associated with AIDS have been intensively investigated. These studies show a fairly stereotyped pattern of abnormality: a low count of lymphocytes, the white blood cells that are crucial in normal immunity; defective functioning of so-called killer cells, a category of T-lymphocytes; and reversal of the normal ratio of two other populations of T-lymphocytes, T-suppressor cells and T-helper cells. T-helper cells (processed through the thymus gland, which itself may be abnormal in AIDS) function in activating the body's response against microbes. T-suppressor cells modulate the activity of the helpers. In a normal, healthy person, helpers outnumber suppressors in a ratio of two to one. In AIDS patients the ratio of helper to suppressor cells is consistently abnormal or reversed. However, as this ratio may also be abnormal in some apparently healthy homosexuals and drug addicts, and in persons with fairly common bacterial infections, this indicator has not provided conclusive diagnostic data in individual cases.

AIDS patients show abnormal responses to tests for delayed hypersensitivity, which is measured by injection into the skin of antigens (*i.e.,* foreign substances) such as tuberculin or mumps antigen. A normal positive reaction indicates previous exposure to a given antigen and demonstrates that this portion of the immune system is intact. The concentration of immunoglobulins (proteins that identify antigens and stimulate appropriate antibod-

*Where orthodox medicine fails to provide a cure, the desperately ill turn to any alternative that provides a source of hope or comfort. This patient has the lesions of Kaposi's sarcoma, one of the opportunistic tumors of AIDS.*

Louise Gubb—Gamma/Liaison

ies) in the blood is usually increased—indicating an ability to produce normal antibodies—and most tests of antibody production show no serious defects in this aspect of the immune system. The complement system, a group of blood proteins also involved in antigen-antibody reactions, functions normally. Scientific interpretation of these findings and of their significance to the etiology of AIDS is still open to question.

## The search for a cause: current theories

Because the discovery of a cure for AIDS is not imminent, the primary efforts of researchers have concentrated on identifying the cause and developing effective means of prevention. So far these attempts have been unsuccessful. The CDC is conducting a major program of case-control studies, in which AIDS patients are exhaustively compared with unaffected controls (*i.e.,* healthy individuals) in an attempt to find epidemiologic clues to the cause of the disease. While these studies have yielded a profile of those individuals at greatest risk, they have yet to uncover evidence of a single, identifiable cause. But, although the case-control studies have not provided irrefutable evidence of person-to-person transmission, they have uncovered several striking instances of networks of sexual contacts among AIDS patients. Based on assumptions derived from these examples of possible transmission, it seems likely that the incubation period of AIDS is long—anywhere from 6 to 18 months, or even as long as several years.

After Legionnaires' disease was identified in 1976, ample evidence of earlier outbreaks soon came to light. Therefore, efforts have been made to find cases of AIDS that occurred before the outbreak of the present epidemic in 1979. A few cases of mysterious incurable immune disorders have been unearthed by retrospective review of innumerable hospital records, but it is impossible to determine if these isolated examples were indeed AIDS. At present, this disease still seems to be a truly new entity.

**The recreational drug theory.** Because the use of recreational drugs such as inhaled amyl nitrite has increased rapidly in the past decade, especially in the gay population, efforts have been made to link AIDS to these agents. There is some experimental evidence that these drugs suppress immunity by various effects on lymphocytes or phagocytes—cells that protect the body from disease-causing organisms. However, the number of AIDS patients who have not used recreational drugs is large enough to cast doubt on this hypothesis, at least as an explanation of the primary cause of AIDS.

**The virus theory.** A number of different kinds of viruses have been isolated from the body fluids or tissues of AIDS patients. These include adenoviruses, parvoviruses, retroviruses, herpes simplex virus, and cytomegalovirus (CMV). Biochemical indicators of the presence of hepatitis B virus and Epstein-Barr virus have also been found in some AIDS victims. All these viruses are currently under investigation as potential factors in the etiology of AIDS.

Much interest has centered on the possible role of cytomegalovirus for several reasons. CMV infection is very common among homosexuals, and live CMV virus has been discovered in laboratory specimens of urine and semen from this group. CMV is known to have immunosuppressive effects; the blood serum of many AIDS patients contains antibodies formed in response

**Public opinion about AIDS***

likely to become epidemic

|  | yes | no | no opinion | not aware |
|---|---|---|---|---|
| national | 33% | 27% | 17% | 23% |
| men | 28% | 31% | 17% | 24% |
| women | 37% | 23% | 18% | 22% |
| 18–29 years | 39% | 22% | 14% | 25% |
| 30–49 years | 34% | 32% | 16% | 18% |
| 50 and older | 27% | 26% | 21% | 26% |

cure imminent (1 or 2 years)

|  | yes | no | no opinion | not aware |
|---|---|---|---|---|
| national | 26% | 35% | 16% | 23% |
| men | 27% | 33% | 16% | 24% |
| women | 24% | 36% | 17% | 23% |
| 18–29 years | 29% | 33% | 13% | 25% |
| 30–49 years | 25% | 40% | 16% | 19% |
| 50 and older | 24% | 30% | 20% | 26% |

*Based on Gallup poll, June 1983.

32

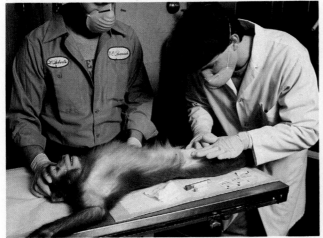 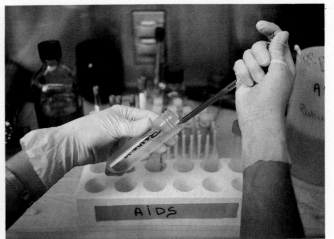

to past or active CMV infection; furthermore, nucleic acids derived from CMV have been identified in Kaposi's sarcoma tissues. On the other hand, there are arguments against a causal role for CMV: it is a common virus in the general population, not a new arrival, and female prostitutes—who are exposed to large quantities of CMV in semen—do not develop AIDS unless they are also intravenous drug users.

Another common virus that could be related to AIDS is Epstein-Barr virus, the cause of infectious mononucleosis. A number of AIDS patients show remarkably high concentrations of antibodies to this virus in their blood serum. Moreover, EBV is related to Burkitt's lymphoma, and the latter occurs in the same parts of equatorial Africa where Kaposi's sarcoma is found. On the other hand, like CMV, EBV is not a new organism.

Hepatitis B is also extremely common in three groups affected by AIDS: homosexuals, recipients of multiple blood transfusions, and drug addicts. This striking epidemiologic association has led some scientists to postulate that the hepatitis B virus might play a predisposing or even a causal role in the development of AIDS. Others interpret the association to mean only that the cause of AIDS, like that of hepatitis B, is transmitted in blood or other body fluids.

Evidence that the human T-cell leukemia virus (HTLV), a retrovirus, may be related to AIDS is perhaps the most promising development in the speculation about a viral cause of AIDS. Retroviruses are of particular scientific importance because they were the first viruses shown to cause malignancies in humans. Now they have been isolated from the T cells of several AIDS patients. Antibodies to antigens that characteristically appear on the surface of T cells after infection with HTLV have been found in 25% of 75 AIDS patients studied but in very few controls. HTLV or a related virus could be the cause of AIDS; if so, the discovery would provide vital insights into the genesis of human tumors and the means by which they evade the body's normal defenses.

**The genetic predisposition theory.** Before the identification of AIDS, Kaposi's sarcoma was known to occur in some kidney transplant patients receiving immunosuppressive drugs. Patients with Mediterranean or Jewish back-

*The first of several outbreaks of an AIDS-like immune dysfunction in nonhuman primates was reported in California in 1969. The disease, now known as SAIDS (simian AIDS), is being studied as a possible animal model for the human syndrome. In the photo at left, a physician at the New England Regional Primate Center, in Southboro, Massachusetts, examines the lymph nodes of a macaque. Although they take special precautions when handling blood or biopsy specimens from AIDS patients, medical and laboratory technicians have been concerned about the risk of exposure to the disease. A very few cases of AIDS have been reported among health care workers, but none of the victims was known to have had any direct contact with AIDS patients or with potentially infectious materials.*

33

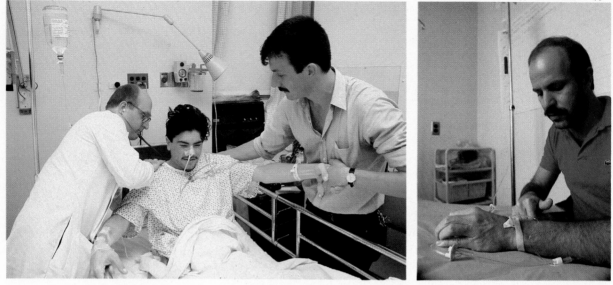

*Because there is no cure for AIDS itself, treatment is necessarily limited to supportive care (above) and drug therapy as indicated by the existing opportunistic infections. The antiviral agent interferon is being used experimentally (above right), thus far with limited success.*

grounds seem to be at higher risk for this particular complication of immunosuppression, suggesting that a certain genetic makeup might be an important predisposing factor. Genetic typing studies show that one genotype (specific genetic configuration) is two to three times more common among AIDS patients with Kaposi's sarcoma than among the general population. Thus, some researchers speculate that a person's genetic constitution could play some role in determining his or her susceptibility to AIDS.

**Evaluation of present evidence.** Many researchers currently believe that by far the most likely cause of AIDS is a virus transmitted in blood or blood products. It could be a known agent such as one of the herpesvirus group, the cancer-causing retroviruses (especially HTLV), the adenoviruses, or the hepatitis B virus. Alternatively, it could be a mutant of one of the known viruses or an entirely new agent. It is possible—even likely—that several factors must act in concert with a virus to produce the disease.

## Treatment

Because the root cause is not yet known, treatment for AIDS patients is necessarily limited to supportive care plus antimicrobial or antitumor drugs. It is possible to treat many, but not all, of the opportunistic infections that plague the victims of AIDS. For example, pneumocystis pneumonia can be treated with the drugs pentamidine or trimethoprim-sulfamethoxazole; thrush, which is a fungal infection, can be treated with nystatin or ketoconazole; and herpesvirus can be treated with acyclovir. Irradiation and chemotherapy are used in cases of Kaposi's sarcoma.

Experimental treatment with interferon—a naturally occurring antiviral agent used in cancer treatment—is under study, based on the possibility that AIDS might be caused by an interferon-sensitive virus. Results have been encouraging, but not all cases respond positively. A team at the Memorial Sloan-Kettering Cancer Center in New York has treated 12 Kaposi's sarcoma patients with one of the several forms of interferon, achieving complete remission in three cases and improvement in two others. This promising line

*Staff members at a Stanford, California, blood bank (below) use a sophisticated computerized device to screen donor blood for abnormalities associated with AIDS.*

of investigation will be pursued to the limit, but it seems likely that specific, effective treatment and prevention of AIDS will come about only through identification of the causal agent—or agents—and complete understanding of the mode of transmission.

## Can AIDS be prevented?

The ever increasing number of AIDS victims has raised legitimate fears among their relatives, friends, and co-workers. In addition, the advent of AIDS-like illnesses among a few infants, children, and spouses of AIDS patients has raised the specter of possible spread within families by intimate, nonsexual contact. Therefore, prevention is a matter of utmost priority.

First, it is important to emphasize that, according to current evidence, most people are *not* at risk for AIDS. Most healthy people and heterosexual and non-drug-using people seem to be immune, even if they come into close contact with the disease. Among medical attendants of AIDS patients, for example, the only clear-cut cases of AIDS have occurred in homosexuals, bisexuals, or drug users. (A few health care workers who fall into none of the high-risk categories *have* developed unexplained cases of AIDS; however, these individuals are not believed to have had any direct contact with AIDS patients or contaminated laboratory specimens.) Children from one year of age through adolescence appear to be virtually immune, and the disease is rare in the elderly. Therefore, although the AIDS epidemic must be viewed as a serious problem, there is so far no cause for panic.

**Blood products: new safeguards.** Because AIDS may be transmitted by blood products, serious and troubling questions have arisen regarding blood transfusions. Should blood donation by homosexuals be outlawed? This controversial and difficult problem remains under intensive debate. Early in 1983 the U.S. Public Health Service, the American Red Cross, the National Gay Task Force, and other interested agencies issued recommendations that members of groups at increased risk for AIDS be asked to voluntarily refrain from donating plasma and/or blood. Severe limitations on donor eligibility could, it should be noted, lead to critical shortages of blood sup-

*Because of the dramatic health threat to homosexuals, the gay community has been in the vanguard of efforts to provide responsible information about AIDS and supportive counseling for patients. In the offices of Gay Men's Health Crisis, Inc., in New York City (below left), volunteers attend a training session on the psychological impact of the disease and its social consequences for the homosexual population in general. In gay bathhouses posters and other educational materials outlining preventive measures are prominently displayed.*

(Left) James Pozarik; (right) Rick Browne—Picture Group

(Top and center) Photographs, Owen Franken—Sygma;
(bottom) Allan Tannenbaum—Sygma

plies. In France the Ministry of Health has initiated a comprehensive donor screening program, and the Institut Pasteur has halted the importation of blood plasma from the United States.

A number of pharmaceutical products are derived from blood pools to which homosexuals have contributed, among them hepatitis B immune globulin, hepatitis B vaccine, and the clotting factors vital for treatment of bleeding disorders such as hemophilia. Some physicians speculate that the hepatitis B vaccine could be a vehicle for transmitting AIDS. The possibility that an unknown infectious agent may lurk in *any* blood product must be recognized, but it is worth noting that the highly purified hepatitis B vaccine is one of the least likely vehicles for an occult infection. Certainly, the risk factor in this vaccine is considerably less than that associated with blood transfusions from homosexual donors. The U.S. Food and Drug Administration is addressing this problem in new guidelines for agencies that collect plasma and blood and for manufacturers of blood derivatives.

**Life-style: personal precautions.** Drug addicts who wish to reduce their risk for AIDS should obviously be advised to stop using all intravenous drugs; certainly those who cannot give up the drug habit should, at the very least, understand the dangers involved in shared needles. Homosexuals and bisexuals can protect themselves by ceasing to engage in promiscuous sexual contact with anonymous partners; they would also be wise to reduce or eliminate use of all nonmedicinal drugs. Heterosexual relationships also may pose some risk, especially if either partner uses intravenous drugs. For medical technologists who handle potentially infected laboratory specimens from AIDS patients, the Public Health Service has issued guidelines emphasizing the need for such precautions as use of gloves while handling blood samples.

## Publicity, rumor, and panic

The AIDS epidemic has generated intense coverage by the news media. But despite responsible journalistic efforts aimed at disseminating important information, the dramatic nature of the disease has stimulated a plethora of rumors and half-truths. Inevitably, certain publications have delighted in sensational speculation, of which one example will suffice: early in 1983 a popular tabloid newspaper proudly announced that AIDS was a disease of the Egyptian pharoahs, transported to the United States in 1976–79 with the traveling exhibition of artifacts from the tomb of King Tutankhamen.

**Public alarm.** As the number of reported AIDS cases has increased—and as new modes of transmission have been postulated—people who come into routine or random contact with AIDS victims have become increasingly fearful, in some cases almost to the point of hysteria. Medical and laboratory personnel, already mentioned, were one of the first groups to become concerned. Subsequently, nurses and ancillary hospital staff voiced similar anxieties. Later, when AIDS was discovered among some prison inmates, guards demanded protective clothing for themselves and isolation of AIDS patients. In some cities police requested mechanical devices to protect them from possible infection while administering mouth-to-mouth resuscitation. With increasing deaths from AIDS, mortuary personnel have demanded

36

*Traditionally festive nationwide Gay Pride parades were marked by a mood of seriousness in the summer of 1983. The banners carried by marchers in New York City (left) typify the new sense of purpose. The grim specter of AIDS is also exemplified in Chicago artist Roger Brown's painting "Peach Light" (below), inspired by the AIDS epidemic.*

government guidelines for the safe handling of victims' bodies.

Inevitably, sensational publicity has generated a flood of telephone calls to local health departments and AIDS hot lines from people worried about sharing public facilities with potential AIDS victims. Because of an unfortunate misunderstanding about the association of AIDS and blood transfusions, U.S. blood banks are reporting a drastic decline in donors, who mistakenly fear that they may get the disease by giving blood. Obviously, since only sterile, disposable needles are used in blood banks, there is absolutely no danger of disease transmission to persons donating blood. Perhaps the most tragic result of such unfounded fears, however, has been the abandonment of AIDS patients by those closest to them, their families and friends.

**Response of the gay community.** In general, the homosexual population tends to be more health conscious and better educated regarding health matters than the population at large. For good reason the AIDS epidemic has generated extreme alarm in the gay community. Many associations, such as Gay Men's Health Crisis, Inc. (GMHC), in New York City, have been formed to help AIDS patients and homosexuals at risk deal with the threat of the disease. In April 1983 the GMHC sponsored an entire performance of the Ringling Brothers' Circus to raise money for AIDS research. Special AIDS clinics have been established by gay physicians, and support groups have been formed to provide some comfort to the critically ill as well as valuable reassurance to the "worried well."

## Questions that demand answers

The central question of the AIDS enigma remains unanswered. What is its cause? Where did AIDS come from? In the past, were men who engaged in homosexual relationships at risk for AIDS? If not, why not? Can AIDS be an entirely new disease? The answers to these questions are of great importance for biology, for medicine, and for all of those at risk. At the present stage of the investigation, developments follow with such rapidity that earlier discoveries may be outdated or superseded almost before they are published. Once the elusive infectious agent is identified, most of the mystifying problems that surround the phenomenon of AIDS should be solved.

*(Opposite) Panic about the spread of AIDS has generated a wave of near hysteria among persons whose work involves contact with actual or potential AIDS victims. Prison guards (top) and police officers (center) were among the earliest to demand protective clothing and equipment. Not surprisingly, the epidemic nature of AIDS in the homosexual population has further incited antigay sentiment and demonstrations.*

# The Riddle
# of the Left Hand
## by Norman Geschwind, M.D.

Left-handedness has been found in a minority of human beings in every contemporary society in which it has been looked for. There is also evidence of left-handedness throughout recorded history in numerous written documents and in art. The Bible specifically refers to the left-handed sling throwers of the tribe of Benjamin in the army of the Israelites—a somewhat paradoxical reference, since the name Benjamin literally means "the son of the right hand." Contemporary researchers Clare Porac and Stanley Coren have calculated the number of individuals who could be identified as left-handed in ancient art, *e.g.,* in Babylonian friezes, by counting those individuals depicted holding a spear or a sword in the left hand. On the basis of these and other findings, it can be concluded that the percentage of left-handed individuals has been roughly the same throughout history—that is, between 5 and 10% of the population.

The effect of the dominant pattern of right-handedness can be perceived in the design of implements throughout history and has even been said to have influenced the design of castles. In the late Middle Ages spiral staircases were designed with a clockwise rotation so that the castle's defenders (predominantly right-handed) could stand concealed behind the central column and swing their swords with the right hand against invaders. A right-handed invader coming up the staircase would have had difficulty swinging *his* sword around the spiral.

## Censure and smirch

In most known societies the use of the left hand has been historically disapproved of to greater or lesser extents. In certain cultures the left hand is used exclusively for the purpose of cleaning after defecation and is never used for eating. Tibetan Sherpas living on the high southern slopes of the Himalayas follow this practice. With the invention of writing it was common to condemn or forbid left-handed use of the pen. In a study of left-handed patients in Austria in the 1950s, it was found that a great majority had been forced early in life to write with the right hand. Even today in many Western countries it is still not rare to find that there is coercion of young people to use

**Norman Geschwind, M.D.,** *is James Jackson Putnam Professor of Neurology at Harvard Medical School, Professor of Psychology at the Massachusetts Institute of Technology, and Director of the Neurological Unit at Beth Israel Hospital, Boston.*

*(Opposite page) Indian figure of Shiva Nataraja. Collection of the Art Institute of Chicago*

the right hand for writing, no matter what their natural tendencies may be.

Through the ages left-handers have often been thought to be devious, evil, and mentally deficient. Many of the terms used to designate the left hand have carried negative connotations, and similarly, many words with an unfavorable meaning have become secondarily linked to the use of the left hand. Obvious examples are the Latin *sinister,* connoting evil, and the French *gauche,* implying social or physical awkwardness. An unfavorable connotation is evident in the English phrase "left-handed compliment." In heraldry, a broad band running from the upper left to the lower right hand corner of a coat of arms indicates an illegitimate child. The Gaelic *cearr* (also *kerr, ker, kar,* and *car*), meaning "twisted, distorted, awkward, or perverse," also came to be applied to the use of the left hand: "carhanded." Interestingly, it has been said, though not firmly documented, that the Scottish clan of Kerr, dating from the late 12th century, has produced an unusually high proportion of left-handed individuals.

Despite overwhelming historical disapproval of left-handedness, the fact that there have always been people who favor the use of the left hand is strong indication of an underlying biological tendency toward handedness. The condemnation of an entire group of humans on the basis of hand preference has resulted in the attempted suppression of this basic biological tendency.

## Cerebral dominance

The first scientific inquiry into left-handedness (or sinistrality) probably came with the work of the 19th-century French physician Paul Broca. He devel-

*Throughout history right-handers have constituted a majority (representing some 90–95% of the population), which is quite evident in most random groups—in the eating scene pictured below, for example. In some societies the right hand has been favored for practical reasons; in Saudi Arabia, where sanitary facilities are lacking and communal meals are eaten with the hands (scooping the repast from a common bowl), the right hand is always used for taking food, the left for attending to toilet functions. To varying degrees in various cultures, left-hand use has been scorned. In some sports use of the left hand has been discouraged or actually prohibited. In Britain and many countries of the British Commonwealth, left-handed polo playing is not permitted, thus forcing left-handers like Prince Charles to play dextrally. Recently the United States Polo Association also banned left-handed play, because it is considered dangerous.*

*Many words with unfavorable meanings have been secondarily linked to the left hand. Sinister is Latin for "left"; in English "sinister" has come to mean hidden, sneaky, underhanded, and evil. The sinister character below may or may not be left-handed. In heraldry the left-handed stripe across a coat of arms (known variously as a bar sinister, bend sinister, or baton sinister) is the mark of a bastard child. The construction of many objects and instruments favors the right hand. In the movie Limelight Charlie Chaplin played a specially strung left-handed violin.*

oped the concept of cerebral dominance; *i.e.,* the greater participation of one of the two hemispheres of the brain in certain learned activities. Broca's discovery came from the investigation of individuals who were suffering from aphasia, the loss or impairment of the ability to express or comprehend language as the result of damage to the brain. Broca found that in the first group of patients studied by him, there was clinical evidence of damage to the left side of the brain, manifested as paralysis of the right side of the body. On examining the brains of these patients at autopsy, he found that the damage producing the language disorder lay in the same location in the left hemisphere. Broca concluded that many important functions—including handedness, since most humans are right-handed—were controlled by a dominant left side of the brain. The right hemisphere in most people then would be subordinate. Thus he argued that in right-handed individuals the regions necessary for the acquisition of language would lie on the brain's left side, and the reverse would be true in left-handed people.

Only since World War II have many of the early beliefs been shown to be incorrect. Thus we now know that while aphasia in right-handers is overwhelmingly the result of damage on the left side of the brain, the situation in left-handers, it turns out, is much more complicated. It has been found that in left-handers who were aphasic the damage lay on the left side in about 60% of cases and on the right side in 40%. This finding at first led to the belief that a small majority of left-handers had speech representation on the left side while the remainder had it on the right side. Subsequent studies, however, have shown that even this formulation is too simple. It now appears likely that left-handers commonly become aphasic regardless of which side is damaged. A. R. Luria examined Soviet soldiers who suffered gunshot wounds to the head in World War II and found support for the idea that left-handers recover better from aphasia than right-handers. This finding is con-

41

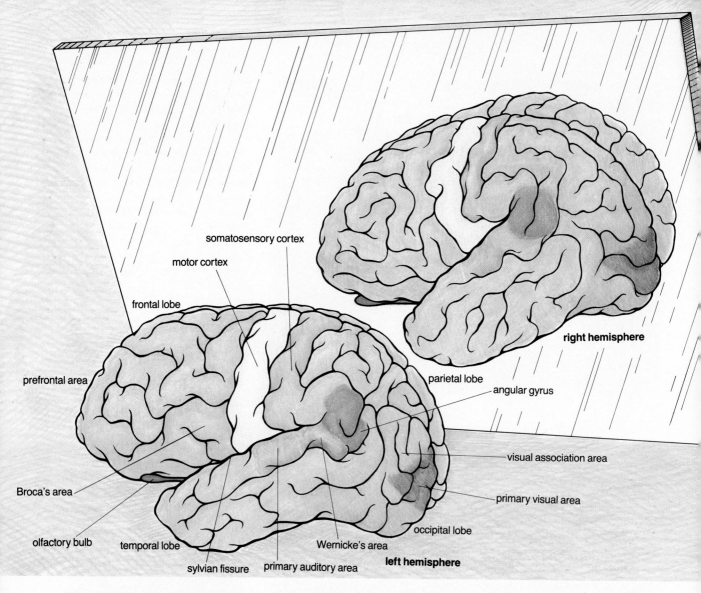

somatosensory cortex

motor cortex

frontal lobe

prefrontal area

Broca's area

olfactory bulb

temporal lobe

sylvian fissure

primary auditory area

Wernicke's area

**left hemisphere**

occipital lobe

primary visual area

visual association area

angular gyrus

parietal lobe

**right hemisphere**

*Map of the left and right hemispheres of the human brain (above) locates major structures and several regions of specialized function. While many specializations are common to both sides of the brain, others are unique to the left side in an overwhelming majority of right-handers. The latter include Broca's and Wernicke's areas, which function in the production and understanding of language; the angular gyrus also plays an important role in writing and comprehending written language. Early investigators believed that the language centers of left-handers would be found on the right hemisphere, but more recent work shows that left-handers do not have a brain organization that is the reverse of right-handers. Rather, their brains are organized according to a different plan.*

cordant with the theory that the left-hander very commonly has representation of language on both sides of the brain. In other words, the brain of the left-hander is at least in some respects more nearly symmetrical in function than is the right-hander's brain. It also appears that certain other bodily asymmetries in structure are less marked in left-handers; *e.g.,* their fingerprints are likely to be more similar on the two sides than those of right-handers. In any case, it has become clear that left-handers generally do not have a brain organization that is the reverse of that of right-handers, but rather their brains are organized in a different fashion.

It was also widely presumed until very recently that cerebral dominance was a property only of the human and not of other animals—a belief reinforced by the repeated finding that there appeared to be no predominant "handedness" in animal populations. Thus, in species as diverse as rats and monkeys about 50% of the animals were found to use the right hand, or paw, preferentially in an obligatory single-handed task. Furthermore, as researcher R. L. Collins, working at the Jackson Laboratories in Bar Harbor, Maine, showed, even if one selectively bred mice that used the right paw for many generations, the offspring were still evenly distributed in paw preference.

Several recent studies have contradicted this view. Fernando Nottebohm of the Rockefeller University has shown left-hemisphere dominance for bird song, and Victor Denenberg and co-workers at the University of Connecticut have shown right-hemisphere dominance for some spatial and emotional functions in the male rat. Even though no one has yet demonstrated a predominant preference for one hand in any animal species, there appears to be a predominance of certain motor activities to one side. Stanley Glick of the Mount Sinai School of Medicine in New York City has found that on injection of amphetamines a rat will typically run in circles to one side. In one of the strains he studied, a small excess of females showed a preference for turning to the right, although the males were more evenly distributed in their preference. The exact relationshp of this apparently sex-related finding in animals to human handedness remains to be determined.

## What determines handedness?

One of the major problems in any research on hand preference is that of establishing good criteria for right- or left-handedness. It is often assumed that the hand with which an individual writes is sufficient to designate him as a right- or a left-hander. The inadequacy of this criterion is, however, evident, as certain individuals will write with the right hand but will favor the left hand in many other activities. Therefore, it has been necessary to devise tests for handedness. The most common test is one in which the individual simply indicates the preferred hand for each item of a list of activities. On the basis of these responses one can calculate a "laterality quotient." Thus, in the widely used test devised by the late Carolus Oldfield of the University of Edinburgh, a score greater than zero indicates preferential use of the right hand, while a score less than zero indicates preferential use of the left hand. Even these tests, however, do not completely resolve the issue of criteria. Oldfield himself argued that anyone who carried out more than a minimal number of activities with the left hand should be designated as non-right-handed. It is likely that more sophisticated batteries of tests will be developed in the near future, and more meaningful methods of scoring will result from the application of knowledge gained in studies of anatomy and function.

Just as most people use the right hand preferentially for most activities, the great majority also use the right leg for such activities as kicking a ball or stamping out a burning object. In general, hand and foot preference go together, but there are exceptions, so that some people are, for example, right-handed but left-footed. Some research is now being carried on that may eventually help to clarify the reasons for these discrepancies.

There have been many theories concerning the cause of left-handedness in an individual, but as yet none has emerged as definitive. It is sometimes argued that hand preference is simply the result of childhood experience since left-handed parents will have more left-handed children than right-handed parents. Yet the majority of left-handers have two right-handed parents.

Other theories try to relate left-handedness to brain structure. One such theory argues that some left-handers are so-called pathological left-handers who have suffered brain damage at birth. Since damage to the brain at birth will occur on the right side in about half of all cases, and since most individ-

*Scientist and statesman Benjamin Franklin became an ombudsman for left-handers. He pleaded with Americans to abandon their prejudices and exhibit compassion and rational understanding for this minority. Franklin, a right-hander, trained himself to use both hands; he signed the Declaration of Independence and the Constitution with his left hand.*

uals are future right-handers, these victims will remain right-handers. In the other half of cases the damage will be on the left. This will lead in many cases to preferential use of the right hemisphere and, therefore, to left-handedness. There is little doubt that this theory is correct in some cases, but the major problem is that of determining what proportion of left-handedness in a population it accounts for. Furthermore, it assumes that brain damage at birth alters some predominant innate tendency to right-handedness, which itself remains unexplained. Marian Annett of Lanchester Polytechnic in Coventry, England, has argued that while such events may account for some cases of left-handedness, they cannot possibly account for the majority, and her view appears to be gaining many adherents in the scientific community.

Another set of theories argues that most handedness is genetically determined. At the first glance this notion is supported by the fact that left-handedness does appear to run in families. Nonetheless, at least in the opinion of many investigators, the data have not fitted adequately with simple Mendelian theory. The finding in many studies that there is an increase of left-handedness among twins of both types, identical and fraternal, is perplexing. Since there is a higher rate of difficulties in delivery of twins, it has often been assumed that the increase in left-handedness is simply the result of birth injury. This explanation might account for some of the cases of left-handedness among twins but not all cases. Many years ago it was shown that there is also an increased rate of left-handedness among the relatives of twins. More recently, Charles Boklage of the East Carolina University School of Medicine has shown that the rate of left-handedness in the parents of twins, both fathers and mothers, is much higher than that found in the general population.

Another curious finding is the distribution of left-handedness in identical twins. Since these individuals are genetically the same, one would expect that every pair would be either both left-handed or both right-handed. In-

*Though left-handers have been excluded from some athletic activities, southpaws and other sinistrals have risen to the top in many competitive sports. Martina Navratilova (below) is one of many left-handed tennis champions on the scene today. Some have surmised that the spin on the ball in tennis affords left-handers an advantage. The Brazilian soccer star Pelé (below, right) is left-footed. Usually, but not always, people who have a dominant right (or left) hand will exhibit the same dominance in a foot.*

(Left) John Russell; (right) Bruce Curtis—Peter Arnold, Inc.

stead one finds that in roughly 80% of cases both are right-handed, while in about 4% both are left-handed and in the remaining 16% they are of opposite handedness. The explanation that the latter are so-called mirror-image twins is also difficult to support, as one does not find in the overwhelming majority of these discordant pairs that the left-handed twin also has a reversal of the position of the heart, the liver, and other internal organs.

Marian Annett has advanced an extremely important concept—that of random dominance. According to this theory, there is a gene that tends to produce left-hemisphere dominance for both language and handedness. She argues that in the absence of this gene the individual's language and handedness are essentially random; *i.e.,* such an individual might have language representation on either side and the control of handedness on either side. Even if one does not accept Annett's exact genetic explanation, it is extremely likely that there is a group of individuals who do have random, or anomalous, dominance. One would, therefore, expect that roughly half of these individuals would be left-handed and half right-handed; further, there is a suggestion here that left-handers should not be viewed as a completely distinctive group. Instead one must consider the larger population of those with anomalous dominance. Annett's theory would imply that the size of the irregular dominance group is roughly twice as large as the number of left-handers; others have surmised that the anomalous dominance group constitutes about 30% of all individuals, of whom roughly one-third will be left-handed.

## Recent progress in solving the riddle

Another approach to understanding the curious nature of left-handedness, and, more broadly, to understanding anomalous dominance, involves biological associations. It has already been noted that left-handers appear to be

45

more nearly symmetrical in certain bodily features such as fingerprints. The higher rate of recovery from focal brain damage leading to aphasia is suggestive that language representation is also more bilateral. Further, in tests of manual skill left-handers on the whole show less difference between the two hands than do right-handers. Another important fact is that most studies have shown that males are more likely to be left-handed than females; *e.g.,* Oldfield in Edinburgh found 6% of the women and 10% of the men he studied were left-handed.

The associations of left-handedness with certain functional impairments provide another potentially important set of data. There is a striking association of left-handedness with the developmental disorders of intellect or emotion in children, sometimes referred to as the developmental learning disorders. Usually included among these conditions are developmental dyslexia, stuttering, hyperactivity, and autism. At the present time all the known conditions of this type appear to have certain properties in common. In the first place, they are much more common in boys than in girls. Secondly, dating from important observations of Samuel Torrey Orton in the 1920s, it has been recognized that there is a marked increase of left-handedness among these individuals with developmental learning disorders, as well as among their unaffected relatives.

The associations to left-handedness, however, go beyond those conditions in which there is some alteration in brain function. There have been many studies demonstrating an elevated frequency of left-handedness in groups with certain disorders. The frequency of left-handedness in children with harelip was found by French investigators in 1944 to be 20%, against 8% in a control population. Similar elevations of left-handedness have also been described in cases of strabismus (the condition of being cross-eyed or wall-eyed) and in certain congenital disorders of the skeleton. But in the absence of a proper theoretical framework into which to fit these findings, until recently they have been generally neglected.

There are additional findings that point to an even wider set of associations of left-handedness with disease. In 1980 I observed that there appeared to be a higher than normal frequency of migraine headaches and certain immune disorders in left-handed individuals and in their families.

It is well known that the body's immune system is extremely important in combating infection. Sometimes, however, the system goes amiss. Thus this elaborately designed set of mechanisms may sometimes marshal the body's defenses in an inappropriate attack on noninfective substances such as ragweed pollen or cat hair. This misguided response leads to allergies such as asthma, eczema, or hay fever. In other cases the immune system may launch an attack on components of the individual's own body. This type of inappropriate response leads to conditions called autoimmune disorders, including lupus erythematosus, myasthenia gravis, ulcerative colitis, regional ileitis (Crohn's disease), rheumatoid arthritis, and various disorders of the thyroid gland. To test these observations of clinical disorders in a controlled manner, Peter Behan of the University of Glasgow and I studied more than 3,000 strongly left-handed and strongly right-handed individuals. We found that immune disorders were two and a half times more frequent in the

*(Opposite page, top left and right) Left-handedness has been associated with the complex learning disorder dyslexia. Dyslexics must work very hard to overcome language and visual-perceptual problems as well as resulting problems of self-esteem. There is wide disagreement about the cause of dyslexia; a considerable amount of research is under way to better understand the precise involvement of the brain as well as the significance of the association with left-handedness. Recent investigations have also found a higher than normal incidence of migraine headaches and certain immune disorders among left-handers. The table on the opposite page compares the incidence of immune and learning disorders in strongly left-handed and strongly right-handed individuals. Several studies have produced similar, statistically significant results.*

46

Photographs, Ira Wyman

strongly left-handed individuals than in the right-handers and were also more frequent in the relatives of the left-handers.

Throughout the history of biology and psychology, important advances have resulted from the specification of the structural basis of some particular function. A familiar example is the discovery of the pigments in the cones of the retina, which led to a deeper understanding of color vision. Some investigators had suggested that the brain was structurally different on the two sides and that this accounted for cerebral dominance, but these views were generally rejected. In 1968, however, Walter Levitsky and I showed that there is a region in the left hemisphere that is larger than the corresponding region on the opposite side. This area is known as the planum temporale and makes up a major portion of the language area of Wernicke, which has long been recognized as one of the major speech zones. It is larger on the left in about 65% of individuals, larger on the right in 11%, and roughly equal in size in 24%. The asymmetry can readily be seen with the naked eye. Working with microscopes, Albert Galaburda of Harvard University and Friederich Sanides of Konstanz, West Germany, have also mapped this brain region on both the right and left sides, permitting more precise specification of their exact sizes. The left-sided region may be as much as ten times greater in size than the corresponding region on the right. In the few cases when the right side is larger, it rarely exceeds the left by more than twofold. These data may provide structural evidence for the concept of random dominance. In the majority of people the left side is distinctly larger and often dramatically so. In the remainder one finds either more nearly equal areas or a slightly larger right side. It is conceivable that this structural symmetry is the basis for the random dominance in a minority of the population, as Annett postulated.

In the late 1970s Galaburda in collaboration with Thomas Kemper of the Boston University School of Medicine studied the brain of a childhood dyslexic who had been killed in an accident. They found that in the region of the

**Disorders associated with left-handedness**

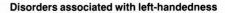

| | 253 left-handers | 253 right-handers | ratio |
|---|---|---|---|
| immune disorder | 10.7% | 4% | 2.8/1 |
| learning disorder | 9.5% | 0.8% | 12/1 |

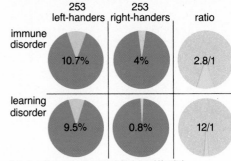

Data from Dr. Norman Geschwind, Beth Israel Hospital, Boston

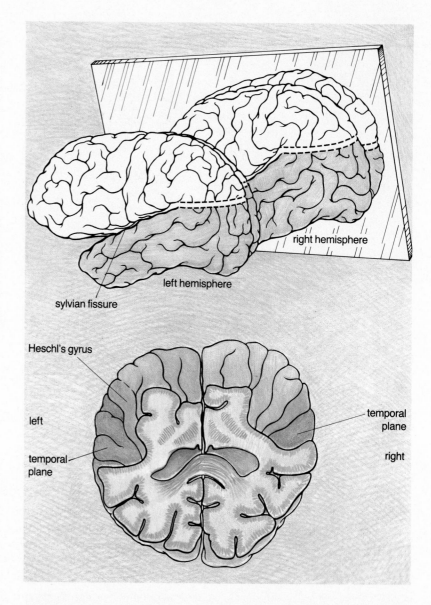

left hemisphere

right hemisphere

sylvian fissure

Heschl's gyrus

left

temporal plane

temporal plane

right

*By removing that part of each hemisphere that lies above the sylvian fissure and above the dotted line (top), one can view the upper surface of the temporal lobes (bottom). On that surface lies Heschl's gyrus, the brain center for hearing. Behind it lies the temporal plane, or planum temporale, which makes up a major part of Wernicke's area, a major speech center. The temporal plane is larger on the left (up to ten times larger) in 65% of the general population; in 11% the temporal plane on the right is larger; in the rest the two structures are about equal in size.*

left planum temporale the pattern of organization of the nerve cells was distinctly abnormal; on the right side no such anomalies were found. These findings have been confirmed in other cases. It thus appears that many cases of dyslexia—a disturbance of the ability to read—may be the result of disturbed development of the normally larger left-sided language region.

Examination of the brains of fetuses provides further information. Even at very early stages in development, one finds the same pattern of asymmetries; *e.g.,* the planum temporale is larger on the left side. On the other hand, the right hemisphere is found to be developing more rapidly than the left. The basic pattern of the human brain is therefore one in which certain regions on the left side are larger. During the course of development in the uterus, there is, however, some influence that tends to slow growth on the left, although in most cases the left-sided regions remain distinctly larger. In some cases, however, the growth on the left is slowed enough so that the two sides of the brain become more nearly symmetrical, or there is even some small advantage for the right side. Recent experimental data in animals support the view that if the development of one part of the brain is impaired, the corresponding region on the opposite side may increase in extent. Thus, the delay in growth of the left hemisphere can lead to compensatory increased development on the right. When the delay of brain growth on the left side is of such magnitude that the developed cortical regions on the two sides are similar in size, there is an increased likelihood of random dominance and, therefore, left-handedness. Moreover, in those cases in which the delay of growth on the left is excessive, there may be an actual disturbance in the formation of the structures of the cortex on the left. In such cases developmental learning disorders such as dyslexia may be produced.

It is obviously necessary to explain why left-handedness is more frequent in males and why the developmental learning disorders are so strikingly male-predominant. It appears likely the factor that tends to delay growth on the left is more often associated with male fetuses than with female fetuses. One speculation is that the male hormone testosterone, which is produced in large quantities by the fetal testes, is often responsible for left-handedness.

Both the male and the female fetus are exposed to some testosterone produced by the mother and the placenta. The female fetus produces very little of this hormone. The production by the male fetus of very large additional amounts of testosterone is known to be essential for the processes that lead to many of the anatomical and structural differences that distinguish males from females.

Any adequate theory of left-handedness and, more generally, of cerebral dominance must also account for their associations with clinical disorders. Possible reasons for the high rate of left-handedness in dyslexia have already been pointed out. The association between left-handedness and immune disorders may also be related to the male hormone testosterone. It has been shown in many experiments that testosterone retards the develop-

*Throughout history a great many of the world's most accomplished artists have been left-handed or ambidextrous. Michelangelo is said to have switched hands frequently to avoid fatigue as he painted his masterpiece on the ceiling of the Sistine Chapel. In this great work Adam extends his left arm to receive the gift of life from God's right arm.*

"The Creation of Adam" by Michelangelo, detail of the ceiling fresco in the Sistine Chapel, Vatican; photograph, Scala/Art Resource

*Leonardo da Vinci has been called the "patron saint of the sinistrals." According to the art historian H. W. Janson, Leonardo "took advantage of his lefthandedness to help along his secretiveness. He wrote in mirror script, which is very easy for a lefthander to do." Neurologist Norman Capener, writing in the medical journal* The Lancet *in 1952 (the 500th anniversary of Leonardo's birth), said: "I am not at all sure that he was properly a left-handed person . . . he was not clearly a right-cerebral-hemisphere-dominant individual. . . ." Capener points out that there is some evidence that the middle finger of Leonardo's right hand may have been crippled by an injury, thus forcing him to use the left. "I believe that for the more dynamic drawing of shape and structure Leonardo probably used his right hand, but for the contemplative aspects of shading and writing he used the left hand," Capener wrote.*

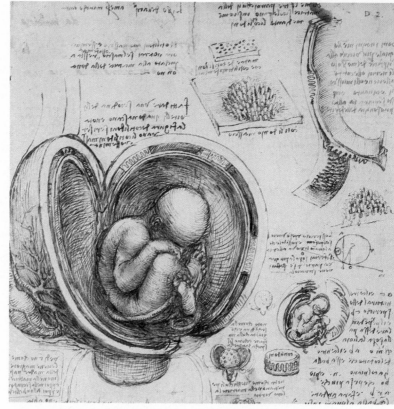

ment of the thymus gland. The thymus is one of the main structures of the immune system. This gland has the major function of processing a certain group of white cells known as lymphocytes for their important immunologic functions. In the course of fetal development there may then be some influence related to the male sex factor that delays the growth of the brain's left hemisphere, thus increasing the frequency of left-handedness. This same factor (which is very likely to be testosterone) also affects the development of the immune system, possibly setting the stage for the later development of immune disorders.

## Are left-handers a disadvantaged group?

The biological study of left-handedness is still in its early stages. Many more experiments must be carried out. The conclusion that there is an elevated frequency of learning disorders and certain diseases in the left-handed population should not be used to support the many historical prejudices concerning sinistrality. Although left-handers are at increased risk for learning disabilities, left-handedness is also found at higher than normal rates among extremely talented individuals in many fields, such as the arts, athletics, architecture, and engineering. Leonardo da Vinci was strongly left-handed; it has been claimed that this was also true of Michelangelo and Picasso; Harpo Marx and Paul McCartney are both well-known left-handed musicians; in baseball the legendary Babe Ruth is among many noted "southpaws"; on the tennis scene today Martina Navratilova, John McEnroe, Jimmy Connors, and Guillermo Vilas are all lefties.

Furthermore, although certain diseases and disorders appear to be more frequent among sinistrals, there is reason to suspect, although firm data are not yet available, that this group is also less susceptible, on the average, than right-handers to many other diseases. One possibility, which needs to be studied experimentally, is that the left-handed population may be less susceptible to certain infections and to many types of cancer.

Left-handedness, and more broadly, random or anomalous dominance, thus *cannot* be regarded as disadvantages. Rather these characteristics are only manifestations of the tremendous biological diversity of humanity. Human survival, moreover, is favored by the allocation of a diversity of talents as well as disabilities among many different individuals in the population.

## The future of research

Only a few years ago the failure to find left-handedness in animals was the foundation for the general belief that handedness, and more generally cerebral dominance, could be studied only in the human. With the increased specification of the biological foundations and associations of handedness and dominance, it is now becoming possible to carry out animal experimentation on a broad scale. It is likely that, as in other branches of biology and medicine, the availability of animal models will accelerate the progress of research into the nature of left- and right-handedness in humans. It is evident that there are many mechanisms producing anatomical asymmetry in animals; several of these may prove to be relevant to the human condition.

A deeper understanding should lead to refinement of our concepts concerning the special capacities of the human mind. It should also eventually favor the discovery of methods of prevention or treatment of the occasional unfavorable accompaniments of anomalous dominance.

FOR ADDITIONAL READING:

Annett, Marian. "The Genetics of Handedness." *Trends in NeuroSciences,* October 1981, pp. 256–258.

Denenberg, V. A. "Hemispheric Laterality in Animals and the Effects of Early Experience." *Behavioral & Brain Sciences* 4 (1981): 1–49.

Galaburda, A. M.; Kemper, T. L.; LeMay, M.; and Geschwind, N. "Right-Left Asymmetries in the Brain." *Science* 199 (1978): 852–856.

Geschwind, N., and Behan, P. "Left-Handedness: Association with Immune Disease, Migraine, and Developmental Learning Disorder." *Proceedings of the National Academy of Sciences* 79 (1982): 5097–5100.

Herron, J., ed. *Neuropsychology of Left-Handedness.* New York: Academic Press, 1980.

Nottebohm, F. "A Brain for All Seasons." *Science* 214 (1981): 1368–1370.

Porac, C., and Coren, S. *Lateral Preferences and Human Behavior.* New York: Springer, 1981.

*Most crabs and lobsters have one claw that is somewhat larger than the other. The male fiddler crab (below) has one disproportionately large claw. If the crab loses the large claw, the smaller claw grows to the size of the former large claw, while a small one grows to replace the lost claw. Until recently it was presumed that cerebral dominance affected only humans. But scientists are now finding many mechanisms producing anatomical and behavioral asymmetries in the animal world as well. Thus it is becoming possible to find animal models and to carry out experiments in animals that may provide important clues to human handedness.*

E. R. Degginger, Bruce Coleman, Inc.

51

# An Enlightened View of Female Destiny

## by Elizabeth B. Connell, M.D.

Whether one views human development as an evolutionary process or as an isolated biblical event, the conclusion is inevitably reached that there are two basic types of *Homo sapiens*—males and females. The distinction is quite clear as regards basic biologic functions; less clear is the nature of the interaction between an individual's genetic endowment and cultural environment in the determination of behavior patterns. Attempts to evaluate the relative importance of these two factors have led to a wide diversity of opinion, ranging all the way from the notion that a person's destiny is determined at the time of conception to the position that the primary determinants of human behavior are sociocultural in origin. As is usually the case where such a diversity of opinion is observed, the truth probably lies somewhere in between, the specific impact of the two components perhaps varying in the case of any particular individual. While considerable information relevant to this subject has been gathered on both sexes, here the focus is primarily on the female of the species, attempting to put into perspective the data on both the biologic and environmental factors that may influence her physical and social development.

Except in very rare instances, the gender of an individual is clearly established as either male or female at the moment that the genetic material from a sperm is functionally joined with similar material inside an ovum. Thus, barring the superimposition of some adverse factor such as infection, trauma, or a fetotoxic substance, a person's basic design—the chromosomal pattern, intelligence, and ultimate bodily dimensions—are all determined at the time of conception.

## Genetic endowment

In order to appreciate the biologic contribution to what we perceive as femininity, it might be well to review briefly the overall structure and function of a female's body, with special emphasis on her reproductive system. Because much of the early work on chromosomal patterns was carried out in institutions for the mentally retarded, it was believed for many years that each human being had 48 chromosomes. The discovery that most people

Elizabeth B. Connell, M.D., *is Professor of Gynecology and Obstetrics at Emory University School of Medicine, Atlanta, Georgia.*

*(Opposite) "Girl Before a Mirror" by Pablo Picasso, 1932, oil on canvas, 64 × 51¼ inches. Collection, The Museum of Modern Art, New York, gift of Mrs. Simon Guggenheim*

*A biblical view of human development
holds that men and women are
descendants of the original couple. Man's
role on this earth is to suffer and toil for a
living and to provide for woman (Adam's
curse), while women are companions to
men—here to fulfill the curse of Eve: "In
pain shall you bring children forth."*

have only 46 of these carriers of genetic material is thus a relatively recent event in medical history.

Every normal individual has two sex chromosomes, either XX in the case of a female or XY in the case of a male. The gender of an offspring is determined at the time of fertilization; an X chromosome is contributed by the mother and either an X or a Y by the father. Therefore, the genetic material in the sperm that penetrates the egg is the deciding factor as to what sex the resulting embryo will be. Inasmuch as this fact has been scientifically well documented, it is interesting to observe that there are still men who divest themselves of wives who produce only daughters.

Numerous studies have been carried out attempting to clarify not only the functional differences between males and females but also the role of the chromosomes in determining these differences. While much of the research has been conducted in apparently normal individuals, a considerable body of information has now been collected on genetically abnormal subjects. This group includes individuals with an XXY (47) chromosomal pattern known as Klinefelter's syndrome, in which the person appears to be a male with small genitalia and increased height but is genetically a female and may have somewhat enlarged breasts. This syndrome is commonly recognized only in adulthood when sterility is apparent. Others in the genetically abnormal group have Turner's syndrome (gonadal dysgenesis), characterized by a single X chromosome and complete or partial absence of the second sex chromosome (XO). These individuals can be identified at birth and are brought up as girls; they usually have small female genitalia, scanty pubic hair, atrophic ovaries, as well as webbed necks and turned-out elbows.

It has been found that the presence of one Y chromosome will result in the production of a testis, even though in some instances it may be abnormal in either structure or function. This is true even when there are as many as three extra X chromosomes; in general, the greater the number of X's, the greater will be the degree of abnormality that results.

Scientists are now learning that, in addition to determining the sex (or apparent sex) of an individual, the sex chromosomes also play a role in the maintenance of health. It has been known for a number of years that females, while physically less strong than males, are biologically superior starting at the moment of fertilization. This may account for the fact that approximately 120 males are conceived for every 100 females. The advantage dwindles to 105:100 even before birth; a disproportionate number of boy babies are miscarried or die before they are born. This same pattern continues into the immediate postpartum period, with male mortality being consistently higher than female mortality.

During infancy and childhood, boys not only are more apt to develop bacterial and viral infections and acute childhood leukemia but also tend to have more serious illnesses and higher death rates. The end result of this accumulated differential in mortality is a most interesting one: boys and girls reach reproductive age in approximately equal numbers, almost as if by design.

Only quite recently has there been a scientific explanation for some of these observed facts. It is now known that the genes that provide immuno-

54

(Left) Burt Glinn—Magnum; (top right) Jim Pozarik—Gamma/Liaison; (bottom right) John Coletti—Stock, Boston

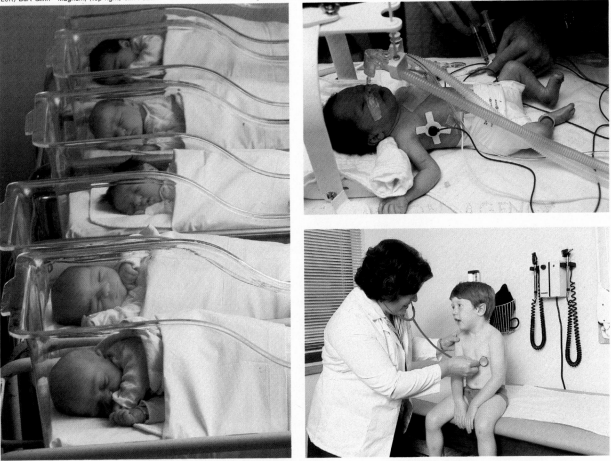

logic protection against disease are located on the X chromosome. There-fore, females, with an XX pattern, have twice the protection that males with their XY pattern are afforded. Later in life, however, this immunologic superi-ority can, on occasion, prove to be damaging; more women than men devel-op autoimmune diseases in which an excess of antibodies attack normal body tissues. These diseases include systemic lupus erythematosus, myas-thenia gravis, and certain thyroid disorders.

Once the genetic sexual pattern has been established, a series of events begins that will eventuate in the formation of either a male or a female. Of pri-mary importance among these events is the differentiation and growth of the gonads, either ovaries or testes. These organs, contrary to what was once believed, are actually functioning at birth; the sex hormone levels in male ba-bies are similiar to those found in 13- to 14-year-old boys. The part of the brain that controls reproduction then suppresses this activity until the time of puberty. Once this block has been removed, the long process of sexual mat-uration begins, resulting in the development of secondary sexual character-istics and, ultimately, in fertility.

In the case of the female of the species, the stages of adolescence, then puberty and menarche (the start of menstruation), and finally full woman-hood are predictable and sequential. The first observable change is noted in

*Approximately 120 males are conceived for every 100 females, but by the time of birth the sex ratio is only 105 to 100, owing to high rates of spontaneous abortion of male fetuses and high male death rates shortly after birth. At every age males are more susceptible to disease and have higher mortality. Boys get more respiratory infections, viral infections of the central nervous system, gastrointestinal diseases, bacterial infections, and leukemia than do girls. Adult males experience more hepatitis, slow viral infections, cancer, heart disease, and alcoholism than do adult women. Women outlive men by an average of eight years. Recent studies have found that women have stronger immune systems and that there are genetic explanations for the long-observed health superiority of females.*

Adapted from A. R. Behnke and J. H. Wilmore, *Evaluation and Regulation of Body Build and Composition*, Englewood Cliffs, N.J., Prentice-Hall, 1974

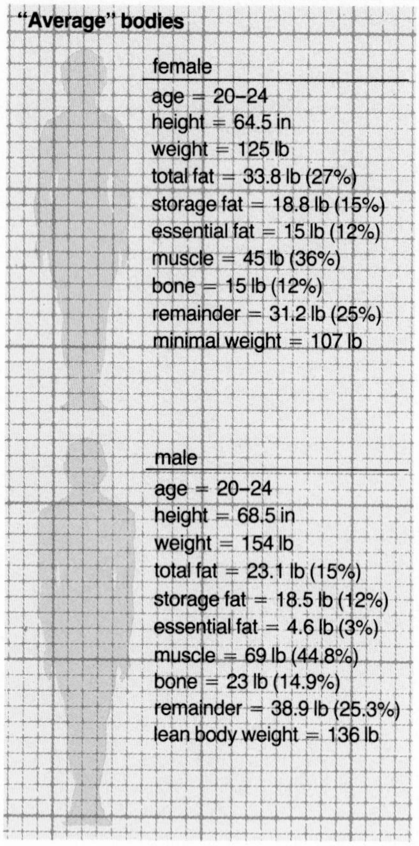

**"Average" bodies**

female
age = 20–24
height = 64.5 in
weight = 125 lb
total fat = 33.8 lb (27%)
storage fat = 18.8 lb (15%)
essential fat = 15 lb (12%)
muscle = 45 lb (36%)
bone = 15 lb (12%)
remainder = 31.2 lb (25%)
minimal weight = 107 lb

male
age = 20–24
height = 68.5 in
weight = 154 lb
total fat = 23.1 lb (15%)
storage fat = 18.5 lb (12%)
essential fat = 4.6 lb (3%)
muscle = 69 lb (44.8%)
bone = 23 lb (14.9%)
remainder = 38.9 lb (25.3%)
lean body weight = 136 lb

*The "reference" man and woman in the diagram above are based on averages compiled by physiology experts from detailed measurements of thousands of men and women in the United States. The woman's shorter height means she has less total muscle mass; thus the man has an advantage in being able to lift heavier weights and to exert greater physical force. This advantage comes into play in certain athletic activities, especially contact sports. A woman has greater muscle endurance and flexibility. She has an advantage in accelerating her body, realized in long-distance running and swimming. Her lower center of gravity helps her maintain balance—an advantage realized in ballet, gymnastics, and skiing.*

*The most significant compositional difference is in body fat. Women have an average of 27% total body fat to a man's 15%.*

the breasts; between the ages of 8 and 13 the young girl's nipples start to enlarge, and a few months later the breast tissue begins to grow. A few pubic hairs can be seen, and she enters into a period of rapid growth. The ovaries are now producing estrogen, causing fat deposits to develop on the hips and thighs, and the slim, angular girl moves steadily toward a more rounded female bodily contour. Meanwhile, her adrenal glands are manufacturing male sex hormones; these play a key role in the development of pubic and underarm hair and make a major contribution to her growth spurt. Unfortunately, these male hormones often stimulate the development of acne, but as the hormonal levels drop toward the end of puberty, acne will tend to improve.

Many view the first menstrual period as the key event in a girl's sexual development. In fact, though, it is the final event, usually occurring between the ages of 10 and 16, two or more years after the entire process is under way. Estrogen causes the girl's reproductive tract to mature, and eventually the thickened lining of her uterus will break down and menarche will occur. During the next year or two, her menses are apt to be irregular; her normal cyclic hormonal pattern has not yet been established, and ovulation is infrequent. Soon after this, however, her menstruation and ovulation cycles will become more regular. Boys, on the other hand, are almost immediately and constantly fertile after puberty.

## Female bodies, male bodies

It has been well established that males, in general, are larger and physically stronger than females. In addition, both sexes have gained in height over the centuries; one has only to watch a group of present-day tourists stooping to get through the doorways of ancient buildings to realize how much taller the human race has become. While improved nutrition and health are cited as major reasons for this change, it has also been pointed out that larger males have been traditionally considered more sexually attractive than their smaller peers and therefore may have fathered a disproportionate number of offspring, leading to progressively larger individuals.

As might be expected, as overall body dimensions increased, so did the size of the various organs. Since men are generally bigger than women, their hearts, lungs, and kidneys are also comparatively larger. It is, therefore, of interest that in the current heredity-versus-environment debate much has been made of the observation that the male brain tends to be bigger than that of the female, which is exactly what would be anticipated. In point of fact, studies have shown conclusively that there is no relationship between intelligence and brain size in essentially normal individuals.

In addition to being basically bigger, men's skeletal and muscular systems tend to be relatively heavier in proportion to their body size. It has been proposed that this is the reason that men have traditionally done the work requiring greater physical strength—fighting, hunting, fishing, farming, and home building. On the other hand, women, with smaller, less powerful bodies, were usually delegated the somewhat less strenuous household activities. Our female ancestors were either pregnant or lactating during most of their adult lives; therefore, the role of homemaker was consistently reinforced by the perpetual need for the provision of child care.

56

While both males and females enter their reproductive years in a somewhat similar fashion, the other end of this era is markedly different. A man's sexual prowess tends to diminish gradually as he grows older, but fertility is usually preserved as long as he lives. Women, on the other hand, must face the fact, either happily or reluctantly, that there will be an end to their childbearing potential. Once the menopause (the cessation of menstruation) is past, the ovaries produce progressively smaller amounts of estrogen. In some women this occurs rather abruptly; in others, over a period of several years. As the estrogen levels decline, all of the signs and symptoms of aging start to appear—regression of the reproductive tract, changes in the skin and bodily configuration, and the gradual demineralization of bone. The final era of a woman's life thus is entered, bringing with it yet another heredity-versus-environment controversy.

Even in death the sexes display markedly different patterns. Men once again demonstrate their basic biologic inferiority by dying at an earlier age, in general, than do women. There is an opposing explanation, however, often presented by the environmentalists, who say that women survive longer than men not because of their genetic endowment but because of their less demanding life-styles.

## The powerful hormones

While there is clear agreement about the role of sex hormones in the growth and development process and about the part they play in human reproduction, there is considerable disagreement as to what other functions they may have. Some investigators believe that they act directly on the brain, inducing so-called feminine and masculine types of behavior; for example, they hold that this is the explanation for the fact that women seem to excel at intuitive thinking whereas men are superior at problem solving.

In support of their position are numerous animal studies showing the induction of "male" traits in females by the administration of male sex hormones. Similarly, tomboyish behavior has been noted in girls who were exposed to abnormally high levels of these hormones, either before or after birth. Even in this situation the social scientists argue that, since they do not appear physically to be normal girls, they are not treated as such, and this is

*There are undeniable physical differences between males and females. But to what extent do these differences shape destinies? Since men are generally larger and stronger, they have traditionally done work requiring great physical strength— fishing, hunting, farming, building houses. Women, with their smaller, weaker frames, usually took on less strenuous household activities. Moreover, without birth control, females in the past often spent most of their reproductive lives pregnant, lactating, or raising children.*

57

(Top) Owen Franken—Stock, Boston; (bottom) Cary
Wolinsky—Stock, Boston

*Behavioral scientists attribute so-called
masculine and feminine behaviors to social
and cultural influences. Rough-and-tumble
play is considered acceptable for growing
boys; for girls, however, it has been
thought more proper to suppress
"aggression" and to develop "nurturing"
behavior. But now there is a growing body
of scientific evidence indicating that sex
hormones and other biologic determinants
also play a considerable role in the
development of early behavior patterns.*

the real reason for their "masculine" behavior patterns.

More recently, studies on brain structure and function in a wide variety of
animals have led to the conclusion that major differences exist between the
brains of the two sexes. Neuroendocrinologists have ascribed the way dogs
urinate and the fact that male canaries sing and female canaries do not to
the influence of sex hormones on specific and identifiable areas of the brain.
However, similar discrepancies have not been identified in humans and,
therefore, there is a danger in extrapolating from animal models to human
behavior.

Once a baby has been born and has been given a sexual identity by society, a continuous stream of impulses is sent out reinforcing the assumed
gender. It has been clearly documented that girl babies are not only dressed
differently but are handled and talked to differently from boy babies. As they
grow older, particularly in traditional societies, it is usually made clear to
them that only certain types of behavior are acceptable and appropriate.
They are given dolls but not trucks to play with; physical aggression is viewed
as unladylike; intellectual achievement is not expected and in some instances is not even desirable; and in most cultures their future roles are
delineated both overtly and covertly, leaving little opportunity for significant
deviations from the anticipated norm.

The events of puberty merely serve to reinforce society's perception of the
female role: a girl's body becomes shapely and sexually attractive; she has
new patches of hair under her arms and over her pubis; and her reproductive
tract has been freed to function—as witnessed by that ultimate in events, her
first menstrual period. She now enters an era in which the nature-nurture
conflict is most violent. When she experiences moodiness and premenstrual
tension, is it because she is helplessly under the influence of what U.S. physician Edgar Berman, serving on a committee on national priorities of the
Democratic Party in 1970, notoriously termed "raging hormones" or because she has received the cultural message that these emotional upheav-
als are bound to occur? When she develops menstrual cramps, is it because
of abnormal amounts of prostaglandins or because her mother has taught
her to expect them? When she is menstruating, does she perceive this as a
normal physiologic event or as an unattractive and disgusting episode that
must be hidden from a generally disapproving society?

Clear, scientifically documented answers to these and numerous similar
questions are hard to find. Some women do seem to be responsive to
hormonal variations, but men, who do not have these cyclic changes, also
have recurrent episodes of moodiness, depression, and anxiety. While excessive uterine contractions that produce cramps can now be measured,
social scientists have carried out a number of fascinating studies showing a
clear relationship between the severity of cramping and the events in a woman's life. Even though a girl is taught that having menstrual periods is entirely
normal, she is still the product of a cultural heritage that has known "menstrual huts"—dwellings to which women are banished at the time of their
periods because they are considered impure and possessed by evil spirits—
and centuries of multilingual verbiage related to this event, almost all of
which is derogatory ("unclean," "polluted," "possessed," and so forth).

58

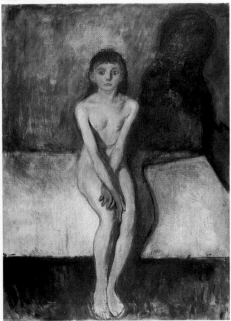

A girl's academic course and career decisions are also fraught with problems. While no one today gives credence to the Victorian edict that women who made excessive use of their brains would divert blood from their sexual organs and impair their fertility, there are still widespread beliefs that there are many areas in our male-dominated culture that women cannot and should not attempt to invade. There have been numerous critiques of male-female studies of basic intelligence, women's desires and abilities to achieve, and their career potentials; these studies, however, frequently exhibit marked sexual stereotyping and have rather remarkable and obvious built-in biases.

## Is biology destiny?

Some of the most difficult decisions women have to make today relate to the choice between traditional roles and the life-styles that are now becoming available to them partially as a result of the women's movement. Although the heredity-environment battle continues unabated, more credence is gradually being given to the evidence that women are quite capable, both physically and mentally, of moving into areas once the private domain of men. Attempts to do this, particularly if successful, place women in a position of great ambivalence; how can they balance the demands of a career and the desire for marriage and children? The truth of the matter is that it is impossible to be a Superwoman and to do both simultaneously without paying the price of being less than entirely satisfied with one's performance in either role. Planning to have fewer children and having them nearer to the end of their reproductive lives help women to solve certain career conflicts but raise a number of medical problems—increasing rates of maternal morbidity and mortality and increasing frequency of Down's syndrome babies.

In addition to the home-versus-career quagmire in which women find

*Puberty can be a time of great physical and emotional upheaval in a girl's life. Society's generally ambivalent attitude toward the menarche, the time of the first menstrual period, probably has a lot to do with a girl's own reaction to this normal physiological event. The monthly cycles of women are the subject of Paul Delvaux's dreamlike painting "Phases of the Moon" (above left), in which women are portrayed as passive sex objects in a man's voyeuristic world.*

59

Roger P. Smith/*American Journal of Obstetrics and Gynecology*

**Painful menstrual contractions**

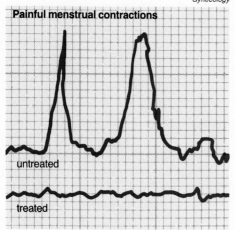

untreated

treated

*Painful menstruation (dysmenorrhea) is a common gynecologic complaint. For a very long time menstrual cramps were generally viewed as psychosomatic— without a physiological cause. Recent research into the chemical changes that take place during the monthly cycle show that women can experience sharp uterine contractions, which are caused by excessive outpourings of prostaglandins. These hormonelike substances are responsible for measurable constriction of blood vessels in the uterine wall at the time of menstruation. Drugs that block prostaglandin formation can decrease the severity of contractions and can eliminate pain for many sufferers. The clearly distinguishable lines in the diagram above show the powerful effect of drug treatment. It was a Victorian belief that complaints about menstrual cramps stemmed from a woman's dissatisfaction with her gender. The Victorians also held that women who used their brains and intellects would divert blood from their reproductive systems and impair their fertility. Though today these attitudes are at best laughable, and virtually all roads in life are open to women, women still must face some tough decisions when it comes to having careers and being mothers. Having fewer children later in life and carefully spacing them has been the solution for many successful professionals. Candace Pert (right) has earned a reputation as one of the most respected researchers in the neurosciences today. She is pictured here at age 35 with her 15-year-old son and is pregnant with her third child.*

themselves today, there continues to be a conflict over their physical capabilities and what constitutes a normal female body. For many years women were viewed as frail, and it was rare to find an outstanding woman athlete; sports were not perceived to be a womanly pursuit, and the opportunities for women in athletics were very limited. As a result, there was a general consensus that females did not have the strength, the stamina, or the competitive spirit required to excel in sports. It was also believed that vigorous exercise would cause the pelvic organs to drop down, causing fertility problems.

It is now well established that most of these concerns are not based upon any scientific evidence; woman have proved themselves to be superlative competitors in many sports. Their health, moreover, is generally improved by physical activity and, contrary to conventional wisdom, exercise has been found to improve muscle tone and thus give better support to their reproductive organs.

With the great increase in the athletic activity of women, however, has come the recognition of a new clinical syndrome—menstrual abnormalities and infertility resulting from strenuous physical exertion. A number of scientific studies have been carried out in recent years documenting this association. Young girls, notably swimmers and ballet dancers, who engage in extensive, vigorous exercise, often experience a one- to three-year delay in their menarche. Women who are having normal menstrual periods and who then begin to participate actively in sports often notice a decrease in flow, sometimes progressing to a complete absence of menses and an inability to become pregnant.

There are currently at least two schools of thought as to the etiology of these reproductive disorders. The first of these is the theory that menstrual function is generally dependent upon body weight and particularly upon fat levels. The body of an average healthy young woman contains 25 to 28%

Joe McNally/DISCOVER Magazine © 1981 Time Inc.

Women athletes have dispelled some of the long-held myths about females being unsuited to pursue strenuous physical activities and being susceptible to injuries. They have proved themselves to be outstanding competitors in many sports. With increased participation of women in athletics has come the recognition of a new clinical syndrome of menstrual abnormalities. The graph below shows some of the disturbances observed in a group of training athletes at the beginning and end of an athletic season. At least two explanations have been proposed for the irregularities: low levels of body fat may be the cause, or the stress of training and performing may be to blame. (Left) Jane Frederick of the United States trains for the women's heptathlon—a grueling seven-event Olympic contest. (Below left) Olga Chenchikova of the Soviet Union dances the part of the Swan Queen with the Kirov Ballet. The 26-year-old ballerina displays a stunning blend of precision, control, and lyrical fluidity.

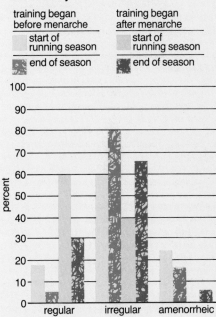

**Menstrual cycles of female athletes**

training began before menarche
- start of running season
- end of season

training began after menarche
- start of running season
- end of season

Adapted from Frisch *et al*, "Delayed Menarche and Amenorrhea of College Athletes in Relation to Age of Onset of Training," *JAMA*, Oct. 2, 1981, vol. 246, no. 14, pp. 1559–63

Michael Abramson—Gamma/Liaison

fat. Levels below 17% appear to delay the onset of menarche; very athletic females are often found to have body fat levels as low as 10%. However, some of these women appear to have entirely normal reproductive functions. In fact, ballet dancers whose periods have ceased have been observed to start menstruating again if they have to stop dancing owing to an illness or injury, long before any appreciable change in body weight or fat has had time to occur.

These observations have led to a second theory; *i.e.,* that menstrual abnormalities are actually due to the stress of training and performing. Support for this theory comes from the observation that both stress and exercise stimulate the brain to produce increased amounts of catecholamines, catecholestrogens, and beta-endorphins—all known to suppress the hormones controlling the female menstrual cycle. Regardless of the etiology, there is no evidence of long-term hormonal damage resulting from these menstrual aberrations.

Finally, there is still great confusion about the balance between physiologic and psychologic factors as regards the signs and symptoms of the time around menopause. The alterations that are induced by the decreasing levels of estrogen are reasonably clear, particularly those in a woman's reproductive tract—irregular menses and, finally, total cessation of menstrual periods, thinning and loss of elasticity of the vaginal walls, and flattening and constriction of the vaginal opening. Functional changes also occur: vaginal secretions diminish in volume, there is a gradual decrease in libido, and orgasms become less intense and sometimes produce very painful spasms of the uterus.

Equally clear are the medical conditions resulting from estrogen loss. Hot flushes, while mild and short-lived in most women, can be severe, long-lasting, and debilitating in a few. Sexual intercourse may become painful, resulting in vaginal lacerations and bleeding. Demineralization of bone leads to pain, the development of a "dowager's hump," and ultimately to an increased incidence of vertebral and hip fractures, the latter carrying a high level of mortality. Fortunately, most of these problems can be prevented, or at least minimized, by the cyclic administration of estrogens and progestins.

Considerably less clear are the psychological events of the menopausal era, particularly those related to alterations in libido. While the overall pattern is one of gradual decline, many women note a rise in sexual desire immediately after their menopause. This has been variously ascribed to the disappearance of the fear of unwanted pregnancy, freedom from the responsibilities of child care, and the sheer joy of having time to devote to themselves and to their own interests.

Conversely, menopause in other women produces a decrease in libido and an increase in emotional problems. These individuals complain of anxiety, depression, nervousness, restlessness, irritability, and feelings of inadequacy. They express fears about their loss of fertility, femininity, and sexual attractiveness. They worry about growing old and becoming physically debilitated and about dying.

It is also essential to note what is going on at the same time in the lives of men their own age. They, too, are experiencing a decline in sexual interest

**Rising lung cancer rates in women**

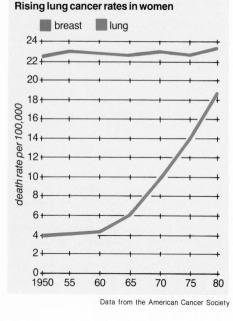

Data from the American Cancer Society

and performance and are starting to develop fears about aging and dying. Many men facing this midlife crisis attempt to deny its existence, at least temporarily, by blaming their failures on their wives. They may begin to have extramarital affairs and ultimately desert their wives for younger women, thus reinforcing the wives' already overwhelming feelings of worthlessness and guilt.

While the role of hormonal changes and the inevitability of aging cannot be denied, the environmental factors in this instance have been found to be of equal if not actually greater importance. Women who are in good health, who have husbands with whom they are compatible, sexually and otherwise, and who are under no severe economic pressures tend to have fewer (or at least less severe) problems of the variety just described. The judicious use of hormone therapy, thoughtful and considerate medical counseling, and the maintenance of health through proper diet and exercise will do much to alleviate the problems of middle age and lessen the inevitable effects of growing older. Above all, it is essential to dispel the societal myth that sexuality in the elderly is, at best, amusing and, at worst, abnormal, immoral, and dangerous.

The argument over the relative importance of heredity-versus-living conditions continues even unto death. The female's biologic advantage over the male has already been alluded to. However, the impact of a great many sociocultural and environmental factors on the longevity of women is currently being documented with increasing clarity. The morbidity and mortality rates related to smoking are rising rapidly among women in a direct-line relationship with their increased use of cigarettes. The injudicious use and abuse of drugs and exposure to occupational hazards are lowering the life expectancy of women. Finally, the pressures of entering the male-dominated marketplace are beginning to exact their toll; women are now starting to develop many of the stress-related diseases that were once the almost exclusive property of men.

Where does all of this controversy and conflicting evidence leave us? Inevitably, somewhere in the middle, between the two groups of extremists. The present biologic evidence is undeniable when based on sound research practices, leading to so-called hard (statistically valid) data. However, there are tantalizing amounts of undiscovered information only hinted at by the current studies, particularly with regard to the anatomy and physiology of the human brain. The behavioral studies, on the other hand, contain a considerable percentage of soft data, including a number of conclusions based primarily on animal observations. Research in these areas must also be expanded, especially in matters related to the human experience. It is of tremendous interest and possible importance that the work done thus far has pointed out that, despite their clear differences, males and females are physically and psychologically quite similar and have become progressively more so in recent times, presumably in response to changes in their surroundings. It would appear that this fact, in and of itself, would be in support of the present majority position that all human beings are the end product of both their heredity and their environment.

*The menopause—literally, the time of the last menstrual period—which marks the end of a woman's reproductive years, is a much maligned and much misunderstood event. Many hormonal changes occur, causing such symptoms as hot flushes, thinning of the linings of the vagina and urinary tract, loss of bone, and depression. These symptoms have been attributed not just to hormonal changes but to a variety of social, cultural, and psychological stresses that converge on a woman at that time. In many women's minds the menopause is associated with a loss of femininity and sexuality and with physical deterioration. A healthy outlook can make all the difference. Women who are in good health, who have compatible partners, and who remain sexually active tend to experience fewer physical and emotional problems. For most women short-term estrogen replacement therapy is considered safe and can minimize the unpleasant effects of physiological changes. An unfortunate phenomenon today is that smoking—an early symbol of women's social emancipation—is now a major threat to their health. Women are rapidly catching up with men in incidence of smoking-related diseases. The graph on the opposite page reflects the rising lung cancer death rates in women, which are soon expected to surpass breast cancer death rates.*

# The New Genetics: Beyond the Lab

## by Harold M. Schmeck, Jr.

**Harold M. Schmeck, Jr.,** *is a science correspondent for the* New York Times.

*(Opposite page) Brian, on the right, is ten years old, but he is the height of a six-year-old, owing to a lack of growth hormone; his nine-year-old companion is of normal height for his age. Now, thanks to a breakthrough in genetic engineering technology, Brian and other short-stature children are receiving injections of synthesized human growth hormone, which will enable them to reach normal or near-normal heights.*
*Photograph, Eddie Adams/*Discover *Magazine © 1982 Time Inc.*

Crouching side by side, the two normal, healthy-appearing white mice looked like parent and child—one twice the size of the other. The surprising fact was that they were from the same litter. The difference in size was attributable to a remarkable feat of the very new science of genetic engineering.

Scientists call the large littermate a 2X mouse because of its double size. Others have called it "supermouse" or Mighty Mouse. The achievements of chemistry and mechanical skill that produced it and others like it show how far research into the chemistry of genetics has come in just a few years. Not long ago it was an exciting accomplishment of recombinant DNA technology, or gene splicing, when scientists were first able to coax bacteria to produce animal or human proteins in the laboratory. Today that process is almost routine industrial technology.

## The creation of a Mighty Mouse

The research that produced the 2X mouse, a collaboration between scientists at the University of Pennsylvania, the University of Washington, the University of California at San Diego, and the Salk Institute, La Jolla, California, illustrates what startling things can be done today with the tools of modern molecular biology. The technique, which involved the transplantation of genes, is still considered basic research and is done only in laboratory animals to learn more about how genes are controlled. The process by which such transplants are done involves removing egg cells from a female animal just after conception. Using a hair-thin hollow glass tube only one one-thousandth of a millimeter in diameter, a scientist then injects copies of the foreign genes into such a fertilized egg cell, which is kept in a laboratory dish. Once the transplantation has been done, the genetically engineered cells are inserted into the reproductive tracts of "foster" mother mice that have been primed for pregnancy. In the experiments that produced the pair of sibling mice of such dramatically different size, one cell had been given an injection of DNA (deoxyribonucleic acid) embodying many copies of the gene for rat growth hormone. The other lacked those foreign genes. The engineered cell and the other grew, multiplied, and developed embryonically side by side in their foster mother's womb. But weeks after the two had been

Recently scientists have realized some stunning successes in the laboratory with gene manipulation. Among the goals of this work: to one day control or cure genetic diseases in humans. A scientist at Yale University (top) prepares a fertilized mouse egg cell for injection with a human interferon gene. A microscopic view (middle) shows the injection procedure, accomplished with micropipettes, in detail. With this technique Yale scientists bred several generations of mice carrying the transplanted foreign gene. Using similar methods scientists have transplanted specially modified genes for rat growth hormone into fertilized mouse egg cells, which were implanted in foster mother mice. The two male mice pictured at bottom are from the same litter. The mouse on the left acquired the gene for rat growth hormone and weighs 44 grams at ten weeks of age. His sibling did not acquire the gene and weighs 29 grams.

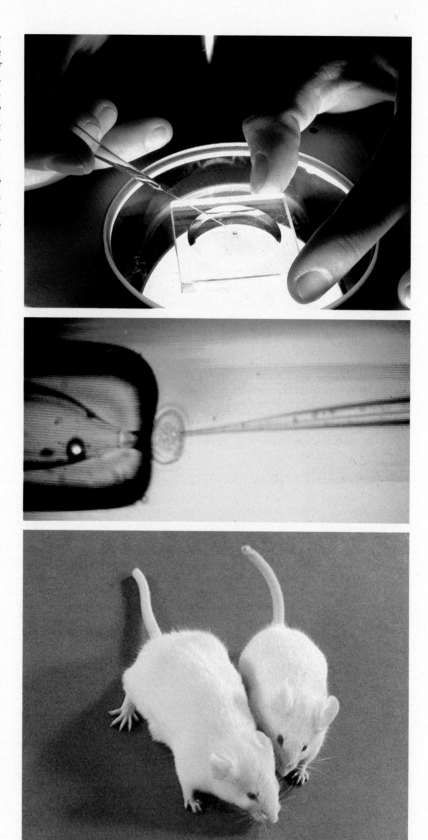

(Top and center) Photographs, Ken Laffal; (bottom) courtesy, Dr. R. L. Brinster, University of Pennsylvania

born, it was clear that the one with the transplanted gene was far outstripping the other in growth. Such a difference could never have been achieved by nutrition alone. The foreign, and extra, rat growth hormone genes were responsible.

Similar gene transplantations have been done by other teams, putting such things as genes for human insulin, for human growth hormone, and for a blood substance of rabbits all into different mice. None of the other experiments has produced such spectacular visible effects as that with rat growth hormone transplanted into mice, but some of the genes have been passed on from one generation of mice to the next, having evidently become incorporated in the chromosomes—the foreign genes thus becoming part of the animals' normal heredity. The work offers the prospect of new strains of laboratory animals carrying specific foreign genes for study of gene regulation in a fashion much more effective than has ever been possible before. A substantial percentage of the engineered embryos survive to develop into living animals.

But the success rate has been far less than 100%. That is one of several reasons why the method is not well suited for use in humans and is not expected to be used in humans in the foreseeable future. In the transplanta-

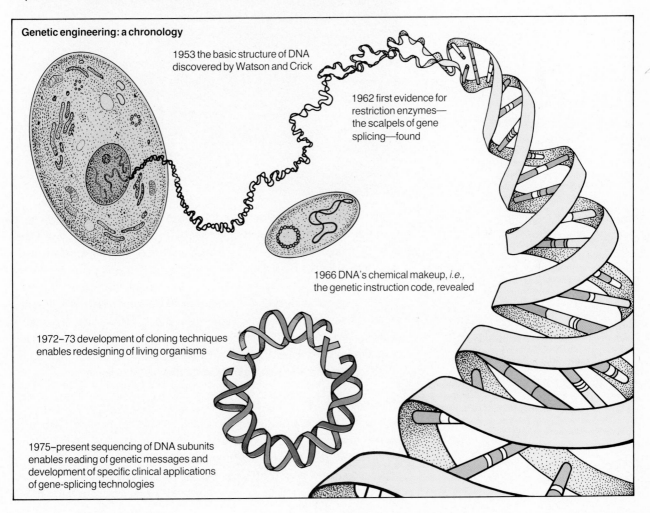

**Genetic engineering: a chronology**

1953 the basic structure of DNA discovered by Watson and Crick

1962 first evidence for restriction enzymes— the scalpels of gene splicing—found

1966 DNA's chemical makeup, *i.e.,* the genetic instruction code, revealed

1972–73 development of cloning techniques enables redesigning of living organisms

1975–present sequencing of DNA subunits enables reading of genetic messages and development of specific clinical applications of gene-splicing technologies

(Top) Courtesy, William H. McAlister, M.D., Mallinckrodt Institute of Radiology; (bottom) Eddie Adams/DISCOVER Magazine © 1982 Time Inc.

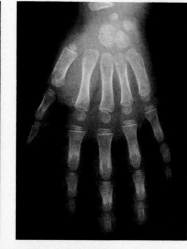

*The hand of a growth hormone deficient five-year-old (left) is compared with that of a normal five-year-old. X-rays of a child's hands reveal bone age and show whether the bone ends have begun to calcify. In adults, the bone ends (epiphyses) normally are entirely calcified. In a child the less calcification, the more room there is for growth still to occur and the more likely he or she is to benefit from growth hormone treatments. The child pictured here was a suitable candidate for such therapy; she is participating in a clinical trial that is being conducted by 11 U.S. universities. Her father administers an injection of synthetic growth hormone; she will have to take these injections three times a week for as long as five to ten years.*

tion experiments with the gene for rat growth hormone, 21 mice developed from the engineered egg cells, 7 carried the foreign gene, and 6 of these grew to abnormally large size. That success rate is splendid for research in mice but obviously far too low to warrant use in humans.

Nevertheless, gene transplantation may have a real future in animal breeding, where a few failures might be justified, especially if the successes produced something valuable. Meanwhile, the current animal research is likely to produce many new insights into the complexities of how genes are controlled and regulated. That was why the studies were done. Gene regulation is one of the key puzzles of modern molecular biology.

## From lab to life

All aspects of molecular biology, including genetic engineering, have been moving forward at a stunning pace during the past few years. While the experiments in gene transplantation are dazzling in performance and in their implications, they are only a small part of the research.

Scientists in laboratories all over the world are manipulating viruses, cell cultures, and fruit flies and are experimenting with laboratory animals in a broad range of studies covering every aspect of the chemistry of life. Meanwhile, a few medical scientists are actually beginning to take the new knowledge to the clinic and the bedside.

The most obvious examples are the new uses of the substances produced on a large scale by genetic engineering. Human insulin produced by gene-engineered bacteria was licensed by the U.S. Food and Drug Administration (FDA) late in 1982, the first medical product of gene splicing to gain such approval. Insulin is used by an estimated two million of the ten million diabetics in the United States. The laboratory-produced product, called Humulin, will offer patients unlimited supplies of pure hormone; previously diabetics depended on hormone taken from animals, which could become scarce in the future.

Human growth hormone, also produced in bacteria, is being tested as a treatment for children whose own growth hormone is either lacking or otherwise ineffective. At least a dozen varieties of human interferon, a natural virus-fighting substance, are being produced on a large scale in bacteria and are being tested in hospitals all over the world as possible aids in cancer treatment. Interferon has become so plentiful that it is even being tested against some of the less serious viral infections that are not life-threatening. Large-scale trials are in progress to see if a nasal spray of interferon could be an answer to the common cold.

In the past, interferon and human growth hormone had always been so scarce, and therefore so expensive, that doctors could hardly use them at all. Now they are abundant and can be tried for any worthwhile purposes their chemistry and biological effects suggest. In fact, just a few years ago human interferon could be used only sparingly in research on the most dangerous diseases. It was not even known that the human substance existed naturally in so many varieties. It was once thought to be a single substance.

Other rare substances including some brain chemicals and factors important in blood clotting are also being produced in bacteria and may soon find important new uses. There are also some less obvious examples of the application of basic genetics research to medical needs. For many of these, doctors are combining recombinant DNA techniques with other new tools such as monoclonal antibodies, giving medical scientists much more sensitive and selective biological probes than they have ever had before.

## One "cured" patient: hope for many

Monoclonal antibodies are produced from single clones of antibody-producing cells. These special antibodies are created in the laboratory by making hybrids from cells that produce a desired type of antibody and cancer cells that arise in the body's immune defense system. The cancer cells render the resulting hybrids virtually immortal and thus capable of producing the antibodies as long as the cell cultures are supplied with nutrients. The cellular antibody factories are called hybridomas.

Antibodies are biological guided missiles of great accuracy and discrimination. Their most familiar function is that of recognizing foreign organisms that

*Crystals of human insulin produced by recombinant DNA technology are pictured below. Insulin, marketed under the brand name Humulin, was the first gene-engineered product to be approved for use in humans by the U.S. Food and Drug Administration. An estimated two million diabetics in the United States require insulin therapy.*

Courtesy, Eli Lilly and Company

69

*Laboratories can now manufacture interferon, a naturally occurring antiviral agent produced by human cells, which is thought to have many potential uses in treating human diseases. A decade ago supplies were extremely limited and prohibitively costly: 90,000 pints of human blood were needed to harvest just 0.014 ounces of interferon; a pound would have cost $22 billion. By 1980 scientists had managed to apply new gene technologies to produce large quantities of the substance in the lab, thus enabling research to accelerate apace. Here, flasks of blood cells used to synthesize interferon are surrounded by white balls of insulating material.*

invade the body, seeking out each invader, and bringing the body's immune defenses to bear against it. Monoclonal antibodies are the most potent and accurate such guided missiles ever developed. Doctors are beginning to use them, together with gene-splicing techniques, for both diagnosis and treatment of disease.

One of the most remarkable recent cases involved a human patient—a man in his late sixties who suffered from malignant lymphoma, an often fatal cancer of the lymphatic system. Doctors at Stanford University Medical Center had been treating him since the late 1970s with an arsenal of conventional anticancer drugs and repeated courses of interferon, but after many ups and downs and a few plateaus, his condition worsened. He suffered from a host of symptoms including night sweats, fevers, extreme fatigue, and anemia. His prognosis was bleak.

At that point Ronald Levy and his colleagues decided to try something new and experimental. Their thought was to use monoclonal antibodies as guided missiles against the cancer. The strategy rested on recent advances in the understanding of lymphomas. The technique of making the monoclonal antibodies themselves, less than a decade old, enabled the physicians to carry out their mission.

For many years scientists have sought in vain for unique chemical markers on cancer cells that might set them apart from the body's normal tissues and therefore offer a clear target for attack. No such unique cancer marker has ever been found, and many scientists have given up hope that such a thing actually exists.

But in their lymphoma patient the medical scientists at Stanford saw an ingenious way of finding a unique identifying characteristic. The patient's disease was of a particular type called a B-cell lymphoma. The B cells are active cells important in the body's immunologic defenses. They are the precursors of the cells that produce antibodies. In this patient's lymphoma it was one clone of B cells that had turned malignant. This meant that the tumor cells carried something on their surfaces that was virtually unique. Every kind of antibody produced in a human or animal is different from all of the others. And each clone of B cells is programed for the production of only one of these. Furthermore, such a B cell will have on its surface a key portion of the specific antibodies that its daughter cells will make. And, of course, all the cells of any single clone of B cells will have the same antibodies on their surfaces. Thus, the patient's malignant B cells did have something unique on their surfaces—*i.e.,* the characteristic and unique antibody produced by the B-cell clone.

So the doctors had the clear target they needed. What could they use to attack that target? They decided to use other antibodies. The art of making monoclonal antibodies is so refined today that technicians can even make antibodies against portions of other antibodies. Levy and his colleagues thus made monoclonal antibodies against the particular antibodies that were present on the surface of the patient's malignant B cells. The antibodies that they made are called anti-idiotype antibodies.

The function of any antibody is to seek out and attach to its special target. Thereafter it sends out a call to the rest of the body's defense system to attack that target. The doctors hoped this would happen in their cancer patient; *i.e.,* the antibodies would seek out the malignant B cells wherever they were and bring on an immune attack against them. In March 1982 they were able to report that the method had worked and that their patient was in remission: "Our patient's tumor response to the monoclonal anti-idiotype antibody was dramatic, and it has persisted. . . ." After eight doses of antibody during a period of four weeks, all evidence of the patient's disease disappeared. The treatment was ended but the remission continued. Those events occurred before the end of 1981; a year and a half later the patient still appeared to be free of his disease.

Theirs has been an exciting success, but Levy and his colleagues caution that no one knows how long the remission will last, or even whether the special antibodies were really responsible. In fact, the group had tried the same treatment earlier in another man of about the same age who also had lymphoma, although of a different type. He too went into remission, but it was only partially successful and it lasted only seven weeks. Thereafter the illness returned and eventually the patient died. That failure simply emphasizes what all cancer specialists know too well: no single success, heartening as it is, can ever prove the worth of a treatment. The doctors at Stanford are continuing their study with a series of further patients. It is too early to say what the results will be.

Even if it does prove as successful as Levy's group hopes, these are cancers of a rather special kind. Furthermore, the monoclonal antibodies for each have to be tailor-made for that one particular patient alone. It is a long, difficult, and expensive process. But none of these obstacles should detract from the worth of what the group at Stanford is attempting. They may already have saved one life, and they hope to save others. Even more important for the long term, they hope and expect to learn ways of making monoclonal antibody treatment more effective and more widely applicable so that it can be used for a broader range of cancer patients.

They are by no means alone in attempts to use monoclonal antibodies in this way. Several other medical research teams are either preparing for or actually trying various strategies using monoclonal antibodies against one or another type of cancer. All of these involve only small numbers of patients. Some of the results seem encouraging, but in diseases as difficult as most forms of cancer, only time and substantial experience will tell.

*Antibodies are the body's natural "guided missiles" that seek out harmful foreign substances, including cancer cells, and help marshal the body's defenses against them. The scanning electron micrographs below dramatically depict one way in which the immune system destroys a foreign cell in the body. In the first, a scavenger cell of the immune system is primed to attack an invader; in the second, the invader—the small globular cancer cell at center—is met by the attacking cell; in the third, the cancer cell's surface holes reveal that its destruction is in progress. Now scientists are using gene-splicing techniques to create more refined and potent missiles that can be used in both the diagnosis and treatment of disease and that can take over when, for whatever reason, the body's own defenses fail.*

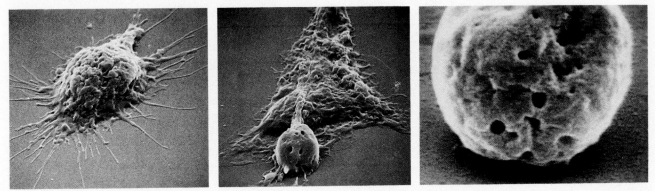

Photographs, courtesy, The Upjohn Company

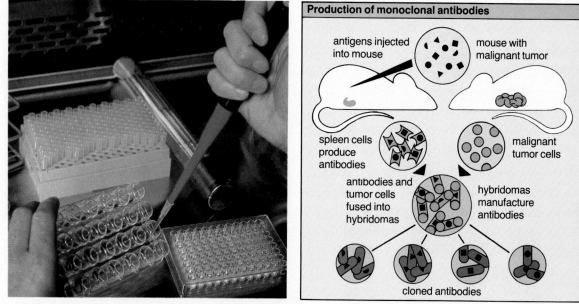

**Production of monoclonal antibodies**

antigens injected into mouse

mouse with malignant tumor

spleen cells produce antibodies

malignant tumor cells

antibodies and tumor cells fused into hybridomas

hybridomas manufacture antibodies

cloned antibodies

*Cells that make monoclonal antibodies are sorted and grown in test tubes. Researchers then analyze the products (above) to select the most promising cultures. The potential uses of monoclonal antibodies are many. They are expected to play a significant role in transplantation success; they have already proved useful in transplants of bone marrow for leukemia patients. Bone marrow can be removed from the patient, all traces of malignant disease destroyed by specially targeted monoclonal antibodies, and the healthy marrow then reimplanted. Or the antibodies can be used to prevent a donor's marrow from rejecting the recipient; they are geared to seek out and destroy T cells in the donor marrow, which are the key agents that cause a marrow graft to attack its adopted body. Steps in a bone marrow transplantation are shown on the opposite page: Doctors withdraw a large quantiy of marrow from a leukemia patient's brother. Through centrifuging, lighter blood cells are separated from the donor marrow. After proper treatment, the marrow is frozen to preserve it prior to transplantation. Meanwhile, the leukemia patient awaiting this gift of life is kept in a protective germ-free environment because her own immune system has been destroyed by high-dose chemotherapy.*

## Targeting drugs

While the medical scientists at Stanford University and at some other medical research centers use monoclonal antibodies alone to attack cancer cells, a different strategy is also being developed in which the antibody is a guided missile that carries a separate warhead. Among the pioneers in this approach are medical scientists at the University of Texas Southwestern Medical School in Dallas, led by Ellen S. Vitetta and Jonathan W. Uhr. They are pursuing an idea that really dates back 75 years to the work of the German medical scientist Paul Ehrlich, who suggested that antibodies might be used as carriers of drugs. But today considerably more is known about antibodies, including, of course, how to make them and how to use them. Far more is known also about the kinds of cell poisons that might be utilized to give specially targeted antibodies more killing power when they reach the cancer cells they have been designed to seek out.

One much-studied poison that has figured in animal research of this kind is the deadly poison made by the bacteria that cause diphtheria. It is this diphtheria toxin, rather than the bacteria themselves, that make the disease so dangerous. Researchers Vitetta and Uhr in their investigations into the use of toxins as carriers of drugs have discovered, however, that the long public health battle against diphtheria that has made the disease a rarity also limits the usefulness of diphtheria toxin as a warhead for monoclonal antibodies. In the United States most people are immune to diphtheria, having been immunized against the disease in childhood.

Another poison, so deadly that it has been used by political assassins who want to kill their targets without being found out, is called ricin and comes from the castor bean. In one case made public a few years ago, espionage agents killed their victims by firing tiny metal pellets filled with ricin from the tip of an air gun disguised as an umbrella. One such pellet, small as the head of a pin, contained enough ricin to kill; the unfortunate victims did not even

72

know they had been shot. So potent a poison makes an ideal warhead for a monoclonal antibody. Part of the ricin molecule can be attached to an antibody under circumstances that will make it deadly when it enters a cell. But, because this tiny biological warhead is not the complete ricin molecule, it is harmless 'elsewhere in the body. The Texas scientists call this combination of ricin and antibody an immunotoxin. Their research has been confined primarily to laboratory work with animals, but the evidence and experience they have gathered have led the scientists to believe there is an important future for immunotoxins in the treatment of some forms of cancer and some other diseases as well.

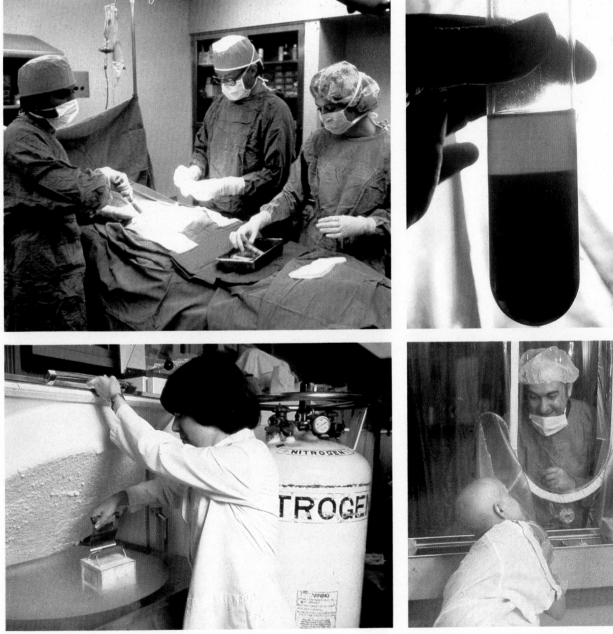

Photographs, Ken Kobre—Black Star

## Improving odds in bone marrow transplants

There is one use of monoclonal antibodies in which the ability to kill selected cells can have profound effects even when the cells have been removed from the patient altogether. This is the case when doctors want to treat a patient's bone marrow to kill cancer cells that lurk within it or when they want to treat donor bone marrow so that the patient who needs a transplant will be able to receive it safely.

In the first situation, involving cancer treatment, doctors may want to "rescue" the patient's bone marrow from the malignant disease. Bone marrow is the body's prime blood-forming tissue and one of the most important factors in the immune defense system. Because of those two closely related roles, properly functioning bone marrow is absolutely indispensable to life. But in some forms of cancer, such as leukemia, the bone marrow may also be the ultimate source of the cancer cells. When successful treatment with chemotherapeutic drugs erases all signs of disease and puts the patient into a remission, a few cancer cells may still lurk in the bone marrow even though they are impossible to detect. These leukemic cells may multiply to bring back the disease. Total destruction of the bone marrow might eliminate the disease, but then the destroyed bone marrow must be replaced or the patient will die of anemia.

There are two ways of dealing with this life-and-death dilemma. Both methods can use monoclonal antibodies and the new knowledge that has been accumulating in recent years through research in molecular biology. The two possibilities are to give the patient a donor bone marrow transplant or to remove some of the patient's own marrow while the disease is in remission and reimplant it in the patient after his or her remaining marrow has been destroyed to eliminate all traces of the disease.

The patient's marrow, stored outside the body awaiting this reimplantation, must be treated to eliminate every last malignant cell so that the vital blood-forming tissue can be restored to the patient without bringing the disease back with it. Monoclonal antibodies designed to seek out the patient's cancer cells are being used to treat this stored marrow to eliminate all malignant cells that may be lurking.

In the situation in which a bone marrow transplant from someone else is the only hope, monoclonal antibodies are also among the possible means of rescuing the patient from disaster. Being a crucial part of the immune defense system, bone marrow is immunologically active. If healthy marrow is transplanted into a person whose tissue type does not match that of the donor, the transplanted tissue views the recipient's entire body as foreign and attacks it. This is called graft-versus-host disease because a transplant is also called a graft and the recipient is often called the host.

When the donor is the patient's identical twin, there is no tissue incompatibility between donor and recipient and therefore no problem. Transplants between two close relatives can also be safe if the tissues are well matched, but in other cases, including virtually all marrow transplants between unrelated persons, graft-versus-host disease is almost certain to develop. It is often fatal. In recent years medical scientists have learned ways of treating bone marrow before transplantation to make it behave neutrally toward the tissues of its adopted body. One of the most widely employed methods is the use of monoclonal antibodies to seek out and destroy the special clones of cells in the marrow that are known to be the main agents of graft-versus-host disease. The cells are called mature T cells. Once they have been removed, the marrow is not likely to cause a graft-versus-host reaction. Patients whose tissues only partially matched the tissue types of the transplanted marrow have been treated successfully.

This method has been used against leukemia and some deadly forms of anemia as well as in children born with severe immunologic deficiencies, who require marrow transplants. Among the leaders in this work are Stuart Schlossman and Ellis Reinherz of Harvard University Medical School and

| Selected single-gene hereditary diseases | | |
|---|---|---|
| disease | cause/clinical features | comments |
| β-thalassemia (Cooley's anemia) | defective synthesis of hemoglobin/ severe anemia; jaundice; leg ulcers; cholelithiasis (mineral deposits in gallbladder and bile ducts); enlarged spleen; cardiac muscle dysfunction | affects persons of Mediterranean descent (autosomal dominant) |
| sickle-cell anemia | malformation of red blood cells/possible growth retardation; acute joint pain | affects blacks |
| hemophilia | insufficiency of necessary blood-clotting factor/tendency to hemorrhage; eventual crippling may result from bleeding into muscles and joints | affects males only |
| PKU (phenylketonuria) (phenylalaninemia) | inability to metabolize the enzyme phenylalanine hydroxylase/ neurologic disorders, sometimes including seizure; may result in mental retardation | affects most population groups but is rare in Ashkenazic Jews and blacks |
| Tay-Sachs disease | deficiency of the enzyme hexosaminidase A necessary for lipid metabolism/progressive fatal degeneration of nervous system; paralysis; cherry-red retinal spot; blindness; dementia | affects Ashkenazic Jews |
| Lesch-Nyhan syndrome (hereditary hyperuricemia) | deficiency of the enzyme hypoxanthine-guanine phosphoribosyltransferase (HGPRT)/progressive nervous system degeneration; incoordination and spasticity; self-destructive behavior (head banging, biting of lips and extremities); mental retardation; excessive uric acid in blood | males only |
| cystic fibrosis | metabolic disorder, exact defect unknown/abnormal function of all exocrine glands; digestive and respiratory malfunctions; marked increase of salt concentration in sweat | the most important congenital metabolic disorder of Caucasians; estimated that one of every 25 North American and European whites is a carrier |
| muscular dystrophy (Duchenne's dystrophy) | exact biochemical defect unknown; evidently related to primary structural defect at cellular level in striated muscle fibers/progressive muscle degeneration; muscular weakness; curvature of spine; susceptibility to respiratory infection | affects chiefly males |

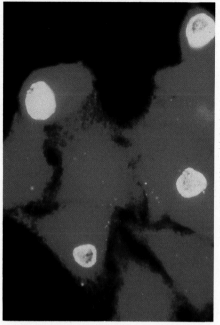

*Traditional laboratory tests that detect sexually transmitted diseases can take up to six days. But with the new gene technologies, scientists now are developing tests that diagnose gonorrhea, herpes, and chlamydia in just half an hour. Monoclonal antibodies are mixed with cell samples swabbed from the genitals of a patient. These antibodies, specially tagged with fluorescent markers, will cling to the organisms that cause infection. Here yellow spots on cells indicate active venereal disease.*

the Dana-Farber Cancer Institute in Boston. At Memorial Sloan-Kettering Cancer Center in New York City, medical scientists have used a different method of preparing marrow for transplantation. It depends on tricking mature T cells into being activated in the test tube under circumstances that tend to make them clump together with the foreign target cells they have attacked. The clumps are then removed, and the bone marrow is repurified and used for transplantation.

## Manipulating genes to conquer inherited disease

The new possibilities offered by gene splicing, monoclonal antibodies, and other advanced techniques have also been put to work for rapid, accurate diagnosis of many kinds of disease. The same new techniques of medical science are also being explored for better weapons against some of humanity's ancient enemies. Among them are malaria and schistosomiasis, parasitic infectious diseases that have always taken a huge toll on health and life throughout the world.

All of the uses discussed so far have been ways of applying new techniques to improve old strategies or to add a new dimension to conventional schemes of treatment and diagnosis. There are other ideas on the horizon that would simply have been inconceivable before scientists learned to read the messages of the genes and compose their own artificial messages in that ancient language of heredity.

For example, many ideas have been advanced in recent years for treating such inherited blood disorders as $\beta$-thalassemia and sickle-cell anemia, but until recently no one ever tried the most dramatic solution of all: to turn on genes that the body had turned off. In fact, until recently scientists had no idea how to turn on any gene. Now they do.

Experts in blood disorders at the U.S. National Heart, Lung, and Blood Institute (NHLBI) and at the University of Illinois College of Medicine put that knowledge to work against a severe case of $\beta$-thalassemia, a disease in which the body's ability to make hemoglobin is seriously compromised. Hemoglobin is the red, oxygen-carrying substance in red blood cells. Any serious defect in a person's hemoglobin is a disaster. A patient suffering from a severe case of thalassemia is likely to have bone deformities, endocrine problems, heart problems, liver problems, anemia, pain, anxieties from all these other difficulties, and not much hope. There is no cure, and life-span is often severely shortened.

A few years ago Martin J. Cline, a medical scientist at the University of California at Los Angeles, attempted to treat two severely affected $\beta$-thalassemia patients, one in Italy, the other in Israel, by transplanting copies of normal genes for the beta globin portion of hemoglobin. This attempt evidently failed. (Cline was later censured by the U.S. National Institutes of Health for violating federal guidelines in failing to obtain permission from his university before trying the treatment, even though the treatments were done abroad with permission from the patients and their local doctors.)

The new strategy of reactivating a native gene was somewhat less ambitious but more effective. It was based on the discovery that a drug called 5-azacytidine can activate repressed genes in cells growing in laboratory cultures. As it had proved true in animals as well as in cell cultures, it seemed it might be a useful strategy against thalassemia owing to one particular function: during their progression from embryos to infants to adults, humans are known to make more than one kind of hemoglobin. During the fetal period they primarily make a kind called fetal hemoglobin. Later the gene for making fetal hemoglobin is turned off, and the body switches to the manufacture of adult hemoglobin. But the genes for making components of fetal hemoglobin still exist in the adult DNA. What would happen then if 5-azacytidine were used in an attempt to turn them back on? That was the strategy tried by Timothy J. Ley and Arthur Nienhuis and a large team of collaborators at NHLBI. They tried the approach first in anemic baboons and were gratified to see that the animals' hemoglobin production improved. Next they tried the same treatment in one human patient who suffered from $\beta$-thalassemia. After seven days of treatment, the patient's hemoglobin production was improved dramatically. The treatment was halted at that point because no one was sure it would be safe to continue, but it was clear that the team had done something remarkable.

An editorial in the *New England Journal of Medicine,* where the report of this achievement was published in December 1982, described the research as "the first encouraging attempts to achieve clinical management of gene expression by molecular manipulation of DNA" in any patient. The authors of the study emphasized that their short treatment of one patient represented early research and that much more would have to be known about the efficacy of the treatment before it could ever be used for long-term management of the disease. But it was clearly a hint of things to come. It showed unmistakably that the era of deliberate gene manipulation is dawning. It seems clear that many health problems might be dealt with more effectively and humanely if the rapidly growing knowledge of the chemistry of genetics could be applied. Hundreds of hereditary diseases are known, each of which occurs because of one or another single error among the possible total of about 100,000 human genes. For some such diseases the specific

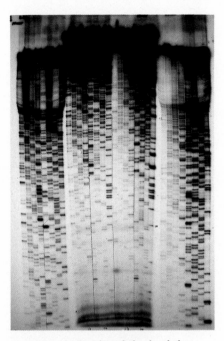

*Rapidly expanding knowledge has led to the "sequencing" of individual genes. (Above) X-ray analyses provide pictures of the several thousand subunits that make up a whole gene, enabling scientists to identify single faulty DNA subunits responsible for human genetic diseases. After sequencing a newly discovered cancer-causing gene and learning that a single subunit differentiated it from a normal gene, researchers were able to transform a normal mouse cell sample (below left) into a cancerous one (right) by transferring fragments of DNA.*

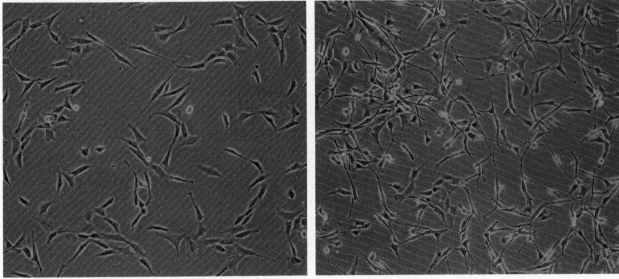

Scientists are very excited about the discovery of certain genes that appear to be linked to human cancers. These "oncogenes" are being investigated with the help of recombinant DNA technologies. The diagram at right outlines several of the steps that may be involved in the cancer process. Each cell contains the coiled genetic material (DNA) that determines physical characteristics. Oncogenes are found in normal cells from birth, together with genes that carry instructions to make organs, tissues, hormones, enzymes, etc. The DNA can be thought of as an uncoiled "tape," containing 50,000 or more bits of information. Each gene has a "switch" that can turn on when the body needs more of a gene product—e.g., when the body needs antibodies, the immunoglobulin (Ig) gene (top panel) is activated. Scientists think oncogenes get switched on by mistake or as a result of another gene switch's going into an "overproduce" mode (middle panel). A number of factors may be responsible for passing on a message to overproduce— radiation exposure, chemicals, viruses, or rare chromosomal translocations. In the latter instance, pieces of chromosomes get misplaced during the normal cell duplication process and end up abnormally close to an oncogene. The oncogene then is mistakenly signaled to produce and thus generates cancerous cells. So far about 15 different oncogenes have been found in the normal genetic material.

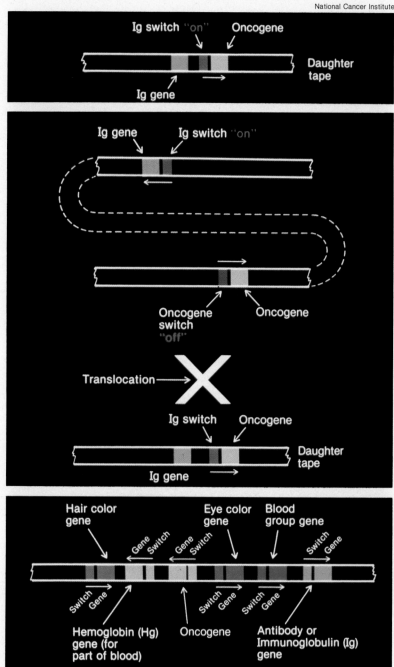

faulty gene has been identified, and the chemical abnormality it produces is known. In a few cases the gene has actually been sequenced; that is, the entire sequence of its DNA subunits has been discovered. In some of these the identity of the genetic error has been narrowed down to a single wrong DNA subunit among several thousand that make up the whole gene.

Thus, with the chemistry of many human diseases so well defined, should it not be possible to devise some way of correcting or countering them? So far, scientists have found the problem to be an immensely difficult one; but they are trying, and that means they believe there is reason for hope.

## The discovery of cancer genes

In another area of molecular biology that has blossomed with the help of the recent recombinant DNA techniques, scientists have identified genes that appear to be linked to human cancers. These are called oncogenes, or cancer genes, because they have been found in human cancer cells and are capable of transforming other cells, growing in tissue cultures, to a cancerous state. Counterparts of some of those so-called cancer genes have also been found in normal cells, a fact that prompted scientists at the Massachusetts Institute of Technology (MIT) and the U.S. National Cancer Institute (NCI) to do experiments in which they spelled out the identities of DNA subunits, called nucleotides, for the entire nucleotide length of one such oncogene.

Led by Robert A. Weinberg of MIT and Edward M. Scolnick of NCI, scientists compared one known cancer gene with its normal counterpart. To their great surprise they found there was only one nucleotide difference between the two genes in their entire 6,000-nucleotide length. The next question, still unanswered but being vigorously pursued, is: What part does that seemingly tiny difference play in the establishment of a cancer?

## A new science—here to stay

With the wealth of new ideas and information coming out of the field, to say nothing of the burgeoning of an entire new biotechnology industry, it would be easy to conclude that all the concerns of prior years about safety and propriety must have evaporated. That is not quite true. It is generally agreed today that most of the original fears concerning the creation of new diseases and monstrous life forms were either totally unfounded or greatly exaggerated. Furthermore, the U.S. Congress has repeatedly considered legislation to regulate genetic-engineering work but has backed off every time.

Yet worries over conceivable future effects of gene splicing remain, along with the hopes. One set of worries is over potential industrial pollution and hazards to workers. Such problems have indeed occurred in many other industries. Meanwhile, there is another set of worries virtually unique to gene splicing; almost by definition, gene splicing offers the future possibility of making changes in the hereditary characteristics of species, including humans. Concerns on this score were summed up in a report, "Splicing Life," issued in November 1982 by a high-level federal panel, the President's Commission for the Study of Ethical Problems in Medicine and Biomedical and Behavioral Research: "Although public concern about gene splicing arose in the context of laboratory research with microorganisms, it seemed to reflect a deeper anxiety that work in this field might remake human beings, like Dr. Frankenstein's monster."

While the commission found these concerns to be exaggerated, their report stated: "As a product of human investigation and ingenuity, the new knowledge is a celebration of human creativity, and the new powers are a reminder of human obligations to act responsibly." The commission concluded that discussion of the powers, benefits, and risks of this extraordinary new scientific technology must become a part of "the conversation of mankind" from now on.

Laboratory dwarf mouse on chromosome charts, Erich Hartmann—Magnum

*Recombinant DNA science—just a few years old—has opened many previously "locked" doors. Already patients are reaping benefits from the new genetics. Hypotheses that were mere glimmers of ideas yesterday are today being rigorously investigated in laboratories and tomorrow may very well enable doctors to offer patients better diagnoses, treatments, and even cures.*

# Mass Hysteria

## by Drummond Rennie, M.D.

Pausanias [Greek traveler and geographer of the 2nd century AD] relates that the malady of the daughters of Proteus, who ran about the country fancying that they were transformed into cows, was common amongst the women of Argos.
—from J. G. Millingen, *Curiosities of Medical Experience*, 1839

The imaginations of women are always more excitable than those of men, and they are therefore susceptible of every folly when they lead a life of strict seclusion, in orphan asylums, hospitals, and convents, the nervous disorder of one female so easily and quickly becomes the disorder of all. . . . [A] nun, in a very large convent in France, began to mew like a cat; shortly afterwards other nuns also mewed. At last all the nuns mewed together every day at a certain time for several hours together. The whole surrounding Christian neighbourhood heard with equal chagrin and astonishment, this daily cat-concert, which did not cease until all the nuns were informed that a company of soldiers were placed by the police before the entrance of the convent, and that they were provided with rods, and would continue whipping them until they promised not to mew any more.

In the celebrated Convent epidemic of the fifteenth century . . . a nun in a German nunnery fell to biting all her companions. The news of this infatuation among the nuns soon spread, and it now passed from convent to convent, through a great part of Germany, principally Saxony and Brandenburg. It afterwards visited the nunneries of Holland, and at last the nuns had the biting mania even as far as Rome.
—from J. F. C. Hecker, *The Epidemics of the Middle Ages*, 1846

At a cotton manufactory at Hodden Bridge, in Lancashire, a girl, on the fifteenth of February, 1787, put a mouse into the bosom of another girl, who had a great dread of mice. The girl was immediately thrown into a fit, and continued in it, with the most violent convulsions, for twenty-four hours. On the following day, three more girls were seized . . . on the 17th, six more. . . . [A]n idea prevailed that a particular disease had been introduced by a bag of cotton. . . . On Sunday the 18th, Dr. St. Clare was sent for from Preston; before he arrived three more were seized, and during that night and the morning of the 19th, eleven more, making in all twenty-four. Of these, twenty-one were young women. . . . [M]ore were infected entirely from report, not having seen the other patients, but, like them and the rest of the country, strongly impressed with the idea of the plague being caught from the cotton. The symptoms were anxiety, strangulation, and very strong convulsions; and these were so violent as to last without any intermis-

**Drummond Rennie, M.D.,** *is Chairman of Medicine at West Suburban Hospital in Oak Park, Illinois, and Professor of Medicine at Rush Medical College in Chicago. He is also Senior Contributing Editor of* The Journal of the American Medical Association *and Medical Editor of* Encyclopaedia Britannica's Medical and Health Annual.

*(Overleaf) Walpurgisnacht; photograph, Mansell Collection, London*

sion from a quarter of an hour to twenty-four hours, and to require four or five persons to prevent the patients from tearing their hair and dashing their heads against the floor or walls. Dr. St. Clare had taken with him a portable electrical machine, and by electric shocks the patients were universally relieved without exception. As soon as the patients and the country were assured that the complaint was merely nervous, easily cured, and not introduced by the cotton, no fresh person was affected.

—*Gentleman's Magazine,* March 1787

These accounts of the bizarre behavior of groups of women in relative isolation who show peculiar and highly contagious psychological symptoms are descriptions of mass or epidemic hysteria. On July 13, 1980, hundreds of excited children began to stagger and collapse during a marching jazz band contest on a hot, humid day in Nottinghamshire, England. The epidemic spread from person to person like wildfire, and the showground soon resembled a battlefield, with loudspeakers blaring out inaccurate and alarming information. As many as 200 were treated on the spot, and a further 412 victims were seen in hospitals. Very few adults were affected by the curious epidemic of staggering and collapsing; recovery in each case was as dramatically rapid and complete as the collapse.

Numerous contradictory official statements were made about the incident; pesticides were immediately blamed, but prompt, exhaustive, and expensive tests of air, earth, vegetation, and gas emanations from the ground and of patients' blood and urine failed to reveal the presence of any toxic chemicals, bacteria, or viruses. When expert physicians labeled the outbreak mass hysteria, they were met first with public disbelief, then with abuse. The organizers of the contest and the parents of the children, asserting there was an official cover-up, proceeded to label the opinion of the experts "rubbish" and set up their own investigation, which proved fruitless. One parent, typically ignorant of hundreds of similar episodes over the centuries, proclaimed of his daughter, "She has suffered convulsions and was doubled up with pain. It certainly was not hysteria."

Over seven days the sober London *Times* devoted considerable front-page coverage to the story; the medical pronouncements of many with absolutely no medical, epidemiological, or toxicological training dominated the news. Finally, officials expressed "disappointment" that it was, after all, due to mass hysteria with its 100% rapid and complete recovery rate rather than to a toxic or infectious organism, which might have maimed or killed at least some victims, but which would have been a more acceptable explanation.

## What is hysteria?

To most of us hysterical behavior implies an exaggerated display of emotion: histrionics under conditions that do not seem appropriately stressful. The word itself, stemming from the Greek for womb, is found in the Hippocratic corpus; "hysterical" has long been applied to women subject to emotional storms. English physician William Harvey in the early 17th century wrote: "In Hysterick Women the Rarity of Symptoms doth oft strike such an Astonishment into Spectators, that they report them possessed with the Devil." In 1755 Samuel Johnson in his *Dictionary* gave this definition: "Troubled with Fits. Disordered in the Regions of the Womb. Fits of Women supposed to proceed from Disorders of the Womb."

As rational medicine and psychiatry gained ground in the 19th century, the original concept of a "wandering womb" was abandoned, in part because

*(Opposite) In the mid-1500s Pieter Brueghel the Elder painted the female pilgrims who on St. John's Day participated in a danse macabre known as St. John's or St. Vitus' dance. These yearly dancing manias, which became a great public menace as they spread through the Low Countries, Germany, and Italy, represented a kind of mass hysteria. Religious, social, and medical influences interacted—probably in response to epilepsy-like seizures of those who at the time were dying from the scourge of the Black Death. The processions probably originated in 1021 when priests, who thought a group of "possessed" dancers in a German village were in the grip of the devil, ordered the raving peasants to sing and dance for a year without pause as a kind of exorcism. Furious dancing that led to complete exhaustion was "observed to produce a good effect."*

Mary Evans Picture Library

*Groups of women who develop peculiar and highly contagious hysterical symptoms have long mystified medical practitioners. For centuries the histrionics of women were attributed to a "wandering womb." Because hysterical symptoms make no sort of anatomic, physiological, or pathological sense, doctors have resorted to all manner of "treatment." At the Charité hospital in Paris, revolving mirrors were used in attempts to quell the exaggerated displays of emotions in female patients.*

men also developed hysteria; hysterical symptoms then were taken to signify physical illness that made no sort of anatomic, physiological, or pathological sense. A great deal of theorizing has now given us the notion of a psychological mechanism—one that is associated with a physical loss of function, unexplained by any rational pathophysiological cause, and one that is associated with the idea of gain. The symptoms and signs are thought to represent an involuntary, uncontrollable expression of inner conflict, and the syndrome has been named "hysterical neurosis, conversion type"—conversion being the manifestation of psychological conflicts through motor or sensory symptoms. Thus a patient develops paralysis, is struck dumb, staggers, has bizarre seizures, becomes blind, or loses sensation in ways that defy any attempt on the part of a neurologist to make sense of or localize an organic cause or lesion.

Two mechanisms have been proposed. In the first the individual achieves so-called primary gain by keeping his inner conflict below the level of awareness—blindness, for example, being a response to seeing something traumatic. The second mechanism—that of secondary gain—implies that by developing a symptom such as paralysis, an individual can avoid some apparently noxious activity, such as leaping out of a foxhole to attack on command. In either case, the symptoms are not under voluntary control; therefore, the patient cannot be said to be malingering.

Hysterical conversion used to be common but is now rarely diagnosed. It tends to be sudden in onset; recovery is variable. There remains no convincing explanation of why, when two people are presented with the same stress, a conversion reaction will occur in one and not the other.

## What is mass hysteria?

"Epidemic" or "mass" hysteria refers to a highly contagious, unorganized, uncontrolled, unusual, and above all spontaneous process that suddenly strikes a community. It does not refer to ritualized, organized religious exercises, such as that of the frenetic whirling dervishes. If it is one "disease," its manifestations vary greatly, from aberrant social movements such as the Children's Crusade to outbreaks of inexplicable and apparently organic disease among hospital nurses.

Because the theory behind the concept of hysteria is so shaky, and also because the term hysteria is outmoded, with its pejorative, inaccurate, and sexist implications, other names have been used: epidemic overbreathing, psychogenic or psychosomatic illness, anxiety state, neurotic reaction, and transient situational disturbance. While these terms are no doubt more appropriate, epidemic or mass hysteria is still the widely accepted, widely used name. For convenience it is used here.

It is not known what, if any, links there are between individual cases of hysteria and the phenomenon of epidemic hysteria, though the same subconscious psychological conversion process has been invoked to explain behavior in both instances. In the epidemic cases there are clearly crowd or community influences, such as general ignorance, uncertainty, and rumor. At the same time, conflicts that have no obvious outlet for open expression may be going on in the subconscious of many individual members of the group.

84

*"Mass hysteria" describes a highly disorganized, uncontrolled, and, above all, spontaneous process that strikes a community. Its manifestations vary greatly. Often the exaggerated yearnings of one person can excite a horde of spirited followers, as in many aberrant religious and social movements. Such was the case in the first Children's Crusade of 1212, in which a French shepherd boy attracted some 30,000 devoted young crusaders in what turned out to be a disastrous effort to conquer the Holy Land.*

The peculiar symptoms that develop en masse in a sense are sanctioned by the group as "preferable" to open acknowledgment of individual powerlessness.

Probably all of us, if stressed enough, will develop hysterical symptoms. Take as an example fear of heights. Most fit people could, without fear, walk along a beam six inches wide and four feet from the ground. A few, however, might exhibit profound and irrational dread of getting on that beam; they might, as such, react to the perceived risk by becoming dizzy, hyperventilating, or displaying any number of other "maladaptive" responses. Raise the beam 20 feet off the ground, and a great many more would show these symptoms. If the beam were 1,000 feet above terra firma, very few would fail to show the symptoms. Thus it would seem there is a threshold of susceptibility to hysteria that varies among individuals, but once the proper convergence of factors occurs or when the stress is great enough (as when the beam hovers at 1,000 feet), most succumb.

Adolescent females are the one group we know from evidence to be inordinately prone to mass hysteria. However, even within this age and sex group it is probable that there are no sharp distinctions between those who succumb and those who do not; the affected proportion may well be some measure of the individually suffered "stresses" the teenaged girls are experiencing—puberty, school conflicts, family battles, intense social pressures, "identity crises," etc.—all common to some degree or other in this group.

Mass hysteria has links with other aberrant forms of collective behavior—which range from disorganized fads to mass movements, such collective behavior being characteristically sudden, volatile, and unpredictable. Typically in crowds of people who are unknown to each other, some sensitization of people to each other and communication among them must first occur, serving to heighten suggestibility, submerge individuality, and reduce the

85

critical faculties of the individual. At first the crowd mills about (indeed, it is called "milling" after the behavior of cattle just before a stampede), and a common mood (impatience, anxiety, anger) develops with a common expectation and a common interpretation of events. News travels swiftly, but since the means to verify facts are lacking, this is mere rumor. Under authoritarian conditions, or when there is a feeling of anxiety and threat to the natural order, rumor is particularly rife, rumors being the more impressive when, as usually happens, they are spread by educated and responsible people who are expressing their need to reach a common understanding of events. As rumors circulate and recirculate, they tend to justify whatever action the crowd takes. Social unrest, milling, and the spread of rumor greatly enhance the gullibility of individuals within the mass.

Collective obsessions may take the form of harmless fads or fashions (roller-skating, CB radios, Rubik's cube, ET paraphernalia, etc.), coming and going over weeks and months. They become harmful when faddism spills over to crazes that afflict, say, the stockmarket—the South Sea Bubble (a speculation mania of 1720 that ruined many an English investor) being a classic, though by no means the most recent, example.

In crowds collective obsessions spread in minutes instead of in weeks, taking an "active" form, as in a race riot, in which aggression focuses on something outside the crowd itself. Violence erupts suddenly, the crowd rampages, and burning and looting ensue. "Expressive" crowds, on the other hand, tend to be caught up with themselves and their own emotional group experience, releasing inner tensions and working off boredom, frustration, or isolation—losing themselves, for example, in a frenzy of singing or dancing. Whether active or expressive, such crowd behavior is a physical manifestation of preexisting attitudes, which now find an outlet.

In the Middle Ages, with the waning of the Black Death, devotees of St. Vitus (who was believed to have special curative powers) participated in ecstatic mass dances. Hundreds of people would leap wildly, screaming with seeming fury and foaming at the mouth. Epilepsylike seizures were common among the participants. St. Vitus' dance, in which medical, social, and religious forces converged, in many ways resembled mass hysteria. In the 17th century, Italy was afflicted by an epidemic disease characterized by nervous symptoms that was presumed to be caused by venomous tarantula bites. Women presumed to have few societal outlets for self-expression were the main victims. To counteract the "poison" they would dance to special music (tarantellas). This orgiastic "illness" is another example of a collective response that has clear links to epidemic hysteria.

At revival meetings in the first decades of the 19th century, hysterialike epidemics were not uncommon. Solid citizens would dance, sing, and laugh in unison, some participants violently jerking and even barking. The great French neurologist Jean-Martin Charcot described cases of hysterical convulsions at such meetings—characterized by delirium, hallucinations, and a spectacular arching of the body. These hysterical convulsions resembled epileptic fits; absent, however, were involuntary loss of control over bladder or bowel and tongue-biting—features typical of true epilepsy. Recovery, Charcot observed, was total.

*The 19th-century founder of modern neurology, Jean-Martin Charcot, was noted for his studious observations of hysterical convulsions. He described spectacular archings of the body, hallucinations, cries, and deliriums—symptoms that were in some ways similar to epileptic seizures.*

"Docteur Charcot" by Renouard, Musée Carnavalet; photograph, Jean-Loup Charmet, Paris

*At various times and in various countries in Europe, frantic dance ecstasies were prescribed as "cures" for inexplicable outbreaks of mass hysteria. "Possessed" women dance around a bonfire on St. John's Day (left). In the 15th, 16th, and 17th centuries, a kind of mass hysteria known as tarantism raged in southern Italy. The strange symptoms were presumed to be caused by the bites of tarantulas. Music and dance appeared to be the only means of combating the disease and calming the victims (top left and right). Couples engaged in quick-paced folk dances, hopping, skipping, and tapping to special tunes called tarantellas.*

Everyone is familiar with today's wild receptions given rock stars and pop entertainers by fans, chiefly girls aged 8 to 15. Typically these girls are crammed together in an auditorium; they share a common motivation—devotion to an idol. They become worked up by a master-of-ceremonies in anticipation, then even more worked up by the appearance of the performer or performers and by the loud, reverberating rhythms of their music. Observers have noted that with wild dancing, hand-clapping, screaming, weeping, overbreathing, and unconscious stimulation of erogenous zones, girls in the audience are sublimating latent sexual desires. It is not uncommon for many to collapse in the frenzy. But again, recovery is rapid and complete. This phenomenon, like the festivals of tarantellas, may be too organized, too ritualized, and even too predictable to be called true epidemic hysteria, but clearly it has similarities. Indeed, distinctions are difficult, and as such there is a wide clinical spectrum of what is considered mass hysteria.

## Modern examples: what lessons?

Late on Sept. 1, 1944, a woman in the small town of Mattoon, Illinois, reported to the police that an intruder had sprayed her with a "sickish sweet-smelling gas," which partially paralyzed her legs. Soon there were other victims in the vicinity experiencing paralysis. In a very short time the newspapers were full of reports of the "anesthetic prowler." Each of 30 victims recovered very rapidly—the four who were seen by physicians were diagnosed as cases of hysteria. Despite intense and continuous patrols, no prowler was ever found; indeed, the pet dogs of the victims had not barked (a fact Sherlock Holmes surely would have found a suspicious circumstance in itself); and then, very suddenly, reports stopped as people began to find the symptoms bizarre and even ridiculous. In this epidemic none of the victims were known to each other. Here the agent or vector was rumor, carried by newspapers not only locally but across the world: "Mad Anesthetist Strikes Again," "State Hunts Gas Madman." Such attention can scarcely have calmed the inhabitants of Mattoon. The victims were 93% women, mostly of a low educational and economic level. It is easy to dismiss the incident as the sort of thing that happens among ignorant people in a provincial community. But, then, why were most people in Mattoon, including children, *not* susceptible? We can only speculate.

In 1954, between March 23 and April 14, newspapers in Seattle, Washington, carried intermittent accounts of damage to automobile windshields. A total of 242 people reported damage to more than 3,000 vehicles, causing the mayor to appeal to the governor and to Pres. Dwight Eisenhower for help. Meteoric dust, sandflea eggs, air pollution, high frequency electronic waves, vandalism, and radioactive fallout from the Enewetak H-bomb tests were blamed. However, some newspapers wondered whether this was not a collective delusion—that people simply were seeing for the first time the everyday pitting of windshields due to cenospheres created by improper combustion of bituminous coal. Then, suddenly, after April 14, calls to police fell to zero. A subsequent investigation questioning a random sample of residents of Seattle showed that the sudden "collapse" of the epidemic was due

*Many religious groups have engaged in practices that have an impassioned, fiery, or even violent character. (Below left) The ceremonies of some radical Shaker sects once involved group dancing, singing, shouting, and shaking. Members of a Russian sect (right) joined together not just in spiritual worship but also in frenzied dance. These religious exercises are highly ritualized and organized, unlike spontaneous and uncontrolled episodes of epidemic hysteria.*

(Left) Historical Pictures Service, Chicago; (right) Jean-Loup Charmet, Paris

not to lack of belief in its reality, despite the absence of substantiation, but to loss of interest either because people thought they knew the cause (*e.g.,* atomic fallout) or because the epidemic had become focused; that is, it enabled people to release diffuse and pent-up anxieties and tensions associated with H-bomb testing. This release was achieved partly by the involvement of the police and the appeals to the president; the hysteria dissipated when people felt assured that something was being done to avert an amorphous but real danger.

In many epidemics of illness, the affected populations seem to share a certain emotional cohesion and homogeneity (often found in schools or the workplace) distinguished by relative isolation, a common bond of frustration, anxiety, and monotony, or by feelings of conflict with repressive authority. In one reported hysterical epidemic in schoolgirls, a generally punitive atmosphere and the fear the girls had of being found to be pregnant and sent to a state correctional school may have accounted for the outbreak. In another a group of nurses developed hysterical symptoms, purportedly because their fear of catching polio was in conflict with their duty to look after their patients.

## Who succumbs?

Numerous characteristics have been suggested as increasing the individual's susceptibility to mass hysteria. Several studies have shown those affected to have below average IQ's, but in an equal number of studies IQ's are above average. Some investigators have found those affected, when compared with those unaffected, to have had a higher incidence of previous emotional and behavioral problems, to be neurotic, or to have experienced traumatic loss in childhood. Just as many have found those affected to be normal in all respects. Thus beyond youth and femaleness modern incidents have provided no clear markers of susceptibility.

## The "index case"

Cases of mass hysteria usually begin in fraught and tense circumstances. Suddenly one of the group—the index case—becomes ill, as often as not with a definite organic illness; for example, a pregnant woman faints in a hot room. Instantly others become ill, but generally only those who share an aspect of identity with the first victim (in 95% of cases, young females). As the epidemic progresses, younger and younger people are affected; parents and teachers rarely succumb. All the physical symptoms are powerfully influenced by those of the index case. A case in point was cited by J. F. C. Hecker, who described an incident in which a 21-year-old woman was reported to have been brought to the Charité hospital, Berlin, in 1801 with convulsions: "At the sight of her violent contortions, six other female patients immediately became affected in the same way, and by degrees eight more were in like manner attacked with strong convulsions. All these patients were from sixteen to twenty-five years of age."

In May 1979, 224 elementary school students, who were gathered for a graduation play, witnessed "a sixth-grade boy, a class leader" become dizzy and fall from the stage, lacerating his chin, which bled profusely. Within minutes large numbers of female students became dizzy and weak, had head-

aches and abdominal pain, and experienced hyperventilation. Of these, 34 were hospitalized, and 50 more were treated on the school lawn.

In an African school the index case was a schizophrenic child; other children subsequently developed catatonic symptoms, hallucinations, delusions, and other bizarre symptoms typical of schizophrenia. One outbreak in London was unusual because the index case, a girl with severe emotional problems, precipitated a classroom epidemic almost deliberately. She later reported: "I enjoyed the attention this [repeated fainting] afforded. . . . I fell again, but this time it was not genuine. I received much attention and fell several more times. I was extremely ashamed of my deceitfulness and it became out of my control and I found it impossible to stop. I used it as an escape from the problems I could not face at home. . . . it was the only thing from which I gained pleasure." The "index" girl later intentionally started an epidemic of pseudopregnancy in a hospital.

## Culture, circumstances, and symptoms

Symptoms manifested in individual epidemics depend upon the historical framework, the culture, and the prevailing mood of the community. In Malaysia reports of an eight-foot-tall man with fangs, white hair, and bloodshot eyes or of demons might seem reasonable precipitants for an outbreak of mass hysteria, whereas in Dade County, Florida, they would seem ridiculous, and toxic gases would more readily come to mind (and recently did). An explosive outbreak of mass hysteria during a high school football game in Monterey Park, California, in October 1982 had nothing to do with poisoned Tylenol capsules or with cyanide, but since these were dominating the national news at the time, it was instantly assumed that they were the cause.

Analysing a Malaysian outbreak at a college, Raymond L. Lee and S. E. Ackerman pointed out that different groups concerned viewed it in very different terms. Students believed they were possessed by spirits; staff, that the students were being disruptive; and townspeople, that the students were being punished for moral corruption.

F. Sirois collected 70 reports of outbreaks between 1872 and 1972. In Malaysia there were 29 outbreaks between 1962 and 1971, 17 of them in 1971 alone—an epidemic of epidemic hysteria. Though reports suggest that the manifestations of mass hysteria are changing to conform with contemporary beliefs, we do not know if the prevalence is actually changing.

## The difficult task of diagnosis

Throughout history the physical manifestations in cases of mass hysteria have been similar. These include nausea, vomiting, faintness, overbreathing (hyperventilation), headache, weakness, itching, abdominal pain, and sometimes convulsions. Diarrhea is very uncommon. In primitive cultures there may be screaming, giggling, laughing, tearing off of clothes, and even climbing of trees. The physician is struck not only by the profusion of individual symptoms (*subjective* indicators of a bodily disorder) but also by the equally spectacular lack of physical signs (*objective* indicators of disorder) and later by the multitude of normal laboratory tests.

Symptoms spread by sight instantaneously; the contagion is greatly aided by the confusion of those in authority, who add to the air of fearful anticipation with dramatic and usually inaccurate public pronouncements. The group's worst fears that they have a serious illness are confirmed by the influx of police, firefighters, television cameras, or investigators wearing protective clothing looking for toxins and bacteria.

Cases of mass hysteria are differentiated from viral or bacterial illnesses, or from chemical poisoning, since such agents attack both sexes and all ages, do so more slowly, and are not transmitted to potential victims merely by the sight of those already affected. Moreover, viruses, bacteria, and toxins will usually result in numerous abnormal physical signs and positive laboratory tests.

Incongruities are notable in hysterical outbreaks. Members of one school class, for example, became ill because of the alleged presence of toxic gases. Everyone had to leave, but another class promptly filed into the empty room, unknowing, and proceeded normally. Unfortunately, it is not usually possible to determine the diagnosis by exclusion at the time when it matters—immediately—as it may take days or weeks to get the results of full toxicological and viral tests.

Recently, fumes forced 2,300 people to evacuate a large school in New York State. Two months later the cause of this sudden epidemic of headache, dizziness, cough, and nausea was still unclear despite an intensive search for toxic substances, possibly because the building had immediately been well aired and the substance proved to be extremely volatile. In this case, administrators and maintenance men as well as students were affected. While the facts seemed to indicate this case was *not* one of epidemic hysteria, there was reason to suspect that an atmosphere of fear may have accounted for the "illness" because two years prior to the event an elementary school less than a mile away was closed after the hazardous chemical

*(Opposite) Adolescent females, more than any other group, seem to be inordinately prone to the influences of crowd-induced, crowd-perpetuated frantic behavior. In 1964 highly excited, dancing, clapping, screaming, and weeping fans greeted the Beatles at John F. Kennedy International Airport in New York (top) and (bottom) gave the British musicians a wild reception outside their Manhattan hotel. At rock concerts and other gatherings where teens devote themselves to "idols," it is not uncommon for girls to get so worked up that they succumb to hysterical symptoms and collapse in the frenzy.*

vinyl chloride, escaping from a sanitary landfill upwind, seeped into the school's heating ducts and *was* detected promptly by chemical tests.

With the recent increasing public awareness of chemical poisons, officials are indeed justified in suspecting toxins and calling in the Environmental Protection Agency and state experts; indeed, they have little choice. Given that mass hysteria manifests itself according to prevailing beliefs, fears, and patterns of behavior, we can expect more "hysterical" outbreaks to be blamed on "environmental toxic gases"—often resulting in very intensive and expensive investigations—not least because the investigators, no matter how assured they are that the epidemic is psychogenic, feel they must protect themselves from criticism.

## Quelling an outbreak

The course of an outbreak of mass hysteria depends to a great extent on the speed and the manner in which the authorities intervene. The majority of epidemics last fewer than 14 days. With strong and appropriate action by physicians, recovery is as instantaneous as the onset of illness. Taking rapid and firm action, however, may not be easy. The physician is usually called to a scene of bedlam, where he receives a jumbled torrent of facts, rumors, and conjectures from highly excited children, teachers, parents, police, and reporters. By failing to diagnose a viral epidemic or to pinpoint a veritable toxin, *e.g.,* vinyl chloride in the heating ducts, he will be villified and probably sued, while correctly diagnosing mass hysteria will make the physician the object of anger and accusation and, no doubt, of suit.

Nonetheless, the responsible physician should note the discrepancy between the dramatic symptoms and absent physical signs and act promptly, calmly, and authoritatively to reassure the badly frightened victims and their parents that there is no organic illness. Johann Weyer, commenting on ways to handle bewitched and demonically possessed nuns in the Rhineland in the 16th century, noted: "It is necessary first of all that they be separated and that each of the girls be sent to her parents or relatives." Today physicians use this "divide and conquer" technique, separating as quickly as possible the affected from each other and from others. This often means shutting down a school or workplace.

At the same time, it is important that a proper and reasoned explanation be given in order to minimize panic. When 35 women working in closely confined quarters in a data processing center, where heavy construction was going on nearby, were suddenly overcome by typical symptoms of mass hysteria and a search for toxins proved fruitless, a team of specialists promptly closed the center and explained that an "atmospheric inversion" was probably the cause of symptoms. All the women quickly recovered as if by tacit agreement.

Can future outbreaks of mass hysteria be prevented? The answer is unclear, but scores of reports of attacks in schools, offices, and factories would suggest that it would be logical as well as humanitarian that authorities in such places pay attention to conditions and morale and that students and workers be given as much freedom as possible.

A recent outbreak of mass hysteria, promptly and positively diagnosed

*On May 11, 1973, a Friday, 95 students and 3 teachers at a rural elementary school in Berry, Alabama, became ill with rashes, headaches, coughs, weakness, sore throats, fainting, vomiting, nausea, diarrhea, and other symptoms. Over the weekend the local newspapers gave prominent coverage to the "mystery" illness. On Monday the 14th almost half of the students stayed home. On Tuesday the 15th, when most returned to school, a second outbreak involving 15 students and 3 teachers occurred, as the graph below indicates. The local health department then temporarily closed the school. But then on May 18th there was a third outbreak affecting some 14 students, which led to the suspension of classes for the remainder of the school year. Over the summer break only two cases occurred. When school resumed in the fall, there were no further cases. An extensive investigation led to a diagnosis of mass hysteria. No mechanism that triggered the curious outbreaks was ever identified.*

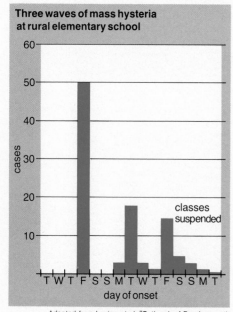

**Three waves of mass hysteria at rural elementary school**

classes suspended

day of onset

Adapted from Levine *et al.,* "Outbreak of Psychosomatic Illness at a Rural Elementary School," *Lancet,* Dec. 21, 1974, no. 7895, pp. 1500–03

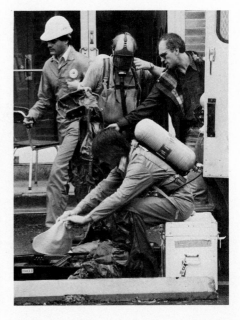

and effectively stopped, was reported by M. E. K. Mofatt of McGill University in Montreal: On Friday, May 29, 1981, a group of 600 7th- and 8th-grade students from southern Ontario were returning home from Quebec City after a four-day cultural exchange. At about 10 PM on a hot and humid evening, groups of children were milling around Montreal Central Station when the index case, a 14-year-old girl, began to feel dizzy and fainted. Very rapidly thereafter other girls began fainting, and many felt weak and dizzy and had headaches, shakiness, tingling in the arms and legs, and abdominal pains. Thirteen girls aged 12 to 14 years were rushed by ambulance to a hospital.

According to one report: "The dramatic series of fainting caused a commotion, and word rapidly spread that a 'mystery illness' was attacking a group of students in the station. Journalists descended on the area. Radio stations began broadcasting special news bulletins. The students themselves became increasingly alarmed. Food poisoning and chemicals leaking from air-conditioning on the train were commonly rumored causes. Chaperones and teachers began to check their charges and asked them to report any symptoms. Within two hours of the index case, there were many other children reporting symptoms, and a further 17 (10 girls and 7 boys aged 12 to 14) were transferred to the hospital."

At the hospital a rapid assessment was made under trying and chaotic conditions. Because the first group of 13 were all girls, many of whom had felt perfectly well until they saw others become ill; because the symptoms were primarily dizziness, abdominal pain, weakness, shakiness, and tingling; because there was a "conspicuous lack of vomiting and diarrhea"; and because physical signs were minimal, a diagnosis of "epidemic hysteria" was made, and the staff calmly dealt with the children so that 11 of the first 13 were cleared for discharge within an hour of arrival. A deliberate, courageous, but correct decision was made not to carry out exhaustive epidemiological investigations. The physicians calmly and firmly explained to the girls

*Beliefs, fears, and prevailing moods of communities seem to have a lot to do with when and where epidemics of hysteria occur and with events that might trigger outbreaks. In some cultures, for example, rumors of sightings of demonlike presences could easily set off an incident. In the United States today the increasing public awareness of chemical poisons and of very real occupational and environmental threats to health makes the climate ripe for such things as "bad smells" to cause large numbers of frightened people to succumb to stresses that manifest themselves as real physical symptoms. In November 1982 a mysterious odor sent dozens of students and teachers from a Long Island, New York, high school to the hospital and forced some 2,300 people to evacuate while scientists from the Environmental Protection Agency investigated (above). In this case unexplained symptoms probably were not hysterical in nature. But unfortunately it is never easy to distinguish the sudden onset of mysterious symptoms caused by toxic poisons from mysterious symptoms that are manifestations of epidemic hysteria. Moreover, a diagnosis of mass hysteria is never a popular one, so experts are often reluctant to proclaim that there is no physical cause for an illness.*

93

Table and graph, data from U.S. Public Health Service; photographs, Sven Nackstrand—Gamma/Liaison

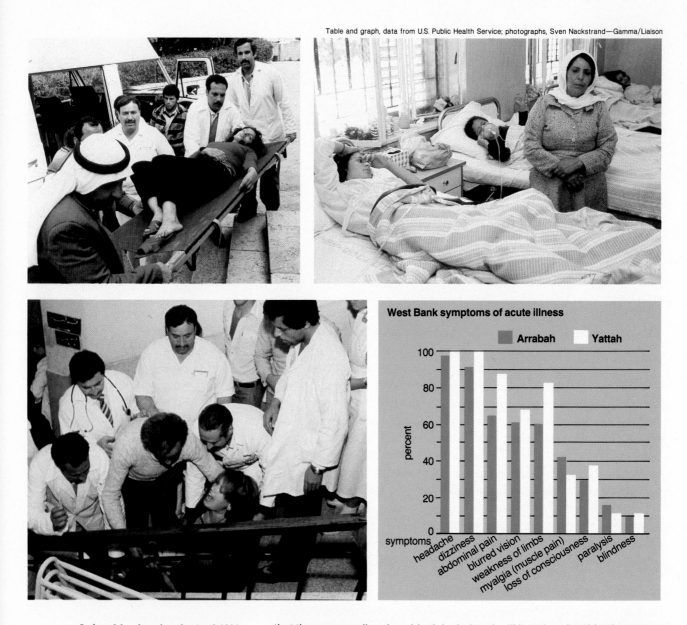

West Bank symptoms of acute illness

In late March and early April 1983, a mysterious outbreak of illness struck the Israeli-occupied West Bank. A total of about 800 West Bank residents, mostly Palestinian schoolgirls, complained of a baffling array of symptoms. Many were so ill they required hospitalization. Several female Israeli soldiers also were affected. At first, poison was suspected; Palestinians accused Israel of waging chemical warfare to drive Arabs from the region and to sterilize Arab girls. But no evidence of environmental toxins was found.

that they were well and could rejoin their train. "Upon hearing this, the two remaining girls got up off their stretchers . . . one of the girls had had severe vertigo only moments before, and the other had had pseudoparalysis which immediately disappeared." Messages were sent to railway employees and chaperones emphasizing the benign nature of the epidemic and asking them to try to calm the crowd and to separate the nonsymptomatic from the others. Very soon all the children were well enough to make an uneventful trip home.

## The mystery lingers

The above episode in many ways summarizes what we know of the strange, ancient, and changing disorder termed mass hysteria. The perplexing nature of some outbreaks may best be illustrated by the 1970 study Colin McEvedy and A. W. Beard made of "benign myalgic encephalomyelitis"—a retrospective analysis of an epidemic that afflicted nurses at the Royal Free Hospital in London in 1955. The epidemic was characterized by severe malaise, headache, sore throat, lassitude, dizziness, neck and back stiffness and pain, motor weakness, and hyperventilation with spasms. The nurses had no fever, and objective neurological signs were absent or were bizarre. For example, lack of sensation in the skin over areas that would be covered by gloves or stockings cannot be explained according to our knowledge of the pathways of nerve impulses but is reasonable to the medically unsophisticated and so is a fairly common "hysterical" finding. It is striking that only nurses—not hospital patients, male members of the staff, or other members of the community—ever caught the disease. McEvedy and Beard saw this epidemic, and 15 other reported outbreaks, 8 of them among hospital nurses, as attacks of mass hysteria occurring in groups of young women under the twin stresses of work and fear of polio. McEvedy and Beard's interpretation of all these outbreaks is a convincing one. And yet the bizarre illnesses occurred in hospitals, among nurses, under the eyes of numerous concerned physicians, and were subjected to the most intensive possible medical investigation. The emotional tone of some of the letters written in response to McEvedy and Beard's published articles from those who had believed in an organic cause emphasizes a reluctance on the part of professionals to accept anything as hazy as a "mass hysteria" diagnosis. Careful follow-up study showed that those who had been affected tended to be more neurotic and to have poorer health than controls. Here retrospective analysis has strongly suggested, not that the emperor had no clothes, but that these clothes were entirely different from what the admiring crowd of experts had imagined at the time.

The fact is, however, that we are still at the descriptive stage and, indeed, very little is really understood about these outbreaks. Baffled observers can only speculate about the psychological processes at work. In his preface to *The Dancing Mania* J. F. C. Hecker bequeathes to us from the 1830s reasons for being interested in these episodes:

[These] diseases . . . afford a deep insight into the workings of the human mind in a state of society. They are a portion of history, and will never return in the form in which they are there recorded; but they expose a vulnerable part of man—the instinct of imitation—and are therefore very nearly connected with human life in the aggregate. It appeared worth while to describe diseases which are propagated on the beams of light—on the wings of thought; which convulse the mind by the excitement of the senses, and wonderfully affect the nerves, the media of its will and of its feelings. It seemed worth while to attempt to place these disorders between the epidemics of a less refined origin, which affect the body more than the soul, and all those passions and emotions which border on the vast domain of disease, ready at every moment to pass the boundary. Should we be able to deduce from the grave facts of history here developed, a convincing proof that the human race, amidst the creation which surrounds it, moves in body and soul as an individual whole, the Author might hope that he had approached nearer to his ideal of a grand comprehension of diseases in time and space. . . .

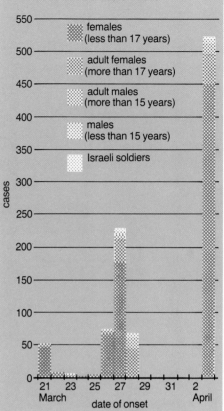

**West Bank cases of acute illness**

*Several international medical teams were dispatched to the West Bank to investigate the mysterious 1983 epidemic. Data collected by epidemic-control experts from the U.S. Centers for Disease Control indicated that either psychological factors or the odor of some nontoxic gas escaping from a latrine at a school in Arrabah triggered the outbreak. But subsequent propagation of the outbreak was mediated by psychological factors, against a background of anxiety probably facilitated by sensationalized mass media reports.*

95

# Shuttle Medicine: Challenges of Space Travel
## by Ralph Pelligra, M.D.

Traditionally, medicine has been concerned with the diseased or abnormal human in a normal environment. Aerospace medicine and its predecessor, aviation medicine, deal with the normal human in an abnormal environment. For the first half of the 20th century, human flight was confined to the Earth's atmosphere. As man endeavored to fly higher and faster within the atmosphere, he became exposed to previously unencountered and sometimes life-threatening conditions that were generated both by the aircraft he piloted and by the characteristics of the sea of air in which he moved. The solutions to the physiologic problems caused by these conditions became the province of aviation medicine. When in the early 1960s rocket technology became sufficiently advanced to propel man to the edge of space, a new field, aerospace medicine, was born. It was a logical extension of aviation medicine since the space voyager would now have to overcome both the hazards of traveling through the atmosphere and those he would meet in space. It seems inevitable that one day we will be able to speak of lunar medicine, planetary medicine, and, perhaps, cosmic medicine.

The challenge to aerospace medicine goes far beyond the need to sustain human life in the near-Earth space environment. Space is not hostile to man; it is indifferent. Aerospace medicine's task is to define human capabilities and limitations in relation to this environment so that the space voyager can function effectively, productively, safely, and happily for prolonged periods, perhaps a lifetime. To appreciate the depth of this challenge, it is necessary to understand those conditions under which man and his progenitors evolved and lived for millions of years—conditions that are not present in

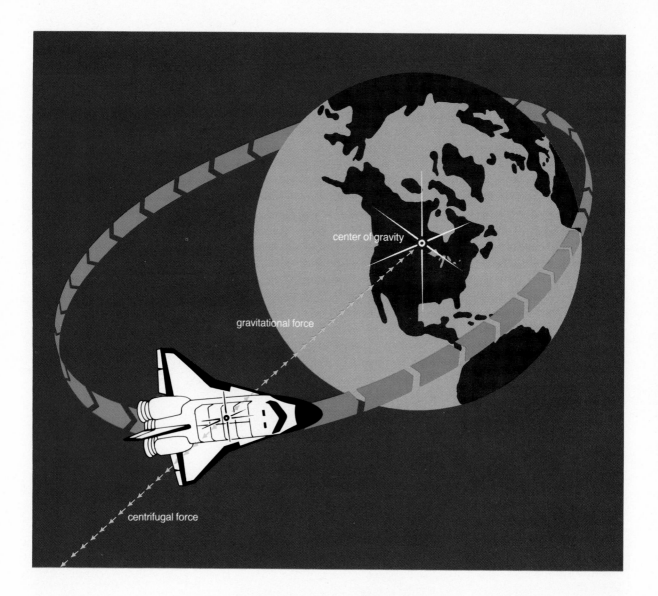

center of gravity

gravitational force

centrifugal force

space. During those formative eons, humans were bound by gravity to the Earth's surface and protected and nurtured by its atmosphere, a blanket of air 100 kilometers (60 miles) thick.

## Gravity: a strange and elusive "force"

Unlike electricity, magnetism, nuclear energy, heat, light, and other natural phenomena, gravity (G) is a "force" that cannot be generated or interchanged at man's will. It cannot be turned on or turned off, interrupted, bent, created, or manipulated. It exists wherever masses exist and exerts its influence on matter, living or inanimate, in every corner of the universe. It can penetrate a shield of lead a billion miles thick or cause steel to bend, and yet it is unimaginably weak. Two fingers holding a pebble lightly between them resist the gravitational pull of the entire $6 \times 10^{24}$-kilogram mass of the Earth.

Gravity has deftly eluded the inquiring human mind and its obsession to control natural forces while it continues to profoundly influence the human

**Ralph Pelligra, M.D.,** *is Medical Services Officer at the National Aeronautics and Space Administration's Ames Research Center at Moffett Field, California.*

*(Overleaf) "40 Pounds of Lead" by Henry Casselli; photograph, NASA*

organism from conception to death. It conspires mercilessly with the ground to maim, cripple, or kill the unlucky human who tumbles from his crib, bicycle, or balcony. It is the cause of much human suffering, contributing substantially to back problems, hernias, prolapses, malposture, certain forms of arthritis, heart conditions, varicose veins, hemorrhoids, shock syndromes, and the sagging skin and organs and bending of bones that accompany old age.

Still, without this paradoxical presence our precious atmosphere would spin away into outer space as the Earth rotates at 1,600 kilometers (1,000 miles) per hour. Rain would not fall or flow down through streams, lakes, and rivers to the oceans. There would be no tides to finely tune nature's ecological balance by flushing wastes and restoring nutrients for other life to feed upon. And just as gravity controls these life-sustaining cycles on Earth, so too does it govern the universe, orchestrating the movements of every cosmic body and the birth and death of every star.

It would appear that gravity offers little benefit to the human body and that any opportunity to live in an environment in which its effects are absent would be highly desirable. This viewpoint provides an interesting and unexpected backdrop to a question of fundamental importance to aerospace medicine: "What are the effects upon the body when the influence of gravity has been nullified?" (The reader may wonder why the question is phrased in this manner. Why not say "when gravity is absent," "in zero gravity," or "in weightlessness"? When spaceflight becomes commonplace, as it most assuredly will in the next decade, many of these terms will become household words, and it is important that they be used properly. It is not accurate to say "when gravity is absent" because gravitation exists, unperturbed and undisturbable, wherever there is matter and therefore throughout the entire universe. The same reasoning argues against the phrase "zero gravity," although it is a very commonly used expression.)

An explanation for the nullified gravity concept is found in one of Albert Einstein's great contributions to science, his "principle of equivalence" theory. He observed that despite gravity's many peculiar properties, it also behaves as a simple acceleration and, most importantly, its effects upon the human body are indistinguishable from those of any other acceleration. For example, when an automobile accelerates as the driver steps on the gas, forces are generated that push his body back into the seat. His eyes are forced deeper into their sockets, and his heart and other organs tug against their attachments as they are moved toward his back.

The body reacts in this same way whether these forces are being generated by an accelerating car (linear acceleration) or, when positioned properly, by the gravitational attraction (acceleration) of the Earth or any other large mass. In fact, the same effects upon the human body would occur if these forces were produced by motion along a circular path (radial acceleration), as occurs in many carnival rides, in a centrifuge, or in a spacecraft orbiting the Earth. Finally, if any combination of linear, radial, or gravitational accelerations are present simultaneously, the resulting forces are added to or subtracted from each other. The net result is a composite of the magnitude and direction of those forces that acts as a single force on the body.

In orbit, then, the centrifugal forces within the spacecraft that result from

*Gravity's influences on the human organism, from birth to death, are profound. Gravity contributes to many of the physical manifestations of aging— sagging skin and organs, bending bones, diminished vigor, decreased immunity, and failing hearts.*

*(Opposite page) When man orbits in space, the force resulting from the gravitational acceleration of his spacecraft toward the center of the Earth exactly counteracts the centrifugal forces within the spacecraft (created by its circular path around the Earth). The result is a situation known as "null gravity," in which the effects of gravity upon the human body are canceled. How the body reacts to null gravity is of fundamental importance to aerospace medicine.*

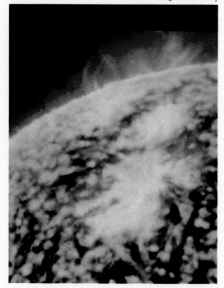

*The challenge to aerospace medicine is to define human capabilities and limitations in relation to the environment of space. Earth's surface features provide the backdrop for the onboard photograph (right) taken through a flight deck window by the crew of the space shuttle "Columbia's" March 1982 flight—man's 83rd venture into space. Intense solar flares, which occur about every decade (above), unleash streams of energetic particles and radiation that could have devastating effects on the crews of spacecraft traveling beyond the Earth's protective magnetic field.*

its circular path around the Earth exactly counterbalance the forces that result from the gravitational acceleration attracting it toward the center of the Earth. Although both forces are very much present, the effects upon the body are canceled, or nullified. Hence the more appropriate term null gravity.

Since the force that results from the acceleration of the body due to gravity is experienced by humans as "weight," loss of this subjective sensation is referred to as "weightlessness." What is often not appreciated is that a person can be "weightless" in the presence of gravity (as in orbit or in a free-fall from an airplane) or can experience weight in a null-gravity environment if an acceleration is applied to him (by a rocket, for example, or by spinning the spacecraft to create a centrifugal force).

## The Earth's atmosphere

It is easy to forget that for every single second of every day, whether we are on a mountaintop or in a cave or closet, we are totally surrounded by an envelope of air consisting of a mixture of gases. It is common knowledge that the ingredient within this mixture of gases most critical to life is oxygen. A dramatic reminder of these facts is to simply cover one's nose and mouth completely. Within as little as ten seconds one begins to experience an uneasy feeling that is soon followed by an overwhelming panic-stricken need to once again inhale this invisible, life-supporting substance.

It is apparent that if man intends to live outside the boundaries of his only readily available source of oxygen, the atmosphere, he must carry his own supply with him. What is perhaps not as obvious is that the oxygen we breathe on Earth is under considerable pressure owing to the sheer weight of the column of air in which it is contained. Although the concentration of oxygen does not change significantly with increasing altitude, there is a marked drop in its pressure. At sea level, air contains about 20.95% oxygen by volume; at 20 kilometers (12 miles) the concentration of oxygen is 20.7%; and at 30 kilometers (18 miles) it is still 20.4%. However, the pressure of oxygen available to the lungs at sea level is 160 millimeters of mercury (mmHg), but it is only 40 mmHg at 11 kilometers (6.6 miles) altitude.

There is a straightforward reason why the oxygen we breathe must be under pressure and why this pressure cannot be below a certain level. Virtually every cell in the body produces two gases, carbon dioxide and water vapor, as end products of its metabolic functions. The lungs are a major outlet for disposal of these waste products, exhaling with every breath the carbon dioxide and water vapor brought to them continually by the circulating blood in the bloodstream. The combined pressure of these gases in the lungs is approximately 87 mmHg. If the pressure of the gases surrounding the body is equal to or less than this pressure (as, for example, at an altitude of 15,000 meters [49,500 feet]), influx of oxygen through the lungs and into the bloodstream is impossible, even if the gas being breathed is 100% oxygen.

So not only must the space traveler take along or somehow provide for an ample supply of oxygen, but the oxygen must also be delivered to his lungs under adequate pressure. Throughout the Mercury, Gemini, and Apollo spaceflights, the space capsule contained 100% oxygen at 258 mmHg

*The traveler in space must somehow receive an ample supply of oxygen delivered to his lungs under adequate pressure. Astronaut C. Gordon Fullerton (below left) dons an ejection escape suit during the flight of the space shuttle "Columbia" in March 1982. This special pressurized garment is worn by the crew at the time of launch and again at reentry. A constant-wear garment is worn for most of the flight when the space cabin provides a proper oxygen-nitrogen atmosphere. In order to leave the protected environment of the orbiting spacecraft, the astronaut must wear a suit that provides a pressurized miniatmosphere that totally surrounds his body and allows for ample movement. During the space shuttle "Challenger's" April 1983 flight F. Story Musgrave floats in space (below), bundled in a thick white space suit known as an extravehicular mobility unit, which he helped design. For about three hours prior to the space walk, in order to prevent decompression sickness, he breathed 100% oxygen to remove all nitrogen from his bloodstream.*

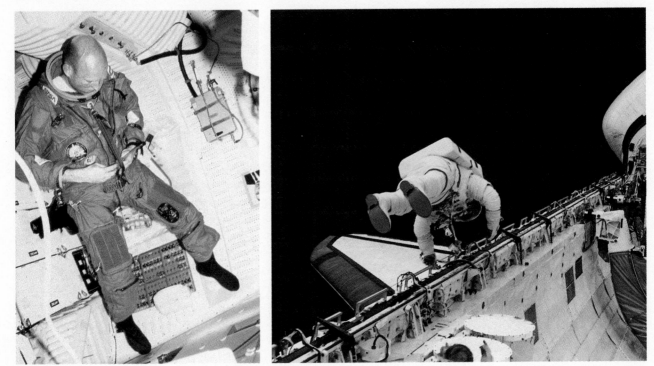

Photographs, NASA

*NASA aerospace engineers are currently designing a new suit that can accommodate increased pressure and still permit functional mobility for space walks. The plastic and metal garment would eliminate the need for oxygen prebreathing before leaving the spacecraft, which is one of its many advantages over space suits that have been used. A prototype is pictured here.*

pressure. This pressure is more commonly expressed as a fraction of the total atmospheric pressure on Earth, or in pounds per square inch (psi). For example, since the atmospheric pressure is 760 mmHg or 14.7 psi at sea level, 258 mmHg pressure can be expressed as approximately ⅓ of one atmosphere ($^{258}\!/_{760} = ⅓$) or as 5 psi (⅓ of 14.7 psi).

A more desirable "shirt-sleeve" environment is provided in the shuttle spacecraft, where air of normal composition (20% oxygen and 80% nitrogen) is compressed to one atmosphere pressure. The reason this was not done in earlier United States spaceflights is that the rockets simply were not powerful enough to carry the required equipment. Larger booster capabilities have enabled the Soviets to use air at one atmosphere pressure since their first manned flight in 1961. In brief, man is now able to take along with him a small chunk of the atmosphere that he is accustomed to at sea level on Earth.

The same approach has been applied to solving the problem of enabling the astronaut to leave the protected environment of the spacecraft while in orbit (extravehicular activity, or EVA). He is provided with a miniatmosphere within the space suit that totally surrounds his body. Ideally, the suit atmosphere would consist of 20% oxygen and 80% nitrogen at one atmosphere pressure, just as in the spacecraft or on Earth. However, pressures of this magnitude would cause unacceptable leakage of these gases from the suit into the vacuum of space, endangering its structural integrity, and they would so inflate the suit that motion of the extremities would be almost completely inhibited. By using 100% oxygen and allowing for a small margin of safety, it is possible to lower the suit pressures to about 211 mmHg (approximately 4 psi or ¼ atmosphere pressure). However, with this compromise a price is paid; there is a potential fire hazard due to the 100% oxygen as well as an increased risk of decompression sickness due to a tendency of nitrogen gas dissolved in body tissue fluids to come out of solution at low pressures. Nitrogen gas bubbles so formed tend to collect and, depending on where they congregate and interfere with blood flow, cause signs and symptoms ranging from mild joint pains to unconsciousness and death. Decompression sickness can be prevented by breathing 100% oxygen for several hours prior to exposure to low pressure literally to wash out, or purge, the body of its dissolved nitrogen. This has obvious limitations in cases of emergency where the astronaut must leave the spacecraft quickly or in the event of rapid loss of pressure within the spacecraft.

The National Aeronautics and Space Administration's (NASA's) Ames Research Center near San Francisco and Johnson Space Center in Houston have begun a collaborative program spearheaded by H. C. Vykukal, an aerospace engineer, to build a space suit that can accommodate a pressure of 414 mmHg (8 psi) and still permit functional mobility. This will reduce the fire hazard by allowing a lower concentration of oxygen to be used and will permit rapid donning of the suit without the need for prebreathing. The concepts that make this protective system possible have been under development at Ames for a number of years. The key element is the unique underlying design of the various joint components and configurations, which allows them to be made of metal and plastic and maintain good seals against gas leakage while permitting a remarkable range of motion of the extremities and trunk. Other features include a variable sizing capability for fitting a range of astronauts and low-cost reproducible manufacturing techniques for producing both the metal and fabric portions of the suit. The prototype is nearing completion and will be evaluated as a possible replacement for the current shuttle suit.

Thus, the space voyager about to depart on a journey beyond the atmosphere must pack his bags with enough oxygen at the right pressure to sustain him until his return. However, there is one feature of the atmosphere that will not fit in his traveling bags, and its absence, while not immediately life-threatening, is potentially lethal. It is the blanketlike protecting effect of the atmosphere and the Earth's magnetic field against the high-energy radiation of space. This galactic radiation that is so devastating to the human cell comes from various sources. Perhaps the most significant for manned spaceflight are the solar flares that, as large clouds of charged particles, stream from the Sun during gigantic eruptions caused by solar storms. Every decade or so, especially intense flares occur; had there been one during the series of U.S. Moon flights in the late 1960s and early 1970s, the astronauts would surely have been killed. These rays, traveling at near the speed of light, reach the vicinity of the Earth within minutes, offering little time to take cover. Spacecraft in near-Earth orbit, unless circling the poles, are within the Earth's magnetosphere and are therefore relatively protected from solar flares. However, when journeys beyond this protected area become commonplace, the Russian-roulette approach will have to be supplanted by technically difficult but not insurmountable methods for protecting the spacecraft by adequate shielding.

## The human response to space

In the early days of the space program, before manned spaceflight, there was concern that the human body would have great difficulty functioning in space because of failure of muscular and postural control and because death might even ensue from circulatory failure due to loss of normal gravitational constraints on blood flow. Could man tolerate weightlessness and speeds more than six times that of a bullet as it leaves the muzzle of a rifle? Would the psychological stresses of confinement and severence from the Earth's gravitational "umbilical cord" lead to psychosis? to delusions of Godlike omnipotence?

Although these fears were based on reasonable theoretical considerations, none of them was realized, thanks to the remarkable adaptive abilities of the human body and mind. As of mid-June 1983, the Americans and Soviets had accumulated a total of 39,834 hours in space since it was first explored by man on April 12, 1961. In December 1982 cosmonauts Valentin Lebedev and Anatoly Berezovoy ended the longest manned spaceflight, which began on May 13 and lasted for 211 days, 9 hours, and 5 minutes. Although full details of their medical conditions may not be realized for quite some time, they appeared to be in good spirits and in good general health immediately after their venture into space. Experience with the crews of previous record-setting flights points to a complete recovery. (The previous long-

103

Photographs, NASA

*The weightless state affects three major body systems: the cardiovascular, the musculoskeletal, and the vestibular (balance). During the November 1982 "Columbia" flight (top), astronaut Joseph P. Allen measures William B. Lenoir's responses to a variety of physiologic functions in the null gravity environment for comparison with earthbound responses. Motion sickness, or space adaptation syndrome, has affected some 30–50% of astronauts to some degree. The best explanation to date is that the sensory information that normally enables man to maintain orientation is disrupted in the null gravity atmosphere. Physicians and astronauts are attempting to glean more precise information about this problem. (Bottom) Lenoir tests his vision during orbit.*

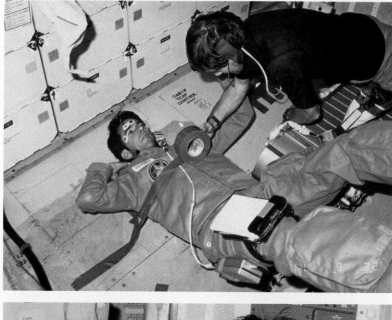

est manned missions were 175 days in 1979 and 185 days in 1980, both by Soviet crews.)

The evidence to date indicates that the body systems most affected by the weightless state are the cardiovascular system, the musculoskeletal system, and the vestibular (balance) system. It should be pointed out that the observed changes do not interfere with function in space after a brief period of adaptation and do not appear to be harmful except in relation to the requirement to return to the 1-G environment on Earth. Stated differently, the adaptive changes that occur in these systems might be inconsequential and conceivably even beneficial for the voyager who has no intention of returning to Earth, although there are still insufficient data to tell. What are the observed changes?

104

*The cardiovascular system.* It is not surprising that the heart, blood vessels, and reflex mechanisms that comprise the cardiovascular system "decondition" when they are no longer required to pump blood in defiance of gravity. By "decondition" it is meant that when the system is called upon to do its job once again during return to Earth, it responds less efficiently; increased heart rate, lowered blood pressure, and fainting are common. The cardiovascular system has more difficulty resisting gravity's attempts to pool blood in the lower body, away from the brain, heart, lungs, and other vital organs.

Concurrent with and contributing to this deconditioning effect in null gravity is a redistribution, or migration, of body fluids from the lower extremities and abdomen into the upper trunk and head. The body interprets this shift as an increase in the volume of circulating fluid and attempts to compensate by instructing the kidneys to increase their excretory activity. This leads to a state of diminished hydration that, while it probably does not interfere with the ability of the astronaut to function in space, can cause problems during reentry and initial readaptation to Earth's gravity.

An example of the detrimental effects of these processes was seen in the second space shuttle flight (STS-2), whose mission was shortened because of technical problems. Astronauts Joe H. Engle and Richard H. Truly, confronted with a contaminated water supply, were unable to drink sufficient amounts of fluids prior to reentry to restore losses. Fortunately, these two highly trained professionals were able to bring Columbia to a smooth and safe landing despite enough impairment of their performance abilities to cause ground controllers to be concerned.

*The musculoskeletal system.* The musculoskeletal system, like the cardiovascular system, is one of man's major allies in his continuing battle against gravity. The alignment of bones and muscles permits the human body to enjoy sustained vertical mobility within the Earth's gravitational field. Under conditions of orbital flight, bones and muscles, deprived of the stressful stimulus of gravity, begin to lose their structural integrity. Whereas deterioration of muscle can be prevented for the most part by proper exercises, an extensive search for more than a decade for measures to prevent bone-mass loss has been unsuccessful.

*"If birds fly over the rainbow, Garber, why, oh why, can't I?"*

*"The boys in research seem to think it has something to do with aerodynamics, Chief."*

In the absence of the stimulus of gravity and for other less clearly understood reasons, calcium leaves the bones and continues to be lost from the body, predominantly through the intestines. Despite the amount of calcium ingested, more is lost than is absorbed, resulting in a negative calcium balance. The negative calcium balance continues to increase in magnitude with duration of exposure to weightlessness. Based on accumulated flight data, it can be calculated that as much as 25% of an astronaut's total calcium pool could be lost in a mission of one year's duration. His bones could become brittle and more likely to fracture with minor impact in space or with weight bearing on return to Earth. Unless effective countermeasures are developed, this anticipated rate of calcium loss may preclude future space missions lasting more than six to nine months for voyagers wishing to return to Earth.

*The vestibular system.* One of the ways that the vestibular system enables man to maintain his orientation in three-dimensional space is by using gravity as a vertical reference. When this guidepost is gone (nullified) in orbital flight, much of the sensory information about the body's position conflicts with previously accumulated and stored experiences. This sensory conflict theory is the best current attempt to explain the very real and mundane problem of space motion sickness, now called the space adaptation syndrome, that affects some 30–50% of astronauts in both the Soviet and U.S. experiences. Symptoms range from mild nausea, pallor, and sweating to severe retching and vomiting. Fortunately, the symptoms are self-limiting and seldom last for more than 24 to 72 hours. However, if, for emergency or other reasons, reentry were required during this period, these symptoms could be incapacitating and potentially dangerous.

Motion sickness sufferers on Earth will attest that during a severe attack they are convinced not only that they are going to die but that a visit from the Grim Reaper would be welcomed just so they could be relieved of their symptoms. Imagine trying to bring back a 90-ton spacecraft from orbit to a pinpoint landing on Earth while feeling this bad.

Of the 12 crew members in the first five shuttle flights, 6 have experienced mild to moderate symptoms of the space adaptation syndrome. Perhaps of even greater concern than the return trip to Earth, many phases of which can be automated, is the possibility of experiencing symptoms while in a space suit during extravehicular activity (EVA). During STS-5 in November 1982, astronaut William B. Lenoir's space walk had to be postponed because of the space adaptation syndrome. Although his symptoms subsequently subsided, the EVA portion of the flight was canceled because of space suit malfunction.

## Aerospace medicine research on Earth

The dilemma that faced early researchers in aerospace medicine and that still poses a significant problem is that sustained weightlessness cannot be reproduced in the terrestrial laboratory. It is possible during certain aircraft maneuvers to provide a null gravitational or weightless state for brief periods of less than one minute. By flying along the path of a vertical parabolic curve, for example, an aircraft generates centrifugal forces that precisely counter-

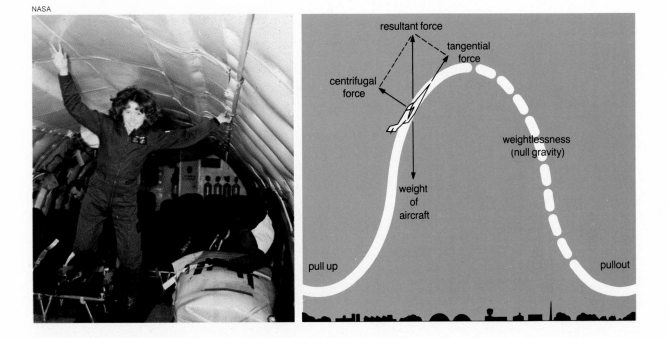

balance the forces resulting from the gravitational attraction between itself and the Earth. However, few meaningful human experiments can be conducted under such severe time and space constraints, and their results are further complicated by the increased forces required to enter and leave the flight maneuver.

Animal orbital flights, a total of 18 by the U.S. and 29 by the Soviet Union, provided important information about the physiologic responses to weightlessness prior to cosmonaut Yury Gagarin's first flight on April 12, 1961. Nevertheless, it would have been reassuring to be able to observe the responses of the human body to weightlessness under controlled laboratory conditions prior to full exposure in orbit. Many of the other potential hazards of the near-Earth-orbit environment, such as the absence of atmospheric pressure, temperature extremes, and radiation effects, have been studied in humans and animals on Earth in altitude chambers and other devices.

However, the closest we have been able to come to duplicating or simulating the effects of weightlessness is to expose human volunteers to prolonged periods of complete bed rest. When the body is resting in the horizontal position, the demands upon the cardiovascular system are markedly reduced because it can now circulate body fluids to all the vital tissues and organs with minimum resistance from gravity. Similarly, the counterbalancing effects of buoyancy when the body is immersed vertically in water partially simulate the changes observed in orbit by causing a headward shift of body fluids. In both these models, bed rest and underwater immersion, various body systems decondition through disuse in much the same manner as occurs in null gravity. However, it should be kept in mind that in both these experimental conditions gravity is present in full force and continues to act upon all the body's cells and tissues. The conditions simulated by bed rest and water immersion, often erroneously referred to as "hypogravity," are in

*One of the problems facing researchers in aerospace medicine is that sustained weightless states cannot be simulated. One approach that has been employed to produce brief periods of weightlessness uses specially flown aircraft. As the diagram above shows, an aircraft is pulled upward into a parabolic flight path. As it approaches the apex of the parabolic curve, the centrifugal and tangential forces increase in magnitude until the resulting force equals the weight of the aircraft, thus creating a short period (about 30–45 seconds) of weightlessness. Astronaut candidate Anna L. Fisher (above left) anchors herself aboard such an aircraft during a training venture at Ellington Air Force Base near Houston, Texas.*

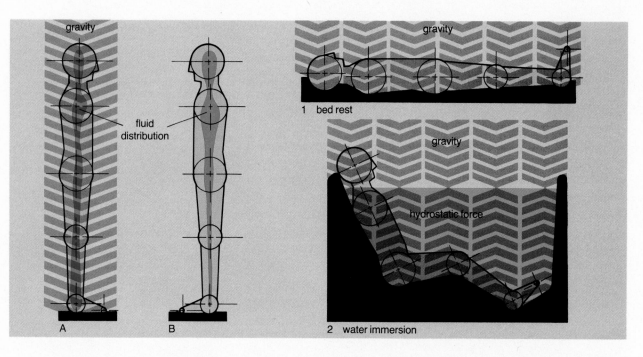

1 bed rest

2 water immersion

*(Above) Figure A shows the normal distribution of body fluids; gravity exerts a downward force on fluids so that they tend to accumulate in the lower extremities. Figure B shows the effect of semiweightlessness; i.e., a shift of fluids toward the upper body, simulated in the laboratory by (1) placing the body in a horizontal position or (2) by counterbalancing hydrostatic forces via immersion in water.*

fact hypodynamic states, or periods of exaggerated inactivity. Nevertheless, they have become useful tools to assess the ability of men and women up to age 65 to tolerate the stresses of the space environment.

As part of their simulated space journey the volunteers are asked to "ride" the centrifuge. Compared with bed rest and water immersion, the centrifuge provides a more nearly accurate and effective simulation of anticipated conditions. As was mentioned earlier, the body's reactions to centrifugal, linear, or gravitational accelerations are identical. To complete the simulation, it is necessary to determine the direction and magnitude of the forces acting on the passengers of a spacecraft such as the shuttle during its journey from orbit (null gravity) to Earth (1 G) and to determine the appropriate rate of rotation of the centrifuge needed to duplicate these forces.

The direction and magnitude of the force acting on the space shuttle passenger results from the combined effects of linear (forward) motion and gravitation. Because of the nose-high attitude of the space shuttle as it reenters the Earth's atmosphere, the direction of the combined forces is along the long axis of the passenger's body; i.e., from head to foot. Although the direction of the force does not change throughout reentry, its magnitude varies with the velocity of the spacecraft. This situation can be accurately duplicated by rotating the centrifuge at appropriate speeds with the test subject positioned properly in the centrifuge cab.

There are a number of investigators in the U.S., Europe, and the Soviet Union who have been attempting to anticipate problems of spaceflight by using bed rest and water immersion to simulate weightlessness and to test susceptibility to fainting (orthostatic intolerance) due to reentry by using various methods such as the centrifuge and lower body negative pressure (LBNP).

Although all the results are not yet in, indications are that neither age (at

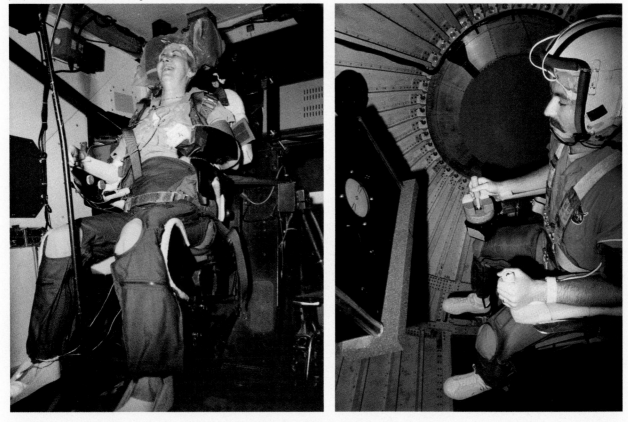

least to 65 years) nor sex should present any insurmountable problems to sending the average, healthy person into space. In fact, most recent research has revealed some interesting surprises. It appears that the older groups and more sedentary subjects tolerate the simulated stresses of reentry somewhat better than younger persons and highly conditioned athletes. The reasons are complex but have to do with increased pliability of the cardiovascular system, which allows blood to pool more easily in the lower body. In the older and more sedentary groups, blood pressures tend to be higher and blood vessels more rigid, which together have the effect of sustaining blood flow to the brain despite the attempt of reentry forces to do the opposite. In general, men have higher tolerance levels than women (possibly owing to the fact that females have smaller heart volumes), but the differences are not so great as to preclude participation of women in all phases of spaceflight.

Two other major areas of current aerospace medicine research deal with the short-term effects of weightlessness (the space adaptation syndrome) and the long-term effects on demineralization of bone. The inconvenience, potential hazards, and high attack rate of space motion sickness have stimulated an intensive and broad-based program of both animal and human research to determine its causes and to develop countermeasures. Various antinausea drugs are somewhat effective but are limited in their usefulness by their side effects, such as drowsiness, which can impair precision perfor-

*(Opposite page) Astronaut Robert L. Crippen is about to be immersed in water in a weightless environment training facility at NASA's Johnson Space Center in Houston, Texas. Simulated bed-rest conditions, which afford minimum resistance from gravity (above left), enable aerospace physicians to study the cardiovascular system when demands on it are greatly reduced. They are thus able to assess the ability of men and women to tolerate the stresses of the space environment. It appears that neither age nor sex is a limiting factor. As part of their training, astronauts ride a centrifuge such as the one at Ames Research Center in California (above). The tests performed enable physicians to predict bodily responses to reentry.*

109

*Astronaut Sally K. Ride records activity of a test specimen for an electrophoresis experiment on board the "Challenger" during the June 1983 mission. Ride was the first U.S. woman to go into space, though many female astronauts were in training and at least seven were scheduled for future flights. The Soviets sent Valentina Tereshkova into space in 1963; in August 1982 Cosmonaut Svetlana Savitskaya was aloft for eight days. Among the questions that have been raised about women as space travelers are: What effects will null gravity have on the menstrual cycle? Will women be more or less prone to the vision loss and fainting that can occur on reentry? Early reports noted that Ride had weathered the flight physiologically as well as her male crewmates.*

mance that is required to operate sophisticated space systems.

A more promising approach to the treatment of the space adaptation syndrome is the combined use of biofeedback and autogenic (self-induced) methods called autogenic feedback training (AFT). Patricia Cowings, an innovator and recognized authority in this field, has used AFT to cure motion sickness symptoms in 80% of the subjects studied in her laboratory at NASA's Ames Research Center. AFT takes advantage of the ability of almost any properly trained person to influence his own body functions, such as heart rate, blood pressure, skin blood flow, and gastric motility. These functions, which are a part of the autonomic nervous system, were previously thought to be beyond willful control. Using AFT a person can reduce the

*The subject (right) is trained in biofeedback to prevent the nausea and other unpleasant or debilitating effects of space adaptation syndrome. Motion sickness is induced in a laboratory setting by a vertical motion simulator.*

response of the brain's vomiting center irrespective of the source of sensory input that is causing it to be overstimulated. Tests will be conducted in Spacelab 3 to see if the benefits of these techniques can be transferred to the space environment. There is good reason to believe that they can be.

As mentioned earlier, the problem that has been most resistant to resolution and that may be the limiting factor in prolonged space travel is the loss of calcium, phosphorus, and protein from human bones that occurs in the absence of gravitational stress. Much of the current study is being done in animal models subjected to prolonged periods of inactivity, but as yet no protective countermeasures have been developed. Unless such measures are discovered, the only solution that will permit prolonged exposure in space may be to provide artificial gravity by rotating the spacecraft to generate centrifugal forces.

## Medical research in space

The highly successful operational flights of NASA's space transportation system that began in November 1982 have demonstrated that routine access to near-Earth orbit is both feasible and practical. These crucial first steps have extended the human sphere of influence into space and have opened a vast new resource. The potential medical benefits are striking. Recognizing that in the unique null gravity, hard vacuum environment of space, crystals and other materials of unprecedented purity can be produced cheaply and efficiently, private industry has invested tens of millions of dollars over the past several years to launch a commercial pharmaceutical production program in space. Their test unit on the fourth shuttle flight verified that a process known as electrophoresis, which separates biological materials from their surrounding medium by utilizing an electrical field, in the absence of the effects of gravity yields 400 times the output and up to 5 times the purity as the same method on Earth. Pharmaceutical concerns

*The most difficult physical complication of space travel is the loss of calcium, phosphorus, and protein from bones. Most of the current studies are being done in animal models subjected to long periods of inactivity. The photographs below show (left) normal bone in a 14-year-old (middle-aged) monkey; (middle) bone after ten weeks of restraint, displaying large cavities of bone erosion; and (right) partially restored bone structure after a 15-month recovery (ambulation) period.*

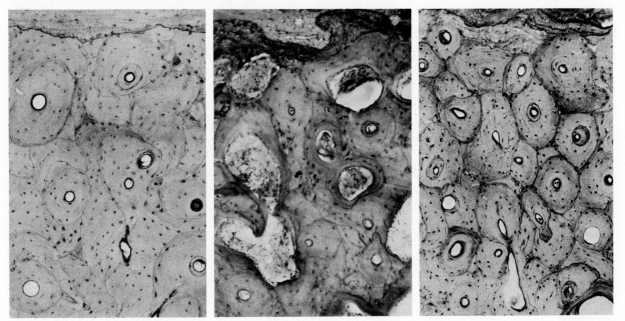

Photographs, Donald R. Young, Ames Research Center, NASA

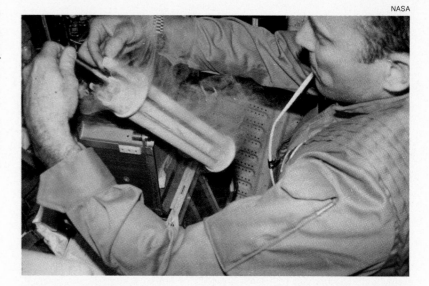

*Before the year 1990, pharmaceutical manufacturers hope to have production facilities in operation in space. The potential to increase yield and purity of drug products in a null gravity environment via the process known as electrophoresis is enormous. Astronaut Jack R. Lousma (right) removes frozen samples of blood cells that have been separated by electrophoresis equipment taken on board the "Columbia's" March 1982 mission.*

foresee an operating production facility in orbit as early as 1987. Just some of the more than 50 anticipated commercially produced pharmaceuticals in space are: (1) beta cells of the pancreas, which, when isolated on a mass basis, could provide single-injection cures for an estimated 3.2 million diabetic patients per year; (2) interferon, a substance that provides the body with immunity from viral infections and has shown promise for its role in the treatment of certain cancers; this drug could offer benefits to 20 million persons yearly; and (3) epidermal growth factors in the skin, important for treating burns and facilitating wound healing in more than one million patients yearly. Approximately another one million patients yearly could benefit from other space-made products such as growth hormone to stimulate bone growth in children with deficiencies of this substance, antitrypsin to limit the progress of emphysema and enhance cancer chemotherapy, and antihemophilic factors to help control a sometimes lethal blood disorder.

On a more speculative plane, it is possible to explore the effects of prolonged weightlessness on human aging and life expectancy. Aging and death are compelling processes to which, in time, all living organisms succumb. But as processes they can be influenced. The detrimental, sometimes devastating, effects of gravity on human anatomy and physiology have already been mentioned. In orbit the potential exists for manipulating forces in order to facilitate and stimulate youthful growth and development while relieving harmful or restricting stresses in infancy and old age. This proposal was first made in 1978 during a symposium on human neurological development sponsored jointly by NASA's Ames Research Center and the Institutes for Achievement of Human Potential, in Philadelphia. The concept's viability is based on a common design feature of the various future space habitats that permits them to rotate about a central axis in order to provide centrifugal forces to the peripherally located living areas. While the intent is to provide a force-field environment comparable to gravitation on Earth, it incidentally offers the opportunity to expose humans for prolonged periods to an infinite range of accelerations between null G and 1.5 G or more. This is accomplished by moving along the radius from the center of rotation where null G

112

conditions exist to the farthest distance out, where, depending on the rate of rotation of the space habitat, forces comparable to 1.5 G or 2 G could be generated.

## A future in space?

It has been said that the need to explore the universe is more than just a matter of curiosity; it is a continuation of the process of human evolution. It is feasible that one day, obviously in the far distant future, it will turn out that only a small fraction of all the humans who were ever born actually lived on the planet Earth. Rather, they will have colonized the far reaches of our galaxy. Our solar system has a finite life-span. In some 5,000,000,000 years our life-giving Sun will suffer the fate of all suns; *i.e.,* extinction.

If for some reason our sciences and technologies are not able to find ways to sustain human life indefinitely beyond the confines of Earth's gravitational field and atmosphere, the eventual demise of the human species and all terrestrial life will be inevitable. This concept is awesome. Nonetheless, it is most exciting to realize that it is our generations that are taking the first critical steps toward meeting this future cosmic challenge to humankind.

Space painting by Tom O'Hara; photograph, NASA

*In the early 1960s when rocket technology became sufficiently advanced to propel man to the outer limits of the atmosphere, aerospace medicine was born to meet the challenges of space travel. Man's accomplishments in space in two decades' time are awesome. It is possible that future challenges will give birth to lunar medicine, planetary medicine, or even cosmic medicine.*

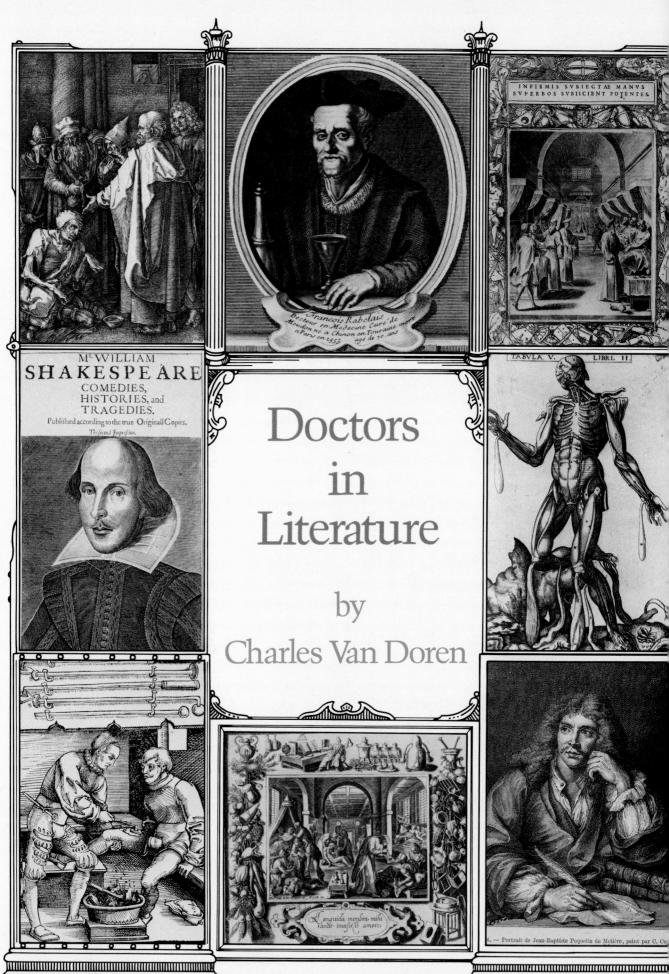

# Doctors
# in
# Literature

## by

## Charles Van Doren

There is an interesting difference between books written by doctors and books written about doctors by authors who are not physicians. We can learn something important from both about medicine and about the world.

William Shakespeare was not a physician, nor are any of his heroes physicians, at least in the modern sense of the term. But there are half a dozen fascinating doctors who play small but important roles in several of his plays. Sometimes these roles are very small; for example, that of the doctor who comes to Macbeth to announce that that dread lady, his wife, has expired. With a shrug, Macbeth, already descended too deeply into evil to feel much, bursts out: "She should have died hereafter!" That is her only epitaph.

Physicians in *King Lear,* in *Pericles,* and in *Cymbeline* have roles that loom larger in the action. Lear, mad and defeated, is more fortunate in his physician than in his daughters; that good doctor's patient care of the frantic old man is a model for all who tend the mentally ill, in or out of institutions. And the actor who plays the part of the doctor is privileged to share in one of the most moving scenes in all of drama, when in Act IV the old king, waking from his long sleep (and from his madness, which the doctor has cured by his calm voice, gentle hands, and soothing medications), recognizes his daughter Cordelia and perceives the deep truth of her love for him, which he has so mightily abused.

The doctor in *Cymbeline* is one of the keys to the play's fantastic, contorted plot. He has tended Cymbeline's vicious second wife and indulged her taste for trying out poisons on cats and dogs. But he fears she will extend her experiments "afterward up higher"—that is, to humans—and so he gives her, instead of a poison, a potion in which there is

No danger in what show of death it makes,
More than the locking-up the spirits a time,
To be more fresh, reviving.

In other words, the potion, even if given with evil intent—which it is, by the queen, to Imogen, the king's daughter and the heroine of the play—will only put her victim into a deep sleep, indistinguishable from death, perhaps, but only for a time. The doctor adds: "She is fool'd / With a most false effect; and I the truer, / So to be false with her." This potion has a key role in the action of the play. Imogen imbibes it, thinking it is a healing medicine; she is taken for dead and mourned by those who love her; but of course she comes back to life when the drug's effect wears off.

A third memorable Shakespearean physician appears in the play *Pericles.* The noble Lord Cerimon, although only an amateur doctor, nonetheless performs a remarkable cure in bringing the maiden Thaisa, later the wife of King Pericles, back to life. Any licensed physician would envy his skill! Cerimon does this with certain "vials and boxes" that he has secreted in his closet, with medicines, in short, that he has prepared himself, after much study. In Act III Thaisa, discovered in a coffin washed up by the sea, seems dead; but eventually, after lengthy ministrations, Cerimon is able to cry out:

She is alive! Behold
Her eyelids. . . . Live, and make
Us weep to hear your fate, fair creature,
Rare as you seem to be!

[*She moves.*]

*Thaisa.*                    O dear Diana!
Where am I? Where's my lord? What world is this?

The attendants applaud, but Cerimon hushes them, adding:

Lend me your hands; to the next chamber bear her.
Get linen: now this matter must be look'd to,
For her relapse is mortal. Come, come;
And Aesculapius guide us!

Certain images of doctors that recur in many classic works by nondoctors are suggested in these three plays of Shakespeare. The calm, affectionate patience of Lear's doctor, never raising his voice, providing moral as well as physical support—that is perhaps what we all hope for in a physician, and is the mark of the "good doctor" in many novels and tales. The action of the queen's physician in *Cymbeline*—in telling his patient less than the truth in order to protect her from herself and for her own good—is also a recurring theme. Here, however, nondoctor writers often protest, either outright or through the words and actions of their characters. Even if it is for the patient's own good, is it ever right for one person, and especially a figure of authority, to lie to or withhold the truth from another? Finally, the doctor as miracle worker, like Lord Cerimon, is a common character in plays and stories—and television dramas!—of our time.

These miracles are not always so mysterious when we are let in on the secret, but what does that matter? A cure is a cure! So it is with Sganarelle, the mock-doctor of Molière's play *Le Médecin malgré lui* (*The Doctor in Spite of Himself*). Sganarelle, an ignorant peasant (but a very wise one), is fascinated by doctors and loves to imitate them, reeling off long paragraphs of what seems, to his equally ignorant hearers, like Latin, and freely dispensing medical advice that always has a kernel of sense in it despite the fantastic forms in which it is offered. Sganarelle's wife, sick and tired of this game, tricks him into putting on a show for certain messengers of the king, who are scouring the kingdom for physicians in the hope that one of them will be able to cure the princess, who has totally lost her power of speech. Sganarelle is terrified when he discovers that, whatever the rewards for a successful cure, there are dire penalties for failure—but there is no backing out now. He fools the learned courtiers with his mock Latin and his medical airs, but not the princess; he manages, however, to have a private interview with her during which he discovers (what his peasant shrewdness has guessed) that her trouble is amatory, not medical at all. She is in love with one young man, but her father has ordered her to marry another. Sganarelle solves the problem, of course, in what is surely one of the funniest plays ever written.

A sick man who often needed medical care and assistance, Molière knew doctors well and expressed his amusement at medical pomposity in this

**Charles Van Doren** *retired from the position of Vice-President, Editorial, of Encyclopaedia Britannica in 1982. He is currently engaged in a number of writing and editing projects and is a member of the Board of Editors of Encyclopaedia Britannica. He resides in Falls Village, Connecticut, and Cortona, Italy.*

Queen. [To PISANIO.] Hark thee, a word.
Cornelius. [Aside.] I do not like her. She doth think she has
Strange lingering poisons.
                                        Act I.  Scene IV.

*"Certain images of doctors that recur in
many classic works . . . are suggested in
. . . plays of Shakespeare. The calm,
affectionate patience of Lear's doctor . . .
providing moral as well as physical
support . . . is perhaps what we all hope
for in a physician. . . . The action of
[Cornelius] the queen's physician in
Cymbeline—in telling his patient less than
the truth . . . for her own good—is also a
recurring theme."*

(Left) Scene from *Cymbeline*, The Mansell Collection, London; (right) William Shakespeare; photograph, The Granger
Collection, New York; (bottom) scene from *King Lear*, Act IV, The Folger Shakespeare Library, Washington, D.C.

(Top) Molière as Sganarelle, in *Le Médecin malgré lui,*
Bibliothèque Nationale; photograph, Bulloz, Paris; (bottom)
Molière, portrait by Paul Mignard; photograph,
Jean-Loup Charmet, Paris

*"What doctors know about disease,
Molière seems to be telling us, or about
nostrums and regimens and therapies, is
not always the most important thing. A
learned physician who is not also a wise
and caring human being may in the end be
both a bad doctor and a fool."*

great comedy. But Sganarelle is not just a pompous fake. He is driven by necessity—indeed, to save his own life—to find a cure for his patient, and he does so by talking to her in a way nobody else does, by showing her that he cares about her and means to protect and support her come what may. In short, Sganarelle's bedside manner is superb, whatever his shortcomings in other respects. He "knows" nothing; after all, his "learning" is all a pretense. What doctors know about disease, Molière seems to be telling us, or about nostrums and regimens and therapies, is not always the most important thing. A learned physician who is not also a wise and caring human being may in the end be both a bad doctor and a fool.

Molière, a great actor as well as playwright, took the lead part in most of his own productions. He was playing Argan, a rich hypochondriac, in *Le Malade imaginaire (The Imaginary Invalid)*—a spoof on doctors' gullibility and the corruptness of their ways—when, during the fourth performance of the play in Paris on Feb. 17, 1673, he collapsed on stage and died.

George Bernard Shaw, to name still another playwright who was fascinated by doctors, was not so generous as Molière. The happy possessor not only of an iron constitution (Shaw lived to be 94 and wrote for the stage until he was well into his 80s) but also of an acid wit, he chastised physicians in many of his works for just those faults that Molière had pointed to in *Le Médecin malgré lui:* for their pomposity and pretense as well as for their fundamental ignorance, no matter how much they *seem* to know, or *say* they do. Shaw's indictment of doctors was only slightly less piercing than his indictment of the even more ignorant public they served, for he realized that even the greatest doctor can seldom move much ahead of the beliefs, no matter how ill-founded, of his patients. In one of his many vitriolic attacks on doctors, Shaw described "the country of the Half Mad" (his readers recognized England, of course), in which there was "a law that when there was sickness in the house the doctor must be sent for, and that if the doctor said that any part of a sick child's body must be cut out its parents must have that done at once whether they approved or not, or else be haled before a magistrate and heavily fined. . . ."

To such powers as this were added extraordinary privileges. For instance, doctors were licensed to commit murder with impunity, provided they did it either by administering poison or by using knives of a particular shape in such a manner that the victim did not die until he or she had been put to bed. Not only was no inquest held and no indictment brought against the doctor, but he was actually paid for his labor, and sometimes invited to the funeral.

The vanity and foolishness of some doctors were further ridiculed in other Shavian works such as his play *The Doctor's Dilemma,* which shows an eminent physician having to face up to a deeply human problem instead of merely a medical one. (Probably all young doctors should read it.)

Gustave Flaubert, in his famous novel *Madame Bovary,* was also less than generous to doctors, a fact all the more telling because Flaubert's father was an eminent physician and hospital director. Charles Bovary, the husband of Emma (the Madame Bovary of the title), is a pathetically ambitious young doctor who has overextended himself to buy a practice in a small town and who, in his desperate attempts to recoup his fortune, sows pain

118

and misery among his patients near and far. It is true that Dr. Bovary has uncommon burdens to bear, his wife being not the least of them; Emma is a silly idealist who demands romance as well as a comfortable living from her husband, and when she does not find it there seeks it in the arms of a lover. This short summary does not, of course, do justice to Flaubert's classic novel of French provincial life, but it does emphasize one facet of the medical profession that deserves note. Charles Bovary has descended upon his little town like a scourge and without so much as a by-your-leave. He has bought the practice, and the townspeople now have no other doctor; nor, in 19th-century France, is there anyone to inhibit Bovary or protect the people from his narrow-minded ambition.

At one point in the novel's action, Bovary, having heard of a new surgical method for curing clubfoot (a condition about which he knows virtually nothing), decides he shall perform such an operation because it is likely to bring him "swift fame." Aided and abetted by the town's apothecary and Emma, he persuades the lame stableboy Hippolyte to undergo the surgery. "You'll feel nothing more than a slight pain at the very most," the unwitting chap is told. The operation is carried out; Bovary is hailed "a magnanimous man of science." But three days later "a livid tumescence ran up the leg," and a specialist had to be summoned to amputate.

A doctor has fearsome powers, as both Flaubert and Shaw remind us; used well, they are a source of great good; used badly, they are a potent force for ill. May the Lord protect us, we may find ourselves saying, from such physicians as Dr. Bovary.

One could wish that Dr. Bovary had been more obedient to the wisdom expressed in the old French maxim: "To cure sometimes; to help often; to comfort and console always." Indeed, in very many cases help, comfort, and consolation are more important, because more possible and realistic, than the illusion of a cure.

Leo Tolstoy, too, was not a great admirer of doctors, although when he dealt with medical matters, his focus tended to fall on the patient rather than on the physician. The famous scenes in *War and Peace* on the battlefield of Austerlitz and in the primitive hospitals of Russia during the Napoleonic invasion of 1812 are memorable for their insights into the hearts and minds of wounded men, not the skill or caring of physicians. Yet even here doctors figure, and the reader is faced with age-old questions that beset the medical profession. How is a doctor, having, as all do, only limited resources, to choose between those he will try to save and those he will not? What shall he say and do to men he knows are dying, even if they do not know? When, and when not, should he inflict pain in order to promote healing, when there is always a chance (in Russia in 1812 a good chance) that the inflicted pain will lead to an even more terrible death? Tolstoy makes us think of these things, but he also places us, with his incomparable literary magic, inside the brain of Prince Andrey as he lies dying in his whitewashed hospital room, nursed by his beloved Natasha, who is no longer real to him. This, which must be considered one of the great scenes in fiction, reminds us of the enormous truth that in the end we die with or without doctors, and our dying is more our business than theirs.

*"George Bernard Shaw . . . chastised physicians in many of his works . . . for their pomposity and pretense as well as for their fundamental ignorance. . . . Shaw's indictment of doctors was only slightly less piercing than his indictment of the even more ignorant public they served, for he realized that even the greatest doctor can seldom move much ahead of the beliefs, no matter how ill-founded, of his patients."*

*"Gustave Flaubert, in his famous novel*
Madame Bovary, *was . . . less than
generous to doctors. . . . Charles Bovary,
the husband of Emma . . . is a
pathetically ambitious young doctor who
has overextended himself to buy a
practice in a small town and who . . . sows
pain and misery among his patients near
and far. . . . Leo Tolstoy, too, was not a
great admirer of doctors, although when
he dealt with medical matters, his focus
tended to fall on the patient rather than
on the physician. . . . From* The Death of
Ivan Ilych *we learn in the most moving
way about the profound dependence of the
dying patient upon his physician—an
emotional tie that so often goes only one
way. . . . Albert Camus was more
sympathetic to and understanding of the
terrible burdens borne by doctors as well
as patients when death intervenes."*

Tolstoy's greatest story, *The Death of Ivan Ilych,* also deals with this theme. The various doctors in the story, both those who succeed and those who fail, both those who care and those who do not, are essentially irrelevant to the experience of Ivan Ilych, which is the experience of facing his own death, and then of dying itself.

Finally, in the end,

The doctor came at his usual time. Ivan Ilych . . . at last said: "You know you can do nothing for me, so leave me alone."

"We can ease your sufferings."

"You can't even do that. Let me be."

Here is more Tolstoyan magic: how can Tolstoy know so much, we wonder, about "that bourne," as Hamlet called it, "from which no traveler returns"?

From *The Death of Ivan Ilych* we learn in the most moving way about the profound dependence of the dying patient upon his physician—an emotional tie that so often goes only one way. When the attending physician comes to examine him,

Ivan Ilych knows quite well and definitely that all this is nonsense and pure deception, but when the doctor, getting down on his knee, leans over him, putting his ear first higher then lower, and performs various gymnastic movements over him with a significant expression on his face, Ivan Ilych submits to it all. . . .

120

Albert Camus was more sympathetic to and understanding of the terrible burdens borne by doctors as well as patients when death intervenes. In his novel *The Plague,* Camus tried to express his feelings about death and life and about commitment to preserving the lives of others even if this costs us our own. Bubonic plague descends upon the city of Oran, in Algeria, where Camus grew up, and Rieux, the young doctor, remains, when others flee, to care for the sick and dying. His friend Tarrou, the philosopher-journalist (who may represent Camus himself), remains with Rieux out of some sense of duty that he can never explain. *Ubi tres medici, duo athei,* goes the old saying: "Where there are three doctors, there will be two atheists." And Tarrou and Paneloux, the priest, are deeply concerned to discover whether Rieux goes on working and risking his own life because he believes in God. But Rieux will not say. Whether or not he is an atheist is beside the point, we come to understand; his dedication to his suffering fellow human beings is sufficient justification. *The Plague* is a profound and disquieting book, with its hero who is a doctor and a great one. It is a book to balance Flaubert and wash the taste of Dr. Bovary out of our mouths.

## Doctors who are writers too

Doctor-writers, of whom there have been many good ones, express different feelings both about medicine and about life from the feelings expressed by writers who are not doctors. For one thing, they often write about or refer to their own medical experience, experience that, of course, is not shared by nondoctors. Somerset Maugham, for instance, practiced medicine for a time but then gave it up to become a writer. In his autobiography, *The Summing Up,* he declared: "I do not know a better training for a writer than to spend some years in the medical profession. I suppose that you can learn a good deal about human nature in a solicitor's office; but there on the whole you have to deal with men in full control of themselves. . . . The interests [the solicitor] deals with, besides, are usually material. . . . But the doctor, especially the hospital doctor, sees [human nature] bare." What in particular did Maugham learn during his career as a doctor? Perhaps he tells us the most important lesson a little later on, when he describes something that happened during his student days.

I have always worked from the living model. I remember that once in the dissecting room when I was going over my "part" with the demonstrator, he asked me what some nerve was and I did not know. He told me; whereupon I remonstrated, for it was in the wrong place. Nevertheless he insisted that it was the nerve I had been in vain looking for. I complained of the abnormality and he, smiling, said that in anatomy it was the normal that was uncommon. I was only annoyed at the time, but the remark sank into my mind and since then it has been forced upon me that it was true of man as well as of anatomy. The normal is what you find but rarely. The normal is an ideal.

That of course is important for any writer to learn. At the same time, the lesson can be a dangerous one, for when we aver that "Truth is stranger than fiction," we are warning the writer not to stray too far from the path of normality, lest we begin to disbelieve him—even if he has seen what he describes with his own eyes!

Lewis Thomas, author of *The Lives of a Cell* and *The Medusa and the*

121

W. Somerset Maugham, detail of a portrait by P. Steegman, National Portrait Gallery, London

*"Doctor-writers . . . express different feelings both about medicine and about life from the feelings expressed by writers who are not doctors. . . . they often . . . refer to their own medical experience. . . .*
*Somerset Maugham . . . practiced medicine for a time but then gave it up to become a writer. In his autobiography,* The Summing Up, *he declared: 'I do not know a better training for a writer than to spend some years in the medical profession. . . . the doctor, especially the hospital doctor, sees [human nature] bare.' "*

*Snail,* has also written with eloquence about the values of a medical education—and about how much better medical education would be if it dealt with the kinds of problems that novelists and poets write about. But in his most recent book, *The Youngest Science* (an autobiography), written after several personal encounters with serious illness, he reveals what he has learned by viewing the medical profession from the viewpoint of the patient. He is disturbed, he confesses, by the distance that has grown up between patient and doctor (a distance, however, that has been complained about for decades if not centuries). Modern doctors, Thomas says, with their wonderful machines and their computerized diagnoses, are losing one of the most important medical arts, "the laying on of hands."

There, I think, is the oldest and most effective act of doctors, the touching. Some people don't like being handled by others, but not, or almost never, sick people. They *need* being touched, and part of the dismay in being very sick is the lack of close human contact. Ordinary people, even close friends, even family members, tend to stay away from the very sick, touching them as infrequently as possible for fear of interfering, or catching the illness, or just for fear of bad luck. The doctor's oldest skill in trade was to place his hands on the patient.

Oliver Wendell Holmes, another great writer-physician, emphasizes what doctors as well as patients may gain from such physical contact. In a remarkable commencement address to the graduating class at Bellevue Hospital in New York in 1871, Holmes described the "educated touch" or *tactus eruditus,* as he called it, that "extends to the mind as well as to the finger-ends."

Book-knowledge, lecture-knowledge, examination-knowledge, are all in the brain. But work-knowledge is not only in the brain, it is in the senses, in the muscles, in the ganglia of the sympathetic nerves—all over the man, as one may say, as instinct seems diffused through every part of those lower animals that have no such distinct organ as a brain. See a skilful surgeon handle a broken limb; see a wise old physician smile away a case that looks to a novice as if the sexton would soon be sent for; mark what a large experience has done for those who were fitted to profit by it, and you will feel convinced that, much as you know, something is still left for you to learn.

In the same address, which is full of useful practical advice, Holmes returns to the point made by the doctor in *Cymbeline:* Don't always tell your patient everything you know. What sort of face should the doctor show to a patient who is seriously ill? Says Holmes, "He should never be able to read his fate in it." He expanded on this advice in a passage from his fine novel *Elsie Venner.* The old Doctor is visiting Elsie in her sick room.

The old Doctor was a model for visiting practitioners. He always came into the sickroom with a quiet, cheerful look, as if he had a consciousness that he was bringing some sure relief with him. The way a patient snatches his first look at his doctor's face, to see whether he is doomed, whether he is reprieved, whether he is unconditionally pardoned, has really something terrible about it. It is only to be met by an imperturbable mask of serenity, proof against anything and everything in a patient's aspect. The physician whose face reflects his patient's condition like a mirror may do well enough to examine people for a life-insurance office, but does not belong to the sickroom.

That is good writing—and good medicine, too.

Finally, two great doctor-writers—strange pair!—who have made good use of their medical knowledge are William Carlos Williams and François

122

Oliver Wendell Holmes, *Vanity Fair*, 1886; photograph, Mary Evans Picture Library

Rabelais. Williams, the 20th-century poet from Paterson, New Jersey, tried to come to grips with his dual life as poet and physician in his *Autobiography*. The brutal, painful, primitive world of the big city hospital, he tells us, is somehow the place where poems are coming to be. "The physician enjoys a wonderful opportunity actually to witness the words being born." Every patient, every sick person, both different and alike (as are well people, too), is trying to say something that he can't quite say. "We begin to see that the underlying meaning of all they want to tell us and have always failed to communicate is the poem, the poem which their lives are being lived to realize."

The poem springs from the half-spoken words of such patients as the physician sees from day to day. He observes it in the peculiar, actual conformations in which its life is hid. Humbly he presents himself before it, and by long practice he strives as best he can to interpret the manner of its speech. In that the secret lies. This, in the end, comes perhaps to be the occupation of the physician after a lifetime of careful listening.

All of this is the highest metaphysics, and we may be accused of straying too far from the "real" world of doctors and hospitals and illness and death when we hear a poem in every word a patient says. But Williams himself can bring us down at any moment to that primal reality. He tells us of a surgeon he once knew "who whenever he'd get into a malignant growth would take a

William Carlos Williams; photograph, Elliott Erwitt—Magnum

"*Oliver Wendell Holmes, another great writer-physician, . . . described the 'educated touch' . . . that 'extends to the mind as well as to the finger-ends. . . . The way a patient snatches his first look at his doctor's face, to see whether he is doomed, whether he is reprieved, whether he is unconditionally pardoned, has really something terrible about it. It is only to be met by an imperturbable mask of serenity, proof against anything and everything in a patient's aspect. The physician whose face reflects his patient's condition like a mirror may do well enough to examine people for a life-insurance office, but does not belong to the sickroom.' . . . William Carlos Williams . . . tried to come to grips with his dual life as poet and physician. . . . 'The physician enjoys a wonderful opportunity actually to witness . . . words being born.' Every patient, every sick person, both different and alike, . . . is trying to say something he can't quite say.*"

*"Rabelais received a medical degree from Montpellier, the best medical school in France in his time. While we do not know whether he ever practiced much medicine, we do know he could not have believed very firmly in 'cures.' Doctors can help us to endure life, he would have preferred to say. . . ."*

*"Lewis Thomas . . . has . . . written with eloquence about . . . how much better medical education would be if it dealt with the kinds of problems that novelists and poets write about. . . . he reveals what he has learned by viewing the medical profession from the viewpoint of the patient. He is disturbed, he confesses, by the distance that has grown up between patient and doctor. . . . Modern doctors, Thomas says, with their wonderful machines and their computerized diagnoses, are losing one of the most important medical arts, 'the laying on of hands.' "*

hunk of it and rub it into his armpit afterward. Never knew why. It never hurt him, and he lived to a great old age."

Williams's account calls to mind another story, told by the American physician Hans Zinsser, who personified the cultivated man. In his autobiography, *As I Remember Him,* which was a best-seller 50 years ago, Zinsser wrote,

One of Dr. Kerr's colleagues from up near Ogdensburg, whom I had met at this time, did a most extraordinary thing. I met him on the river one day when we were both fishing off the head of Watch Island. Just as I came in sight of him as I rounded the point, he pulled out a magnificent pickerel.

"Good for you, doctor!" I shouted to him.

"What d'ye think, young feller?" he called back. "I caught that fish with a nice fat appendix I took out this mornin'."

Stories like that would have pleased Rabelais, the author of the strange and wonderful *Adventures of Gargantua and Pantagruel,* who lived in France nearly 500 years ago. The tales of Zinsser and Williams would have made him nod and say, Yes, that's the way it is, that's the wisdom of the physician.

Rabelais received a medical degree from Montpellier, the best medical school in France in his time. While we do not know whether he ever practiced much medicine, we do know he could not have believed very firmly in "cures." Doctors can help us to endure life, he would have preferred to say, and they can help us to understand it. The best way to understand, as well as to endure, is to laugh. It is a curious conclusion, and probably not an incorrect one. There is such a thing as a "Rabelaisian" view of life and, as everyone knows, it includes mostly laughter with generous portions thrown in of good food and good wine. Rabelais would not mind being remembered in this way.

Jumping again to contemporary times, yet another writer—this one *not* a doctor—who has taught many readers much about both doctors and books is Norman Cousins. Cousins's own nearly mortal bout with illness some years ago has become very well known through his *Anatomy of an Illness*

124

"Professor Henri Vaquez at la Pitié Hospital" by Édouard
Vuillard, 1921, National Academy of Medicine, Paris;
photograph, Rapho/Photo Researchers

*"One could wish that Dr. Bovary [and a
good many other physicians in literature
and in life would be] more obedient to the
wisdom expressed in the old French
maxim: 'To cure sometimes; to help
often; to comfort and console always.'"*

*as Perceived by the Patient.* Cousins began to be cured, he wrote, the day
he began to laugh again.

Such insights led to a medical school faculty appointment for Cousins. The
great men of medicine who above all respect their patients are the models
for his courses. But in his lectures he is also quick to castigate the all too
many doctors who presume to wield mighty powers. Cousins has published
an anthology of writings by and about doctors—a testament to the fact that
the subject of the doctor in literature offers a wealth of very good and useful
medicine for the spirit.

The American physician Walter B. Cannon once wrote a book called *The
Wisdom of the Body.* Rabelais would have appreciated it, but he probably
would have changed the title to "The Goodness of the Body." Above all, Ra-
belaisianism involves acceptance—of our bodies and of ourselves. Let's not
stand on circumstance, Rabelais would have said; let's admit that we all
have the same needs, of intake and output. Another great Frenchman,
Michel de Montaigne, made the same point when he said that the greatest
king in the world, on the highest throne, is still sitting on his own backside.

The backside of man, as of life, amused Rabelais, as it amused William
Carlos Williams, and Hans Zinsser, and Somerset Maugham, and Norman
Cousins. And this amusement, which is coupled with acceptance of the body
as it is, is what distinguishes these writers and doctors from the others. The
best doctors are the earthiest of humans; as it was said long years ago, of
the earth are we made, and to earth we shall return. When we remember
that, we are remembering something very important about medicine, about
literature, and about life.

FOR ADDITIONAL READING:
Cousins, Norman, ed. *The Physician in Literature.* Philadelphia: W. B.
Saunders Co., 1982.

Starr, Paul. *The Social Transformation of American Medicine.* New
York: Basic Books, 1983.

# The Science of Successful Weight Loss

## by Peter D. Wood, Ph.D., D.Sc.

The problem of obesity—carrying more body weight than is considered desirable by the overweight individual or by the society in which he or she lives—is without question a major preoccupation in the United States and in many developed countries. There are two aspects of overweight that cause concern: the shape and size of the overweight person in relation to "desirable" shapes and sizes at a given place and time, and the health consequences of a given degree of overweight. Perceived beauty and fashion are fickle and changeable; the degree of "obesity" of the female bust and buttock generally held to be desirable has fluctuated historically over a wide range. And although biologically illogical, the desire to attain the fashionable shape has long been a powerful one, and failure to achieve it a frequent cause of distress.

Our views of the health consequences of overweight have also evolved over the years. Currently, a proposed liberalization of weight/height standards for optimal health is receiving considerable attention and some criticism. But extreme obesity is clearly detrimental to health and longevity, while lesser degrees of overweight worsen the prevalent conditions—high blood pressure and diabetes—and predispose to gallstones. By any standard, some 25 million to 50 million men and women in the U.S. are undesirably overweight, and the great majority would prefer to be slim. As a consequence, a vast weight-loss industry has grown up. Billions of dollars change hands in a frequently futile attempt to lose weight permanently; each month sees a new, more exotic but frequently less scientific treatise on weight loss; and frustration grows among the overweight and their medical advisers.

## Body composition

"Overweight" means too much body mass relative to one's height, body build, and sex. It can be a very subjective matter. When inspecting our friends and neighbors, with or without clothes, we are not in a strong position technically to assess the problem. We see a shape, and we register "skinny," "fat," "out of condition," or "sexy" as the case may be and as our cultural background dictates. We are aided in our judgment by tables, in particular the much-used weight/height tables of the Metropolitan Life Insur-

**Peter D. Wood, Ph.D., D.Sc.,** *is Professor of Medicine at Stanford University School of Medicine and Deputy Director of the Stanford Heart Disease Prevention Program, Stanford, California.*

*(Opposite page) Jack Sprat and his wife, illustration by Arthur Rackham for an edition of* Mother Goose; *photograph, The Granger Collection, New York City*

(Top left) "The Three Graces" by Peter Paul Rubens, Museo del Prado, Madrid: photograph, Art Resource, New York; (top right) The Bettmann Archive; (bottom) from Soemmering, *Über die wirkungen der Schnürbrüste*, Berlin, 1793; photograph, National Library of Medicine, Bethesda, Md.

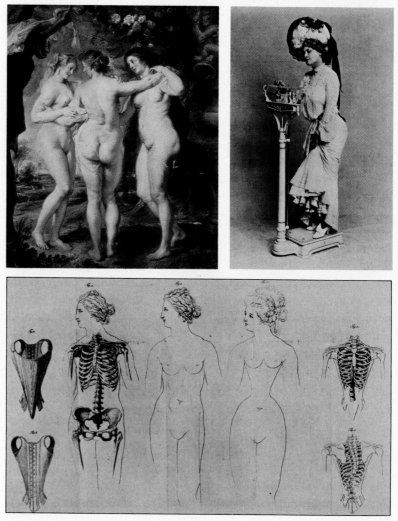

*In the 17th century Rubens painted well-fleshed female figures whose richly hued bodies were composed of subtle hollows and swells and curves, epitomizing sensuous beauty. Perceived ideals of body shape vary according to prevailing standards of fashion and beauty. The desire of women to attain a fashionable shape has long been a powerful one—failure to achieve it, a great source of distress. Often what is considered attractive is not natural or healthy. To achieve a 19th-century ideal, women wore corsets that shaped their torsos to desired proportions. These viselike undergarments squeezed waists to tiny sizes, accentuated hips, and pushed up bustlines. This unhealthful practice could cause anatomical disfigurement and displacement of internal organs—not to mention discomfort.*

ance Co. (old and new versions), which indicate "desirable" body weight for a given sex, height, and body build, based on certain actuarial data. In a general way, these tables have been a very useful guide to overweight, but they inevitably fail to take account of the composition of the excess weight. Is it fat? muscle? bone? water? Unfortunately, simple, generally available methods to assess body composition are not available, although the determination of body density by weighing the subject in air and under water (hydrostatic weighing) is a reasonably accessible scientific tool. Using this procedure, we now know that the vast majority of the "overweight" in the United States are in fact "overfat." But we should bear in mind that muscularity is different from adiposity: the 5-foot 10-inch, 200-pound muscular football player is quite different from the 5-foot 10-inch, 200-pound flabby, sedentary businessman. Their metabolisms are different, and their silhouettes are different.

It is worth noting that ready accumulation of body fat has conferred biological advantages upon our forebears. Survival during hard winters and famines has depended until relatively recently upon entering the period of deprivation, like a hibernating bear, with ample body fat. It seems probable that we have arrived at the easy-living 20th century genetically selected for ready storage of body fat. But suddenly, comforted by well-stocked freezer and neighborhood food store, we do not need this evolutionary asset any more. Of course, modern man occasionally faces his old adversary, inadequate calories, in the concentration camp or on the wilderness trek. But most of the time the enemy is overready accumulation of body fat.

## The paradox: eating less but getting fatter

Overfat individuals are usually not prominent in the populations of less developed, poorer nations, except among the wealthy minority. This clearly relates to the availability of food and the characteristic activity levels of the population. A study of the population changes in the U.S. in the past 80 years is instructive. Height and weight data, accurate and easily obtained, have been regularly recorded, and it is clear that the population has become fatter. At the same time, the evidence shows that per capita food consumption has *fallen* in the United States. What has happened is this: physical work has been replaced progressively by machines—cars, conveyor belts, ditch-digging machines, electric golf carts. Labor saving has been touted as desirable and a symbol of prosperity and wealth. We have become addicted to foods rich in fat and sugar—calorically dense foods—so that the bulk of food required to meet our diminished energy needs has fallen. As we get older, the situation deteriorates. We are less inclined to dance all night or play touch football and more inclined to sit and watch television. We can afford to eat out more often, but we no longer have the luxury of satisfying a ravenous appetite as we did in our twenties. And so, many people in the U.S. and other developed nations accumulate one or two pounds of fat year after year from age 20 to age 50, and thus arrive at middle age with 20–50 pounds of excess fat that they would like to dispose of. What errors did all these people commit? There was a minute error in calorie intake. Over the years they ate 14.4 calories per day more than they expended (for an annual fat gain of a

*In 1983 new standard tables of "desirable weights" were released for the first time since 1959. The new numbers, which represent averages associated with lowest death rates, have been revised upward by an average of seven pounds. Desirable-weight tables can be useful general guides, but they have limitations and flaws. For instance, they fail to reflect the composition of excess weight. The new tables are based on weights for persons 25–59 years old in indoor clothing (five pounds for men, three pounds for women) and in shoes with one-inch heels.*

| Revised "ideal" weight tables | | | | | | | |
|---|---|---|---|---|---|---|---|
| | men | | | | women | | |
| height | small frame | medium frame | large frame | height | small frame | medium frame | large frame |
| 5 ft 2 in | 128–134 | 131–141 | 138–150 | 4 ft 10 in | 102–111 | 109–121 | 118–131 |
| 5 ft 3 in | 130–136 | 133–143 | 140–153 | 4 ft 11 in | 103–113 | 111–123 | 120–134 |
| 5 ft 4 in | 132–138 | 135–145 | 142–156 | 5 ft 0 in | 104–115 | 113–126 | 122–137 |
| 5 ft 5 in | 134–140 | 137–148 | 144–160 | 5 ft 1 in | 106–118 | 115–129 | 125–140 |
| 5 ft 6 in | 136–142 | 139–151 | 146–164 | 5 ft 2 in | 108–121 | 118–132 | 128–143 |
| 5 ft 7 in | 138–145 | 142–154 | 149–168 | 5 ft 3 in | 111–124 | 121–135 | 131–147 |
| 5 ft 8 in | 140–148 | 145–157 | 152–172 | 5 ft 4 in | 114–127 | 124–138 | 134–151 |
| 5 ft 9 in | 142–151 | 148–160 | 155–176 | 5 ft 5 in | 117–130 | 127–141 | 137–155 |
| 5 ft 10 in | 144–154 | 151–163 | 158–180 | 5 ft 6 in | 120–133 | 130–144 | 140–159 |
| 5 ft 11 in | 146–157 | 154–166 | 161–184 | 5 ft 7 in | 123–136 | 133–147 | 143–163 |
| 6 ft 0 in | 149–160 | 157–170 | 164–188 | 5 ft 8 in | 126–139 | 136–150 | 146–167 |
| 6 ft 1 in | 152–164 | 160–174 | 168–192 | 5 ft 9 in | 129–142 | 139–153 | 149–170 |
| 6 ft 2 in | 155–168 | 164–178 | 172–197 | 5 ft 10 in | 132–145 | 142–156 | 152–173 |
| 6 ft 3 in | 158–172 | 167–182 | 176–202 | 5 ft 11 in | 135–148 | 145–159 | 155–176 |
| 6 ft 4 in | 162–176 | 171–187 | 181–207 | 6 ft 0 in | 138–151 | 148–162 | 158–179 |
| weight in lb at ages 25–59 based on lowest mortality | | | | | | | |

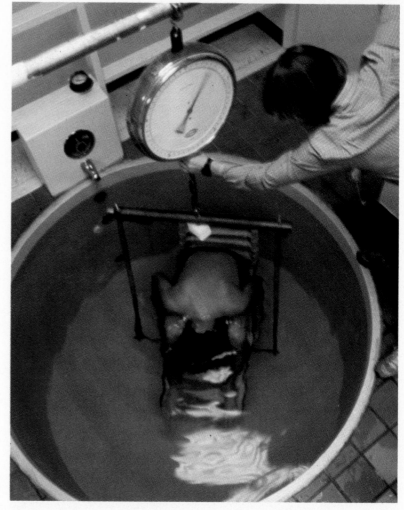

*There are a number of ways to determine individual fat composition. One method uses calipers (left) to measure fat thicknesses at various sites on the body. Another employs the ancient underwater technique of Archimedes; this hydrostatic weighing (right) is based on the low specific gravity of fat tissue. Fat is lighter than water, while muscle and blood are slightly heavier.*

pound and a half). This amounts to about one-fifth of a banana too much each day for 30 years. We begin to see that gluttony can hardly be blamed for the problem; for most fat people the eating control mechanism is only slightly off, but the result is the inexorable accumulation of fat. But all these people committed a major error in energy expenditure. They became, under social and cultural influences, much less active than they had been as youngsters and so moved into a region of energy input-output where their calorie input control was *slightly* faulty, with consequent slow accumulation of fat.

## Fat people versus slim people: surprising differences

Ingrained in our society at all levels is a belief that the overweight state in humans is due to overeating. This underlying belief expresses itself in the diet book's preoccupation with eating less, in the newspaper doctor's advice to the overweight reader, and even in the prestigious professional committee's recommendation to the overweight public to eat less. This view goes far back into history. Shakespeare's Prince Hal says to the grossly overweight Falstaff: "Leave gormandizing; know the grave doth gape/ For thee thrice wider than for other men." He does not instruct: "Start exercising."

It is true that in some circumstances overweight people suffer from overeating disorders characterized by high calorie intake relative to slim people with similar physical activity levels. But the evidence is that the majority of overweight people eat no more—and in fact they frequently eat *less*—than slim people. Several large population studies—for instance, one of 1,485 London civil servants—have shown that recorded food intake tends to decrease with increasing fatness. There is a great deal of individual variation, including measurement error, but the evidence shows that generally the fat eat less than the slim. Some studies have shown that this may not be true at the sedentary end of the activity spectrum, where fat sedentary people eat more than thin sedentary people. The point is that there are relatively few thin sedentary people, especially in the U.S.

Study of the eating habits of very active and very sedentary people shows what we might intuitively expect: the active consume more calories than the sedentary. In groups of middle-aged runners (male and female), calorie intake is higher than in a random sample of the population that is presumed to be relatively inactive. Calorie intake per kilogram of body weight is some 40 to 56% greater in the active groups. In a study of tennis-playing women (averaging ten hours per week of singles play), an average daily intake of 2,417 calories was recorded, compared with the intake of only 1,490 calories by a control group of sedentary women. These differences are quite substantial, but reasonable, since extra exercise clearly demands extra fuel. But in both groups—the runners and the tennis players—the active individuals were also much leaner than the sedentary controls.

Might we expect, then, that if fat people become more active and lose weight they will eat more? In a study conducted at Stanford University, 32 middle-aged, sedentary men volunteered for a one-year program of progressive physical conditioning based on running. They were not asked to attempt to lose weight or modify their food intake. Measurements of body fat and calorie intake were made at the beginning and end of the year. None of the men went on a low-calorie diet. The data showed a *negative* correlation between the mileage run by the men and the change in percentage of their body fat: the more miles the men ran, the more fat they lost. There was a *positive* correlation between miles run and change in calorie intake: the more miles the men ran, the more they increased their calorie intake. And most interestingly, there was a *negative* correlation between change in percentage of body fat and change in calorie intake: the more body fat the men lost, the more they increased their calorie intake. At the end of the one-year period, the men who had successfully become more active had lost body fat and increased their calorie intake simultaneously.

The fact that the active slim eat more than the sedentary overweight has at last shed some light on the best approach to the overweight problem in developed countries. In the face of these findings, it is curious that the overweight person attempting to lose weight typically decides (1) to remain sedentary and (2) to eat less. In studying the noted differences between the slim and the fat, the scientist looks at those who already have the desired

*"When I tell him, he'll hit the ceiling . . . but he needs the exercise!"*

*Exercise adjusts the caloric equation—i.e., it raises the rate at which calories are burned, thus favoring weight loss or easier weight control. The exerciser who is exposed to cold temperatures—swimmer, skier, skater, winter jogger—benefits from extra calorie usage because the body has to expend more fuel to maintain its temperature. It is not surprising that active people tend to consume more calories than inactive people. As the table on this page indicates, calorie intake for groups of middle-aged runners is substantially greater than for nonrunners. The figure on the opposite page shows the relationships between miles run per week, change in percentage of body fat during one year, and change in calorie consumption during that year for 32 sedentary men who voluntarily entered a one-year exercise program at Stanford University.*

characteristic: What are they like? How do they behave? Dieting actually makes the fat person even more *unlike* the slim person; he or she is simply a fat person reluctantly eating less, and the transformation into a true slim person has not occurred. It is not at all surprising, then, that the "eat less" approach to weight loss and permanent weight control has not worked.

## Important mechanisms in weight loss: new insights

In order to maintain life, the human body needs to expend a certain amount of energy even in conditions of complete rest. This energy, measured in calories per minute, is required to sustain metabolic processes in the cells and to maintain body temperature. This expenditure is known as resting metabolic rate (RMR) or basal metabolic rate (BMR) and is roughly one calorie per minute for an average-sized individual, or 1,440 calories per day. This figure is affected by a number of influences and can vary considerably from person to person. Muscular activity above rest involves additional energy expenditure. An extremely sedentary person may add only 200 or 300 calories per day to his RMR, to about 1,700 calories per day. An average person may use a total of 2,200 calories per day, and an extremely active person (a lumberjack or a marathon runner) probably uses as many as 3,000–6,000 calories per day.

What influences RMR? It varies with sex and age. Exposure to cold increases RMR since the body has to burn more fuel in order to maintain its temperature. Body composition affects RMR since muscle and fat tissue have different energy requirements at rest. Thyroid hormone and certain drugs (*e.g.,* caffeine) also influence RMR. Any influence that increases our underlying RMR is likely to favor weight loss or easier weight control—and vice versa, since extra energy taken in as food must be used to sustain RMR, whereas it might otherwise be stored as body fat.

We can now examine how the typical life-styles of the slim and the overweight influence RMR. It has been clear for many years that reduction of calorie intake (*i.e.,* dieting) is soon accompanied by a *decrease* in RMR. This effect is quite apparent when calorie intake is abruptly reduced to very low

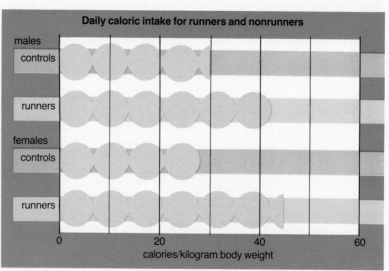

Adapted from S. N. Blair *et al*, "Comparison of Nutrient Intake in Middle-Aged Men and Women Runners and Controls," *Medicine and Science in Sports and Exercise*, vol. 10, no. 5, pp. 310—315

levels, as happened to millions of Europeans during World War II. Clearly this is a valuable defense mechanism for the body, which senses that hard times have arrived and economy must prevail. The metabolic fires are banked down in anticipation of more deprivation to come. No doubt this mechanism served our ancestors well during famines and hard winters and enabled some inmates to survive the starvation diets of concentration camps. But the body's defense mechanism cannot tell the difference between the first month in Belsen and the first month on the latest exotic low-calorie weight-loss diet. So down goes the hopeful but unsuspecting dieter's RMR as the body starts to economize, often sabotaging heroic efforts to cut calories. In an extreme, hypothetical example, a reduction in calorie intake of 600 calories per day that simultaneously reduced RMR from 1,400 to 1,000 calories per day would produce a net deficit of only 200 calories per day, with correspondingly disappointing weight loss.

The opposite effect is also seen, so that attempts by the thin person to eat more and fatten himself up tend to be thwarted by the body's ability to *increase* RMR with caloric excess. It should not be thought that it is impossible to gain or lose weight by altering calorie intake. Clearly this is not the case, but the body does have quite effective mechanisms that have a tendency to maintain fat levels in spite of fluctuations in food intake.

## Some stunning effects of exercise

A fascinating and incompletely understood influence upon RMR is exercise. It is apparent that vigorous physical activity acutely raises metabolic rate. For instance, if a resting individual suddenly runs a mile in five mintues, his metabolic rate may go from one calorie per minute at rest to 20 calories per minute during the run (a total of 100 calories used to run one mile). We might

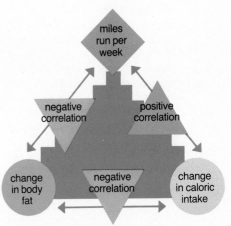

Adapted from Peter D. Wood *et al,* "Increased Exercise Level and Plasma Lipoprotein Concentrations . . . " *Metabolism,* vol. 32, no. 1, pp. 31–39, 1983

133

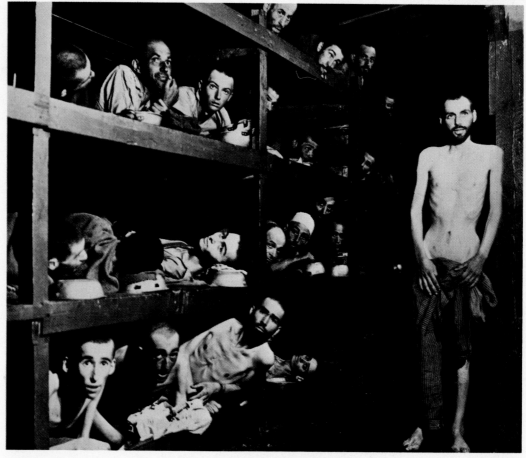

*The cells' response to a caloric cutback is to reduce their activity, thus conserving energy to protect themselves against death by starvation. The more drastic the diet, the more drastic the drop in resting metabolic rate (the rate at which calories are used by the body at rest). This defense mechanism has been a biological advantage in times of deprivation and famine. Much was learned about the metabolic effects of starvation and the body's apparent ability to adjust to severe circumstances in concentration camp inmates during World War II. Such understanding has helped explain why low-calorie diets alone can be self-defeating or even counterproductive. The body reacts to the latest exotic quick-weight-loss scheme as it does to any starvation diet.*

think (indeed, we usually have thought) that the extra cost of running the mile is 95 calories (*i.e.,* 100 calories *less* 5 calories for the RMR). But what is the metabolic rate for the minute *after* the mile is completed? What is the rate after an hour has passed? After 12 hours? Indications are that RMR is somewhat elevated for several hours after vigorous exercise. The topic is a difficult one experimentally because the increase in RMR is small, and it is difficult to detect and measure accurately a change of RMR from, say, 1.0 to 1.1 calories per minute. In spite of the small magnitude of the increase, exercise-induced elevation of RMR may be very important because it probably operates for a long period of time. To return to the runner, let us suppose that after the run his RMR is 1.1 instead of 1.0, which it had been, and that this 10% elevation is maintained for 17 hours. The extra energy used *after* the run is approximately 100 calories, so that the true cost of the mile run would be 95 calories (during the run) plus 100 calories (during the following 17 hours) for a total of 195 calories. This hypothetical example indicates that active people might have a much greater expenditure of calories than has generally been believed, by virtue of their regular exercise. Slim, active people have frequently been credited with "different metabolisms," compared with sedentary, overweight people, and this is probably true; but we must remember that physically active thin individuals probably have a different, more

134

profligate energy economy by virtue of the extra exercise they get.

It seems reasonably clear that regular exercise, especially of a vigorous nature, does increase RMR for some hours, probably by increasing body temperature and by speeding up certain metabolic processes. The magnitude of this effect in different circumstances is not clear at present, and much further study is required.

"Migrant Mother, Nipomo, California," 1936, by Dorothea Lange; photograph, Library of Congress

The regular exerciser has a denser body than the sedentary person. He has retained muscle over the years and stored relatively little fat. This gives him an advantage when it comes to calorie burning because a greater proportion of his body is energy-burning (muscle) while a smaller proportion is heat-insulating (fat). Again, the active person is a big spender of energy but a poor conserver. As we have seen, exercise is associated with eating more, and eating more calories is associated with an *increased* RMR. One of the few advantages of the overweight person is the higher mass of his body. A given amount of exercise (*e.g.,* walking a mile) will cost the 240-pound man more calories than the 160-pound man because more mass has to be propelled over the distance.

A seldom-mentioned calorie-using opportunity often enjoyed by the regular exerciser is more frequent exposure to low temperatures. More calories must be used to maintain body temperature in cold water by the swimmer and in cold weather by the jogger. In both cases the body is often relatively lean and not well insulated against heat loss.

These energy-using consequences of regular exercise have not been well recognized in the past, perhaps partly because a rather small proportion of people (especially older people) in our society have been vigorously active until comparatively recently. In addition, the effects, though potentially very important in relation to weight control, are small and difficult to measure with confidence. On the other hand, the caloric profusion provided by our food supply has been highly visible and easy to measure. Advice to the overweight has thus advocated restricting dietary intake, while the increased use of calories through exercise has been relatively neglected. Popular dieting advice has emphasized caloric restriction because presumably vast amounts of exercise are needed to reduce weight: 50 miles of running are needed to burn a pound of fat, and so on. This statement may be true but it is also misleading. The body is amazingly efficient; it can be propelled over 50 miles on one pound of fat, while an average car requires some 20 pounds of gasoline. But even a low-level runner, jogging 10 miles per week, covers a distance of 50 miles in five weeks and uses the equivalent of one pound of fat. In a year he has run off the equivalent of ten pounds of fat. But as we have seen, the majority of overweight people in developed countries are putting on fat at a rate of only one to two pounds per year.

We can conclude then that increased exercise is an excellent way to reverse the prevalent fat-accumulating trend of most middle-aged people in the U.S. It is probably the most important part of the change of life-style that truly converts a fat person into a slim person. It is true that a person who accumulated 60 pounds of surplus fat over the years has a large task ahead. The tendency has been to abandon increased exercise as an aid in this task because "you have to run 3,000 miles to burn 60 pounds of fat." So all

135

attention is devoted to calorie intake reduction, but since the resting metabolic rate is turned down as well, dieting becomes an equally daunting solution to the problem. The conclusion for many overweight people has been that nothing really works and that they are destined to remain heavy.

## The scientific combination: exercise and dieting

A number of studies now indicate that weight loss is most rapid—and, more importantly, is best maintained—when increased exercise accompanies caloric restriction. Clearly the two techniques exert a push-pull effect. They are complementary in several ways: dieting reduces RMR, decreases calorie intake (by definition), and tends to decrease muscle mass; exercise increases RMR, increases calorie intake, and tends to increase muscle mass. It seems very probable that the dieter's arch enemy, lowered RMR, can be considerably offset by regular exercise. It is certainly clear that the traditional loss of

136

*Without exercise, nearly all attempts to lose weight and, more importantly, to keep it off are doomed. Physical activity has specific advantages for the dieter: exercise itself uses up calories; it speeds up metabolism of muscle cells; it burns fat for fuel; it builds muscle; and it tends to bring appetite into scale with energy expenditure. Some exercises are better than others for expending energy. The best are endurance (aerobic) activities that elevate heart and lung function and speed up metabolism, such as running, cycling, cross-country skiing, swimming, walking at a brisk pace, aerobic dancing, stair climbing, and rope skipping. Exercises that do not require continuous motion are not as good. Singles tennis, then, is only a moderately effective adjunct to the dieter, assuming the player has the skill to keep the ball in play. The leisurely, stop-and-go pace of golf—even for the person who walks rather than rides around the course—renders it quite ineffective for meaningful weight loss.*

muscle tissue during dieting can be largely reversed by adding endurance, or aerobic, exercise to caloric restriction. This combined approach appears to have been used by millions of overweight individuals in recent years as they joined one or another regiment of the exercise revolution and combined moderate dieting with jogging or tennis or cycling. It is true that large, controlled studies of this effect were not performed as this was happening, but the anecdotal evidence is overwhelming, and the slimmed-down product is to be seen—still exercising—in swimming pools and on tennis courts and in the streets and parks across the U.S.

There are several important points about this powerful weight-loss combination. First, the exercise should be adopted very gradually. Overweight people are almost invariably in less than optimal physical condition. For a 5-foot 10-inch, 230-pound man of 45, jogging five miles at a time may be a year away. Some months of walking first a quarter mile, then a half mile, and

From *Physical Fitness for Practically Everybody: The Consumers Union Report on Exercise.* Copyright 1983 by Consumers Union of United States, Inc., Mount Vernon, N.Y.

## Estimated calorie costs of various activities

| activity | cal/min/lb* |
|---|---|
| aerobic dance (vigorous) | .062 |
| basketball (vigorous, full court) | .097 |
| bathing, dressing, undressing | .021 |
| bed-making (and stripping) | .031 |
| bicycling (13 mph) | .071 |
| canoeing (flat water, 4 mph) | .045 |
| chopping wood | .049 |
| cleaning windows | .024 |
| cross-country skiing (8 mph) | .104 |
| driving a car | .020 |
| eating while seated | .011 |
| gardening: digging | .062 |
| hedging | .034 |
| raking | .024 |
| weeding | .038 |
| golf (twosome carrying clubs) | .045 |
| handball (skilled, singles) | .078 |
| horseback riding (trot) | .052 |
| ironing | .029 |
| jogging (5 mph) | .060 |
| kneading dough | .023 |
| laundry (taking out and hanging) | .027 |
| mopping floors | .024 |
| painting house (outside) | .034 |
| peeling potatoes | .019 |
| piano playing | .018 |
| plastering walls | .023 |
| rowing (vigorous) | .097 |
| running (8 mph) | .104 |
| sawing wood (crosscut saw) | .058 |
| shining shoes | .017 |
| shoveling snow | .052 |
| snowshoeing (2.5 mph) | .060 |
| soccer (vigorous) | .097 |
| swimming (55 yd/min) | .088 |
| table tennis (skilled) | .045 |
| tennis (beginner) | .032 |
| walking (4.5 mph) | .048 |
| writing while seated | .013 |

*Multiply weight by figure in second column to get estimated calorie cost per minute for an exercise or activity.

finally a mile, with slow but constant progression, are indicated. The muscles, tendons, and ligaments, weakened by years of inactivity, need at least a few months to regain their former glory. Gradualness is the key. The type of exercise is important: walking, jogging, running, cycling, swimming, and cross-country skiing are the big calorie users; bowling, weight lifting, and golf are not. The exercise should also be enjoyable.

Second, moderate caloric restriction is much preferable to extreme restriction for several reasons: (1) Extreme restriction of calories has an extremely depressing effect on RMR; (2) the weight loser feels better with a reasonable intake of food, especially carbohydrate, and so is better able to do the essential exercise; (3) very low-calorie diets are frequently deficient in vitamins and minerals and almost always low in fiber and bulk; and (4) life on very low calorie intakes is restrictive and unpleasant, socially and physiologically. The dieter is likely to give up, and the regimen fails.

Third, it should be remembered that caloric restriction plus increased exercise, with attendant fat loss, cannot go on forever. Caloric restriction should be regarded as a temporary therapeutic measure to help correct the fat accumulation of years. "Low-calorie eating" should not be presented, as it frequently has been, as a desirable, healthy, modern way of life; in fact, it can be quite undesirable from several health standpoints. The weight loser adopting this technique should therefore anticipate that as his or her exercise level increases over the months, food intake can and should gradually increase. The goal should be the transformation of the fat person to a slim person, and as we have seen, this involves an evolution to a slimmer person exercising more but also eating more.

The modern weight-loss prescription, then, will read as follows for the majority of mildly to moderately overweight adults (excluded are individuals who are extremely overweight—80 pounds or more—and those who were clearly overweight as children; professional advice is important in these cases): (1) Think in terms of a year, not a few weeks; (2) seek a new life-style, not a temporary "fix"; (3) adopt a moderately low-calorie diet that is nutritionally desirable (for most people, this will be in the region of 1,200–2,200 calories per day); (4) devise a very gradual, progressive, and enjoyable program of play activities of the aerobic type, each month increasing the amount of daily activity; (5) find a companion to share your exercise program; (6) be prepared to increase your food intake gradually so that after a year you are no longer consciously restricting calories; and (7) before adopting any regimen, discuss your plans with your medical adviser, particularly if you suffer from cardiovascular, lung, or orthopedic problems.

## The side effects of exercise: many benefits and a few risks

A program of regular exercise brings with it many other well-recognized and some presumed health benefits. Regular aerobic exercise produces a good level of fitness, which improves performance in many of life's activities and makes them more enjoyable. The conditioning effect is the result of improvements in heart and lung function and increased efficiency of the working muscles, which have increased concentrations of energy-producing enzyme systems. Studies in England and the United States strongly suggest that,

138

*Many companies make cosmetic changes in their advertising symbols to reflect the times. As fitness has become fashionable and its health benefits recognized, the Campbell's Soup kids of the 1920s (left) have gotten less pudgy and more athletic.*

compared with more sedentary counterparts, men who regularly engage in physical activity, particularly of the more strenuous variety, at work or during leisure, are protected, relative to sedentary men, from heart attack. Regular exercise tends to increase the concentration of high-density lipoproteins (HDL) in blood plasma. These minute circulating particles are strongly associated with reduced risk of coronary heart disease. At the same time, regular exercise and its attendant leanness result in lower concentrations of low-density lipoproteins (LDL), particles that are clearly implicated in the process of atherosclerosis, the artery-wall disease underlying heart attacks. Regular exercisers tend not to smoke. This concomitant of the active life-style is, of course, of major health benefit.

It is not clear at present that exercise of various types has any effect, good or bad, on the risk of developing arthritis, the most disabling disease in the United States and some other developed nations. But it is clear that regular use of joints improves function in most people who have arthritis. There is also evidence to suggest that loss of bone mineral with age, leading to osteoporosis and weakened bones, is slowed and possibly reversed by regular exercise. Another probable contributor to osteoporosis is inadequate intake

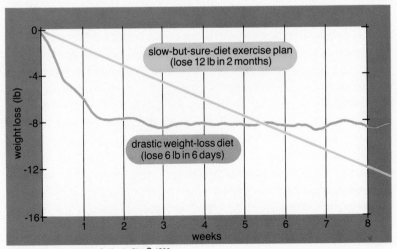

slow-but-sure-diet exercise plan
(lose 12 lb in 2 months)

drastic weight-loss diet
(lose 6 lb in 6 days)

weight loss (lb)

weeks

Adapted from Peter Wood, *California Diet* © 1983

*As physiologists have gained insights into the specific bonuses afforded by exercise, they have learned that the primary source of body energy during vigorous physical activity is fat—not water, muscle protein, or sugar. Thus it is increasingly clear that weight loss through exercise, though gradual, is real, and therefore it is likely to be permanent.*

# Don't Be Too Fat

Don't ruin your stomach with a lot of useless drugs
and patent medicines. Send to Prof. F. J. Kellogg,
1866W. Main St., Battle Creek, Michigan, for a free
trial package of a treatment that will reduce your
weight to normal without diet or drugs. The treatment is perfectly safe, natural and scientific. It takes
off the big stomach, gives the heart freedom, enables the lungs to expand naturally, and you will
feel a hundred times better the first day you try this
wonderful home treatment.

*Studies in England, the United States, and
Puerto Rico strongly suggest that men
who engage in physical activity regularly
not only are trimmer but also eat more
and are relatively protected against heart
attack when compared with sedentary
counterparts, as the table below indicates.*

| Daily caloric intake | | |
|---|---|---|
| community studied | heart disease victims (sedentary) | survivors (physically active) |
| U.K. bank and businessmen | 2,656 | 2,869 |
| Framingham, Mass. | 2,369 | 2,622 |
| Puerto Rico | 2,223 | 2,395 |
| Honolulu | 2,149 | 2,319 |

of calcium in the diet of older people. Again, regular exercise helps since older exercisers eat more, including more calcium. Constipation also appears to
be much less common in active individuals, probably owing partly to the stimulating effect of exercise on the gastrointestinal tract and partly to the larger
food intake of the exerciser, with its greater bulk and fiber content.

A feeling of well-being, not scientifically documented but frequently reported by regular exercisers, is perhaps the greatest single health benefit of
exercise. The most frequent response to the question "Why do you exercise?" is "Because it makes me feel better." Recently scientists have measured endorphins (naturally occurring substances that produce pain-free
states) in the plasma of individuals after vigorous exercise. They have found
elevated levels of these opiumlike compounds released by the brain. The so-
called runner's high and other exercise-induced euphoric states may be
related to outpourings of these body chemicals.

There are, to be sure, some risks associated with regular exercise as with
almost all worthwhile activity. For the most part they may be minimized by
taking common-sense precautions. All exercisers using the roads (walkers,
runners, cyclists) share an increased risk of collision with motor vehicles; this
risk may be reduced greatly by avoiding use of the roads at night, not
exercising two or more abreast, and (for walkers and runners) facing oncom-
ing traffic. Undue loss of body water, leading to dehydration and possibly
heat stroke, is a risk associated with strenuous exercise in hot weather and
can be minimized by drinking plenty of water. Athletic injuries are not uncommon in regular exercisers—more so in runners and tennis players, less so in
walkers and swimmers.

Investigators have recently noted that some men who devote themselves
to running, often in order to lose weight, become "obligatory runners"; they
develop an exercise compulsion and follow very strict diet regimens. A
similar phenomenon has been observed in young women who exercise
excessively and also fall victim to anorexia nervosa. Neither group can ever
see themselves as fit or lean enough. In rare cases their dieting and exercise
fanaticism is taken to the point of starvation and death.

## Challenging accepted ideas about dieting

An entrenched revulsion toward overeating and gluttony has made it difficult
for most people to accept that eating more may, in some circumstances, be
more healthful than eating less. At one end of the food intake spectrum, the
pathologic preoccupation with leanness seen in anorexia nervosa often
involves life-threatening regimens of dieting and exercise. But even among a
large number of "average" women in the United States, the measured
calorie intakes are surprisingly low (1,500–1,800 calories per day). At these
levels the risk of inadequate intake of critical nutrients is high, particularly for
iron and calcium. The advantage of the exerciser's higher food intake is
clear: he or she is more likely to take in adequate amounts of all nutrients.
There is evidence that increased intake of dietary fiber would be beneficial to
a large portion of the population, and here too eating more can only be
beneficial, provided some thought is given to the source of the extra calories.
It seems unlikely that the gastrointestinal tract of a sedentary 50-year-old

woman who remains overweight on a miserly 1,600 calories per day of low-bulk, calorically dense food can really be functioning well.

There is another, rather neglected, aspect of calorie intake in relation to health. At least four prospective community studies have shown that people reporting higher calorie intakes have less risk of developing heart disease in future years than those reporting lower intakes. From these remarkably consistent results we conclude that a high calorie intake predicts less heart disease in the future. Although this does not necessarily mean that increasing food intake will lower risk of heart disease, it certainly does not suggest that decreasing calorie intake, as has been widely advocated, is a wise public health trend. It is probable that the increased food intake is reflecting a more active life-style, and this increased activity is what is actually protective.

The traditional view that overweight is due to overeating and that the cure is to reduce food intake is becoming a less well-accepted concept and, in fact, is probably an erroneous one when examined carefully. For many people the idea that to be slim and fit one must be forever vigilant about restricting calories not only is unattractive but leads to obsessive preoccupation with dieting—and very often to unnecessary self-deprivation, failure, and lifelong self-deprecation. Food, after all, is energy, and energy gets things done. An active slim population, eating robustly and leading productive and rewarding lives, surely is preferable to a sedentary slim population, unhappily nibbling celery and gazing at the television screen.

FOR ADDITIONAL READING:

Bennett, William, and Gurin, Joel. *The Dieter's Dilemma: Eating Less and Weighing More.* New York: Basic Books, Inc., 1982.

Brownell, K. D., and Stunkard, A. J. "Exercise in the Development and Control of Obesity." In Stunkard, A. J. (ed.). *Obesity.* Philadelphia: W. B. Saunders, 1980.

Fries, James F., and Crapo, Lawrence M. *Vitality and Aging: Implications of the Rectangular Curve.* San Francisco: W. H. Freeman and Co., 1981.

Gwinup, G. "Effect of Exercise Alone on the Weight of Obese Women." *Archives of Internal Medicine* 135 (1975): 676–680.

Katch, Frank I., and McArdle, William D. *Nutrition, Weight Control, and Exercise.* 2nd ed. Philadelphia: Lea & Febiger, 1983.

Kusinitz, Ivan, *et al. Physical Fitness for Practically Everybody: The Consumers Union Report on Exercise.* New York: Consumers Union, 1983.

White, Philip L., and Mondeika, Therese (eds.). *Diet and Exercise: Synergism in Health Maintenance.* Chicago: American Medical Association, 1982.

Wood, Peter D., *et al.* "Increased Exercise Level and Plasma Lipoprotein Concentrations: A One-Year, Randomized, Controlled Study in Sedentary, Middle-Aged Men." *Metabolism* 32 (1983): 31–39.

Wood, Peter D. *The California Diet and Exercise Program.* Mountain View, Calif.: Anderson World, 1983.

**Refused; On Account of His Shape.**

Obesity is a disease. Dr. Schindler-Barnay, of Vienna, has made it a life-long study. His writings are quoted in all medical text-books on this disease. Dr. Schindler's Marienbad Reduction Pills mailed upon receipt of $2.50. His treatise on obesity free upon application. EISNER & MENDELSON Co., Agents, New York. The genuine Marienbad Pills must have Dr. Schindler-Barnay's signature on every box.

*Obesity is well recognized as having serious health drawbacks as well as being aesthetically displeasing and interfering with social acceptance. The overweight have long been a group easily lured by the promise of effortless, "overnight" weight loss. Indeed, an enormously thriving industry has grown out of the perpetual public concern for weight control. But while new dieting gimmicks are born daily—most of these based on premises that suspend the laws of nature— fortunately medical science is making great strides in understanding the mechanisms of successful weight loss. It should be reassuring to perpetual reducers that notions of painfully restrictive dieting regimens, long held as the keys to slimness and health, are now being overturned.*

# CAT's Kin:
# New Windows on the Body

## by John A. Correia, Ph.D., and Ian L. Pykett, Ph.D.

**John A. Correia, Ph.D.,** *is Associate Director of the Physics Research Laboratory at Massachusetts General Hospital and Assistant Professor of Radiology at Harvard Medical School in Boston.* **Ian L. Pykett, Ph.D.,** *is President of Advanced NMR Systems, Inc., in Needham, Massachusetts, and former Director of the NMR Research Program at Massachusetts General Hospital.*

*(Overleaf) Nuclear magnetic resonance scan of the head and neck of a human subject. Photograph by Howard Sochurek—Woodfin Camp.*

Since the early 1970s a revolution has occurred in the ability of the doctor to see inside the human body. Although for nearly a century conventional X-ray techniques have served well at this task, yielding remarkable diagnostic information, the flat, ghostly images of internal structure captured on film often have proved to be of limited value. Moreover, even in small doses X-rays carry some risk of doing physiological harm. Modern imaging methods are remedying these deficiencies to a large extent; they are safer and can produce cross sections or even three-dimensional images of the anatomy with unprecedented clarity. But more than that, some of the new techniques can actually probe the biochemistry of the tissue under study to provide information about function as well as structure, consequently allowing doctors to better discriminate between healthy and diseased tissue and to improve their understanding of normal physiological processes.

## The foundations of modern imaging methods

Developments in medical imaging parallel similar developments in other fields of high technology. Perhaps the most important was the development of sophisticated electronic and digital-computer technology during the late 1960s and early 1970s. Traditionally most diagnostic images have been produced by exposing photographic film to X-rays that have been sent through the body or by photographing images from some other X-ray conversion system such as a fluoroscope. Once a film image is formed it is extremely difficult, if not impossible, to manipulate it or to extract further information. Thus, until the 1970s radiological diagnosis consisted mainly of viewing film images and evaluating them visually. At that time a diagnostic imaging instrument appeared that changed the nature of the diagnostic process.

In 1972 the first successful X-ray computerized axial tomographic (CAT) scanner (also called a computed tomographic, or CT, scanner) was constructed by Godfrey Hounsfield in England from a design based on his own work and that of physicist Allan Cormack and others. Hounsfield and Cor-

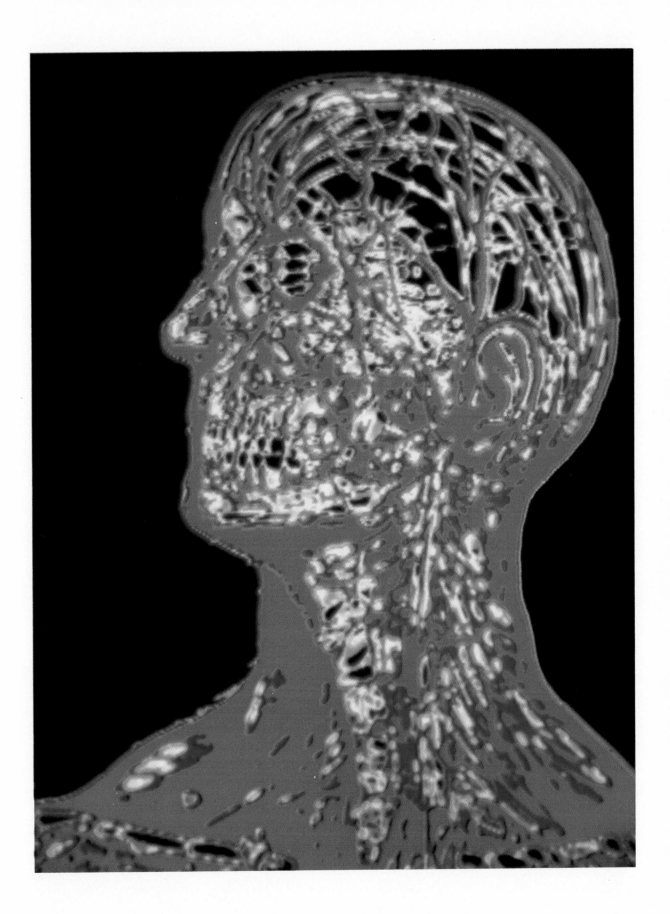

mack shared the 1979 Nobel Prize for Physiology or Medicine for their development. Their device consisted of a conventional X-ray source, a set of X-ray detectors, and a digital computer that read the electronic outputs of the detectors. The source and detectors were moved about the human head (later the whole body), collecting measurements of X-ray transmission from many directions. This measured information was then "reconstructed," or unraveled, by the computer to provide images of structures in "slices," or planes, through the head. For the first time, physicians could view cross sections of the body noninvasively (*i.e.*, without direct entry into the body). What made this feat possible in large part was the availability of computers with great computational ability. The success of the CAT scanner in its first few years of application (between 1973 and 1976) stimulated the pursuit of other computerized imaging methods and led to the revolution that is still going on today.

Three of the most promising of these new techniques are nuclear magnetic resonance (NMR), positron emission tomography (PET), and digital X-ray imaging. Each technique addresses a different aspect of the diagnostic problem; they are, therefore, largely complementary. Nevertheless, they are all computer-based techniques that generate images of the body and other data related to its structure, function, or both.

The distinction between structure and function is an important one. The CAT scanner and almost all previously invented radiological imaging techniques make pictures of structure, or morphology. When one is dealing with living organisms, though, this type of information is only part of the story. One must also know how they function, both physiologically and in their underlying biochemistry.

An analogy will illustrate this point. If one looks inside a radio and notes the sizes, shapes, and materials of all its components as well as their spatial relationships to one another, one will characterize the "anatomy" of the radio. But in order to totally describe the radio, one also must understand how electrical signals are received and processed by its various structural elements to reproduce sound; *i.e.*, the "physiology" of the radio.

In humans early stages of disease often show aberrations in function but no immediate changes in structure. Frequently structural changes occur only some time after the physiological changes. There are also some diseases, such as major psychoses, in which there appear to be physiological abnormalities in brain tissue that is structurally normal.

Of the three new techniques mentioned above, NMR and PET have the potential to give physiological and biochemical information as well as structural information and, thus, are likely to extend the field of diagnostic imaging to new areas. The third, digital X-ray imaging, has some potential for physiological evaluation but, perhaps more importantly, it has the potential to expand what can be learned from traditional X-ray studies while substantially lowering radiation exposures and other risks.

## Nuclear magnetic resonance imaging

Like CAT, nuclear magnetic resonance techniques generate images of thin slices of the body. But what makes NMR exciting to clinicians and scientists

*The photographic image of the hand of Wilhelm Röntgen's wife, one of the first X-rays ever taken, suffers from the same limitation that marked traditional diagnostic imaging for the next 75 years: once the image is formed, it is almost impossible to view it any other way or to extract further information. In the late 1960s and early 1970s the computer and electronics revolutions effected a dramatic change in the imaging process. X-ray transmissions through the body could be collected and recorded electronically and then reconstructed to provide unprecedented views of internal structure. This development, computerized axial tomography, has stimulated the pursuit of several other computerized imaging methods with unique diagnostic capabilities.*

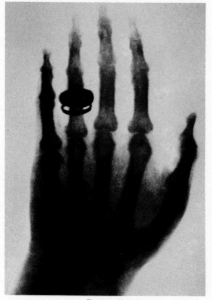

The New York Academy of Medicine

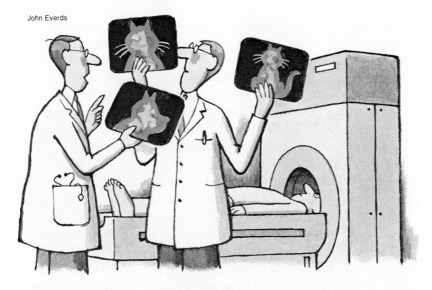

John Everds

*"I have the feeling our new CAT scanner is going to be of limited usefulness."*

*CAT scanners typically provide images of living tissue in the form of cross-sectional slices. A CAT scan of the brain of a normal individual (below) is compared with one of a person with a malignant brain tumor (bottom). Whereas CAT scanners have had great success in making pictures of normal and abnormal structures, some of the newer imaging methods have the potential for providing physiological and biochemical information as well.*

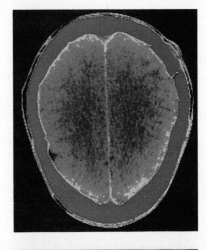

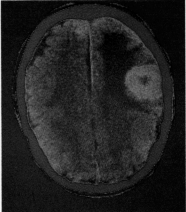

Photographs, Dan McCoy—Rainbow

alike are its differences. Some of them relate to its already demonstrated superiority in the diagnosis of certain diseases, while others relate more to its still unproved potential.

The basic principle of NMR has been exploited by physicists and chemists for nearly 40 years to investigate the magnetic properties of nuclear and subatomic particles and to unravel complex molecular structures. But only recently have its applications extended to the study of biological systems. In 1971 physician Raymond Damadian, then at Downstate Medical Center, State University of New York, Brooklyn, noted that information supplied by NMR could be used to distinguish some tumor tissues from corresponding normal samples. Other research groups at the time were using NMR to study metabolism in animal organs such as the heart and kidney. All of these early studies, however, were *in vitro,* or test-tube, experiments. More significantly, conventional NMR techniques could not produce images; the information obtained contained no spatial information. Even if the whole human body could have been examined in this way, the NMR signals, while they conceivably might have been able to indicate the presence of a disease, could not have located it.

In 1973 Paul C. Lauterbur of the State University of New York at Stony Brook produced the first NMR images. He had found a way to encode the signals so that their origin in space could be determined. Very soon afterward several other laboratories in the United States and Europe generated their own images using modified conventional NMR systems. Before long, images of human fingers and wrists (all that could be accommodated in these early machines) were published, and their remarkably high quality immediately excited the medical world. Some advantages of this new technology were readily apparent. The different nuclear magnetic resonance "signatures" obtained from normal and abnormal tissue might permit the sensitive and noninvasive diagnosis of many diseases, including cancer. As a bonus, the technique used no X-rays or ionizing radiation of any kind and appeared to be free of hazard.

During the next few years, as the technique underwent numerous refine-

145

Photographs, courtesy Francis Smith, Royal Infirmary, Aberdeen, Scotland

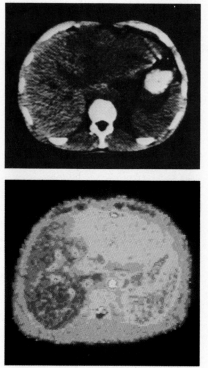

*A CAT scan (top) and an NMR scan (bottom) of a liver tumor are compared. Both images were made in the same plane through the torso, with the patient's back at the bottom. In the CAT scan the tumor appears as a dark gray region on the right; in the NMR image the tumor is yellow-orange, while undiseased liver tissue is blue.*

ments, several of its limitations also became obvious, not the least of which was its very high cost. Current NMR imaging systems cost about $800,000 to $1.6 million, somewhat more than the price of a CAT scanner. In addition, although it is difficult to believe from a look at state-of-the-art images, the detected NMR signal is extremely weak. In practice this means that scanning times are long compared with CAT studies. While enough information to generate a CAT scan is now collected in just a second or two (it used to take much longer), a diagnostically useful NMR image with corresponding spatial resolution (picture sharpness) requires a minute or so of signal collection. For regions of the body that can be held fairly still (for example, the head and limbs), a minute's time is not a problem. But many other organs, such as the heart, lungs, and intestines, are continually moving. Since many such movements are under the control of the autonomic ("automatic") nervous system and cannot be stopped voluntarily, image detail can be blurred. Special techniques, however, are being developed to circumvent these problems.

NMR elicits signals directly from atomic nuclei. For medical purposes the nuclei most commonly probed are the nuclei of ordinary hydrogen (single protons) in tissue. In practice the signal comes almost entirely from the protons in water and lipids (fats) in the body.

To be sensitive to detection by NMR, the atomic nuclei must have certain physical properties: electric charge and angular momentum, or "spin." Together these properties make each nucleus behave like a tiny bar magnet. Ordinarily, these tiny magnets point in random directions. But when an external magnetic field is applied, they preferentially align with the lines of magnetic induction (lines of "force"), just as a magnetized compass needle points along the north-south axis of the Earth's magnetic field. A drop of water placed in a magnetic field becomes temporarily magnetized as its hydrogen "nuclear magnets," on average, point in the direction of the field. This bulk magnetization is lost when the field is removed.

In NMR this magnetization is detected with a second, much smaller mag-

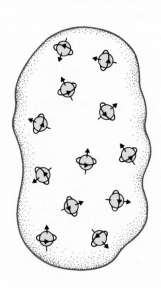

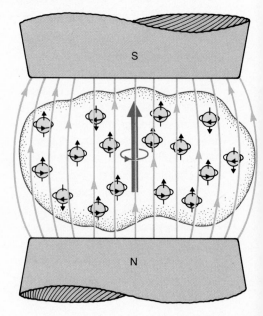

netic field, which is applied at right angles to the first field. The second field tends to tip the magnetization direction of the tissue under study away from its initial, or "equilibrium," position. By analogy, one can bring a small bar magnet close to a compass needle so as to tip it away from its orientation with the Earth's field. But because the nuclei in matter are spinning, they do not behave exactly like a compass needle. In fact, the magnetization behaves more like a spinning top aligned with the Earth's gravitational field in that it wobbles, or precesses, about the direction of the main field.

In practice, radio waves, which have a magnetic component, are used to generate the second field. This radio-frequency (RF) energy is delivered by means of a coil of wire wrapped around the tissue. A short pulse of radio waves will cause the bulk nuclear magnetization of the tissue to precess; in doing so, it will generate a small, detectable voltage in a detector coil. The precessional motion thus detected is the genesis of the nuclear signal.

The nuclei "ring" in response to an RF pulse just as a bell rings when struck with a hammer. Over a period of time the sound of the bell dies away; similarly, the nuclear signal decays in a characteristic time. In addition, following application of an RF pulse, the bulk magnetization direction is gradually reestablished as the nuclei orient themselves once again with the main magnetic field; there is another time characterizing this realignment as well. These two "relaxation" times are affected by the presence and distribution of nearby atoms. Coupled with NMR information on hydrogen concentration, they afford a picture of a nuclear environment that can vary significantly between normal and abnormal tissues.

As its name implies, NMR is a resonance phenomenon. This means that it will occur only if the applied RF pulse is "tuned" to the natural resonance frequency of the nucleus in question. The nuclei of different elements—hydrogen, phosphorus, and sodium, for example—have different natural resonance frequencies and, hence, respond to significantly different frequencies of radio waves. The natural resonance frequency of any given nucleus also

*Basic principles of NMR imaging are depicted in the diagrams on the opposite page and below. The proton nuclei of hydrogen atoms and other NMR-sensitive nuclei in a sample can be likened to tiny spinning magnets, which ordinarily point in random directions (a). When the sample is placed in a magnetic field, the nuclei tend to align with the field lines of "force," creating a bulk magnetization in the sample (b). This magnetization is detected with a second, smaller magnetic field generated by pulses of radio waves from a coil surrounding the sample (c). The second field tips the bulk magnetization out of alignment, causing it to precess, or wobble. This motion induces a minute voltage in the coil—the NMR signal—that can be detected and amplified. Like a struck bell, the nuclei "ring" in response to the radio pulse, and with time the NMR signal dies away (d). The frequency with which they ring is proportional to the strength of the main field that they "feel." If the main field is graded so that its strength increases from one end of the sample to the other, the nuclei will ring with different "notes" depending on their position in the sample (e). In this way the NMR signal is coded with spatial information.*

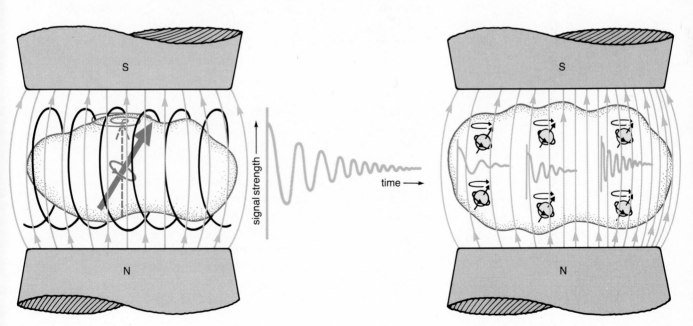

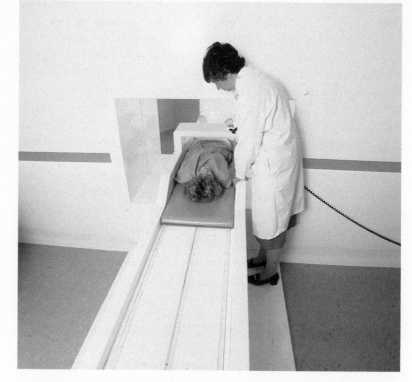

*A patient undergoing NMR imaging lies within a large magnet, which temporarily induces a slight, harmless magnetization of the body tissues. Brief pulses of radio waves are sent to the atomic nuclei, which respond with signals of their own. These nuclear signals are detected and analyzed by a computer, which displays the final image on a television screen.*

increases in proportion to the strength of the applied main magnetic field. Hydrogen nuclei have been used most extensively in NMR imaging studies to date. The NMR signal from ordinary hydrogen is intrinsically greater than that from any other stable isotope. In addition, hydrogen is present in very high concentrations in tissues—largely as water, which comprises about 75% of human body weight. Thus, the observation of other nuclei, although a prospect of great diagnostic potential, will require longer imaging times and result in images that are less sharp.

The foregoing discussion has described how NMR signals can be elicited from the atomic nuclei of tissue but not how they can be related to the position of the nuclei. How, for example, can one distinguish among signals arising from different regions in the brain? This step requires that the main magnetic field be graded so that it is not of uniform strength but rather increases slightly in strength from one side of the sample to the other. Because the resonance frequencies of the nuclei are proportional to the applied field strengths, they will "ring" with different "notes" depending on their position in the sample.

In practice this concept is applied in many different ways, each of which employs a somewhat different scheme for applying the required magnetic-field gradients and for altering their magnitude and direction in carefully controlled sequences. The most common methods record nuclear signals arising either from single, two-dimensional planes or else simultaneously from whole regions of the body. The first method requires that the physician select a particular slice for imaging before the scan is done, just as in CAT scans. In the second method, known as the three-dimensional or whole-

148

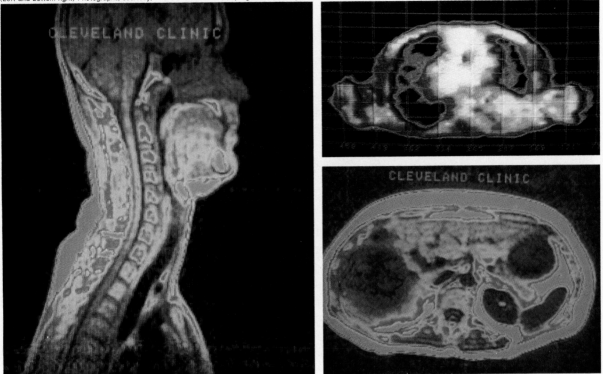

volume method, the computer can select any two-dimensional plane for display after the scan is complete. Both methods have their advantages and limitations; the choice must take into account such factors as the organ system under study and the imaging speed and sharpness required.

The intensity, or brightness, of any given element in the image depends on the NMR properties of the tissue at that point—principally the hydrogen concentration and the nuclear relaxation times. With appropriate techniques one or more of these properties can be highlighted; in effect, the NMR technique can be tailored to the tissue under study or the type of disease being sought. For example, because the nuclear relaxation times alter significantly when tissue becomes diseased or when it is deprived of its blood supply (ischemic), NMR images can accurately define such abnormal areas. Indeed, NMR appears to detect tumors more easily than any other current diagnostic technique. It also clearly shows multiple sclerosis plaques (areas in which the insulating myelin sheath surrounding nerve fibers of the brain has been destroyed), hitherto extremely difficult to detect. Ischemic tissue found, for example, in the brain following a stroke and in cardiac muscle after a heart attack often can be detected at an earlier stage by NMR techniques than by X-ray methods.

In addition, NMR techniques are able to provide images of parts of the body hitherto difficult to view with other methods; for example, the lower regions of the head and brain (posterior fossa), where large amounts of bone often produce undesirable streaks on CAT scans, and the spine, where X-ray examination can be time-consuming and uncomfortable for the patient. Moreover, the ability to manipulate the intensity of the NMR signal coming

*NMR techniques provide images of parts of the body that are difficult to view with other methods and show great sensitivity in differentiating between diseased and normal tissue. The image of a sideways, or sagittal, slice of the head and neck of a normal individual (left) shows the spinal vertebrae as a vertical stack of bright square patches as well as the disks between them. The spinal cord appears just to the left of the vertebrae. Transverse scan through the upper chest and shoulders (above top) reveals internal structures; with NMR, clearer distinctions can be made between lung cancer and normal tissue that might otherwise be mistaken for a tumor. A cross-sectional NMR slice of a torso (above) discloses a liver tumor, which appears as a large blue region on the left. NMR appears to detect tumors more efficiently and accurately than any other current diagnostic technique.*

149

from blood flowing in the major arteries and veins may make it possible to measure blood-flow velocities in this way.

It is important to note that NMR studies are totally noninvasive. Nothing is injected into the patient, while in CAT studies contrast media that are opaque to X-rays are frequently required in order to visualize or differentiate some abnormalities. Nevertheless, NMR contrast agents, known as magnetopharmaceuticals, may be used in the future to help increase further the sensitivity or specificity of diagnosis.

NMR has already proved its worth through its sensitivity in detecting diseased tissues. Various research programs are now under way to increase its specificity and, hence, its absolute diagnostic capability. Several groups are also developing the somewhat different techniques required to image the phosphorus-31 nucleus. Phosphorus is a constituent of the compounds adenosine triphosphate (ATP) and phosphocreatine, which sustain energy-transfer processes within the cell. In this application it is necessary to extract the conventional NMR spectrum of phosphorus from relevant regions of the image. The spectrum is a graph that will typically show five or six principal resonance peaks whose heights correspond to the concentration of the individual phosphorus metabolites. Knowledge of these concentrations allows estimation of the metabolic status of the internal organs. Experimental phosphorus scanners large enough to accommodate limbs have revealed some of the chemical changes that occur in a healthy muscle as it becomes fatigued from exercise as well as biochemical abnormalities in the muscles of patients who experience premature muscle fatigue. As mentioned earlier, however, the anticipated problems of lengthy scan times and poor spatial resolution must be dealt with satisfactorily if the potential benefits of this test are to outweigh the drawbacks.

The most imposing component of a whole-body NMR imaging system is the magnet, several types of which are being tried. Resistive electromagnets consume about 60 kilowatts of electric power to generate the magnetic field but are relatively inexpensive to build. Permanent magnets also require a relatively modest capital outlay but need no power supply to maintain the field. They are, however, very heavy—up to 100 tons. Superconducting magnets are much more expensive than either permanent or resistive systems but can generate much higher magnetic-field strengths, which in turn can provide somewhat faster imaging times and better spatial resolution. More important, the high magnetic-field strengths and field stabilities afforded by superconducting systems will be virtually mandatory for the study of nuclei other than hydrogen. Although superconducting coils do not require a supply of power to maintain the magnetic field, they must be maintained at a very low temperature (about −264° C, or −443° F), which requires the use of cryogenic fluids such as liquid helium and liquid nitrogen.

Rather than the depiction of simple anatomy, future developments in NMR imaging will probably move toward the inclusion of biochemical, functional, and metabolic information. It is possible that advanced machines will routinely allow doctors to trace the flow of body fluids and measure their flow rates, observe the swelling and shrinking of inflamed tissue in response to disease and healing processes, and watch the reaction of a tumor to anti-

Leo Cullum © 1983

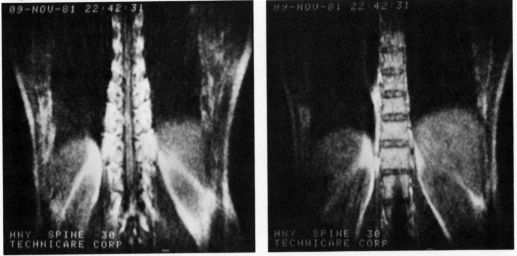

cancer drugs. In this regard NMR may have more in common with PET or nuclear-medicine studies than with CAT investigations. In any event, it is certain to become an increasingly useful diagnostic tool.

## Positron emission tomography

The success of CAT scans for anatomic imaging prompted researchers to develop physiological-imaging techniques based on a similar approach. One general method for studying organ physiology is to introduce a tracer-labeled compound into the organ in some way. Ideally, this compound would take part in some physiological process while not perturbing the process it traces. Furthermore, the location of tracer atoms in the system should be measurable in some way.

A very useful approach when studying living systems is to use radioactive atoms (radioisotopes) as tracer labels. If these atoms emit hard (penetrating) radiation such as gamma rays or other photons, one may in principle follow the behavior of tracer atoms with external monitoring equipment. The concentration of tracer in a given organ at any time is usually related to physiological quantities such as organ blood flow, metabolism of oxygen, glucose, and other materials, or synthesis of such compounds as amino acids. This relationship can be expressed through a mathematical model. Such a model is an abstraction, or simplification, of the underlying physiological processes in the form of equations that describe the behavior of tracer atoms within the system. This scheme of describing physiological systems is called tracer kinetics.

Nature has been helpful in providing a class of atoms that not only are biologically important but also emit useful radiation and, thus, turn out to be good tracer substances. An important subgroup of these "ideal" radioisotopes consists of artificially produced proton-rich nuclei that decay by emitting positrons, the antimatter counterpart of electrons. Positron-emitting isotopes can be produced by bombarding naturally occurring nuclei with a beam of accelerated protons or deuterons (heavy hydrogen nuclei, each consisting of one proton and one neutron).

*The lumbar region of a human spine is pictured in two distinct planes reconstructed from a single three-dimensional, or whole-volume, scan. On the left the spinal cord can be seen in the spinal canal. In the right-hand image the plane is shifted a few centimeters to reveal the intervertebral disks. A three-dimensional NMR scan collects nuclear signals simultaneously from whole regions of the body; afterward the computer can select any two-dimensional plane within that region for display.*

151

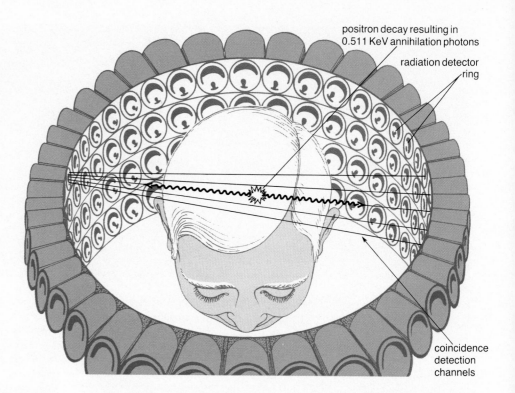

*The collection unit for a practical PET imaging device consists of several stacked rings of photon detectors. Each detector is electronically paired with several detectors on the opposite side of the ring and thus views a number of lines, or coincidence channels, through a given plane. Positrons emitted from radioactive tracers in the tissue under study quickly encounter electrons and annihilate to yield pairs of high-energy photons traveling in opposite directions. Each photon pair that arrives at a pair of opposing detectors within a fraction of a second constitutes a valid signal and defines the line along which the annihilation event took place. From a record of many such signals a computer can reconstruct pictures of the radioactivity distribution in the form of slices through the scanned region.*

Positrons are short-lived in a world of ordinary matter. After traveling a short distance (a few millimeters at most), the emitted positron encounters an electron, and the two particles annihilate each other to produce two highly penetrating photons traveling in approximately opposite directions. It is these paired photons that are detected in PET imaging.

These pairs of photons can be detected as coincident events. That is, if the two photons arrive at a pair of diametrically opposed radiation detectors within about a hundred-millionth of a second of each other, they can be attributed to a single annihilation event, and the line along which the original nuclear decay took place becomes defined.

Detecting pairs of photons in coincidence has a number of physical advantages over other types of photon detection. The system responds exclusively and uniformly to radioactivity within its field of view, and its resolving ability is likewise uniform. Moreover, the system detects a comparatively large fraction of the emitted radiation—a desirable property when one is striving to limit the amount of radiation exposure to the patient. Coincidence detection also allows simple corrections for such effects as absorption of photons within the body. Taken together, these advantages allow PET to quantitatively measure the concentration of radioactivity in small volumes of tissue in the living body. To date, PET is the only method with this ability.

Practical PET imaging instruments consist of several rings of radiation detectors stacked together. Each ring may contain more than a hundred individual detectors, which are usually bismuth germanate or sodium iodide scintillators coupled to photomultiplier tubes. The detectors are usually arranged so that each one pairs up with any of several detectors on the opposite side of the ring and thus views many lines through a given plane in different directions. Many detector pairs view each plane, and often there are several planes in an instrument. The detectors can also be moved to provide additional measurements through the planes of interest.

The signals collected by the positron imaging device for all measurements through a given plane are sorted out, or reconstructed, with a digital computer to give pictures of the radioactivity distribution in the form of slices through the scanned region. Typically, structures about one square centimeter in area (about the area of the head of a thumbtack) can be distinguished, and adjacent structures of this size having differences of 5% or more in radioactivity concentration may be resolved.

Other advantages of PET lie in the kinds of isotopes that are positron emitters. These include carbon-11, nitrogen-13, oxygen-15, and fluorine-18, with half-lives of 20, 10, 2, and 110 minutes, respectively. All of these isotopes are artificially produced in a particle accelerator. Because of their short half-lives they must be made at the site where they are to be used. They cannot be shipped any great distance. An isotope production "factory," usually a small but complex and expensive cyclotron, must be located at or near the facility in which PET is being used.

From these biologically active isotopes a host of tracer compounds may be synthesized. These range from simple substances like water labeled with oxygen-15 for the study of organ blood flow to complex compounds like 2-fluoro-2-deoxyglucose, an analogue of glucose labeled with fluorine-18 for studying the brain and heart as their cells metabolize glucose for energy. Producing such compounds routinely for hospital use requires automatic chemical-synthesis facilities connected to the cyclotron facility.

When a patient receives a PET scan, a tracer-labeled compound is administered by injection, inhalation, or some other route, and its behavior in a given organ system is followed over time. This usually means that the regional concentration of radioisotope in tissue at various times is determined. For a given compound these measurements are related by computer to some physiological event through a mathematical "physiological model," ultimate-

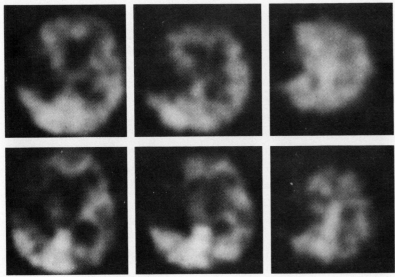

Courtesy, Dr. Ian Pykett and Dr. John Correia

*PET imaging techniques have been used experimentally to trace the course of ischemia, or abnormally decreased blood flow, in the brain. The PET images at the left, made with tracers containing radioactive oxygen-15, are of a patient experiencing an acute stroke due to blockage of the right middle cerebral artery. The top row depicts blood flow at three levels of the brain, while the bottom row shows metabolic uptake of oxygen by brain tissue. Decreases in both blood flow and metabolism, indicated by the dark regions in the left of each image, are easily seen.*

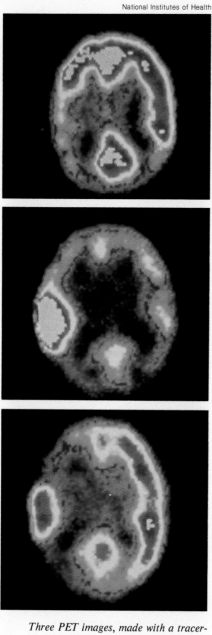

*Three PET images, made with a tracer-labeled glucose analogue, give a direct view of metabolic abnormalities in the brain of an epileptic patient. High levels of metabolic activity appear in reds and light blue. Between seizures (top), activity in the left temporal cortex (left edge of the image) is low compared with the same area on the right. During a severe seizure (center), activity is high in the left temporal cortex but depressed elsewhere. During a more moderate seizure (bottom), metabolism is less affected overall.*

ly yielding cross-sectional images of physiological processes such as organ blood flow and metabolism.

Quantitative images of function or physiology are valuable in a number of medical diagnostic problems. One important class of situations involves decreased blood flow in the heart and brain. Such ischemia is an event that ultimately results in anatomic changes stemming from tissue death. PET has the potential to find and evaluate the event before much or any structural damage is done and in time to reverse it with drugs, physiological manipulation, or other therapy. In fact, PET can be used as a research tool to evaluate the effectiveness of therapies in such situations.

To date, researchers using positron emission tomography have begun to trace the course of ischemia in both the brain and the heart. For example, mismatches between the flow and uptake of oxygen, glucose, or both in ischemic brain regions have been observed. The nature of this mismatch, in fact, appears to be predictive of stroke; decreased metabolism leads to stroke, while increased metabolism often leads to a resolution of the metabolic abnormality without stroke.

PET may have its most exciting uses in the future in studying diseases that present physiological but no anatomic abnormalities. To date, the most intensive work has been carried out in the brain. For example, PET has allowed doctors to see, for the first time, metabolic abnormalities during and between seizures in epileptic individuals. PET also has shown that individuals with major psychotic illnesses such as schizophrenia and bipolar (manic-depressive) illness have abnormal patterns of brain blood flow and glucose metabolism. In both epilepsy and psychosis the brain is often anatomically normal.

Another future application of PET is in the study of normal physiology, both to benefit basic science and to better understand disease. Again, the majority of work to date has been carried out in the brain. The brain is an organ composed of regions—many with different sections specialized for different tasks. With PET one may study which areas of the brain are activated (*i.e.,* increase their metabolic activity) when a person sees light, hears sounds, reads, listens to speech, and performs other sensory and cognitive tasks. Thus, one can map the physiological correlates of various brain functions. Researchers at the University of California at Los Angeles, for example, have correlated the metabolic activation of sensory areas of the brain during various tasks involving vision and hearing. Other studies, involving more subtle brain activations, such as those evoked by cognitive processes (for example, listening to music or working a mathematics problem), are under way at a number of centers throughout the world.

To date, PET has demonstrated its ability to observe physiological abnormalities in the brain and, to some extent, in the heart that either precede structural abnormalities or occur in the presence of normal structure. In the future, PET may diagnose and monitor the course of disease, observe the patient's response to therapy, help evaluate new treatments, and add to basic knowledge of normal and abnormal physiology. But PET is still very much an experimental tool, and appreciation of what it can reveal about human beings in both health and disease is in its infancy.

154

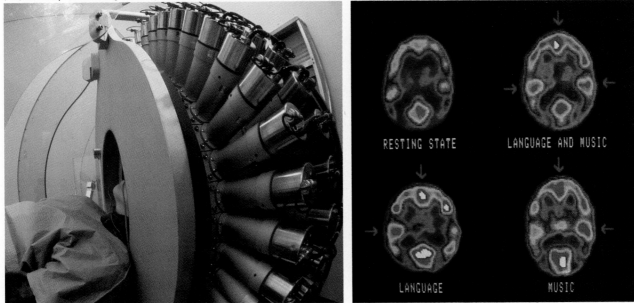

## Digital X-ray imaging

The computer revolution, while making nuclear magnetic resonance imaging and positron emission tomography possible, has also had an effect on the more traditional areas of radiography. Conventional X-ray imaging, which also might be called static radiography, is a process wherein an image of some organ or structure is produced on film by X-rays passing unabsorbed through the body. The quality of the film image depends on the number of X-ray photons absorbed at each point on the film. To increase the number of photons that reach the film, one must increase the radiation dose to the patient by sending more photons through the body. Films have very low efficiency; typically they stop less than 5% of incoming photons. Converter screens used as intermediate image-formation devices have had some suc-

*Rings of photon detectors surround a patient undergoing a PET imaging study (left). PET images of brain glucose metabolism (above) are of normal right-handed subjects given various listening tasks. Listening to language, for example, correlates with increased brain activity in the language area of the left hemisphere, while listening to music causes activation on the right. Such maps of neural activity during sensory and cognitive tasks offer exciting prospects for studying normal physiology.*

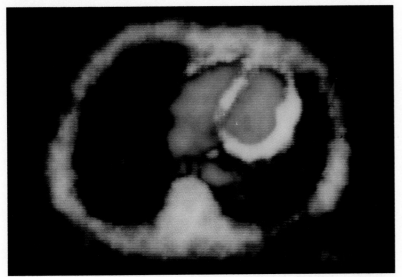

*The cross-sectional image of the heart and chest at left is a composite picture constructed from three separate PET scans. Red areas, measured with a carbon monoxide tracer labeled with carbon-11, show the blood volume within the heart's chambers. Yellow areas, traced with a fatty acid labeled with carbon-11, show fatty acid metabolism in the heart muscle. The blue image outlines the chest. The view is from the feet looking up; hence, the heart appears on the right side.*

From "Diagnosis of Cardiovascular Disease by Digital Subtraction Angiography," Charles A. Mistretta and Andrew B. Crummy, *Science*, vol. 214, no. 4522, p. 764

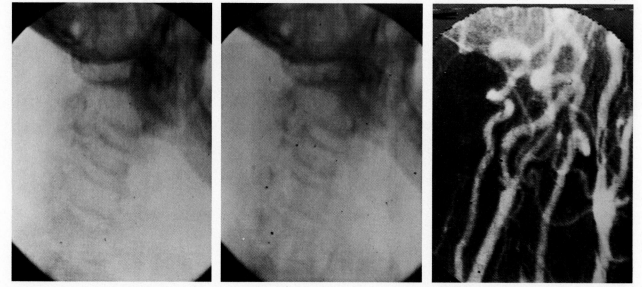

*Digital subtraction angiography, or DSA, a safe and relatively inexpensive approach to the X-ray imaging of blood vessels, takes advantage of the computer's ability to store and manipulate fluoroscopic images recorded with a television camera. The sequence of images above, made in the region of the carotid arteries outside the skull, illustrates the technique. Before the injection of X-ray contrast material, a "mask" X-ray image of the area of interest is recorded (left). This mask is then electronically subtracted from one or more images taken during the passage of contrast material through the area (center). The result (right), formed only of regions containing contrast medium, is an image in which the blood vessels stand out dramatically.*

cess in raising the efficiency of static radiography. Traditional radiography also suffers from the effect of scattering; some X-ray photons are deflected in their course through the body and strike the film at skewed angles. These scattered photons decrease the contrast range of the image and thus obscure fine details. Methods for suppressing this scattering effect are only partly effective.

Another type of traditional X-ray imaging, developed during the past 30 years, couples an electronic radiation-detection device called an image intensifier with a television camera to give so-called real-time X-ray images that can be recorded on videotape. Alternatively, one can obtain real-time images by making a rapid sequence of film images directly. One application of this approach, called angiography, allows the physician to inject X-ray-opaque substances into the artery supplying a given organ and watch its transit through the organ's vessels.

Traditional angiography of this kind has several drawbacks. First, in order to place enough X-ray contrast material in the vessels of interest, doctors usually must insert a long hollow tube, called a catheter, into the arterial system at a peripheral artery and thread it, under fluoroscopic observation, to the artery feeding the organ to be studied. This surgical procedure usually requires an overnight stay in the hospital. Second, the contrast agent itself, usually an iodine-containing compound, can cause allergic reactions or other complications. Finally, once images are stored on film or videotape, they cannot be easily manipulated, changed, or processed to extract further information.

The advent of high-speed electronic circuits that allow the acquisition and storage of fluoroscopic images by digital computer has drastically changed the way in which angiographic studies are carried out. Until the mid-1970s the main limitations to such a system were the very fast transfer speed and large storage requirements imposed by X-ray images being produced at TV rates by a fluoroscope.

In the early 1970s attempts to improve the contrast in fluoroscopic images stored on videotape and videodiscs led workers at the University of Wisconsin to experiment with systems based on digital computers. Between 1976 and 1980 this group and an independent group at the University of Arizona showed that angiographic information could be obtained with simple intravenous injections of small amounts of contrast material and a digital image acquisition and processing system. Their technique consisted of collecting a "mask" X-ray image of the tissue of interest before injection of contrast medium and then electronically subtracting this mask image from each of a sequence of images taken during the passage of the contrast material through the tissue. Subtracting the mask image effectively leaves only regions containing contrast medium, causing the image of the vessels to stand out dramatically. The name of the technique, digital subtraction angiography (DSA), comes from this subtraction process.

The ability of DSA to get useful information with an intravenous injection of a relatively small amount of contrast material eliminates the risk to the patient from catheterization and reduces the possibility of adverse reactions to the contrast medium. In addition, DSA usually does not require hospitalization.

A drawback of DSA imaging arises from the fact that the signals destined for digital manipulation and storage are taken directly from the TV camera in a fluoroscopic imaging system. The screen images formed with TV equipment standard in the United States consist of 525 scan lines, which sets limits on resolving power. The resolution of an X-ray field of moderate size imaged with DSA is low compared with direct film angiography. One way of minimizing this effect is to image only a small field of view that encompasses only part of an organ.

Several important applications of DSA have already emerged. One involves evaluation of the carotid arteries, the main arteries feeding the brain.

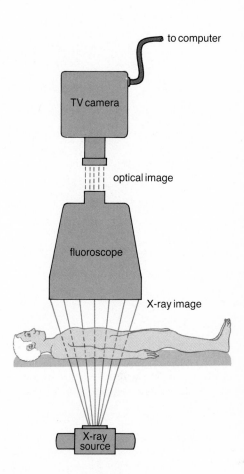

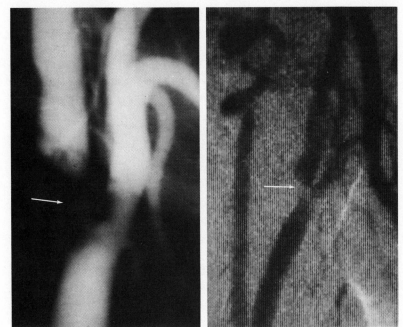

*The diagram above depicts a typical image-collection system for digital subtraction angiography. Fluoroscopic images are converted to electronic signals by means of a television camera and sent to a computer for storage and later manipulation and display. At left, two images of the carotid arteries in the neck of a patient are compared: one made with traditional angiography (far left) and the other with less invasive DSA (left). Arrows indicate the buildup of atherosclerotic plaque in the internal branch of the carotid artery as it leaves the common carotid. Although the DSA image is of lower resolution, the obstruction is clearly visible.*

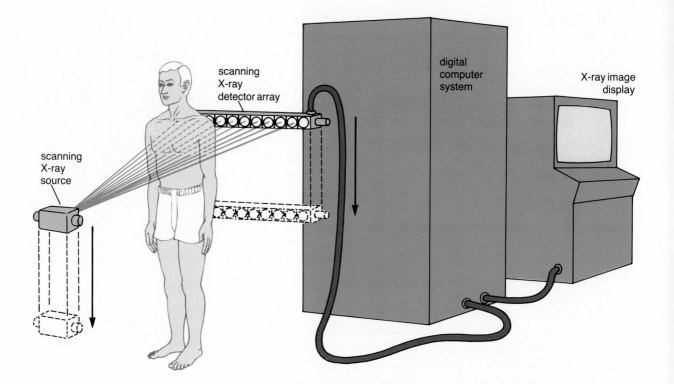

scanning
X-ray
detector array

scanning
X-ray
source

digital
computer
system

X-ray image
display

*Digital radiography is a computerized imaging technique in which the film or fluoroscope is replaced by a linear array of detectors that is scanned synchronously with a source of X-rays over the region of the body to be studied. Output from the detectors is transmitted to a digital computer, which constructs an image from the signals. Digital radiography exposes the patient to substantially lower doses of X-rays and uses magnetic media for image storage, rather than more expensive silver-based film.*

If physical examination and other tests suggest that a patient has deposits of plaque on the insides of the carotid artery walls, the physician may consider surgery to prevent a possible stroke. The final decision is made after determining the extent and status of the plaque deposit. In the past such a patient would have been subjected to an angiographic study, including an overnight stay in the hospital and arterial catheterization. Today, however, DSA offers a less traumatic and less expensive means of screening patients for the more dangerous procedure. Patients who ultimately go to surgery still have conventional angiographic studies, but a large number of others are spared on the basis of DSA results.

Another application of DSA is in the study of cardiac status, particularly the status of the left ventricle, the high-pressure pumping chamber of the heart. DSA can measure the pumping efficiency of the left ventricle as well as other indicators of its status. Much of this information previously has been obtained by an angiographic procedure involving arterial catheterization.

DSA has also been used to monitor patients requiring a sequence of evaluations over periods of days or weeks. Such situations include monitoring the condition of the arterial connections to transplanted kidneys and the detection and monitoring of pulmonary embolism (sudden blockage of the pulmonary artery or one of its branches). In both cases the less invasive, less risky DSA procedure can be applied as often as needed in lieu of a more dangerous angiographic study.

DSA has potential in other situations, including imaging of abdominal vessels, peripheral vessels, and vessels within the brain. Even with the improvements in spatial resolution expected from more advanced TV technology, it is unlikely that DSA will replace traditional angiography, but it will almost certainly reduce the number of angiographic procedures done and, thus, significantly reduce patient discomfort, risk of complications, and health care costs in general. Furthermore, medical scientists expect a host of new uses for digital subtraction systems in accessing and processing image data.

A less-developed but potentially important marriage of computer technology with X-ray-imaging technology is digital radiography (DR). In this approach the film or fluoroscope is replaced entirely by an array of solid-state radiation detectors that scan or move synchronously with an X-ray source across the region of interest. The detectors are directly linked to a digital computer, which assembles the collected electronic signals into an image.

Digital radiography has a number of advantages over traditional radiography, including, for a given image quality, substantially lower X-ray exposure to the subject and the ability to store images for later recall and processing. X-ray dosage is reduced because only that segment of the body being viewed by the detector array need be irradiated at any given time. This drastically reduces the number of scattered X-ray photons contributing to the final image and results in vastly improved image contrast. Although digital radiography is in its infancy, in the future most traditional X-ray units may well be replaced by DR units, not only because of lowered risk to patients, but because it is cheaper to store images on magnetic disks and tape than on silver-based film. During the next two decades the trend toward computerized imaging may result in entirely digital radiology departments, in which all images and patient data are collected, stored, and retrieved by computer.

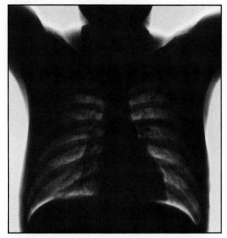

*This X-ray image of a human chest was produced with digital radiographic techniques. Stored on a magnetic disk, the image—or a magnified section of it—can be called up on a television monitor and easily photographed to provide a hard copy. It can also be displayed in the familiar positive mode (e.g., light bones) or reversed to the negative mode (dark bones) for particular diagnostic purposes.*

# Health and Fitness
# in the White House
## by William M. Lukash, M.D.

**Rear Admiral William M. Lukash, M.D.,**
*first became a member of the White House medical staff under Pres. Lyndon B. Johnson. He served as official White House physician to three presidents—Richard M. Nixon, Gerald R. Ford, and Jimmy Carter—before retiring from the post in January 1981. He is currently medical director of preventive medicine at the Scripps Clinic and Research Foundation, La Jolla, California.*

*(Opposite page) The author and President Ford; photograph, The White House*

The health of the president, like many other aspects of his personal life, is an acknowledged matter of public interest and, some feel, a consideration of his fitness for office. In 1975 Gerald R. Ford, the 38th president of the United States, caused some controversy when he authorized his personal physician to make a public disclosure of his health status; many people—including a few doctors—disagree strongly with the notion that presidents (and candidates for the office) are not entitled to the same confidentiality extended to other patients. Nonetheless, today's presidents are public figures, and their private lives and habits are the object of much curiosity. And many recent presidents, in satisfying that curiosity, have gone to great lengths to project images of themselves as healthy, vital individuals eager to undertake the burdens and responsibilities of high office and fully prepared to withstand the attendant pressures.

It has not always been so. In the early years of the United States, publicity about a president's personal life was scant, and news—even of a president's death—was slow to reach the outer fringes of the population. Few people know that George Washington, Thomas Jefferson, and Andrew Jackson suffered from a number of chronic disorders; all three, for example, were subject to recurrent episodes of malaria. Washington's wooden dentures are a clue to another source of suffering, although news reports of the day did not carry regular bulletins about his chronic toothaches. Thus, the health of past presidents has been largely a subject of interest to only a few rather specialized historians. And because of changes in medical terminology and advances in diagnostic techniques, it is not always possible for these specialists to discern the exact nature of vague complaints chronicled in the diaries, letters, and other documents that, in many cases, provide the only basis for such research. One conclusion seems justified, however: the earlier presidents of the United States, whatever their individual talents and abilities, were hardly examples of robust health.

*In 1919 two devastating strokes left Woodrow Wilson, whose health was precarious throughout his presidency, a temporary invalid. Nevertheless, Wilson completed his term of office, retiring to private life in March 1921. The above photograph, taken in December 1921 on his 65th birthday, shows Wilson still partially paralyzed.*

As the office of the presidency grew in importance and responsibility, presidential illnesses—particularly health problems that might affect the individual's ability to govern or the public's perception of his strength and effectiveness—gradually became carefully guarded secrets. In 1893, for example, during the first year of Grover Cleveland's second term of office, his physician discovered that Cleveland had a cancerous growth in his mouth. During July of that year, the president twice underwent secret surgery in which a part of his upper left jaw was removed and replaced with a vulcanized rubber prosthesis. Less than a month after the second operation, Cleveland resumed his public appearances, and there was evidently no public disclosure of his ailment.

The grave illnesses of presidents Woodrow Wilson and Franklin D. Roosevelt were shielded from public knowledge for many years, the true facts coming to light only after their deaths. In both cases the presidents' physicians, as well as their closest advisers, played crucial roles in helping to suppress information about the seriousness of their patients' conditions. Wilson, who had always been somewhat frail, returned from the Versailles Peace Conference in extremely weakened health. Nevertheless, against his doctor's advice, he embarked on a grueling cross-country train trip to win public support for ratification of the World War I peace treaty. During the course of the trip he suffered two strokes, the second paralyzing his left arm and leg. He remained a virtual invalid during the rest of his term in office, the knowledge of his true condition kept from the public by his physician, one or two close aides, and his wife—who, also unbeknownst to the public, assumed many of the president's executive responsibilities.

In contrast to Wilson, Roosevelt was strong and vigorous when he first en-

(Top) Keystone—EB, Inc.; (bottom) Brown Brothers

*After a bout of poliomyelitis, Franklin D. Roosevelt wore leg braces (left) for the rest of his life. Nonetheless, as president he was determined to project an image of robust physical health; he made his public appearances in a standing posture, always arranging for rostrums, lecterns, and even speaking platforms on trains (opposite page) to be equipped with some form of physical support.*

tered office, despite—or perhaps because of—his fight against a crippling bout of poliomyelitis. Although he could not stand without leg braces, he was determined not to be seen in public in a wheelchair; even the fact that he was physically handicapped was not universally known. In 1944 Roosevelt's determination to seek a fourth term as president, along with general concerns about national security in time of war, contributed to the secrecy regarding his deteriorating condition. During the 1944 election campaign, the president's physician stated unequivocally that Roosevelt was in excellent health. Later reports showed that he was already suffering from hypertension and heart failure and may even have had cancer. The secrecy surrounding his final illness was so complete that the public reaction to his death in April 1945 was a mixture of shock and disbelief.

*At Yalta (above) in 1945, Roosevelt appeared as a frail, gaunt, unresponsive specter of a man. It is difficult to understand how the drastic decline in his mental and physical state—so evident in the many photographs taken at the time—remained virtually unknown to all but his family, physicians, and closest advisers.*

163

## Health of recent presidents

The openness and publicity that have characterized the health problems of recent presidents represent a significant break with tradition. The first such disclosure was the announcement in 1956 that Pres. Dwight D. Eisenhower had suffered a serious heart attack. The entire world was shocked by the news, and many feared that the attack would necessarily prevent him from fulfilling the rigorous duties of his office. Fortunately, the president's cardiologist, Paul Dudley White, was a pioneer in early ambulation (*i.e.,* encouraging the patient not to remain bedridden) and exercise in the rehabilitation of cardiac patients. White, himself in his seventies, preferred a brisk walk to a ride in the car and never took an elevator when he could climb stairs instead. His promotion of the concept of early ambulation initiated a new outlook for heart attack victims, who had traditionally been viewed as virtually disabled; many recovering heart patients were advised by their physicians to retire from work and reconcile themselves to leading relatively inactive lives. Under White's care, however, Eisenhower recovered from his attack and even underwent subsequent abdominal surgery—and still was able to complete two terms in office.

Lyndon Baines Johnson suffered a massive coronary thrombosis when he was Senate majority leader in 1955. Johnson's background showed several major risk factors associated with a predisposition to cardiac disease: all of his male relatives had died of heart disease before the age of 60; he was a heavy smoker, was overweight, and lacked an adequate program of physical

*A month after suffering a serious heart attack, a convalescent Dwight D. Eisenhower poses for his first public picture-taking session at Fitzsimons Army Hospital in Denver, Colorado. His red pajamas, a gift from the White House press corps, bear the legend "Much Better Thanks"; to the five gold stars of his general's rank has been added a single silver star for "good conduct," awarded by the president's cardiologist, Paul Dudley White.*

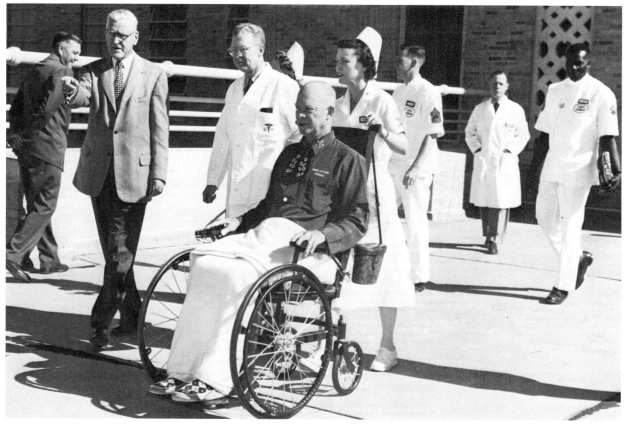

UPI

exercise; and because of the demands on him as majority leader, he did not allow enough time for relaxation or recreation. Like Eisenhower, Johnson fortunately experienced a complete recovery. He subsequently modified his living habits, giving up smoking and cutting down on the amount of fats in his diet. He lost 30 pounds and began a program of daily swimming, which he continued during his term as president. His health remained stable despite the tremendous strains and pressures of the Vietnam war.

Pres. John F. Kennedy played an important role in pioneering the physical fitness movement in the United States. Kennedy believed that every U.S. citizen needed a healthy body in order to make a creative contribution to society. The spirit of youth and vigor that became associated with his presidency was reflected in Kennedy's personal interest in sports; he was a varsity swimmer at Harvard, played golf, and was an avid sailor. The family games of touch football made the sport fashionable in Washington, D.C., at that time. Many have forgotten that the president suffered chronic back pain as the result of a serious injury incurred during World War II. To provide some relief from the pain, the medics assigned to the White House during his presidency gave Kennedy daily physiotherapy; he also followed a schedule of regular exercise and swimming.

Richard M. Nixon enjoyed general good health while in office, although he was hospitalized for viral pneumonia and had a serious attack of phlebitis during a crucial Middle Eastern foreign policy mission. Nixon and Egyptian Pres. Anwar as-Sadat were scheduled to make a three-hour train trip be-

*The now famous Kennedy rocking chair provided more than homespun charm at the White House—it was part of a regimen of treatment prescribed for John F. Kennedy's chronic back problems by his physician, Janet G. Travell. After one particularly painful flare-up, the Air Force had to use a special power lift to facilitate Kennedy's descent from a jet plane returning him to the capital.*

(Top) Wide World; (bottom) UPI

tween Cairo and Alexandria. The trip was considered a key event of the visit, and millions of Egyptians were assembled to greet the two leaders along the route. Unfortunately, Nixon, who had experienced a previous bout of phlebitis, again developed acute superficial phlebitis involving his leg. He was advised that the prolonged standing required on the train trip could seriously jeopardize his health, possibly even resulting in an embolus, or blood clot, in a lung. Although well aware of the potentially serious complications, he felt that the importance of his visit with Sadat and their public appearance together necessitated his taking a considerable personal risk. He was advised to remain seated whenever possible during the course of the trip and to keep the leg elevated. He was also treated with moist heat packs, a surgical support stocking, and anti-inflammatory drugs. His recovery at that time was without complications.

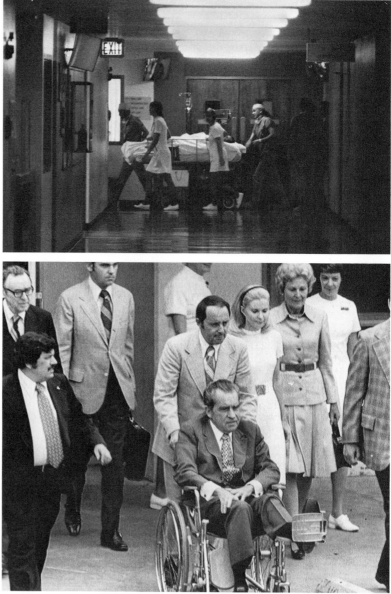

*After suffering intermittent episodes of phlebitis while in office, Richard M. Nixon experienced a series of recurrences during the three months after his resignation from the presidency. On Oct. 4, 1974, after nearly two weeks of diagnostic tests and anticoagulant therapy, an exhausted-looking Nixon (right) left Memorial Hospital Medical Center of Long Beach, California, to recuperate at his San Clemente home.*
*Later that month, however, the development of life-threatening blood clots in his left leg and lower abdomen required that the former president be rushed into emergency surgery (above).*

(Top) Tony Korody—Sygma; (bottom) UPI

After leaving office, however, Nixon suffered another episode of phlebitis, which progressed to deep vein thrombosis and ultimately developed into a pulmonary embolism that required surgery. Many persons have speculated that the stress of the Watergate affair and his subsequent resignation from office had something to do with the recurrence of phlebitis. Certainly it cannot be denied that stress can aggravate any medical condition. But to the White House physicians, who had ample opportunity to be with the president at Camp David and Key Biscayne, where he was able to escape the pressures of Watergate, Nixon demonstrated no evidence of significant emotional or psychologic deterioration. Like most presidents, he was able to focus on day-to-day matters of office without becoming overwhelmed by their cumulative weight and seriousness. Nixon's family and close friends were also instrumental in providing the emotional support necessary for him to carry on the functions of the presidency while confronting the pressures of a political scandal that eventually proved disastrous to his administration.

Pres. Gerald R. Ford was also subjected to extreme stress, assuming the office of the presidency under the unusually tense circumstances of the Nixon resignation and as one of the few men to succeed to the office without having been elected. Nonetheless, he enjoyed general good health during his term. Although he had chronic arthritis in both knees—the result of college football injuries—he maintained a daily program of swimming 20 laps every morning and every night in the White House pool. Ford also managed to carry on the responsibilities of the presidency when his wife suffered a serious health crisis. In 1974, after a routine physical examination revealed that she had a malignant tumor, Betty Ford underwent an emergency mastectomy. Like the Nixons, however, the Fords were a close family and a source of emotional strength in times of stress. Certainly his wife's courage at this time also helped the president to maintain his stability.

Jimmy Carter was reported to be in excellent health when he assumed office. Carter did have a history of a chronic hemorrhoidal condition—a common problem that afflicts some 15 million people in the U.S.—and suffered

David Kennerly/TIME Magazine © 1974 Time Inc.

*Gerald Ford's physical and emotional resilience served him well during the personal crisis of his wife's emergency breast cancer surgery. In the photograph, taken at the first lady's hospital bedside, Ford looks on as she views an official "get well" message signed by all 100 members of the U.S. Senate. Betty Ford's courage and composure at this time were an inspiration to mastectomy patients everywhere.*

one acute attack that forced him to cancel his official appointments for a day. He responded to conventional treatment, and the pain gradually resolved. The condition was treated by means of rubber-band ligature, a highly effective but relatively simple procedure that usually results in prompt healing. Because of the publicity surrounding this event, many people with hemorrhoids became less hesitant about seeking medical care. In addition, information on how to treat and prevent hemorrhoids became a subject of much attention in the news media.

Carter will be remembered as another president who gave enthusiastic support to the physical fitness movement. He was a member of the cross-country team while a midshipman at Annapolis, and during the Camp David peace summit in 1978 he decided to take up jogging for relaxation. The rigorous schedule of the summit process, involving separate daily meetings with both President Sadat and Israeli Prime Minister Menachem Begin, did not allow him much time to relax and unwind. Observing that a perimeter road around Camp David gave him a significant amount of privacy from the rest of the staff, Carter decided to start jogging. Following the Camp David summit, he became an avid jogger; both he and Mrs. Carter ran almost every evening. Despite his excellent conditioning program, however, the president suffered from heat exhaustion while competing in a ten-kilometer race sponsored by the National Park Service. The excitement and adrenaline surge at the starting line and the president's competitive instinct probably contributed to his overheating. After fluid replenishment and appropriate cooling, he recovered completely and was able to present the awards to the winners.

168

## Day-to-day care of the president

Historically, since 1813, the majority of presidential physicians have been military doctors; this arrangement allows the president to take advantage of military medical facilities, where previously established security measures are less disruptive than those that would be required in a civilian hospital. (The military tradition went unbroken until President Kennedy named a civilian, Janet G. Travell, M.D., as his personal physician. Similarly, Pres. Ronald Reagan also appointed a civilian doctor, Daniel Ruge, M.D., to serve as official White House physician.)

**Medical care in the White House.** A fully equipped medical facility located in the White House is funded by the Department of the Navy. The staff consists of a senior physician, two assistant physicians, three nurses, two physicians' assistants, and three hospital corpsmen. The president's personal physician has an office and treatment room on the ground floor of the White House, directly across from the elevator to the presidential living quarters. The White House clinic has complete emergency and life-support equipment, including a portable cardiac defibrillator, as well as a pharmacy. A similar facility is located in the Executive Office Building. Health care is provided for each of the 1,500 persons associated with the White House. Day-to-day care is provided for the entire staff. Those individuals with more serious problems are referred to their private physicians. (Senior staff, Cabinet officers, and members of the first family are also eligible for medical care and hospitalization at military hospitals in the Washington, D.C., area.)

The White House medical staff must remain on duty during evening hours and at social functions such as state dinners. In addition, on presidential trips they are expected to provide care for all persons who travel with the president, an entourage that may consist of as many as 600 people, including military and diplomatic personnel, the security staff, and members of the communications media.

*(Opposite top) Even while on a foreign policy mission in Israel, Jimmy Carter kept up his jogging program; he is shown accompanied by physician Lukash and national security adviser Zbigniew Brzezinski. Despite excellent conditioning, Carter succumbed to heat exhaustion in a much-publicized ten-kilometer race in September 1979 (bottom).*

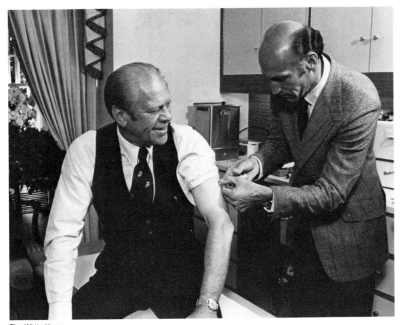

The White House

*The chief executive receives all of his primary medical care in the office of his personal physician, which is located in the White House just opposite the elevator to the presidential living quarters. Gerald Ford and William Lukash usually had a brief visit there every day. In the photograph (left), Lukash gives the president a flu shot.*

The president's personal physician supervises his diet and exercise programs, accompanies him at public appearances and on foreign and domestic trips, and even attends church with the president. It is also his responsibility to be available at all times to members of the first family. He is provided with a car that has a direct telephone line to the White House, and White House signal phones are installed in his home. Basically, he is on call 24 hours a day, seven days a week, and can anticipate phone calls and house visits on a reasonably frequent basis.

**Hospitalization.** The designated hospital for the past five presidents has been the National Naval Medical Center at Bethesda, Maryland. A nine-room presidential suite was modernized at the naval hospital during President Johnson's term in office. An elaborate communications system was installed to enable the president to respond to a possible security crisis in any part of the world. Secret Service measures required bulletproof windows. The suite was designed not only for the president's medical needs but also to accommodate the day-to-day business of government. A large dining room area was equipped to hold a full Cabinet meeting. A presidential sitting room was designed for private visits and relaxation, and a bedroom was made available for the first lady if she desired to stay at the hospital. When a president is hospitalized, members of the White House medical staff remain on duty around the clock, working in cooperation with the hospital medical and nursing staff. Walter Reed Army Medical Center also has a similar presidential suite. Both presidents Truman and Eisenhower received their medical care there. As the commander in chief the president is entitled to hospital care essentially free of cost. It has been the custom, however, for presidents to use their third-party health insurance and to be charged fees comparable to those of a civilian hospital.

*While recovering from gallbladder surgery, Lyndon Johnson conducted the business of office—including regular visits with Vice-Pres. Hubert Humphrey—from the presidential hospital suite at the National Naval Medical Center in Bethesda, Maryland. In addition to elaborate security measures, the Bethesda facility is equipped with a special communications center (shown on table, left) linking the president to the White House and all key government officials.*

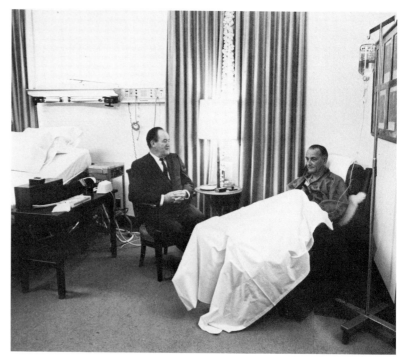

# Presidential travel

**The threat of assassination.** In view of the elaborate precautions that surround the president's movements today, the evident lack of regard for the safety of past presidents seems both incredible and naive. Four presidents died at the hands of assassins, and five others (Andrew Jackson, Franklin D. Roosevelt, Harry S. Truman, Gerald Ford, and Ronald Reagan) were the objects of unsuccessful attempts. All were outside of the White House at the time of the attack, and several were making scheduled public appearances that had been well publicized in advance. Three of those assassinated had no physician in immediate attendance.

The first, Abraham Lincoln, was shot while he and Mrs. Lincoln, accompanied by friends, sat in the presidential box at Ford's Theatre. There were no security personnel close by, with the exception of the bodyguard assigned to secure the door to the box—who had evidently left his post unattended. The provisions for medical emergency were equally casual. A few soldiers carried the wounded president to a boardinghouse across from the theater. He died there early the next morning.

The fatal shooting of Pres. James A. Garfield occurred in a Washington, D.C., railroad station. Garfield was taken back to the White House, but the team of physicians who attended him was unable to locate and remove the assassin's bullet; the president finally died of blood poisoning 80 days after the shooting.

The assassinations of presidents William McKinley and John Kennedy took place under somewhat similar circumstances. In both cases an atmosphere of tension surrounded their last public appearances, which had been widely publicized and drew large crowds of spectators. Again, in both cases, fear for the president's safety prompted unusually strict security measures but did not prevent fatal injury.

Today, maximum security measures and advance medical precautions are necessary not only to ensure the protection of the president but also to allay increased public anxiety about his safety. The Secret Service prepares an extensive intelligence survey of all areas to be visited and establishes security measures for every presidential trip and public appearance. As many observers have noted, however, nothing can guarantee a president total protection against a determined assassin. This fact was amply demonstrated in the attacks on presidents Ford and Reagan. In 1975 Ford, while traveling in California, was attacked twice within a period of several days; in both instances the presidential physician was present, and the instantaneous response of the Secret Service prevented a potential tragedy. Reagan, who was shot and wounded after making a public appearance at a Washington, D.C., hotel only 70 days after taking office, also owes his life to the rapid response of the security and emergency medical personnel who accompanied him on that occasion.

**Preparation for medical emergencies.** Because of the ever-present possibility of assassination, accident, or sudden illness, White House physicians now accompany the president any time he leaves the executive mansion, whether he remains in the Washington area or travels to a foreign country. Prior to any public event, a member of the medical staff and the Secret

*The first attempt on the life of a U.S. president took place in January 1835 when a deranged man fired at Pres. Andrew Jackson (right) on the steps of the Capitol. Abraham Lincoln, the first president to be assassinated, died in the Petersen house (below), a boardinghouse on Tenth Street across from Ford's Theatre, where the fatal shooting had taken place. Although Lincoln was mortally wounded, no fewer than 16 doctors gathered, helpless, during the night-long vigil at the president's bedside.*

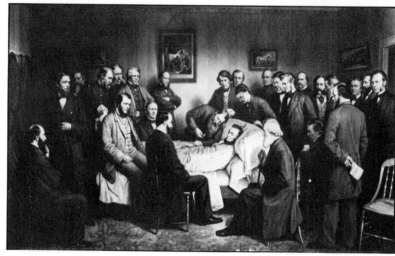

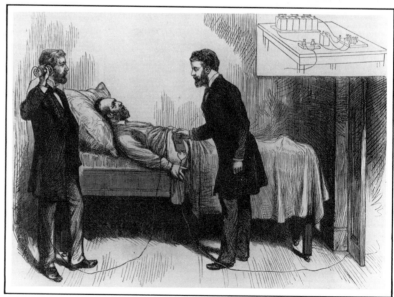

*Unable to find the assassin's bullet, the physicians attending Pres. James A. Garfield called upon Alexander Graham Bell (right), who attempted—without success—to locate the bullet by means of a rudimentary metal detector powered by a battery-circuit breaker assembly (inset) and attached to a telephone.*

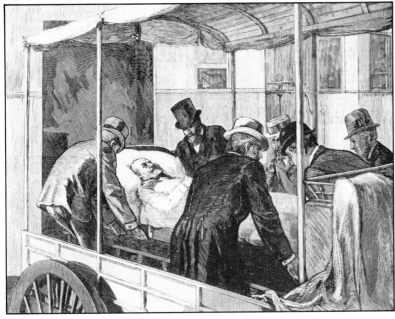

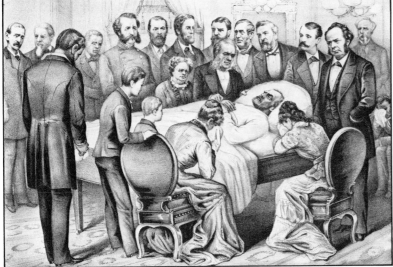

*Garfield was shot on July 2, 1881. In addition to Bell's electronic search, exploratory surgery was also performed three times during the 80 days the wounded man lingered alive; the bullet was finally recovered during the autopsy. In the meantime, because of the extreme heat of Washington, D.C., it was decided early in September to move the injured president (top) to the New Jersey seaside, and a special ice-cooled train car was fitted to transport him. Although he rallied briefly after arriving at Elberon, Garfield died (center) of blood poisoning on Sept. 19, 1881. The assassination of Pres. William McKinley (below left) occurred while the president was attending a public reception at the 1901 Pan American Exposition in Buffalo, New York. He was rushed by ambulance (below) to a nearby hospital but died eight days later.*

*The tense atmosphere that surrounded John F. Kennedy's November 1963 visit to Dallas prompted tighter than usual security measures, but these were not enough to prevent the tragedy of his assassination. A photograph taken moments after the fatal shots were fired shows a Secret Service agent climbing into the hospital-bound presidential limousine.*

Service accompany an advance team that determines the availability of a capable medical facility equipped to handle any health problem that might befall the president and also establishes an elaborate evacuation plan in the event of any medical disaster or threat of presidential assassination.

Emergency medical facilities, including an ambulance and paramedical team, are available at any location where the president is to make a public appearance and every hotel where he is a guest. These facilities remain active and prepared as long as the president is in residence. In the case of presidential trips, hospitals for emergency use are specifically selected in advance, both in the United States and abroad. Highly qualified professional care and quick accessibility not jeopardized by traffic are the prime requirements for hospital selection.

Within a single city, two or three hospitals may be chosen in order to ensure that immediate medical care will be available from the airport and all locations to be visited in the city. Direct communication lines are established between the Secret Service detail accompanying the president and each of the selected hospitals. It is, of course, necessary that these hospitals have full surgical and anesthetic capabilities. Blood of the president's type must be on hand, and a specific surgeon, anesthesiologist, and internist are designated to care for him during his stay in the area. Over the past several years specifically designated hospitals have been used repeatedly on return trips, especially to major metropolitan cities; this has enabled the establishment of prompt, routine procedures for safeguarding the president's health and safety during any visit.

On presidential trips abroad, a member of the medical unit accompanies the advance team to assure that appropriate medical care and designated physicians will be available to assist the presidential medical staff with any illness or to perform any surgery that may be required. Emergency care is sometimes marginal in the less developed countries of Southeast Asia, Africa, or the Middle East. In such cases, in addition to preparing hospital facilities in the host country, it is sometimes necessary that a navy ship— equipped with an operating suite and fully staffed surgical team—cruise a few miles offshore of the president's closest destination. Helicopters are ready at all times to transport him aboard.

Even the most comprehensive planning and preparation cannot anticipate every situation. When, for example, President Carter and his family took a three-day raft trip down the Snake River through rugged mountain terrain in Idaho, security problems were more challenging than usual and medical evacuation plans more critical. Evacuation helicopters were situated on mountaintops at appropriate intervals along the river. The White House physician rode with the president, and a nurse followed in a backup raft. A security detail in kayaks preceded the three rafts. Only essential portable medical equipment could be stored aboard the rafts. Fortunately, the trip was completed without any serious mishaps.

## Dealing with the pressures of office

**Privileges of the presidency.** While most people are aware of the heavy burdens of the presidency, perhaps less is known about the ways in which a

*Relaxation, leisure-time hobbies, and physical fitness routines help the president withstand the awesome responsibilities of office. Gerald Ford (bottom) was one of several presidents who enjoyed a daily swim. A working vacation was rancher Lyndon Johnson's idea of relaxation (below), while Ronald Reagan—who also enjoys the role of part-time ranch hand— is equally adept at the "nonworking" vacation (left).*

president's life is made easier and less complicated than that of the average citizen. The president is provided with the most convenient and efficient surroundings imaginable to help him relax. The White House staff cares for all the personal needs of his family. An outdoor swimming pool, a bowling alley, tennis courts, and beautiful gardens are available within the privacy of the White House grounds, providing relaxation and recreation during any periods of leisure time that he can arrange. Transportation is always prompt and with police escort; there are never any traffic jams. No president must wait in line for theater tickets or for a table at a crowded restaurant. Presidential helicopters and Air Force One are at his disposal at all times, and takeoff begins at the moment the president buckles his seat belt. While on a long flight, he can dine with aides or family members, work, make calls anywhere in the world, or relax and watch television.

Most presidents prefer to spend their weekends at Camp David, a tranquil mountain retreat surrounded by Catoctin Mountain Park only a 30-minute helicopter flight from the capital. Camp David is an installation administered and run by the Navy. All the comforts of the White House are available in addition to seclusion from the public and the press. Presidential families traditionally become much closer at Camp David, where they obtain relief from the fishbowl scrutiny of official life. This reinforces their ability to meet the demands of a public that expects them to be responsive, open, and gracious at all times.

The Ford and Carter children often brought their friends to Camp David. Recreational resources are unlimited, including everything from archery to snowmobiles. Now there are saddle horses for the Reagans. Guests invited by the president see the latest movies and are free to use any of many hiking trails or to play tennis or swim. Few other places provide a better opportunity for the presidents to relax and spend time with their families in an atmosphere free of the pressures of the White House.

**Keeping fit.** In addition to these special recreational facilities, most recent

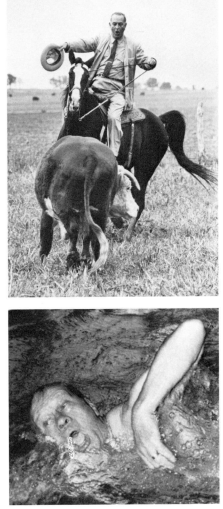

presidents have had their own programs of physical fitness and their own hobbies or individual forms of relaxation. President Johnson took a daily swim in the White House swimmming pool. President Nixon had an early morning calisthenic program, and in addition to weekends at Camp David he enjoyed inviting friends on brief trips to his homes at San Clemente, California, and Key Biscayne, Florida. At these retreats he would swim daily in the ocean for as long as an hour and would enjoy two- or three-mile walks along the beach with Mrs. Nixon. President Ford developed an aerobic exercise program consisting of swimming twice a day. He also enjoyed golfing and skiing. Like Nixon, Ford also was concerned with watching his weight. The White House physician, in collaboration with the chef, prepared a diet regimen tailored to his personal needs. In addition to jogging, President Carter liked playing tennis and fishing.

Each president also has techniques for relaxation that help him unwind and regenerate his energy to meet the heavy responsibilities of office. President Nixon listened to symphonic music. President Ford relaxed in the late evening by visiting in the private quarters with Mrs. Ford and his children. President Carter, an avid fly-fisherman, enjoyed the challenge of making his own dry flies, which required total concentration. While engaged in this activity he felt completely relaxed and thus was able to insulate himself, for a while at least, from the burdens of the presidency.

**The effects of stress.** There is considerable public concern about how any president can deal with so many different kinds of problems and cope with the day-to-day responsibilities of his high office. I can truthfully say that during my years as White House physician a day did not pass during which the president was not faced with a serious problem or a decision of enormous magnitude. Obviously, he receives advice from the members of his Cabinet and from the Congress, and certainly he has access to the nation's most knowledgeable experts on every subject. Ultimately, however, the final decision rests with him alone.

In general, I saw no unusual clinical manifestations of excessive presidential stress or strain. Those individuals who achieve the office of the presidency seem in the course of their careers to acquire effective methods to deal with stress. Basically these methods consist of an ability to face problems one by one as they arise, to make full use of brief periods of relaxation as well as longer vacations away from the White House, and a certain special ability to thrive under pressure. Even during the most intense crises, they retain the capacity to be diverted and amused and to get sufficient rest. Needless to say, the development of personal routines that promote good general health—especially regular exercise and appropriate eating habits—plays an integral part in the maintenance of a president's mental and physical fitness.

# The World of Medicine

# Contributors to The World of Medicine

**George J. Annas, J.D., M.P.H.** *Health Care Law.* Edward Utley Professor of Health Law, and Chief, Health Law Section, Boston University Schools of Medicine and Public Health.

**Edward L. Applebaum, M.D.** *Ear Diseases and Hearing Disorders.* Professor and Head, Department of Otolaryngology, University of Illinois College of Medicine, Chicago.

**Norman R. Bernstein, M.D.** *Pediatrics Special Report: The Burned Child.* Professor of Psychiatry, University of Illinois, Chicago; Consultant, University of Chicago Burn Center.

**Walter G. Bradley, D.M.** *Neuromuscular Disorders.* Professor and Chairman, Department of Neurology, University of Vermont College of Medicine, Burlington.

**Carroll M. Brodsky, M.D., Ph.D.** *Occupational Health.* Professor of Psychiatry, University of California School of Medicine, San Francisco.

**John P. Bunker, M.D.** *Health Care Technology Special Report: The Costs of Medical Innovation.* Professor of Anesthesia, and Professor of Family, Community, and Preventive Medicine, Stanford University School of Medicine, Stanford, Calif.

**Bertram W. Carnow, M.D.** *Environmental Health.* Professor of Occupational and Environmental Medicine, University of Illinois College of Medicine, Chicago; President, Carnow, Conibear & Associates, Ltd., Chicago.

**Edward P. Cohen, M.D.** *Infectious Diseases.* Director, Office of Research and Development, and Professor of Microbiology and Immunology, University of Illinois, Chicago.

**Edward Cotlier, M.D.** *Eye Diseases and Visual Disorders.* Professor, Department of Ophthalmology and Visual Sciences, Yale University School of Medicine, New Haven, Conn.

**Ronald G. Crystal, M.D.** *Lung Diseases.* Chief, Pulmonary Branch, National Heart, Lung, and Blood Institute, National Institutes of Health, Bethesda, Md.

**Alan H. DeCherney, M.D.** *Gynecology and Obstetrics.* Associate Professor, Department of Obstetrics and Gynecology, and Director, Division of Reproductive Endocrinology, Yale University School of Medicine, New Haven, Conn.

**Leon Eisenberg, M.D.** *Death and Dying Special Report: The Tragedy of Childhood Suicide.* Chairman, Department of Social Medicine and Health Policy, Harvard Medical School, Boston.

**Stephen E. Epstein, M.D.** *Heart and Blood Vessels* (in part). Chief of Cardiology, Cardiology Branch, National Heart, Lung, and Blood Institute, National Institutes of Health, Bethesda, Md.

**Fred H. Frankel, M.B.Ch.B., D.P.M.** *Mental Health and Illness Special Report: Hypnosis.* Professor of Psychiatry, Harvard Medical School, and Director of Clinical Psychiatry, Beth Israel Hospital, Boston.

**William F. Fry, Jr., M.D.** *Human Physiology Special Report: Laughter and Health.* Psychiatrist in private practice, Menlo Park, Calif.; Associate Clinical Professor, Department of Psychiatry, Stanford University School of Medicine, Stanford, Calif.; Director, Gerontology Institute, Nevada City, Calif.

**Vincent A. Fulginiti, M.D.** *Pediatrics.* Professor and Head, Department of Pediatrics, University of Arizona College of Medicine, Tucson.

**Charles S. Green, D.D.S.** *Dentistry* (in part). Professor of Oral and Maxillofacial Surgery, and Research Coordinator, Temporomandibular Joint and Facial Pain Research Center, University of Illinois College of Dentistry, Chicago.

**Fred. H. Hochberg, M.D.** *Occupational Health Special Report: The Ailments of Musicians* (in part). Assistant Professor of Neurology, Harvard Medical School; Staff Neurologist, Neurology Service, Massachusetts General Hospital, Boston.

**Warren A. Katz, M.D.** *Arthritis and Connective Tissue Disorders.* Division Chief, Division of Rheumatology, Department of Medicine, Medical College of Pennsylvania and Hospital, Philadelphia.

**Matthew J. Kluger, Ph.D.** *Human Physiology.* Professor of Physiology, Department of Physiology, University of Michigan Medical School, Ann Arbor.

**Mary Jane Koren, M.D.** *Aging.* Assistant Professor of Medicine, Division of Geriatrics, Albert Einstein College of Medicine, Bronx, N.Y.; Assistant Medical Director, Department of Home Care and Extended Services, Montefiore Medical Center, Bronx, N.Y.

**Robert J. Krane, M.D.** *Human Sexuality.* Professor and Chairman, Department of Urology, Boston University School of Medicine.

**Lynne Lamberg.** *Skin Disorders* (in part); *Sleep Disorders.* Free-lance medical writer, Baltimore, Md.

**Stanford I. Lamberg, M.D.** *Skin Disorders* (in part). Associate Professor of Dermatology, The Johns Hopkins University School of Medicine; Chief, Department of Dermatology, Baltimore City Hospitals, Baltimore, Md.

**Daniel M. Laskin, D.D.S.** *Dentistry* (in part). Professor and Head, Department of Oral and Maxillofacial Surgery, and Director, Temporomandibular Joint and Facial Pain Research Center, University of Illinois College of Dentistry, Chicago.

**Robert D. Leffert, M.D.** *Occupational Health Special Report: The Ailments of Musicians* (in part). Associate Professor of Orthopedic Surgery, Harvard Medical School; Chief, Department of Rehabilitation Medicine, Massachusetts General Hospital, Boston.

**Martin B. Leon, M.D.** *Heart and Blood Vessels* (in part). Senior Investigator, Cardiology Branch, National Heart, Lung, and Blood Institute, National Institutes of Health, Bethesda, Md.

**Nathan W. Levin, M.D.** *Surgery and Transplantation.* Head, Division of Nephrology and Hypertension, Henry Ford Hospital, Detroit; Clinical Professor of Internal Medicine, University of Michigan Medical School, Ann Arbor.

**Mortimer B. Lipsett, M.D.** *Endocrinology.* Director, National Institute of Child Health and Human Development, National Institutes of Health; Clinical Professor of Medicine, Uniformed Services University of Health Sciences, Bethesda, Md.

**Melvin H. Marx, Ph.D.** *Mental Health and Illness.* Research Professor of Psychology, University of Missouri, Columbia.

**Lisle A. Merriman.** *Occupational Health Special Report: The Ailments of Musicians* (in part). Research Assistant, Neurology Service, Massachusetts General Hospital, Boston.

**Oglesby Paul, M.D.** *Medical Education.* Professor of Medicine, Harvard Medical School, Boston.

**Edmund D. Pellegrino, M.D.** *Medical Ethics.* John Carroll Professor of Medicine and Medical Humanities, Georgetown University Medical Center, Washington, D.C.

**Ricki L. Rusting.** *Diet and Nutrition Special Report: Bulimia: An Eating Disorder.* Managing Editor, *Diabetes Forecast,* American Diabetes Association, New York City.

**Omar Sattaur.** *Endocrinology Special Report: Prostaglandins: New Keys to Disease and Health.* Bioscience Editor, *New Scientist,* London, England.

**Barry A. Shapiro, M.D.** *Health Care Technology.* Professor of Clinical Anesthesia, and Director, Division of Respiratory/Critical Care, Department of Anesthesia, Northwestern University Medical School, Chicago.

**Edith T. Shapiro, M.D.** *Death and Dying.* Psychiatrist in private practice, Englewood, N.J.; Clinical Associate Professor of Psychiatry, College of Medicine and Dentistry, New Jersey Medical School, Newark.

**Peter Steinglass, M.D.** *Alcoholism.* Professor of Psychiatry and Behavioral Sciences, George Washington University School of Medicine, Washington, D.C.

**Myron Winick, M.D.** *Diet and Nutrition.* R. R. Williams Professor of Nutrition, Professor of Pediatrics, Director, Institute of Human Nutrition, and Director, Center for Nutrition, Genetics, and Human Development, Columbia University College of Physicians and Surgeons, New York City.

# Aging

"Even when the correct diagnosis is made, the aged are frequently improperly treated through our ignorance of the action of drugs upon the senile organism." This quotation appeared in the April 20, 1912, edition of the *Medical Record.* If this statement was apt in 1912, it is even more apt today. Persons over the age of 65 currently account for about 11% of the people in the United States, or as many as 23 million. By the year 2000 this figure will probably increase to anywhere from 15 to 20% of the total population. Life expectancy for men is now 69, for women 77. An understanding, therefore, of the rational use of medications becomes a critical issue for this group. A heightened awareness of how drug therapy is complicated by the aging process lets both physicians and consumers participate in the team effort needed to optimize treatment and diminish untoward effects.

One of the difficulties in any discussion of "the elderly" is that like any other segment of the population joined only on the basis of age, they are in most respects heterogeneous. From the standpoint of religious beliefs, politics, socioeconomic status, and personal prejudices, they are as diverse as any other age group. Even the process of aging itself is often gradual, and physiological age need not exactly parallel chronologic age. Therefore, to call everyone over the age of 65 "old" is to be unduly simplistic. There are, however, certain physiological changes that do occur as part of the normal aging process that make the elderly, as a group, highly at risk for the overuse and adverse effects of medications.

## Drugs and the elderly

Older people experience more illnesses than do younger people; 86% of people over the age of 70 have at least one chronic illness (*e.g.,* arteriosclerotic heart disease, diabetes mellitus, chronic lung disease, osteoarthritis, and so forth), and 50% have two or more concurrent illnesses. It is this simultaneity of illnesses that is one of the hallmarks of geriatric medicine. Also, not only are multiple chronic illnesses the rule, but even minor acute illnesses, when they occur superimposed on a chronic condition, can rapidly become life-threatening. Further, these diseases necessitate more frequent hospitalization, for longer periods of time (65% of all patients in acute care hospitals in the United States today are over the age of 65), and may in 15 to 20% of the population lead to long-term institutional care. Owing to these facts, a greater fraction of personal income is spent by the elderly on health care; in fact, in the U.S. the older population accounts for 25 to 30% of all health care expenditures.

Given this background of vulnerability, the elderly often take a staggering number of medications, a situation that gives rise to a problem called "polypharmacy." It is a problem not only engendered by physicians but often exacerbated by patients themselves. Take the case that follows as a typical clinical example:

Mrs. Y is an 80-year-old widow living by herself in an apartment in an urban area. She has a daughter living close by. Mrs. Y had a bleeding ulcer some 20 years ago and a heart attack 10 years ago and sometimes is bothered by shortness of breath from congestive heart failure. Irregularly she sees a cardiologist who gives her a diuretic (a pill to eliminate excess fluid from the body), digoxin (to help the heart work more efficiently), and nitroglycerin (for occasional attacks of angina). She also has arthritis, for which she takes aspirin, but since it upsets her stomach, she frequently takes an antacid as well. Recently the problem with her stomach became so bad that she went to a doctor whose office is in her building, and he gave her another pill for her stomach, cimetidine (which decreases acid production in the stomach).

Mrs. Y's diet is very poor; she largely subsists on tea and toast. She was once told by a doctor in the emergency room that she was anemic, so on her daughter's advice she takes vitamins and iron. This has made her quite constipated, so she also takes a stool softener and a laxative.

She has had some trouble sleeping, which is helped by a sleeping pill. Also, because she is often nervous (the neighborhood has been getting quite bad), she sometimes takes some diazepam (Valium), given to her by her daughter. Her family thinks she may need to go to a nursing home soon because she has started to fall frequently and is often confused and very forgetful.

## The problem of overmedication

Mrs. Y, on 13 different medications, soon to be declared senile and put in a nursing home, is a victim of

*The problem of polypharmacy, or overmedication, is a serious issue in geriatric medicine. One solution currently being tested by some California practitioners is a program that allows physician-supervised pharmacists, working directly with patients, to adjust and monitor medication.*

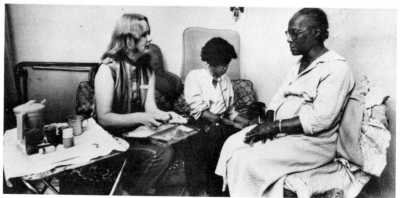

*The elderly often take a stunning number of medications. Often these are prescribed by many different physicians, who may not know what other drugs the patient is taking.*

polypharmacy. Her predicament can be used to illustrate some of the problems facing geriatric pharmacology; namely, those factors predisposing to polypharmacy, drug side effects and toxic effects, drug interactions, and the effects of diet, smoking, and alcohol on a patient's response to medication.

First, why is Mrs. Y on so many medications? She does have several medical illnesses: (1) she has had a heart attack and currently has arteriosclerotic cardiovascular disease that occasionally causes congestive heart failure and angina; (2) she also had an ulcer at one time; and (3) she has considerable pain and stiffness from osteoarthritis. However, because Mrs. Y is going to several physicians and each is trying to treat different aspects of these illnesses, each unbeknown to the other, her care is uncoordinated, and the medications she is receiving may be inducing other illnesses in her or causing what is called iatrogenic disease. Some of the complaints that she treats herself and that her well-meaning family and friends are also helping to treat may in fact be induced by some of her medications. For example, her stomach pain, her mild nausea, and perhaps her poor appetite might well be due either to digitalis toxicity, to the doses of aspirin she is taking for her arthritis, to the potassium supplement she is taking with her diuretic, or perhaps to the iron she is taking for her anemia. Her insomnia and bad dreams may again be due to digitalis or perhaps to all of the tea and coffee she drinks. Her constipation may have several etiologies. Some antacids can cause constipation, as can iron-containing preparations; very low-fiber diets, inadequate hydration, and a very sedentary lifestyle may contribute as well. Her nervousness and seeming dementia may also be drug induced; cimetidine, sleeping pills, aspirin, and Valium often act synergistically to cause confusion, lethargy, and forgetfulness in the elderly. The anemia could be from bleeding gastritis (slow, diffuse bleeding of the stomach), caused by her frequent doses of aspirin, which is a major stomach irritant. The recent increase in the number

of falls that she is having may be due to postural hypotension (low blood pressure brought on by standing up) caused by her diuretics or perhaps by her nitroglycerin, which is taken under the tongue for chest pain and can cause sudden drops in blood pressure. So, it can be seen that several of Mrs. Y's illnesses are in fact merely the side effects of some of the medications that she is being treated with for some of her real diseases.

## Adverse effects of drugs

From this background of vulnerability arises the problem faced by so many elderly patients who take many medications—that of the side effects and toxic effects produced by drugs. Side effects are undesirable effects related to the major pharmacological action of the drug itself. Toxicity, on the other hand, is an undesirable effect not actually related to the principal drug action. The exact distinction here is unimportant, but the idea that drugs used to combat real illnesses in and of themselves may cause life-threatening conditions, or may cause other symptoms and signs that very closely mimic entirely new and unrelated illnesses, is a key problem facing geriatric medicine today.

As can be seen from the case of Mrs. Y, her so-called senility—perhaps caused by her Valium, her sleeping pills, or her cimetidine—might well have caused her to be placed in a long-term care facility; her diuretics and nitroglycerin might have caused a fall, an accident that can sometimes result in incapacitating head trauma or hip fractures, either of which could lead to the demise of an elderly individual. Moreover, these types of adverse drug reactions, like systemic illnesses themselves in the elderly, may be very difficult to recognize. Studies have shown the prevalence of adverse drug reactions of 12 to 17% in patients aged 70 to 90, as opposed to 3% in those aged 10 to 30 years.

## Drug interactions

A further problem resulting from drug use in the elderly is that drugs may interact with each other or alter the

Adapted from Troy L. Thompson et al., "Psychotropic Drug Use in the Elderly," The New England Journal of Medicine, Jan. 20, 1983, vol. 308, no. 3, pp. 134–137

| Effects of common drugs in the elderly | |
|---|---|
| *physiological change* | *pharmacokinetic effect* |
| distribution in body | |
| decreased lean body mass and total body water | increased plasma concentration of water-soluble drugs |
| increased total body fat | decreased plasma concentration and slower elimination of fat-soluble drugs |
| decreased serum albumin | higher percentage of unbound, metabolically active drugs |
| elimination of drug | |
| decreased hepatic enzyme activity and blood flow | decreased effectiveness of metabolism of foreign substances |
| decreased renal function | decreased renal excretion; prolonged effects of drugs that are excreted primarily unchanged |

action that one or the other has. One drug can, for instance, interfere with the absorption of another; one can interfere with the binding of another drug to plasma proteins; one can change or modify the metabolism of another drug; and a competing drug can interfere with the action of a drug at its receptor in the target organ. Mrs. Y's apparent dementia might well have been due to the interaction of cimetidine with some of the sleeping pills or tranquilizers she was taking. Drug interactions may range from purely theoretical to frankly fatal. Conversely, they may produce a desirable effect. This is the case, for example, with certain antibiotics that, when used in combination, have an enhanced efficacy greater than their additive effects (*i.e.*, $2 + 2 = 5$). Sometimes the effect of the interaction may not be a toxic reaction but rather a loss of desired effect (*e.g.*, if the antibiotic tetracycline is taken simultaneously with an antacid, which prevents the absorption of the tetracycline into the body, no antimicrobial action can take place).

There are now several computer-based systems to evaluate and monitor potential drug interactions. These systems can be used to try to gain new information about potentially serious or harmful drug interactions. Most clinicians are familiar with the common drug interactions that cause difficulties in patients. Many times, though, even with known drug interactions, the two drugs may be necessary and can in fact be given simultaneously if the patient is monitored carefully for any side effects that may occur.

Not only is it possible for drugs to interact with each other, but diet can also influence the workings of some medications. Mrs. Y's diet of tea and toast (the elderly typically have poorer nutrition than other age groups) could cause significant protein malnutrition as well as contribute to her anemia, weakness, and fatigue. In addition to these general effects, there are certain known drug-food interactions that can cause problems in the elderly. For example, people on diuretics often

have an anginalike syndrome, a tightening of the chest and often a flushing of the face when they eat food containing monosodium glutamate (MSG), a substance commonly used in Chinese cooking. People taking medications containing monoamine oxidase inhibitors—drugs such as Nardil (phenelzine), Parnate (tranylcypromine), or Marplan (isocarboxazid), all used in certain psychiatric illnesses—can, because of enzyme inhibition when eating foods containing tyramine (such as aged cheeses, Chianti wine, chicken liver, or pickled herring), have a resultant hypertensive crisis or may develop a syndrome that simulates a pheochromocytoma, a condition in which there is an excess secretion of epinephrine (adrenaline) and related hormones by a tumor of the adrenal medulla or related tissues. Tuberculosis, an infectious disease occurring with increased frequency in the elderly, is often treated with isoniazid, which can cause vitamin $B_6$ deficiencies if supplements are not taken. Alcohol consumption also can change the metabolism of drugs in the liver by affecting some of the enzyme systems responsible for drug biotransformations. Heavy cigarette smoking is less frequent in the geriatric population since early mortality of smokers tends to select against this population group; however, heavy smoking is known to stimulate the enzymes in the liver responsible for metabolically clearing drugs from the blood and so can sometimes decrease the effect of certain drugs.

## Patient compliance problems

Yet another difficulty, which was not actually illustrated with Mrs. Y but is frequently a problem in the elderly population, is that of patient compliance with therapeutic regimens; *i.e.*, getting patients to follow the exact instructions of physicians about taking drugs—how many, how often, for how long, etc. At any age, compliance can be as low as 25% and is often no better than 60%. The elderly as a group are influenced by several factors that can make the carrying out of medication plans additionally problematic. Since understanding the pharmacokinetics and prescribing rationally are futile if the medications are not taken or are taken incorrectly, factors that lead to noncompliance need to be assessed.

First, as has been said, the elderly are often beset by multiple simultaneous conditions, all requiring some sort of treatment. These regimens, however, are occasionally conflicting and usually are quite complex, with some medications being taken once a day or every other day, some two to four times a day, some only at certain times of the day (*e.g.*, before bed or after meals), and some only as needed in response to specific symptoms. Add to this schedule the difficulty encountered by many older persons in hearing clearly and getting the instructions correctly from the physician, the possibility of visual impairment (which makes reading labels difficult or impossible), the presence of a physical disability (such as severe arthritis of the hands) that leads to great difficulty in opening medication containers, or hand tremors permitting liquids to spill from the spoon before they can be ingested, and it is evident that even a person with the best intentions in the world may take medications incorrectly.

Also, the social and economic position of many of the elderly may necessitate choices between needed food and costly drugs. Moreover, in attempting to hold on to previous independence, many may reject much needed help from family, friends, or social agencies. Denial of the need for assistance, or sometimes denial that a medical problem even exists, can cause treatment plans to be ignored by those needing them most. Additionally, some illnesses may be "silent" (such as hypertension) in that they produce no immediately discernible signs or symptoms, while treatment may produce disagreeable side effects (such as impotence, sedation, or weakness), thus discouraging the person from complying with a therapeutic plan. So, recognizing these problems and getting the elderly patient to participate in care can be the difference between the success and failure of medical treatment.

## Understanding how drugs work

Getting the proper medication at the correct dosage becomes more difficult as people age because of the interplay between normal physiological changes that occur with advancing age and the pathological or disease-specific changes that become more frequent as people age. In order to begin to appreciate how many variables there are, it is necessary to look at two major systems: pharmacodynamics and pharmacokinetics.

Pharmacodynamics involves the actual drug receptor sites on body cells as well as age-related changes in both number and sensitivity to specific types of drugs, thus explaining the differences observed clinically between the responses of old and young people. Pharmacokinetics, or the handling of drugs by the body, can be affected by age changes also. Initially, when drugs are ingested, absorption is controlled by gastrointestinal function. The process of getting the molecule of drug from the lumen of the gut into the blood can be either active, in which instance the lining cells have to expend energy to move the molecule, or passive, in which the drug diffuses from one side of the gut wall into the blood on the other side. The decrease in old age of some of the active transport mechanisms affects some substances, such as calcium, iron, and thiamine, but most drugs use the passive diffusion process and are thus not affected by age to any degree of clinical significance.

Once a drug has entered the blood, it is rapidly distributed into many body tissues. How fast the process occurs and into what organs the drug is transported depends to a large degree on whether the drug is more soluble in water or in lipids (fats). Changes occur in the

elderly that alter the availability of the drug for its pharmacological effects as well as for how long it remains in the body, because as people age the composition of their bodies changes. There is a decrease in the total body water, including the volume of plasma (the liquid part of blood in which the blood cells are suspended) and the extracellular fluid (fluid in the interstices of cells in tissues), and a higher proportion of the body's total weight is fat or adipose tissue. Even with no change in actual weight, 36% of the body's composition becomes fat in men; in women it goes to 48%. Therefore, there is even a sex-related difference in the way drugs are distributed. This means that drugs like diazepam that are lipid-soluble can move into peripheral depots of body fat, and the amount of drug present in the bloodstream is therefore only a small fraction of the total amount in the body. The plasma protein albumin, manufactured in the liver, also decreases in amount with increasing age. This protein, however, and ones similar to it, are often chemically bound to molecules of drug in the blood and serve to keep them within the vasculature instead of letting them diffuse out of the blood vessels. In the elderly, who have less albumin to bind drug molecules, there will be a higher fraction of drug that remains unbound or free. The exact effect of decrease in protein binding is not entirely clear, but it seems that because various drugs and medications can escape more quickly to the site of action or to the kidney or liver for clearance, the therapeutic and toxic levels for different drugs that have been reported by surveillance laboratories are often lower in the elderly than they would be in younger persons.

The metabolism of a drug, or how it undergoes biotransformation from one chemical structure to another, occurs primarily in the liver. The hepatocytes (liver cells) are capable of performing many different types of reactions on the chemicals presented to them. In so-called phase I reactions (e.g., oxidations, reductions, and hydrolysis) the drug usually remains pharmacologically active. Phase II reactions (or hepatic clearance) usually involve conjugation of an active drug to a larger molecule, which very often renders it inert and is a preliminary step for final excretion, usually via the kidney. As people grow older, their livers decrease in size and receive a lesser proportion of an already diminished cardiac output. Additionally, the microsomes that produce the enzymes necessary to perform the multiple processes carried out in the liver seem to be less active or perhaps fewer in number, and it is also more difficult to stimulate or induce higher enzyme production with drugs such as phenobarbital or alcohol. Because of the diminished blood flow and enzyme changes, hepatic processes are usually slowed, but it is difficult to predict any reliable age-related decline that holds for all elderly people or multiple drug types. About the best that can be said is that phase I reactions (especially oxidations) do seem to be prolonged, and that phase II reactions seem considerably less affected in any predictable way.

The primary organ of drug excretion is the kidney. An organ can excrete only as much of a drug as is brought to it. Thus the diminished renal perfusion that occurs with age as well as the decrease in the rate substances are filtered through the glomerulus (a tuft of capillaries located in the kidney that filters from the blood fluids and chemicals that eventually become urine) means that as people age, they have more difficulty eliminating drugs from their bodies. Drugs can accumulate in the body and produce toxic effects if given to an elderly person at the same dosage and interval as to a younger person.

Two terms frequently used when explaining excretion of drugs from the body are *total body clearance*, a hypothetical volume of blood that can be completely cleared of a drug in a given period of time, and the *half-life* of a drug (expressed as $t\frac{1}{2}$). The latter process depends not only on the clearance of the drug but on its volume of distribution (*i.e.*, in which tissues the drug may be stored as well as its concentration in the blood). As mentioned, because of changes in body composition between young people and the elderly, the $t\frac{1}{2}$ is a parameter of limited value when estimating drug levels or predicting dosage schedules. The way the body copes with the many drugs given to it is therefore a very complex process that needs to be understood fully to utilize medications correctly.

It can be concluded then that the chemistry of drugs, coupled with the physiology of the aging process, marked as it is by individual variation in both chronology and degree and further complicated by the personal ability or desire to comply with drug therapy, makes geriatric pharmacology a most inexact science. It is, however, one that requires increasing study to effectively and safely handle the acute needs of the elderly now and in the future.

*—Mary Jane Koren, M.D.*

# Alcoholism

Popular and scientific conceptions of alcoholism have undergone dramatic transformations in the past three decades. Some 25 years ago the public tended to hold stereotyped views of alcoholism and alcoholics: those homeless men seen on downtown street corners asking passersby for some loose change to "buy a cup of coffee," "skid-row" derelicts, etc. The average physician was aware of cirrhosis of the liver and other alcoholism-related medical conditions, but he too would probably have in mind the same inner-city vagrants as his lay counterpart.

Today, however, we know that skid-row residents represent at most from 3 to 5% of the adult alcoholic population in the United States. A series of extensive surveys about drinking practices carried out by re-

search teams at the University of California at Berkeley and George Washington University in Washington, D.C., have been instrumental in making physicians and the public aware of the incidence rates of problem drinking and alcoholism in the adult population (12% of men and 3% of women questioned in a 1979 survey reported drinking five drinks or more on an average of at least ten occasions per month). These studies have also made us aware of the magnitude of adverse social consequences associated with drinking (9% of male drinkers and 5% of female drinkers reported incidences of inappropriate behavior in social settings or of major difficulties at work directly attributable to problem drinking). At the same time, these surveys have also made it clear that despite these extremely high rates of problem drinking in the adult population, only a very small percentage of people surveyed indicated they had undergone marital separations or divorces directly related to alcoholism. If we were, therefore, to look for the "average" alcoholic individual, we would be most likely to find him or her living in an intact family.

Marital intactness, however, does not necessarily mean that life in such families is sanguine. Alcoholism has been demonstrated to be associated with significantly higher rates of family violence (both spouse and child abuse), has been implicated in substantial numbers of homicides involving family members, produces major economic difficulties for the family, is associated with significantly higher rates of psychopathology in children, and so forth. In fact, a Gallup Poll carried out in 1982 reported that 33% of respondents answered yes to the question "Has drinking ever been a cause of trouble in your family?" (This figure represented an 11% increase over the affirmative response rate from a survey taken only one year previously and double the rate in 1976.) Thus despite the adverse consequences of alcoholism, the fact remains that most alcoholic individuals are married and that most of these marriages manage to survive despite the presence of an alcoholic member, but the long-term consequences of chronic alcoholism for the family are substantial indeed.

## Family factors influencing onset and course of alcoholism

For many years treatment for alcoholism was primarily individual oriented. Whether the treatment was directed at combating the medical consequences of alcoholism or at trying to change behavior patterns, it focused on the alcoholic only. More recently, an alternative view, which looks at alcoholism from a family perspective, has been gaining influence. The family is seen as a social environment that can affect both the likelihood of alcoholism's occurring in an individual family member and the course and pattern of drinking once it has reached alcoholic levels. A corollary to the family perspective is that treatment approaches should involve not only the alcoholic individual but the family as well.

*While it may not cause the breakup of the family unit, alcoholism is associated with increased rates of domestic violence and childhood behavioral problems. Treatment of the problem drinker alone is not as effective as therapy that actively involves other family members in the rehabilitation process.*

Why has this family perspective been gaining influence? First and foremost this is attributable to the familial nature of the condition itself. Individuals growing up in families in which one or both parents are alcoholic have a dramatically increased likelihood of developing alcoholism themselves (*e.g.,* men having alcoholic fathers are seven times more likely to develop alcoholism than men whose fathers are nonalcoholic). Whenever such familial patterns are found to occur, two possible explanations have been proposed: a genetic one and a social-environmental one. Substantial evidence indicates that both these factors play a role in the familial incidence of alcoholism.

The genetic evidence has been gleaned from two research strategies. In identical twin studies monozygotic (identical, one-egg) twins are compared with dizygotic (fraternal, two-egg) twins. Higher rates of alcoholism in monozygotic twins support a genetic hypothesis. In studies of children of alcoholic parents who have been adopted by nonalcoholic parents, compared with nonadopted children of alcoholic parents, a genetic cause is implicated if both sets of children have comparable alcoholism rates. Thus far, data from both types of studies have been supportive of a genetic hypothesis, especially for the more severe forms of alcoholism.

Researchers looking for evidence of social-environmental factors have compared behavioral characteristics of alcoholic and nonalcoholic families. Significant differences in communication patterns, in levels of conflict, in marital cohesiveness, in daily routines, and in family rituals have been observed. However, most of these studies have been unable to tease out cause and effect. That is, we do not know whether family problems are reactions to the presence of an alcoholic member or whether family behavior is itself either causing or perpetuating chronic alcoholism.

Because of these various findings, current thinking is that both genetic and social-environmental factors are powerful; genetic factors are most important as risk factors predisposing an individual to alcoholism, and

social-environmental factors both influence the likelihood of alcoholism's actually occurring given a predisposition and determine the long-term course of the condition once it has emerged. It follows that a therapy approach aimed at the family can have important preventive aspects—*i.e.,* decreasing the incidence of alcoholism in genetically prone individuals. It can also help attenuate the effects of existing alcoholism.

## Family therapy

Family therapy is a term encompassing a wide range of technical and theoretical approaches. Sometimes, for example, a family therapist will focus exclusively on the relationship between husband and wife; other therapists will insist on involving all the children in the family, regardless of age; still others are interested in exploring multigenerational themes and patterns and will be inclined to include at least three generations of a family in therapy sessions. Yet another approach is to bring together several different couples or families in group therapy, thus enabling families to compare problems and strategies for dealing with them. Sometimes "family" groups are not limited to blood relatives but involve concerned or significant others; thus roommates, close friends, and lovers may be included.

Despite the heterogeneity of specific approaches, all family therapists share a conviction that techniques intended to alter patterns of family behavior will also produce dramatic and lasting changes in individual behavior. Furthermore, they contend that family therapy approaches are more efficient and more rapid than individual approaches. And finally, they feel that family therapy is in many cases a more responsible approach to the treatment of serious behavioral problems in that it tries to work out solutions beneficial to all members of a family, rather than solely to the index patient. (It is not uncommon, however, to see improvement on the part of the behaviorally disturbed individual coincident with deterioration in the behavior of other family members.)

Family therapy approaches to alcoholism are still

Beautyful Homes are Destroyed by Alcohol

*For a child, the emotional consequences of living with an alcoholic parent can be devastating. The drawing above eloquently expresses one such youngster's distress.*

relatively new, having come into common use only during the past 15 years. Nevertheless, family therapy represents the single most innovative change in alcoholism treatment during the past decade. Three major approaches have gained widespread acceptance and have demonstrated their efficacy when used in controlled studies comparing them with more traditional forms of alcoholism treatment.

The first of these is known as concurrent group therapy. This form of therapy treats alcoholic individuals and their nonalcoholic spouses in separate but concurrent groups. The alcoholic patient groups tend to focus on emotional factors contributing to drinking and on effective behavioral techniques intended to achieve and maintain sobriety, while spouse groups focus on identification of patterns of behavior that tend to facilitate uncontrolled drinking in the spouse and on ways of altering that behavior. Attempts are made to break down persistent and pernicious behavior patterns of spouses that—although often believed by the nonalcoholic spouse to be efforts at helping the alcoholic stop drinking—in the opinion of the therapist perpetuate the problem.

Concurrent group therapy is most frequently part of a residential treatment program for alcoholism. In these instances the severity of alcoholism warrants hospitalization of the alcoholic for detoxification and an initial phase of psychotherapy. Therapists advocating this approach underscore the need to separate husband and wife initially in order to maximize therapeutic benefits. But the involvement of spouses as early as possible tends to encourage the efforts of the alcoholic to

persist in the difficult recovery process. Since premature dropout from treatment has been a major problem in the psychological treatment of alcoholism, the finding that engagement of other family members in the treatment process decreases dropout rates gave a powerful boost to advocates of family therapy approaches. Studies have also noted considerable improvement in marital harmony when spouses participate in concurrent group therapy.

Al-Anon, a self-help organization for families of alcoholics, which arose in the early 1950s as a separate but similar approach to Alcoholics Anonymous (AA), is based on a concurrent group therapy model. There are currently some 19,000 Al-Anon groups in some 75 countries. Al-Anon is similar to AA in that it fosters a fellowship of peers sharing a common problem. Al-Anon participants are spouses, children, and close relatives of alcoholics who are usually (but not necessarily) AA members. In discussion groups Al-Anon members learn coping strategies based on "loving detachment"; the family provides understanding and support to the alcoholic, who must learn abstinence on his own—most often in AA. Both AA and Al-Anon emphasize acceptance of personal responsibility as critical to successful coping. Family members are helped to accept their fundamental helplessness to alter the behavior of the alcoholic family member.

A second family approach is conjoint therapy, in which a single family is treated as an integral unit. Many family members participate in the therapy sessions. It is the most widely used approach to general family therapy but has been used less frequently for the treatment of alcoholism. Conjoint therapy is most frequently carried out in out-patient settings. Therapy focuses on interaction, communication, performance of specific problem-solving tasks, and redefinition of alcohol-related problems in the family and thus applies traditional family therapy techniques to the specific problem of alcoholism. Owing to the enthusiastic reports to date on the use of conjoint family therapy for alcoholism, it is likely that this approach will gain influence as more and more family therapists receive additional training in alcoholism as a specialty area.

A third approach is multiple-couples group therapy, which combines both family and group psychotherapy techniques. Three or more married couples meet together for a group therapy session that focuses on couple dynamics, delineation of marital difficulties, and alteration of behavior. In a variant of this technique, three or more families (including children and grandparents) meet conjointly, and family, rather than marital, behavior patterns become the focus.

Once again, controlled studies of the use of the latter technique have suggested that it is an extremely successful treatment. For example, in one such study 40 couples were recruited and randomly assigned to one of two groups: an immediate treatment group and a

*Contributing to the development of the family perspective on the treatment of alcoholism is the growing recognition that there are familial patterns associated with the condition; children of alcoholic parents are much more likely than other children to become alcoholics themselves.*

waiting-list group, in which they continued with a traditional treatment program but did not engage in the outpatient multiple-couples group. Six-month follow-up results were striking: 9 alcoholics in the couples therapy remained abstinent, 4 were doing some drinking, and 7 had relapsed completely. Among the waiting-list group, however, only 2 were abstinent, 5 were drinking moderately, and 13 had completely relapsed.

Despite the many advances in our understanding of family factors as they relate to alcoholism and in the use of family treatment techniques, it is clear that we have only begun to scratch the surface. As we look at the major research questions in the alcoholism field that are currently capturing the interests of the scientific community and the public, the role of the family comes up over and over again. The fetal alcohol syndrome, teenage drinking, domestic violence, the transmission of alcoholism from generation to generation, and the effect of alcoholism on children are all areas of major concern. None of these areas can be divorced from a consideration of family issues. Thus it is likely that the role of family factors in alcoholism will continue to be vigorously investigated over the next decade.

In like fashion, the enthusiastic early reports about the efficacy of family treatment approaches for alcoholism ensure that more and more clinicians will be receiving specialty training in this area. Alcoholism treatment programs will be increasingly in a position to offer comprehensive services to families as well as to alcoholic individuals.

*— Peter Steinglass, M.D.*

# Arthritis and Connective Tissue Disorders

The musculoskeletal system bears a major brunt of the aging process. Muscle strength and responsiveness diminish. Tendons and ligaments stretch and degenerate. Cartilage in the joints and disk pads between the spinal vertebrae show evidence of biochemical and

structural deterioration. Loss of resiliency, flexibility, and stability of the joints in turn leads to a wear-and-tear arthritis called osteoarthritis. Furthermore, as the body ages, the immune system responsible for fighting foreign invaders withers. Immune surveillance is weaker, a phenomenon that probably heightens the susceptibility of older people to cancer, infection, and several forms of arthritis.

As more people survive to older ages, the problems of arthritis and other rheumatic diseases in the aged are becoming increasingly recognized. In the early 1980s, 11% of the U.S. population was over the age of 65, and in 20 years that figure is likely to more than double. The practical issues of arthritis in the aged concern both diagnosis and management.

## Diagnosing arthritis in the elderly

Most diagnostic problems of the aged are actually the same as those of younger patients. The elderly, however, not only are more predisposed to rheumatic disease but also are likely to have more than one condition. A combination of shoulder bursitis and chronic low back pain, for example, is quite common. Of course, nonrheumatic diseases also are more common in the elderly. Arthritis, infection, diabetes, heart disease, and hypertension often coexist in the same patient.

The results of certain tests designed to help diagnose a variety of rheumatic disorders have different meanings in older and younger patients. For instance, the erythrocyte sedimentation rate (ESR), a blood test measuring the degree of inflammation, may be elevated in the elderly whether or not they have any rheumatic disease. An ESR distinctly abnormal in a 25-year-old man may be unremarkable in an 80-year-old woman. The latex fixation test for rheumatoid factor, a protein element in the blood of most patients with rheumatoid arthritis, is apt to be positive in an elderly person without the disease.

X-rays of bones and joints must be interpreted differently as well. Because in some people osteoporosis, a

Pfizer, Inc.

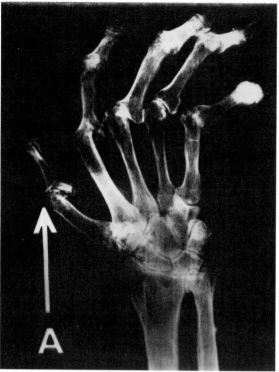

*An X-ray of an elderly patient's hand shows advanced rheumatoid arthritis—with severe dislocation of the finger joints—as well as osteoarthritis of the thumb.*

thinning out of bone substance, is a normal part of the aging process, it usually is less significant in an older person than in a younger person. Certain conditions, such as deterioration of the disk pads in the neck (cervical spondylosis), are present in almost everyone over 60; therefore, the physician might have great difficulty differentiating this condition from other painful neck syndromes.

Senility, organic brain syndrome, depression, and faulty senses may cloud an elderly person's medical evaluation because the physician may not be able to obtain a thorough and completely accurate medical history. An uncooperative patient may make a detailed examination difficult. Finally, patients who are depressed may hurt all over or complain simply of "heavy legs," leaving the physician with the frustrating and often expensive task of differentiating organic from psychiatric illness.

### Rheumatic diseases common in the elderly

Certain rheumatic diseases are almost exclusively confined to the elderly. Osteoarthritis, the prototypical rheumatic disease in this category, is characterized by cartilage deterioration that causes pain, stiffness, and limited motion in a limited number of joints. A single major injury, a series of minor injuries, or congenital musculoskeletal abnormalities may prompt osteoar-

thritis to develop sooner. X-rays show joint narrowing, spur formation, and thickening of the adjacent bones.

Pseudogout is an inflammatory condition resembling gout in which one or perhaps a few joints are acutely inflamed and contain deposits of calcium salt crystals. The pain is usually exquisite and disabling. Pseudogout may be associated with certain metabolic diseases such as diabetes, hemochromatosis (increased iron deposition in tissues), and hyperparathyroidism (overproduction of calcium in the body). Except when it occurs in families because of genetic disturbances, it almost always strikes older people.

Polymyalgia rheumatica is a common, yet frequently overlooked, condition associated with patients over 50. It usually produces generalized achiness especially in the neck, shoulders, upper arms, low back, pelvis, groin, buttocks, and thighs. Many such patients seemingly have rheumatoid arthritis because of multiple joint inflammation, morning stiffness, fatigue, and an elevated ESR. In polymyalgia rheumatica, however, most symptoms appear in or near the spine rather than in peripheral joints like the hands. Joint destruction does not occur. Other features of polymyalgia rheumatica are inflammation of the blood vessels in the head and depression and dramatic improvment with small doses of cortisone. Biopsy of the temporal artery, a large blood vessel in front of the ear, may be needed to confirm the diagnosis. Polymyalgia rheumatica, which has been recognized as a disease entity for only about 25 years, is highly treatable once the diagnosis is established.

Paget's disease does not often affect young people. It is characterized by bone thickening particularly in the pelvis, legs, collarbone, and skull. Bowing of the legs, loss of body height, and deafness are features of the condition. Products of accelerated bone production are found in blood (alkaline phosphatase) and urine (hydroxyproline). X-rays showing dense whitening of bones confirm the diagnosis.

In osteoporosis the bones thin out excessively because there is deterioration of the network upon which calcium is deposited. The vertebrae of the spine are most likely to be affected and in the severest cases may actually fracture without injury. Victims may become bent over (dowager's hump) and lose considerable height because of fractured vertebrae.

### Rheumatic diseases of special concern in the elderly

Few differences exist between rheumatoid arthritis in the young and old. Aged patients suffer more often from fever and vasculitis (inflammation of blood vessels) and from shoulder involvement. The ESR tends to be more elevated in patients over 60, and some studies show a higher blood level of rheumatoid factor. Older patients respond better to treatment with gold salts than younger ones but have more problems with nonsteroid anti-inflammatory drugs and cortisone.

Gout is more likely to affect several joints in the elderly and is associated with fever. Its incidence is also greater in older people.

Systemic lupus erythematosus (SLE) is often regarded as a disease of young people, but lupus can occur at any age. Lupus is one of the so-called connective tissue or collagen diseases that affect not only joints but any organ that has lining tissues, such as the kidneys, heart, lungs, and brain. It is the prototype of a group of immune disorders in which, for reasons unknown, the body reacts against itself (autoimmunity). SLE in the aged, as in the young, may strike without apparent cause, but in the elderly it is usually drug-induced. For example, certain medications such as procainamide, used to control abnormal heart rhythms, somehow alter the immune system if taken for many months. Fortunately, drug-induced lupus usually improves after the responsible agent is discontinued.

Dermatomyositis, another connective tissue disease, may cause inflammation of muscles with resultant weakness even in children, but with age the likelihood of a coexistent malignancy, usually cancer of the lung, increases. The reason for this association is not clear, but all polymyositis patients older than 50 years are checked for an undiagnosed tumor.

Certain types of infectious arthritis, especially those caused by staphylococcal bacteria, are indeed more common in the elderly, whereas others, such as those caused by gonococcal bacteria, are distinctly unusual. Conversely, nongonococcal infectious arthritis is found primarily in middle-aged or young patients who have another serious systemic illness or preexisting joint disease.

Other conditions that may develop at any age but are more common over age 50 include carpal tunnel syndrome (pinched nerve at the wrist), bursitis, low back syndromes, tendon tears, and cancer that has spread to bone, where it may mimic a variety of rheumatic disorders. The importance of precise diagnosis in the elderly to distinguish arthritis from the many other diseases that may affect this group cannot be overstated, for improper diagnosis leads to improper treatment.

## Managing arthritis in the elderly

Patients of any age with rheumatic disease must be approached from a comprehensive point of view, but this is especially important in the elderly. A multidisciplinary approach may involve drug therapy, physical medicine and rehabilitation, psychosocial and sexual counseling, orthopedic surgery, and a variety of other disciplines that ease the road to recovery. Each of these modalities poses both advantages and disadvantages for the elderly. Without paying attention to other aspects of treatment, the physician who uses drugs alone will cheat his patient.

*Drugs.* There are several classes of medications that can be used for arthritis: pain killers (analgesics), agents not in the cortisone family that reduce inflammation (nonsteroid anti-inflammatory drugs), cortisone administered orally as a tablet or injected into the joints, and drugs that modify the disease process rather than simply relieve symptoms (remittives). Either singly or in combination they can be effective in treating most rheumatic diseases.

As beneficial as drugs are, there are problems—especially in the elderly. In patients over 70 years old, 21% show side effects, compared with less than 5% in patients under 20 years. Drug toxicity in the elderly is related in part to a slowing of cardiovascular, kidney, and liver metabolism. Output of blood from the heart drops by half, and most patients will have some decreased kidney function depending upon coexisting diseases and drugs. Some of the nonsteroid anti-inflammatory drugs are excreted more slowly by the kidneys and therefore build up to excess in the body. Toxicity is related to the number of drugs given: the greater the number of drugs, the higher the incidence of unwanted adverse reactions. Since it is unusual to find an older patient with arthritis taking only one drug, the older arthritic is more likely to suffer side effects.

Surprisingly, many of the drug problems in elderly Americans stem from U.S. Food and Drug Administration (FDA) regulations. One problem relates to a regulation setting the upper age limit for drug trials with nonsteroid anti-inflammatory agents at 65 or, in certain studies, 70. Yet when the drug reaches the market, it is administered frequently to patients over these ages because they are the ones most likely to develop arthritis. Furthermore, as stated above, it is the elderly who take numerous drugs in the face of cardiac, kidney, and liver impairment in contrast to the healthy volunteers who are studied in premarketing investigations. It is suspected that this was one of the major sources of difficulty that forced the recall of Oraflex (benoxaprofen) in August 1982 as a result of deaths in aged patients (*see* below).

Aspirin, one of the most commonly used drugs in any age group, has been used effectively in the treatment of rheumatoid diseases much longer than any other nonsteroid anti-inflammatory agent. There is no reason to question its efficacy in the elderly, but there are a number of side effects that are probably more common in this age group. They include dizziness, hearing loss, ringing in the ears, forgetfulness, lethargy, gastrointestinal blood loss, and bleeding beneath the surface of the skin. More serious adverse reactions, albeit rare, are acute asthma, severe metabolic disturbance, coma, and death. Aspirin may intensify the anticoagulation effect of coumarin and related drugs that are used to prevent the formation of blood clots; such a combination may result in severe excessive bleeding from many sites in the body.

Because other nonsteroid anti-inflammatory drugs

189

*Preserving maximum flexibility is one goal of arthritis treatment. Mild exercise in a heated pool, where the buoyancy of the water prevents further trauma to already damaged joints, is ideal for maintaining freedom of movement in joints that are painful and swollen.*

also reduce joint pain, heat, and swelling, they are effective in treating arthritis in the elderly. But because these drugs tend to induce fluid retention, high blood pressure may be worsened. Diuretics will reduce fluid accumulation, but when given to the elderly with some anti-inflammatory drugs, they pose an added risk for kidney failure.

Corticosteroids, drugs of the cortisone family, are potent anti-inflammatory agents, but they cause complications at any age. In certain diseases the beneficial effects are dramatic and sometimes lifesaving, but the greater the dose and the longer the duration of therapy, the more likely are side effects. One could argue that toxicity is greater in older individuals because they may have cataracts, hypertension, diabetes, congestive heart failure, osteoporosis, and increased susceptibility to infection, all of which can be aggravated by corticosteroids. Injections of cortisone preparations into the joints are relatively safe and effective if only a few joints are involved. A major advantage of this technique is that it avoids systemic effects.

Intramuscular injections of gold salts, usually reserved for patients with rheumatoid arthritis, may be more effective in the elderly, although the evidence for this is anecdotal. Toxicity is about the same at any age. Like gold, antimalarials (chloroquines) and penicillamine are remission-inducing drugs. There have been some single case reports of their being dangerous and less helpful in those over 65 years, but scientific documentation is lacking.

*Physical approaches.* Physical medicine and rehabilitation includes physical therapy, occupational therapy, recreational therapy, and vocational rehabilitation, all of which pose special problems in the elderly. In addition, certain aspects of daily living such as transportation, travel, and dress must be included in the therapeutic picture.

Heat treatments such as hot packs, whirlpool baths, and heated pools have a tonic effect; that is, they make people feel better. But heat can aggravate some cardiovascular problems, making precautions necessary for certain patients. Exercise and sports are important to both young and old arthritic patients. Almost any physical modality or exercise used in the young can be and should be used, with appropriate care, in older people. For the elderly a more gradual increase in activities and longer warm-up periods are necessary, their extent depending on the individual. Swimming is ideal because the buoyancy of the water helps those with weight-bearing problems. Manipulation and massage are permitted, but the therapist must be more deliberate.

Although some older arthritic patients are content to settle into a sedentary life-style, they should be encouraged to keep active in order to avoid joint contractures and deconditioning. Encouraging people to walk is much easier to accomplish in a hospital than at home. Assistive devices like canes and walkers may not be accepted by the patient, but they are invariably helpful. For many patients, using a cane is an admission that they are getting older. Regardless of coexisting medical illnesses, most patients can participate in rehabilitation and physical fitness programs provided that the limitations are recognized beforehand. Slowing the pace, premedicating, bracing, and offering assistive devices are ways of working within these limitations. The benefits of physical fitness in arthritic patients regardless of age have only recently been recognized. A study carried out in Finland indicated that after five years participating patients with rheumatoid arthritis who became involved in an active exercise program not only felt better physically but also had a better sense of mental well-being; they also exhibited less evidence of arthritis on examination.

190

*Surgery*. Today surgery for arthritic problems is commonplace, offering much pain relief and return of function. In order for the surgery to be successful, however, the physician must select the candidate for surgery carefully, perform a full presurgical evaluation, and conduct close observations afterward for surgery-related or general complications. Age itself is not a barrier to arthritis surgery. Quite the opposite: surgery may be mandated under certain circumstances. That older arthritics, previously racked with pain and confined to bed, can live out their remaining years walking and caring for themselves is one of the miracles of modern medicine.

For a patient with heart disease, elective joint surgery carries special concerns, but cardiovascular disease in itself does not rule out surgery. In fact, for some patients with severe arthritis of the hip or knee, the labor of walking places a greater strain on the heart than an operation would.

In certain cases surgery may not be the best choice. For example, an older person who is otherwise healthy but who is confused, depressed, or suffering from dementia should not be pushed into elective surgery because he or she may not be able to cooperate with the rehabilitation program. The overwhelming majority of elderly patients, however, do well in the postoperative period and suffer few complications. Few regret having surgery, but many regret not having it sooner.

*Psychosocial and sexual issues*. The many problems related to arthritis peak in the later years of life. Senility and organic brain syndrome, of course, have their highest incidence in the aged. Sometimes the confusion, memory loss, and bizarre behavior that characterize these maladies prevent any significant treatment of arthritis. In the hospital many otherwise healthy elderly people become disoriented, and in certain patients there may be frank psychosis. Frequent family visits, interaction with the members of the treatment team, and careful monitoring of drugs will usually control these problems.

As people age, depression becomes more common. Much of it stems from chronic illness, isolation, despair, loneliness, and disfranchisement of human rights. Depression and related forgetfulness can interfere with the arthritis treatment program. Patient counseling, socialization, and antidepressant drugs are able to combat depression in most instances. In a hospital setting most patients respond to a team approach that calls for interaction not only with the primary physician but also with the orthopedist, resident staff, nurses, physical therapist, occupational therapist, psychologist, and social worker.

Sometimes the stress that patients endure because of surgery, coexisting medical illnesses, family problems, and similar situations can be handled by the primary physician, but a psychiatrist or psychologist may be needed. Stress can aggravate preexisting arthritis

and, if undetected, may obviate the benefits of surgery. Some older patients apparently are unable to recognize stress or consider it unmanageable.

Somehow the sexuality and sexual needs of older people often go forgotten. Although in some relationships sexual interaction is not important, in many it is. Unfortunately, many physicians are hesitant to discuss sexual problems with their patients. In some otherwise healthy people there are problems of impotency, orgasmic dysfunction, and premature ejaculation. In the patient with arthritis there are added factors of musculoskeletal pain, limited motion of the extremities, deformity, and fatigue, any of which may cause a loss of sexual interest or preclude sexual intercourse. Patients with sexual problems may be counseled about communicating with their mates, timing of sex, pain-reduction techniques, improved positions for sexual intercourse, and sexually gratifying alternatives to intercourse.

*Patient education*. Education is important in providing patients with an awareness of their disease, informing them of what to expect from the treatment program, and helping to ensure their compliance. Patient compliance is a problem at any age. One cannot expect drugs to work if the patient does not take them regularly; nor will exercises help if they are not properly performed. Compliance is probably poorest among the elderly because they are more likely to be confused, have other illnesses, or have poor concentration. The older patient may have a number of diagnosed disorders, each treated with a variety of drugs. Some studies have shown that after two weeks, fewer than half of elderly patients take their prescriptions as ordered. Repetition of instructions, readable direction sheets, and proper packaging of drugs improve compliance.

## Recall of Oraflex

Oraflex is the trade name in the U.S. for a nonsteroid anti-inflammatory drug called benoxaprofen. The drug is one of several compounds designed to reduce inflammation, notably in rheumatoid arthritis and osteoarthritis. Most of these drugs vary in their efficacy but are usually equivalent to aspirin. The range of side effects, however, does vary from one to another.

For many years double-blind controlled studies of drugs have been carried out by specialists to determine their benefits and toxicity. In the U.S. such studies of Oraflex were performed under the scrutiny of its manufacturer, Eli Lilly and Co., and the FDA. After hundreds of patients had been investigated, the results seemed clear. Oraflex demonstrated the same degree of anti-inflammatory activity as other such agents. The gastrointestinal tract was sometimes affected, resulting in abdominal pain, nausea, and vomiting, but these reactions are seen with other drugs. A unique side effect of Oraflex was its ability to induce sensitivity to sunlight, which manifested itself as a rash and brittleness of the fingernails. Use of a sunscreen lotion obviated this side effect in most instances. It was noted during the study period that liver toxicity had occurred in a significant number of patients with rheumatoid arthritis. But few problems were noted in normal healthy volunteers, who for the most part were young people taking no other medication.

In the spring of 1982, Oraflex was released with a great deal of publicity. Many patients pressured their physicians for the drug, and in the first 12 weeks of its availability physicians wrote an estimated 500,000 prescriptions. But concern over the drug soon began—not in the U.S. at first but in Great Britain, where benoxaprofen had been on the market since 1980 under the trade name Opren and where medical reports had begun to note a high incidence of side effects, notably deaths related to toxic reactions in the liver. By August 1982 a flood of similar reports describing adverse reactions prompted the British government to suspend sales of the drug. Almost immediately thereafter Eli Lilly withdrew benoxaprofen worldwide.

It is reasonable to question why a drug that had been so thoroughly investigated under controlled studies would cause such difficulties when introduced to the general market. In clinical practice anti-inflammatory drugs, like many other medications, are prescribed not for healthy younger people but for older sick people, including those with liver, kidney, and heart diseases, for which a variety of medications are used. It has been suggested that, in some patients who died, kidney function had been impaired before they took Oraflex; as a result toxic levels built up and caused an adverse effect on the liver. As of mid-1983 Oraflex was not available for general use. The drug is being reevaluated and those people who took part in the original studies reexamined. Whether Oraflex will be released again is not known.

—*Warren A. Katz, M.D.*

# Death and Dying

An 11-year-old girl began to cry uncontrollably after the funeral of her grandmother because she realized that one day "there would be no more me." Her panic subsided after she prayed with the rest of the family and shared a meal with them, and after she was reassured that *she* would not die for a long time. Her fear and its resolution are a characteristic kind of reaction to a death.

Between the ages of 8 and 11 we grasp the fact that death is personal and inevitable. Man alone among the species knows that death is his destiny. For that reason, as expressed by Albert Camus, man, far from being at the summit of evolution, is fragile and unhappy. For coping with the dilemma of death man has developed both individual defense mechanisms and societal death systems.

We do not experience our own death but infer it from deaths of others. Claims made by some people that they died and returned are questionable because irreversible tissue damage did not occur. Reports that have described benign to ecstatic experiences, including out-of-body sensations, being in long tunnels with lights at their end, and encountering deceased family members and deities, may describe coma or even dying but not death itself.

People who knew that they were dying have often described their feelings. Individuals who have worked with the dying have also extrapolated information from what they have observed, but contrary to some of their assertions, it is obvious that no living person has ever "shared" in another's dying since dying is a completely private and subjective experience. While mystics, poets, and others claim to have grasped the meaning and experience of death (and life) in an irrational, intuitive, or emotional mode, scientists are now beginning to bring more objective criteria to the understanding of dying and death.

## What is death?

Death is the disintegration of cell structures, the cessation of protoplasmic activity. *Algor mortis, livor mortis,* and *rigor mortis* (loss of body heat, stagnation and settling of the blood, and postmortem rigidity) are the postmortem changes that define organ death. Current discussions about the precise moment of death generally have to do with reversibility of certain comatose states, not with death. A number of medicolegal and ethical problems have been raised by modern technology, which imposes critical decisions about the prolonged use of life-support systems and the removal of vital organs for transplantation before they deteriorate. It is generally considered repugnant to let a salvageable human being die—but it is equally repugnant to maintain a formerly human (*i.e.,* conscious) organism in a vegetative condition. For many people it is unthinkable to waste organs that might maintain a sentient human life, yet it is not possible to remove a vital organ from a living individual.

## Death fears

Sigmund Freud said that man cannot conceptualize his own death and that death anxiety is really anxiety about separation or castration. Others have said that all fear is ultimately fear of death; yet others, that there are several fears rather than a single death fear.

In the mid-1960s, in a major work on man's mortality, Jacques Choron described four fears: fear of what comes after death, fear of the event of dying, fear of ceasing to be, and fear of the dead. Different fears come to the foreground according to personality type: those who worry about tomorrow may worry most about life after death; those who fear suffering in general may fear dying the most; and so on. In the early 1970s researchers Robert Kastenbaum and Ruth Ai-

*Ideas about the human fear of death were debated in philosophy, expressed in poetry and prose, and portrayed in the visual arts long before they became a subject of scientific inquiry. "The Old Man and Death" (c. 1774) was painted by the English artist Joseph Wright of Derby.*

senberg published *The Psychology of Death,* in which they subdivide death fears into the fear of dying itself, of what the afterlife will bring, and of extinction—all relating to personal death—and the fear of the deaths of others. Thus, fear of dying may mean fear of suffering and indignity for oneself and fear of vicarious suffering and vicarious disintegration when other people die. In the afterlife we fear punishment and rejection for ourselves and retaliation and loss of relationship from the passing of friends. For some people personal suffering is easier to bear than the suffering of others; for them fear of rejection by God may be more potent than fear of nonbeing.

Fear of the fear of death is another reaction that has been described. This fear creates an additional burden, particularly for those in imminent danger of dying. The fear of nonbeing (*i.e.,* the fear of ceasing to be, or "existential" fear), illustrated by the 11-year-old child described above, is considered by many people to be the basic death fear.

### Individual defenses

According to some authorities, death is "natural" and fear of death is "learned," but others say that when we look past individual and societal defenses, fear of death is always present. Freud thought that death was natural in a different way. He had postulated the existence of Eros, the life instinct, as the driving force of existence. After he observed the carnage of World War I, certain abnormal psychological states, traumatic neuroses, and sadism and masochism, he inferred that there was a second instinct, death-seeking Thanatos. People disagreeing with him say that pathological phenomena are aberrations of life, sicknesses of Eros,

rather than manifestations of an innate lust for death, or else they are failures of societal death systems whose purpose is to safeguard life.

Ernest Becker, who has written widely about modern man and death, says that death is and always was frightening to man and that we spend our lives repressing that fear, putting it out of consciousness. Repression is one psychological mechanism that is always utilized and works, but there are others. Several are said to work even better. Those who say that there is no innate (existential) fear of death, but that fear of death is acquired through learning, may be utilizing denial or projection, two primitive psychological defense mechanisms in a hierarchy that puts intellectualization higher and sublimation highest. In denial we reject the obvious, while in projection we say that other people are responsible for problems that originate within ourselves.

### Societal defenses: death systems

Some authorities say that the fear of death is present in all human societies as well as in individuals but that societal coping mechanisms also vary. Becker insists that the indifference to death characteristic of certain Eastern cultures is actually mass use of defense mechanisms, especially denial. Coping tactics in a society change in response to environmental events and probably also along with shifts in ideas and feelings accumulated throughout history that reside in a culture through myths, customs, and rituals.

Wars, epidemics, and scientific discoveries are some of the environmental, or extrinsic, factors. Intrinsic factors may be exemplified by what the French historian Philippe Ariès has called themes and classi-

193

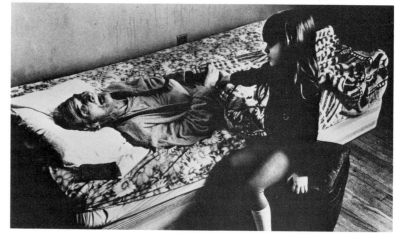
Mark and Dan Jury/The New York Times

*Though death is the inevitable outcome of life, fear of death for most people is profound. Between the ages of 8 and 11 most children are able to grasp the concept of ceasing to be and to begin to develop personal ways of coping.*

fied as "awareness of the self," "defense of society against untamed nature" (ecstasy of love as well as agony of death), "belief in afterlife," and "belief in the existence of evil." "Spontaneous" shifts in these categories mold history and, with it, thinking and behavior toward death. In the view of Ariès, only in prehistory, and again recently, have death systems been inadequate, and only rarely did death systems fail altogether. Death was a *malheur,* a misfortune, but "tame," not a horror, for much of human history. In prehistory, he says, death was feared because it was perceived as external and malevolent, caused by evil spirits. (In psychological language this is considered mass use of projection.) Tribal (group) consciousness and identity were stronger than the sense of the individual, and emphasis was on reconstituting society and maintaining it against the savagery of nature. Thus, the dead were rejected and contacts were forbidden—taboo. Afterlife did not figure.

The first millennium of the Christian era continued attitudes toward death that had their origins in Greco-Roman times. Death was seen primarily as a disruption of the social fabric. After about the 11th century the individual became increasingly important. Dying was a shadowy but safe time, and death was perceived to be a sleeplike state with vague expectation of resurrection. Deathbed farewell scenes and elaborate mourning developed and satisfied both individual and society. As self-consciousness grew still more, there came a split between body and soul. The fate of the body was still unclear, but the soul became radiantly immortal. Toward the end of the 19th century, life was perceived as a way station for death; deaths of beloved others were the main concern, and the focus was on reunion in the hereafter.

But modern science was being born in the 17th century; new attitudes were germinating. Social bonds were weakening, the beyond became of little interest, and fear of evil was being replaced with social theory. It was the individual who was extolled, while technology

gave him an increased sense of control over nature. It appeared that death itself would be vanquished; hence, death could be acknowledged to be a frank adversary. But death refused to die, thus threatening the new scientific omnipotence; it then became an irrelevancy, something to be hidden, dismissed, and denied. The dying were again shunned and abandoned; death systems were becoming inadequate.

We are now entering still another era. It is increasingly plain that while the human life-span will most certainly continue to increase, death will remain the inevitable outcome of life. As the intractability of individual death is rediscovered, we find our secular culture caught short, unprepared to cope. At this time both scholars and the public are engaged in debate about death. Death again has become relevant; it even threatens to become a "fad" as an example, perhaps, of a counter-phobic defense mechanism. In a recent article in *Harper's* magazine entitled "Turn On, Tune In, Drop Dead," Ron Rosenbaum exposes the excesses of a so-called love-of-death movement, which include séances and coitus with persons allegedly returned from the dead. Premature suicides to avoid death and the increase of criminality and drug abuse in our time have been compared to the cruelties of Nero and Caligula in Roman times and to the Inquisition, flagellants, witches, and vampires of the Middle Ages; they are said to illustrate the collapse of societal death systems, with death-seeking behaviors running rampant and threatening individuals and all humanity.

### Dying: recent observations

Common descriptions of dying patients during final days and hours include uncanny feelings, a sense of invasion by an alien force, and "the familiar distorted by the unfamiliar." Some patients have described losing the feeling of "things going on" (*i.e.,* the dynamism that is characteristic of life). "Everything would be the way it is," "the future has already happened," and "trapped in reality" are direct quotations expressing

194

the sensations of individuals very close to death.

The work of Elisabeth Kübler-Ross with the dying is well known, but others have also made important contributions both in support of and in disagreement with her conclusions. Kübler-Ross describes dying as an orderly sequence of steps with shifting defense mechanisms and the emergence of undisguised feelings, beginning with denial and isolation (it's not happening and I have no feelings about it), anger (why me?), bargaining (I'll do this or that if. . . .), depression, and ultimately acceptance.

Russell Meares says that it is trivial to characterize dying as a syndrome, but he, too, proposes stages: detachment, disengagement, exhaustion (or depression), followed by acceptance. Kastenbaum and Aisenberg say that people who know that they are dying are afraid but the fear is self-limiting and is followed by the emergence of coping mechanisms, which include planning for legacies, producing lasting works, and providing for children. Many investigations have noted that initially death is experienced as an intruder, but later a sense of participation emerges. Until more research is conducted, however, about the most that can be said is that dying is as idiosyncratic as living and that people usually cope with death in ways similar to the ways they coped with life.

## Coping

How can the fear of death be transcended? Both the individual and society must share the work of confronting and resolving the fear of death. To accomplish this it is necessary to acknowledge the dual nature of man, the physical and the symbolic. It is also essential to admit the paradox that, in spite of his capability of abstract thought and his knowing about death, man is still destined to die. The revulsion caused by that thought can be contained through the psychological defense mech-

*Children with terminal illnesses need special help in coping with their fears. A dying boy's drawing, below, expresses his perception of the disease process.*

From *There Is a Rainbow Behind Every Dark Cloud*, published by Celestial Arts

anisms that best promote a full life. The individual is helped by utilizing the more mature defense mechanisms, such as sublimation (for example, building monuments, producing works of art, being creative and altruistic) or intellectualization (reasoning, philosophizing, etc.). An attempted solution that is one-sided, all physical or all spiritual, is not likely to be valid. Thus, extremes of asceticism or sensuality do not successfully minimize the fear of death.

Some new societal death systems have emerged recently, which include both philosophies and tactics. The concept of "death with dignity" and the hospice movement promote the need to accept death and suggest practical means for discerning the best moment and the best circumstances for the departure from life. However, the hospice movement has been criticized for allegedly promoting a false idea that dying can be totally benign. Rosenbaum has noted that the success of the hospice in Great Britain may be due to the availability of heroin as a component in the Brompton cocktail (a potent pain-medication mixture) as much as to other factors. However, the superiority of heroin over other opiates has not been demonstrated in scientific studies.

Harold Y. Vanderpool, who has written about the ethics of terminal care, suggests that the dying should be given every possible consideration, including participation in decisions affecting them, treatment of pain, care for the body, and satisfaction of even the most trivial needs. But he says that the notion of death with dignity is absurd because the physiological events that surround terminal illness are intrinsically undignified. He proposes instead that we strive for "dying with a sense of worth," which comes if the individual feels he has lived his life well, has accepted his mortality, and, at the conclusion of his life, is confident that society will invest in him whatever resources are appropriate to prolong his life. Modern medical technology frequently places the dying among strangers, away from the traditional supports of home and religion (which, in any case, may be faltering as institutions).

Kenneth Chandler, who worked extensively with dying patients and the staff who cared for them, discovered that discussing their fears eased dying for both patients and caretakers, as demonstrated by a marked reduction in "acting out"; *i.e.,* outbursts of inappropriate behavior due to bottled-up feelings. People who have come to terms with their own mortality often can be of more help to others.

Finally, a most encouraging speculation comes from writer, physician, philosopher, and medical researcher Lewis Thomas. He is optimistic that death is biologically programmed to be painless. He has postulated that the body's natural painkillers, the endorphins, or endogenous opiates, are involved in palliating the transition from life to death.

*— Edith T. Shapiro, M.D.*

# Special Report:
# The Tragedy of Childhood Suicide
## by Leon Eisenberg, M.D.

Few of us go through life without at least fleeting thoughts of suicide. Confrontation with its cold actuality makes us shudder at ourselves. Suicide is a disorder for which there can be no treatment, for the act is final. Suicide imposes a triple burden on the family: grief at loss, as with any death; rage at desertion, for this was a deliberate death; and guilt, at having failed the victim. When the person who commits suicide is a child or an adolescent, the distress among the survivors is all the greater; we are shaken to be forced to recognize that the despair of youth can be so profound. All are frightened.

The disciplines of religion, law, and medicine agree it should be prevented. But "should" is not the same as "can." The problem is daunting: Is prevention possible? In order to try to answer the question, we must put the problem in epidemiological perspective by examining data on rates and trends in suicide among young people. So informed, we can then consider the opportunities for effective intervention to reduce the increasing toll of tragic deaths.

## The problem of defining "suicide"
Suicide is defined in both medical and general dictionaries as the intentional taking of one's own life. Thus, evidence of intentionality is required before a death is reported as suicide. The relative difficulty of establishing intentionality limits the accuracy of suicide statistics. If the deceased leaves behind a note establishing intent or has told others who report his statements of intent, then the attribution of cause is straightforward.

However, there may be no message, or it may have been destroyed by family members in the hope of avoiding disgrace; witnesses may fail to report what they know. Some adolescent suicides may have been impulsive decisions taken while driving at high speed; intentionality may not be distinguishable from accident. We have good reason for suspecting that some one-car "accidents" are concealed suicides by the driver because individuals who have survived automobile crashes sometimes report that they wanted to die and regret that the so-called accident was not fatal. One method for attempting to discover in retrospect whether an otherwise unexplainable death was a suicide is what has been called the psychological autopsy. Review of all of the ascertainable facts about the mental state of the individual through diaries, letters, and interviews with relatives and friends may lead to the presumptive diagnosis of suicide, though such a diagnosis never can be unequivocal.

Religious proscriptions against suicide that deny burial in hallowed ground to its victims give families good reason for concealing the facts from the official records. At times, financial motivations are at stake when death benefits on insurance policies pay differentially for accidental death and preclude payment for deliberate death. Intent may be difficult to establish in patients with chronic disease. For example, the diabetic patient who is aware of how dependent his life is on insulin and diet and who knows the danger associated with infection may deliberately induce an infection and neglect its treatment in order to end his life. This motivation has been established by interviews with survivors of such attempts.

There is one further complexity. Jumping off a tall building or hanging oneself may represent instances of planned and deliberate suicide, while placing oneself in a high-risk situation where death is likely, though not certain, is far more difficult to establish as suicide; yet the latter risk may have been taken deliberately by a person who did not believe life was worth living. Official figures on suicide, thus, are almost certainly an underestimate of the actual number of suicides because of the instances that go unrecorded.

## Suicide in children
Suicide occurs so rarely before the age of ten that the vital statistics reports of the United States do not include rates for this age group. U.S. findings are similar to those for all other countries reporting suicide statistics. What can be said about those prepubertal children who do commit suicide? In a restrospective study of child suicides in the United Kingdom, it was found that antisocial behavior patterns were far more common in the histories of those children than severe depression, contrary to findings among adult suicides. The most common precipitating events included disciplinary crises, loss of face with peers, and arguments within the family.

It is not until early adolescence that death is under-

*Many children feel isolated, lonely, and unable to cope with social and parental pressures. An attempted suicide is a desperate cry for help.*

stood to be an irreversible event. Suicide attempts in children are usually intended to "change things"; the child has the fantasy that his parents will regret the error of their ways and that he or she will be treated more lovingly after the attempt. The thought process may be like Tom Sawyer's in his fantasy of attending his own funeral; after he is dead, young Tom believes, his folks will be sorry they were so mean to him. Of course, he expects to be there to witness parental remorse and to benefit from it. Yet, however unrealistic the premises of the fantasy, when a child attempts suicide, he is making a statement of personal agony. Moreover, the attempt does carry a risk of death because younger children tend to be poor judges of the lethality of the methods they use. The relative rarity of suicide in preadolescents reflects limited access to lethal means, less ability to plan ahead and to make use of highly lethal instruments, and fewer long periods of despondency. Take the following case as an example:

Lucy R., who was ten years old, left school at noon, walked to a nearby church, and shot herself with a .38 caliber revolver. She had written notes to friends stating that she did not want to live. She had attempted suicide with pills a month earlier. The pediatrician and the psychiatrist who examined the child after the attempt strongly advised Lucy's mother to place her

in a residential school, but the mother would not agree. She "needed time to think about it."

Lucy had been born out of wedlock. The home situation had been extremely unstable. During her early years Lucy moved from foster home to foster home, from her mother to her father, and then back to foster care when one parent or the other proved unable to care for her. Her last foster placement was terminated because of frequent runaways in search of her mother. Lucy and her mother were reunited (physically if not psychologically) for the last 18 months of her life.

Despite turbulence in family life, she was a capable student in school but was isolated and withdrawn. Her teacher reported that "she seemd to live in a fantasy world, unaware of what was going on around her." The police investigation of her death showed that the revolver she used to kill herself belonged to her mother, who had bought the gun "to protect herself."

Lucy R.'s tragic story illustrates at least some of the background factors associated with child suicide: a broken and turbulent family, social isolation, repeated runaways in the search for an idealized parent, repeated warnings of intent that were ignored, and the availability of a weapon in the home despite the obvious danger to the child.

## Adolescent suicides

Although the health of adolescents in the U.S., as measured by most indicators of morbidity and mortality, improved rapidly between 1900 and 1960, mortality rates among those between 15 and 24 have risen by 11% during the past 20 years. This is principally because of increasing deaths from violence, *i.e.*, accidents, homicides, and suicides. Together they account for a very high proportion of all deaths in this age group. Among whites, accidents (two-thirds of them vehicular) are the leading cause of death; among nonwhites, deaths from homicide surpass deaths from motor-vehicle accidents. These few data make abundantly clear the close links between behavior, social environment, and mortality in adolescence.

Between ages 15 and 24, suicide is the third leading cause of death among males and the fourth among females. Table 1 summarizes male suicide rates per 100,000 between ages 10–14, 15–19, and 20–24. Over the three decades from 1950 to 1979, the latest year for which U.S. data are available, suicide rates more than tripled for the adolescent and young adult age cohorts. Table 2 summarizes female suicide rates in comparable age groups over the same time period. Rates for 1979 are about double those for 1950 but remain at about one-quarter of the rates for males. Both white and nonwhite suicide rates have increased at about the same pace over the past 25 years; between ages 15 and 19, nonwhite rates are about half of those for whites, but between 20 and 24, they are about the same.

The marked increase in rates between 1950 and 1977 is a source of great concern. Fortunately, the figures for 1978 and 1979 suggest (but do not prove)

| Table I: Male suicide rates per 100,000 in U.S. | | | |
|---|---|---|---|
| year | age group | | |
| | 10–14 | 15–19 | 20–24 |
| 1950 | 0.5 | 3.5 | 9.3 |
| 1960 | 0.9 | 5.6 | 11.5 |
| 1970 | 0.9 | 8.8 | 19.3 |
| 1975 | 1.2 | 12.0 | 25.9 |
| 1977 | 1.6 | 14.0 | 29.2 |
| 1978 | 1.2 | 12.6 | 26.8 |
| 1979 | 1.1 | 13.4 | 26.5 |
| Source: National Center for Health Statistics. | | | |

| Table II: Female suicide rates per 100,000 in U.S. | | | |
|---|---|---|---|
| year | age group | | |
| | 10–14 | 15–19 | 20–24 |
| 1950 | 0.1 | 1.8 | 3.3 |
| 1960 | 0.2 | 1.6 | 2.9 |
| 1970 | 0.3 | 2.9 | 5.7 |
| 1975 | 1.4 | 2.9 | 6.7 |
| 1977 | 0.3 | 3.3 | 7.1 |
| 1978 | 0.4 | 3.0 | 6.3 |
| 1979 | 0.5 | 3.2 | 6.3 |
| Source: National Center for Health Statistics | | | |

that the trend is moderating. However, we will need more information from subsequent years before we can take much comfort from the most recent findings.

The problem posed by rising rates is twofold. First, and most immediately, they represent needless deaths today. But second, and no less important, they suggest that rates will be higher in the years ahead for today's 15–24-year-olds when they enter their late twenties and early thirties. This dire prediction is based on several studies that have compared succeeding "birth cohorts" in Canada and the United States. "Birth cohort" is the term applied to all individuals who are born within a given year (or, for statistical convenience, a given five-year span).

When the suicide rate for a given cohort aged 15–19 proved to be higher than that for a similar age cohort five years previously, then the later cohort was more likely to experience a higher suicide rate at ages 20–24 than did the preceding cohort. Whatever the causes of this cohort effect, the findings indicate a persisting impact of early influences on later behavior. The findings emphasize the importance of developing better methods for suicide prevention as a matter of high priority for public health.

*Males versus females.* In all age groups, in most countries, and for all periods for which data are available, males consistently outnumber females by about 3 to 1 in completed suicides. The major exception to the male preponderance is found in Asian countries. In Japan the male/female ratio is only 1.4 to 1, similar to data for Hong Kong, Singapore, and Thailand.

Suicide rates among adolescents and young adults in Japan have become a source of great national concern in the past decade. Rates among females aged 15 to 19 are not only much higher than those for the United States but almost as high as those among males. Certain discernible trends in suicide behavior in Japan, such as high female rates, a higher incidence of suicides in rural than in urban areas, high rates among youth, and excessive rates among workers in certain industries, indicate the importance of cultural factors in determining differences in behavior among populations.

*Suicide attempts.* Whereas males have consistently outnumbered females in completed suicides, reports of attempted suicide are uniformly higher for females in about the same ratio. Reports of attempts are based primarily upon records from hospital emergency rooms. Therefore, they understate the prevalence in the community, since attempts managed out of hospital are not caught in the statistical net. Estimates of the ratio of attempts to completions in adolescents range from 10 to 1 to 100 to 1.

What is also unclear is the extent of the overlap between the population of suicides and that of suicide attempters, sometimes called "parasuicides." That is, while many of those who kill themselves have made prior attempts, many have not; the reversal of sex ratios between parasuicides and suicides indicates that many parasuicides are at low risk for fatality. How to distinguish high-risk from low-risk groups of parasuicides is currently under active investigation. Rates of repeated attempts within one year have varied from 6% in one survey to 16% in another. Like completed suicides, suicide attempts among adolescents have shown a sharp increase. Recorded suicide attempts peak between ages 15 and 19 and show a steady decline thereafter.

*Suicide at college.* Is it true that selection pressures and demands for academic performance make college students, particularly those at elite institutions, vulnerable to suicide? Major evidence for this hypothesis has been provided by a comparison of suicide rates between 1945 and 1955 at Oxford, Cambridge, and University College in England—all elite institutions—with those at the so-called red-brick universities, which have less restrictive admissions policies. Table 3 summarizes these findings. Despite a limited sampling frame, statistical analysis indicated a significantly high incidence of suicides among the "Oxbridge" students. A more recent study of suicides among Oxford students from 1966 to 1976 reported rates of 10 for males and 13 for females, one-third the earlier figure. These reported rates are suggestively but not reliably in excess of those for young Britons as a whole (5.1 for males and 2.6 for females between ages 15 and 24).

With the important exception of one study—from the University of California at Berkeley for the years 1952 through 1961, which found more than double the expected rate among 15–19-year-old students—such data as can be assembled from U.S. and Canadian sources do not substantiate the British findings (Table 4). Suicides known to the health service at Yale University over a 25-year period showed no difference between rates at Yale and those for young men of the same age in the general population. Unpublished data from the university health service at Harvard University over a six-year time span reveal rates similar to those in the earlier Yale study. In contrast to British data of 30 years ago, U.S. statistics provide no evidence to support the belief that college students in general or college students at Ivy League institutions are at higher risk for suicide than other late adolescents. However, problems in the ascertainment of suicide when students are off campus, failure to break down the data by sex, and uncertainties in the precise definition of the population denominators limit the accuracy of the available information.

Although suicide rates are distressingly high from a medical perspective, they are very infrequent as statistical events. In a coeducational university with as many as 10,000 students, no more than one or two suicides would be expected in a given year. Simply by random variation the statistical properties of such distributions will result in years with none and others with as many as four or five deaths. In consequence, the evaluation of a suicide-prevention program on a single university campus is extraordinarily difficult.

## Can teen suicides be prevented?

Indeed, because of the low frequency of suicide (just under 30 per 100,000) in the population that is at highest risk (males aged 20–24), the statistical problems in assessing a community prevention effort even on a statewide basis are formidable. The size of the sample necessary to recognize a therapeutic effect depends on three factors: (1) the magnitude of the change we wish to be able to detect; (2) the criterion considered to be of prime significance, *i.e.,* having a probability of 5% or less; and (3) the "confidence" level at which we wish to be sure that we are not missing a real effect if it is present, a level often set at 95%. If we anticipate that a given intervention might succeed in reducing the suicide rate from 30 to 25 per 100,000, and if we employ the probability value of 5% and the confidence interval of 95%, then we would require an experimental sample of 2.9 million males in the appropriate age range and a control sample of the same size!

Even an unusually powerful screening test would be of dubious value. For example, suppose that we had something not yet achieved in medicine, a test with a sensitivity of 100% (that is, able to identify *all* potential suicides) and a specificity of 99% (that is, yielding only one false positive in every 100 normals). This phenomenal measure, if administered to 100,000 young males between the ages of 20 and 24, would identify all 30 true positives at the cost of labeling 1,000 false positives (that is, 1% of the sample of 100,000), a ratio of 33 false positives to every true positive. Consider the results if the hypothetical test had the same precision as that of an excellent existing diagnostic procedure, the liver scan; *i.e.,* a sensitivity of 90% and a specificity of 63%. A suicide prediction of similar power would yield, for the same population, 27 true positives (90% of 30) and 36,989 false positives (37% of 100,000 minus 30); the ratio of false to true positives would be 1,370 to 1! Since the label "high risk for suicide" would warrant vigorous intervention (including hospitalization as an option), such a screening test would be unsuitable as a public health measure because of an unacceptable risk/benefit ratio.

However, if the same test were applied to 1,000 parasuicides, in whom the expectation of a repeated attempt is on the order of 10%, it would yield, when applied to a population of 1,000 parasuicides, 90 true positives (90% of 100) as against 333 false positives (37% of 1,000 minus 100). The ratio of false to true positives would be 3.7 to 1, but the information would spare us the need for following up 577 parasuicides who are at no risk of repeat at the cost of missing only 10 actual repeaters. Such a test does not exist, but if it did it would be useful only in those who had tried suicide already.

*High adolescent suicide rates in Japan are attributed in part to the highly competitive academic system. This student's headband reads "Sure victory in exam."*

| Table III: Student suicide rates — U.K. (1945–55) | | |
|---|---|---|
| population group | rate/100,000 | 95% interval |
| Oxford | 30.5 | 17–49 |
| Cambridge | 21.8 | 12–37 |
| University College | 22.9 | 6–58 |
| "red brick" | 7.8 | 4–14 |
| all males (20–24) | 6.0 | 5.4–6.5 |
| students | 15.7 | 11.3–21.2 |

| Table IV: Student suicide rates — U.S. | |
|---|---|
| population at risk | rate/100,000 |
| Yale (1920–1955) | 13.0 |
| Harvard (1969–1976) | 14.0 |
| survey (1971–1974) | 8.7 |
| 1:1/male:female | 11.9 |
| 3:1/male:female | 15.4 |

"Survey" represents an annual rate computed from data accumulated by the American College Health Association from a group of cooperating universities with a population-times-years-at-risk of more than a million. The rates were not reported by sex; therefore, for comparison purposes "expected" rates have been computed for the population between 17 and 21 by interpolating from available national data and by calculating separately for a 1:1 or a 3:1 male-female ratio in the college population.

## Ways to intervene

Restricting access to the means of committing suicide, even though absolute control is clearly not possible, can make an important difference. Suicide rates in England and Wales declined between 1960 and 1975; almost all of the decline is accounted for by the elimination of suicide by domestic-gas poisoning. This secondary public health benefit resulted from a change in the sources of the domestic-gas supply from an almost total dependence on coal gas to almost total substitution of the much less toxic natural gas.

From 1971 to 1976 in the United States, there was a decline by almost half in the number of suicides ascribable to barbiturates; over the same interval, the number of barbiturate prescriptions written by physicians declined from 40 million to 20 million. A similar pattern was reported from Australia after controls were imposed to restrict the size of single prescriptions for barbiturates. However, in the United States patterns of multiple drug use (particularly in combination with alcohol) have resulted in an offsetting increase in other drug-related deaths. Nonetheless, it is evident that more careful drug-prescribing practices by physicians can have the effect of decreasing suicides with controlled drugs.

Deaths from suicide (as well as homicide) from the use of firearms by 15–24-year-olds in the U.S. doubled between 1966 and 1975. Therefore, gun-control legislation can be expected to diminish deaths from both causes. The common argument that "gun control will not stop criminals" may well be true, but in the case of suicide it is entirely irrelevant, because the lethality of guns increases the "success" rate of suicide attempts and converts assaults against family members and acquaintances (which account for the majority of homicides) into murders instead of nonfatal attacks. Given the fact that ropes, knives, high places, automobiles, and other means of committing suicide are so ubiquitous, it may seem against common sense to believe that restricting access to coal gas, drugs, and guns would deter would-be suicides. But this commonsense view overlooks the following important considerations: (1) many suicides are impulsive and depend on the availability of means immediately at hand; (2) despite suicidal intent, many who use one method are frightened by or disdain other methods; and (3) many who attempt suicide are ambivalent.

In England the Samaritans have been providing volunteer hot lines and emergency counseling services for persons contemplating suicide during the period in which suicide rates have fallen sharply. Although one study comparing towns with and without Samaritan services was interpreted as indicating a significant favorable difference, more rigorous evaluation conducted subsequently has not borne out this finding; similar negative findings have been reported in assessing U.S. suicide prevention centers. This does not deny the usefulness in other respects of such services to troubled persons, only a minority of whom will, in any event, attempt suicide.

Another proposal emphasizes the importance of controlling what has been termed the Werther effect. In Goethe's romantic novel *The Sorrows of Young Werther* (1774), a gifted young man is torn by hopeless passions and shoots himself in the head. The book was believed to have inspired a wave of imitative suicides in impressionable young people and was banned by the authorities in several countries. Reexamining the Werther effect with contemporary data, sociologists have demonstrated an increase in suicides and in motor vehicle fatalities, considered to be disguised suicides, in the interval following newspaper-publicized suicides; additional force is provided for the thesis by the demonstration of a significant correlation between the extent of the increase in deaths and a measure of the amount of publicity. Similar effects have been shown for television coverage. The data do not enable us to distinguish between two equally plausible possibilities: earlier triggering of a suicide that would have occurred in any event or precipitation of a death that would never have happened in the absence of publicity. The findings do suggest a public health benefit from minimizing sensationalized reporting of suicides. However, it is not immediately evident how this could be accomplished without violating constitutional guarantees of a free press.

When we turn from populationwide measures to the individual case, the frame for decision making changes markedly. For one thing, the odds are quite different when we are faced with a decision, not about adolescents in general, but about one person in particular— one who has made a threat or an attempt and for whom the risk is significantly higher. For another, we cannot defer an answer while awaiting a definitive study; we must act on the basis of the best understanding available. Furthermore, although preventing suicide is a primary consideration, it is not the only one. An intervention that is "unnecessary" in the sense that the risk for suicide may have been low may promote health and therefore be warranted if it succeeds in enabling both patient and family to develop a coping style more mature than threat and confrontation.

## The depressed teenager

Depression is the most common psychiatric antecedent of adolescent and adult suicide. The long-term risk in a patient with a clinical depressive disorder is estimated to be 10 to 15%. Since depressions are for the most part "treatable" conditions, this is a particularly tragic figure.

Depression is characterized by a persistent blue mood and by a loss of interest and joy in usual activities; the depressed teenager feels sad, hopeless, empty, and helpless. Commonly, appetite is diminished and weight is lost. Sleep disturbances are prominent and sexual drive is decreased. Patients complain they cannot concentrate, and making the simplest decisions is difficult. They exhibit low self-esteem, reproach themselves for minor faults, and express guilt for past misdeeds. The inner feelings of the depressed patient have been graphically portrayed by the French poet Charles Baudelaire in his poem "Spleen." (Translation by Geoffrey Wagner, *Selected Poems of Charles Baudelaire*. New York: Grove Press, 1974.)

When the low and heavy sky presses like a lid
On the groaning heart, a prey to slow cares,
And when from a horizon holding the whole orb
There is cast at us a dark sky more sad than night;

When earth is changed to a damp dungeon,
Where Hope, like a bat,
Flees beating the walls with its timorous wings,
And knocking its head on the rotting ceilings;

When the rain spreads out vast trails
Like the bars of a huge prison,
And when, like sordid spiders, silent people stretch
Threads to the depths of our brains,
Suddenly the bells jump furiously
And hurl to the sky a horrible shriek,
Like some wandering landless spirits
Starting an obstinate complaint.

—And long hearses, with no drums, no music,
File slowly through my soul: Hope,
Conquered, cries, and despotic atrocious Agony
Plants on my bent skull its flag of black.

There are many effective, specific treatments available for depressions today. Though medication may be appropriate for the severely depressed patient, it has little place much of the time; the treatment of choice— care and understanding—is not to be found in the pharmacopoeia. Also, drug therapy can be counterproduc-

*Feelings of rootlessness and alienation from parents and peers drive many youngsters to consider suicide. Hot lines and crisis centers respond to troubled teenagers by taking their cries for help seriously.*

Ben Weaver—Camera 5

tive by shifting focus away from the essential task of modifying family relationships and life stress.

What is crucial is a therapeutic context that permits the rebuilding of hope and the reestablishment of healthy ties among family members. Because the patient feels unloved and unworthy of love, the task of treatment is to convey a sense of caring and to restore faith in the possibility of a satisfying future.

## Critical factors

Suicide and suicide attempts are more likely in the presence of a major psychiatric disorder, alcohol or drug abuse, prior attempts, a turbulent family situation, a history of suicide in the family, and recent changes in behavior (despondency, inability to concentrate, onset of truancy, and antisocial behavior). There is usually an identifiable precipitant: rejection by or loss of a person important to the patient, unwanted pregnancy, a threat of imminent punishment, a family crisis, or failure at school. Particularly ominous is the availability of weapons in the home that have not been removed even after the patient has made intent obvious.

Most patients give ample warning of suicide in the days and weeks before the event, although impulsive suicides are more frequent during adolescence than at other ages. While we may rejoice that most who talk about it do not try, and that most who try fail, the warning must be heeded; the danger is not only that suicide is a fatal disease but that suicide attempts can leave the patient crippled, even when less lethal means are used. Moreover, if the distress that led to the contemplation of suicide evokes a family response manifesting itself in love and concern, there is a new opportunity for personal growth and for the restoration of psychological equilibrium.

The first decision facing the physician is to determine whether hospitalization is necessary for behavioral reasons after the successful resolution of the medical consequences of the attempt. Some recommend admission to an adolescent inpatient unit for at least a brief period in order to provide sanctuary for patient and family as well as time for developing an individual plan of care. This may well be useful where a suitable facility is available and the community is willing to sustain the cost. Whether it leads to a better outcome than selective hospitalization remains to be determined; clinical experience indicates that many patients can be treated successfully on an outpatient basis.

Hospitalization is essential when history and examination justify a diagnosis of psychosis, particularly if the attempt has been made in response to a hallucinated command. Most often, the adolescent is *not* psychotic, and the task of the clinician in planning care is to assess two crucial factors: the risk/rescue ratio and the psychosocial resources of the patient's family.

Most suicides are ambivalent; along with the wish to die, there is the hope of being saved. The force of the intent to die (that is, the risk) can be inferred from the lethality of the means the patient has chosen. Thus, the use of guns, a rope, or poison indicates a more lethal intent than the use of aspirin or superficial cuts at the wrist. However, there is an important caveat: One must not mistake a scientific assessment of lethality for the patient's subjective intent and judgment; ignorance of hazard may dictate a misleading choice. Furthermore, the patient who, after an attempt, is dismayed at his "failure" and announces a commitment to "succeed" should be promptly hospitalized.

If the means of suicide indicates severity of intention, the strength of the wish for rescue can be estimated from the amount of warning given and the choice of circumstances that enhance the likelihood of discovery in time. The patient who, without prior warning, chooses a moment when the family is away clearly has less wish for rescue than the one who, after many forewarnings, makes a noisy and dramatic gesture with her or his parents in the next room.

If the weight of the risk/rescue ratio is on the rescue side of the fraction *and* the parents show understanding and concern, counseling on an outpatient basis is feasible. On the other hand, if the parents are indifferent and, worse, if they are angry, show no understanding of the distress represented by the attempt, and are unable to be supportive, then hospitalization will be necessary despite a favorable risk/rescue ratio. Failure of the gesture to bring about an affirmation of genuine concern may serve to confirm the patient's worst fears of being unloved; the parent who belittles the adolescent as a faker may make it necessary for the youngster to try again in order to save face.

## The importance of human ties

Suicide is the ultimate expression of alienation. It is best conceptualized as a deficiency disease, a deficiency of social connections. The aim of treatment is to restore to the patient the sources of emotional sustenance on which all of us depend for our survival.

In *Hamlet,* Shakespeare's young hero, bereft by his father's death, unmanned by his mother's betrayal, and enraged by his uncle's treachery, epitomizes the inner crises that lead to the contemplation of suicide—an intention Hamlet thrusts aside consciously even as he ensures his own death by his impulsive acceptance of Laertes's challenge to a duel. In his 29th sonnet, which begins, "When, in disgrace with Fortune and men's eyes," Shakespeare with equal vividness portrays the human tie that permits a life-affirming resolution of the depressive crisis:

Yet in these thoughts myself almost despising,
Haply I think on thee, and then my state,
Like to the lark at break of day arising
From sullen earth, sings hymns at heaven's gate,
　For thy sweet love remember'd such wealth brings
　That then I scorn to change my state with kings.

# Dentistry

The temporomandibular joint (TMJ) is the connection, or hinge, between the lower jaw (mandible) and the base of the skull. It has been estimated that in the United States as many as ten million people suffer from disorders of this joint. Although the number of sufferers probably has not increased, in recent times there has been an increasing public awareness of TMJ conditions. This is due, in large part, to the greater emphasis placed on their recognition by the dental and medical professions. But even more so, it is because of the considerable attention that has been given to the subject by the various public media. Unfortunately, much of what has been presented to the public has been based on opinion rather than fact. It is important, therefore, to review the scientific facts about the various disorders that affect the temporomandibular joint.

## Anatomy and function

To understand the problems that may arise in the temporomandibular joint and associated structures, it is first necessary to understand something about structure and function. The TMJ consists of a movable portion—the condyloid process of the lower jaw—and a socket located at the base of the skull. The parts are held together by ligaments and a capsule, and the jaw is moved by the muscles that attach to it. This joint differs from most other joints in the body by having a disk, which acts as a shock absorber, interposed between the bony parts. Also, the contacting surface of the condyloid process contains a specialized tissue (cartilage) that contributes to the growth of the lower jaw as well as to its function. This is an important distinction because any disease process or injury that damages this cartilage in a growing person not only will cause jaw dysfunction but also will result in facial deformity.

The TMJ is a very mobile joint that moves freely in all directions. It is also a very adaptable joint and is constantly beng remodeled in response to normal functional stresses. In humans, opening the mouth involves not only a hinge movement (as is the case in most animals) but also a gliding movement. In animals with a lower jaw that is parallel to the ground and to the backbone, hinge movement is unimpeded. In man, pure hinge movement would result in the lower jaw hitting the neck and interfering with breathing. To accommodate to the human upright position, the lower jaw slides forward at the same time that it rotates.

## Diseases and disorders of the TMJ

The temporomandibular joint is susceptible to all of the disease processes that affect other joints of the body. Thus, even at birth the joint may be absent, underdeveloped, or deformed. Congenital defects also produce secondary facial deformities, characterized by crookedness and underdevelopment of the lower jaw. Trauma to the jaw joint during childhood and adolescence also affects subsequent growth of the face. In adults, fractures, dislocation, disk displacement, tissue tears, and compression of nerves and blood vessels following trauma can produce pain and interfere with normal function. The scarring and abnormal bone formation that may follow a traumatic injury can also lead to restricted movement (ankylosis). The TMJ is also the occasional site of both benign and malignant tumors.

The disease that most commonly affects the TMJ is arthritis. A person who has a generalized form of arthritis, such as rheumatoid or gouty arthritis, may experience pain and limited movement in the TMJ as well as in other parts of the body. However, one can also have a localized form of arthritis, such as osteoarthritis or degenerative arthritis, occurring solely in the jaw joint. In older persons degenerative arthritis of the TMJ can be considered part of the aging process, and it is generally relatively asymptomatic. In younger people, however, where localized arthritis in the TMJ is caused by trauma or excessive stress on the joint, both pain and dysfunction can be significant.

The problem most frequently referred to simply as "TMJ" or "TMJ syndrome" is actually initiated in the jaw muscles rather than the jaw joint and is more accurately described as myofascial pain-dysfunction (MPD) syndrome. It has been estimated that 80 to 90% of so-called TMJ problems are actually of this type. It is similar to lower back pain, where arthritis of the spine or a slipped disk can be present, but most often pain is associated with muscles and tendons.

It is difficult to determine accurately how widespread TMJ problems are because there are no reliable statistics. Several surveys have estimated that as many as 50 to 80% of the general population have some type of TMJ problem; 10 to 20% is probably a more reasonable estimate. The majority of patients seen in clinics

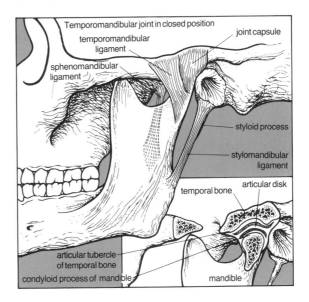

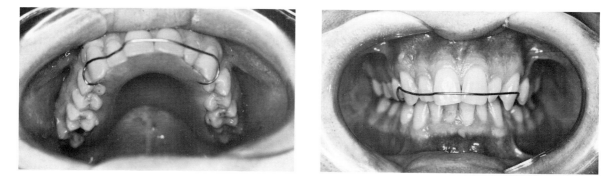

One type of oral appliance is a plastic form molded to fit against the palate; a wire is sometimes added to keep teeth from shifting. In the closed position (right), the appliance separates the posterior teeth, thus preventing the patient from engaging in habitual grinding or clenching of the teeth.

and offices are adult women between the ages of 20 and 40 who are suffering from MPD syndrome. There has never been a satisfactory explanation for the preponderance of women over men, which may be as high as seven to one. Among older patients seen, degenerative disorders are most common, but these can affect younger patients too.

## Symptoms and diagnosis

True problems of the temporomandibular joint are usually characterized by dull, aching pain in the area of the ear—pain that increases with wide opening of the mouth, chewing, or talking. Use of the jaw may produce clicking, popping, or grating sounds heard during function. Arthritis should be suspected when the jaw joint is painful and tender. A person who has arthritis in other joints should be especially aware of the possibility of TMJ involvement if facial pain develops.

A person who has limited movement of the jaw; dull, aching, radiating pain in the region of the temporomandibular joint, as well as the ear, cheek, and temple; tenderness in one or more of the jaw muscles on one side; and minor clicking in the joint when the jaw is moved probably has myofascial pain-dysfunction syndrome.

If there are loud clicking or popping sounds, if the jaw gets stuck during opening or closing, or if the jaw cannot be opened more than an inch, the problem may be a displaced disk. The latter often begins suddenly after an accident involving the jaw or as a result of wide opening, biting on a hard object, or extraction of a lower tooth under general anesthesia. It may also be a sequel to long-standing MPD syndrome.

Many people experience minor or transient symptoms related to the temporomandibular joint for which they do not seek professional help. Simple home remedies such as aspirin, resting the jaw, application of heat, and a soft diet relieve the symptoms in a great number of cases. However, because of the large variety of serious conditions that can produce facial pain and jaw dysfunction, and because many disorders can become worse if neglected or improperly treated, self-diagnosis is risky. It is best to seek professional help when symptoms persist or recur.

The dentist is the person who will most often make the diagnosis of a TMJ disorder. However, patients with facial pain frequently consult a variety of medical specialists. While many dentists and physicians are knowledgeable and competent in dealing with TMJ and MPD disorders, there are some who inappropriately tend to attribute the cause of a variety of medical disorders to so-called bad bite relationships or to TMJ problems; moreover, they may routinely recommend very aggressive, radical, or unconventional forms of therapy. Patients who have long-standing complaints of facial pain, headache, and other chronic symptoms that do not appear to be jaw or muscle related should be especially wary of doctors who proclaim that all the problems stem from a TMJ disorder and that they can be alleviated by proper alignment of the teeth and jaws.

The diagnosis of TMJ and MPD disorders can be difficult because signs and symptoms may mimic or be similar to those of a variety of other, unrelated conditions. For example, an infected lower wisdom tooth can cause pain in the ear, tenderness of the jaw muscle, and difficulty in opening the mouth. The final diagnosis is usually based on a thorough history, a careful general and oral examination, and appropriate X-rays. When a disk displacement is suspected, special X-rays called arthrograms—which use a contrast medium that allows the disk to be seen on film—are used to confirm the clinical impression.

## Causes of TMJ disorders

The question of what causes a particular disease is always at the center of any medical discussion; regrettably, clear answers often are not forthcoming. While a virus may cause a cold, or distinct bacilli may cause tuberculosis, it is not so easy to isolate the cause of a headache, high blood pressure, arthritis, diabetes, and many other conditions. In the case of painful joint and muscle syndromes, as well as chronic pain problems in general, it is especially difficult to isolate a specific causative factor. Many of these disorders seem to arise from a functional overload of the system. The bony surfaces of the joint wear out prematurely; the jaw muscles become fatigued, inflamed, and go into spasm; and ligaments become stretched and permit the disk to be displaced. There are those, however, who believe that a structural abnormality or anatomical change is the underlying basis for such problems. This function-versus-structure argument is the major controversy today in the area of TMJ disorders.

Many dentists believe that malocclusion (abnormality in the coming together of the teeth) and misalignment of the jaws are the principal factors responsible for the onset of TMJ symptoms, and they advocate treatment designed to correct these anatomic features. Recent studies, however, have tended to minimize the importance of such anatomic factors. Although many patients may have anatomic relationships of the teeth or jaws that are imperfect in some way, that does not mean they are the cause of the pain problem, nor does it mean that they must be corrected. There are no studies that offer conclusive evidence showing a significant difference in dental features such as inappropriate tooth contacts, malocclusion, and missing teeth, as well as in jaw position, between those who do and those who do not develop TMJ problems. There are many recent studies, however, that have shown that anxiety and stress, along with the frequent habits of clenching and grinding the teeth that accompany these states, are important factors in producing the increased muscle tension and fatigue, as well as the functional overload of the joint structures, that lead to both TMJ and MPD disorders. Thus, MPD syndrome is now considered a psychophysiological disease similar to ulcers, colitis, and low back pain.

## Treatment of TMJ disorders

The therapies for disorders of the temporomandibular joint can be divided into two categories: procedures to treat diseases and derangements of the joint itself and procedures aimed at correcting problems involving the jaw muscles (MPD syndrome). The treatment for most diseases involving the temporomandibular joint, such as congenital deformities, traumatic injuries, tumors, and ankylosis, is surgical. Although both degenerative arthritis and rheumatoid arthritis are usually managed medically, surgery can also play a part in their therapy. Degenerative joint disease that fails to respond to more conservative treatment may require smoothing of the rough surfaces, and the limited jaw movement occurring in patients with rheumatoid arthritis may require the creation of an artificial joint. Although some internal disk derangements lend themselves to dental treatment, many also require surgical correction.

The treatment of MPD syndrome has not been as clearly defined as that for the diseases of the temporomandibular joint. Some doctors believe that the patient

must have a structural change to get better, while others do not. A recent survey of dentists and physicians found that more than 50 different methods were advocated for the management of this problem. Moreover, clinical reports claim a high degree of success with a number of widely varying approaches.

The earliest approaches to treatment of TMJ problems were based on the concept that the jaws could be "overclosed" when most of the back teeth were extracted, and that this overclosure could cause the TMJ to shift and press on neighboring nerves and blood vessels, causing pain and degenerative changes in the joint structures. Even symptoms such as ringing or stuffiness in the ears and hearing loss were blamed on this jaw shift, and the recommended treatment was to "open the bite" with crowns or dentures. This concept has now been disproved. Later versions blamed the problem on inappropriate tooth contacts, and treatment included bite-adjustment methods, known as equilibrations, in which the teeth were ground or filed to produce a "correct" bite. Orthodontic treatment also has been used to change tooth positions. Although a large number of patients appear to have benefited from these treatments, recent research has shown that a large percentage of this apparent success can be explained in other ways: TMJ conditions sometimes get better spontaneously; placebo or mock versions of these treatments also produce a high level of positive response; and other forms of therapy unrelated to the teeth produce equally good results. These findings have raised doubts about the efficacy of bite-changing treatments.

Amid the unresolved controversies about traditional bite-changing methods, a new generation of major jaw-repositioning treatments has emerged. These treatments are based on the general concept that the lower jaw is misaligned or improperly positioned in patients with TMJ disorders, and that the task for the dentist is to analyze and correct this problem by repositioning the jaw and then rebuilding the bite. Some practitioners use X-rays to determine where the TMJ is positioned and where it ought to be, while others use measurements on the patients or on models of their teeth to compute the "correct" jaw relationships. All of these methods are based on the assumption that a jaw can be misaligned and, therefore, the misalignment can be detected and fixed. Most authorities in dental anatomy and anthropology, however, find little basis for making such an assumption; they find great variations in normal jaw anatomy and function among human beings, and in general they consider geometric clinical analyses to be without scientific validity. Thus, many patients are undergoing major jaw repositioning that may be inappropriate and, in some cases, harmful.

A more logical approach to the treatment of MPD syndrome is grounded in the notion that it is actually a psychophysiological disease. Therapy based on this concept tends to be more conservative, using such things as muscle-relaxant drugs, oral appliances, heat, massage, and a soft diet. Appreciation of the roles that stress and anxiety can play in causing this problem also leads to such treatments as biofeedback or conditioned-relaxation training and even psychological counseling in certain treatment-resistant cases. No attempt is made to change the anatomy of the teeth or the position of the jaw, although routine dental adjustments, fillings, bridges, and dentures may be made as needed after the symptoms are controlled. Recent studies have shown that this approach to treatment works well, not only on a short-term basis, but also over long periods of time. In general, there is no difference in treatment outcome if more aggressive and radical treatments are used; this is a powerful argument for using the most conservative approach to therapy for TMJ conditions.

In addition to the many dentists and physicians who treat disorders of the TMJ, there are a number of specialized clinics or centers that concentrate on these problems. Most of the clinics are based in dental schools or hospitals, and some are funded by government grants to conduct research in this field. There are also many groups of dentists and physicians with a special interest in TMJ disorders, but this interest does not necessarily give them automatic credentials as experts. People who are seeking expert advice about TMJ problems should be aware that no standard body of information exists at this time. Patients, therefore, need to be cautious about whom they consult and how much they permit to be done when seeking care for conditions they believe to be TMJ disorders.

### Future considerations

Despite the progress that has been made in the last two decades, there are still many gaps in our knowledge regarding both the diagnosis and the treatment of disorders of the temporomandibular joint. Part of the problem relates to a lack of certain basic scientific information in such fundamental areas as functional anatomy, pathophysiology, and neurophysiology of the TMJ. Failure to understand the causes of many TMJ problems has also limited progress in therapy. Moreover, the accuracy of clinical diagnosis has been hampered by the similarity in signs and symptoms produced by the many unrelated conditions that affect this area of the body, and there is a dire need for more objective means of confirming clinical impressions. Although sophisticated instruments that measure and record such phenomena as muscle activity, jaw movements, and biting sounds have been developed, generally these have failed to provide consistently useful information with specific clinical applications.

Currently there is intensive research being conducted in many areas. Already, computerized axial tomography (the CAT scan) is being used as a noninvasive

means of viewing the disk, and one of the newest developments in diagnostic imaging, nuclear magnetic resonance (NMR), promises to provide a more sensitive non-X-ray technique for viewing the tissues of the TMJ. Radionuclide scanning (injecting radioactive materials into the body) for evaluating the joint structures and immunoassay techniques (observing a substance's capacity to act as an antigen) for analyzing the components of the lubricating joint fluid are other diagnostic procedures being explored more fully.

In addition to the improvement in clinical diagnostic procedures, the future should also bring about new research that should lead to greater understanding of joint biomechanics and lubrication, as well as muscle function and dysfunction, as they relate to the etiology of degenerative arthritis, internal derangements, and MPD syndrome. With such improvements will come rapid advances in the management of TMJ disorders.

*— Daniel M. Laskin, D.D.S.,*
*and Charles S. Greene, D.D.S.*

# Diet and Nutrition

For thousands of years we have been adding substances to our food supply to help in its preservation and to improve its taste, color, or odor. The New World was discovered in an attempt to find a short route to the spices of the Orient, which were needed to keep food palatable before the days of refrigeration. With the advent of mass production, distribution, and processing of food, more and more of these substances have been added.

Some food additives are chemicals synthesized in the laboratory. Others are found naturally in certain plants not traditionally considered foods, and still others may be found in small quantities in a variety of foods that we normally consume. Prime examples of substances in the last two categories are caffeine, found in the cola nut, coffee bean, certain tea leaves, and other plants not considered foods; and salt (sodium chloride), found in small amounts in almost all meats and dairy products and in many fruits and vegetables.

Caffeine is a pharmacologically active agent—a true drug—that will elicit a response very rapidly when given in sufficient amounts. It is totally foreign to the body. Salt is a necessary constituent of our body fluids; it is essential for life and even in relatively large amounts it will not evoke an immediate response within the body. Caffeine is added to foods and beverages or consumed in foods made from caffeine-containing plants in order to evoke its response. It is a drug added to food to produce a stimulant effect; if it did not produce that effect, it would not be added. Caffeine is tasteless and odorless and has no preservative function. By contrast, salt is added to food to improve taste and in some cases as a preservative. It is not added with the expectation of its having any effect on the physiological functions of the consumer. Both of these very different substances added to the food supply may have major implications for the health of the population.

## Caffeine

Caffeine is a central nervous system stimulant, and its major effects, both positive and negative, derive from this action. Positive effects that have been described in people who use caffeine include improved motor performance, decreased fatigue, enhanced sensory activity, and increased alertness. These positive effects may partly explain the compulsion of many adults to consume coffee or other caffeine-containing beverages as part of the morning ritual of awakening. However, the same level of intake that produces "positive" effects in many people induces negative effects in many others. These may include irritability, nervousness or anxiety, tremor, jitteriness and jumpiness in children, headache, insomnia, and withdrawal headaches. In adults these responses frequently occur at levels of intake between 200 and 300 mg (approximately two cups of drip coffee) and sometimes at levels of less than 150 mg (one cup of coffee). In children they may occur at even lower levels.

It should be noted that drinks typically consumed in large quantities by children, such as colas, naturally contain significant quantities of caffeine. In addition, many soft drinks not made from cola nuts have caffeine added to them, presumably to give them an extra "kick" by producing the "desirable" central nervous system effects. Some noncola soft drinks contain more caffeine than the cola drinks (up to 57 mg per 12 oz).

Over and above the increasing number of foods and beverages to which caffeine is added are the many medicines, prescription and nonprescription, that contain caffeine not as their main ingredient but for an extra stimulatory effect. Cough medicines and common cold remedies often fall into this category.

Thus both adults and children are exposed to relatively large quantities of caffeine. This exposure has raised some important health questions regarding both short-term and long-term use of caffeine. Can the short-term effects of caffeine result in hyperactivity in children? Does long-term exposure increase the risk of cancer and birth defects? These questions are areas of intensive investigation, and much more work needs to be done before any definitive answers are forthcoming. However, certain things are already known.

Animal experiments have shown that relatively small

### The common sources of caffeine

| soft drinks | caffeine (in milligrams) | | | | |
|---|---|---|---|---|---|
| Diet Mr. Pibb | 57 | Pepsi Cola | 37 | Sprite | 0 |
| Mountain Dew | 54 | Royal Crown Cola | 36 | Diet 7-Up | 0 |
| Mello Yello | 51 | Diet Rite Cola | 36 | RC-100 | 0 |
| Tab | 45 | Diet Pepsi | 34 | Diet Sunkist Orange | 0 |
| Sunkist Orange | 42 | Coca-Cola | 45 | Patio Orange | 0 |
| Shasta Cola | 44 | Mr. Pibb | 41 | Fanta Orange | 0 |
| Dr. Pepper | 43 | Cragmont Cola | * | Fresca | 0 |
| Diet Dr. Pepper | 43 | 7-Up | 0 | Hires Root Beer | 0 |

| coffee | | tea | | cocoa and chocolate | |
|---|---|---|---|---|---|
| drip (5 oz) | 146 | one-minute brew | | cocoa beverage | |
| percolated (5 oz) | 110 | (5 oz) | 9 to 33 | (water mix, 6 oz) | 10 |
| instant, regular (5 oz) | 53 | three-minute brew | | milk chocolate (1 oz) | 6 |
| decaffeinated (5 oz) | 2 | (5 oz) | 20 to 46 | baking chocolate | |
| | | five-minute brew | | (1 oz) | 35 |
| | | (5 oz) | 20 to 50 | | |
| | | canned ice tea | | | |
| | | (12 oz) | 22 to 36 | | |

| nonprescription drugs | | | |
|---|---|---|---|
| stimulants (standard dose) | | diuretics (standard dose) | |
| Caffedrine Capsules | 200 | Aqua-Ban | 200 |
| NoDoz Tablets | 200 | Permathene H₂Off | 200 |
| Vivarin Tablets | 200 | Pre-Mens Forte | 100 |
| pain relievers (standard dose) | | cold remedies (standard dose) | |
| Anacin | 64 | Coryban-D | 30 |
| Excedrin | 130 | Dristan | 32 |
| Midol | 65 | Triaminicin | 30 |
| Plain aspirin, any brand | 0 | weight-control aids (daily dose) | |
| | | Dexatrim | 200 |
| | | Dietac | 200 |
| *Trace amount as reported by the manufacturer. | | Prolamine | 280 |

doses of caffeine will produce behavioral abnormalities resembling hyperactivity. Carefully controlled studies have not been done to determine whether similar behavior can be elicited in children. However, clinical observation suggests that certain hyperactive children may improve when foods containing caffeine are removed from their diets. Although caffeine may contribute to hyperactivity in some children, it is clear from the studies that have already been done that it is not the major cause of this disorder.

The only evidence presently available linking long-term exposure to high levels of caffeine with cancer is an epidemiological study relating heavy coffee consumption to cancer of the pancreas. This study, although provocative, is far from conclusive, first because pancreatic cancer is fairly uncommon and hence an extremely large population must be studied in order to collect enough cases. The larger the overall population, the greater the chance for other variables not considered by the investigators to be important to exert an effect. For example, it is possible that people who consume large quantities of coffee have different eating patterns than those who do not. Or they may smoke or drink more. Or they may exercise less. Or a host of other differences may be present. Some of these were considered by the investigators; others were not. Second, the increased incidence of pancreatic cancer was at best quite small, raising the question of just how important caffeine or coffee really is in the genesis of the disease. Certainly exposure to caffeine is nowhere near as important as exposure to alcohol in this disease. Whether exposure to both may increase the danger even more is an intriguing question that has not yet been investigated.

From the evidence so far presented, caffeine can hardly be considered a major health risk. However, the effect of chronic exposure to caffeine, mainly from soft drinks, in children and adolescents has not been studied, particularly in respect to subtle behavioral effects that may not be obvious but that in aggregate could affect school performance as well as other important functions.

Recently a serious health concern has been raised regarding chronic exposure to large amounts of caffeine in a particular population—pregnant women and their unborn offspring. Birth defects can be produced in animals by exposing the mother to high doses of caffeine early in pregnancy. Even later in pregnancy, lower doses of caffeine can retard fetal growth and result in stunted newborn animals. Perhaps even more significant, in experiments in which coffee or a comparable amount of caffeine was added to the drinking water of the mother throughout pregnancy, not only was fetal growth retarded but behavioral abnormalities could be demonstrated in the offspring, abnormalities that, though they disappeared eventually, persisted for about a month.

Staff Davis

*A study involving 123 Seventh-day Adventist high school students showed that reduced sodium intake had little impact on adolescent blood-pressure levels.*

Studies in human populations have been few and inconclusive. There is some evidence that the incidence of spontaneous abortions may be slightly higher in women who consume large amounts of caffeine. Other studies raise the possibility of retarded fetal growth. No studies have demonstrated an increase in congenital malformations. Studies of behavior of offspring of heavy caffeine users have not been done. The evidence presently available would suggest that caffeine in amounts generally consumed even by heavy users is not a major cause of birth defects or fetal growth failure. Its contribution to spontaneous abortion, while probably real, is minimal.

How do we translate these findings into realistic recommendations for pregnant women? Certainly the moderate coffee or cola drinker has little to fear. Based on the animal data and on the few human studies discussed above, the heavy consumer (eight cups of coffee—*i.e.,* more than one gram per day) might prudently reduce her intake. This may not only reduce her risk for the complications noted but will also increase her own peace of mind during the pregnancy.

## Salt

In many ways the problem of adding salt to our food supply is much more serious and much more complicated than that of adding caffeine. One reason is that salt is added to an enormous amount of processed foods whereas caffeine is restricted to just a few. Salt adds flavor that is desirable to a large segment of the population—the habit of salting food being well established in many cultures.

Salt consumed in large amounts over long periods of time has been associated with hypertension (high blood pressure), an extremely serious health problem that afflicts millions. It is this association that has raised the question of reducing salt intake, and therefore it is worthwhile to examine the evidence on which it is based.

Hypertension, or high blood pressure, is a condition in which the pressure exerted by the blood on the vessels through which it circulates is greater than it should be. The heart must pump with extra force against this pressure, and the walls of the larger and smaller arteries must in turn resist this pressure. Prolonged sustained high blood pressure can therefore lead to heart failure or to disease of the wall of arteries, leading to clogging of the vessels and to coronary or other artery disease. Finally, a vessel that is no longer able to resist the increased pressure may burst. If this occurs in the brain, a serious cerebral hemorrhage (stroke) can occur. Unfortunately, high blood pressure often is not accompanied by serious symptoms; thus many people have high blood pressure and do not know it until some catastrophic event—such as a heart attack or stroke—occurs.

Hypertension runs in families and is much more common in certain ethnic and racial groups. For example, it is particularly prevalent in blacks in the United States and to a lesser extent in eastern European Jews. By contrast, in the black populations in Africa where American blacks originated, hypertension until recently was very rare. Thus there is a genetic component to hypertension; certain populations are innately more susceptible than others. But this genetic disposition must be catalyzed by a particular environmental circumstance, a high exposure to salt (sodium chloride), or particularly to the sodium in salt.

The data supporting the above thesis come from both animal experimentation and human studies. Most rats cannot be made hypertensive no matter how much salt they are exposed to. However, certain strains of rats, while usually normotensive (having normal blood pressure) throughout their lives, can be induced to show hypertension when chronically exposed to large quantities of salt. In some of these strains the hypertension, once induced, will remain even after the excess salt is removed from the diet. Intensive investigation has at least partially revealed the mechanism by which sodium increases blood pressure in susceptible animals.

As previously discussed, sodium is an essential constituent of all body fluids. The amount of sodium in the body is regulated by the kidney. When sodium is scarce the kidney reabsorbs most of the sodium that filters through it. When sodium is excessive, the kidney filters more from the blood and allows it to pass into the urine. The efficiency with which the kidney is able to filter sodium and many other materials depends in part on the pressure of the blood entering the glomerulus (the small arteries involved in filtration). The pressure within these arteries in turn depends to a major extent on the blood pressure as a whole. The kidney has a very sensitive hormonal mechanism that is able to detect the amount of sodium in the blood. When sodium levels are high, hormone levels are changed and the blood pressure increases so that more sodium can be filtered. In laboratory animals the level of sodium in the blood needed to evoke this response will vary depending on the genetic strain. In certain strains the kidney can filter enough sodium, even with excess intake, without raising the blood pressure; in other strains it cannot. It is these latter genetic strains that develop hypertension when exposed to large amounts of sodium in their diets.

Although the same hormonal mechanisms are operative in humans, their sensitivity in different genetic populations with greater or lesser propensities for hypertension has not been tested. However, a number of other studies in human populations indict dietary sodium as an important factor in the cause of hypertension.

In populations that consume little sodium, blood pressure does not rise with age, and hypertension is very rare. By contrast, in populations consuming relatively high amounts of sodium, blood pressure increases with age and hypertension is quite common.

*In the United States hypertension is prevalent among blacks; dietary changes and reduction of salt intake can help these patients lower blood pressure.*

Thomas S. England/TIME Magazine

For example, among Greenland Eskimos, Australian Aborigines, Polynesians, African bushmen, and American Indians, hypertension is virtually unknown, and blood pressure remains constant throughout life. As these populations begin to acculturate to Western societies, blood pressure rises. The major factors involved in the development of their hypertension appear to be the increased incidence of obesity and the increased consumption of salt.

An interesting study was carried out in a group of Samburu from northern Kenya. Traditionally these nomadic people consume a diet consisting of meat and milk, which is low in sodium content. A group was followed after being drafted into the Kenyan Army, where the ration consisted of cornmeal and other foods that increased their sodium intake fivefold. During the second year of service the blood pressure of these men began to increase and continued to increase throughout their six years of service. By contrast, their weight remained relatively constant throughout their tour of duty. Thus increased sodium consumption without increase in weight resulted in higher blood pressure values in this population.

A second line of evidence implicating dietary sodium in human hypertension has been accumulated by studying people who already have high blood pressure. The pressure can often be lowered by drastically curtailing the intake of sodium. Since such a low-salt diet is difficult to maintain in our society because of the widespread use of salt in food processing, diuretic drugs—which induce the kidney to excrete more water and with it more sodium—have been used in treating high blood pressure. The success rate has been impressive. Thus if the amount of sodium consumed is drastically reduced or the amount of sodium excreted is markedly increased, blood pressure will usually fall in individuals with hypertension.

The combined animal and human data build an impressive case against sodium excess in our diet. The problem is that food processing is such that extra sodium is almost everywhere. Salt is added to flour and to most baked goods; canned peas may contain 100 times as much sodium as fresh peas; pickled or smoked foods are soaked in brine until they are saturated with salt. Although moderate salt reduction can be achieved by not adding salt in cooking, not using a salt shaker at the table, and reducing consumption of smoked or pickled foods, whether such reduction would be sufficient to reduce our high incidence of hypertension is presently unknown. Even if such moderate efforts were partially successful, who would benefit from their use? Would this make a medically important dent in the high incidence of hypertension among the most susceptible populations, such as blacks and people with a strong family history of hypertension?

All of these questions must be answered more fully before precise recommendations for lowering our salt intake can be made. At present we can say only that a prudent approach would be to reduce our salt intake, particularly if our genetic background suggests that we may be at increased risk for hypertension.

## Unanswered questions

Caffeine and salt, two very different food additives, raise a number of important social issues regarding our food supply and the protection of public health. Should a drug be permitted to be added to foods with the express purpose of producing its pharmacological effects even though certain possibly harmful side effects can and do occur? Should sodium in the form of salt be added simply to enhance the taste of food when overall sodium consumption is clearly too high for major segments of our population?

There are no easy answers; probably the solution lies in an informed public that is able to choose from an adequate number of alternatives. Thus foods should be labeled with their caffeine or sodium content. If either of these substances (as well as many others) is added by the manufacturer, the public has a right to know. Only then can the average consumer decide whether one product is better than another if he or she is trying to limit the amount of salt or caffeine in the diet. Manufacturers have the responsibility of offering a wide enough variety of foods so that real choice is available, even within food classes. As the public becomes more informed, people will demand such options.

Already we are seeing the result of consumer pressure with both caffeine and sodium. Soft drinks are advertising that they are caffeine free, and more and more of them are reducing the quantity of caffeine added or eliminating it altogether. Now salt-free foods are being advertised increasingly, and foods with no added salt are becoming more available. Even the baby-food manufacturers have responded to consumer pressure by removing added salt from their products. This is a positive development, since the taste for salt is believed to be acquired. Most research indicates that young infants do not innately favor salty foods; rather they develop such preferences only upon exposure.

For the present, then, it is important for consumers to be aware of the proved and potential health hazards of too much salt or caffeine so that they may take these hazards into consideration when choosing foods. The more informed the consumer, the more realistic the choices. To be sure, the food manufacturers watch those choices and react very rapidly by making available more foods that reflect what is being chosen. If the public wants a food supply that contains less caffeine and less salt, the best way to ensure getting it is to buy foods with the quantity of these two additives in mind. The food industry will get the message.

—*Myron Winick, M.D.*

# Special Report:
# Bulimia: An Eating Disorder
by Ricki L. Rusting

Once I start on one cookie or a donut, I end up having a feast of foods! I have used laxatives excessively and tried throwing up. I quit eating only when I am actually bloated, depressed, and upset. This happens at least six times a week. I have tried without success to end this habit. . . .

This graduate student, who says she has eaten two loaves of bread and whole pies in a sitting, is one of thousands of young women who have symptoms of bulimia, a newly recognized and potentially deadly eating disorder. "Bulimia," which means "ox hunger" in Greek, refers to episodic binge eating that the individual feels is uncontrollable. A large portion of bulimics follow these binges by vomiting or taking large doses of laxatives and/or diuretics and by rigid dieting or fasting. However, technically, the binges need not be alternated with such behaviors to be considered bulimic.

## Dietary chaos

Despite the eating jags and the self-destructive actions after it, bulimics tend to look healthy and to be of normal, or near normal, weight. But beneath their facades they are tormented by conflicts about eating. Taking to heart the messages of a society that tells its women to be thin but bombards them with pressures to eat, they are terrified of becoming fat yet constantly think about food and feel that their lives are controlled by it. Many report that if they take one bite of what is for them a forbidden food, they cannot stop from embarking on a full-fledged binge.

Bulimics are in some ways like victims of anorexia nervosa in their intense fear of fat and determination to control their weight. However, unlike anorexics, they do not have the willpower to starve themselves for so long that they lose 25% or more of their body weight. Bulimics, some of whom have a history of anorexia, also tend to be slightly older, more sexually experienced, and more extroverted. To meet them at school or in the office, one might have no idea they had any problem at all—with food or otherwise.

Bulimic behavior is not a new phenomenon. The ancient Romans were famous for their food orgies during which participants forced themselves to vomit and returned for more food. But it was only in the late 1970s that several studies revealed binge eating and its associated purges to be a serious problem for a surprising number of college-age women. And it was only in 1980 that the American Psychiatric Association included bulimia as a bona fide syndrome in its *Diagnostic and Statistical Manual of Mental Disorders* (*DSM-III*). *DSM-III* lists the following criteria for the diagnosis of bulimia:

A. Recurrent episodes of binge eating (rapid consumption of a large amount of food in a discrete period of time, usually less than two hours)
B. At least three of the following:
  (1) consumption of high-caloric, easily ingested food during a binge
  (2) inconspicuous eating during a binge
  (3) termination of such eating episodes by abdominal pain,

*Bulimia is characterized by food binges—episodes of uncontrolled eating—often followed by some form of purgative behavior such as self-induced vomiting or abuse of laxatives.*

Anthony Wolff

sleep, social interruption, or self-induced vomiting

(4) repeated attempts to lose weight by severely restrictive diets, self-induced vomiting, or use of cathartics or diuretics

(5) frequent weight fluctuations greater than ten pounds due to alternating binges and fasts

C. Awareness that the eating pattern is abnormal and fear of not being able to stop voluntarily

D. Depressed mood and self-deprecating thoughts following eating binges

E. The bulimic episodes are not due to anorexia nervosa or any known physical disorder.

Many patients with anorexia nervosa develop bulimic symptoms, sometimes severely. They tend to be extremely difficult cases to treat. *DSM-III* also points out that most bulimics have periods of normal eating between binges (or periods of normal eating and fasts), although some skip the normal periods altogether. The manual does not define what is meant by "large amounts" of food in criterion A, but in a study of 316 bulimics, Craig L. Johnson, director of the Eating Disorders Clinic at Michael Reese Hospital and Medical Center in Chicago, along with colleagues, found that the average caloric intake of people who binged for up to two hours was 4,800 (a range of 1,000 to as many as 55,000 cal), principally from sweet or salty carbohydrate foods.

## Current understanding of bulimia

In 1980, when *DSM-III* was published, much was unknown about the prevalence and predisposing factors. Today the disorder is better recognized, but investigators still have reached no definite conclusions about many aspects of bulimia and do not have an established treatment protocol. However, their work does offer glimpses into the scope and origins of the problem.

Bulimia was once thought to be an occupational hazard primarily of female athletes, models, and actresses who had to be ever vigilant about maintaining slim figures. But it seems to have "spread" to an increasing number of female students in high school and college. Clinicians have estimated that 5 to 20% of college-age women engage in some degree of bulimic behavior, but the number who meet all the *DSM-III* criteria is probably lower than 20%.

In a 1983 survey of 1,355 college freshmen, Richard L. Pyle and James E. Mitchell found that 7.8% of the females met the *DSM-III* criteria but that when a once-a-week criterion was added for binge eating, the number dropped to 4.5% of the females. Johnson and colleagues found similar numbers in a 1983 survey of 1,268 female high school students between the ages of 13 and 19. In the latter case 8.3% of the young women met all the *DSM-III* criteria, but only 4.9% met the full criteria plus were binge eating as often as once a week. Many, however, who did not meet all the criteria were binge eating, purging, or both to some degree

From "Bulimia: A Descriptive Survey of 316 Cases," Craig L. Johnson, Ph.D., *et al*, *International Journal of Eating Disorders*, vol. 2, no. 1, p. 9

### Binge/purge behavior

| frequency | eating binge | self-induced vomiting | laxative abuse |
|---|---|---|---|
| more than daily | 26.7% | 36.4% | 9.9% |
| at least daily | 24.8 | 22.8 | 14.6 |
| at least weekly | 41.8 | 28.6 | 30.2 |
| a few times a month | 5.7 | 5.5 | 26.6 |
| monthly or less | 1.0 | 6.7 | 18.8 |

each week. Of the women surveyed, 21% binged at least weekly, 4% induced vomiting, and 3% used laxatives.

Bulimia is also found in men (particularly wrestlers and other athletes) and in younger and older women, but the disorder is primarily one of women who develop binge eating (and purging) behaviors between the ages of 15 and 25. Various studies indicate that bulimics tend to be single white women in their early twenties who have had at least some college education. The average age at onset is about 18. Usually the women who have been studied also have been from upper- or middle-class families, although the disorder can occur at any socioeconomic level.

Even bulimics who meet all the *DSM-III* criteria can vary in the extent of their involvement with binge eating, vomiting, and abuse of diuretics and laxatives. In a study of 40 patients, for instance, Pyle and Mitchell found that while some binged once a week, the frequency for others went as high as 46 times. Most vomited each time they binged; others did not.

In addition, bulimics may become caught up in the syndrome via different routes. However, typically the bulimic behavior first begins after a susceptible woman has engaged in the great American pastime: dieting. Psychologist Marlene Boskind-White, at Cornell University in Ithaca, N.Y., reported in 1977 that in each of more than 100 subjects with bulimic symptoms, "the young woman's efforts to perfect herself through dieting had led to her first eating binge." (Boskind-White, then a doctoral student, drew the attention of the public and an increased number of health professionals to bulimia with her early work. She named the binge-vomiting syndrome "bulimarexia.")

That binge eating would follow strict dieting is not surprising. A considerable amount of research has shown that people who diet are caught on a seesaw—wanting to eat on the one hand and fighting the urge on the other. The ones who restrict themselves most severely are most prone to binge in a big way when some trigger snaps their self-control. Such a trigger might be emotional distress (*e.g.,* depression, loneliness, anger, sexual difficulties, loss or separation from a loved one, going away to school, and other life transitions) or even severe hunger.

Whatever the immediate cause of the first binge, it generally does not take long until the diet breaker feels guilty and worried about her lapse and decides to try vomiting or taking laxatives—weight-control techniques she has very likely learned from a friend or relative (or lately, the media). She is initially thrilled that she has "gotten away" with a binge without having to pay for it with weight gain.

Nonetheless, the young woman returns to her dieting, which eventually leads to another binge and another purge. After all, she tells herself, the last episode caused no harm. But before long a cycle begins: the binges and purges occur frequently, and the woman feels powerless to stop.

Most bulimics manage to continue with work or school, albeit with difficulty. But many become so enmeshed in the bulimic behavior that they start to isolate themselves from friends and give up their normal activities—steps that may well increase their involvement with bulimia.

Bulimics generally recognize that their behavior is abnormal, but embarrassment keeps them from seeking help. In Johnson's study of 316 bulimics, most reported having engaged in the bulimic behavior for about five and a half years. The fortunate victims seek help themselves or accept a helping hand from alert friends, relatives, or physicians. But a few die before they can be reached.

## Roots of the problem

What makes some young women susceptible to this disorder while others escape it? Part of the answer may simply be hunger from dieting. Also, certain characteristics have been found to occur with some frequency in bulimic women, and some of these characteristics may increase susceptibility to bulimia. Among them are difficulty handling stress, problems with interpersonal relationships, low self-esteem (often despite attractiveness and accomplishment), and vulnerability to impulsive behavior and substance abuse. According to *DSM-III,* bulimics may also exhibit "undue concern with body image and appearance, often related to sexual attractiveness, with a focus on how others will see and react to them."

Other roots of the disorder are unclear. Nonetheless, a number of possibilities—social, individual, and familial—have been suggested, each of which may carry varying degrees of relevance in various individuals. Boskind-White believes that social pressures play a major role. She cites the high incidence of female victims as indication that socialization into the so-called

female role (*i.e.,* thin and passive) predisposes young women to become obsessed with their weight and attractiveness to men. Bulimics, she wrote in a 1978 report, are trying "desperately to fit themselves into stereotyped feminine roles both in their relentless pursuit of thinness and in their passive, accommodating, and helpless approach to life."

Johnson and others agree with the view that social pressures drive many women to diet, thus putting them

| Profile of 30 bulimic patients | |
|---|---|
| **sex** | |
| female | 29 |
| male | 1 |
| **marital status** | |
| single | 22 |
| married | 6 |
| divorced | 2 |
| **religion** | |
| Jewish | 11 |
| Protestant | 11 |
| Catholic | 8 |
| **family income** | |
| $ 8,000 | 0 |
| $ 8,000–$14,000 | 1 |
| $14,000–$22,000 | 5 |
| $22,000–$45,000 | 13 |
| $45,000 + | 11 |
| **birth order** | |
| only child | 2 |
| oldest child | 10 |
| 2nd child | 8 |
| 3rd child | 7 |
| 4th child | 2 |
| 5th child | 1 |
| **parents' marital status** | |
| married | 19 |
| divorced | 8 |
| widowed | 3 |
| **family psychiatric history (first-order relatives)** | |
| alcoholism | 10 |
| affective illness | 3 |
| **family history of obesity (in at least one parent)** | 11 |
| **family history of death or chronic physical illness (in at least one parent)** | 15 |

From "Bulimia: The Secretive Syndrome," David B. Herzog, M.D., *Psychosomatics,* vol. 23, no. 5, p. 481

at risk for bulimia. In his report on high school students, he notes that the "increased emphasis on thinness over the last two decades . . . appears to have created a standard for body size among women that has resulted in an increase in the incidence of prolonged restrictive dieting and more drastic measures for weight control." (It is an interesting phenomenon that between 1959 and 1979 "ideals" for women in the U.S. reportedly became increasingly thinner—as measured by the weights of beauty contest winners and *Playboy* playmates—while the average woman under 30 became progressively heavier.)

Some clinicians further note that bulimics are often perfectionists and that this might be one of the psychological factors that makes them prone to the disorder. The women never feel as if they measure up—in school, work, or social life—and these feelings somehow get translated into the belief that if they were thin, all would be well.

Michael Pertschuk, associate director of the Center for Behavioral Medicine at the University of Pennsylvania, has observed, "These women see the world in black and white terms, and if they're less than perfect, they're bad." For some, he notes, "the bulimia confirms their badness," which in turn perpetuates the disorder because the women seek to comfort themselves with food.

Several researchers, including David B. Herzog, director of the Eating Disorders Clinic at Massachusetts General Hospital in Boston, have found a high incidence of depressive symptoms among their subjects. Clearly, women can develop depressive symptoms in *response* to bulimia. But depression may also *contribute* to bulimia. In a study of 30 bulimics (reported in the May 1982 issue of *Psychosomatics*) Herzog found, along with high incidences of depressive symptoms, family histories of affective illness and of death or chronic illness (50% had at least one parent who had died or had a history of serious physical illness). Bulimia, he concluded, may thus be a variant of depressive illness.

Family histories also offer possible evidence that family-wide problems with addictive substances, such as drugs and alcohol, or with obesity may make women prone to bulimia. However, to date, these patterns have not been explored in well-controlled studies with age-matched "normal" subjects. It has been suggested that women who become "addicted" to binge eating apparently turn to food abuse in part because food is cheap and easily available. Also, the women tend to see themselves as "good," not renegade, and binge eating carries less of a stigma in their minds than would, say, alcohol or illicit drug use.

Another cause of bulimia might be a physical disturbance in the brain. But this possibility, based on reports of electroencephalogram (EEG) abnormalities in some people, is controversial.

## Consequences of bulimia

What is known is that women who become caught up in binge eating and purging—for whatever reasons—can suffer devastating side effects. *DSM-III* notes that bulimia "is seldom incapacitating, except in a few individuals who spend their entire day in binge eating and self-induced vomiting." For people who vomit or use laxatives and diuretics excessively, however, bulimia can lead to dehydration and severe electrolyte imbalances, which in turn can lead to hypokalemia (low levels of serum potassium). Potassium is needed for normal cell function, and its loss can cause depression, irritability, tetany (mineral imbalance often involving muscle spasms), urinary infections, fatigue, and extreme muscle weakness. One woman, for instance, became so weak that she was unable to climb the stairs of a bus. In the extreme, hypokalemia can also lead to kidney and heart failure. At least one death due to heart failure from excessive vomiting has been documented. Vomiting can also lead to severe dental erosion, irritation of the esophagus, swollen salivary glands, and chronic sore throat.

Laxative and enema abuse can cause chronic constipation because the bowel loses its ability to respond normally. Such abuse can also lead to rectal bleeding and inadequate absorption of nutrients, including essential fats and proteins. Other side effects of bulimia include liver damage, stomach rupture, ulcers, and hernias. And occasionally some women stop menstruating.

Not surprisingly, for people who have concurrent diseases the dangers of bulimia increase. In diabetics, for example, binges may cause blood sugar levels to soar. This is dangerous because uncontrolled diabetes, aggravated by purging, can lead to such acute emergencies as diabetic coma. Further, chronically elevated blood sugar is believed to contribute to the long-term complications of diabetes (including blindness, kidney failure, and poor circulation at the extremities). Some insulin-dependent diabetics may try to reduce blood sugar after a binge by taking extra insulin and, in so doing, overdose and throw themselves into a state of hypoglycemia (extremely low blood sugar). Low blood sugar is corrected with sweets, and sweets can actually trigger another binge. There have also been reports of insulin-dependent diabetics who have resorted to cutting back on their doses of insulin to lose weight. When no insulin is available, blood sugar soars and the body begins to break down its own tissues, causing weight loss but also potentially causing diabetic coma and death.

But the consequences of bulimia are not all physical. Binges can be economically devastating. One subject reported that she spent an entire week's salary on food. Some bulimics resort to stealing food. Also, although bulimic women are sometimes characterized as outgoing, the ones who become totally preoccupied with binge eating and purging can, indeed, become alienated, lonely, and very depressed. Johnson has noted that food may become the bulimic's "closest companion," to the degree that she may opt to stay home and binge rather than be with friends or family. In extreme cases bulimics have become suicidal.

## Treatment of bulimia

Whether bulimia is more difficult to treat than anorexia nervosa is open to question. It does appear, however, that the earlier bulimia is treated, the better the chances are for a cure. Unfortunately, the behavior is usually well established by the time the victims overcome their shame over their behavior and seek treatment.

In spite of this, clinicians do not consider bulimia to be untreatable if the patient is motivated to change. Health professionals experienced in treating eating disorders have reported many successes with a wide variety of treatment approaches. In general, treatments are aimed at helping women to stop the bulimic behaviors, to regain a sense of control over themselves, to define their worth in terms other than weight, and to cope constructively with stress. For some people therapy focuses primarily on controlling the binge eating; for others the emphasis is on controlling the purging.

Among the therapies used are nutrition counseling, behavioral training, cognitive therapy, psychotherapy, group therapy, and medication. Patients suffering from physical side effects of bulimia also need concurrent medical treatment. Psychotherapy is considered to be an important treatment but may not be sufficient by itself. It is generally most successful when coupled at least with behavior therapy and, ideally, with nutrition counseling.

Nutrition counseling teaches the bulimic the rationale for a balanced diet. Often women are surprised to learn that many of their symptoms are like those of the undernourished—preoccupation with food, irritability, anxiety, and depression—and that expanding their repertoires of "allowed" foods might actually make resisting binges easier.

Behavior therapy is aimed at identifying the triggers of binges and purges and teaching women new ways of reacting. The woman learns to note the specific triggers of a binge and the emotions involved, often recording this information so she can use the information to make plans for coping better the next time. (Record keeping also helps bulimics to pay attention to their behavior instead of grabbing for food automatically.)

Other behavioral activities include setting weekly targets (such as cutting down to two binges a week from five), stimulus control (such as limiting access to cues by keeping favorite binge foods out of the house), and response delay (such as taking a walk when the urge to eat hits, although doctors have to be careful about recommending exercise as an alternative behavior be-

cause some bulimics have a tendency to overdo strenuous exercise). In addition, behavior therapy can include assertiveness training (to help bulimics gain more control over their worlds) and relaxation training. The women are also helped to relearn their body signals for hunger and fullness and to distinguish between hunger and such emotions as anger and anxiety.

Cognitive therapy is essentially aimed at giving bulimics a new perspective on themselves—for instance, helping them to stop viewing their weight as the yardstick for measuring their worth—while psychotherapy's role is to help the bulimic unearth and work on her underlying emotional problems, such as depression and low self-esteem. With a therapist's support, bulimics who isolate themselves can be aided to gradually expand their horizons and gain self-confidence.

Many bulimics find group therapy and such self-help groups as Overeaters Anonymous to be quite valuable. However, self-help groups are unlikely to work magic on their own. These groups do, nevertheless, lend important social support to bulimics and can make them feel less alone.

Drug treatments—with antidepressants or anticonvulsants—have been used with some success in some bulimics. However, the value of such medicines is still being investigated.

Many bulimics are treatable on an outpatient basis. Those who are seriously endangering their health may need to be hospitalized for a time to stop their destructive behaviors and to initiate behavioral and other therapies in a controlled environment.

People who recognize that they are in trouble and want help can turn to a variety of resources. Among the voluntary organizations in the United States aimed at helping those with bulimia or anorexia are: ANAD (National Association of Anorexia Nervosa and Associated Disorders), in Highland Park, Ill.; AANA (American Anorexia Nervosa Association) in Teaneck, N.J.; and NAAS (National Anorexic Aid Society) in Columbus, Ohio.

Bulimia is a distressing and sometimes hard-to-treat eating disorder. But it is finally being recognized as a serious problem. Today clinicians and researchers are striving to find successful treatments. Bulimics can find hope in the successes that fellow sufferers have had; some bulimic patients reportedly have conquered the problem within a few months after beginning treatment.

Of course, in their struggles to overcome compulsive eating and vomiting or laxative abuse, bulimics will have slips now and then. And many will never be totally cured. But those who want to change and are patient can generally be helped. They can gain control over their actions. They can be helped to avoid becoming totally lost each time they trip up. And they can be taught to examine the causes of their lapses, to learn from such reflections, and to pick themselves up and go on with their lives.

# Ear Diseases and Hearing Disorders

The two inner ears are the essential organs of hearing and equilibrium. They are located in the temporal bones of the skull and connected to the brain by the auditory and vestibular divisions of the eighth cranial nerves. These labyrinthine structures can be affected by a number of diseases, disorders, and syndromes, which cause balance and hearing problems of varying degrees of severity.

In 1861, in an article in the *Medical Gazette* of Paris, the physician Prosper Ménière described patients who experienced bouts of severe dizziness that often resulted in their falling to the ground but with no loss of consciousness. Although this problem had been considered to be similar to a stroke, Ménière was the first to associate the dizziness with complaints noted by these patients of hearing loss and noises in the ear. He concluded that it was the ear and not the brain causing the problem.

The condition known as Ménière's disease is not common in the general population. The hearing loss and dizzy spells, however, are often severe enough to be disabling to those affected. Its cause is unknown. Although symptoms similar to those of Ménière's disease may develop years after a severe blow to the head or after an ear infection, more often there is no detectable antecedent. Further, there is no evidence that the condition is inherited or contagious. Children may develop Ménière's disease, but the illness is rare in that age group. Young adults and older persons are those typically affected. Generally the disease is unilateral; *i.e.*, in about 90% of cases it affects only one ear. The illness does not appear to be of a systemic or generalized nature and, excluding accidents that the victim may suffer during an attack, does not result in a fatal outcome.

## Symptoms of Ménière's disease

Although there are variations in the symptomatology, the usual patient with Ménière's disease complains of dizzy spells, hearing loss, and ear noises. The dizzy spells are episodic and are typically characterized as a sensation of vertigo—a sensation (or hallucination) that the environment is spinning about the patient or that the patient is spinning in the environment. A vertiginous episode is similar to that brought on intentionally by children at play when they suddenly stop after whirling around rapidly or being spun around in a circle. In Ménière's disease the vertigo is more severe and prolonged, usually lasting minutes to hours. During an attack the vertigo may be so severe that the patient cannot remain upright and seeks a reclining position with eyes closed. Nausea, vomiting, and sweating may accompany a severe vertiginous episode. An attack of Ménière's disease may resemble a convulsion by its

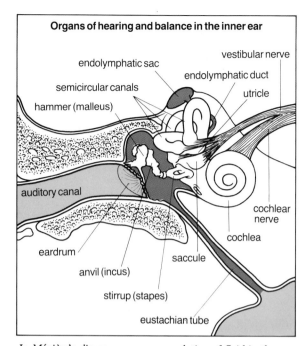

**Organs of hearing and balance in the inner ear**

*In Ménière's disease an overaccumulation of fluid in the spaces of the inner ear causes balance and hearing problems. In some patients this condition can be surgically corrected with a shunt to divert fluid from the delicate inner ear structures.*

sudden onset and the disorientation that it causes the patient but, unlike most seizure disorders, there is no loss of consciousness. An uncommon variation of the vertigo experienced by some patients with Ménière's disease is the so-called drop attack. These also occur without warning, and the patient suddenly loses balance and falls to the ground without the rotary sensation of vertigo.

The frequency of occurrence of the dizzy spells in Ménière's disease varies greatly from patient to patient and often within the same patient during the course of the disease. Although most patients have episodes only every few weeks or months, some have attacks several times a week. A patient may become functionally incapacitated when dizzy spells strike daily or a number of times every week.

Most patients with Ménière's disease also develop a hearing loss in the affected ear. The majority of cases involve only one ear, but some patients will have both ears affected. Early in the course of the disease the hearing loss fluctuates, with deterioration during the dizzy spells but improvement after the attack has passed. As time goes on and the disease progresses, the hearing loss often progresses to a degree of severity that compromises communication, and it ceases to fluctuate. An inability to discriminate speech sounds makes the use of a hearing aid less effective than would be desired.

Ear noises, or tinnitus, are usually present in Ménière's disease. The tinnitus varies from a low-pitched buzzing sound to a high-pitched hiss. It often worsens as the hearing loss progresses and can become highly disconcerting to the patient.

The three hallmark symptoms of Ménière's disease—vertigo, hearing loss, and tinnitus—are frequently accompanied by a fourth symptom, fullness in the ear. This pressure sensation is often described as similar to the feeling resulting from water or excessive ear wax blocking the ear canal. In Ménière's disease the sensation of fullness exists without any evident cause that can be detected by examining the patient. The ear canals are free of obstruction.

## The variable course of the disease

Predicting the natural history or prognosis of a patient with Ménière's disease is difficult. The disease is capricious and runs an unpredictable course. Episodes of vertigo may return at approximately equal intervals, or they may steadily increase in frequency to the point at which the patient becomes incapacitated. In others, for no apparent reason, the attacks may cease for many years or entirely, as if the disease somehow had burned itself out.

Examination of the inner ears of patients who have died and who had Ménière's disease has revealed the pathologic changes that take place in these ears (but not their cause). Under the microscope it can be seen that the delicate fluid-containing spaces of the inner ear have become distended, evidently owing to the excessive accumulation of fluid. Both the hearing and balance portions of the inner ear are affected, and there is degeneration of some of the sensory cells comprising the hearing mechanism. Usually no abnormality is found in the eardrum.

## Diagnosis of Ménière's disease

Since the pathological changes are limited to the inner ear, the diagnosis of Ménière's disease cannot be made by a physical examination, but such an examination is necessary to rule out the presence of other ear disorders that result in similar symptoms but produce changes in the eardrum. The disease is suspected when a patient has a history of symptoms typical of the disorder. At this time there is no single test that can prove that a patient has Ménière's disease. Rather, a battery of hearing, balance, blood, and X-ray examinations is usually necessary to exclude the presence of other disorders with similar symptoms. The abnormalities detected on various tests of hearing and balance function may be typical of those usually found in Ménière's disease and, coupled to a classical history of the symptoms, will lead the physician to a correct diagnosis. In general, a physician specializing in disorders of the ear (otologist or otolaryngologist) should be consulted if Ménière's disease is suspected.

## Medical management of Ménière's disease

Because of its unknown cause and unpredictable natural course, the treatment of Ménière's disease is difficult. Mild cases, with infrequent attacks, may need no treatment at all—only periodic examination by the physician. Unfortunately, no known medication will predictably and consistently prevent the major symptoms. In the past it was believed that a low-salt diet had a beneficial effect. Many physicians still prescribe such a diet as a possibly useful aid for this condition since there is no single effective treatment. Many and various types of drugs are prescribed, including hormones, diuretics, tranquilizers, and vitamin derivatives. Each medication has its advocates, but none has been proved to be of certain value. Probably the most widely prescribed and apparently effective drugs are those tranquilizers and antimotion-sickness drugs that are known to exert an influence on the inner ear. These drugs may not prevent attacks, but they can lessen the severity of the vertigo. They may be prescribed to be taken daily or at the first sign of an attack.

## Surgical methods

If medical management is ineffective, and if the severity of symptoms warrants it, then surgery may be considered. As in medical therapy, there is no uniformity in the surgical management of Ménière's. During the past two decades a variety of operations have been devised either to alter the function of the diseased ear or to destroy it. Various surgical approaches attempt to eliminate abnormal inner ear function while preserving useful hearing. Ultrasound irradiation and application of extreme cold (cryosurgery) to the inner ear have been used in this attempt but have been abandoned by most ear surgeons because of inconsistent results and unpleasant complications.

Surgery to shunt the inner ear fluid and prevent its accumulation would seem to be a reasonable approach to surgically managing Ménière's disease, and several operations have evolved to accomplish this end. The obstacles to devising a successful operation on the inner ear are its deeply recessed location within solid bone, the minute amounts of fluid it contains, and its fragility to surgical intervention. The shunt operations attempt to divert the excess inner ear fluid to the nearby spinal fluid, the recesses of the mastoid bone behind the ear, or from one portion of the inner ear to another. Some require the insertion of a tiny shunt tube or valve to control the fluid movement. The most common shunting operation performed today attempts to divert fluid from the endolymphatic sac (an inner ear structure that apparently acts as an absorber of inner ear fluid) to the spinal fluid or the mastoid. It is hoped that such an operation will prevent vertigo and progressive hearing loss while preserving the hearing that is present. In some cases the hearing may even improve following this type of surgery.

Unfortunately, none of the surgical operations that attempt to ameliorate the symptoms while preserving hearing produces consistent and predictable results. Approximately two of three patients operated on will be helped, but some will relapse and again develop symptoms as time passes. For those patients who do not respond to the more conservative surgical approaches, and for those with no inner ear function worth preserving, relief may be obtained by surgical operations that are of a more destructive nature. Labyrinthectomy is the surgical destruction of the inner ear, and it produces a complete loss of hearing and balance functions in the ear that undergoes surgery. Vestibular nerve section is another destructive surgical operation that cuts the nerve from the balance portion of the inner ear, thus eliminating the abnormal impulses sent to the brain from an afflicted ear. The hearing portion of the ear can sometimes be spared by a vestibular nerve section. For patients with incapacitating symptoms due to Ménière's (fortunately, a small minority), labyrinthectomy and vestibular nerve section offer the hope of symptomatic relief in approximately nine of ten cases, but loss of inner ear function is an inescapable result.

Currently, patients with Ménière's disease can be managed by supportive measures, conservative (shunting) operations, or destructive surgery to the inner ear and its nerves. Ongoing research is directed toward determining the cause of this disease and finding better surgical operations to control the disturbing symptoms while preserving the ear's function. In the 120 years that have intervened since Prosper Ménière described the disease, progress has been made in understanding the pathologic changes of the inner ear, but the cause of these changes and their definitive cure unfortunately remain elusive.

— *Edward L. Applebaum, M.D.*

# Endocrinology

Thirty-five years ago the pituitary gland was assumed to be the master gland of the human body. It produces hormones that control the functions of the thyroid and adrenal glands and of the ovaries and testes as well as hormones that are necessary for growth and lactation. But even at this time an English endocrinologist, Geoffrey Harris, was finding that when the pituitary gland, which lies below the base of the brain, was isolated from the brain, the pituitary hormones were either not secreted or secreted inaccurately in response to need. Consequently, he postulated that there must be substances that regulate pituitary gland function and that these substances are produced in the hypothalamus and carried to the pituitary through a system of small blood vessels. The hypothalamus is a small region of the brain lying just above the pituitary. It took medical scientists almost 30 years to isolate some of these substances from the hypothalamus and to explore their

clinical usefulness. Some of these hypothalamic hormones have been shown to induce the manufacture and secretion of pituitary hormones; others inhibit pituitary hormone release.

Recently two new releasing hormones of the hypothalamus have been characterized and tested. One is corticotropin-releasing factor (CRF); its function is to regulate the release of adrenocorticotropin (ACTH), the pituitary hormone that stimulates the adrenal gland to make and release cortisol (hydrocortisone). The other is growth hormone-releasing factor (GRF), which directs the pituitary to secrete growth hormone, the hormone that causes children to grow. A third substance, gonadotropin-releasing hormone, which was first structurally elucidated in 1975, has become a valuable agent for treating several serious disorders.

## A new insight into stress

The investigation of corticotropin-releasing factor has shed some light on an additional element of the human reaction to stress. Although it is difficult to define stress, most people recognize it intuitively and can appreciate what constitutes it at physical and emotional levels. Stress often results in a discharge of cortisol from the adrenal gland, setting in motion a variety of biochemical and physiological changes needed for the body to cope with emergencies. This effect of stress arises from the interpretation of stress by the brain and its resulting neural signals to the hypothalamus, which responds by releasing CRF.

The structure of CRF was deciphered in 1981 by Wylie Vale and his collaborators at the Salk Institute for Biological Studies in La Jolla, Calif. It was the third of the hypothalamic releasing hormones to be identified. Thyrotropin-releasing hormone, which ultimately controls thyroid gland function, and gonadotropin-releasing hormone, which regulates ovarian and testicular function, were isolated first and proved to be small peptides containing 3 and 12 amino acids, respectively. (Amino acids are the building blocks of protein, and small proteins are called peptides.) CRF, however, turned out to have 41 amino acids.

Once the structure of such a peptide is known, chemists can modify it. They can determine what portion of the peptide is necessary to carry out its action, prolong its effect by modifying the structure, and create antagonists and other substances capable of modifying or redirecting its effects. Such studies of CRF have been under way since its identification.

Some applications of this research are immediately apparent. First, CRF can be used to test the pituitary's ability to release ACTH. Several kinds of illnesses reduce this ability and, consequently, the body's ability to handle stress. Disastrous results might occur if severe stress such as surgery were imposed on such patients without the physician's knowledge of the problem. Second, the availability of CRF will make it possible to

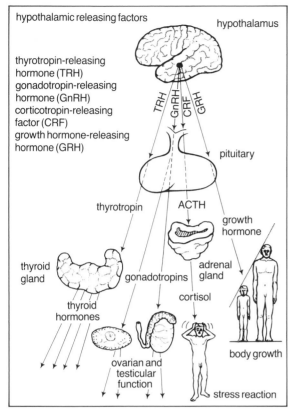

hypothalamic releasing factors      hypothalamus

thyrotropin-releasing
hormone (TRH)
gonadotropin-releasing
hormone (GnRH)
corticotropin-releasing
factor (CRF)
growth hormone-releasing
hormone (GRH)

TRH   GnRH   CRF   GRH

pituitary

thyrotropin    ACTH

growth
hormone

thyroid
gland     gonadotropins    adrenal
gland

thyroid
hormones

cortisol

body growth

ovarian and
testicular
function

stress reaction

*The brain regulates the release of a number of important hormones of the pituitary gland by means of factors secreted from the hypothalamus. The diagram above lists the four most important of these factors and summarizes the physiological effects of the pituitary hormones under their control.*

probe several illnesses, such as severe depression, and some types of schizophrenia in which the stress reaction is inexplicably activated. Third, CRF research may allow doctors to modify reactions to stress. It is known that when ACTH is released from the pituitary by CRF, some of the body's own opiates, the opioid peptides, are released simultaneously. These peptides have many functions, but one of them is to decrease the perception of pain and emotional stress. A modified CRF might emphasize opioid peptide release, thereby mitigating some of the effects of stress. Finally, the availability of synthetic CRF makes it possible to study the intricacies of the brain's regulation of stress reactions in a way never before possible.

## Hormonal control of growth

The proper amount of growth hormone, produced by the pituitary gland, is necessary for normal growth. In its absence a child fails to grow normally and becomes a dwarf. When a child develops a tumor of the pituitary gland that produces excess growth hormone, excessive growth in stature, or gigantism, results. In the adult

oversecretion of growth hormone produces acromegaly, a condition marked by enlargement and deformity of various parts of the body.

When endocrinologists developed the ability to measure small amounts of growth hormone in the blood, they soon found that this pituitary hormone also was regulated from the hypothalamus and that a putative growth hormone-releasing factor was the signal for that release. But the identification of GRF did not come easily. Unlike CRF, which was isolated from hypothalamus tissue collected from hundreds of thousands of sheep, GRF proved impossible to isolate from this source although its presence could be detected by biological tests. The breakthrough in this quest came with the realization that on rare occasions some cancerous growths unrelated to the pituitary gland caused acromegaly and did so by pouring a substance into the bloodstream that stimulated the pituitary gland to release excessive amounts of growth hormone. Cells from such cancers were induced to grow in tissue culture, providing an almost inexhaustible supply of their own growth hormone-releasing factor.

In 1982 Roger Guillemin, who received a Nobel Prize in 1977 for isolating thyrotropin-releasing hormone, and Vale, a previous collaborator of Guillemin, independently and almost simultaneously announced the isolation and structure of GRF. The two structures were not identical, although they were very close; one contained four more amino acids than the other. But this discrepancy does not mean that either scientist is wrong. Tumors manufacture and process proteins in a somewhat disorderly fashion compared with normal tissue, and their final products are not always identical to the products that are manufactured in the appropriate tissues. Furthermore, each tumor may vary in its processing actions. It is not yet known which, or indeed if, either structure is the same as that normally produced in the hypothalamus, but all the evidence suggests that they are closely related. The peptides con-

*The isolation of growth hormone-releasing factor has led to better understanding of the many types of dwarfism that affect some 60,000 in the U.S.*

Members of Little People of America; photograph, Wide World

tain either 40 or 44 amino acids; thus, GRF is about the same size as CRF, although it differs markedly in structure. An active GRF peptide has already been synthesized and tested in humans.

Much still needs to be learned about the mode of secretion of GRF. Medical scientists do know that growth hormone is secreted episodically and that the number of these secretory episodes increases at the beginning of sleep and with such stimuli as exercise, hypoglycemia (abnormally low levels of sugar in the blood), and a variety of drugs. It is presumed that each secretory episode of growth hormone is caused by a similar release of GRF from the hypothalamus.

As with CRF, the availability of GRF is leading to new diagnostic tests and perhaps will result in new forms of therapy. For example, it had never been known whether the ordinary, so-called pituitary type of dwarfism (there are many other types) was due to hypothalamic failure to make or release GRF or to pituitary problems in the manufacture of growth hormone. By analogy with other diseases, it was suspected that the first hypothesis was correct. Synthetic GRF has been administered to pituitary dwarfs, following the logic that if growth hormone in the blood increases after injection of GRF, the pituitary gland must be able to manufacture growth hormone after all. Most pituitary dwarfs that have been so tested have been shown in fact to be hypothalamic dwarfs because the pituitary gland can secrete growth hormone once GRF is provided.

Such studies have given some insight into a longstanding clinical problem. Some children who come from seriously disturbed home and family environments stop growing and show low levels of blood growth hormone. When they are placed in an environment where they feel secure and loved, blood growth hormone rises and growth resumes. This condition, which has been termed psychosocial dwarfism, is an extraordinary example of the way in which the brain can affect certain endocrine functions. When some of these stunted children were tested with GRF, the pituitary gland responded, showing that it can make growth hormone. It thus appears that the part of the hypothalamus making GRF is turned off by mechanisms of the central nervous system that are not yet understood.

Because there are many types of dwarfism, the coming availability of large amounts of growth hormone by means of genetic engineering techniques makes it imperative for the physician to be sure who will benefit from growth hormone treatment. This task will be accomplished in part with studies involving GRF.

GRF itself may prove to be a satisfactory treatment for dwarfism and is being tested for its usefulness in children with growth problems. Chemical modifications of GRF should result in more potent, longer acting preparations that will induce growth hormone release from the pituitary in a way that cannot be duplicated with exogenous growth hormone.

## Hormonal control of sexual function

The pituitary gland releases two hormones, called gonadotropins, that play major roles in controlling both male and female reproductive function. Their release is regulated in turn by gonadotropin-releasing hormone (GnRH), which is produced in the hypothalamus. In recent years investigations have shown that GnRH is normally secreted in pulses and that regular frequency of these pulses is essential if gonadotropins are to be released in a way that maintains the function of the ovaries and testes. GnRH given continuously to experimental female animals, for example, blocks ovulation by disrupting these pulsed signals to the pituitary, and longer acting synthetic derivatives of GnRH have been shown to exert the same effect in humans.

These findings are already proving useful in treating several diseases and have initiated a series of clinical trials of GnRH analogues as contraceptives. Women with endometriosis, a disease in which uterine tissue migrates out of the uterus and is displaced in the abdomen, suffer pain each month when estrogen hormones are produced by the ovaries. Stopping the ovarian secretion of estrogen has required either surgical removal of the ovaries or administration of drugs such as steroids that have unpleasant side effects. The long-acting analogues of GnRH can cause reversible cessation of ovarian function without side effects.

Puberty is believed to result from a maturing of the sexual control centers of the hypothalamus, during which time it begins to release GnRH. Some children go through puberty at a very early age, an event that can lead to such physical problems as short stature as well as psychological stress. Although several causes for precocious puberty are known, there has never been a successful treatment. In tests involving more than 50 children, GnRH analogues proved successful in reversing the process without any residual damage to the ovaries, testes, or pituitary.

Men with prostate cancer that has spread respond about 70% of the time to either castration or estrogen therapy. The first treatment, being mutilating, is unacceptable to some men, whereas the second treatment causes enlargement of the breasts and an increased risk of heart attack. Both treatments have in common the suppression of the secretion of the male hormone testosterone, which stimulates prostate cancer cells to grow more rapidly. Testosterone is produced by the Leydig cells of the testis. Since these Leydig cells are under the control of pituitary gonadotropins, it is possible to turn off the secretion of testosterone in men with prostate cancer by administration of long-acting GnRH. This result has led to a new successful treatment nearly free of side effects and available to men with advanced cancer of the prostate. Like its predecessors, however, this treatment makes testosterone unavailable to the body and thus causes impotence.

*—Mortimer B. Lipsett, M.D.*

# Special Report:
# Prostaglandins: New Keys to Disease and Health
by Omar Sattaur

Prostaglandins are often described as local hormones. Although they were discovered more than 45 years ago, it is only since the early 1970s that scientists have begun to understand the remarkably wide range of physiological roles that they play in the body. For the three key scientists of prostaglandin research, Sune Bergström, Bengt Samuelsson, and John Vane, the road to this understanding culminated in the 1982 Nobel Prize for Physiology or Medicine. For the world a biochemical treasure chest has been unlocked, in which some of the secrets of heart disease, pain, inflammation, and allergy have lain hidden for so long.

### Early prostaglandin research

The story begins in the mid-1930s, when it was discovered that human seminal fluid caused strong contractions in excised strips of uterine tissue. In 1936 a Swedish researcher, Ulf von Euler, found that the active substance of seminal fluid lowered blood pressure when injected into laboratory animals. Further experiments led him to propose that the active ingredient had the properties of a fatty acid, a member of a group of long carbon-chain molecules that serve as the building blocks of fats. He called the substance prostaglandin because he thought that it originated in the prostate gland.

At the renowned Karolinska Institute in Stockholm, Euler encouraged Bergström to determine the chemical structure of prostaglandin. Bergström found that prostaglandin is not one substance but a family of related ones. By 1963 he had discovered four members of the family, designated $PGE_1$, $PGE_2$, $PGF_{1\alpha}$, and $PGF_{2\beta}$. One year later Bergström and Samuelsson and, independently, D. A. van Dorp demonstrated that prostaglandins are made from fatty acids.

This fact accounts for the ubiquity of the prostaglandin family. The membranes of all cells in the body are composed primarily of molecules called lipids, which in turn are built from fatty acids absorbed from the diet. Thus, every cell in the body is potentially capable of making prostaglandins. Which prostaglandin is made depends partly on the particular fatty-acid precursor. Arachidonic acid is the most common fatty acid in cell membranes, and so its metabolites are the most widely studied.

For some time it was thought that arachidonic acid was converted directly to its prostaglandin end products and that $PGE_2$ and $PGF_{2\alpha}$ were the most important members of the prostaglandin family. But in 1974 Samuelsson managed to show the existence of two highly unstable intermediates called prostaglandin endoperoxides, which later proved to be of far more physiological importance than the stable prostaglandins.

The slightest stimulation, be it chemical, thermal, or mechanical, will persuade a cell membrane to part with some of its arachidonic acid. Once released, arachi-

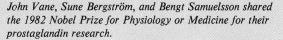

*John Vane, Sune Bergström, and Bengt Samuelsson shared the 1982 Nobel Prize for Physiology or Medicine for their prostaglandin research.*

Michael Grecco—Picture Group

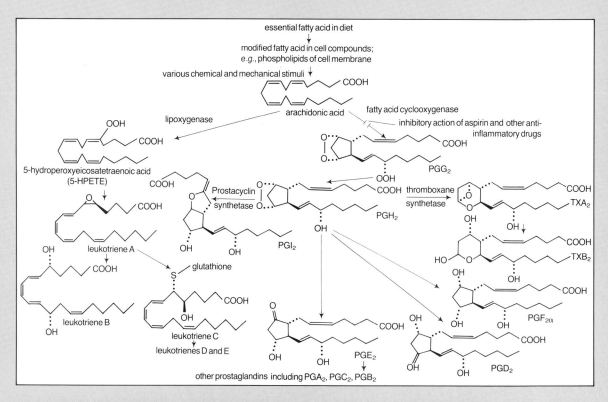

essential fatty acid in diet

modified fatty acid in cell compounds;
*e.g.*, phospholipids of cell membrane

various chemical and mechanical stimuli

arachidonic acid

lipoxygenase

fatty acid cyclooxygenase

inhibitory action of aspirin and other anti-inflammatory drugs

OOH

COOH

5-hydroperoxyeicosatetraenoic acid
(5-HPETE)

COOH

$PGG_2$

Prostacyclin synthetase

OOH

COOH

thromboxane synthetase

COOH

$TXA_2$

$PGH_2$

COOH

$TXB_2$

OH

leukotriene A

COOH

$PGI_2$

OH

OH

OH

$PGF_{2\alpha}$

OH

COOH

glutathione

OH

leukotriene B

OH

S

COOH

OH

leukotriene C

leukotrienes D and E

COOH

OH

OH

$PGE_2$

COOH

OH

OH

$PGD_2$

other prostaglandins including $PGA_2$, $PGC_2$, $PGB_2$

*The pathways leading to the synthesis of members of the prostaglandin family from arachidonic acid are diagramed. The fatty acid cyclooxygenase pathway leads to the endoperoxides $PGG_2$ and $PGH_2$ and on to prostacyclin, the thromboxanes, and several prostaglandins. The lipoxygenase pathway leads to the leukotrienes. Anti-inflammatory drugs such as aspirin bind chemically to cyclooxygenase, thus interfering with the production of all substances that lie on that enzymatic pathway.*

donic acid can be metabolized by either of two enzymes, lipoxygenase or fatty acid cyclooxygenase. Lipoxygenase begins the conversion of arachidonic acid to a family of substances known as leukotrienes. These are powerful mediators of the immune response and are thus of great importance in inflammation and allergy. Fatty acid cyclooxygenase converts arachidonic acid to the endoperoxides $PGG_2$ and $PGH_2$, which can then be converted to any of several prostaglandins. Moreover, these endoperoxides can be transformed by enzymes into two other highly potent and perhaps even more remarkable substances: prostacyclin ($PGI_2$) and thromboxane $A_2$ ($TXA_2$).

## The discovery of two potent substances

This last-mentioned junction of the prostaglandin pathway forms an important border between disease and health. Prostacyclin and $TXA_2$ have opposing properties, especially in their effects on blood platelets. Platelets are tiny disklike blood cells, and their aggregation at the site of an injury is crucial to the clotting process. Whereas $TXA_2$ causes platelets to stick together, prostacyclin is the most potent inhibitor of platelet aggregation known.

The first hint of $TXA_2$ emerged in 1969 when Vane and Priscilla Piper (then a colleague of Vane at the Royal College of Surgeons in England) discovered a substance released from the lungs of guinea pigs that caused strong contractions in strips of rabbit aorta. True to the style of scientists, they called the substance rabbit-aorta-contracting substance (RCS). In 1973 other researchers showed that RCS was released when platelets clumped together in the test tube. Originally it was suggested that the active substance was an unstable prostaglandin endoperoxide, $PGH_2$, but further studies of the properties of $PGH_2$ convinced Samuelsson that the degree of activity of RCS could not be wholly attributed to $PGH_2$. One year later he discovered $TXA_2$, which he found to cause strong contractions in rabbit aorta and to be a potent inducer of platelet aggregation as well. The mystery was solved: RCS turned out to be a mixture of prostaglandin endoperoxides and $TXA_2$.

In October 1975 another breakthrough was in the making. Vane, together with Salvador Moncada, Stuart Bunting, and Ryszard Gryglewski, began to look for $TXA_2$ in the walls of blood vessels. They reasoned that a substance so powerful in causing platelets to clump must somehow be involved in the events leading to the formation of blood clots. But they soon found that $TXA_2$ was not produced by vessel walls. Instead they discovered a substance, which they referred to as PGX, that had exactly the opposite effects of $TXA_2$.

Rather than constricting the muscles of the blood-vessel walls, PGX relaxed them and inhibited platelet aggregation more powerfully than any substance so far discovered. In fact, it was found to be the major metabolite of arachidonic acid in vascular tissue. In 1976, in close collaboration with scientists from the Upjohn Co. in Kalamazoo, Mich., Vane's group elucidated the structure of PGX. They renamed it prostacyclin and gave it the abbreviation $PGI_2$.

The discovery of the $TXA_2$ and prostacyclin pathways was exciting. Here was a neat illustration of the inherent beauty of nature. In the two related substances, with their opposing effects, scientists at last had a base from which to probe further the secrets of vascular diseases and, more importantly, the way in which the body of a healthy individual manages to stave off those diseases.

But the excitement by no means ended there. In 1971 at the Royal College of Surgeons, Vane found that he could explain the mechanism of action of aspirin, one of the oldest drugs known to Western medicine. Moreover, the discovery revealed a whole new area in which prostaglandins are involved.

Plant substances closely related to aspirin have been used for centuries as medicines. A popular folk remedy for pain relief, for example, was to drink the liquor in which strips of willow bark had been steeped. In the 70 years or so that pharmaceutical companies have been manufacturing a derivative of the active ingredient of willow bark as aspirin tablets—for treating a wide variety of afflictions from headache to chronic inflammatory diseases such as rheumatoid arthritis— no one had an inkling of how it worked.

Vane was able to show that aspirin inhibits fatty acid cyclooxygenase, the enzyme responsible for converting arachidonic acid to the prostaglandin endoperoxides. Aspirin, then, blocks the synthesis of both prostacyclin and $TXA_2$ and all their breakdown products.

## Links to human health and disease

The work linking aspirin and the prostaglandins implied that prostaglandins were important in all of the manifestations of disease that aspirin could treat, including pain, inflammation, and thrombosis (the formation of a clot in a blood vessel). Headaches are mostly caused by constriction of the blood vessels in the brain. It is easy to appreciate that inhibition of $TXA_2$ synthesis would be beneficial in treating headaches, because $TXA_2$ causes blood vessels to constrict. Yet the drug also blocks production of prostacyclin, which relaxes blood-vessel walls. So how does aspirin contrive its overall vasodilatory effect in the cerebral blood ves-

sels? The explanation has to do with the fact that the various sites of prostaglandin biosynthesis do not function the same way.

The distribution of the enzymes and other biosynthetic machinery needed for prostaglandin manufacture is such that different tissues will preferentially produce different prostaglandins upon stimulation. The cells of the blood-vessel wall—endothelial cells—do not contain thromboxane synthetase, the enzyme that converts $PGH_2$ to $TXA_2$, and so the major metabolite of arachidonic acid in endothelial cells is prostacyclin. Conversely, platelets lack prostacyclin synthetase, and so they preferentially synthesize $TXA_2$.

Platelets, like red blood cells (erythrocytes), are devoid of nuclei. Platelets have none of the genetic material normally present in the nucleus of every other cell type in the body, and consequently they are unable to make enzymes and other proteins. At the time of their production they are provided with a particular array of enzymes that lasts them the rest of their lives, which is about ten days.

Aspirin works by chemically binding to the active site of fatty acid cyclooxygenase, thus physically stopping the enzyme from reacting with arachidonic acid. Aspirin neutralizes the platelet's lifetime supply of the enzyme, making it unable thereafter to produce $PGH_2$, the precursor of $TXA_2$. Conditions are different, however, in the endothelial cell. The effects of aspirin last only as long as it takes the cell's protein-synthesis machinery to produce more cyclooxygenase. The net result is that prostacyclin and its vasodilatory effects continue after aspirin therapy, but $TXA_2$ production in the platelet ceases.

The anticlumping effects of aspirin on platelets have been recognized for some time, and many trials of aspirin as an antithrombotic agent have been carried out. But the drug has not proved very satisfactory, possibly because aspirin blocks only one of the pathways to platelet aggregation. The ideal antithrombotic agent would be a substance that directly inhibits $TXA_2$ or stimulates prostacyclin production.

Despite the elucidation of the prostaglandin pathways, scientists are still unable to describe how the delicate balance of $TXA_2$ and prostacyclin is maintained in health or any details of the cause of imbalance in cardiovascular disease. Recent research, however, has begun to point them in the right direction.

For example, Polish researchers have reported that platelets from rabbits with arteriosclerosis and from human beings who have survived a heart attack produce more $TXA_2$ than is normal. Their platelets are also abnormally sensitive to substances that stimulate aggregation. There is some evidence that the blood vessels of diabetics produce less prostacyclin than those of normal subjects, a finding that could help explain the circulatory disorders that arise as complications of diabetes.

The fatty plaques laid down on the vessel walls in atherosclerosis have been shown to contain large amounts of substances called lipid peroxides. Moncada and colleagues have demonstrated that one particular lipid peroxide is a potent and specific inhibitor of prostacyclin synthesis. Experts now feel that lipid peroxides in plaques could cause the formation of blood clots by blocking prostacyclin synthesis in the vessel wall without interfering with TXA$_2$ production by platelets.

Eskimos have long been known to have a remarkably low rate of heart disease, and much effort has been made to determine whether this is due to their diet. The fat consumed by Eskimos is rich in a fatty acid called eicosapentaenoic acid (EPA). EPA has been shown to inhibit platelet clumping in the test tube. Recent research has shown that Caucasians fed a mackerel diet for one week (mackerel is a rich source of EPA) had modified platelet activity. Their platelets clumped less readily, and they produced less thromboxane. Other researchers have confirmed the findings; for example, supplementing the diet with cod liver oil decreased platelet clumping and thromboxane synthesis. There is no longer any doubt that the prostaglandins play an intricate role in the development of arteriosclerosis and such afflictions as angina pectoris that involve a reduction of blood supply to the heart muscle. Many researchers are studying the effects of dietary supplementation with EPA on prostacyclin and TXA$_2$ metabolism.

Though the role of prostaglandins in the inflammatory response is not fully understood, it is clear that they are important. White blood cells (leukocytes), which collect at sites of inflammation in large numbers, produce TXA$_2$ and prostaglandin endoperoxides. Interaction with vessel walls could stimulate them to produce prostacyclin, and Vane's group has suggested that prostacyclin may be important in regulating the activity of leukocytes in inflammation. Stable end products of TXA$_2$ may have the ability to recruit cells of the immune system to the site of infection, thus facilitating the fight against invading cells. In autoimmune diseases such as rheumatoid arthritis, however, this is a hindrance rather than a help. Here there is no infection to fight, and the body in effect is harming itself. Aspirin and other agents that reduce inflammation are believed to work by inhibiting the synthesis of TXA$_2$ and its end products, thereby lightening the load of cells migrating to the inflamed area.

## Prostaglandins as therapeutic agents

Prostacyclin itself has been used therapeutically to treat peripheral vascular disease, which encompasses a number of conditions characterized by sluggish circulation, cold extremities, and pain. One problem with prostacyclin, however, is that it cannot be taken orally because it is metabolized long before it reaches its site

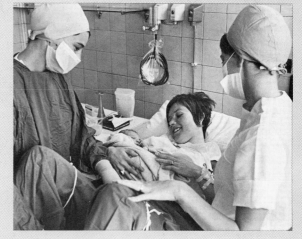

of action. Infusions of prostacyclin have given patients relief from their often disabling symptoms. Prostacyclin has been shown to relieve the pain in patients with angina, presumably by dilating their partly blocked coronary arteries and thus improving blood flow. Prostacyclin has also been suggested as a possible therapy for stroke, in which its ability to prevent platelet aggregation may prove useful.

One prostacyclin infusion already on the British market is known as Flolan. It is used primarily to prevent blood from clotting in machines that are used to bypass certain parts of the circulation; for example, in cardiopulmonary bypass operations, hemodialysis, and charcoal hemoperfusion.

The more "classic" prostaglandins are also being explored as therapeutic agents and tools in treating diseases of the heart and blood vessels and of other organs. One pharmaceutical company produces PGE$_1$ for use in treating peripheral vascular disease. PGE$_1$ is also being given to babies with congenital heart defects to improve their chances for surviving corrective surgery. Normally in the fetus a blood vessel known as the ductus arteriosus forms a temporary connection between the pulmonary artery and the aorta, allowing blood to bypass the nonfunctioning lungs. After birth, however, the ductus closes, partly in response to changing prostaglandin levels. In newborns with certain congenital heart problems, normal blood flow to the lungs is partially or completely blocked, and the ductus becomes the only way enough blood can get to the lungs. Administration of PGE$_1$ keeps the ductus open and prevents the baby's blood-oxygen level from becoming dangerously low until the defect can be corrected surgically.

Drug companies have also capitalized on the earliest property of prostaglandins to be recognized, that of causing uterine muscle to contract. PGE$_2$ is currently marketed for use in inducing labor. The drug is extremely effective, causing contractions gradually and inducing labor within 24 hours of administration.

224

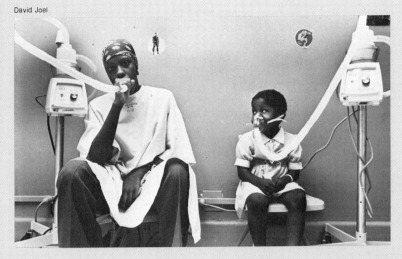

*Prostaglandins, which cause uterine muscles to contract, can be used to induce labor in pregnant women. As powerful mediators of the immune response, these substances may also prove useful in treating asthma and allergies.*

$PGF_{1\alpha}$ and $PGE_2$ are produced by the cells that line the stomach and reduce the amount of gastric acid produced there. The discovery of this function for some of the prostaglandins also explains why aspirin has such undesirable effects in the stomach, sometimes leading to peptic ulcers. While searching for a prostaglandin analogue that would inhibit platelet clumping but would be long lasting and orally active, scientists at the Wellcome Research Laboratories in the U.K. stumbled across a compound that shows great promise as an antiulcer drug. The compound seems to retain the inhibitory effects of prostacyclin on gastric-acid secretion but has lost all ability to modify platelets.

## Mediators of immune response

The other branch of the arachidonic-acid pathway, the one brought about by lipoxygenase and deftly elucidated by Samuelsson and Elias Corey at Harvard University, leads to the leukotrienes. Leukotrienes are known to be powerful mediators of the immune response. Therapeutically their major use may lie in fighting allergies, asthma, and chronic inflammatory diseases.

Leukotrienes are produced by cells of the immune system, especially those known as mast cells. Mast cells are particularly concentrated in the tissues of the lung and are intimately involved in hypersensitivity to allergens (irritating substances) such as pollen, which causes hay fever, and dusts and animal dander, which give rise to asthma. Hypersensitive individuals produce abnormally large amounts of a particular antibody known as immunoglobulin E (IgE), which comes to coat the outer surfaces of mast cells. Mast cells contain a gamut of highly potent chemicals that, upon release outside the cells, have profound effects on blood-vessel size, bronchial-airway size, heart rate, and other variables. A critical point is reached when enough allergen has found its way to the lungs to swamp the mast cells. The reaction of allergen with surface antibodies causes a conformational change in the mast cell membrane, the end result being the release of chemical mediators that produce the well-known symptoms of particular allergies. For example, one mediator called histamine causes bronchial airway constriction and is one of the reasons why asthmatics wheeze.

By the late 1930s biochemists knew that mast cells contain a powerful substance that causes some hypersensitive individuals to suffer a life-threatening condition known as anaphylactic shock. Anaphylaxis is characterized by a dramatic fall in blood pressure, impaired respiration, collapse, and finally death. They called the element responsible for anaphylactic shock slow reacting substance of anaphylaxis (SRS-A). Forty years later it was Samuelsson who showed that SRS-A was in fact a mixture of leukotrienes C, D, and E.

Some leukotrienes show chemotactic properties; that is, the ability to recruit to the site of infection other immune-system cells that engulf and destroy invading foreign cells. Since that discovery scientists have been looking for a compound that would inhibit both the lipoxygenase and cyclooxygenase pathways and so prove useful in combating inflammatory diseases. Scientists at the Wellcome Research Laboratories have synthesized a compound they believe has the desired properties, but the drug must undergo further tests before it can be marketed.

## A bright outlook

After decades of research, prostaglandins have shown themselves to be among the body's most transitory yet most potent agents, producing a broad array of effects that involve virtually every biologic function. Inhibition of their natural production is now known to be the mechanism of action for some of modern medicine's most widely used drugs, knowledge that can be applied to the design of even more effective pharmaceuticals. A few prostaglandins are now on the market, and scientists in institutes and drug companies around the world are investigating a much larger number, including synthetic analogues, that might be better suited to particular therapeutic purposes.

225

# Environmental Health

Dioxin, an undesirable by-product in the manufacture of herbicides, disinfectants, and other chemicals, is the most toxic of all man-made substances. Compared with the most powerful naturally occurring poisons, it ranks fourth, just below the bacterial toxins responsible for botulism, tetanus, and diphtheria. A portion of Seveso, an Italian town near Milan, has been cordoned off since 1976, when a chemical-plant explosion contaminated the area with dioxin. Recently more than a hundred sites in Missouri have been found or are suspected to have dioxin-contaminated soil. The most publicized of these locations, the small town of Times Beach, has been purchased by the U.S. government, and its citizens offered the option of relocation. Dioxin has also been detected in fish and in river water from Michigan, in other U.S. communities, and in Vietnam. The extraordinary toxicity of this chemical, its high stability, its insolubility in water, and its widespread presence make the problem of protecting people especially serious and difficult.

## What is dioxin?

Although the term dioxin has become a popular synonym for one specific dioxin, 2,3,7,8-tetrachlorodibenzo-$p$-dioxin, technically it refers to any of a group of chemical compounds called dibenzo-$p$-dioxins. Structurally the dioxins consist of two benzene rings connected by a pair of oxygen atoms. Each of the eight carbon atoms on the rings that are not bonded to oxygen can bind with hydrogen atoms or atoms of other elements. By convention these positions are assigned the numbers 1 through 4 and 6 through 9. The dioxins of greatest concern carry chlorine (Cl) atoms at these positions. Theoretically, 75 possible combinations, called isomers, can be formed by adding one or more chlorine atoms. There are 22 possible arrangements for dibenzo-$p$-dioxins that contain four chlorine atoms; these 22 isomers constitute the family of tetrachlorodibenzo-$p$-dioxins (TCDD's). The most toxic dioxin is a member of this group, with chlorine atoms at the 2, 3, 7, and 8 positions. This isomer, 2,3,7,8-TCDD, is extremely stable chemically even at temperatures as high as 700° C (1,290° F), possibly because of its symmetrical structure. Moreover, this isomer is virtually insoluble in water and in most organic compounds but is soluble in oils. It is this combination of properties that allows dioxin in soil to resist dilution with rainwater and causes it to avidly seek and enter fatty tissue in the body if it is absorbed.

Dioxin serves no useful purpose but is formed as an undesirable by-product during the synthesis of 2,4,5-trichlorophenol and some other useful compounds. For example, if the mixture of reactants used to synthesize 2,4,5-trichlorophenol exceeds 180° C (360° F), an exothermic (heat-generating) reaction occurs, and some

*When Environmental Protection Agency workers tested the soil in Times Beach, Mo., they found dioxin levels so high that the U.S. government offered to buy the town's 800 homes and relocate its 2,000 frightened residents.*

dioxin is formed. In fact, many accidental releases of dioxin have resulted from such overheating, producing a runaway explosive reaction. 2,4,5-trichlorophenol serves as a raw material for making the herbicides Silvex and 2,4,5-T (2,4,5-trichlorophenoxyacetic acid). The latter compound is a major active ingredient of Agent Orange, a defoliant formerly used in Vietnam by the U.S. military and in the U.S. on railroad, highway, and power-line rights-of-way and in forested areas to kill unwanted vegetation. 2,4,5-trichlorophenol is also used in the production of hexachlorophene, an antibacterial agent formerly used in deodorants and soaps but banned since 1972. If 2,4,5-trichlorophenol is contaminated with dioxin during manufacture, then dioxin appears in these end products.

The toxicity of dioxin renders it capable of killing some species of newborn mammals and fish at levels of five parts per trillion (or one ounce in six million tons). Less than two millionths of an ounce will kill a mouse. Its toxic properties are enhanced by the fact that it can pass into the body through all major routes of entry, including the skin (by direct contact), the lungs (by inhaling dust, fumes, or vapors), or through the mouth. Entry through any of these routes contributes to the total body burden. Dioxin may affect the skin upon contact, then enter the blood and move into the fat and fatty tissues of many organs. An autopsy of a resident of Seveso who died some months after exposure showed the highest concentrations in fat tissue, with decreasing levels in the pancreas, liver, lungs, kidneys, and brain. In animals dioxin also appears to enter the thymus and the adrenal gland, and it has been found in human breast milk.

## What makes dioxin so toxic?

A great deal of scientific information on the mechanisms of dioxin's toxicity has been gathered from numerous studies of laboratory animals and human exposure victims. One productive approach in these studies has been to look at the way in which dioxin enters a cell and what it does once it gets in. Contained in cell membranes are protein molecules, called receptors, that normally function to move substances into the cell. Dioxin avidly binds to these receptors and, as a result, is rapidly transported into the cytoplasm and nucleus of the cell, where it causes changes in cellular processes. Experiments in animals suggest that after entering the cell, dioxin affects tiny protein strands called smooth and rough endoplasmic reticula. These structures participate in the synthesis of a large number of enzymes that, in minute quantities, regulate important chemical reactions in the body, including the production, conversion, and storage of proteins, carbohydrates, and fats. Called mixed-function oxidases, these enzymes are also responsible for the breakdown of some sex hormones, drugs, and other substances, thus enabling their removal from the body.

Mixed-function oxidases are produced in many organs of the body, including the liver, skin, kidneys, lungs, and those white blood cells called lymphocytes. They appear only when they are needed and are "turned on" by the presence of various other chemicals called inducers. Dioxin is the most potent enzyme inducer known. It has long been recognized that increased production of some of these enzymes greatly increases the cancer rate in animals exposed to carcinogens. Another potent enzyme inducer, 3-methylcholanthrene (3-MC), has been used for years in cancer research because of its potency as an inducer. Dioxin is 30,000 times more potent an inducer than 3-MC, and its effect is many times longer lasting—further reasons for its extraordinary toxicity. In addition, the presence of chlorine atoms at key locations in dioxin's structure apparently protects it from some of the major biochemical breakdown processes by which the body disposes of toxins.

The flood of enzymes stimulated by dioxin leads to the malfunction of many organs and to the excessive destruction and excretion from the body of certain essential chemicals such as estrogens. On the other hand, chemical building blocks pile up in the body because some basic processes cannot go forward to completion. For example, iron and compounds called porphyrins, both of which are components of hemoglobin, may accumulate in the blood and tissues.

## Significance of animal studies

Because information about the direct effects of dioxin on people has been limited primarily to studies of victims of inadvertent exposure, investigators have relied heavily on monkeys, guinea pigs, rats, mice, and other laboratory animals to gain a better idea of what dioxin does to the human body. While results from animals vary somewhat among various species because of differences in enzyme systems or in the degree of enzyme induction, many common effects have been found. These consistencies increase the likelihood that other species, including human beings, may be similarly affected.

In most species, except in cases in which very large doses were administered, the effects of dioxin appeared only after considerable delay, possibly because of the time needed for enzyme induction to occur. In

Allan Tannenbaum—Sygma

*In the summer of 1983, high levels of dioxin were discoverd in a Newark, N.J., neighborhood near a chemical plant that once produced the deadly herbicide Agent Orange. A local swimming pool was closed because of dioxin contamination, and agents from the EPA went door-to-door collecting household refuse to be analyzed for the possible presence of dioxin.*

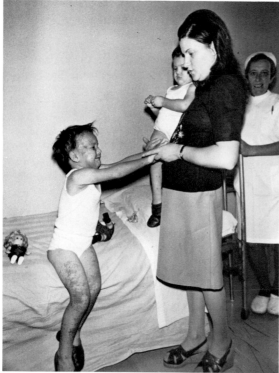

*In 1976 an explosion covered the town of Seveso, Italy, with a toxic dioxin cloud. Today former Seveso residents continue to suffer from a variety of skin disorders.*

every species studied, dioxin destroyed testicular tissue and tissue of the thymus gland. In some animals the skin, liver, and kidneys and the endocrine, gastrointestinal, cardiac, and central and peripheral nervous systems were affected. In some animals the immune defense system was suppressed. Birth defects, particularly cleft palate and neural tube abnormalities; embryotoxic effects, including abortion, miscarriage, and resorption of the fetus; and mutagenic effects appeared in a number of species. Many species experienced a striking increase in cancer incidence, particularly when dioxin was administered with chemicals known to be cancer initiators.

That dioxin increases the chances of cancer, birth defects, and genetic mutations in any species is of particular concern. It is often difficult, if not impossible, to determine the least amount of a substance sufficient to cause genetic abnormalities because of the long latent period between exposure and the appearance of disease. Consequently, the question shifts from finding a level of exposure where no one is affected to finding a socially acceptable level. The Centers for Disease Control (CDC) in Atlanta, Ga., has recommended that exposure to dioxin be limited to less than one part per billion, based on an estimate that a group of one million people exposed to this concentration in their lifetimes would experience one excess cancer death.

## Human experience with dioxin

Most people known to have been heavily exposed to dioxin have been the victims of industrial mishaps involving the explosion of a reactor vessel or a blown safety valve. Workers in the vicinity at the time of the incident or who came in afterward to clean up were usually exposed for a short time to high concentrations. In the past 30 years more than 200 such episodes have occurred worldwide. The first happened at a Monsanto plant in Nitro, W.Va., in 1949, when 228 workers were reported to have been exposed following an explosion of a reactor vessel.

Other accidents include those in the BASF plant in Ludwigshafen, West Germany, in 1953; the Rhone Poulenc plant in Grenoble, France, in 1956 and again in 1966; and Coalite & Chemical Products Ltd. in Derbyshire, England, in 1968. Another such incident occurred at the Philips-Duphar plant in Amsterdam in 1963. Decontamination was apparently impossible at the BASF and Philips-Duphar plants, which were dismantled, put into ships, taken out into the Atlantic Ocean, and sunk. In another instance a plant was dismantled and buried after more than two years of attempts to remove the dioxin. Later a large stainless steel vat salvaged from that plant was installed at a new site over a three-day period by two workers who had never entered the old plant. Both of the workers developed disease due to dioxin, and the son of one worker acquired a severe skin disorder called chloracne, one of the manifestations of dioxin-caused disease, from wearing his father's scarf.

Other workers exposed to lower levels of dioxin over longer periods of time—ranging from months to many years—have been examined and also were found to have disease. They include groups from the Diamond Alkali plant in Newark, N.J., a plant in Spolana, Czech., the Dow Chemical plant in Midland, Mich., and the Monsanto plant in Nitro, W.Va.

A report of dioxin-induced disease in three laboratory workers in England was published in 1975. Their exposure was only to dioxin, and they knew of its toxicity. In spite of the fact that they took extreme precautions, which included the use of ventilation hoods and protective clothing, all three developed various symptoms and findings associated with dioxin exposure, including abdominal pain, excessive fatigue, decreased ability to concentrate, irritability, blurred vision, decreased muscle coordination, and excessive oiliness or severe acne of the skin. In addition, all experienced elevated serum cholesterol levels that persisted for at least three years. One showed no symptoms until three years after exposure, a delay also noted in some of the Czech workers.

In January 1979, 47 railroad workers sent to clean up a chemical spill in Sturgeon, Mo., came in contact with chemicals that included phenol, orthochlorophenol, and dioxin. The dioxin was present in concentrations

228

ranging from 22 to 36 parts per billion, and exposure ranged between 8 hours and 90 days. Several extensive examinations over a three-year period uncovered disorders of all major organ systems. Laboratory abnormalities were similar to those found in other exposed groups, and again in some individuals disease did not appear until more than two years after exposure.

Perhaps the most publicized industrial accident involving dioxin occurred in 1976 near Seveso, Italy. The source was a chemical factory belonging to Hoffman-La Roche that produced trichlorophenol. An accidental rise in temperature in a reactor vessel caused a safety valve to open, sending a cloud of dioxin-contaminated trichlorophenol into the air. Within three weeks 700 residents had to be evacuated after thousands of small animals, birds, and insects were found dead. More than two-thirds of these people showed signs of dioxin poisoning. Contaminated crops within a region extending five miles south of the plant were burned. The area around the plant was divided into three zones based on the levels of contamination thought to be present. As of 1983 the most heavily contaminated zone remained fenced in and uninhabited.

Of more imminent concern than the occupational exposures is the growing realization that land sites and entire communities have been contaminated by the improper disposal of chemical waste containing dioxin. In 1971 waste oil was sprayed in several horse arenas in eastern Missouri to keep down dust. Within weeks hundreds of rodents, insects, dogs, cats, and birds were found dead in and around the arenas. More than 80 horses that had stood or were ridden in the arenas became ill, and within 16 months most developed multiorgan disease, became paralyzed, suffered extraordinary wasting, and died. Children and adults also appeared to be affected.

The oil was eventually recognized as the source of the problem, and several inches of topsoil were removed from the arenas. By the time dioxin was identified as the toxic agent (one arena showed a concentration of 33,000 parts per billion), some of the excavated soil had been used as landfill for homes in other areas of Missouri. In addition, the same dioxin-contaminated oil was sprayed on dusty roads in Times Beach and apparently hundreds of other areas in Missouri. It was later found that the waste oil had been mixed with thick, oily, dioxin-contaminated sludge from a plant that had manufactured herbicide and hexachlorophene. In 1983 Times Beach residents were told that the U.S. government would purchase their 800 homes from a "superfund" established in 1980 to finance toxic-waste cleanups.

Dioxin has also been found in soil and streams surrounding a waste-disposal plant in Arkansas and has been detected in fish taken in parts of New York and in fish and water from the Tittabawassee and Saginaw rivers in Michigan. High dioxin levels continue to plague the Love Canal area of Niagara Falls, N.Y., a residential community built on land used as a chemical-waste dump in the 1940s and 1950s. In 1979 the U.S. Environmental Protection Agency identified 31 cities whose chemical industries were likely to be a source of dioxin-contaminated waste.

## Dioxin and Vietnam

About 20 million gal of phenoxy herbicides were among those used to defoliate vast areas of tropical forest in Vietnam between January 1962 and September 1971 in an operation called Ranch Hand. Various combinations of the phenoxy herbicides 2,4-D (2,4-dichlorophenoxyacetic acid) and 2,4,5-T, the latter contaminated with varying amounts of dioxin, received names according to the color coding on the barrels in which they were shipped. Approximately 276,000 gal of Agents Green, Purple, and Pink were spread over 2.5 million ac of forest between 1962 and 1964. The measured levels of dioxin were as high as 45,000 parts per billion in some samples.

From 1964 until 1971 the major defoliant used was Agent Orange and a modification called Orange Two. During this time 11,250,000 gal of Orange were spread over five million acres of land. The stated military objectives of forest defoliation were both offensive and defensive: to increase visibility for air strikes and monitoring of enemy troop movements and to clear land along highways, loading zones, and military bases used by U.S. and South Vietnamese forces. A third objective was to destroy crops in order to reduce food sources in areas controlled by Viet Cong.

About 2.6 million U.S. military personnel served in Vietnam between Jan. 1, 1965, and March 31, 1973, the time of heaviest use of Agent Orange. Those likeliest to have been exposed include crew members of helicopters used for spraying and those who loaded, unloaded, and serviced the crafts. In addition, soldiers spraying from backpacks, boats, and trucks had potentially heavy exposure. Because of the persistence of

| Variation among species of lethal dioxin dose | |
| --- | --- |
| animal | LD$_{50}$ ($\mu$g per kg body weight)* |
| guinea pig | 1 |
| rat (male) | 22 |
| rat (female) | 45 |
| monkey | less than 70 |
| rabbit | 115 |
| mouse | 114 |
| dog | more than 300 |
| bullfrog | more than 500 |
| hamster | 5,000 |
| *LD$_{50}$ = median lethal dose | |

Poland and Knutson, *Annual Review of Pharmacology & Toxicology*, 1982

dioxin, personnel in camps where perimeters were sprayed and others on foot and in vehicles in forested areas that had been sprayed were also exposed.

The effect of exposure to dioxin on the health of Vietnam veterans has yet to be adequately assessed. Various governmental agencies have been given responsibility for carrying out a study. Most recently this responsibility has shifted from the Veterans Administration (VA) to the CDC. Meanwhile, more than 16,000 veterans have filed with the VA for disability benefits for health problems claimed to be related to exposure to Agent Orange. Studies to examine the effect of Agent Orange on the Vietnamese people are also being carried out.

## How dioxin affects human health

The first human health problem from dioxin to be noted was chloracne, a particularly unsightly form of acne with large whiteheads and blackheads, pustules, and sometimes abscesses. Although chloracne was initially thought to be an essential manifestation of dioxin poisoning, more recent studies in Seveso and of the Sturgeon railroad workers revealed that only about 15% of those affected developed chloracne, usually younger people and especially those with a history of teenage acne. This condition can be very persistent; some victims of the 1949 Nitro accident who developed chloracne still had it 34 years after exposure.

Other skin effects include increased pigmentation and increased facial hair. Skin cancer has also been reported. In the railroad workers, for example, 15% developed one or more skin cancers within three years after exposure.

The liver is a major organ for the synthesis and processing of proteins, fats, and carbohydrates. It also plays a major role in detoxifying and removing unwanted substances from the body. For these reasons it is particularly affected by dioxin. Many studies have revealed abnormal enzyme elevations resembling those seen in hepatitis; in some cases these abnormalities persisted for years. A disturbing finding in studies of both humans and other animals was the profound derangement of lipid metabolism with raised levels of triglycerides and cholesterol, both of which can be harmful. Also noted were decreases in high-density lipoproteins, which are beneficial to the body. Individuals with this lipid pattern are much more prone to atherosclerosis, or hardening of the arteries, stroke, and heart disease.

Dioxin also seriously affects human reproductive organs and their function. Although few studies exist of dioxin's effects on male reproduction, some men, including Vietnam veterans, have reported impotence and loss of libido. More than 40% of the Sturgeon railroad workers were found to have abnormally low sperm counts and high percentages of inactive sperm. Eighteen of the 47 workers had abnormally low levels of testosterone, the male hormone responsible for libido and secondary sex characteristics.

Studies of the offspring of people exposed to dioxin-containing herbicides in Vietnam and Australia revealed increased abnormalities of extremities, particularly fingers and toes; neural tube defects; and other birth abnormalities. Abnormal births have been reported among the families of exposed U.S. Vietnam veterans. One study of women exposed to herbicides in a town in Oregon revealed abnormally high miscarriage rates: 130 per 1,000 births, compared with 46 per 1,000 births for a similar town not exposed and used as a control. These rates peaked dramatically each June for six years, about two to three months after the spring spraying of 2,4,5-T in the area.

In studies of the Sturgeon workers, the genitourinary system also appeared to be affected. Some of these abnormalities might have been related to the toxic effects of phenol and orthochlorophenol present with the dioxin. Difficulties included inflammation, obstructed urine flow from the bladder, and, in some persons, loss of sensation of the need to urinate.

Studies carried out in Seveso and among the Sturgeon railroad workers revealed suppression of the immune system in both groups. In a large percentage of Sturgeon workers, activity of white blood cells called T-lymphocytes was particularly suppressed. T-lymphocytes play a major part in the development of immunity against disease and in preventing cancer by destroying newly formed cancer cells.

The central and peripheral nervous systems are also major targets of dioxin. Many of the reports of exposures document symptoms of increased and long-lasting irritability, severe headaches, profound fatigue, sleep disturbances, and in some cases seizures. A major symptom in these groups was depression, which appeared to be chemically mediated and not of psychological origin. Memory loss was also a significant finding in some of the studies. An extensive battery of neurobehavioral tests given to the railroad workers revealed many with central nervous system dysfunction.

Effects on the peripheral nervous system manifested themselves as numbness and tingling in the fingers and toes. Nerve damage, evidenced by slowed and impaired transmission of electrical impulses in the nerves, was found in some people along with abnormal reflexes and weakness of the extremities.

Joint stiffness and weakness of the muscles also were common in many dioxin victims. Loss of muscular strength, particularly in the extremities, after brief work suggested impaired energy transfer mechanisms, which are essential to muscle function. One component of the cell affected by dioxin is the mitochondrion, a structure that has responsibility for processing chemicals to provide ready energy to muscles. In experimental animals mitochondria were shown to be swollen and damaged after exposure to dioxin, a finding that may

From a study of dioxin-exposed railroad workers by S. A. Conibear and B. W. Carrow, 1982

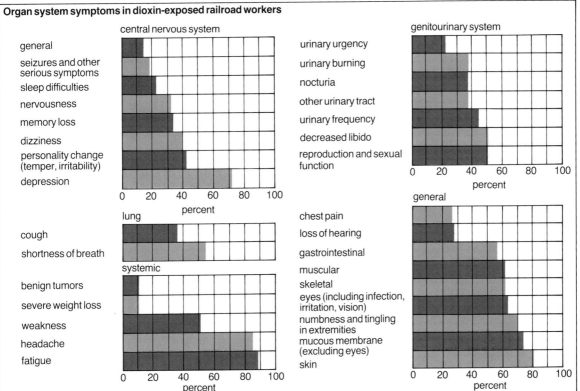

**Organ system symptoms in dioxin-exposed railroad workers**

help explain the reason for muscular weakness.

Other organs and tissues affected by dioxin include the blood, heart, lungs, kidneys, and mucous membranes of the eyes and nose. In some exposed groups pancreatic function appeared to be impaired, resulting in an increased incidence of diabetes.

Dioxin also appears to be linked to an increased incidence of cancer in exposed humans. One study carried out in Vietnam showed an increase in primary liver cancer. A significant increase in soft-tissue sarcoma, a form of cancer, was found in Swedish workers exposed to 2,4,5-T. An increase in cancer rates among BASF workers was also noted years after the accident there. Because cancer frequently has a long latency period between the time of exposure and the appearance of disease, long-term observation of exposed populations is necessary, particularly in view of animal studies showing dioxin's potency as a cancer promoter and its ability to suppress the immune system.

### The work ahead

Dioxin's stability, toxicity, and potential for wide dissemination in the environment make decontamination a difficult problem. Two proved methods, irradiation and incineration, are workable only under certain circumstances. Stores of Agent Orange and Orange Two that remained after the Vietnam conflict were eventually taken to Johnstown Island in the Pacific, put on an in-

cinerator ship, taken out to sea, and burned. This method was costly and was possible only because the chemical was in a reasonably concentrated, liquid form. Incineration is not practical for treating contaminated water, buildings, or tons of soil. Chemical degradation methods are being explored but are still in the laboratory stage. There is currently no good, acceptable method for disposing of or neutralizing dioxin in most situations.

Much more information needs to be gathered regarding nearly every facet of the dioxin problem. Efforts are being made to identify other communities that may have been exposed to dioxin so that measures can be taken to protect individuals living in them. In the U.S., administrators and legislators at various governmental levels are under pressure to toughen inspection and enforcement programs aimed at the producers and transporters of hazardous waste and to improve methods for identifying sites where dioxin is likely to be created.

A better elaboration of toxic pathways may ultimately enable medical researchers to block or neutralize dioxin or remove it from the body. For example, it has been found that animals placed on low-iron diets appear to be somewhat less affected than those with normal iron stores. Current treatment is supportive and consists mostly of attempts to protect those organs that have been affected or may be affected in the fu-

231

ture. Dioxin victims have been advised to stop smoking and to avoid excessive exposure to sunlight in order to lower their cancer risk. Doctors have also recommended diets low in cholesterol and triglycerides to reduce the levels of these lipids in the blood. Such preventive medicine is seen as a stopgap until such time as measures to block or remove dioxin can be developed.

*— Bertram W. Carnow, M.D.*

# Eye Diseases and Visual Disorders

Optically the eye is like a camera. In order to focus images on film a camera requires a lens. The eye likewise contains a transparent lens, called the crystalline lens, to focus clear images on the retina. The transparency of the crystalline lens is essential to vision; the loss of lens transparency is caused by a cataract. There are really two definitions of cataract: any opacity in the crystalline lens, or one or more opacities in the axial, or visual, part of the lens causing decreased vision. The first is a broader, structural definition; the second is actually the definition of cataract disease and refers to visual impairment due to progressive clouding of the visual portion of the lens.

Most cataracts develop as a part of aging; these are commonly called senile cataracts. Decreased vision due to cataracts (less than 20/30 visual acuity, *i.e.,* seeing at 20 ft what a normal eye can see at 30 ft) was found in 41% of individuals 75 years old or older who were tested in an extensive study of the population of Framingham, Mass., conducted by the U.S. National Institutes of Health. Other types of cataracts, such as those present at birth or in young adults, are rare.

## Diabetes and cataracts

Diabetes mellitus, characterized by abnormally high levels of glucose in the blood, occasionally causes cataracts in young individuals. More often, however, diabetes accelerates the development of senile cataracts such that they appear at an early age. The natural progression of senile cataracts has been determined by classifying the various cataract stages, which range from a mild initial stage through several degrees of advancement to complete opacity. When this classification was applied in studies of nondiabetic and diabetic persons, it was found that nondiabetic cataracts advance from the initial stages at an average age of 61 years to a very advanced stage at age 75. Diabetic cataracts appear earlier, at an average age of 58, and progress faster to dense cataracts by age 66. Thus, accelerated development of diabetic cataracts results in earlier visual impairment and the need for surgical intervention at an earlier age.

In juvenile diabetes in humans and in diabetic animals, lowering blood glucose levels with insulin delays or prevents the formation of cataracts. In older humans with diabetes, however, the risk of developing cataracts increases with the duration of the diabetes and to some extent with increased blood glucose levels. Because of the chronic nature of diabetes it is recommended that blood glucose levels be controlled consistently (kept under 150 mg per 100 ml of plasma) to prevent cardiovascular, retinal, or nerve complications. Adequate diabetes control with insulin injections, oral hypoglycemic agents, or diet may actually prevent most complications of diabetes, including cataracts.

Specific drugs have been shown to delay or prevent the formation of cataracts in diabetic animals. These agents prevent the buildup of sorbitol, a toxic sugar alcohol derived from glucose, by inhibiting the enzyme that normally brings about this conversion. Several such inhibitors have been found well-tolerated by humans: aspirin, indomethacin, oxyphenbutazone, and sulindac. Their clinical efficacy against diabetic senile cataracts remains to be determined. In one recent study diabetics in the 60–85 age group who received high dosages of aspirin for prolonged periods of time developed fewer cataracts (20% prevalence) than those who did not receive aspirin (78% prevalence).

## Visual disorders caused by cataracts

It is unusual for senile cataracts to develop equally in both eyes. If a cataract is present in only one eye, it may not be noticed unless the unimpaired eye is covered accidentally or during an eye examination. In an individual whose occupation does not require vision with two eyes for depth perception, a cataract in one eye may represent only a mild nuisance at work or while driving. Because senile cataracts progress slowly, it may be several years before vision is sufficiently impaired in both eyes to require surgery. However, when cataracts do affect both eyes, they may impair daily work, reading, and even manual coordination and spatial orientation. Viewing in bright light may accentuate the impairment, and thus individuals living in tropical sunny regions or reading under strong illumination may notice the problem comparatively early. This stage is reached when visual acuity in the affected eye falls below the 20/70–20/100 level.

Advanced cataracts must be removed surgically. Such optical devices as eyeglasses, contact lenses, or surgically inserted lens replacements (intraocular lenses) must be used if clear vision is to be restored. None of these corrections, however, can perform as well optically as the natural crystalline lens, even when slight opacities are present. Furthermore, their use presents new visual problems, including color and space distortions and optical aberrations.

## Surgical removal of cataracts

There are two types of operations for cataracts. In the first the entire lens is removed, including its surrounding elastic capsule (intracapsular extraction). In the

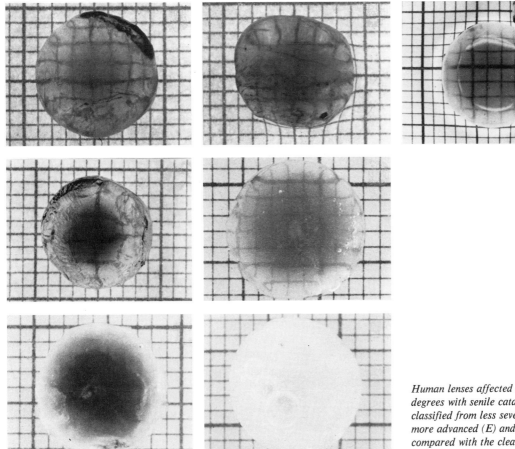

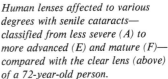

*Human lenses affected to various degrees with senile cataracts—classified from less severe (A) to more advanced (E) and mature (F)—compared with the clear lens (above) of a 72-year-old person.*

second the lens is removed but the capsule is left in the eye (extracapsular extraction). The risks associated with both types of surgery are similar, and excellent visual results are obtained in more than 90% of cases. Before surgery the patient is given either general or local anesthesia. Local anesthesia consists of injection behind the eyeball of a short-acting anesthetic such as Xylocaine. In the absence of pain a small speculum (spreader) is placed to separate the eyelids and expose the eyeball.

Intracapsular removal of the cataract consists of several stages: (1) an incision on the external coat of the eye (either on the cornea or on the border between the cornea and sclera) and placement of thin sutures; (2) a small cut on the iris, the pigmented part of the eye; (3) removal of the lens through the corneal incision; (4) closure of the incision with additional sutures; (5) administration of antibiotics to prevent infection; and (6) bandage applied to the eye. Because of improved surgical techniques and suture material, there is little inflammation associated with this type of cataract surgery. Intracapsular removal of cataracts is the procedure of choice worldwide because it is effective and comparatively simple to perform. A postoperative recovery period of two to three weeks is needed, and resumption of everyday activities takes one to four weeks.

Extracapsular removal of a cataract varies from the above description in step 3. At this stage an opening is made in the capsule, and the contents of the lens are removed from the eye. Several devices exist that allow the lens to be fragmented with an ultrasonic beam and the pieces sucked out of the eye with a hollow needle. This procedure is termed phakofragmentation or phacoemulsification. Because the incisions required for extracapsular removal are smaller, fewer sutures are needed and the postoperative healing period is reduced. Consequently this small-incision procedure is especially suitable for patients in their fifties or sixties and those physically active or requiring early rehabilitation. The equipment for fragmentation and aspiration of cataracts is cumbersome and expensive and requires operating-room personnel with suitable training. These disadvantages have slowed widespread acceptance of this procedure. Furthermore, the capsule, which normally is transparent after extracapsular removal, may develop wrinkles or become opaque at a later time, requiring additional surgery.

Some patients show an increased risk of certain postoperative complications (poor healing of wounds, detachment of the retina, or inflammation of the retina) associated with intracapsular removal. For these patients, extracapsular extraction of cataracts is recommended.

## Optical correction after cataract surgery

Aphakia is the lensless condition of the eye after the cataract has been removed. To focus images on the retina the aphakic eye requires an optical device: eyeglasses, a contact lens, or an intraocular lens. To correct an aphakic eye, a magnifying lens of about ten diopters in strength (100-mm focal length) is required. Larger eyes, in which the lens-to-retina distance is greater than normal, require somewhat weaker lenses—*i.e.,* lenses with a longer focal length—whereas smaller eyes require stronger lenses. In addition, changes in the curvature of the cornea (astigmatism) may accentuate optical distortions in the aphakic eye. Furthermore, optical correction for near vision requires a bifocal segment of even higher strength.

When the lenses of both eyes have been removed, eyeglasses, although necessarily thick and heavy, can in most cases be satisfactory if the resulting visual acuity is 20/30 or better. This degree of correction is considered more than adequate for elderly patients with decreased occupational and physical activities. Contact lenses, however, particularly the extended-wear type, are better suited to more active or younger patients.

Currently three types of contact lenses are available: hard lenses, soft lenses, and extended-wear lenses. Hard and soft lenses must be removed daily, whereas the extended-wear variety can be worn for several days or weeks. The latter, however, are a very recent

*Development of cataracts from stage A through stage D is plotted according to the ages of the diabetic and nondiabetic patients in whom they were found. The broken lines from point O represent estimates of the average age at which cataract formation probably began. In diabetics cataracts begin earlier and progress more rapidly than in nondiabetics.*

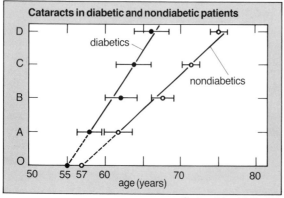

development and have not been extensively tested.

All types of contact lenses are suited to patients who have had only one cataract removed while the other eye retains its natural lens. Although the optical image formed by the aphakic eye wearing a contact lens is larger than that formed by the intact eye by about 6%, in some patients images from both eyes will be fused together into one by the brain. In most patients, however, the images from each eye are processed separately, and the brain selects only the clearer or more natural one. In such a case the intact eye, even if an early cataract is present, may be preferred to a surgically treated eye equipped with a contact lens.

An intraocular lens may be placed in the eye at the time of surgery to replace the natural lens. Such an insert, which is made of polymerized methyl methacrylate plastic, can be located in front of the iris, roughly on a plane with the iris in the pupillary space, or behind the iris. In many cases it does an excellent job of correcting aphakia in the immediate postoperative period, avoiding the optical distortions caused by glasses or contact lenses. Intraocular lenses are thus better suited for patients with aphakia in one eye only.

However, intraocular lenses are associated with long-term problems that may lead to loss of vision or the need for additional surgery. In some cases cloudiness or opacity of the cornea develops after several years. The major problem associated with some intraocular lenses however is a low-grade inflammation that results in retinal edema (fluid accumulation) and decreased vision. This complication tends to diminish the visual advantages of intraocular implants. Although several reports attest to the short-term tolerance of the eye to intraocular lenses, long-term evaluation is needed to determine their value.

## Medical therapy for senile cataracts

In the search for causes of senile cataracts, investigators have found aggregations of opaque, denatured protein material in the lens. The white coagulated mass that results when egg white is cooked is a common example of protein denaturation. Heating the egg proteins causes these normally coiled chains of amino acids to unfold and cross-link with each other to form a hardened gellike structure. Among the proteins in the natural lens, denaturation and hardening are likewise the result of cross-links, although the cause is biochemical rather than thermal. As lens protein becomes more denatured and cross-linked, cataracts in humans acquire a yellow or brown color. Such browning can be duplicated in the test tube by treating clear lens protein with substances like those believed to participate in protein denaturation in senile cataracts.

Some drugs that prevent certain kinds of cross-linking also have been found effective in the laboratory in preventing denaturation of lens protein. One such drug is salicylate, which is derived from aspirin. In studies

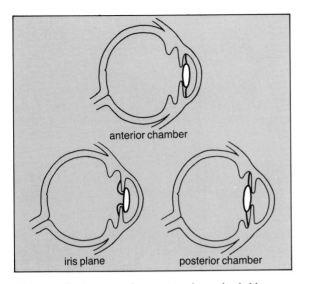

*An intraocular lens to replace a natural one clouded by cataract can be surgically implanted in one of three locations: in the anterior chamber in front of the iris (top), roughly on a plane with the iris (bottom left), or in the posterior chamber behind the iris (bottom right).*

conducted in victims of rheumatoid arthritis or osteoarthritis who had taken aspirin in high dosages for many years, it was found that the formation of senile cataracts was delayed or prevented. Because salicylate given in high dosages penetrates into the cataract and is retained by the lens, it is possible that a "coating" of salicylate prevents lens protein from cross-linking.

Other investigations into the medical therapy of senile cataracts are necessary. Several drugs are currently being evaluated.

*— Edward Cotlier, M.D.*

# Gynecology and Obstetrics

In July 1978 the first infant conceived by means of *in vitro* fertilization was born. The event represented the culmination of eight decades of scientific experimentation and, for the new parents and their physicians, the fulfillment of a human dream. For childless couples *in vitro* fertilization, or IVF, offers a new hope; for humankind in general it opens new prospects for the understanding of human conception and development.

## IVF statistics

The number of so-called test-tube babies already born is difficult to ascertain, but estimates as of June 1983 indicated that about 150–200 babies born had been conceived in this fashion, with another 100 due in the next six months.

The number of clinics and centers having *in vitro* programs throughout the world cannot be counted exactly, as there are centers at all levels of development.

In the United States alone, there are more than ten existing *in vitro* programs and at least six institutions that have engaged in successful IVF procedures. These include Eastern Virginia Medical School at Norfolk (the first IVF program in the United States); University of Southern California in Los Angeles; University of Texas in Houston; Vanderbilt University in Nashville, Tenn.; University of Pennsylvania in Philadelphia; and Yale University School of Medicine in New Haven, Conn. About 50 more U.S. institutions have established IVF centers or announced plans to begin IVF programs in the near future. Throughout the world, countries reporting successful *in vitro* programs include England, Australia, Israel, France, and Austria. The ratio of success (*i.e.,* number of pregnancies) corresponds well to the length of time that each institution performing the procedure has been in operation.

There are approximately 60 million reproductively active women in the United States alone; of these, 7%—or some 4,200,000—are infertile, and 40% are infertile solely because of female reproductive disorders. The rest are infertile either because of couple problems, meaning that the husband and wife are both subfertile, or because of medical problems affecting the male partner alone. Of the women suffering from reproductive disorders, it is estimated that about 500,000 are unable to become pregnant because of blocked or absent fallopian tubes. Such was the case with the first successful IVF birth, in England, in which the patient's severely scarred fallopian tubes had made normal conception impossible. Theoretically, all such women are candidates for IVF. Others who could eventually benefit from the technique are wives of males with low sperm counts (oligospermia) and patients whose infertility remains unexplained. In fact, if one projects the future possibilities for this technique, a woman unable to carry a fetus could donate an egg to be fertilized by her husband's sperm and implanted in a surrogate during pregnancy.

## Historical background

The first experiments involving *in vitro* (literally "in glass") fertilization and embryo transfer date to the late 19th century, when embryos were flushed from pregnant rabbits and implanted into recipient rabbits. Subsequent work with rabbit embryos yielded documented proof of cleavage (*i.e.,* cell division), demonstrating that a sperm could penetrate an egg and initiate embryogenesis outside of the body. The work continued, using rats and mice as subjects; little experimentation was done on subhuman primates, although IVF was successfully performed in the squirrel monkey in 1973.

Thus, in these early animal experiments, the goals of *in vitro* fertilization and embryo transfer were realized. These two processes were then successfully applied to the commercial breeding of livestock. In 1944 an attempt was made at *in vitro* fertilization of human ova,

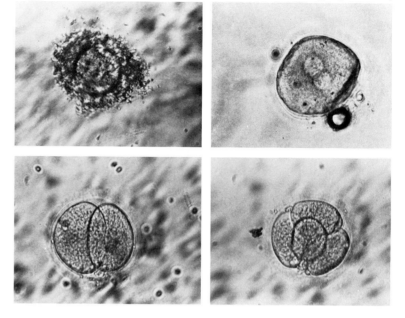

*This sequence of photographs shows a human egg, or ovum (top left), immediately after laparoscopic recovery; a pronuclear egg (top right) with egg and sperm nuclei beginning to unite, thus initiating the first stage of cleavage; a two-cell embryo (bottom left); and (bottom right) a four-cell embryo.*

but because parthenogenesis (division of the cell without penetration by sperm) could have occurred, evidence of fertilization was not substantiated.

## Methods of IVF

To date, only slight variations have been made in the original scientific protocol that resulted in the first human *in vitro* birth, in England in 1978, although the procedure involves several steps—patient selection, control and monitoring of ovulation, ovum recovery, sperm preparation, fertilization, embryo transfer, and pregnancy maintenance—all subject to minor alterations. The initial assessment for patient selection requires a normal menstrual cycle in the woman and a normal sperm count in the man. Occasionally a patient may have to undergo surgery prior to ovum collection in order to make sure that the ovary is accessible to surgical laparoscopic manipulation and ovum capture. Patients are selected at the end of an exhaustive infertility evaluation, and it must be understood that *in vitro* fertilization is a last-step treatment, generally performed only after other therapies have failed.

Because the egg must be captured at a time close to maturity (*i.e.,* at the time of actual ovulation, or as close as possible) in order for fertilization to occur, the timing of ovum recovery is critical. There are variations in approach to ovulation monitoring, induction, and recovery at the different centers practicing IVF, but these variations are not of great magnitude. In England, for example, the woman's natural menstrual cycle is not manipulated or altered; in Australia, and at some U.S. centers, various fertility drugs are used to stimulate and regulate the cycle. Among such drugs currently in use are Pergonal, a mixture of naturally occurring pituitary hormones, and clomiphene, a synthetic antiestrogen.

Manipulation of the menstrual cycle has the advantage of precise timing with less rigorous monitoring. If the natural cycle is followed, it must be closely monitored in order to predict when ovulation will occur; this is accomplished through analysis of the urine level of luteinizing hormone (LH), the substance that stimulates release of the mature egg from the follicle. This natural-cycle method produced the first successful pregnancy from *in vitro* fertilization.

Ovulation may be induced by means of an injection of human chorionic gonadotropin (HCG); release of the ovum will occur approximately 36 hours after the injection. Levels of serum estradiol (an estrogen) and natural surges of LH must be monitored, since they will indicate if ovulation has already occurred. It should be emphasized that the use of natural or synthetic hormones for ovulation induction not only offers more precise timing but also stimulates the release of more eggs per cycle; thus more than one embryo can be implanted, increasing the likelihood of a successful pregnancy. Ovulation is also monitored periodically by ultrasound, which provides a measure not only of the number of developing follicles but also of the size, shape, and acoustic density of each follicle. When the follicle reaches the critical stage at which release of the egg is imminent, the laparoscopy for ovum capture is planned.

Laparoscopy is a surgical procedure in which a small, cold-light telescope, called a laparoscope, is passed through the umbilicus allowing visualization and manipulation of the abdominal cavity contents and particularly, in this instance, the pelvic organs. The patient is given a short-acting general anesthetic. The ovum, along with its follicular fluid, is aspirated with a needle through a separate puncture site and sent to the laboratory for evaluation. A simple suction trap is employed to capture the ovum.

In the laboratory the recovered eggs are first graded as to maturity, an evaluation based on the compactness of surrounding cells called the cumulus oophorus and its component granulosa cells. These tissues have a characteristic microscopic appearance by which the egg's degree of development can be judged. Once identified as preovulatory, the eggs are incubated for 8 to 24 hours—depending on their stage of maturity—in a special culture medium. The preparation of the culture medium is one of the most sensitive parts of the procedure. A number of substances have been tried; some contain umbilical vein serum and others consist of pooled female serum. After incubation the eggs are exposed to the sperm; fertilization, if it occurs, initiates the actual *in vitro* portion of the procedure.

The man's semen is obtained by masturbation, and the sperm cells are separated from their fluid component, the seminal plasma, either by washing and centrifugation or by allowing the motile sperm to swim from the seminal plasma into a culture medium not unlike the culture medium in which fertilization takes place. This prepared sperm is then added to the egg. Fertilization usually occurs within 12 to 48 hours, resulting in an egg with two pronuclei, one from the ovum, the other from the sperm head, which eventually unite to form a single nucleus. The movement of the pronuclei toward each other initiates the first cleavage, or division, of the zygote (fertilized egg).

The potential embryo is then removed from the original medium and placed in a growth medium, where it is observed periodically for division into a two-cell embryo and then into the four-cell stage. These divisions usually occur approximately 38 to 46 hours after fertilization. Embryos at the two-, four-, or eight-cell stage are then implanted into the uterus. As mentioned above, if several embryos have been fertilized, all may be implanted. Each embryo is carefully inspected before insertion into the uterus to assure that the initial

*Using a laparoscope for visualization of the pelvic organs, the* in vitro *team captures and removes a mature egg ready for fertilization.*

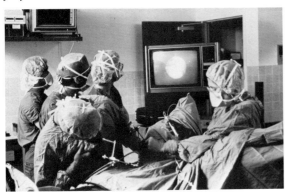

Michael Alexander

phases of development are proceeding normally.

The embryo is transferred to the uterus by introducing a small metal catheter through the cervical canal, which is entered through the vagina; a plastic cannula, or tube, is then passed into the uterus. The embryos are flushed into the uterus, using their growth medium as a carrier. The catheter is checked after embryo transfer to make sure none of the embryos have remained in the instrument.

Once implantation has occurred, the patient undergoes frequent hormone testing to ensure that ovarian function is adequate. If pregnancy is achieved, the fetus is carefully monitored to rule out genetic problems.

### Reasons for failure

Successful implantation seems to be the major factor affecting the number of successful pregnancies initiated by IVF. Ova are recovered from approximately 95% of patients, and 85% of the eggs collected will cleave and become embryos; the ultimate success rate of 10–20%—measured in number of normal, full-term pregnancies (and compared with an average of 14–23% in naturally occurring pregnancies)—implicates the implantation phase as the weakest link in the process. It is possible, however, that abnormal embryo development might be a contributing factor, as the normal milieu of fertilization and early embryonic growth is altered in IVF. The most popular current explanation for failure of embryo implantation is that the *in vitro* embryo develops at a slower rate than the embryo *in vivo* (*i.e.,* within the body). Hence, the growth of the *in vitro* zygote and the development of the endometrial tissue within the uterus are not perfectly synchronized. Attempts at altering the receptivity of the endometrium with progesterone given after implantation have not as yet been successful.

The most important naturally occurring biological problem after implantation is spontaneous abortion. It should, perhaps, be emphasized that this very same problem is also the most common cause of failure in pregnancies produced by *in vivo* conception. The fact that about 80% of normally fertilized embryos do not result in full-term pregnancies indicates that research in this field is necessary for an understanding of the problems related to pregnancy loss and failure of implantation in IVF.

### Risks

Certain risk factors must be considered in a critical evaluation of this procedure. Certainly, some risk is associated with the surgical procedure of laparoscopy, although such hazards are basically secondary to the use of a general anesthetic. Ectopic pregnancies—those in which the fertilized egg becomes implanted outside of the uterus—have occurred in some patients during implantation; in other cases there may be migration of the embryo into one of the fallopian tubes.

*The birth of Louise Joy Brown in July 1978 was a medical miracle—she was the first human infant conceived by means of* in vitro *fertilization. Now Louise has a baby sister, also conceived in vitro. Today thousands of childless couples have renewed hopes of parenthood.*

The risk of failure and its psychological effects must be considered, particularly the disappointment of the couple if pregnancy does not occur, since IVF may represent their last opportunity for parenthood. Most couples have extensive counseling both before and after IVF. Probably the greatest sustaining psychological factor for the patients who enter an IVF program is the relationship of mutual support that develops among the couples as each goes through the testing and various steps in the procedure. Another considerable asset to patients in such a program is the close interaction of the health care professionals themselves, which helps to create a reassuring atmosphere.

The possibilities of congenital malformation in babies conceived *in vitro* has also been a subject of much concern. To date, however, genetic problems have not been demonstrated to be more common in IVF than in normal conception. Of the 150 or so babies conceived throughout the world by *in vitro* methods, all have been essentially normal, with the exception of two sets of twins, one born in Australia, the other in the U.S. In each case one twin was born with a congenital heart defect that could not be definitely attributed to the fertilization process. One infant with severe genetic defects aborted in the middle trimester. In fact, the rate of chromosomal abnormality is quite high in naturally conceived embryos, and about 99% of such abnormal fetuses are eliminated by spontaneous abortion. While the incidence of spontaneous abortion itself does seem to be somewhat greater for IVF patients, based on current statistics, this apparently higher rate may be a reflection of earlier determination of pregnancy in these carefully monitored patients.

The cost of *in vitro* fertilization—from $3,000 to $5,000 per treatment cycle—is another problematic aspect. Such expense is prohibitive for many couples, and it raises the ethical issue of the cost to society for one individual life or for the treatment of one couple's problem.

## Benefits

The benefits of IVF to the infertile couple are immeasurable. In addition to solving the problem of damaged or absent oviducts, it could in the future be applied in cases of oligospermia and unexplained infertility; it may also provide a remedy for patients with uterine abnormalities or immunologic infertility. Equally important are the gains to be made in scientific understanding of human reproduction and development. As IVF techniques are studied and refined, research will inevitably contribute to knowledge about follicular activity, the dynamics of embryonic implantation, the initiation of embryonic differentiation, and the development of normal and abnormal cells. The practical applications of this knowledge will probably lead to safer and more effective family planning techniques and, ultimately, to methods of correcting genetic defects at the earliest stages of human life.

There are also ethical issues that must be addressed; risk–benefit ratios, the process of patient selection, and fetal outcome have already been partially examined. Without doubt, however, the ethical issue of paramount importance and greatest potential controversy is that of experimentation with human fetuses. Techniques for ectogenesis (maintenance of the embryo *in vitro* beyond the implantation stage), developments in cryobiology allowing the freezing of eggs or embryos for future implantation (at least one successful human conception has already been accomplished through this technique), and manual fertilization by injection of sperm heads into the substance of the egg are only a few of the possibilities likely to promote ethical and religious debate.

## The future of IVF

Over the next few years the number of centers performing the procedure is expected to increase as IVF becomes relatively routine and readily available. Some centers undoubtedly will close because of the tremendous investment of resources, both human and technological, required for an IVF program.

With the use of techniques similar to those employed today, pregnancy rates eventually should approach approximately 20% per cycle, although it may take many attempts for a patient to achieve a pregnancy—if she is able to attain one at all. The safety of IVF and the efficiency of the method employed remain open to question, and only long-term studies can resolve the uncertainty about normal growth and development of children conceived *in vitro*. Changes in technique, especially in the timing of ovulation and method of implantation, also will occur over time. It is clear, nonetheless, that IVF is now a relatively acceptable and soon-to-be accessible clinical tool that will offer help to many infertile patients. The developments of the next decade promise to be exciting.

— *Alan H. DeCherney, M.D.*

# Health Care Law

Modern health law controversies are usually products of modern medical technology, but there are exceptions. Surrogate motherhood is one. Its use is recorded in Genesis: Sarah offered Abraham her handmaid to bear them a child because Sarah herself was infertile. Contemporary interest in surrogate motherhood stems largely from the difficulty that infertile couples, most of them white, have in obtaining healthy white infants to adopt. In the United States there has been increasing promotion of this method of procreation by some attorneys and physicians. Though no accurate statistics are available, probably no more than 1,000 surrogate pregnancies have resulted. Nonetheless, the practice raises many important questions.

### The surrogate contract

Those who are most interested in hiring a surrogate mother are couples who are unable to have their own child because of the wife's infertility. In a typical surrogate contract, a woman agrees to be artificially inseminated with the sperm of the husband of an infertile woman. The surrogate agrees to carry the child to term and agrees that after the child is born she will give it up for adoption to the couple. Alternatively, she may agree simply to relinquish her parental rights in the child, leaving the biological father as the sole legal parent. The contract may also provide for life insurance and amniocentesis for the surrogate and restrictions on her use of drugs and alcohol during the pregnancy.

The term surrogate mother is somewhat misleading. A surrogate is a substitute, someone who serves in place of another. Wet nurses, neonatal intensive care units, and baby-sitters are thus surrogate mothers. A woman who carries a child for another does not act as a substitute "mother" for the child but as a substitute "bearer" of the child. Accordingly, "surrogate child-bearer" would be a more accurate descriptor. Nevertheless, because "surrogate mother" has become a popularly accepted term, it is used here.

## Motivations and questions

The cases of two surrogate arrangements have received considerable attention in the United States recently. One involves Patricia Dickey, a single, 20-year-old woman who had never borne a child and who agreed to carry one and give it up without any compensation. She was recruited by a Michigan attorney who had made a reputation for his television appearances in which he said that for a $5,000 fee he would put "host mothers" in touch with childless couples. Dickey explained her own motivation to become a surrogate mother as follows: "I had a close friend who couldn't have a baby, and I know how badly she wanted one. . . . It's just something I wanted to do."

Better known is the case of one of the first women to complete her obligations under a surrogate contract. Elizabeth Kane (a pseudonym) was married and the mother of three children when she agreed to carry a child for $10,000. The arrangement was negotiated by a Kentucky physician who reportedly has more than 100 surrogates who are willing to perform the same service for compensation, and who claims to have no "moral or ethical problems with what we are doing." Kane described her relationship to the baby by saying, "It's the father's child. I'm simply growing it for him."

These brief sketches raise fundamental questions: Should the surrogate be married or single? Should she have other children or have no children? Should the couple meet the surrogate? (The couple in the second case were in the delivery room when Kane gave birth.) Should the child know about the arrangement when he or she grows up? (In the latter case the couple plans to tell their child, a son, about Kane when he is 18.) To what extent is monetary compensation the real issue? What limitations should there be? (In the first case the sperm donor agreed to give Dickey *more* sperm if she wanted to have another child of her own.) What kind of counseling should be given to all parties? What records should be kept? In the U.S. where more than a million and a half abortions a year are performed, shouldn't there be an attempt to get women who are already pregnant to give birth and place their children up for adoption instead of inducing those who are not pregnant to undertake the surrogate role?

## Objections to surrogacy

Four basic objections have been raised to the practice of surrogate motherhood: (1) risks to the surrogate, (2) risks to the offspring, (3) confusion of family relationships, and (4) a general moral concern over tampering with nature. On the basis of the limited evidence available to date, there does not seem to be an unreasonable risk to the surrogate mothers either physically or psychologically. The risks to the offspring remain uncertain and are discussed later. Confusion of family relationships is a real issue but probably not different in kind from that encountered in the widely used practices of adoption or artificial insemination by donor. But the moral concerns are very pressing, since surrogacy is, in effect, "commerce" in children. Moreover, many questions are raised by the potential that arises for "redefining" the family as an entity.

Thus far, legal debate has focused on "baby selling." Is the surrogate in fact selling a child or is she only selling her ovum and thereafter "renting" her womb? Some have argued that surrogacy can be distinguished from baby buying because one of the parents (the father) is biologically related to the child, and the surrogate mother is not pregnant at the time the deal is struck (and so is not under any compulsion to provide for her child). Because of these differences, the child is protected by having one biological parent, and the surrogate is protected because she is under no psychological pressure to give up her child at the time she enters the agreement.

Surrogate motherhood could be viewed as independent adoption arranged prior to conception, but in that case the question arises whether the court will grant the adoption. Some such adoptions have been granted, but the only legal opinions rendered to date suggest that compensation for this form of adoption is illegal. Courts in Michigan and the attorney general of Kentucky have both viewed contracts to bear a child for compensation as baby selling.

## Court challenge in Michigan

In the mid-1970s most states in the U.S. passed statutes making it criminal to offer, give, or receive anything of value for placing a child for adoption. These statutes were aimed at curtailing a major black market in babies that had surfaced, with children selling for as much as $20,000. Anticipating that Michigan's version of this statute might prohibit him from paying a surrogate for carrying a child and giving it up for adoption, the Michigan attorney Noel Keane, who instigated the first case described above and who has arranged many surrogate births, sought a declaratory judgment. He argued that the antibaby-selling statute was unconstitutional because it infringed upon the right to reproductive privacy of the parties involved. But a lower court concluded that "the right to adopt a child based upon the payment of $5,000 is not a fundamental personal right and reasonable regulations controlling adoption proceedings that prohibit the exchange of money (other than charges and fees approved by the court) are not constitutionally infirm." The court characterized the state's interest as one "to prevent commercialism from affecting a mother's decision to execute a consent to the adoption of her child." The court went on to argue that "mercenary considerations" in-

volved in creating "a parent-child relationship" strike at the "very foundation of human society" and are "patently and necessarily injurious to the community."

This decision was affirmed on appeal, and the U.S. Supreme Court has refused to review it. Accordingly, surrogate mothers in Michigan and other states with similar laws cannot charge a fee for bearing a child. The court rulings do not, however, forbid surrogates from bearing children out of love or compassion or for their own personal reasons.

## Kentucky ruling

On Jan. 26, 1981, Steven Beshear, the attorney general of the Commonwealth of Kentucky, issued an opinion to a Louisville newspaper reporter that contracts to bear a child are, in fact, illegal and unenforceable in that state. He based his opinion on Kentucky statutes and "a strong public policy against 'baby buying.' "

Specifically, Kentucky law invalidates consent for adoption or the filing of a voluntary petition for termination of parental rights prior to the fifth day after the birth of a child. The purpose of these statutes, according to the attorney general, is to give the mother time to "think it over" before giving up the child. Thus, any agreement or contract she entered into before the fifth day after the birth would be unenforceable. Moreover, Kentucky, like Michigan (and almost every other state), prohibits the charging of a "fee" or "remuneration for the procurement of any child for adoption purposes." Even though there is no similar statute regarding the termination of parental rights, the same public policies regarding monetary consideration for the procurement of any child stand: "The Commonwealth of Kentucky does not condone the purchase and sale of children." The attorney general has filed suit to enjoin the Kentucky physician who has made a specialty of surrogate births and his corporation from making any further surrogate mother arrangements in Kentucky.

## Protecting would-be children

The would-be parents and the surrogate mother are usually represented by legal counsel, undergo at least minimal psychological counseling, and enter into an elaborate written contract that spells out their respective rights and obligations. The "missing person" in this negotiating process is, of course, the would-be child. Is the would-be child adequately protected in surrogate contracts? And does society have any obligation to see to it that the would-be child's interests are adequately represented?

A complex case that illustrates potential problems for the child occurred early in 1983. A New York man, Alexander Malahoff, contracted with Judy Stiver, 26, married, of Lansing, Mich., to be inseminated with his sperm and bear him a child. Malahoff was separated from his wife and hoped the baby might reunite them. The child, a boy called Baby Doe by the court, was born

*Sarah's handmaid, who bore Abraham a child, was the first "surrogate mother." Today surrogate arrangements are facing many legal snarls; such was the case of Judy Stiver (above with husband [left] and Alexander Malahoff).*

on Jan. 10, 1983, with microcephaly—a condition in which smallness of the head is usually associated with mental defects. Stiver disavowed responsibility for the child, claiming he was not hers. Malahoff likewise refused to take custody, claiming the child was not his. Blood- and tissue-typing tests later proved that Malahoff was not, in fact, the father. Prior to the insemination, the parties had entered into a contract—the only instrument that in any way defined their rights and responsibilities, and one that all lawyers involved in writing surrogate contracts believe is probably not enforceable in court. The contract specified that Stiver was to refrain from having intercourse with her husband for 30

days after the insemination but, remarkably, mentioned nothing about the days prior to the insemination. Malahoff complained: "Instead of a baby, I end up with a lawyer." Ultimately Stiver and her husband agreed to accept the child as their own, as indeed he was. But what if neither party had wanted the "defective" child? How could the child have been protected? The original contract used by the physician called for the child to become his (the doctor's) if the contracting parents refused it. According to writer Roger Rosenblatt, in a commentary on the so-called Baby Doe case in *Time* magazine (Feb. 14, 1983), "A procedure has been devised in which a human being is literally conceived as a manufactured product. Therefore, consciously or not, all the participants in that procedure tend to regard the product either as the flower of a growth industry or, if a flaw appears, as industrial waste."

Others have argued, on the contrary, that we need not be overly concerned about the would-be child's interests. The reasoning is twofold: (1) since no child has the luxury of choosing its own environment, there is no "right" to any particular family arrangement; and (2) since without the surrogate arrangement the child would not have been born at all, it is almost always better off being born under even a poorly constructed or poorly executed surrogate agreement. These arguments do carry a certain degree of force and may prevent courts from permitting children to sue their surrogate mothers or the contracting couple for physical or psychological damages (on the basis that they are better off alive and in the surrogate situation than they would be not having been born at all and that, in any event, it would be impossible to calculate the monetary value of their "injury"). But they do not speak to society's obligations to children. Society must do what it can to protect unborn children as well as living ones. We can do so by encouraging the type of family structures we believe are in the best interests of children and by discouraging those we believe are not. Few would go so far as to legally prohibit surrogate arrangements (although such statutes have been introduced in Michigan and Alabama), but many believe regulation is reasonable.

## Legislation

Legislation to protect everyone involved in surrogate contracts has been introduced in a number of states, including Alaska, Michigan, South Carolina, and California. A proposal introduced by state Rep. Richard Fitzpatrick of Michigan in February 1983, for example, called for specific clauses in a surrogate motherhood contract that would be enforceable in court, legal representation of all parties, tissue typing of the sperm donor and child to determine paternity, and insemination by a licensed physician. For up to 20 days after the birth of a child, the surrogate could revoke her consent and initiate an action for custody of the child, although the sperm donor and his wife would retain custody during the proceedings.

## Whose baby?

Many surrogate mother issues revolve around fundamental value considerations and our view of the family. Accordingly, they will ultimately have to be decided in the legislatures. Nevertheless, there is at least one major issue that does have a clear legal answer: Whose baby is it? Legally it is the surrogate, or "womb," mother's baby, and if she wants to keep it, she almost certainly can. Indeed, under the proper circumstances she may even be able to keep the child and sue the sperm donor for child support. On the other hand, it is also the biological child of the sperm donor. In all states, children born in wedlock are presumed to be the legitimate children of the married couple. If the surrogate is married, therefore, the child will be presumed (usually rebuttable only by proof beyond a reasonable doubt) to be the child of the couple and not of the sperm donor. The donor could bring a custody suit if he were able to prove beyond a reasonable doubt that he was the real father, and then the court would have to decide to which parents it would be in the child's "best interests" to grant custody. In a California case a sperm donor sued the surrogate mother for custody or visitation rights. The case was settled out of court; the surrogate kept the child but acknowledged the donor as the father on the birth certificate.

In many states that have laws relating to artificial insemination, the sperm donor has no right to the child. This provides an interesting legal twist. To protect sperm donors, the Uniform Parentage Act states that "the donor of semen provided . . . for use in artificial insemination of a woman other than the donor's wife is treated in law as if he were not the natural father of a child thereby conceived." The saying "Mama's baby, papa's maybe" aptly describes the current legal reaction to a surrogate who changes her mind and decides to retain the child. The Uniform Parentage Act is a suggested model statute that many states have adopted.

## Surrogate mothers and test-tube babies

Surrogate childbearing is currently relevant only to a small group of individuals who wish to utilize this method of bearing a child. It is, as previously noted, not new and is not based on modern technology. Modern surrogacy requires only the minimal intervention needed for artificial insemination. It can be done at home, without the involvement of either physicians or lawyers. The issue has become public only because doctors and lawyers became involved as "middlemen" and advertised for surrogates on television and in the newspapers. There is, however, a new medical technology that can in the future make surrogate childbearing a much more universal issue: *in vitro* fertilization (IVF) and embryo

transfer—also known as test-tube conception. Using these techniques (currently available primarily in the United States, Australia, and England), a woman can have her ovum removed and fertilized outside her body with her husband's sperm and then have the fertilized ovum, or embryo, "transferred" to the uterus of a surrogate childbearer. This woman would then nurture the fetus and give birth to the child, with whom she would have *no* genetic link. Theoretically at least, women might utilize surrogates in this manner because they themselves have no uterus (*e.g.,* due to a hysterectomy), have an abnormal uterus, or simply prefer, for personal or career reasons, not to undergo the physical experience of pregnancy.

Such an arrangement would make the question of who the legal mother is problematic. The legal presumption in favor of the "womb" mother should, however, continue to apply. This not only would provide certainty of identification at birth (a protection for both mother and child) but would also recognize the biological fact that the womb mother has contributed more than the genetic mother to the child and, therefore, has a greater interest in it. This has led some futurists, such as Isaac Asimov, to suggest that IVF surrogates are not likely to prove very popular because mothers would give up a large part of their biological link to their children: "A baby is not, after all, a matter of genes only. A great deal of its development in the fetal stage depends upon the maternal environment; upon the diet of the host-mother, the efficiency of her placenta, the biochemical details of her cells and bloodstream."

Whether surrogate motherhood is ultimately popular or not, the issues provide society with the opportunity to reexamine its view of the family and the extent to which the state should become involved in restricting the ways in which individuals are able to obtain children to rear. Because these are extremely personal questions about which most individuals have very strong feelings and beliefs, they are likely to be the subject of public debate for some time to come.

*—George J. Annas, J.D., M.P.H.*

# Health Care Technology

A century ago the present capabilities of medicine and surgery would have been thought impossible. Miraculous though they are, many of these techniques and treatments could not succeed were they not supported by a very specialized kind of physician and nursing care available in the modern hospital. Indeed, some circumstances demand continuous, careful observation of the patient; frequent determinations of various rates, pressures, volumes, concentrations, and other indicators of vital functions; and the availability of equipment to support these functions should it become necessary.

Hospitals traditionally have grouped patients according to medical specialty (for example, medicine, sur-

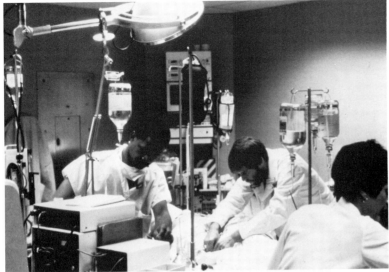

*Advances in medical technology have vastly improved the chances of survival of critically ill patients.*

gery, or pediatrics) primarily for the efficiency of the nursing staff and other hospital necessities. During and following World War II, advances in therapy for the acutely ill—for example, prolonged and intricate surgical procedures—required the development of expertise in artificially maintaining physiological stability before, during, and after the therapy. Such demands introduced the concept of grouping patients in the hospital according to the intensity of care they required.

The earliest intensive care units (ICU's) were the respiratory wards for polio victims established in the 1930s. Most present-day ICU's, however, evolved during the 1950s from one of two kinds of facilities: postanesthesia recovery rooms that expanded into 24-hour surgical care units or coronary care units (CCU's) that developed because of advances in electrocardiographic monitoring of heart patients. By 1970 the concept of patient grouping in the hospital according to the intensity of care required had become well established.

Today critical care medicine (CCM) is recognized to extend beyond the ICU. It is a multiprofessional endeavor concerned with patients who are experiencing or are at risk of experiencing an acute, life-threatening failure of one or more organ systems due to disease or injury. In its broadest meaning CCM includes treatment and support at the scene of onset of the critical illness or injury, during transportation, in the hospital emergency room, in the operating room, and finally in the ICU. The common factor is that the patient's condition eventually necessitates minute-to-minute therapy or observation in an ICU.

## Critical care personnel

CCM has recently become a subspecialty within the medical disciplines of anesthesiology, general surgery, internal medicine, and pediatrics. Physicians may subspecialize in CCM following residency training in any of these four fields. Their subspecialty training concentrates on knowledge and skills specifically required in caring for the critically ill patient. Importantly, the critical care physician, often referred to an an intensivist, is trained in coordinating care among numerous medical consultants and allied health personnel and in the administrative demands of the ICU.

Nurses in the ICU provide most of the moment-to-moment bedside care. Registered nurses with at least one year of postgraduate clinical experience are eligible for comprehensive orientation and on-the-job training in the ICU. After significant experience and participation in appropriate continuing-education courses, an ICU nurse must pass national examinations to be designated a critical care nurse.

In cooperation with the patient's physician, the critical care physician and nurses work in concert to assure coordinated care. Additionally they must accept primary responsibility for the continuous monitoring, support, and intervention required by critically ill patients.

The allied health profession of respiratory therapy encompasses the technological skills necessary to monitor and support the very essence of physiological life—oxygenation and ventilation. Therefore, respiratory therapy is an essential component of care to most critically ill patients. Registered respiratory therapists must complete at least two years of approved college training and pass national exams attesting to their competency in this complex and demanding field. Other allied health professionals such as physical therapists, radiology technologists, dieticians, and pharmacists also play a vital role in the care of many ICU patients.

## Support technology

Although there is no universally accepted definition for critical illness, all definitions acknowledge that a critically ill patient probably will die without aggressive therapeutic intervention. Thus the subspecialty of CCM specifically concentrates on diagnosing the need for treatment and life-support technology in the critically ill and providing these supports with appropriate monitoring. Present-day capabilities of supportive care in CCM include the following:

*Pulmonary support.* The lungs serve primarily to supply the blood with oxygen and to remove carbon dioxide, a process referred to as respiration. Respiratory failure is a common occurrence in critically ill patients. Regardless of the reasons for respiratory failure, adequate respiration can be maintained for days or weeks with the aid of mechanical ventilation, most commonly in the form of a respirator, or breathing machine. Placing and maintaining the patient on a respirator requires a host of special skills—for installing an airway tube through the nose or mouth or surgically into the trachea, for establishing an adequate breathing cycle by mechanically raising and lowering the airway pressure, for supplying the lungs with the correct amount of oxygen, and for protecting the respiratory system from complications of treatment.

In conjunction with the ability to accurately monitor blood levels of oxygen and carbon dioxide (blood-gas analysis), the technology of respiratory support has advanced to such a degree that death due to respiratory failure alone is uncommon. In fact, such support can be continued far beyond any hope of salvaging a meaningful life. In such circumstances the term pulling the plug is often used to refer to discontinuance of ventilatory support, and consequently many ethical questions are raised concerning today's pulmonary support capabilities.

*Cardiovascular support.* The heart and blood vessels together make up the cardiovascular system, the main function of which is to keep blood circulating through the body tissues. Whereas adequate circulation is often threatened in critical illness, it can be maintained by administering medications, blood, blood substitutes, and saltwater solutions if accurate information concerning cardiovascular function can be obtained. The pulmonary artery catheter can provide many of the precise measurements needed for proper support. A plastic tube with one or more channels (lumens) is introduced into a large vein and directed through the right side of the heart to the pulmonary artery. Once in place such a catheter can be used to sense pressures, withdraw blood for analysis, and measure blood temperature.

In certain circumstances heart function can be temporarily supported with a machine called the intra-aortic balloon counterpulsator. A catheter tipped with a balloon that can be rapidly inflated and deflated is introduced into the femoral artery in the groin and threaded to the aorta in the chest. The inflation cycle of the balloon is synchronized with the electrocardiogram so

*These children have been kept alive in the hospital since birth by sophisticated and extremely costly mechanical support systems.*

that it matches the periods of systole (emptying of the heart chambers) and diastole (filling of the heart chambers). At the onset of systole the balloon collapses, allowing the heart to eject blood against reduced resistance and thereby decreasing the energy required by the heart muscle. At the onset of diastole the balloon reexpands, pushing blood against the closed aortic valve and augmenting blood flow through the coronary arteries. Such support helps a transiently weakened heart muscle supply a nearly normal output of blood to the body while keeping the heart muscle itself adequately supplied.

*Kidney support.* Functioning kidneys are essential for the excretion of metabolic waste products. They also maintain fluid and electrolyte balance by regulating the excretion of water and various ions (*e.g.,* sodium, potassium, and chloride). The kidneys normally receive 25% of the total blood flow through the body and are extremely vulnerable to damage when this flow is inadequate. The kidneys often react to critical illness by temporarily shutting down (renal failure) or functioning at a suboptimal level (renal insufficiency). Both renal insufficiency and failure can be supported by dialysis, the cleansing of the blood of waste products by artificial, mechanical means.

Two kinds of dialysis are available, hemodialysis and peritoneal dialysis. Hemodialysis requires direct access to the circulation, usually by means of a pair of tubes surgically placed in an artery and vein of the patient. Blood is routed through an artificial kidney machine, which cleanses it of waste products, and is then returned to the body. Peritoneal dialysis is technically simpler to perform and does not require access to the bloodstream, but it takes considerably longer to remove comparable quantities of waste substances. A catheter is placed through the abdominal wall, and the abdominal cavity is filled with a special dialysis fluid. Waste substances diffuse through the membranous lining (peritoneum) of the abdominal cavity and into the fluid, which is periodically drained and replaced with a fresh supply.

*Brain resuscitation.* Automatic reflexes within the blood vessels of the brain normally assure an adequate blood supply to brain tissue even though it may be insufficient elsewhere in the body. However, in situations in which the blood supply to the brain *is* diminished, fluid tends to accumulate in the brain cells; this results in swollen tissue (cerebral edema). Acute injury to the brain usually results in dilation of the cerebral blood vessels, allowing the brain to become engorged with blood.

Critically ill patients may experience swelling of the brain because of a reduced cerebral blood supply, a head injury, or both. Since the skull cannot expand, the pressure within it may rise to such an extent that it destroys brain cells and further impairs blood flow. When conditions warrant, a device can be surgically placed within the cranium to continuously measure the intracranial pressure. This information allows the physician to monitor the effects of various drugs and mechanical respiration patterns and to adjust them in order to safely lower intracranial pressure.

*Nutritional support.* The body's normal metabolic requirements for glucose, protein, and fat are supplied in the diet. Nutrients in excess of short-term needs are stored, a process called anabolism. In the presence of physiological stress such as acute illness, metabolic requirements increase, and the new demand must be filled from body stores, a process called obligatory catabolism.

A critically ill patient cannot ingest an adequate diet. Thus, even when nutritional stores are depleted, the patient will continue in a catabolic state, consuming essential tissue protein, unless adequate nutrients are provided. Further, a patient recovering from critical illness is hypermetabolic, requiring greater than normal cellular energy for reparative processes. This hypermetabolic state necessitates hyperalimentation—increasing caloric intake together with appropriate proteins, sugars, and fats.

If the patient's gastrointestinal tract is functioning, a tube placed through the nose to the stomach or small bowel can deliver the necessary nutrients. In many critically ill patients, however, gastrointestinal function is poor, necessitating placement of a catheter into a large vein in the chest for intravenous administration of the nutrients. This procedure is called parenteral hyperalimentation.

## Present and future problems

An iatrogenic illness is one that has been introduced inadvertently in the course of medical treatment. The grouping together of critically ill patients, with the application of sophisticated technology, presents many such hazards. For example, potential undesired effects of the types of therapy discussed above are numerous. Incidence of these complications is minimized by highly trained and dedicated personnel, the greatest single factor in the high cost of CCM. Further, ICU's inevitably harbor bacteria that have developed resistance to many antibiotics. It is thus an irony that those patients most susceptible to overwhelming infection are cared for in hospital areas where virulent and difficult-to-treat bacteria are prevalent. Obviously the benefits of intensive care must outweigh the risks before a patient is placed in an ICU.

There is overwhelming evidence that ICU's have made a significant contribution to lowering the incidence of death for many kinds of illnesses. Nevertheless, there is also convincing evidence that ICU's are being overutilized for terminally ill patients and underutilized because of failure to admit patients who need respiratory and other supports. The costs of intensive care are too great to waste on those who cannot benefit, while its effectiveness is too great to deny admission to those who may benefit. Much of this problem is due to the lack of accurate information upon which these decisions can be based. Many medical groups, including the U.S. National Institutes of Health (NIH), are seeking answers through clinical research.

In March 1983 a Consensus Development Conference on CCM, sponsored by the NIH, brought together biomedical investigators, critical care physicians and nurses, medical specialists, technologists, consumers, and representatives of public interest groups to address and formulate a draft statement on a number of issues affecting the future course of critical care medicine. It considered such questions as the effectiveness of CCM; the kinds of patients likely to benefit most; the skills, staffing levels, and organization necessary to assure the best care for the patients most in need; and directions for future research in CCM.

The greatest problem of all in determining the appropriate use of ICU's is society's attitudes toward death and dying. In the U.S. the Judeo-Christian ethic for the sanctity of all human life has been coupled for centuries with the credo of "the best medical care at all costs." The clarity of these time-honored beliefs has been blurred by certain realities—that the capabilities of critical care medicine can be used equally effectively either for saving lives or for prolonging death and that people, individually, can no longer afford the best medical care at all costs. The task facing society is to accept the responsibility of using medicine's best resources to the advantage of everyone.

—*Barry A. Shapiro, M.D.*

# Special Report:
# The Costs of Medical Innovation
## by John P. Bunker, M.D.

In fulfilling their responsibilities as healers, it is not enough for physicians to apply existing knowledge. Where no effective treatment exists, society expects its doctors to invent new ones. The challenge to invent new treatments is one to which physicians and other medical scientists respond with enthusiasm and energy—and with frequent and spectacular success. Witness the outpouring of dramatic technological advances of the past few years, such as coronary-artery bypass graft, total hip replacement, computerized axial tomography (the CAT scan), and plasmapheresis.

However, not all proposed or attempted treatments or diagnostic procedures are successful. It is estimated that about a third of new surgical treatments represent improvements over existing methods. Perhaps a sixth are marked successes, and the rest are no better, and in some cases less effective, than those we already have. Many entail large costs in dollars, and many also are associated with substantial costs in suffering. It is exceedingly difficult to balance the expected benefits of a new medical or surgical treatment in terms of its potential to enhance quality of life or to prolong life against the costs in dollars and in risks.

### The artificial heart: economic, social, and ethical questions

Consider the artificial heart. Are the potential benefits, measured in terms of modestly prolonged life, worth the enormous costs in dollars? Does the uncertain quality of life afforded by this innovation justify the costs? On Dec. 2, 1982, the name Barney Clark became known throughout the world when an operation was performed at the University of Utah Medical Center in Salt Lake City in which the two lower chambers of his dying natural heart were replaced with an artificial heart—the first to be implanted in a human being. The trials and tribulations that he endured during his subsequent 112 days of life were followed with intense interest. His death, which followed a great many medical crises, raises a number of difficult questions that the medical profession and the public at large must now address: Was the operation a success or a failure? Was it done prematurely? Or was it simply the wrong operation, as two world-renowned heart surgeons, Denton Cooley and Norman Shumway, have suggest-

ed? Was it worth the money it cost—an estimated quarter of a million dollars? Can society afford such expensive medical technology? Are there more important social needs, such as improved primary care, disease prevention, or basic education?

Surgeon William DeVries, who performed the operation, when asked whether the operation was a success, replied that only Clark himself could give the answer. Ultimately, and despite the multiple complications he suffered and the subsequent operations he had to undergo, Clark did say that it was worth it. "Yes, it has been hard," Clark said early in March 1983, but, he added, "All in all, it has been a pleasure to be able to help people." Even after his death, Clark's family (including a son who is a surgeon) said that they were glad the operation had been done, and they were grateful for the additional three and a half months of life that the artificial heart had afforded. But what kind of "life" did Clark have during those months? And even disregarding the four operations, three of them emer-

*Barney Clark became known throughout the world when his dying heart was replaced with an artificial heart—the first such implant in a human patient.*

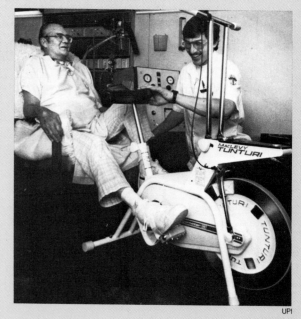

UPI

gencies to deal with complications from the original operation, what kind of life would it have been if he had survived, tethered by a hose to the large tanks of compressed air, weighing 170 kg (375 lb), that were necessary to drive the artificial heart?

Whether or not Barney Clark's operation is judged a success, it must be considered a remarkable accomplishment. More to the point, it is important to consider it in the perspective of the history of other major medical and surgical innovations. Only 14 of the first 30 patients who underwent closed mitral valvotomy operations in the late 1940s survived. The first 100 total hip replacements carried out in England in the early 1960s had to be repeated when it was discovered that the wrong cement had been used. These operations—now widely performed and generally considered safe and effective—might well be judged failures, based on the early results; their ultimate success was made possible only through the experience gained by the "failures." Whether the artificial heart will be judged a success will become apparent only after many additional test cases.

## Progress versus safety

The question whether Barney Clark's operation was premature is a critical one. Should additional research in animals have been carried out, as some physicians have suggested? It can be argued that a better and more convenient power source than a large tank of compressed air is necessary before a clinically feasible operation can be considered to have been achieved. It is anticipated that such a refinement—a mechanical heart with a totally implantable power source—will be available in about a decade. In fairness to the research team in Utah, however, it must be acknowledged that the Jarvik-7, the device implanted in Clark, and earlier models had been tested in several hundred calves, that survival in one calf for as long as nine months had been achieved, and that the program of artificial-heart research from which the plastic and aluminum Jarvik device emerged had extended over a period of more than two decades.

The more important general question is: Should medical innovations be encouraged to move rapidly in order to achieve maximum benefits for the public, or to go more slowly in order to minimize the inevitable risks that accompany new technologies? The former philosophy was epitomized by the statement of a member of the U.S. Congress who, in urging the appropriation of funds for the artificial-heart program in 1965, stated that we should not defer the program for one moment if, by so doing, we would condemn a single person unnecessarily to death. Other advocates of more rapid introduction of new drugs, devices, and procedures argue that society must be willing to accept modest risks—even large ones—in the pursuit of economic growth and continuing improvement in our standard of

*Early models of the artificial heart Barney Clark received were tested in several hundred calves; one calf survived for nine months.*

living. For them, progress should receive first priority. For others, the avoidance of risk is paramount, and a slower pace is considered necessary since risks in medicine—particularly in the use of drugs—may become apparent only with the passage of considerable years. The appearance of vaginal cancer in the daughters of women who had been given diethylstilbestrol (DES) during pregnancy some 15 or more years previously is a notable recent example.

The champions of medical innovation are usually the physicians and other medical scientists who introduce new treatments, and the industries that manufacture new drugs or devices. It is on the government that the public must rely for protection against possible risks—in the United States the major responsibility being housed in the Food and Drug Administration (FDA). In the performance of its responsibilities, the FDA has erected an elaborate set of obstacles designed to prevent the introduction into medical practice of drugs or devices that pose significant risk. Once a new drug or device has been released and is publicly available, the FDA loses nearly all control (its limited authority of recall is almost never invoked); as a result, extraordinary (and, what seems to industry and the profession, often unreasonable) precautions are taken prior to initial approval.

The rationale for such protection is, of course, that not all innovations do what they are supposed to do, nor are they always as successful as their proponents anticipate and claim. Indeed, many have harmful side effects. Medical innovators themselves frequently overestimate the benefits and underestimate the risks of the new treatments they advocate. The history of medicine in this century is replete with examples of new treatments introduced with great enthusiasm only to be shown, often years later and at the expense of substantial iatrogenesis (injury caused by the treatment itself), to do more harm than good.

In the power struggle between the forces of progress and those of protection, the latter, represented by the

*Clinical trials cannot always uncover all of a new drug's potential side effects. Very serious complications have resulted from several large-scale vaccination programs.*

FDA, have apparently gained ascendancy. Certainly, in comparison with other advanced nations, the United States has, through the FDA, placed a higher priority on preventing the introduction of risky drugs and devices and has made less effort to detect drug- or device-induced injury after their release for general use. Great Britain, by contrast, allows greater freedom in the introduction of new drugs. The British justify this policy on the basis of close surveillance and control of drugs following their release.

How realistic are these two approaches? While it can hardly be doubted that it is preferable to avert the use of a dangerous drug prior to introduction than to withdraw it after widespread use, there are major difficulties in the attempt to identify all risks in advance. First, as we have seen, adverse effects, such as those associated with DES, may become apparent only many years later—and not even in the recipients of the drug itself. Second, the effects of a treatment under the tightly controlled conditions of a prerelease clinical trial may be very different from those of widespread general practice.

For example, the numbers of patients or experimental subjects in a clinical trial may be too small to detect a serious but rare complication, as was the case in the federally sponsored swine flu vaccination program of 1976. The complication, known as the Guillain-Barré syndrome, a very serious neurological illness causing paralysis and occasionally death, occurred in 532 cases among the 48 million people in the U.S. who re-

ceived the vaccine, an incidence of approximately one case per 100,000 administrations. To detect a complication so rare in the field trials that preceded the release of the vaccine would have required that several hundred thousand subjects be tested. The field trials had, in fact, been limited to approximately 7,000 subjects.

Thus, premarketing tests cannot realistically be expected to detect late-occurring, or relatively infrequent, complications of treatment. A more rational approach would seem to be the careful testing for serious acute toxicity before marketing and general usage, coupled with the development of a strongly enhanced long-term surveillance designed to detect chronic toxicity and rare adverse reactions.

## Can we afford medical innovation?

It is now apparent that the medical profession can provide more treatment than the public can, or is willing to, pay for. Treatment of end-stage renal disease, for which the Medicare amendments of 1972 provided universal entitlement, cost Medicare $1.8 billion in 1982. Plasmapheresis, an established procedure in which whole blood is removed from a patient, the plasma extracted by centrifugation, and the rest of the blood components reinjected into the body—an experimental treatment for myasthenia gravis, rheumatoid arthritis, multiple sclerosis, and a wide variety of the so-called autoimmune diseases—costs as much as $1,000 per treatment, with individual patients undergoing from 10 to 200 treatments. Total costs, if and when plasmapheresis becomes standard medical practice, could easily exceed those of end-stage renal disease treatment. It was estimated in a recent report published by the U.S. Congressional Office of Technology Assessment that the artificial heart, if successfully developed for general medical application, will cost as much as $3 billion annually.

An endless stream of equally promising and equally expensive new medical innovations can be anticipated. Robert Wilson, president of the Utah State Medical Association, while acknowledging that the implantation of the Jarvik-7 into Barney Clark was a technical achievement, attempted to halt the Utah artificial-heart program on the basis of its expense. In his opinion the public could not afford it. The U.S. government clearly has its own concerns. While encouraging the development of new technology in general, the government has tended to erect formidable obstacles to the introduction of many new medical technologies, obstacles that seem intended more to avert cost than to guard against risk.

It is not easy, however, to prevent the use of new medical technologies after they have been developed, particularly when individual lives might be saved by their use. Alternatively, society may choose not to embark on the development of a new technology in the first place. This would be an easier ethical decision to make, as law professors Guido Calabresi and Philip Bobbitt have pointed out in their book *Tragic Choices*. As a practical matter, however, it is hard to see how this could be accomplished, since medical advances usually emerge from many years and many separate lines of basic scientific research rather than from specific targeted research aimed, for example, at conquering one disease and, therefore, may not be the result of a formal planning process. A decision not to fund the development of the artificial heart could, of course, have been made by the government at the time of the appropriation hearings, but while undoubtedly delaying its development, the government's decision not to fund would not have prevented the use of private funds for this purpose. Furthermore, a decision not to develop a technology in the U.S. in no way affects its development in other countries; indeed, two of the most important medical technologies of this century that are widely used in the United States, the artificial kidney and computerized axial tomography, were invented in Europe.

Public policy, then, is more likely to determine how rapidly a new medical technology will be made available and in what volume. Once a lifesaving treatment is available, if it is in short supply, society faces the immediate and profound ethical problem of who will be saved. When hemodialysis for the treatment of kidney failure became available in Seattle in the early 1960s and there were insufficient facilities to meet the need, a committee was appointed to decide who would receive the treatment. The ethical dilemmas encountered were resolved only with the passage of the Medicare amendments of 1972, by which the government accepted full fiscal responsibility for all costs of treatment of kidney failure, and for all patients.

Private sources primarily funded the research and development of hemodialysis. By contrast, public money was the primary source of support for research and development of the artificial heart. As a result, it has been strongly urged by medical ethicists and others that, if perfected and made available to anyone, it should be made available to everyone. It would be unfair and "un-American" if only those who could pay were to have access. Yet even at this early stage of research, this is exactly the situation at the University of Utah following the implantation of an artificial heart in Barney Clark at a cost of nearly a quarter of a million dollars. Future patients, the university now states, will have to demonstrate the ability to pay.

Part of the difficulty at Utah is that the operation is obviously still experimental, and neither insurance companies nor the government through its Medicare and Medicaid programs is willing to pay for new treatments in the experimental stage. Even if and when the artificial heart is shown to be safe and effective, it is by no means certain that the government or third-party payers will be able or willing to assume the enormous costs that will be incurred. And the problem is by no means limited to the artificial heart. The potential costs of other medical technologies currently in the research or development process may be equally large.

## Containing costs

If the public is in favor of the continuing encouragement of medical innovation and wants access to those inno-

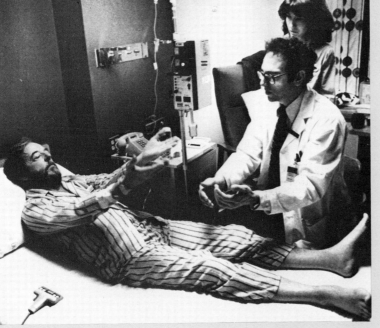

*Medical science has the ability to provide very promising new treatments. But the costs of these innovations raise serious social and ethical questions.*

vations that are successful, how will society be able to pay for them? Allowing the rapid escalation of medical costs to continue is presumably not an acceptable option, since the current expenditure for medical care of over 10% of the gross national product is considered intolerable by most economists and, presumably, by the public.

However hopeless the task of controlling expenditures for new medical technologies may seem, there are, in fact, a number of things we can do to lessen the economic burden. The first is to lessen the need. In the case of the artificial heart, anything that can be done to decrease the incidence of heart disease will obviously decrease the potential demand. The incidence of heart disease has fallen rapidly during the past decade, presumably as a result of the public's healthier life-styles, and it can be assumed that continuing preventive efforts and research in prevention will result in further decreases in heart disease.

Second, if we are to be able to afford new medical procedures, we must make sure that we pay only for those that work. If only a relatively small proportion of innovations actually accomplish their intended purpose, we must determine, at as early a time as possible, whether or not they are effective. To do this will require a considerably enhanced national investment in cost-effectiveness studies of medical procedures and in long-term surveillance. In the past the funding for more rigorous evaluation has been inadequate and inconsistent. With the recent termination of federal funding of the U.S. National Center for Health Care Technology, which had been established in 1978, in part, to serve that purpose, the responsibility now appears to fall on the private sector. It is the private sector, notably large industrial employers, that is increasingly the purchaser of health care for employees, and it is perhaps on industry as well as on the government that the responsibility should fall. Toward this end the Institute of Medicine, a nongovernmental agency within the National Academy of Sciences, is currently attempting to bring together a consortium of health professionals, insurance companies, employers, health officials, and members of the public to establish such an institute for health care evaluation in the U.S.

Finally, if we are to be able to pay for new treatments, we must look at old treatments to determine which ones should be discarded and which ones retained. Reducing or even stopping some current medical procedures will provide some of the savings necessary to support new medical innovation costs.

## Making decisions about new technologies

The decisions about the spending of public moneys for research, development, and evaluation of new medical technologies must be made in consideration of other uses of public funds and, in particular, of needs for other social services. A greater investment in medical care may necessitate a smaller one for education, for example. The public's role in the spending of public money for research and development is to a large extent delegated to their representatives in the Congress, but the public can, through special-interest groups, exert considerable influence on health legislation. The population at large can influence the speed at which innovation is made available via demands on insurance companies and other third-party payers.

A larger, and possibly more useful and effective, role for the public is at the local level as medical innovations are first applied to individual patients. A hospital board might not seem a likely body to consider such matters, but it was the lay board of trustees at the Massachusetts General Hospital in Boston that made the decision not to do heart transplants at that institution. The so-called institutional review boards (IRB's), the committees that review the procedures by which new treatments are introduced in individual hospitals and medical centers, are required by federal regulation to include at least one member of the public. The IRB has traditionally limited its attention to the safety of the proposed experimental treatment and to the process of informed consent, by which patients are told of the potential risks involved. It is argued that in carrying out this responsibility, the IRB should also assess the scientific quality of the proposed experiment on the basis that all experiments carry some risk and that no risk is justified if the science itself is bad. With such an expanded responsibility, the IRB can thus become a partner in the experimental decision process. The review board at the University of Utah demonstrated this during and following Barney Clark's operation. It now finds itself in the dual role of protector of the interests of future recipients of the artificial heart at the medical center and of protector of the interests of the institution itself; in the process, it has undertaken the additional task of considering the overall social and fiscal costs of the experimental procedures that come under its purview.

Scientists and others have argued that members of the public have neither the ability nor the right to participate in scientific decisions. Whatever limitations the nonscientist may have in understanding the purely technical aspects of science—and they may be less than generally assumed—it is to the economic, social, and ethical issues of medical innovation that the public must devote its special attention. The public has not only the right but the obligation to set social and ethical priorities implicit in biomedical innovation and to determine how much of the nation's resources it wishes to invest in biomedical innovations instead of in other social goods and needs.

# Heart and Blood Vessels

Over the past 15 years there has been an important reduction in the frequency of morbid events associated with cardiac illness. The reasons for this improvement are not completely understood but probably relate to increased public awareness, which has resulted in behavioral adjustments extending to diet, stress management, exercise programs, and earlier recognition of the signs and symptoms of heart disease. Medical advances have probably also contributed; these include new diagnostic techniques to help image the heart noninvasively, significant refinements in surgical procedures, and a dramatic expansion in the availability of new drug therapies.

Despite such encouraging trends, the epidemiological, social, and financial impact of coronary artery disease (disorders affecting the large arteries that supply blood to the heart) remains the most significant health care problem in the United States today. Perhaps one of the most exciting areas of research in cardiology involves extending our ability to reduce blockages within coronary arteries through the use of nonsurgical techniques. Catheters (long, flexible hollow tubes composed of synthetic materials) can be inserted into peripheral arteries in the arm or leg and advanced to the heart for the purpose of disrupting blockages that impede the normal flow of blood in coronary arteries. The use of nonsurgical catheter-facilitated procedures to "remodel" the internal channels of coronary arteries has already found direct clinical application and promises to be an important adjunct to traditional therapeutic approaches.

## Manifestations of coronary artery disease

The heart muscle (myocardium), heart valves, and specialized electrical conducting tissue all receive continuous nourishment in the form of oxygen that is transported in the blood by the coronary arteries. The coronary arteries originate from the aorta (the main artery carrying blood from the heart to the rest of the body) as two distinct subdivisions, the left and right coronary arteries. The left coronary artery consists of an "early" portion (the left main coronary artery), which divides (bifurcates) into two large branches. These two branches of the left coronary artery, combined with the right coronary artery, supply blood to the main pumping chamber of the heart (the left ventricle).

Atherosclerosis is the process whereby the smooth inner space of arteries (lumen) is disrupted by the formation of an atheroma, a complex lesion consisting of fatty deposits, calcium, blood clot, and other materials. When the architecture of coronary arteries is critically violated by the presence of atheromatous lesions to such an extent that lumen diameter is reduced by 50%, then clinical manifestations are often present. Most patients with coronary artery narrowings have no symptoms under normal resting conditions. However, when metabolic demands of the body increase, for example, during the stress of exercise, there is a commensurate augmentation in cardiac function. While myocardial blood flow normally increases three to four times, blood flowing through a partially occluded coronary artery cannot increase appropriately, and a supply-demand imbalance results.

Ischemia is the term used to describe the physiological consequences of inadequate coronary blood flow to portions of the myocardium in relation to its metabolic needs. Ischemia results in impaired pumping function of the myocardium and bears as its clinical marker a distinctive form of chest tightness or discomfort known as angina pectoris. As atheromatous lesions become more severe and impinge further on the vessel lumen, angina will appear during lower levels of exercise or even at rest. The sudden total occlusion of a coronary artery or one of its major branches by a blood clot (thrombus) results in complete interruption of blood flow to a region of the myocardium, a process

*Balloon angioplasty uses catheters and inflatable balloons to expand occluded coronary arteries. Shown in the diagram at right: (A) guiding catheter, (B) balloon-tip dilatation catheter, and (C) steerable guide wire. Arrows mark improvement in the right coronary artery of a man with severe angina (left and center) after successful balloon angioplasty treatment.*

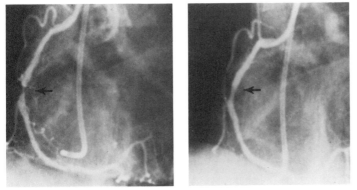

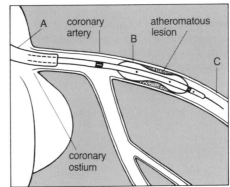

G. Lee, R. M. Ikeda, D. Stebbe, et al., "Laser Irradiation of Human Atherosclerotic Obstructive Disease . . . ,"
*American Heart Journal*, January 1983, vol. 105, no. 1, p. 163

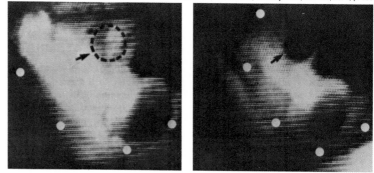

*The encircled target area shows an atheromatous lesion of the iliac artery in a cadaver before it is vaporized by experimental argon laser treatment (right).*

called myocardial infarction (commonly known as a heart attack).

Some patients appear to have angina predominantly at rest with almost no angina during exertion. In this curious circumstance, muscle cells normally present in the middle layer of coronary artery walls have the capacity to contract inappropriately, thereby constricting the vessel lumen in the absence of atherosclerosis. Such coronary artery "spasm" can cause severe ischemia by markedly decreasing blood flow. Although the triggering mechanisms for coronary artery spasm are poorly understood, the resulting chest pain occurs predominantly at rest and has been called variant angina. Some patients have angina at varying exercise thresholds and also at rest; this is often caused by a combination of atheromatous lesions and superimposed coronary artery spasm.

## Standard therapies

Proper therapy for coronary artery disease requires a multifaceted approach. Specific "risk factors" favoring the development of atherosclerosis, such as high blood pressure, diabetes, and elevated blood-lipid levels, should be controlled with careful diet and medications as needed.

Medical therapy for symptoms of angina involves the use of drugs that help to correct the myocardial oxygen supply-demand imbalance created by narrowed vessels. The oldest and most commonly used class of drugs is the nitrates, one well-known member of which is nitroglycerin. These drugs relieve angina by lowering blood pressure and reducing heart size; this diminishes the pressure against which the heart must pump and thereby reduces myocardial oxygen needs. In addition, nitroglycerin can dilate coronary arteries, an action that may increase blood flow and oxygen delivery in patients with coronary artery spasm and, to a lesser extent, in patients with atheromatous lesions.

Beta-adrenergic blocking drugs also reduce myocardial oxygen requirements by lowering heart rate at rest and during exercise. These drugs do not change the caliber of coronary arteries and have no beneficial effects in patients with coronary spasm. Beta-adrenergic blockers can be used alone or in combination with

nitroglycerin; the latter results in additional antianginal efficacy in patients with effort-induced angina.

Finally, a new class of drugs called calcium-channel blockers has been shown to be effective in all forms of ischemic chest pain syndromes. By inhibiting the flow of calcium ions across membranes, these drugs have been shown both to reduce myocardial oxygen demands (by lowering heart rate, blood pressure, and the force of myocardial contraction) and to increase coronary blood flow via primary vasodilating influences.

In the majority of patients with exertional or rest angina, the judicious use of medications will result in a salutary response. However, some patients continue to experience severe life-style-limiting symptoms despite medical therapy. Such individuals require a more aggressive approach.

Coronary artery bypass graft surgery has become an accepted alternative for those patients with atheromatous lesions and anginal symptoms refractory to medical therapy. The bypass operation involves removing portions of veins from the lower extremities and forming a reconstructed conduit from the aorta to a coronary artery beyond the site of blockage. Successful implantation of bypass grafts will greatly increase blood flow to areas of jeopardized myocardium and diminish the clinical manifestations of ischemia. Most patients have a significant reduction in symptoms, and with improved surgical techniques the operative risks to life are only 1 to 2%. Furthermore, there are data that indicate that, in addition to improving the overall quality of life, in certain patients (those with left main coronary artery narrowing and some with narrowing in all three coronary arteries) surgery will favorably affect the longevity of life.

## Balloon angioplasty

The accurate diagnosis of specific cardiac disorders often requires cardiac catheterization. Patients are taken to a catheterization laboratory (a semisterile environment with complex X-ray and monitoring equipment), where catheters approximately 2 mm (0.08 in) in diameter are introduced into blood vessels and advanced to the heart. Pressure measurements are taken within and around the heart, and dye is injected through the catheter, enabling X-ray pictures to be obtained of various cardiac structures, including the coronary arteries. The data derived from catheterizations are often critical in determining the need for specific therapeutic interventions.

More recently, investigators have been employing the catheterization laboratory not merely as a diagnostic tool but also for therapeutic purposes. Percutaneous transluminal coronary angioplasty (PTCA), or balloon angioplasty, is the process whereby catheters, modified by the insertion of inflatable balloons at their tips, traverse a partially occluded coronary artery. Once in position, the balloon is inflated and mechanically expands the vessel lumen.

Current state-of-the-art catheter systems consist of a guiding catheter with a relatively large bore, through which is placed a smaller dilatation catheter. At the tip of the dilatation catheter is a polyvinyl balloon 2 cm (0.8 in) in length, which can be inflated to diameters varying from 2 to 3.7 mm (0.08 to 0.15 in). The dilatation catheter has two channels, one for balloon inflation and the other with an orifice at the tip (beyond the balloon) used for injecting dye and measuring pressure. Modern catheters are also equipped with "steerable" guide wires, which can pass through this second channel to help negotiate tortuous arteries or difficult-to-traverse lesions. The guiding catheter is carefully inserted into a diseased coronary artery, and the dilatation catheter is further advanced until the deflated balloon segment is centered around the stenotic segment. Correct positioning of the dilatation catheter is confirmed by dye injections and the measurement of a drop in pressure as the catheter tip passes beyond the narrowed area. Next, the balloon is inflated to its full diameter for several seconds. Typically, there is an area of indentation in the balloon contour corresponding to the location of the obstructing lesion, which expands or flattens with successful dilatations. The process is repeated several times with increasing inflation pressures. The result is a wider vessel opening that permits significant increases in coronary blood flow.

In 1979 the National Heart, Lung, and Blood Institute (NHLBI) in the U.S. established an international registry for the purpose of rapidly accumulating data pertaining to the efficacy and safety of PTCA. The NHLBI registry now has data from over 100 contributing centers in the United States and Europe, comprising over 3,000 patients. Although long-term follow-up information is available for only a small fraction of these patients, published reports detailing the results from the first 631 patients are sufficient to draw several general conclusions. The overall initial PTCA success rate (defined as a 20% or greater increase in lumen diameter) was 59%; average coronary stenosis was reduced from 83 to 31%. Unsuccessful dilatations most commonly resulted from inability to pass the balloon segment of the catheter across the lesion and accounted

for 29% of cases. An additional 12% of cases were failures due to incomplete dilatation despite correct positioning of the balloon catheter. After successful PTCA, patients demonstrated significant improvement in symptoms and generally manifested a reduction in all objective measures of ischemia. However, approximately 20% of patients had an early return of symptoms, and repeat cardiac catheterization revealed recurrent narrowing at the site of the original lesion. A second attempt at dilatation is usually successful in such patients. Many centers with a large number of experiences are now reporting primary PTCA success rates as high as 85 to 90%.

The frequency of serious complications caused by PTCA has been carefully monitored by the NHLBI registry. In the first 1,500 patients enrolled, there were 72 myocardial infarctions (4.8%), 102 emergency coronary artery bypass graft operations (6.8%), and 16 in-hospital deaths (1.1%). Factors influencing the occurrence of complications include the presence of unstable angina prior to PTCA, the magnitude of lesion stenosis, success or failure of PTCA, and the experience of those performing the procedure.

Patient selection for PTCA is extremely important and is usually confined to those individuals with a history of severe angina refractory to standard medical therapy who would otherwise be candidates for coronary artery bypass graft surgery. Furthermore, owing to the potential complications associated with PTCA, a fully equipped surgical team must be prepared for the possibility of emergency bypass surgery. The majority of patients (approximately 80%) have single-vessel disease (narrowing in one of the three major coronary arteries). Lesions most amenable to successful dilatation are in the proximal, or early, portion of the vessel. As familiarity with PTCA increases and technical acumen improves, the clinical indications have correspondingly grown. There are now ongoing studies examining the efficacy of PTCA in patients with multiple lesions in a single vessel, double- and triple-vessel disease, left main coronary stenosis, and bypass graft stenosis.

## Lasers: a potential new treatment

Although none would dispute the real and potential contributions of PTCA to the management of coronary artery disease, even the most optimistic estimates project that only 25% of patients considered for coronary artery bypass graft surgery would be candidates for this procedure. Thus, investigators have searched for additional ways to use catheters to help a broader spectrum of patients. The most promising of these involves the use of lasers to burrow holes through atheromatous lesions in blocked arteries.

The medical use of lasers (a term derived from "light amplification by stimulated emission of radiation") is a natural extension of the ancient concept of heliotherapy (whereby the health-giving properties of sunlight were prescribed for a wide variety of illnesses). Since the invention of the first ruby laser in 1960, more refined laser systems have found selected medical uses, including the stoppage of bleeding at the site of bleeding ulcers, repair of retinal detachments, and joining of arterial segments in microsurgery. The emission from a laser contains high-density photons that form a single, narrow beam of intense light, which allows precise microdot focusing despite relatively low energy inputs. Lasers can blast a hole in a steel plate without containing enough energy to boil an egg; in eye surgery they are routinely focused on spots 0.1 mm in diameter.

Lasers also have the property of coherence; *i.e.,* all the light waves are exactly in step with one another or have the same phase. This property is important because it helps to eliminate interference effects and results in absolute uniformity as well as amplification of the light beam. Finally, laser light is monochromatic; that is, the light waves are derived from a very narrow bandwidth of wavelengths. This is in sharp contrast to conventional light, which is composed of a broad spectrum of wavelengths. Laser beams are preferentially absorbed by materials with similar wavelengths. After laser light is absorbed by molecules in tissue or other biological substances, part of the energy is converted to heat, which can be so profound that the substances are boiled or vaporized. The potential application of lasers to the treatment of coronary artery disease derives from their ability to induce controlled thermal injury and subsequent vaporization of atheromatous lesions.

There are several theoretical advantages of laser angioplasty compared with currently available PTCA. Atheromatous lesions containing calcium cannot be dilated using balloon-tip catheters because they are too rigid; these lesions would likely be susceptible to laser techniques. Patients with total or nearly total blockage caused by an atheromatous lesion are generally not considered candidates for PTCA. Such individuals may be ideally suited to laser-induced thermal penetration of the lesion with at least partial restoration of blood flow. Correspondingly, patients with acute total occlusion of a vessel caused by a thrombus and resulting in heart attack may also benefit from early treatment using lasers. Finally, since thermal damage caused by lasers can be precisely controlled and well localized, it is possible that laser angioplasty may result in more complete dilatations with less injury to the underlying and surrounding vessel wall.

Thus far, research efforts to explore the feasibility of laser techniques in coronary artery disease are in their embryonic stages. The three most frequently used laser sources in these experiments are $CO_2$ (carbon dioxide), Nd-YAG (neodymium-yttrium, aluminum, garnet), and argon. To couple a laser with a catheter system requires the introduction of an optical fiber that

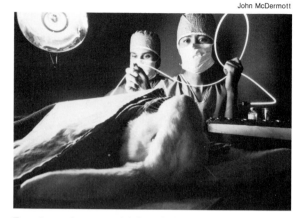

*Experimental surgery with laser light is being performed to clear cholesterol from clogged arteries in a rabbit; laser treatment has resulted in significant reductions of artery narrowings in about half of animal test subjects.*

will conduct the laser energy from the source to the target. Such optical wave guides resemble polished glass rods approximately 0.5 mm in diameter and are usually composed of monofilament quartz.

Experiments examining the effects of various laser systems on diseased coronary arteries from human cadaver specimens have been performed by several investigators. In these studies, successful penetration of atheromatous lesions depended on the type of laser used, total energy of the laser systems (duration of exposure × input power), and conditions of lasing (dry, under saline or blood, or stained with dyes to increase absorption). Vaporization of lesions was not influenced by their composition; hard, calcified lesions were as easily vaporized as softer lesions composed of fatty substances, thrombus, and fibrous or scar tissue. The process of laser vaporization did not result in the formation of loose debris but rather was associated with the generation of microbubbles probably consisting of carbon dioxide and water vapor. Microscopic examination of laser-induced changes in the region of the atheromatous lesion reveals three zones of injury: a superficial crater of tissue vaporization (the depth and diameter of which are directly proportional to the total energy applied), a zone of thermal-induced charring called coagulation necrosis, and a more diffuse region of acoustic or shock injury.

Studies using animal models have attempted to simulate more realistic conditions. Data from an experiment using rabbits fed high-cholesterol diets to create atheromatous lesions in large arteries demonstrated that laser penetration could be achieved in approximately half the cases, with a reduction in average lumen-diameter narrowing from 84 to 20%. Unfortunately, vessel-wall perforation occurred in one-third of cases. Blockages caused by artificial blood clots implanted in the arteries of dogs and rabbits were more easily vaporized without evidence of vessel perforation. Investigations designed to assess the subacute effects of lasers aimed at normal blood vessels were performed in dogs; they revealed partial healing of the laser-induced thermal injury in 9 days and complete restoration of normal vessel appearance in 30 days.

A provocative area of new research that may accelerate the practical application of laser techniques in coronary artery disease includes the development of catheters suitable for direct visualization of the inside of arteries. Tiny illumination fibers, packed within the core of a catheter, provide adequate light to allow viewing of the internal vessel lumen via a large fiberoptic viewing port. A second channel in the catheter is used to advance a fiberoptic wave guide attached to an external laser source. Thus, laser energy can be introduced into an intravascular site under direct vision. These prototype catheter systems are still in an early developmental stage. However, experiments have already been conducted using such a dual fiberoptic catheter to vaporize atheromatous lesions in leg arteries from human cadavers.

The future of laser coronary angioplasty as a viable therapeutic tool still remains highly speculative. The immediate and long-term effects on surrounding vessel walls caused by a level of laser energy sufficient to vaporize an atheromatous lesion are unknown. Research directions in the future are likely to include techniques to steer the laser beam accurately, preferential absorption of laser energy by the lesion through the use of different laser sources, and the combination of laser-equipped catheters with inflatable balloons so that once the lesion is penetrated it can be further dilated.

—*Martin B. Leon, M.D.,*
*and Stephen E. Epstein, M.D.*

# Human Physiology

At the onset of a fever a person experiences chills and feels very cold. The normal response of the body to this feeling is to elevate its internal temperature, a response similar to readjusting a household thermostat. A fever occurs when the set point of the body's thermostat is raised. A fever does not indicate that body temperature is out of control, but merely that it is being regulated at an elevated level.

Unlike a house, which relies simply on an increase in heat production from its furnace, the human body has many ways to raise its temperature. For example, the amount of warm blood pumped from the core of the body to the skin can be decreased. This adjustment, called peripheral vasoconstriction, conserves heat at the body core and accounts for coldness of the skin. Such behavioral responses as adding more blankets, raising the temperature in the room, and huddling also help. If these strategies are inadequate, the body may shiver. Shivering, the rhythmic contraction of the skeletal muscles without accomplishing external work, re-

sults in an increase in the body's metabolic heat production. In conjunction with heat conservation strategies, shivering may send the deep-body temperature from 37° C (98.6° F) to 39° or 40° C (102.2° or 104° F) or occasionally even higher. Once body temperature arrives at the febrile temperature, the person generally no longer feels as cold as in the rising phase of fever. The body is now in a steady-state condition in which internal heat production again equals net heat loss, the only difference being that the regulated deep-body temperature is higher than normal.

Defervescence, the term used to denote the end of a fever, results in the return of the body's set point to its original level. With its core temperature now higher than its set-point temperature, the body responds in numerous ways, an event sometimes called crisis or flush. Sweating produces considerable heat loss via evaporative cooling. Peripheral vasodilation, the increase of blood flow to the skin, carries heat to the external surfaces for dissipation to the environment. The body feels hot and responds by kicking off the blankets, removing garments, and craving a cool drink.

## What causes fever?

A fever is usually the result of contact with some harmful organism. Infection with viruses, bacteria, fungi, or other microorganisms often begins the sequence of events that raises the body's thermoregulatory set point. An early response to contact with a pathogenic organism is the inflammatory response. Within minutes of invasion, white blood cells enter the site of inflammation and begin to phagocytose, or eat, the infective agent. Among the many types of circulating white blood cells, the monocyte is currently thought to play a

*Fever begins when the set point of the body's thermostat is raised. In response, the body conserves heat and generates additional heat, causing the deep body temperature to climb, typically over a period of several hours, until it reaches the new setting. At the end of a fever, the body's set point drops to its normal value. The body responds by giving off excess heat until its core temperature returns to its original level.*

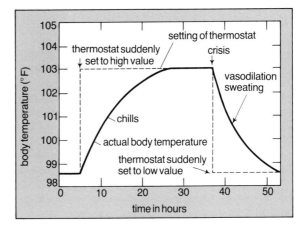

vital role in the fever process. As monocytes engulf the invading organisms, they produce and release a small protein molecule called endogenous pyrogen (EP). EP appears to initiate not only fever but also many other host responses to infection and may play a part in the body's normal thermoregulatory process as well.

EP enters the blood circulation within minutes of its release and travels to the hypothalamus, a region at the base of the brain. A phylogenetically ancient structure, the hypothalamus is essential to the control of many physiological and behavioral functions including sleep, reproduction, food and water intake, and the regulation of body temperature. It is thought that EP acts indirectly on the anterior hypothalamus to raise the thermoregulatory set point. The action of EP on the hypothalamus appears to be indirect because there is no evidence that EP can actually cross the blood-brain barrier (a system of cells and capillary walls that retards the passage of substances in the blood to brain tissue) to enter the brain at this site. Most experts speculate that there are receptors for EP near the hypothalamus but that the specific signal for raising the thermoregulatory set point comes from a group of biologically ubiquitous substances called prostaglandins.

Prostaglandins are fat-soluble chemicals produced by many tissues; they have a wide range of biologic activity including effects on the heart and blood vessels, smooth muscles, hormone secretions, kidneys, and pain pathways. Support for a role for these substances in the initiation of fever comes from a variety of sources. Prostaglandins do occur naturally in the hypothalamus, and their concentrations have been shown to rise during infection. Injection of small amounts of prostaglandins into the anterior hypothalamus of laboratory animals produces fever. Further, antipyretic drugs (drugs that lower the elevated set point) such as aspirin and acetaminophen are also potent inhibitors of prostaglandin synthesis. Many studies have shown that a small amount of an antipyretic drug injected into the hypothalamus is more effective in reducing fever than a much larger dose taken orally or intravenously. Nevertheless, despite the strong evidence linking prostaglandins with the development of fever, some experiments seem to show that prostaglandins may not be involved in all fevers.

While little is actually known about the precise events leading from the production of EP to the development of fever, even less is known about the factors responsible for returning the elevated set point to normal. Some studies indicate that the kidneys participate in the removal of EP from the circulation, and others show that the liver degrades EP. It is possible that the central nervous system itself inactivates EP and therefore participates in defervescence.

Many fevers are cyclical in nature, and virtually nothing is known about what is responsible for these swings. Regardless of pattern, however, most fevers in

human beings are limited to 41° C (105.8° F). This maximum has obvious survival value since a sustained body temperature above 41° C causes cell degeneration and is ultimately fatal. Evidence exists for the natural occurrence of substances that lower normal body temperature and attenuate fevers. These endogenous antipyretics, or cryogens (in contrast to pyrogens), may prove to play an important role in the normal fluctuations in body temperature observed in both health and disease.

## The role of the body's thermostat

The ancient Greeks believed that fever was a beneficial sign during infection. This idea apparently had its origins in the Empedoclean doctrine that the roots of all matter were earth, air, fire, and water. Hippocrates and others expanded these concepts to correspond to the four bodily humors—blood, phlegm, yellow bile, and black bile. Disease was the result of an imbalance in one of these humors. Fever was a response of the body to the production of the excess humor and resulted in its being "cooked" and eventually evacuated from the body. Some ancient physicians believed that a fever helped evacuate excess humors from the sick person by inducing some combination of vomiting, diarrhea, and sweating.

The idea that an excess of humors caused disease led to the simplification of ancient medical practice. The physician could "cure" a patient by administering drugs that were sudorofics (sweat-inducing agents), emetics, or purgatives or that raised body temperature—all effects that would help the body evacuate excess humor. Additionally the physician could use such physical means as warming the patient externally, a practice that came to be known as fever therapy, or bloodletting to remove some of the excess humor directly.

So strong was the belief in the scholarship of the ancients that the concept of fever as beneficial to an ill person persisted for centuries. For example, in the late 17th century the famed English physician Thomas Sydenham wrote that "fever is Nature's engine which she brings into the field to remove her enemy." Carl Liebermeister, a German physician of the late 1800s who first accurately defined fever as the regulation of body temperature at a higher level, believed that fevers were generally beneficial. He did warn, however, that excessively high or long fevers were harmful.

Despite the lack of hard scientific evidence on the value of fever, by the early 1900s many physicians were advocating that fevers be reduced. This turnabout correlates with the appearance of the first commercially available antipyretic drugs such as aspirin and may have been encouraged by the fact that most antipyretic drugs are also analgesics; that is, they reduce pain associated with infection. Whereas a purely antipyretic drug would have no effect on the pain ac-

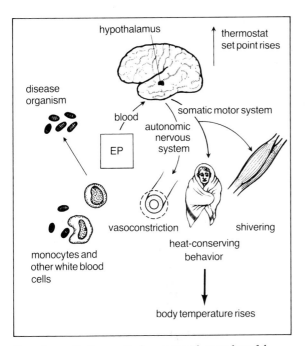

*Fever is usually the result of contact with some harmful organism. As part of the inflammatory response, monocytes and other white blood cells attack the invader; in the process they produce and release a protein called endogenous pyrogen (EP). EP travels through the blood to the hypothalamus, where it is believed to raise the set point of the body's thermostat, thus initiating the physiological and behavioral responses needed to elevate the deep body temperature.*

companying most infections, a dual-function drug such as aspirin could have convinced physicians that their patients reported feeling better because their fevers were reduced.

During the past decade another type of historical approach has helped vindicate the ancient belief of a useful purpose for fever. This approach does not trace the recorded history of writings on fever and disease; rather it looks at the phylogenetic or evolutionary history of fever.

Research from numerous laboratories has shown that virtually all species of vertebrates develop fevers in response to infection, from cold-blooded species of fish and reptiles to warm-blooded birds and mammals. It is reasonable to wonder how a cold-blooded animal can develop a fever. As mentioned above, the regulation of body temperature involves both behavior and physiology. Warm-blooded species (often called endotherms) rely on such physiological responses as internal generation of heat, changes in skin blood flow, and sweating as well as on an enormous array of behaviors. Many cold-blooded vertebrates (ectotherms) also regulate their body temperature—but almost exclusively by behavior. Fish, amphibians, and reptiles have not evolved the metabolic machinery necessary to gener-

ate the substantial amounts of heat necessary to regulate body temperature. Nevertheless, they often maintain a remarkably constant deep-body temperature by moving into and out of the sunshine, by swimming to a warmer or cooler area of the pond, or by subtle changes in body posture relative to the Sun or some other heat source.

Investigations into the central nervous control of thermoregulation have shown that the nerve cells that sense temperature and those that integrate this thermal information are similar in cold- and warm-blooded vertebrates. In the early 1970s some researchers speculated on this similarity, predicting that a cold-blooded animal such as the desert iguana would develop a fever and therefore seek a warmer environment when infected. Their experiments showed that, following inoculation with bacteria, iguanas indeed did choose a warmer region of a simulated desert environment set up in the laboratory. As a result, the lizards' deep-body temperature rose several degrees Celsius. Subsequent studies from several laboratories revealed that a variety of species of fish, amphibians, and reptiles also develop "behavioral fevers" when they are infected.

The above experiments have several important implications. Once again they reaffirm earlier assertions that fever is simply the regulation of body temperature at a higher level. The only way an ectotherm can raise its body temperature is through behavior. Contact with some disease organism clearly raises its thermoregulatory set point, the proof being that the animal actively seeks out a warmer environment.

Another implication is that fever appears to be a response that has been around for hundreds of millions of years. The similarities between the febrile responses of, for example, reptiles and mammals are too many to be simply the result of chance. Both groups of vertebrates develop fevers in response to similar stimuli. The antipyretic drug sodium salicylate lowers the set point in both groups. In addition, an endogenous pyrogenlike protein has been isolated from both groups. Since reptiles and mammals have been phylogenetically distinct for well more than 200 million years, the genes necessary for the fever response must have existed prior to that divergence.

Phylogenetic studies of fever have also provided some insights into the biologic role of fever in disease. One is that fever represents an expensive energy loss to the animal. Regardless of whether an organism is cold- or warm-blooded, a rise in body temperature results in a substantial metabolic increase and therefore in energy expenditure. For example, a rise of 2° or 3° C (3.6°–5.4° F) usually means an increase in energy expenditure of about 25%. There is obviously no selective pressure for waste. Because fever has apparently existed throughout the vertebrates for millions of years without diminishing in magnitude, it must confer some survival advantage; that is, fever must be a component of the host organism's immune defense system.

The discovery that cold-blooded animals can develop fever has also provided excellent animal models for investigating the biological role of fever. One of the difficulties in any such study involving a warm-blooded animal—for example, the laboratory rabbit—is that of controlling the deep-body temperature of the animal. A reasonable experimental design would be to infect a group of rabbits with bacteria in an amount known to kill about half the animals. Some infected animals would be allowed to develop a normal fever; the others would be prevented from doing so. The percentage of survivors in each group would be compared and conclusions drawn. The major problem with this design is the near impossibility of suppressing fever in an infected warm-blooded animal without making the experiment difficult to interpret. For example, suppose one prevented some rabbits from raising their body temperature by placing them in an ice bath and found that the death rate was higher in that group than in an unmanipulated group. Can one be certain that the difference was due to the effect of the ice bath on body temperature or to some side effect of this obvious stress?

By contrast, manipulating the body temperature of cold-blooded animals is considerably easier. Scientists working with infected desert iguanas and infected goldfish, for example, had little difficulty maintaining the animals' body temperatures at normal or febrile levels simply by placing the animals in constant-temperature environments set at different temperatures. When in their natural habitat, cold-blooded animals can select a preferred environmental temperature. But place these animals in an unnatural constant-temperature environment, and their temperature will be within 0.5° C of the environmental temperature.

The results of studies on cold-blooded animals infected with disease bacteria have shown that fever is advantageous. A significantly higher percentage of animals forced to remain at febrile temperatures survived the infection. For example, on its own an infected desert iguana will choose an environmental temperature of 40°–42° C (104°–107.6° F). Prior to infection these lizards chose a temperature near 38° C (100.4° F). When groups of infected lizards were forced to be at either 42° C or 38° C, the percentage of survivors was 75 and 25%, respectively.

One group of warm-blooded animals shares some of the characteristics of cold-blooded animals—newborns. Many young mammals tend to be thermolabile; that is, their body temperature is affected to a large extent by environmental temperature. Consequently, newborn mammals have been used in several studies designed to probe the role of fever. In three studies all involving viral infections, it was found that placing dog pups, mice pups, or piglets at a warmer environmental temperature resulted in a higher deep-body temperature (similar to fever in the adult animals) and a higher survival rate.

If fever is beneficial, then would the use of antipyretic drugs be harmful? Several studies suggest that this may be the case. When infected lizards received aspirin, the lizards selected a cooler environmental temperature, resulting in a significantly higher mortality rate. Partially blocking the fever with drugs in bacterially infected rabbits resulted in a significant increase in mortality rate. And suppression of fever with an aspirin-like drug in ferrets, the animal model used most often for influenza research, led to an increase in the amount of viruses in their upper respiratory system.

## When is fever beneficial?

When considering possible mechanisms behind the adaptive value of fever, one must compare the host defense responses at normal and febrile body temperatures in order to make some statement about the effects of fever on mechanisms of resistance. There is evidence accumulating that many components of the host defense system are assisted by small elevations in temperature. For example, white blood cells are considerably more mobile at temperatures found during fever. Not only can these cells get to the site of infection faster, but they also seem to be more effective in phagocytosing and digesting the invading microorganisms at febrile temperatures. Interferon, a natural cellular product that has become recognized in recent years as a potential antitumor and antiviral agent, has also been shown to be more effective at elevated body temperatures.

Despite strong evidence that fever has evolved as a host defense mechanism, there are times when its detrimental effects make it advisable to use drugs or physical means (e.g., sponge baths) to lower body temperature during an infection. Patients for whom the risk of fever might outweigh its benefits include young children, some of whom may be predisposed to febrile convulsions; pregnant women, because of the potentially harmful effects on the fetus; and elderly or debilitated persons, because of the general stress of an elevated temperature on weakened organs and systems.

Although fever appears to have remained of value to animals over hundreds of millions of years of evolution, as host defense systems evolve so do disease organisms. Selective pressures are continually reestablishing some dynamic equilibrium between host and pathogen. For fever to have remained an active response to virtually all infections, it is likely that fever is beneficial in a majority of infections. In other words, fever is generally, but not always, a nonspecific host defense response. One important task now facing biomedical investigators is to determine more precisely when fever is beneficial and when it is not.

—*Matthew J. Kluger, Ph.D.*

# Special Report:
# Laughter and Health
## by William F. Fry, Jr., M.D.

*Members of the human race develop individual styles of laughing and displaying mirth; (above) the archbishop of Canterbury and Nancy and Ronald Reagan show theirs.*

On the face of it, there are few topics that would seem more inappropriate for scientific discussion than humor, mirth, and laughter. But there are aspects of humor and its attendant emotions and behaviors that deserve careful appraisal regarding their potential contributions to health and the healing sciences. There is indeed some emerging evidence that the roots of humor and mirth strike deep in human biology. The effects of humor are complex both upon individual functioning and on the relationships between individuals. Further, human physiology appears to be stirred in many ways by the physical components of laughter; evidence is available for effects in most of the major physiological systems. Information revealing this spectrum of impacts comes from diverse sources that have provided both laboratory data and clinical observations. Information has been gleaned from many disciplines, including medicine, psychology, and even anthropology.

## Humor: inherited or acquired?

For decades debate had swirled around the question of whether the human sense of humor has inherited biological origins or is acquired by environmental exposure. Persuasive information favors the view that members of the human race are born with the potential for developing a sense of humor as one component of their inherent psychological development. This view is supported by infant and child development studies that focus on early responses to various stimuli, including appreciation of humor. These developmental studies are corroborated by anthropological data indicating that there are no ethnic groups anywhere in the world that lack individual or group humor.

Whereas heredity is strongly implicated in the potential for developing a sense of humor, environmental influences are widely believed to be predominent in shaping and guiding the content of each individual's sense of humor. The strongest influences appear to be parental and familial. Peer and cultural influences are also very active.

Regarding the humor-associated behaviors—smiling and laughing—the potential for developing these responses appears to be inherited; their specific occurrences, however, as well as individual "styles," are dictated by environmental influences. Since each human has a somewhat different array of environmental exposures, it is not unexpected that every individual's "mirth repertoire" is different.

An interesting study demonstrating the inheritance of smiling was based on D. E. Freeman's observations of infants who are blind, deaf, or both blind and deaf. All of these infants were found to manifest "reflex" smiling behavior early in life. The operation of environmental influence was illustrated in the finding that blind infants were markedly retarded in their smiling responses. Visual facilitation was concluded to be a critical element in this deficiency. Support for the view that there are both inherited and environmental influences for the smiling response is provided in studies by other investigators as well, who have demonstrated that within the first 36 hours of life, sighted human neonates are capa-

259

ble of discrimination and imitation if presented with facial expressions, including smiling.

The biological origins of humor, *e.g.,* for manifesting one's appreciation of situations with laughter, etc., are related to two other inherited elements of human functioning—the capacity for playing and the capacity for experiencing ambivalence. The spirit of play establishes a frame for the occurrence of humor; *i.e.,* play establishes a context for interpreting and responding to forms of communication—verbal or nonverbal—intended to be "humorous." Without this context or frame, the communication presumably intended as humorous would appear inconsequential, bizarre, or incongruous. Likewise, the human ability to tolerate the experience of ambivalence is a necessary part of our sense of humor. The two (or more) simultaneous and contradictory attitudes or feelings that compose ambivalence provide the potential for the acceptance of humor. If humans could not experience or tolerate ambivalence, the otherwise humorous experience would be perceived as inconsistent or conflictual.

The question of whether other creatures experience humor and "laughter," or whether humans are the only creatures so blessed, has long puzzled investigators. Until recently it has largely been viewed as a moot question because communication could not be established between humans and other creatures to certify adequately that other animals experience what could be described as "humor." Primatologist and psychologist Lawrence Pinneo, however, has demonstrated a breathy, paroxysmal, climactic respiratory behavior of chimpanzees in response to their being tickled. This same response to tickling has been verified in gorillas and orangutans. Parallels between the physiological aspects of human laughter and respiratory paroxysms in the higher primates are marked. Moreover, the unique genre of stimulation—tickling—is productive of similar behavior in humans and primates. Further, it is an equally desired, sought after, and presumably enjoyed response by all four animals.

Further evidence of a sense of humor in primates has come from the study of two gorillas, Koko and Michael, who have been taught to communicate with sign language and studied by Francine Patterson. These gorillas manifest a sense of humor that includes practical joking—which is differentiated from simple play by measures of coherent actions calculated to build to a climax. Practical joking by primates has also been described by scientists Jane Goodall and Dian Fossey in their observations of the behavior of chimpanzees and gorillas in the wild. Koko and Michael, through the vehicle of sign language, also have demonstrated an ability to engage in other more cognitive forms of humor, such as puns, word "games," sarcasm, and ridicule.

## The study of humor and laughter

Physicians and other health professionals have manifested an empirical understanding of the values of humor in health and healing for centuries. This understanding has been expressed, for example, in conceptions of what a good "bedside manner" entails—not just caring and compassion but also joviality and optimism. Healers of the past were well aware of the beneficial effects—for even the sickest patient—of a smile or jest or gentle laugh shared between them. The tendency to trivialize humor and mirth, however, has prevented the emergence of a scientific system for utilizing their empirical values therapeutically.

The well-publicized case of writer Norman Cousins, who "laughed himself back" from a serious illness, has but a modest standing in the annals of medical re-

*Chimps and gorillas respond to tickling with breathy respiratory paroxysms that are quite similar to human laughter. Tickling appears to be both desired and enjoyed by primates.*

*"I'm sorry, but I don't laugh out loud."*

search. Nonetheless, his recovery, which he partially attributes to "deep belly laughter," has aroused the interest of many investigators who believe that the positive emotions may indeed produce beneficial chemical changes in the body. Thus far the physiological effects of laughter on health have not been studied or validated sufficiently to satisfy scientific rigor.

## What do we know about laughter?

Laughter is essentially a respiratory act, composed of the same basic elements as normal, cyclic breathing—namely, expiration and inspiration of air and an abundance of pauses. Cyclic, regular breathing patterns have been shown to be greatly disrupted by laughter. While there is a wide range of individual laugh patterns, most laughs are characterized by a varying degree of expiratory predominance. Consequently, it can be shown that laughter of several cycles' duration affects the normal residual air volume, resulting in an increase of pulmonary ventilation beyond that achieved during normal breathing. Despite this expiratory predominance, peripheral blood oxygen concentrations are not greatly disturbed and maintain stability even during prolonged laughter of pronounced intensity.

The most well-studied physiological phenomenon is an increase in heart rate that accompanies laughter. This effect appears to be a reflex mechanism, involving pulmonary-cardiac functions. The increase of rate has been shown to be directly proportional to intensity and duration of laughter. This increase is also observed in other respiratory activities representing a change from normal breathing, such as talking and coughing. This heart-rate increase is followed by a brief decrease in heart rate below the previous normal baseline rate.

Laughter-induced alterations of arterial blood pressure show brief, but sometimes large, increases of both systolic and diastolic pressure. Again, these increases are directly proportional to intensity and duration of laughter. Following cessation of laughter, there is a short-lived drop of pressure below the norm.

Another system known to be greatly influenced by laughter is the musculoskeletal system. Mild mirth (smiling, chuckling, chortling, etc.) produces modest degrees of activity of facial, neck, scalp, and shoulder muscles. More substantial laughter produces effects that can be measured in muscles of the respiratory apparatus, including intercostal muscles (situated between the ribs), abdominal muscles, and the diaphragm. Increasingly greater degrees of laughter are accompanied by greater numbers of muscle groups being affected and greater intensities of muscle activity. "Convulsive" laughter appears to involve most of the body's skeletal musculature. These observations have been substantiated in varying degrees by laboratory procedures. Electromyographic readings have revealed the presence of a brief period of muscular relaxation following cessation of laughter.

While it is presumed that the central nervous system (CNS) is activated during mirth and laughter, few actual laboratory studies have confirmed this. Muscle "noise" interference with brain-wave testing creates technical difficulties for measuring such responses. A few studies have recorded general CNS effects, but specific patterns of activation for the most part have not been revealed. There have been a few reports that, in rare cases of susceptible patients, laughter can precipitate epileptic seizures, laughter convulsions, and cataplectic seizures (the sudden loss of muscle power following a strong emotional stimulus).

The impact of humor and mirth on the human endocrine system remains even less explored than that of the CNS. Clinical observations—such as Norman Cousins's experience of varying periods of diminished pain following extensive laughter—suggest endocrine effects, but these have not yet been substantiated by laboratory studies. One exception: laughter's stimulatory effect on the body's production of circulating adrenaline has been observed by one investigator. This finding has been supported by the demonstration that persons are more "humor-responsive" when injected with adrenaline. These studies, however, have not been carried out recently or confirmed with refined technology now available. There is considerably more to be learned about the effects of humor and mirth on various components of the endocrine system, which physiologists believe may be extensive.

## Clinical implications

A few explorations of clinical uses of humor are in progress, the field of psychological treatment currently the most active. At the 1983 convention of the American Psychological Association, a team of California researchers that has been studying types of humor and personality revealed several preliminary findings, among them that a lively sense of humor indicates flexibility and healthy mechanisms for coping with life's difficulties.

Several practitioners, through successful clinical experience, have come to view humor's therapeutic powers as a major instrument for psychological change. These pioneers have seen the value of humor as a force that can offer hope and even liberation from compulsive, self-defeating behavior. Humor is also an antidote to some depressions. The California psychologists emphasized humor in psychotherapy as a means of furthering the patient's sense of identity and self-understanding.

The beneficial role of humor in psychotherapy has suggested that there may also be specific roles for utilizing mirth and laughter in institutional settings such as nursing homes, convalescent hospitals, and retirement homes. These institutions can be cheerless, sterile, gloomy, and oppressive places. The benefits of introducing cheer into the lives of residents seem obvious. At the Andrus Gerontology Center in Los Angeles it was found that a humor "program" increased morale, general activity level, and socialization among the patients. One program format included puppetry, a mock "fashion show," exchange of jokes and cartoons, and playful uses of music and musical instruments. A crucial factor for the success of any such humor program is the direct participation of institution residents.

## Exercise-laughter parallels

In recent years extensive investigation of physiological effects of exercise has demonstrated a wide variety of presumed health benefits, from prophylactic and rehabilitative values for coronary heart disease to the discovery that exercise may increase the vitality of the immune system, which protects the body from a vast number of diseases, possibly including cancer. There appears to be good reason to hope that physical fitness achieved through regular aerobic (vigorous) exercise that stimulates the circulatory system and activates muscle groups promotes strength, flexibility, and endurance. There is good reason to believe, likewise, that the physiological mechanisms of laughter, which also stimulate circulation and activate muscles, have similar beneficial effects. Other presumed benefits of aerobic exercise are also seen with laughter. One is a sense of well-being. Another is pain relief, possibly

attributable to increased levels of endorphins, the body's natural opiates, which are released into the bloodstream. Indeed laughter can be said to give the body a miniworkout and has been compared to stationary jogging.

*Circulatory system effects.* With laughter, heart rate is increased and blood pressure is elevated. Peripheral blood oxygen concentration is maintained at normal levels. These effects result in stimulation of circulation with imputed increases in blood-borne dissemination of high-density lipoproteins (HDL's), associated with low rates of heart disease. This circulatory stimulation has, in rare instances, proven detrimental, even fatal. A few cases of strokes (brain hemorrhages) have been reported during laughter, presumably precipitated by the increase in arterial blood pressure. However, despite the often profound increase of heart action accompanying laughter, heart attacks are *not* likely to occur during bouts of laughter.

*Respiratory effects.* Normal cyclic breathing leaves a body of air behind in the lungs—the so-called residual air. Moisture concentrations of residual air can build up, making the lungs a more favorable environment for microorganism colonization. Mirthful laughter, with its attendant excess expiration, invades the residual air volume and quickens its exchange with external air, thus enhancing aeration. Further, laughter can activate the respiratory process whereby purulent discharges in the tracheobronchial tree, associated with such clinical conditions as bronchitis and emphysema or with heavy smoking, are raised and expectorated.

*Emotional health effects.* Psychosomatic medicine has established etiologic or precipitating roles for emotions in several disease conditions. Anger and fear are suspected of being associated with higher rates of coronary heart attacks—either attributable to acute episodes, sometimes occurring at the time of emotional outbursts, or to the chronic buildup of fear or anger, which may set the stage for an attack.

It is proverbial that humor minimizes the intensities of both fear and anger. Those two emotions cannot exist in full force while mirth is experienced. And in many instances, fear and anger are totally dissipated by a cultivated sense of humor.

## The future

Psychiatrist George Vaillant followed the personal development and psychological health of a group of male college graduates for nearly 40 years. In his analysis of their "adaptation to life," he described humor as one of the five mature human coping mechanisms.

It is reasonable to assume that there are many as yet unexplored physiological and emotional effects of laughter and humor on health. Gelotology, "the science of laughter," obviously is emerging as a new field of study. There is much work to be done to fill in many important gaps in this science.

# Human Sexuality

The term impotence is often used loosely to denote any disturbance in male sexual function, including libido (sexual drive), erection, ejaculation, or orgasm. A more nearly accurate definition of male impotence, however, is the persistent inability to obtain or maintain a penile erection suitable for sexual intercourse. This definition implies that the mere presence of penile erection does not preclude the diagnosis of impotence. Indeed, we now recognize that primary impotence may exist, referring to a situation in which penile erections have been insufficient for sexual intercourse throughout a man's life. In contrast, secondary impotence defines a situation in which erectile ability was adequate previously but is no longer so. Impotence may also be separated by primary cause into two main categories: psychogenic and organic. Psychogenic impotence implies a lack of erectile ability arising from psychological causes such as emotional conflict, anxiety, or depression. Organic impotence is secondary to a physical cause, which will usually involve the vascular, neurologic, or hormonal systems of the body.

It is estimated that between five million and ten million males in the United States suffer from some degree of erectile dysfunction or impotence. It had been previously held that up to 90% of these men had an underlying psychological problem as the primary cause. Newer diagnostic techniques have shown that this proportion is probably closer to 50–60%, meaning that at least 40–50% of men with impotence are suffering from an underlying physical disorder. For the understanding of the current approach to correction of erectile impotence, a brief discussion of normal and abnormal erectile function is necessary.

## Normal erection

Several factors are required for the production of a normal erection. The nervous, the vascular (blood vessel), and the hormonal (glandular) systems all contribute to the process. The nerves that control the penis come from the last part of the spinal cord (sacral cord). These nerves are part of the parasympathetic nervous system. The sacral parasympathetic nerves interact with a second nerve to innervate, or supply the penis with nerves, in order to effect an erection. At present the nature of the second nerve remains unknown, and much investigative work is being performed in order to identify its neurotransmitter—the messenger substance that it secretes to alter penile function. Knowledge about the final neurotransmitter may play an important clinical role in the development of suitable medical therapies for erectile dysfunction.

The blood supply to the penis comes through the internal pudendal arteries. The penis contains two large potential blood channels called corpora cavernosa. Blood supplied through the internal pudendal artery

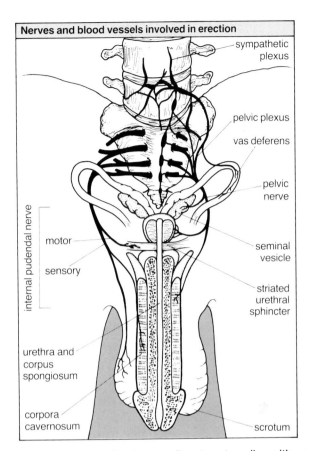

**Nerves and blood vessels involved in erection**

- sympathetic plexus
- pelvic plexus
- vas deferens
- pelvic nerve
- seminal vesicle
- striated urethral sphincter
- scrotum
- corpora cavernosum
- urethra and corpus spongiosum
- internal pudendal nerve
- motor
- sensory

eventually enters the deep penile artery, traveling within each corpus. During sexual stimulation, the blood enters the potential corporal spaces, fills the corpora, and is then "trapped" as certain critical veins constrict within the corpora. This mechanism is the basis of the formation of an erection. It is, therefore, a neurovascular event and requires integrity of both the nervous system and the vascular tree.

Three other factors are important in the mechanism of erection: suitable hormonal environment, a healthy psychological outlook, and normal corporal tissue. Abnormal erectile function, then, can result from causes that are psychological, hormonal, vascular, or neurological or from those involving end-organ, or penile, disorders.

It is not uncommon for a short-lived period of impotence to occur in a man's life. These periods are usually self-limited and improve without professional help. Patients who seek medical advice regarding impotence will usually have had a problem for at least six months.

## Psychogenic impotence

At present it is estimated that impotence secondary to psychological causes accounts for about 60% of all cases of erectile dysfunction. Essentially, psychogenic impotence is suspected when no evidence for an organic disorder is found. However, it is important to remember that the emotional problems connected with impotence may at times be the effect of the disorder rather than the cause. Various factors that play a role have been determined, including anxiety or fear of failure, hostility and resentment toward one's partner or toward women in general, shame (usually secondary to one's upbringing), and guilt (usually secondary to religious views). For example, "widower's syndrome" is a well-known situation in which men who have recently suffered the loss of their wives, who often died following a prolonged illness, cannot perform sexually. This presumably is secondary to some degree of guilt. Other causes of psychogenic impotence include latent homosexuality and, of course, recognized psychiatric disorders such as depression and psychosis.

## Hormonal impotence

A wide variety of endocrine disorders may affect potency, including acromegaly, pituitary insufficiency, thyroid dysfunction, Addison's disease, and adrenal neoplasias. Impotence associated with these disorders, however, is rarely the main problem for which the patient seeks medical attention.

The majority of patients suffering from hormonally induced impotence will fall into one of three categories. The first is characterized by a decrease in the level of the male hormone testosterone. This occurs most commonly because the testes, where testosterone is made, are incapable of manufacturing testosterone (hypergonadotropic hypogonadism). More rarely, the pituitary gland, which stimulates the testes to make testosterone, cannot do so (hypogonadotropic hypogonadism). The third mechanism for hormonally induced impotence involves a small pituitary tumor that secretes a hormone called prolactin. High levels of prolactin are associated with lowered levels of testosterone and impotence (as well as with male infertility).

## Neurogenic impotence

As an erection involves all levels of the nervous systems, from the brain to the peripheral nerves, lesions anywhere along the path may be responsible for erectile failure. Brain tumors, Parkinson's disease, and multiple sclerosis (MS) are the more common neurologic diseases associated with impotence. Diabetes mellitus is probably the single most common disease associated with erectile failure. It has been estimated that close to 50% of diabetic males have some degree of erectile dysfunction. Diabetes, a metabolic disease with vascular and nervous system complications, may affect both the blood supply to the penis and the nerve supply to the penis. Neuropathies (disorders of the nerves) are commonly seen in many diabetics, and when these involve nerves to the penis, impotence may ensue. Other causes of peripheral neuropathies such as alcoholism may also produce this disorder.

## Vasculogenic impotence

During the process of erection, there is approximately a fivefold increase in the blood flow to the penis. For maintenance of an erection, the blood flow to the penis is only slightly increased over normal. If there is any obstructive process in the arteries leading to the penis, an increase in blood flow becomes impossible. This process is the basis of vasculogenic impotence. Disease of the penile blood vessels is affected by the same risk factors that pertain to other vascular diseases, including diabetes mellitus, hypertension, and cigarette smoking.

In addition, many patients who are being treated with medicines to decrease their blood pressure often suffer from impotence. This is probably due to a drug-induced lowering of blood pressure in vessels leading to the penis that are already compromised by disease. Diabetes mellitus may, as stated above, involve both the nerves and blood vessels throughout the body and is thus a major cause of vasculogenic impotence. Blood flow to the penis may be interrupted by trauma to the pelvic region, causing arterial obstruction. Surgical procedures involving the pelvis, such as radical cystectomy (removal of the bladder for bladder cancer) and Miles' resection of the colon (removal of a cancerous lower large bowel) can also cause arterial obstruction and thus impotence.

## Penile (end-organ) impotence

Inability of the corpora to fill completely with blood is rare. There are two diseases, however, in which this inability is almost always seen. The first is Peyronie's disease, which involves the formation of scar tissue (plaques) on the covering (tunica albugenea) of the corpora. These plaques may cause marked distortion of an erection making intercourse impossible. In addition, the plaque may also obstruct the normal flow of blood within the corpus itself.

The second end-organ problem is priapism. Priapism is an abnormal state of constant erection that is not due to sexual stimulation. It may be caused by certain injuries to the penis or secondarily by obstruction to the normal outflow of blood (through the dorsal vein) at the root of the penis. A surgical procedure is usually required for relief. However, many patients will be impotent following an episode of priapism, perhaps because of permanent scarring in the corporal spaces.

## Finding the cause of impotence

Over the last decade there has been considerable progress in our ability to determine the etiology of impotence. The initial step is to determine whether it is of a psychological or organic origin. The patient's history still remains one of the best means of determining basic cause. For example, a classic history for organic impotence usually involves an insidious onset and a prolonged course with gradual diminution in erectile

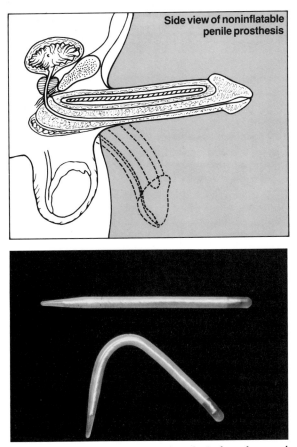

**Side view of noninflatable penile prosthesis**

*In cases of erectile dysfunction with a physical, nonhormonal cause, a prosthetic device that consists of paired, flexible silicon rods (above) can be surgically implanted in the corpora. The penis is constantly erect but can assume an inconspicuous resting position under clothing.*

capacity. Initial symptoms might include decrease in rigidity that progresses to inability to maintain an erection. With time, erections become less and less rigid until no erections occur. Typically, patients with organic impotence will not awaken in the morning with a normal erection, but this is not always the case.

Conversely, patients with psychogenic impotence usually have a relatively abrupt onset of their problem, often associated with an important event in their lives, such as a wife's death or a divorce. Patients with psychogenic impotence will usually arise in the morning with a normal erection. During sleep a man will normally have four to five well-sustained erections, almost always associated with dream states. An erection upon awakening is merely one of these normal nocturnal erections that is coincidental with arising. Therefore, if a man awakes with a well-sustained erection, the doctor's diagnosis is usually psychogenic impotence, as this indicates that the neurovascular input to the penis is adequate—*i.e.*, the mechanics for erection are normal.

These two categories of psychogenic and organic impotence are not necessarily mutually exclusive. There are patients who are affected by both types of impotence. In addition, physicians cannot always distinguish satisfactorily between the two groups.

Various specialized examinations are necessary in order to fully evaluate a patient with erectile dysfunction. Levels of various hormones such as testosterone and prolactin are usually measured. Impotence secondary to hormonal disorders is considerably less common than had long been thought. When present, however, it usually can be treated by appropriate medications. In patients with low testosterone levels an endocrinologic workup is in order and, if appropriate, treatment with testosterone given intramuscularly every three to four weeks is usually effective. Patients with prolactin-secreting tumors are treated either with surgery or more commonly with the prolactin-suppressing drug bromocriptine. In one survey of nearly 1,000 impotent patients, only 4% suffered from true hormonal disorders that could lead to impotence. Most patients whose testosterone levels are low will have a decrease in desire (decreased libido) rather than a true lack of erectile capabilities.

The blood pressure in the penis can be measured with the use of a Doppler device. A tourniquet that is able to stop blood flow to the penis is placed at the base of the organ. When the tourniquet is released, the physician can determine the pressure at which blood flow returns to the penis. This is essentially the same way that blood pressure is measured in the arm. The diagnosis of vasculogenic impotence is made by measuring penile blood pressure and at the same time recording the blood pressure in the arm. These pressures are compared, and usually if the pressure in the penis is less than 80% that of the arm, some degree of vascular insufficiency to the penis is present.

It is also worth noting that patients with vasculogenic impotence will almost always still be able to ejaculate since ejaculation is a purely nerve-mediated event. More specialized testing such as arteriography may also be performed to clearly delineate the area of vascular disease. This test is performed by placing a small catheter or tube within the appropriate region of the arterial system itself in order to visualize the vessels to the penis. A contrast medium is injected through the catheter to outline these vessels on X-ray film. This method is generally reserved for patients who are being considered for vascular operations in order to cure their problems.

Neurogenic impotence usually accompanies obvious neurologic disease such as MS, spinal cord injury, or an alcoholic disease; it is also evident in some cases of juvenile diabetes mellitus. Examinations known as evoked potential studies can be performed to evaluate the nerves going to and coming from the penis. In these studies an electrical stimulus is applied to the penis, and a response is recorded at either the bulbocav-

265

ernosus muscle (a muscle between the scrotum and anus) or the brain. The time between the stimulus and the recording of the response is measured. Knowing the normal values for this response, the physician can determine whether there is nerve disease present. These tests have largely been reserved for patients in whom it has become important to document the presence of an underlying nerve disease.

A final test in the evaluation of male impotence is the nocturnal penile tumescence examination. As discussed previously, a man will normally have four or five well-sustained erections during a night's sleep. The nocturnal penile tumescence examination is able to determine the presence or absence of these erections during sleep. The exam itself is carried out by having a strain gauge placed around the penis and attached to a monitor. Changes in circumference during sleep are therefore recorded, and one can determine the erectile activity during the period. Obviously, if there is no erectile activity whatsoever or only partial erectile activity over several nights, the presence of organic impotence can be surmised. Conversely, should there be completely normal erectile activity over several nights, impotence of psychological origin is the likely explanation. The underlying premise of this exam is that in the psychogenically impotent patient normal erections during sleep will not be suppressed, while they will be suppressed during periods of stress. As mentioned before, this is quite similar to the presence or absence of a normally sustained erection upon arising.

The diagnosis of psychogenic impotence is often made by exclusion when no underlying organic disorder can be found. In addition, psychometric tests such as the Minnesota Multiphasic Personality Inventory or the Beck-Zung Inventory, which are sometimes administered, can aid in the diagnosis.

## The treatment of impotence

There are three major therapeutic approaches for impotence. If patients are found to have hormonal abnormalities, appropriate medications can be used as described above. Patients with psychogenic impotence should in most instances be treated with some type of psychological therapy. In the last decade, sex therapies that employ behavioral approaches such as the techniques pioneered by William Masters and Virginia Johnson in the 1970s have become quite popular. The basic premise of behavioral therapies is that sexual problems can be "unlearned" and normal sexual function "learned." Patients with more severe psychiatric disorders will not be appropriate candidates for this type of therapy, however, and will need more intensive psychiatric therapy. The behavior modification techniques usually produce about a 70–75% initial success rate, especially in well-motivated couples. In patients with more prolonged psychogenic impotence (five years or more), the success rate is considerably less.

| Selected drugs reported to cause temporary impotence |
|---|
| alcohol abuse |
| amphetamines |
| atenolol (Tenormin) |
| baclofen (Lioresal) |
| chlorpromazine (Thorazine and others) |
| chlorthalidone (Hygroton) |
| cimetidine (Tagamet) |
| clofibrate (Atromid-S) |
| clonidine (Catapres) |
| desipramine (Norpramin, Pertofrane) |
| dichlorphenamide (Daranide and others) |
| digoxin |
| disopyramide (Norpace) |
| ethionamide (Trecator) |
| fenfluramine (Pondimin) |
| guanethidine (Ismelin) |
| haloperidol (Haldol) |
| heroin abuse |
| homatropine methylbromide (Homapin and others) |
| hydralazine (Apresoline and others) |
| hydroxyprogesterone caproate (Delalutin) |
| isocarboxazid (Marplan) |
| lithium (Eskalith and others) |
| marijuana abuse |
| mepenzolate bromide (Cantil) |
| methadone (Dolophine) |
| methantheline bromide (Banthine) |
| methazolamide (Neptazane) |
| methyldopa (Aldomet) |
| naproxen (Naprosyn) |
| nitrous oxide abuse |
| norethandrolone |
| norethindrone (Norlutin and others) |
| nortriptyline (Aventyl, Pamelor) |
| PCP |
| perhexilene maleate (Pexid) |
| phenelzine (Nardil) |
| prazosin (Minipress) |
| progesterone |
| propantheline bromide (Pro-Banthine and others) |
| propranolol (Inderal) |
| protriptyline (Vivactil) |
| reserpine |
| spironolactone (Aldactone) |
| thiazide diuretics |
| thioridazine (Mellaril) |
| timolol (Blocadren, Timolide) |
| tranylcypromine (Parnate) |

In patients with a physical, nonhormonal reason for their erectile failure, some form of surgical therapy is usually considered. The most common type of surgical intervention for impotence is the implantation of a penile prosthesis. As has already been described, an erection involves the relative entrapment of blood within the corpora cavernosa of the penis. In order to simulate an erection, a prosthetic device can be placed in both corpora. These devices are basically of two varieties: noninflatable and inflatable. Noninflatable devices are paired silicone rods placed within the corpora. The penis is therefore constantly "erect." However, the rods themselves are malleable and therefore may be bent so that they are inconspicuous under clothing.

Several improvements over the initial simple silicone rods have been made. At present, a noninflatable prosthesis (known as the Jonas Silicon-Silver Penile Prosthesis) constructed with an inner core of braided silver wire permits a downward and upward position to be obtained. The implantation of noninflatable devices is relatively simple, and it usually requires less than half an hour.

The inflatable prosthesis is more complicated and contains several components: the cylinders placed within the corpora are the inflatable components; there is an inflate-deflate pump that is placed below the skin in the scrotum; and a reservoir of fluid usually is placed behind the abdominal muscles. These three components are connected by tubing. The device works by the man's pumping the scrotal pump, thereby allowing the fluid in the reservoir to fill the cylinders. The deflate valve is then used for detumescence.

The main complication with either type of prosthesis is infection—a problem encountered when any prosthetic device is placed in the body. In the case of the inflatable devices, complications such as leakage and component failure have also occurred. Newer devices that combine the simplicity of paired silicone rods with the ability to inflate are forthcoming.

The newest addition to the surgical armamentarium for impotence problems is revascularization of the penis. This type of surgery is reserved for patients who have vasculogenic impotence. The operation itself is similar to other vascular bypass operations in which a good artery (in this case the inferior epigastric artery of the abdomen) is connected to an artery that supplies blood to the corpora. This type of surgery is performed in only a few select medical centers in the U.S. More time will be required before it can be considered a nonexperimental procedure. Thus far success rates appear to be much higher for younger patients with arteriosclerotic or traumatic vascular disorders than for older men with generalized arterial disease.

There is no doubt that in the last ten years we have seen a marked increase in the therapeutic options available to the man with impotence. More sophisticated and specialized diagnostic tests have been perfected to properly evaluate and determine the etiology of the problem. Treatment with hormones and drugs, surgical intervention, and behavioral sex therapy have brought about cure or improvement rates of close to 90%.

Future therapeutic advances will probably be in the areas of nerve stimulation techniques and drug therapy. The former may take the form of an implantable nerve stimulator or a transrectal nerve stimulator. Research is now being done in order to improve understanding of the neurologic control of erections. Thus it is hoped that new drugs can be formulated that will be able to alleviate impotence.

—*Robert J. Krane, M.D.*

# Infectious Diseases

Antibiotics are chemical substances that interfere with the growth and proliferation of microorganisms that are sensitive to their action. Their great advantage is that they are selective, killing or interfering with the growth of bacteria and other infectious organisms (except viruses) at concentrations that do not affect normal cells and organs of the body. Some antibiotics are bacteriostatic; *i.e.*, they inhibit the growth of microorganisms as long as they are present. Others are bacteriocidal; *i.e.*, they kill the organisms directly by interfering with a vital function.

Although antibiotics have undoubtedly earned their reputation as "miracle drugs" countless times over, they present several dangers that can result from their excessive or indiscriminate use. The emergence of antibiotic-resistant infectious bacteria is a particular and growing concern.

## Development and use of antibiotics

The use of natural chemical substances to treat infection began at least 2,500 years ago when the Chinese discovered the curative properties of moldy soybean curd applied to boils, carbuncles, and similar afflictions. In early English folk medicine, plasters of moldy bread were recommended for sores. During the mid-1600s the Spanish conquerers observed Peruvian Indians administering a beverage of cinchona bark, which contains quinine, to victims of malaria; in fact, this centuries-old "antibiotic treatment" is still used in certain parts of the world.

In 1935 prontosil, a dye developed by I. G. Farbenindustrie in Germany, was found to cure infections of the throat, skin, and other organs caused by *Streptococcus* bacteria. The bacteria, usually transmitted from another infected individual, enter the tissues of the upper respiratory passages and infect the mucosal linings of the throat, nose, and mouth. Strep throat is a widely known and common illness, especially in young people. Prontosil, a bacteriostatic drug, has no effect upon the growth of streptococci in the test tube; it is metabolically converted in the body to the antibiotic known as sulfanilamide. Although prontosil is no longer used in treatment, derivatives of sulfanilamide are still frequently called upon to combat a variety of bacterial infections. They are especially useful in treating infections of the bladder (sulfisoxazole) and of the lower intestine (sulfadiazine). Today strep infections are usually treated with penicillin, which is more effective and less likely to cause side effects.

Many antibiotics now in common use were discovered first as the products of microorganisms themselves. Penicillin, produced by the mold *Penicillium notatum*, was discovered in 1928 by Sir Alexander Fleming, who found that *Staphylococcus aureus* bacteria growing in culture were killed by the mold present as a contaminant along with the bacteria. Subsequent research revealed that the active agent, penicillin, was effective against a wide range of bacterial species and strains.

Penicillin and its numerous chemical derivatives are bacteriocidal. They kill directly by interfering with the synthesis of the bacterial cell wall. In some cases the result is a wall-less bacterium surrounded only by a thin membrane and highly susceptible to destruction by host defenses. In most instances the bacterium dies because its abnormal cell wall ruptures, releasing the contents of the cell. In its usual therapeutic dose penicillin has no significant effect upon normal cells of the body. The surrounding membranes of the body's cells are synthesized through metabolic pathways that are distinct from and independent of those involved in bacterial cell-wall synthesis. Today penicillin is synthesized using established chemical methods, a simpler, more reliable, and less costly way of obtaining the drug than isolating it from penicillin-producing molds.

Soil microorganisms known as actinomycetes also have proved to be a rich source of many different antibiotic substances. Streptomycin, a member of the aminoglycoside family of antibiotics and first isolated from *Streptomyces griseus,* is a notable example. Streptomycin has found widespread use in treating tuberculosis and other infectious diseases that at one time were serious public health problems. Aminoglycoside antibiotics kill bacteria by upsetting the protein synthesis mechanism of the bacterial cell, causing a misreading of the genetic code and the production of abnormal proteins.

A single antibiotic substance like penicillin or streptomycin is not effective against all types of bacteria. Penicillin, for example, works best against microorganisms, like *Streptococcus,* that stain positively with gram stain, a procedure used to distinguish broad classes of bacterial types. Others, like *Escherichia coli,* which do not stain positively with gram stain (gram-negative types), ordinarily are not affected by penicillin. They may be killed by different types of antibiotics.

Some antibiotics, called broad-spectrum agents, are able to kill a variety of both gram-positive and gram-negative microorganisms. Tetracycline and chloramphenicol, both originally isolated like streptomycin from soil actinomycetes, are two examples of broad-spectrum antibiotics. Both kill by inhibiting protein synthesis in the bacterial cell.

## Antibiotic resistance

One serious consequence of the widespread use of antibiotics has been the emergence of antibiotic-resistant bacteria. Once sensitive to a particular antibiotic, such bacteria now possess the ability to proliferate in its presence. Like other living organisms, bacteria are capable of evolving biochemical mechanisms to help them survive in a hostile environment. In

the case of antibiotic resistance, drug-resistant organisms appear under the selection pressure of prolonged exposure to antibiotics.

The most notable example of such induced resistance is that which has developed in staphylococci exposed for long periods to penicillin. Resistant staph bacteria synthesize an enzyme known as penicillinase, which cleaves and inactivates penicillin. Most resistant strains begin producing penicillinase after a brief exposure to penicillin, although some produce it even in its absence. Doctors treating patients with staph infections are aware of the possibility that penicillin may not be effective. In these instances they turn to penicillinase-resistant forms of the drug; for example, cloxacillin or methicillin. Other examples of enzymes that confer antibiotic resistance are chloramphenicol acetylase, which degrades chloramphenicol; streptomycin phosphotransferase, which degrades streptomycin; and kanamycin acetyltransferase, which degrades kanamycin.

In most instances, microorganisms develop antibiotic resistance through a process of genetic mutation and natural selection. Bacteria undergo division at about 30-minute intervals. Each replicates the DNA present in its genetic makeup along with other cellular constituents and divides to form two daughter cells. Bacteria thrive in large numbers in infected tissues of the body. A common skin infection such as a boil may have as many as ten billion staphylococci proliferating rapidly in the rich environment. By random chance the genes of one or two bacteria present may alter slightly, giving the mutated organisms the ability to form an enzyme that degrades the antibiotic used for treatment. Continued treatment of the patient with this antibiotic allows these few resistant bacteria to survive as the others are killed. Because the mutation is inherited and passed on to daughter cells, the culture quickly converts from a sensitive one to one that is resistant. Hence, the infection persists in the face of antibiotic treatment.

In addition to their ability to create antibiotic-resistant populations through direct inheritance, resistant bacteria can transfer bits of genetic material containing resistance genes to sensitive ones, enabling them to degrade antibiotics as well. These resistance, or R, factors are contained in plasmids, pieces of DNA that exist apart from and are replicated independently of the bacterial cell's own genetic material. This remarkable feature enables antibiotic resistance to spread throughout large numbers of previously sensitive bacteria, complicating antibiotic therapy. The recipient organisms need not undergo mutation since resistance is provided from external sources.

Antibiotic-resistant organisms may spread from person to person. Penicillin-resistant staph infections are especially prevalent in hospitals where the antibiotic is commonly used. So are infections from pentamycin-

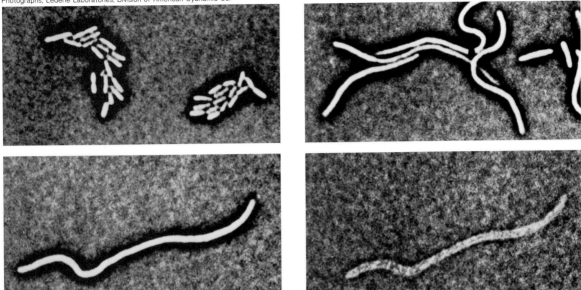

*Piperacillin is a fourth-generation penicillin. Its broad-spectrum antibiotic properties make it effective*
*against even very stubborn intestinal microbes. (Above) Gram-negative bacilli in lab dish; bacilli elongate*
*after drug is added; bacilli walls weaken and rupture; organism dies.*

resistant organisms such as *Pseudomonas* in hospitals where pentamycin is commonly used. Fortunately, alternative antibiotics such as cefotaxime, one of the so-called third-generation cephalosporins, are effective, although forms resistant to these newer agents are likely to appear as well if they are used extensively. To keep ahead of the resistance problem, pharmaceutical researchers are active in developing even more advanced generations of antibiotics and in seeking new ones from natural sources. Also under investigation are combinations of existing antibiotics with substances that deactivate penicillinase and other antibiotic-degrading enzymes.

Antibiotics are only one means for combating harmful and infectious microorganisms. For the most part, the body's natural defenses against infection—white blood cells, antibodies, and the like—are capable of dealing with both resistant and sensitive organisms. Patients whose natural immunity is weakened, however, because of illness or other reasons are especially at risk. For them, infections with large numbers of antibiotic-resistant microorganisms can be a life-endangering problem.

The potential for creating large, rapidly multiplying populations of antibiotic-resistant microorganisms gives sufficient cause for doctors to prescribe antibiotics only when absolutely necessary. Common, trivial infections that the body's defenses are capable of handling should be treated with heat, rest, and other conservative measures. Patients with virally caused colds and upper respiratory infections that will run their course in a few days are not helped by antibiotics. More

serious illnesses such as bacterial pneumonia, however, must be treated vigorously with the appropriate antibiotic drug.

Infections caused by viruses are unaffected by antibiotics that kill bacteria. Unlike bacteria, viruses replicate within cells of the body, taking control of the cell's metabolic machinery for their own purposes. Few virally specific agents have been developed because most agents that might interfere with viral replication would also destroy the cells of the host. The use of antibiotics for viral illnesses such as the common cold is without benefit and potentially harmful, increasing the risk of creating resistant bacteria that may then invade virally damaged tissues. Secondary bacterial infections—for example, a bacterial infection of the sinuses following a viral upper respiratory infection—are treated with antibiotics if necessary.

Controlling bacterial resistance to antibiotics is not a problem for the medical and pharmaceutical professions alone. Individuals routinely dose themselves with antibiotics left over from a previous illness in vain attempts to head off a cold or other viral infection. In many countries, particularly third world nations, antibiotics are sold over the counter, encouraging people to take them for afflictions that do not require their use. In the U.S. and elsewhere tetracycline and penicillin are added in subtherapeutic doses to animal feed to prevent disease and promote growth in livestock, thus allowing farmers to raise large numbers of animals in confined feedlots. In fact, nearly half of the antibiotics sold in the U.S. are used for this purpose. Growing international concern with such abuses was reempha-

269

sized at a recent meeting of the World Health Organization, which urged that antibiotics be controlled worldwide by prescription. It also recommended better education in the proper use of antibiotics for both doctors and patients and called on countries to restrict the use of antibiotics as animal-feed supplements.

## Determining antibiotic sensitivity

Since resistant organisms are common, especially in hospitals and other settings where antibiotics are frequently used, doctors attempt to determine the antibiotic sensitivity of the infectious organisms before beginning treatment. This is accomplished first by obtaining a sample from the infected site, often with a sterile culture swab. The sample is then cultured in the laboratory with appropriate nutrients to identify the specific bacterial type involved. In the case of a severe sore throat, the doctor swabs the throat to pick up a sample of the organisms causing the illness and places it in a container of nutrients that can support the growth of a variety of different types of bacteria. Infectious organisms that are present are subcultured by placing them in a second container, often a low, round glass or plastic petri dish, that has been coated with nutrients. When the culture has spread across the surface of the dish, small paper disks each containing a particular antibiotic are placed on the culture. A zone of inhibition or localized killing appears around the disks that contain antibiotics to which the bacteria are sensitive. The entire procedure, which takes about 48 hours, indicates the antibiotic that will be most therapeutically effective. This test does not indicate whether resistance will develop subsequently but only whether it is already present.

The precise concentration of the antibiotic necessary to kill the infectious bacteria may be determined by placing samples of the culture into test tubes containing nutrient medium plus varying concentrations of the antibiotic to be tested. Bacterial organisms may proliferate at lower concentrations but not at higher ones. The level of antibiotic required for effective treatment can be readily determined and the appropriate dose given to the patient.

In some instances it is critically important to determine the cause of the patient's illness in the shortest possible time. Treatment of patients with meningitis, an infection present in the tissues lining the brain and spinal column, or of patients with septicemia, a widespread infection carried in the blood, must begin within hours to minimize the risk of death or permanent damage. In such cases a preliminary determination of the type of bacteria causing the disease often can be performed quickly by microscopic examination. Bacteria have characteristic shapes and sizes that aid in identification. Other studies involving the use of antibodies that are specific for various types of bacteria also can be performed. Although antibiotic sensitivities cannot be obtained with this approach, broad-spectrum antibiotic therapy can begin while antibiotic sensitivities are determined.

## Antibiotic treatment

To obtain high concentrations of antibiotic throughout the patient's body in the shortest possible time, most drugs can be given intravenously. For patients who do not need rapid administration or who are being treated at home for less serious infections, antibiotics taken by mouth or given by intramuscular injection are sufficient. Since absorption of the antibiotic from the gastrointestinal tract may vary, the blood levels obtained from antibiotics taken orally cannot always be predicted. For intramuscular injection the antibiotic may be mixed with an agent to slow its absorption, providing sustained levels for longer periods at the site of infection.

Some patients require preventive therapy with antibiotics to maintain health—one notable example: children who have had rheumatic fever, a disease of the heart and connective tissue that is the aftermath of an infection with streptococci. For such children the chances that another strep infection will lead again to rheumatic fever are increased about 150 times. Consequently, to prevent further strep infections doctors prescribe penicillin, either as a pill taken daily or as a monthly intramuscular injection. Fortunately, emergence of penicillin-resistant streptococci in patients taking penicillin over long periods is rare. Such patients, however, do carry other penicillin-resistant bacteria as part of the body's normal complement of microorganisms.

## Adverse effects of antibiotics

In general people tolerate antibiotics well, but occasional adverse reactions do occur. Severe allergic re-

*In many third world nations, antibiotics are sold over the counter, encouraging people to take them when their use is neither required nor helpful.*

Peter Menzel—Stock, Boston

action (anaphylaxis) is one common example. Typically an individual is given an initial injection of penicillin with no apparent ill effect. Weeks later a second injection of penicillin soon produces wheezing, difficulty in breathing, and perhaps even vascular collapse and death. These signs of generalized anaphylaxis are often preceded by the appearance of less severe reactions including hives, swelling of the lips and other parts of the body, and a red itchy rash that may last for weeks. Other antibiotics can also cause severe allergic reactions and such toxic effects as bone marrow failure and kidney damage.

Fortunately, allergy to one antibiotic does not necessarily preclude the use of another. Patients with penicillin allergy may be able to take tetracycline without ill effect. But patients with penicillin allergy sometimes have allergies to a variety of drugs and other environmental substances, complicating treatment.

Doctors determine whether an allergy to an antibiotic exists by asking patients if they experienced allergic symptoms following prior drug therapy. Where there is any doubt, presence of an allergy to the drug can be confirmed by injecting a small amount of it under the patient's skin. If an allergy exists, a localized hive results.

Ironically, in the process of suppressing one infection, antibiotics sometimes encourage another. This problem, called suprainfection, results when the antibiotic treatment upsets the population balance that is normally maintained by competition among the various species making up the body's natural microbial complement. The antibiotic kills off large populations of sensitive bacteria, freeing nutrients and space for the proliferation of other, harmful organisms that are not sensitive to the antibiotic. A woman being treated for a throat infection with a broad-spectrum agent like tetracycline, for example, may develop a vaginal yeast infection and thus require an antifungal agent. To reduce the chance for suprainfections doctors choose the antibiotic that is most specific for the type of infection present and avoid prolonging antibiotic therapy longer than necessary.

—*Edward P. Cohen, M.D.*

# Lung Diseases

Emphysema is a common, disabling, and often fatal disorder of the lung characterized by destruction of the walls of the air sacs (alveoli). Since the alveoli are the site at which the body transfers oxygen from the air to the blood, individuals with emphysema typically become short of breath with exertion, are forced to limit their physical activities, and often suffer strokes or heart attacks, the consequences of oxygen starvation of vital tissues.

Emphysema is a disease of adults, usually individuals who are more than 50 years old. It does not occur suddenly but rather slowly, with alveoli being lost progressively over many years. The affected individual, however, does not sense this ongoing destructive process. First, there are no nerves in the alveolar walls to signal the brain that the destruction is occurring. Second, the human lung is quite redundant; unless an individual engages in activities that demand a high rate of oxygen transfer from air to blood, at least one-third of the lung's 300 million alveoli can be lost without the individual's sensing that there is a problem. Furthermore, emphysema is irreversible. Like Humpty-Dumpty, once the wall of an air sac is destroyed, it cannot be rebuilt or a new one regrown.

It has been known for some time that people who smoke cigarettes have a greater incidence of emphysema than nonsmokers. Furthermore, among smokers the risk and severity of the disease increase with the number of cigarettes smoked. However, the knowledge that smoking is a major risk factor for the development of emphysema does not answer the more fundamental question: Why are the air sacs destroyed? The answer to this question is now known and is centered on a protein called $\alpha_1$-antitrypsin.

### The key to emphysema

The major breakthroughs in emphysema research started with a serendipitous finding by investigators who were not interested in emphysema at all. In 1963 two investigators, C. Laurell and S. Eriksson, were studying blood proteins at Malmö General Hospital in Sweden; they observed that 3 of the 1,500 individuals in their study were deficient in a protein called $\alpha_1$-antitrypsin. When they examined the clinical records of these patients they made a striking observation: all three of the individuals deficient in $\alpha_1$-antitrypsin had developed emphysema at a relatively early age, usually in their thirties or forties. It was soon recognized that the form of emphysema linked to this deficiency of $\alpha_1$-antitrypsin was an inherited disorder, in which the inherited inability to have normal blood levels of $\alpha_1$-antitrypsin was associated with a high risk for the development of emphysema.

A sugar-containing protein, $\alpha_1$-antitrypsin is made by liver cells (hepatocytes) and secreted into the blood. In normal individuals $\alpha_1$-antitrypsin is maintained at a level of approximately 150 to 250 mg per 100 ml of plasma. The importance of $\alpha_1$-antitrypsin is in its function as an antiprotease—a molecule with the ability to combine with and inhibit proteases, a class of enzymes that are proteolytic, or protein destroying. While $\alpha_1$-antitrypsin inhibits many proteases, its vital function is to inhibit elastase, a broad-spectrum, powerful protease capable of degrading most structural proteins that form the extracellular support structures of tissues. The most important source of this elastase is the neutrophil, a blood cell frequently recruited to the site of tissue damage in response to injury or infection.

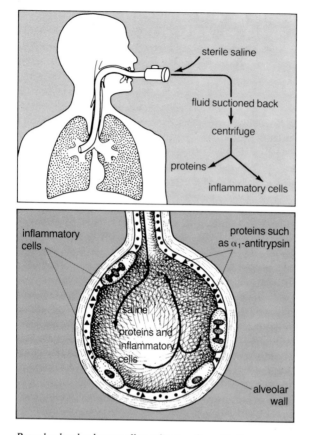

*Bronchoalveolar lavage allows the sampling of inflammatory cells and protein constituents of the fluid lining the air-exposed surfaces of the lower respiratory tract. A bronchoscope is wedged into a distal branch of the bronchial tree (top). Sterile saline fluid is infused and suctioned back, and inflammatory cells and proteins are separated by centrifugation. (Bottom) A view of the inside of an air sac.*

In regard to the finding by Laurell and Eriksson, the deficiency of $\alpha_1$-antitrypsin in the blood meant that the affected individuals had markedly reduced antielastase activity in their blood. While this does not seem to be very important for most organs, for several reasons it has major consequences for the lower respiratory tract. First, the alveolar walls are thin, fragile tissues comprised of structural proteins that are highly susceptible to attack by elastase. Second, the lower respiratory tract is a common site for blood neutrophils to accumulate. Third, when a large amount of elastase is placed in the alveoli of experimental animals, the animals rapidly develop a lung disease indistinguishable from human emphysema; this leads to the conclusion that an excess of elastase activity in the lung can lead to destruction of the alveolar walls.

Considered together, these observations lead to what is commonly referred to as the protease-antiprotease (or the elastase-antielastase) theory of emphysema. This theory, for which there is now over-

whelming evidence, states that while the lung is susceptible to attack by elastases, the alveolar walls are normally protected from destruction by antielastases. In the normal human this antielastase screen is provided by $\alpha_1$-antitrypsin molecules that are produced by the liver and diffuse from the blood through the alveolar structures. Thus, under normal circumstances any elastase that may gain access to the alveoli is immediately inhibited by $\alpha_1$-antitrypsin before it can injure the structural proteins of the alveolar wall. However, in circumstances in which the elastase burden increases significantly or, as in the case of $\alpha_1$-antitrypsin deficiency, the antielastase protective screen of the alveoli is markedly reduced, the balance is shifted in favor of the elastases, resulting in unimpeded destruction of the alveolar walls; *i.e.*, the disorder we call emphysema.

The importance of the elastase-antielastase theory goes far beyond $\alpha_1$-antitrypsin deficiency disease (a relatively rare disorder affecting approximately one in 3,000–4,000 individuals), as it also forms the basis for understanding how cigarette smoking causes emphysema. In this context, it is now clear that the destruction of the alveoli caused by cigarette smoking is also associated with an imbalance of elastase and antielastase activity in the lower respiratory tract, an imbalance shifted in favor of elastase.

## Structure, physiology, and genetic variants of $\alpha_1$-antitrypsin

The $\alpha_1$-antitrypsin molecule is a protein that comprises a single string of 394 amino acids with three side chains of complex sugars. The liver of a typical individual produces about two grams of $\alpha_1$-antitrypsin every day. A typical $\alpha_1$-antitrypsin molecule stays in the blood for five days. Because of its size, the $\alpha_1$-antitrypsin molecule is only slightly impeded as it diffuses through body tissues. In the lung, for example, the $\alpha_1$-antitrypsin concentration in the epithelial fluid lining the surfaces of the alveoli that come in contact with air is approximately 10% of that of the $\alpha_1$-antitrypsin concentration in the blood.

The $\alpha_1$-antitrypsin molecule functions as an antielastase by virtue of its ability to combine with neutrophil elastase to form a tight complex. The $\alpha_1$-antitrypsin molecule performs this function at a part of the molecule called the active site, a region of the amino acid sequence 358 amino acids from the beginning of the molecule. The center of this active site is the amino acid methionine; this amino acid binds to the elastase and, together with the other amino acids forming the active site, renders the elastase ineffective as a protease.

The $\alpha_1$-antitrypsin molecule is highly polymorphic; more than 40 variants are known, all thought to be due to a single substitution in the amino acid sequence of the protein. The variants of $\alpha_1$-antitrypsin are typed by what is called the Pi (protease inhibitor) system, a classification that is based on the charge differences of the $\alpha_1$-antitrypsin variants when they are placed in an electric field under conditions of an acid gradient. The nomenclature used for the Pi variants assigns different letters to each variant. The specific types of $\alpha_1$-antitrypsin that every individual has is defined by inheritance, with one variant of the molecule inherited from each parent. Current evidence suggests that the human genome contains only one gene for $\alpha_1$-antitrypsin, with the gene residing on chromosome 14. Thus, each individual inherits two $\alpha_1$-antitrypsin genes, one from each parent.

The most frequent $\alpha_1$-antitrypsin gene codes for an M-type $\alpha_1$-antitrypsin molecule. If, as is quite common, an individual inherited an M-type gene from each parent, that individual would be a homozygote for the M protein and would be classified as Pi type MM (commonly referred to as PiM). The $\alpha_1$-antitrypsin variant most commonly associated with emphysema is called the Z variant. An individual who inherits the Z gene from both parents is referred to as a PiZ homozygote. It is this individual who is deficient in $\alpha_1$-antitrypsin in the blood and who develops emphysema at an early age. Epidemiological studies have demonstrated that the Z gene is found in 1 to 2% of the U.S. population. Thus, there are approximately 50,000 PiZ homozygotes in the U.S. and approximately two million to three million PiMZ heterozygotes (*i.e.*, persons in whom the Z gene is inherited from one parent and the more common M gene from the other).

The sequences of the M and Z $\alpha_1$-antitrypsin proteins are known. Furthermore, the M and Z $\alpha_1$-antitrypsin genes have been isolated and sequenced. Whereas amino acid number 342 of the M protein is glutamic acid, in the Z protein it is lysine. Sequence studies of the M and Z forms of the $\alpha_1$-antitrypsin gene have shown that the change from glutamic acid to lysine is due to a cytosine (C) residue in the gene being changed to a thymine (T) residue (*i.e.*, in the M gene, the code word for glutamic acid is CTC; the cytosine-to-thymine change alters this code word to TTC, which codes for lysine).

The consequences to the $\alpha_1$-antitrypsin molecule of this single substitution in the gene sequence and, hence, in the protein sequence are profound. Even though the Z-type molecule is as good an antielastase as the M-type molecule, the change in this one amino acid causes the $\alpha_1$-antitrypsin molecule to fold in an abnormal fashion when it is being synthesized within the hepatocyte. Because of this, the hepatocyte cannot add the normal types of sugars to the protein and, consequently, the secretory apparatus of the hepatocyte does not secrete the $\alpha_1$-antitrypsin into the blood. Thus, an inherited difference in a single amino acid in the molecule causes a deficiency of that protein in the blood.

### Inherited emphysema

Proof of the concept that emphysema results from an imbalance of elastase and antielastase in the alveoli in favor of elastase demands direct evidence that such an imbalance actually exists in the human lung. It became possible to search for such proof with the development of a technique called bronchoalveolar lavage. This technique utilizes the fiber-optic bronchoscope, an instrument that enables investigators to easily visualize the upper airways with little discomfort to the patient. After local anesthesia with a spray of xylocaine (similar to the type of medication used for pain relief by dentists), bronchoalveolar lavage entails the insertion of the bronchoscope until it is wedged into an airway. Since the instrument is six millimeters (about ¼ in) in diameter, this usually means a fourth or fifth branch of the bronchial tree. A sterile salt, or saline, solution is then infused into the bronchoscope and immediately suctioned back. The purpose of this is to recover the epithelial-lining fluid of the alveoli and, with it, proteins (such as $\alpha_1$-antitrypsin) as well as inflammatory cells (such as neutrophils) that may be present. This procedure is simple to carry out and is safe; more than 2,000 have been carried out at the U.S. National Heart, Lung, and Blood Institute without any serious effects.

By means of this lavage procedure, it has been possible to directly evaluate the elastase-antielastase theory in both inherited $\alpha_1$-antitrypsin deficiency and acquired emphysema associated with cigarette smoking. The concept of the pathogenesis associated with $\alpha_1$-antitrypsin deficiency rests on the hypothesis that a reduction in the level of blood $\alpha_1$-antitrypsin is reflected by a reduction in the level of lung $\alpha_1$-antitrypsin. Direct evaluation of the epithelial-lining fluid of PiZ individuals has shown that this is the case. These patients have markedly reduced blood levels (less than 50 mg per 100 ml of plasma) that are paralleled by markedly reduced lung levels (less than 5 mg per 100 ml of alveolar epithelial-lining fluid). Furthermore, the lavage analyses have shown that these patients have neutrophils in their alveoli and that active neutrophil elastase is present in their alveolar epithelial-lining fluid. Thus, individuals with $\alpha_1$-antitrypsin deficiency clearly have an imbalance of elastase and antielastase in the alveolar structures that is shifted in favor of the elastase. Since an excess of elastase placed into the lungs of experimental animals leads to emphysema, it is no wonder that a genetically inherited deficiency of $\alpha_1$-antitrypsin is associated with the development of emphysema at an early age.

### Smoking-induced emphysema

The pathogenesis of the acquired form of emphysema associated with cigarette smoking is somewhat more complex, but the results are the same—an imbalance of elastase and antielastase in the lung in favor of the elastase. Lavage analyses of PiM individuals who

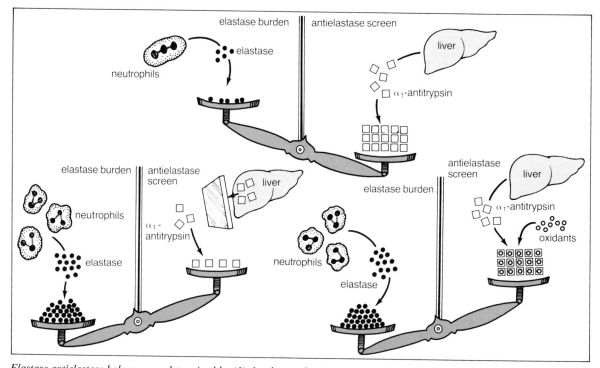

*Elastase-antielastase balances are determined by (1) the elastase burden, which reflects the presence of blood neutrophils in the lower respiratory tract, and (2) antielastase screens, provided by $\alpha_1$-antitrypsin that is produced by the liver and transported to the lung, where it combines with and inhibits neutrophil elastase. (Top) Elastase-antielastase balance in a normal nonsmoker; antielastase screen far outweighs elastase burden. (Middle) Elastase-antielastase balance in a person with an $\alpha_1$-antitrypsin deficiency; burden outweighs screen; elastase released by neutrophils acts destructively and causes emphysema. (Bottom) Elastase-antielastase balance in a smoker; burden outweighs screen; oxidants in lung cause normal $\alpha_1$-antitrypsin to be ineffective, allowing destruction of alveolar walls.*

smoke cigarettes demonstrate that while they have normal amounts of $\alpha_1$-antitrypsin in their alveolar epithelial-lining fluid, the $\alpha_1$-antitrypsin that is present is functionally inactive. The mechanism for this functional impotence lies in the fact that the amino acid at the active elastase-combining site of $\alpha_1$-antitrypsin is methionine, an amino acid with a sulfhydryl group that is easily oxidized, thus converting the methionine to methionine sulfoxide. When this occurs, the rate at which $\alpha_1$-antitrypsin can combine with elastase is markedly reduced; *i.e.*, the $\alpha_1$-antitrypsin is intact but functionally impotent to inhibit elastase. In this regard, studies have shown that: (1) in the test tube, cigarette smoke can cause $\alpha_1$-antitrypsin to become functionally inactive; (2) the methionine in the $\alpha_1$-antitrypsin recovered from the lungs of cigarette smokers is oxidized; and (3) the $\alpha_1$-antitrypsin in the epithelial-lining fluid of PiM cigarette smokers cannot combine with elastase at a normal rate. Furthermore, the functional impairment of the $\alpha_1$-antitrypsin of PiM cigarette smokers is limited to their lungs; *i.e.*, the blood $\alpha_1$-antitrypsin is functionally normal. This suggests that cigarette smoking causes what is functionally equivalent to a genetic-deficiency disease localized to one organ.

Cigarette smokers not only have a functional deficiency of the antielastase screen of their lower respiratory tract but also have a burden of elastase at the same location. Recent studies have shown that cigarette smokers have neutrophils in their lungs, and neutrophil elastase can be detected in the epithelial fluid lining the alveoli. It is likely that blood neutrophils accumulate in the alveoli because they are attracted by chemotactic factors, mediators that form a chemical gradient that attracts living cells. These chemotactic factors are present because cigarette smoke contains particulates that stimulate lung macrophages (another inflammatory cell in the alveoli) to release a chemotactic factor specific for neutrophils. Thus, cigarette smokers have an elastase-antielastase imbalance within their lower respiratory tract.

The observation that cigarette smokers with the PiM $\alpha_1$-antitrypsin phenotype have elastase-antielastase imbalance in their alveolar structures leads to an obvious conclusion: if smoking causes a functional $\alpha_1$-antitrypsin deficiency in the lungs, then cigarette smoking must be an added risk factor for PiZ homozygous individuals who have the inherited form of $\alpha_1$-antitrypsin deficiency. There is convincing evidence to support this concept. While 20% of nonsmoking individuals with the PiZ phenotype have died by the age of 50, 70% of PiZ individuals who smoke cigarettes are dead by the same age.

## The treatment of emphysema

At present there is no therapy to halt the progressive destruction of the alveolar walls in either $\alpha_1$-antitrypsin deficiency or emphysema caused by cigarette smoking. However, since emphysema results from an elastase-antielastase imbalance in the lower respiratory tract in favor of elastase, therapy to halt the further destruction of the alveolar walls would logically include a reduction in the elastase burden, an enhancement of the antielastase protection, or both. At this time, other than stopping cigarette smoking there is no way to achieve the former. However, recent studies suggest that, at least for $\alpha_1$-antitrypsin deficiency, reestablishment of the antielastase screen of the alveolar structures may be possible.

Studies performed at the U.S. National Institutes of Health have demonstrated that weekly injections of partially purified human $\alpha_1$-antitrypsin can reestablish amounts of $\alpha_1$-antitrypsin in blood and lung to levels thought to provide protection against potential elastase attack in the alveolar structures. Furthermore, when $\alpha_1$-antitrypsin is infused into PiZ $\alpha_1$-antitrypsin-deficient patients, the active elastase that is present in the epithelial-lining fluid disappears; i.e, it is inhibited by the $\alpha_1$-antitrypsin that has diffused into the alveoli. Thus, one approach to the treatment for PiZ $\alpha_1$-antitrypsin deficiency is to utilize frequent infusions of purified $\alpha_1$-antitrypsin to reestablish the elastase-antielastase balance.

Unfortunately, $\alpha_1$-antitrypsin is not an easy protein to purify, and large amounts are needed. Current estimates are that four grams of $\alpha_1$-antitrypsin will be needed each week for each patient. Several tons of pure $\alpha_1$-antitrypsin may be needed yearly in the U.S. alone, where there may be as many as 50,000 PiZ individuals. There are, however, several possible solutions to this problem.

First, although the task is difficult, the protein can be purified from pooled human plasma. Thus, if technical problems can be overcome, this may be a future source.

Second, genetic engineering techniques, i.e., recombinant DNA technology, may provide the needed protein. The human gene for $\alpha_1$-antitrypsin has been isolated and inserted into yeast and bacteria; these organisms have then been induced to make copies of the human $\alpha_1$-antitrypsin protein. While there are many problems to solve before such material can be produced in huge quantities and used clinically, this approach is clearly feasible.

Third, it is possible to synthetically produce small molecules that can combine with and inhibit neutrophil elastase. Such molecules—for example, compounds called chlormethyl ketones—have already been tested in animals and have been shown to be effective. While the molecules that have been investigated so far are too dangerous to give to humans, this approach is theoretically possible.

Fourth, replacement therapy from any source may be combined with drugs that stimulate the liver to secrete more $\alpha_1$-antitrypsin. For example, when patients with PiZ $\alpha_1$-antitrypsin deficiency are treated with the drug danazol, an analog of the male sex hormone testosterone, the blood levels of $\alpha_1$-antitrypsin are raised by approximately 10 to 20 mg per 100 ml of plasma in 70% of those treated. Thus, while danazol itself does not elevate $\alpha_1$-antitrypsin levels to normal, it might be used in conjunction with $\alpha_1$-antitrypsin infusions to reduce the frequency at which replacement therapy is needed.

While a practical, rational treatment of emphysema is not yet available, major breakthroughs have been made in the understanding of the pathogenesis of this disease. It is a remarkable story of how a chance finding—that a deficiency in a blood protein was associated with a lung disease—led, in only 20 years, to an understanding of what causes this disease and how it may be treated.

*—Ronald G. Crystal, M.D.*

# Medical Education

Since World War II, medicine has become a very popular career choice for young people. This may be due in part to the increasing interest in science present at all levels of society, in part to the attractions of a well-paid and socially acceptable profession, and in part to the prospects for a useful and important service to mankind. Young physicians have been much sought after by hospitals, clinics, group practices, and communities, and the opportunities for an interesting, remunerative career have been many.

Although the number of positions in entering medical school classes has risen sharply over the past 30 years (from about 7,000 to 17,000), and the number of applicants has increased proportionately less (from about 22,000 to 34,000), there have been many disappointed applicants who have not been able to enter medical school. Members of this often vocal group and their parents and sponsors have held many misconceptions about the whole process of admission to a medical school. While every medical school has its own admissions policies, and these may differ considerably, there are some generalizations that can be made about the selection process.

## The selection of medical school students

Fortunately for medicine, a great many well-qualified young men and women have selected it as a career.

**Medical education**

A. R. Tarlov, "Shattuck Lecture—The Increasing Supply of Physicians . . .," *The New England Journal of Medicine*, May 19, 1983, vol. 308, no. 20, p. 1237

There is no magic to being admitted, and the qualities sought are those reasonable for any person entering a lifelong career charged with responsibility for human life and welfare. The last 30 years have witnessed an increasing diversity of entering classes; today approximately one-third of the students are women, and the percentage of minority students is in the range of 5 to 15%. An increasing number of students enter medical school several years after completing their college education.

The caliber of the applicants has been remarkably high. One of the problems for most admissions committees, which, one should mention, do their work with the utmost dedication, has been selecting a class from among many very attractive applicants. In the process, some good applicants necessarily do not get admitted to the most competitive schools. It should be understood—as it often is not—that an earnest desire to become a physician and an attractive personality are not, in themselves, enough. The public deserves—and indeed must have—in its doctors a high level of intelligence, dedication, judgment, personal stability, and integrity. That there are occasional individuals in the profession who lack these attributes makes it all the more important that the process of selecting men and women for medicine, imperfect though it may be, must be conducted as carefully as possible.

One area of misunderstanding surrounds the statistics. It is often said that a medical school admits only, say, one out of 20 or so applicants. This, in essence, may be true. Overlooked, however, is the fact that every applicant applies to many schools—an average of about 10 but often as many as 20 or even more—thus, overall in the United States approximately one out of every two applicants will be admitted to some medical school. As indicated above, there are approximately 17,000 positions currently available in the entering classes, and in the 1982–83 academic year there were almost 34,000 applicants. In some tax-supported state medical schools, which limit the student body essentially to state residents, the odds for admission may be even more favorable. The peak number of applicants (42,000) was seen in the United States in 1974. A decline of about 22% has occurred since that time, influenced especially, no doubt, by the rising cost of a medical education. It is to be hoped that we shall never come to the time when anyone may be enrolled in a medical school regardless of qualifications. This has occurred in some European countries, such as Italy and Greece, with catastrophic consequences.

During the admission year 1982–83, approximately 22,000 males and 11,000 females filed applications for admission to the 127 U.S. medical schools. The applicant group included almost 1,300 black males and 1,200 black females. Residents of California were the most numerous, followed by those of New York, Texas, Pennsylvania, Illinois, Ohio, and Michigan.

| Enrollment of first-year students in U.S. medical schools | | | |
|---|---|---|---|
| year | schools | students | increase from previous year |
| 1965 | 94 | 9,018 | |
| 1966 | 97 | 9,255 | 2.6% |
| 1967 | 100 | 9,823 | 6.1% |
| 1968 | 104 | 10,261 | 4.6% |
| 1969 | 107 | 10,846 | 5.7% |
| 1970 | 110 | 11,792 | 8.7% |
| 1971 | 115 | 12,748 | 8.2% |
| 1972 | 119 | 14,380 | 12.8% |
| 1973 | 121 | 14,760 | 2.6% |
| 1974 | 123 | 15,484 | 4.9% |
| 1975 | 123 | 15,912 | 2.8% |
| 1976 | 126 | 16,350 | 2.8% |
| 1977 | 134 | 16,700 | 2.1% |
| 1978 | 139 | 17,376 | 4.0% |
| 1979 | 140 | 17,682 | 1.8% |
| 1980 | 140 | 18,068 | 2.2% |
| 1981 | 141 | 18,208 | 0.8% |
| 1982 | 142 | 18,248 | 0% |

Several thousand young men and women who are United States citizens and who were not admitted to any U.S. schools are living abroad studying medicine. Especially popular are the several Caribbean schools. It is very difficult for a foreign national to be enrolled in British or Scandinavian medical schools or in most of the better European schools. Attendance at a foreign medical school—most notably the so-called offshore Caribbean schools catering almost exclusively to U.S. nationals—is accompanied by serious problems. Among them are the usually inferior education offered by the institutions, the difficulty of classes and textbooks in a foreign language, the considerable expense of living abroad plus the costs of tuition and travel, and the uncertainty of reentry into the U.S. medical system for high-quality residency training and practice. Before embarking on such a course, a student rejected by all U.S. schools should be sure that medicine is, after all, the appropriate career for his or her talents. An applicant should take stock of his own strengths and weaknesses, based on advice obtained from experienced admissions officers, and he should strive to correct areas of deficiency. It is possible to be admitted on reapplication if the career choice is sound, the student is highly motivated, and there is demonstration of some positive features in the renewed application.

## Criteria for admission

There are no fixed criteria that determine which students will be selected. The four broad areas considered are those of academic achievement, Medical College Admission Test (MCAT) scores, nonacademic activities, and personal qualities. In order to gain insight into these areas, admissions committees utilize academic records, MCAT scores, information provided by the student in the application (which usually includes an essay), letters of recommendation, and personal interviews. High grades in college (grade-point averages of 3.5 to 4.0) are obviously helpful, although they do not in themselves guarantee acceptance; poor grades (averages of 2.5 or below), on the other hand, will make acceptance very unlikely. The same is true for MCAT scores. While some admissions committees do automatically screen out applications exhibiting poor grade-point averages or poor results in the MCAT, usually some allowances are made; for example, for grades that may have been adversely affected by hours that the student spent in outside employment to cover college expenses.

Today most committees are interested in evidence of a broad education, both in science and in the liberal arts, and they especially value indications of achievement in extracurricular activities, including athletics, the arts, student government, journalism, paid work experience, and religious participation. In 1983 the Johns Hopkins University School of Medicine launched a new type of admissions program aimed at reversing the trend toward early specialization and overemphasis on science as preparation for medical careers—the so-called premed syndrome. Under the new admissions plan students will gain acceptance into the medical school when they are juniors in college so that they will not feel pressure to abandon or steer away from a liberal course of study while completing their last years of undergraduate work.

It is not necessary to have worked in a research laboratory, a hospital emergency room, or on hospital floors, but many students take on such work both to obtain experience in the areas of science and health and to try to improve their chances of acceptance. Insofar as these are often mere "window dressing," they probably are not helpful.

The essay, in which the candidate manifests his or her skills of self-expression, receives important attention, particularly with "borderline" candidates. Letters of recommendation have been found to be of limited value. Their authors all too often become unabashed advocates for the students recommended and carefully omit any references to unfavorable traits or limitations. Such documents have been referred to recently as a "farce"—"the fantasy land of letters of recommendation"—in an article in the prestigious *New England Journal of Medicine.* Most would agree, however, that this interpretation is by no means correct for *all* such letters. Students who are the sons or daughters of alumni do not automatically gain admission, as many have presumed, but usually they do have a slight advantage.

It is not necessary or wise for a student who wishes to follow a "premed" course to select an area of specialization before going to medical school. It is quite enough to be sure of the professional career choice. Whether one becomes a practitioner or a laboratory investigator, a teacher or an administrator, or chooses to be a neurosurgeon, a cardiologist, or a primary care physician is best decided later. Very often, the preliminary thoughts of the student are changed after two or three years of medical school with the practical experience and observation permitted by that interval of maturation.

## A more diverse student body

There has been in the past 30 years a healthy trend to a more diverse student body. It seems highly probable that before long the number of female medical students will equal the number of male students. Minority representation has also greatly increased in this interval, although the number of minority applicants has changed little in the last decade.

One of the trends detectable recently has been that of older applicants. At Harvard Medical School, for example, during the past ten years the number of students accepted over age 24 has more than doubled. In 1970 no student over age 29 was accepted, but in 1980 nine students over 29 were enrolled. Today these applicants are looked upon favorably since they may be particularly mature, have often had a wide range of experiences in life, and may clearly have superior motivation. Some wish to enter medicine after several years in research; some enter with career experience in business, nursing, pharmacy, dentistry, or law; and a good many women have made the decision after they have begun families and their children have started school. It is essential that the applicant who is older fully understand that four years of medical school and

*Students rejected by U.S. medical schools who then enroll in Caribbean programs to obtain M.D. degrees are likely to encounter many problems.*

at least one year of residency—and more likely three or more—are ahead before the practice of medicine is possible. It is also important for the applicant to be prepared to be a full-time student again, competing with bright young men and women who are well accustomed to the rigors of disciplined study. Older applicants who have ricocheted from career to career have a slim chance of acceptance.

## High costs and other influential matters

A major current issue affecting medical school attendance is the cost of medical education. Most expensive are the privately supported schools, where tuition is in the range of $10,000 to $19,000 per year with living expenses adding $5,000 or more to this figure. Much less expensive (perhaps half as much as the private schools or less) are the state-sponsored, tax-supported schools, but these are essentially limited to students from that state. But state legislatures, too, have been forced to increase tuition costs as total institutional budgets have risen. Federal, state, and private loan funds are available, and although relatively high interest rates discourage potential borrowers, the majority of students have no alternative. Scholarship funds have not increased with the demand, and money earned during medical school must be modest, as students have minimal time away from their studies. Loans thus constitute the major portion of most financial-aid packages. Despite these problems, financial-aid committees do make it possible for thousands of middle- and low-income students to complete their education, although often at the price of considerable long-term indebtedness. In 1982 the mean debt of graduating medical students was $20,000.

With increasing signs that the acute shortage of physicians is over, the stimulus to open more new medical schools and increase enrollment has disappeared. It is the view of some that an oversupply of doctors is imminent, and there is a distinct possibility that the size of entering classes will be reduced during coming years. Meanwhile, the more generous number of physicians has had a healthy effect in introducing medical manpower to areas previously completely lacking it, and in providing competition where at times none previously existed.

It has at times been suggested that changes in medical practice, with increasing emphasis on group rather than solo practice, the spread of prepaid medical plans (health maintenance organizations and the like), the trend toward more and more technological approaches to medicine, the burgeoning and complexity of medical scientific knowledge, and the intrusion of governmental restraints all might make medicine less attractive as a career than in the past. But these factors, if at all influential, have not had any major impact in reducing the interest in medical school applications. Doubtless, too, they have been offset by the excitement and at-traction of medicine as a lively and rapidly developing field and by the high income of physicians.

It is clear that medicine continues to appeal as a career to a very large number of bright young men and women. The chances of admission are actually good, as approximately one out of every two applicants may expect to be admitted to a United States medical school. The selectivity of the admissions process has its rewards in that more than 90% of matriculating students will graduate. The high cost of a medical education remains a serious and difficult issue, usually met by the assumption of loans to be repaid during years of practice. An excellent source of detailed information regarding medical schools and the admissions process, *Medical School Admission Requirements,* is published annually by the Association of American Medical Colleges.

*—Oglesby Paul, M.D.*

# Medical Ethics

Democratic societies cannot thrive without access to timely and accurate information upon which to base personal and political decisions. This is acutely the case with the results of scientific research, especially new biomedical discoveries, which can so profoundly affect the lives of all.

How quickly, in what detail, through what agency, and under what controls for accuracy should the results of medical research be made available to the public? What are the relative roles and responsibilities of researchers, professional journals, and the communications media? What moral obligations bind those people who generate, and those who disseminate, medical information?

## The reporting of medical information

These questions have been increasingly vexatious for some time. They were brought to a head a decade or more ago when the prestigious *New England Journal of Medicine* formulated what is known as the "Ingelfinger rule." Named after Franz Ingelfinger, the journal's redoubtable editor from 1967 to 1977, a policy was formulated that excludes from publication material that has been reported or submitted elsewhere. The rule is known to authors beforehand, and they sign a form that says the manuscript is submitted solely to the *Journal.* Exempted are abstracts and formal presentations at scientific meetings, press reports based solely on these public presentations, and information of immediate public health importance.

Two reasons have been adduced for this policy: the desire of the *New England Journal of Medicine* to maintain its enviable reputation in the medical field for originality and newsworthiness and the necessity of peer review to assure accuracy of reporting. Since its adoption, the merits of this argument have been debated widely within the biomedical community and between that community and the news media.

Those who defend "freedom of the press" as absolute view the so-called Ingelfinger rule as a "gag order," which gives the *Journal*'s editors unjustifiable powers of censorship. They view all news as news and any delay in its release as unacceptable. Others interpret the policy as evidence of the academic proclivity for secrecy to protect the priority of a discovery or to assure that physicians get information before their patients do. Still others see a conspiracy among the profession to maintain a monopoly over all treatments, suppressing those that might disadvantage physicians' self-interests. Still others worry about the victimization of the investigator who must subject himself to censorship of unorthodox ideas that are not acceptable to the academic establishment.

Proponents of the rule defend it as a necessary means to protect the public and the profession from irresponsible, false, misleading, or inadequately assessed data—or even deliberate hoax. Peer review cannot assure certitude, but it does assure critical review of the design, methods, and cogency of the conclusions, without which nonexperts could be seriously misled. Accuracy is therefore placed against timeliness since the review process must, of necessity, be time-consuming in order to be thorough.

Timeliness is, of course, essential when a new treatment or preventive measure is discovered. To get such information too late to help victims of a disease or prevent a public health disaster is tragic. The most elementary ethical principles of beneficence dictate that useful information be available as soon as possible. Timeliness is, therefore, a moral obligation binding scientific investigators and those who report their work to the public. What must be balanced against this obligation, however, is the equal obligation to be sure that the information on which a treatment is based is as accurate as possible. Proponents of the rule point out that the time that elapses from conception of an idea, through applying for a research grant and carrying out the actual research, to actual submission of a paper for publication is often five or more years. Thus a six-week or so delay for peer review is a relatively trivial one.

Accuracy is a much more difficult thing to assure than the public, the news media, or even the majority of physicians appreciate. Biomedical research today uses sophisticated methods of laboratory and clinical investigation that require equally sophisticated methods of statistical design for proper interpretation. In clinical investigation, *i.e.,* the evaluation in patients of the cause of an illness or a new treatment, the whole matter is vastly more complicated. Trials of new treatments are among the most difficult to design, carry out objectively, and interpret soundly. Humans are notable for the individuality of their responses to illness, of their responses to the effects and side effects of drugs, and of

their capacity to perceive the success or failure of a treatment. Conclusions drawn from clinical trials are, therefore, among the most difficult data to assess.

Often the differences between "new" treatments are marginal and demand careful sampling and the most refined statistical designs. The temptation of investigators to seek favorable, and suppress unfavorable, results is well established. Often the side effects of new treatments take time to manifest themselves. Truly effective medications are likely to have toxic effects, so dosage, modes of administration, and interactions with other medications must be carefully evaluated before a treatment is offered for general use.

## The dangers of misinformation

The recent history of therapeutics is replete with false starts, collapsed expectations, unexpected side effects, and useless treatments, a fact that illustrates the dangers of premature release of inadequately evaluated treatments. In the United States no small part of the annual multibillion-dollar expenditure for medications, medical devices, and operations results from public and professional reliance on uncritical enthusiasm for the "latest and the best."

Appealing as they may be, anecdotal testimonials by physicians or satisfied patients about the effectiveness of the latest therapeutic triumph are, more often than not, erroneous. Equally dubious and more suspicious are the media "hype" and promotional hyperbole that accompany the latest "wonder" drug. In today's technological society few of us can critically evaluate all the information crowding our senses from so many sources. Some scrutinizing filter is necessary if we are not to be overwhelmed by information or misled into dangerous decisions.

*"Eureka! A breakthrough! A boon to mankind! But first, an article in the New England Journal of Medicine!"*

Sidney Harris

But even when data are carefully scrutinized by competent peers, they may be difficult to report accurately. Most statements about medicine are probability statements. Differences in effectiveness between new and old treatments or discoveries of new causes of illnesses must be interpreted within definite restraints imposed by the design of the experiments. Under the omnipresent pressures of television cameras, skillful media interlocutors, and the public taste for sensational news, even the skilled science writer and the investigator himself may be tempted to extract more than what should be concluded from the data.

The dangers of misinformation are painfully obvious: false expectations, dashed hopes, money wasted, and—more seriously—dangerous side effects, toxicity, and even deaths. One needs only to think of the recent media stimulus of public demand for Oraflex, a drug for arthritis. The drug's manufacturer launched an extraordinary promotional campaign for the prescription drug directly to the public, via television and other media, in effect urging patients to pressure their physicians to prescribe the new nonsteroid anti-inflammatory pill. Oraflex was on the market for only about 12 weeks when serious side effects and fatalities began to appear, and the drug had to be withdrawn. Public demand had unwittingly provided the expanded sample size needed to uncover the toxicity of the drug. The recent history of therapeutics is replete with similar examples of ineffective, costly, and dangerous treatments for the often desperate victims of such chronic disorders as cancer, multiple sclerosis, schizophrenia, heart disease, arthritis, and senility. Even cautious physicians can be tempted to draw unwarranted conclusions because of the intractable nature of such diseases and the desire to "do something" for their sufferers.

As mentioned above, evaluation of the efficacy and safety of treatments is an unavoidably painstaking and time-consuming process. What is not sufficiently appreciated, however, is that the most effective treatments usually manifest themselves rather quickly. Antibiotics for pneumonia, bacterial meningitis, subacute endocarditis, tuberculosis, and meningitis, for example, were easy to assess because of the high mortality of the untreated disease. It is treatments that show only marginal improvements that usually cause difficulty— and it is precisely these that require the longest time to assess. Delays in introducing the latest treatment are usually less damaging than premature introduction of experimental or partially evaluated medications or procedures. Those who promote and those who rush to use a new treatment may be unknowingly enrolling themselves and others in an uncontrolled experimental protocol.

## Timeliness, accuracy, and freedom of the press
None of these comments can justify withholding medical information that is well assessed as long as what is not known and what dangers may follow are stressed. The moral obligations of the researcher are clear: to conduct his research in the most meticulous manner, to subject it to peer criticism, and, consistent with these two obligations, to report it as soon as possible. Editors of scientific journals do a needed public service by monitoring the review process that balances to some degree the normal tendency of authors to want to see their work in print.

Nothing undermines the credibility, and therefore the social utility, of science and the media more than sensational, erroneous information. The result in matters of public health can be a dangerous cynicism that leads to equally dangerous passivity. Public skepticism about such matters as the relationship between dietary fats and heart disease, food additives and cancer, or pesticides and health are cases in point. Careless investigation and premature reporting of complicated issues can only frustrate the very reason for the free flow of information in democratic societies.

Public cynicism about the news media is already widespread. The pathetic gullibility of European publications that recently fell victim to the forged "Hitler Diaries" shows clearly where avarice and sensationalism can lead. Surely one of the rudimentary principles of any ethics of transmitting information is to assure the reliability of the "expert" sources.

The real danger of peer review is not so much its inhibitive effect as the possibility of public sanctification of the information it finally approves. In a free society we must guard against the uncritical acceptance of the opinions of experts. In a technological society we are all susceptible to the tyranny of experts who extrapolate their expertise into social prescriptions. Peer review and technical authority do not confer social, political, or moral authority. The British political scientist and social reformer Harold Laski put it well many years ago: "... expertise consists in such an analytic comprehension of a special realm of facts that the power to see that realm in the perspective of totality is lost. ... There is no illusion so fatal to government as that of the man who makes his expert insight the measure of social need."

Here is the most important function of a free press— to subject the product of peer review to critical analysis, debate, and close examination. The assurance of accuracy does not guarantee accuracy nor the wise applications of knowledge, no matter how reliable. Public decisions can safely be made only in the public realm. The containment of expertise by public debate is our safeguard against the dangers Laski so well pointed out. The debate will be more sensible if it is based on well-examined fact. Peer review followed by open and free criticism is the mainstay of responsible policy decisions in a democratic society.

Insistence on accuracy should not in principle violate the cherished doctrine of freedom of the press. That freedom is accorded because an uncensored and unmanipulated press best serves the interests of a democratic society. That freedom surely must be preserved. But like all freedoms, it is not absolute. Freedom implies the duty to use it responsibly and for the purposes for which it has been granted. When that freedom defeats those purposes, as is the case with the proliferation of inaccurate information, then it is in danger of being lost.

The requirement for peer review of medical findings is a far cry from government censorship. The process of peer review, the criteria used, the people involved, and the correspondence between medical journal editors and authors reporting new data are available for inspection should suspicions of censorship be raised. Moreover, there are some 8,000 or more medical publications that provide numerous alternative opportunities for publication if one journal chooses not to accept a submission. A scientific journal, no matter how prestigious, would soon lose that prestige if it practiced even subtle censorship. This contrasts sharply with the total impotence of the press and society in countries with a government-dominated press.

Some argue that the damage done by premature or inaccurate reporting is less than the damage done by even the slightest restriction of the absolute freedom to publish without delay. There are at present no facts that permit quantification of the relative damages. It would be difficult to measure the damage to the expectations of patients, the disability and mortality, and the economic loss caused by misinformation about new drugs, surgical procedures, the effects of food additives, diet, or pesticides. The question must remain moot. But it is not a moot point that the surest way to assure freedom of the press is to use that freedom wisely and with some sense of the moral obligations it imposes.

### Ethical standards and the public interest

On balance then, something like the Ingelfinger rule, responsibly implemented, can serve the public interest. This means that the peer review process must be more carefully documented and subject to ethical standards aimed at protecting the rights of the author and the public. Properly implemented, the peer review process should be welcomed by media cognizant of their own moral responsibilities.

In fact, neither the media nor the scientists can fulfill their obligations without a serious cooperative effort. They must develop an unprecedented sensitivity to the ethical dimension of their functions in society. Self-restraint, the development of mutually agreed-upon ethical guidelines, and a proportionate respect for the tremendous power of information in a technological society are in order.

Democratic societies do indeed depend on the free flow of information for survival. But survival also depends on information that is both accurate and timely. That dependence imposes moral obligations on the producers and the processors of information. These obligations are painful and difficult to fulfill. But the alternatives are equally painful—public cynicism and confusion on the one hand and censorship and regulation on the other. Neither is compatible with a free and democratic society.

The debate over the Ingelfinger rule is not a parochial dispute between academics and the press but another crucial arena for adjusting our freedoms and our duties in such a way as to assure a free and humane way of life. Making that adjustment in so many spheres of life may be the most delicate and serious domestic challenge of our times.

*—Edmund D. Pellegrino, M.D.*

# Mental Health and Illness

Within the past few years there has been a remarkable surge of pet ownership based in part upon the assumption that the establishment of a warm human-animal bond makes for improved human mental and emotional adjustment. Mental health considerations have thus come to be a significant supplement to the traditional motivations for having pets. At the same time, in orthodox psychoanalytic circles a resurgence of interest in Freudian theory and its connection with the personality of Freud himself has been stimulated by the publication of some long-suppressed personal correspondence between Freud and some of his closest confidants.

### Pets as therapeutic agents

Reduction of loneliness and depression as well as an increase in empathy and self-esteem are often claimed as benefits of pet ownership. Most of the emphasis in the mental health field has been upon older people whose opportunities and abilities for social interaction are often diminished. In one recent study, however, measurements of interpersonal trust and empathy were found to be higher among college students who were pet owners than those students who were not. The cause-and-effect relationships—that is, the degree to which pet ownership is a determinant of such differences—can be established only by further and more specific research projects.

In 1981 the University of Pennsylvania's Center for the Interaction of Animals and Society sponsored the First International Conference on the Human/Companion Animal Bond. Conferences of this type attract a surprisingly wide range of participants. Typically the major conferees are veterinarians and psychologists, but also attracted are physician-specialists—psychiatrists, pediatricians, and gerontologists—officers of humane societies, ethologists, anthropologists, social workers, physical and occupational therapists, pet breeders, and pet store owners.

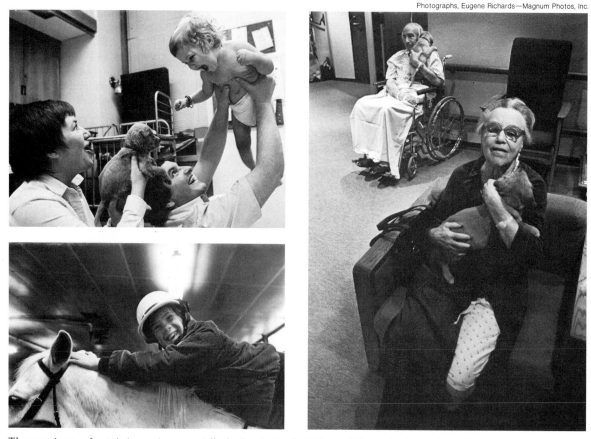

*Therapeutic use of pets is increasing, especially for hospitalized children and for geriatric residents of nursing homes. At Cheff Center for the Handicapped in Augusta, Mich. (bottom left), horseback-riding therapy provides stimulation of muscles and an enormous emotional boost to paraplegics and other handicapped individuals.*

Consideration of the therapeutic role of pets in the psychological well-being of older persons is a major objective of such conferences. Because they provide both direct emotional support and the sense of being needed, so lacking in the lives of many elderly people, pets can be a simple and relatively economical means of countering feelings of isolation and loneliness.

There is a growing body of empirical data in support of these propositions. For example, in 1974 Roger Mugford, a British researcher in animal behavior, conducted an experiment in Yorkshire, England, in which one-half of a group of older people (average age, 73) who lived alone were given a parakeet as a pet; the other half of the group received a begonia. Social workers then made semiannual assessments of social adjustment and psychological health and at the end of three years reported that the pet owners were distinctly better adjusted than the plant owners.

In the United States, psychiatrist Aaron H. Katcher, chairman of the University of Pennsylvania conference, conducted an investigation to determine the efficacy of various social factors influencing the health of heart patients. An unexpected finding of this study was that pet ownership was the most significant social influence identified. More than half of the 93 patients in the study had pets; after one year only three of these patients had died, compared with one-third of those who did not own pets. This evidence certainly justifies the planning and execution of better controlled and more extensive scientific investigations of morbidity and mortality as they are affected by the human-animal relationship.

Across the United States, staff and volunteers in hospitals, nursing homes, and public and private agencies are undertaking joint efforts to introduce animals into the lives of people confined to institutions. In Chicago, personnel from the local Anti-Cruelty Society (ACS) take puppies and kittens for periodic visits to a health center for elderly persons. The ACS also sponsors a similar program at the city's Children's Memorial Hospital. Many of the individuals involved in such programs are volunteers—many, in fact, are relatives of the sick children and of the elderly nursing-home residents. All of them have had firsthand experience of the joyful nature of these human-animal encounters.

Obviously, pets provide no universal panacea. They

seem to work best with older people but are also proving to be of great value in the treatment of emotionally disturbed, physically handicapped, and retarded children and have evoked positive responses among inmates in institutions for the criminally insane.

Psychologist Leonard J. Simon has pointed out some of the negative aspects of pet ownership. After a year of interviewing pet owners and their families, he concluded that pet ownership entails a potential for psychological harm as well as help. The harm is most likely to occur when pets are used as substitutes for human affection in situations where the possibilities for human interaction exist. For example, Simon found a number of couples with marital problems in which the purchase of a pet merely postponed—or in some cases actually exacerbated—the interpersonal problems between the husband and wife. Thus, pets should be considered with some caution as therapeutic agents. Moreover, before one makes the decision to acquire a pet as a solution to a problem of adjustment, due consideration must be given to the cost of maintenance, both physical (food, litter, veterinary costs) and psychological (*e.g.,* possible jeopardy to pleasant neighborly relationships).

The use of animals in another role, that of human helpers, has also been receiving a great deal of recent attention. The American Humane Society has initiated a program in which "hearing-ear" dogs are being trained as companions for the deaf. The dogs learn to alert their human companions to certain meaningful sounds, such as telephones or fire alarms. The Tufts-New England Medical Center Hospital in Boston has started a program to train monkeys to aid severely disabled persons. For example, a capuchin monkey has learned to perform a variety of tasks—from feeding to changing phonograph records—for a young quadriplegic. Although there was considerable difficulty during the adjustment period, the monkey eventually became a true and effective companion. In return for getting food and drink from the refrigerator, the monkey was rewarded with food pellets, provided by the paralysis victim with a laser beam manipulated by means of a mouth control on the patient's wheelchair.

Although it is apparent that many problems will be encountered in the development of this kind of human-animal relationship, the potential for effective service by the animals is very high. Moreover, some of the emotional benefits of pet ownership—feelings of companionship and connectedness—should also accrue to the human participants in these programs.

## Reevaluation of Freudian theory

Sigmund Freud, the founder of psychoanalysis, who radically altered prevailing views of human nature, has been a long-time figure of controversy. A revival of interest in the man and his theories is particularly noteworthy in light of the widespread apathy that had developed in the 1960s and '70s with respect to psychoanalysis. According to many contemporary therapists, psychoanalysis is widely viewed as an outdated, inflexible idea whose time has passed. Even among analysts themselves, there appears to be a diminished confidence in both analytic theory and method.

Reports of the death of psychoanalysis, however, appear to be premature. One indication of the renewed interest in Freudian ideas among psychologists has been the establishment of a new psychoanalytic division within the structure of the American Psychological Association. In addition, there has been an active reevaluation of Freud's thinking and a striking revival of interest in his private life and close personal relationships. Another area of renewed controversy concerns questions now being raised about central doctrines of Freudian theory—in particular the radical reversal of his original proposition that adult neuroses are the product of childhood incestuous experiences.

*New emphasis on Freud's humanism.* Viennese-trained analyst and child psychologist Bruno Bettelheim has recently launched a far-reaching attack on what he sees as unfortunate distortions and misinterpretations—among psychiatrists and psychoanalysts themselves as well as others—of Freud's fundamental ideas. The major thrust of Bettelheim's critique is that the humanistic aspects of Freud's thinking and writing have been grossly neglected. These concerns Bettelheim considers to be much more important in Freud's work than the strictly scientific aspects of Freudian theory.

Difficulties and omissions in English translations of

*Researchers are interested in the interactions of healthy people and pets. An investigator measures the blood pressure of this woman as she pets her dog.*

Toby Sanford/DISCOVER Magazine © 1983 Time, Inc.

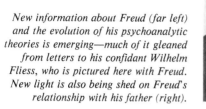

*New information about Freud (far left) and the evolution of his psychoanalytic theories is emerging—much of it gleaned from letters to his confidant Wilhelm Fliess, who is pictured here with Freud. New light is also being shed on Freud's relationship with his father (right).*

Freud's writings are held to be primary factors in these distortions. The humanistic orientation of the original German terminology has apparently been lost in translation; for example, Bettelheim has noted that *Seelentätigkeit,* or "activity of the soul," is typically rendered in English as "mental activity." In partial defense of the erring translators, it should be noted that there is a certain natural ambiguity in many of the German words that Freud used to represent his ideas. Moreover, Freud seems to have deliberately exaggerated this ambiguity. For example, he never attempted to define the key term soul. Bettelheim concedes that the understandable motivation to express terms as clearly as possible in English translation has been responsible for a substantial amount of the distortion.

Although alleged mistranslations may not seem to be especially troublesome in single or isolated cases, the pervasive nature of such errors is held by Bettelheim to have resulted in a generally fallacious view of Freud's thinking. Freud's primary objective, according to Bettelheim, was to enable the individual to better understand himself or herself by eliminating unnecessarily self-destructive tendencies—the dark side of the psyche that has been so much emphasized at the expense of the more positive facets of society and selfhood.

*Experimental testing.* In stark contrast, superficially at least, to this humanistic orientation toward Freud are the various new experimental, laboratory-based investigations of some of his central ideas. The most controversial of these, a research program begun in 1962 by psychologist Lloyd H. Silverman, has used subliminal presentation of presumably wish-related stimuli, and Silverman's more recent positive results have been interpreted to demonstrate the power of unconscious motivation in the laboratory setting. In this research subliminally presented stimuli designed to generate aggressive motives (for example, a picture of a snarling man or the written message "Cannibal eats person") were reported to have produced transient increases in "ego pathology." The more frequently used subliminal stimulus, "Mommy and I are one," is said to have relieved the negative behavioral symptoms of subjects in a variety of different experimental situations. Silverman

interprets this effect as an indication of the powerful influence of the unconscious fantasy of gratification that is produced by the stimulus.

Silverman's results have been considered quite startling and highly controversial. Apart from the several reports of failure by other investigators to replicate his findings, Silverman's experimental techniques are open to a number of crucial questions. For example, there is the length of the message. Experimental psychologists working in the field of subliminal perception generally have difficulties in ensuring adequate control, as of partial conscious perception, even with stimuli comprising short words or single letters. Thus, there is considerable skepticism concerning the effective subliminality of relatively long strings of words. Nevertheless, Silverman's work is important because, as he himself has pointed out, the time is long overdue for psychoanalytic theory to be modified on the basis of experimental and empirical, rather than merely theoretical, grounds.

Another long-standing research program, using more traditional laboratory methodology, has been conducted by psychologist Howard Shevrin and his associates at the University of Michigan Medical Center. Their research, involving both subliminal stimulation and psychophysiological measures, evaluates the so-called evoked potentials of the brain. Using a combination of stimuli, both electronic and sensory, evoked potentials can be measured and quantified in data that reflect the ability of the nervous system to acquire and process sensory information. Evoked potential examination has proved of value in the diagnosis of physiological abnormalities and has also produced results generally in accord with Freudian theory.

*Freud the man: a new look.* A wealth of newly released material bearing on Sigmund Freud's development of psychoanalysis has recently become available to scholars and researchers. The result has been a searching reanalysis of Freud's personal relationships and professional life.

Most prominent among these new materials are the unexpurgated texts of the 284 known letters that Freud wrote to his mentor-confidant Wilhelm Fliess, a Berlin physician, over the 15-year period of their close friendship. Following a decision by Freud's heirs, publication over the next several decades of these and other long-restricted or "unaccounted for" Freudian materials has recently been arranged by the Harvard University Press. Until now, only 168 of the letters to Fliess have been published, often substantially cut to protect the confidentiality of certain personal and professional matters—in many cases, of course, exactly the sort of material most valuable to scholars.

The Sigmund Freud Archives has also reached an agreement with the U.S. Library of Congress to open its vast store of materials to the public over the next several years. There is to be a complete cataloging of the approximately 150,000 items in the collection, plus 400 taped interviews with surviving friends and patients recently added to the collection. Also under way is the initial publication of Freud's letters to a close teenage school friend and the first full publication of his letters to disciples Karl Abraham and Ludwig Binswanger.

Finally, awaiting compilation for subsequent publication are the 2,000 letters exchanged between Freud and his future wife, Martha Bernays, during their engagement (only 100 of which have been published previously) and the 1,500 letters exchanged between Freud and Sandor Ferenczi, a patient and one of Freud's most brilliant, and critical, disciples.

*Childhood sexual trauma: real or fantasized?* Perhaps the most pressing and persuasive reason for the search into Freud's own life and mind is the conviction that further biographical detail can shed light on the most mysterious of his theoretical revisions. The focal issue that has absorbed Freudian scholars over the past several years concerns his dramatic reversal of his original hypothesis that sexual trauma during childhood is responsible for adult neurosis. Freud's vacillation over and ultimate rejection of this hypothesis are vividly represented in the newly released correspondence with Fliess, beginning with the letters that followed the death of Freud's father in 1896. On Sept. 21, 1897, for example, Freud wrote Fliess that he no longer believed in his sexual seduction theory. In December 1897, however, Freud wrote Fliess about a case that "speaks for the intrinsic authenticity of infantile trauma." Nonetheless, by 1905 Freud had definitely renounced the sexual-trauma hypothesis and had reinterpreted neurosis on the basis of fantasized rather than real trauma.

Freudian scholars attribute this radical turnabout to two major factors. First, they speculate that Freud was tired of his professional isolation, which largely stemmed from the failure of many of his colleagues to accept his innovative ideas. There had been an especially hostile reaction from the prominent sex pathologist Richard von Krafft-Ebing, who is quoted as having labeled the childhood-seduction hypothesis "a scientific fairy tale." According to Jeffrey Moussiaeff Masson, a psychoanalyst and Freudian scholar and archivist, who was apparently instrumental in persuading Freud's daughter Anna to release the remainder of his letters to Fliess, the criticism and peer pressure were overwhelming to Freud and caused him to abandon his long-held theory.

The second factor in Freud's turning to fantasized rather than actual sexual trauma in the etiology of neurosis is said to be an attempt to absolve his own father, Jakob, of any charge of sexual abuse. The true facts of the father-son relationship remain murky, although this subject has been actively explored by many of the scholars determined to penetrate the intimate secrets of Freud's familial relationships. The interpretation is lent some credence by certain parts of the Fliess correspondence; *e.g.,* Freud's short phrase "not excluding my own" following the statement that blame was typically placed on fathers in memories of childhood sexual trauma.

Interestingly, much support for the original Freudian hypothesis of actual sexual trauma is now being advanced. There seems to be a growing consensus that a great deal of abuse, both sexual and nonsexual, really does occur in childhood. The latest in a series of prominent Freudian critics to speak to this point is psychiatrist Karl Menninger, who founded the Menninger Institute in Topeka, Kan. In an article for a professional journal, Menninger has written, "Why oh why couldn't Freud believe his own ears? Why did he knuckle under to those who said, 'Oh, people don't do those dreadful things to children.'. . ." Then, with regard to the Menninger facilities for troubled adolescents, he added: "Seventy-five percent of the girls we accept . . . have been molested in tender childhood by an adult. And that is today in Kansas! I don't think Vienna in 1900 was any less sophisticated."

Another reason for the criticism of Freud's turnabout on this pivotal issue is the feeling that the emphasis on fantasy has simply not been productive. Thus Masson, in an address at Yale University, stated that "Freud began a trend away from the real world that, it seems to me, has come to a dead halt in the present-day sterility of psychoanalysis throughout the world."

Whatever the outcome of these questions and criticisms of Freud, it is clear that the view of Freudian psychoanalysis will never be quite the same and that historical judgments about Freud himself are still very much in the making. It would be ironic indeed if future developments identify the childhood period as crucial in neurosis on the basis of abuse—physical and psychological especially, even more than sexual—real or fantasized. Certainly, increasing experimental investigation of nonconscious mental phenomena, combined with the renewed emphasis on early environmental factors, promises to provide a much sounder, more empirically grounded basis on which to assess Freud's contributions.

*—Melvin H. Marx, Ph.D.*

Special Report:

# Hypnosis
## by Fred H. Frankel, D.P.M.

As you sit comfortably in the chair, permit yourself to focus on my voice at the same time as allowing yourself to relax. Let your eyes close when they are ready as you allow yourself to slow down; feel your breathing slow down, your body slow down, and your mind slow down. Feel the sense of relaxation and calm spread from the top of your head all the way down to the tips of your toes, spreading to displace all the tensions right out of your body. As you continue to relax, disconnect your working mind from the everyday world around you, and focus it deep down on the sense of inner calm within you. As you become deeply relaxed, will you kindly let me know by nodding your head?

Sometimes when people are as deeply relaxed as you are now, they can, by focusing their attention on the feelings in their forearm and hand, permit themselves to experience very different sensations in that limb. I am not sure which arm will be selected, nor of the sensation that will develop. It could be a wooden feeling, a heavy feeling, a tingling feeling, or a light feeling. If light, it will get lighter and lighter, permitting the hand and forearm to lift up from the armrest and float in an upward direction toward an upright position.

When a patient consents to the use of hypnosis as part of his treatment plan, his physician or therapist offers the above induction procedure or one of many other similar versions. The hand and forearm might indeed float into an upright position, or by signals elicited from the patient, the physician or therapist will know that the patient is experiencing a very heavy limb, a tingling limb, or a wooden feeling in that limb. Whichever sensation occurs is encouraged as the patient becomes more and more involved in the experience of the altered perception, to the almost total exclusion of other aspects of awareness.

It is at this stage of the proceedings that the therapeutic strategy is introduced. This could entail suggestions to increase self-esteem; to relieve the discomfort of an asthmatic attack, or migraine, or the nausea associated with the treatment of cancer; or to relive past relevant experiences. The strategy might include the repetition of helpful ideas related to relinquishing a habit such as smoking, or it might encourage the patient to create vivid images of himself or herself succeeding at a task that has, up until now, been overwhelming.

The induction of the event of hypnosis might follow one of very many forms other than that cited above, including simply having the patient focus attention on the memory of a peaceful scene. The goal is to achieve a state of disconnectedness from the pressures of the real world, a trance or state of altered awareness, which then paves the way for the unfolding of the therapeutic plan. This is a brief glimpse of modern therapeutic practice involving hypnosis.

### Historical context

Although considerably altered in many ways, the contemporary practice of hypnosis is the successor to the practice of animal magnetism introduced by Franz Anton Mesmer into Vienna and later into Paris in the 1770s. Mesmer believed he could transmit a "universal fluid" or "animal magnetism" through his body to a suffering patient by physical contact or by merely motioning with his hands or eyes. He conducted his séances in a theatrical setting complete with drapes and music. By holding on to metal bars extending from a wooden tub filled with water, ground glass, and iron filings, among other things, the patients were exposed to the reparative magnetic forces. They were similarly convinced of Mesmer's power and would experience convulsive seizures called crises, which ostensibly had a benign and healing effect. A commission appointed by King Louis XVI to carry out a scientific investigation of this animal magnetism emphasized the role played by the imagination in the therapeutic process. Although the commission's findings were a blow to Mesmer and many of his followers, we, two centuries later, are largely in agreement. The altered physical sensations experienced by those patients are comparable to the altered state of awareness that is the essence of the modern-day hypnotic experience.

After the unfavorable report of the royal commission, little was heard of animal magnetism until the mid-19th century. It reappeared then under a new name, hypnosis, enjoying a revival of interest. In addition to the "mental healers" who practiced the art in Europe and then in the United States, several physicians became interested in its use in the practice of medicine. Notable

*"You certainly may not try to hypnotize me."*

Drawing by Frascino; The New Yorker Magazine © 1983

*In the late 1700s Franz Mesmer developed a system of therapeutics known as mesmerism, which was a forerunner of the modern practice of hypnosis. In sessions resembling séances, Mesmer attempted to transmit reparative magnetic forces through his own body to suffering patients.*

among these were James Esdaile, John Elliotson, and James Braid in the 1840s and Jean-Martin Charcot, Ambroise-Auguste Liébeault, Hippolyte Bernheim, Pierre Janet, and Sigmund Freud during the latter part of the last century. Although the Portuguese Abbé Faria was probably the first to comment on it, Braid was the earliest English writer to emphasize the importance of the mental mechanisms of the patient as opposed to the "magical" qualities of the hypnotist in producing the event of hypnosis.

Subjectively quite remarkable to some individuals experiencing it for the first time, hypnosis can contribute to dramatic clinical effects. Regrettably, both charlatans and stage entertainers have had completely free access to the technique in most countries of the Western world and have used it to demonstrate the extent of their hypnotic powers; audiences are amused by the comical antics of the hapless volunteers.

## Laboratory studies

For the past century and longer, reports of the clinical successes with hypnosis have been numerous and at times fascinating. Even when published in medical and clinical psychology journals, however, the great majority have been anecdotal and not persuasive to discerning colleagues eager for a more convincingly scientific appraisal. For almost a half century now, experimental psychologists have devoted increasing energy and attention to the study of hypnosis in the laboratory. Significant advances include the development of a series of standardized scales (the most noteworthy being the Stanford Hypnotic Susceptibility Scales and the Harvard Group Scale) to measure the hypnotizability of subjects and sophisticated methods for studying the event. The use of the scales, standardized so that all subjects tested on them are given the same instruc-

tions in the same manner, has affirmed what clinicians have long suspected—not all people are equally responsive to hypnosis. Consistently among all laboratory subjects, approximately 5 to 10% respond extremely well, about 25% respond poorly or not at all, and the remaining 65% are distributed on a bell-shaped curve. This means that the manner in which subjects experience a light feeling in the forearm when this is suggested to them differs from individual to individual. With some the arm feels rapidly lighter and floats with ease into the upright position; with others there is absolutely no sensation of lightness at all, and the forearm never feels like floating involuntarily into an upright position. For the majority the experience is somewhere in between. It seems that the level of a person's response remains stable.

Furthermore, although the scales have provided clear-cut findings that neither the sex nor the educational level of the subject influences the extent to which he or she responds, the capacity to respond tends to diminish somewhat with age. Whereas personality profiles determined on tests such as the Rorschach Inkblot Test, the Thematic Apperception Test, and the Minnesota Multiphasic Personality Inventory seem not to correlate with the level of hypnotizability, other data remind us that hypnotizability does correlate with the extent to which individuals can become involved or absorbed in their own imagination. Highly hypnotizable individuals are highly imaginative and are able to live deeply in their imaginings.

The rating scales paved the way to the development of an impressive investigative methodology. By observing and studying the behavior of individuals who are known to be highly hypnotizable, we have come to appreciate the rich nature of their experiences. They can truly be encouraged to experience themselves,

287

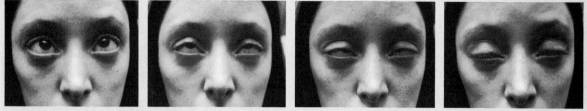

Bernard Gotfryd/*Newsweek*

*Standardized scales that measure hypnotizability are enabling scientists to study hypnosis. One scale calls for a patient to roll the eyes back and lower the lids. The more white exposed, the higher the score.*

their bodies, and their environment as different. For example, the highly hypnotizable can experience themselves as very small or very large, their skin as warm or cold, and their lives as highly successful and accomplished regardless of their shortcomings in reality; these individuals can be persuaded not to see the minute hand on the clock, to hallucinate a person at the same time as that individual continues quite obviously to be seen by them in another spot in the same room, and to provide and tolerate the most blatantly illogical judgments.

By comparing the behavior and experiences of highly hypnotizable subjects with those of consistently poor hypnotic responders, investigators have demonstrated conclusively that the hypnotic experience is a genuine event that follows clear-cut rules. Highly hypnotizable subjects who have had no means of communicating with one another provide accounts of hypnotic experiences and behaviors in hypnosis that are consistently similar to one another. Poorly hypnotizable subjects told to fake hypnosis in blind studies (*i.e.,* in studies in which the investigator does not know who among the subjects are highly hypnotizable and who are not) all show behaviors that are similar to those of other poorly hypnotizable subjects but distinctly different from those of the highly hypnotizable subjects.

## The hypnotic state

Hypnosis has been defined and understood in many different ways. The most widely accepted definitions and descriptions at this time emphasize the altered state of awareness experienced by the hypnotized individual, or the altered perception, cognition, and mood that contribute to the essence of the experience. Most authors and clinicians appreciate the importance of the setting in which the hypnotic event or altered state of awareness occurs. They recognize that an induction procedure succeeds only if there is a positive relationship between the hypnotizer and the subject and if the individual is motivated to participate. Others emphasize the importance of the manner in which the subject pays attention.

A clear understanding of the mental mechanism that permits an adult individual to experience his arm as lighter than air, or to have the vivid experience of reliving his tenth birthday party, is elusive. Attempts have

been made, however, to provide possible explanations. The hypnotic state has been described as a withdrawal of attention from the surroundings of the everyday world, and a redirection of that attention to an imagined experience. The generalized reality orientation constantly available to us, should we wish to check where we are and what date it is, is pushed further and further to the periphery of consciousness; ultimately, although we are vaguely aware of its existence there, we are totally absorbed and persuaded by what we are imagining. In some way we continue to observe ourselves at it.

Another method of describing the event is in terms of "dissociation"; the term reflects some form of divided consciousness. For instance, one might be driving along the highway, focusing almost all one's attention on mentally reliving an important event while still controlling the vehicle with the necessary care. It is as if the driving is assigned to an automatic pilot sensitive to environmental shifts and changes, while the bulk of the attention is focused on the important reverie. One might reach a point in the road and have no recollection of how in fact one arrived there. While this experience of divided consciousness is not necessarily hypnosis, it provides a model from which one may conceptualize what can take place in hypnosis.

## Hypnosis as a treatment

Laboratory studies are undertaken on normal healthy adults, most often youthful and drawn from college populations. By contrast, the patient population is likely to be of all ages, many considerably older, and suffering from symptoms and discomforts. The question is often asked whether the data from the former population are applicable to the latter. While care must be exercised in extrapolating the findings from laboratory to the suffering patient, the knowledge accumulated in scientific studies can be of considerable value in understanding clinical events.

It is generally accepted that many patients respond to hypnotic techniques—more perhaps than the laboratory statistics allow us to expect. Several clinicians claim that they virtually never fail to achieve some improvement in almost all their patients, many of whom must fall in the group who score low on the laboratory scales. Rather than negating the validity of the labora-

*Progressive relaxation is one technique for inducing hypnosis. In deep relaxation the patient may experience sensations suggested by the therapist; e.g., that her arm is weightless and floating effortlessly upward.*

tory findings, this observation might well mesh with them.

The hypnotic technique generally begins with a good relationship between therapist and patient, optimistic expectations, and the achievement of relaxation. While these three items contribute to the context in which hypnosis is to occur, they are not the essential ingredients of hypnosis per se. Indeed, most effective interpersonal therapies depend upon a good patient-therapist relationship, optimistic expectations, and a reduction in the patient's anxiety. Poorly hypnotizable subjects might well achieve some degree of relief from pain or discomfort by being exposed to a warm, comforting, reassuring relationship. Highly hypnotizable subjects are able to add to that emotional comfort the actual alteration of their perception of the pain, which can be transformed, for example, into a numb, cool, or tingling feeling.

Certain clinical behaviors quite reliably predict a higher mean hypnotizability rating among patients than among controls. There is also evidence that such heightened hypnotizability seen in patients might itself lead to the development of symptoms. Part of the treatment process for some highly hypnotizable individuals includes learning to control the ease with which they unknowingly slip into hypnoticlike states.

## The uses of hypnosis

Traditionally, hypnosis has been used clinically to relieve or remove symptoms, to modify habits, or to aid in the uncovering of past experiences. However, the more insightful use of hypnosis requires that the therapist be sensitive to the psychological forces surrounding or even creating the problems in the first place. If, for instance, the patient needs the increased attention

that he gains from his stubborn symptoms, suggestions for their relief might fall on deaf ears or can create considerable anxiety. Unwittingly, patients sometimes not only experience their physical problems in an exaggerated way but might even psychologically generate physical symptoms such as paralysis or pain. In practice, such symptoms should be approached with caution; they are not infrequently more difficult to dislodge than those that arise on a purely physical basis.

Much of the work with hypnosis is focused on helping patients learn how to induce hypnosis on their own. The self-induced hypnotic trance is especially helpful as it enables the patient to practice what he learns in the therapy, thereby gaining confidence in his own ability to master situations.

It should be clearly stated that hypnosis, at its best, is an adjunct to treatment and rarely a treatment in its own right. It provides a facilitating factor or context within which the primary treatment mode can be carried out. The practice of using hypnosis as if it were an independent discipline is questionable. It is an easy matter to hypnotize a responsive patient. To do justice to the situation, the treatment strategy must then invoke techniques that are part and parcel of the accepted psychological therapies. Individuals who lack the basic training in psychotherapy provided by accredited educational programs probably practice hypnosis without the necessary competence to do so.

## Future directions

Many investigative studies on the uses of hypnosis remain to be done. In view of the recent trend toward the forensic use of this technique to find facts, the role of hypnosis in facilitating the recall of events is commanding considerable attention.

Despite numerous efforts, we still have no evidence that there is any neurophysiologic or chemical event in the body that is uniquely associated with hypnosis. The metabolic accompaniments of relaxation are, of course, often found, but these are not peculiar to hypnosis. Further work in this area to determine whether physical correlates of hypnosis do indeed exist is indicated. The role of hypnosis or hypnotizability in influencing human behavior, and in relation to the success of the persuasive religious cults that have arisen in recent years, is a similarly inviting area of study.

Clinicians and laboratory investigators recognize with increasing conviction that they are mutually dependent on each other. Clinical work, without the underpinnings of a basic science derived from laboratory studies, will continue to meet with skepticism. Laboratory studies, to be relevant, must take their cues from the challenges of clinical experience. One is the lifeblood of the other.

# Neuromuscular Disorders

Baseball hero Lou Gehrig died in 1941, struck down at the age of 32 by a neuromuscular disorder that has come to be called Lou Gehrig's disease. To the physician the disease is known as amyotrophic lateral sclerosis (ALS). To both the patient and the neurologist ALS is a frustrating, distressing, progressively crippling, and eventually lethal disease for which, at present, no effective therapy is known. Recent research, however, is beginning to provide important clues about the basis of this enigmatic disorder.

## Clinical features of Lou Gehrig's disease

Lou Gehrig's disease, or ALS, generally affects older individuals; the older the population, the higher the incidence of the disease. There are two specific features of the disease, wasting and spasticity. The wasting and weakness of muscles is due to death of the motor nerve cells, or motoneurons, in the spinal cord that send the messages to drive the muscles. The spasticity is due to death of the upper motoneurons running from the brain to the lower motoneurons in the spinal cord, causing a lack of control of the voluntary muscles and spinal reflexes. The disease may affect any or all of the limbs, the respiratory muscles, and the muscles controlling swallowing and speech. Typically, the disease starts in one area and gradually spreads to affect almost all of the body. It always remains restricted to the motor system and never involves any sensory or higher mental functions.

A typical case might be a man of 60 who begins to notice a weakness in his grip and wasting of the muscles of his hands. The hands begin to become clawlike, and about this time he notices a flickering in his muscles (fasciculations). Weakness gradually spreads to other muscles in the body, and his legs begin to stiffen when walking. At about this time he is referred to a neurologist, who finds that in addition to the wasting and weakness of the muscles there is spasticity (increased stiffness) in the lower limbs with increased tendon reflexes (ascertained by examining the knee- and ankle-jerk reflexes). Over the next two to three years, as the condition spreads to involve the muscles of respiration and swallowing, the patient becomes severely incapacitated.

## Epidemiology and causes

The annual incidence of ALS is about one to three cases per 100,000 population in all parts of the world, with the exception of three isolated areas in the western Pacific: the island of Guam in the Mariana Islands, the Kii Peninsula in Japan, and a small area in Irian Jaya (West New Guinea). The incidence of ALS in these three areas is about 100 times greater than in the rest of the world; this striking difference has offered some clues about the nature of ALS. The condition has

Terrence McCarthy/*The New York Times*

*Since 1979 former New York senator Jacob K. Javits has suffered from the debilitating neuromuscular disease known as ALS (amyotrophic lateral sclerosis).*

been particularly well studied in Guam, where there is also a high incidence of a Parkinsonlike neurological disorder marked by tremors and weakness and of a progressive dementia (mental deterioration) similar to Alzheimer's disease. Sometimes two or three of these conditions occur in the same patient. Studies of the nerve cells of dying patients in Guam have shown abnormal collections of fibrillary proteins, known as neurofibrillary tangles. Under the electron microscope these tangled collections of protein appear as pairs of tubules twisted one upon the other in a helical formation; they appear to be extremely insoluble. Those neurofibrillary tangles are also a common feature of Alzheimer's disease in patients in other parts of the world but are generally not seen in ALS patients. Their presence, then, in ALS victims in Guam seems to offer a clue to the cause of the disease; researchers are currently trying to understand the precise biochemistry of these abnormal proteins and to learn exactly how they are formed in the neurons.

Up until recently there have been a great many suggested causes for ALS. Recent work is beginning to suggest a common basis upon which each of these different causes may produce degeneration of the motor nerve cells.

One theory of the cause of motoneuronal degeneration is that it is due to premature aging of these neurons. It seems that there is a programmed biological clock in every cell that defines its maximum life-span. This biological clock is responsible for the aging and eventual death of the organism. It is suspected that the mechanism of action of this clock resides in each cell's nucleus. Presumably, if such a clock could be turned off, the organism would live forever. Such a process appears to occur in cells that have become cancerous. When the cause of cancer is eventually identified, it may well provide an understanding of the cause of normal aging and cell death. In regard to ALS, the suggestion has been made that a faulty mechanism programs the motor nerve cells for an unnaturally early death. Exactly how this works is not clear. The reason may relate to damage to the nucleic acids, which is discussed below.

Another major theory of the cause of ALS is that it is due to the effect of one or more toxins upon the motoneurons. Lead intoxication has been known since the days of the Romans and often produces a clinical picture similar to that seen in ALS. In a few patients, treatment of ALS with chemicals that remove lead from the body has resulted in improvement of the disease. In the majority of patients, however, this approach has not been effective. Some work suggests that once there is an accumulation of lead in the central nervous systems of ALS patients, the damage is irreversible.

Another toxic element that is now considered of some relevance is aluminum. It has been found that in patients with Alzheimer's disease and in the Guamanian ALS-parkinsonism-dementia complex of diseases, aluminum accumulates in the nerve cells. Investigations of the soil and water in Guam have revealed unusual amounts of certain trace elements, including aluminum. Certain elements, or minerals, are known to perform a wide variety of vital functions in the body. These are needed in only very tiny amounts and are derived from food sources. The most common such trace elements are iron, zinc, selenium, manganese, molybdenum, copper, iodine, chromium, and fluorine but not aluminum. It is suspected that alterations in the trace-element nutrition in patients in Guam might be responsible for the disease. When aluminum is injected into the central nervous system of animals, it produces an accumulation of neurofillamentary material that is not dissimilar to the neurofibrillary tangles seen in the Guamanian type of ALS. Research is currently being directed to investigate the exact basis of the toxic effect of aluminum on neuronal nuclei.

A third major hypothesis of the cause of ALS is that it is due to a virus infection. The motor nerve cells of the spinal cord are particularly susceptible to certain viruses; the poliomyelitis virus causing infantile paralysis is a good example of such a pathogen. Research indicates that the motor nerve cells have specific receptors for the polio virus, which probably form the basis for the virus specifically attacking these cells. The infection produces acute damage and death of the cells, unlike the slow degeneration of the motoneurons seen in ALS. Though chronic virus infection is a possible cause of the motoneuronal degeneration in ALS, to date it has not been possible to transmit the disease to animals in the laboratory or to find direct evidence of a specific virus infection.

However, recent studies of other chronic degenerative diseases in humans and animals have demonstrated that there is a new class of viruslike structures, termed slow viruses, that previously was not recognized. Slow viruses have yet to be seen under the electron microscope and are clearly of a structure different from the classic, well-known viruses. Nevertheless, the diseases they cause can be transmitted experimentally from one animal to another or from a human to an animal. One disorder caused by a slow virus is Creutzfeldt-Jakob disease, a rare condition causing rapidly progressive dementia. Another is kuru, a condition that affects a tribe in New Guinea that practices cannibalism; transmission of the virus is believed to result from cannibalism of diseased patients.

A long-standing theory of the causes of a number of different neurological degenerative conditions holds that they are due to nutritional deficiencies. The paradigm for such a condition is the nervous system degeneration associated with vitamin $B_{12}$ deficiency, which also causes pernicious anemia. Many years of research have demonstrated that the degeneration of the spinal cord and other parts of the nervous system in patients with pernicious anemia is due to the lack of a factor secreted by the stomach that allows the absorption of vitamin $B_{12}$ by the body. Thus, even when foods such as liver that are rich in $B_{12}$ are ingested, the body does not process the essential vitamin. We now know that this disorder arises from immunologic damage to the lining of the stomach, preventing the secretion of what is known as intrinsic factor, which aids the absorption of vitamin $B_{12}$ in the terminal part of the small intestine. The link between the disease and the vitamin deficiency probably would never have been discovered if research had focused solely on investigating the central nervous system itself. There always remains the possibility, then, that other neurological diseases such as ALS may be due to a deficiency of some as yet undiscovered vitamin or nutrient. However, attempts so far to find such nutritional abnormalities in ALS have been unconvincing.

The application of new "microtechniques" in the laboratory has enabled scientists to study the metabolic functions of the motor nerve cells. Recent investigations—one utilizing the absorption of light by dye-stained ribonucleic acid (RNA) in the motoneurons and another involving the dissecting out of single nerve cells from the spinal cord, weighing them on microbalances made from single fibers of quartz, and determining the concentration of RNA in each cell by miniaturized chemical assays—suggest that there may be insufficient protein and insufficient RNA in the neurons of ALS patients. There may also be abnormalities of the deoxyribonucleic acid (DNA) of the motoneuronal nuclei. These studies suggest that the DNA of the nerve cells may be the primary site of damage in ALS.

Until recently the diseases connected with alterations in the DNA were genetic disorders and some cancers. In genetic conditions there is an abnormality of one particular part of the DNA, a mutation of a gene, which leads to the production of abnormal or deficient RNA and to damage to the cell's function, which is then passed on to offspring. It is thought that for certain cancers damage to the DNA of cells causes unregulated growth and proliferation of abnormal cells. It is now becoming clear that the DNA undergoes a spontaneous degradation and also is susceptible to damage by X-rays, ultraviolet light, and certain chemicals. The normal cell has enzymes capable of repairing the damaged DNA, thus preventing damage to the cell metabolism as a whole. A number of rare diseases have been linked to specific deficiencies of some of these DNA repair enzymes. Several of these disorders are associated with neurological degeneration. It has been suggested that ALS may be due to spontaneous degeneration or a deficiency of repair of damaged DNA in the motor nerve cells. This might explain why the disease occurs so much more frequently in the older population; more spontaneous degeneration of or damage to the DNA can occur over time.

At present none of these suggested etiologies has been confirmed, and thus we still do not know the cause of ALS. Research in many different centers is actively proceeding in hopes of clarifying these possibilities.

### Treatment of ALS

Since the exact cause of the disease has not yet been determined, it has not been possible to design a treatment to circumvent this cause. Nor is there at present any treatment that is known to slow the progression of the disease. There have been many trials of drugs, but to date none has been effective in halting the progressive degeneration. Recently it has been reported that thyrotropin releasing hormone (TRH) can improve some of the symptoms in ALS patients. An experimental study was undertaken with intravenous infusions of this hormone; the observed benefits lasted for only a brief time after completion of the intravenous infusion. Since TRH is localized in nerve endings on the motor neurons in the spinal cord, this therapeutic response may suggest an effect on the disease. However, it appears more likely that this agent is reducing spasticity rather than preventing nerve cell death, which is the primary problem of the disease. Moreover, the intravenous infusions produce significant side effects. Further work is needed before the significance of these observations can be judged.

There are, however, many ways of circumventing the effects of the rapidly fatal disease. A health care team of neurologists, gastroenterologists, pulmonary specialists, orthopedic surgeons, physical therapists, respiratory therapists, and social workers can aggressively intervene in order to circumvent the effects of the disease.

A wide range of mechanical aids, from simple appliances such as splints and wheelchairs to complex experimental computerized walking machines that are now being tried, can help the ALS patient remain active and productive. Because speech can be severely affected by this disease, there is a great need for special communication devices; it is hoped that microcomputers can aid in the production of speaking devices so that ALS patients can better cope with loss of normal speech function. Many advances in modern medical technology now allow ALS patients to be sustained whatever the degree of their weakness. It is possible to circumvent the difficulty in swallowing with feeding tubes leading directly to the stomach. It is also possible to prevent the loss of breathing capacity through the use of respirators. It is even possible to nurse patients and sustain life when total paralysis has set in.

Medical bioethical questions thus become extremely relevant to the ALS patient. Does he or she want to have life supported by machines? Is the quality of life on these machines worth the discomfort or the expense? Who has the right to make these decisions? Should the patient be forced to accept life support when such life becomes intolerable?

ALS, or Lou Gehrig's disease, is a terrible affliction because its onset is so rapid and the physical debilitation so extreme. Average life expectancy is two to three years, but as many as 30% of patients may survive for eight to ten years. While research continues on many fronts for an understanding of this mysterious killer, it is essential that ALS victims receive active treatment to minimize the pain and anguish of symptoms and to sustain the highest possible quality of life.

—*Walter G. Bradley, D.M.*

# Occupational Health

Stress can be broadly described as an unpleasant awareness of one's internal or external environment. Work stress is an unpleasant awareness experienced on the job, when anticipating going to work, or when reflecting on one's work. In any given work organization, the level of stress created by working conditions will vary from hour to hour and will be perceived differently by each person in the workplace.

There are physical work stresses, which can be measured; *i.e.,* in weights lifted, movements required during a given time period, number of rest periods, and so forth. The subject's experience of physical stress will correlate with his own strength, stamina, and concerns about being strained by the physical demands. There are also psychological work stresses, which are the worker's responses to and interpretation of the meaning of events at work; the more negative his reading, the greater the stress.

A worker does not necessarily react to stress in a negative way; certain individuals, for example, may enjoy the pressures of competition and achievement and not experience them as stressful, although they may suffer mental or physical harm as a result.

There are short-term and long-term work stresses. Ordinarily, short-term stress results from an unexpected occurrence, such as an explosion or fire at the workplace or, in the case of a taxi driver or subway conductor, a collision. Short-term stress can also be produced when an important document has been lost, after an argument with a co-worker, or by the sharp criticism of a superior. The event producing the discomfort might last for minutes or only seconds; ordinarily, there are no consequences. If the worker believes that the event might predict future danger or discomfort, however, it can then be the beginning of long-term work stress. In other words, the psychological consequences of an experience vary according to the evolving meaning of the event. Take the example of an explosion in which workers feel the physical force and smell malodorous fumes produced by the accident. A worker who suffers no physical harm might conclude that he is a "lucky guy" or that bad things happen to others but not to him. For another worker the meaning might be that the job environment is dangerous and that he could have been overcome by toxic fumes or even maimed or killed; no matter how hard he tries, he cannot stop feeling he came very close to very real danger.

Personality factors and characteristic modes of perceiving and coping with external events contribute to one's reaction to a particular event. Social roles can affect how one interprets the meaning of events at work; the father of a young child might be far more concerned about his own health and safety than he was before he had the emotionally charged responsibility of being husband, father, and provider. Before he had these responsibilities, he might have witnessed a major accident at his workplace with no apparent emotional consequences; now, however, he panics when he is present during a minor accident at the factory where he is employed, and he continues to feel anxious and threatened long afterward.

## Implications of long-term work stress

Considerbly less is known about long-term work stress and its consequences than about short-term stress.

*Fear of bodily injury is a prominent source of psychological stress for those who work with potentially dangerous equipment.*

However, there are many reasons to study long-term occupational stress. It makes people unhappy and diminishes the quality of their lives; it probably reduces productivity; in some cases it harms workers physically, producing physiological dysfunction, disease, and premature disability and death; in some cases it produces anxiety states or depression so severe that it might lead to suicide; in some cases, psychiatrists believe, stress might overload the mind of a person who is prone to schizophrenia and therefore result in active psychosis. Ultimately, the reason for studying long-term work stress is to reduce or eliminate its undesirable consequences.

This author's experience with more than 2,000 patients seen over an 18-year period has yielded information about the cumulative effects of jobs on workers. Most of those studied came from middle and lower socioeconomic classes, the groups that constitute most of the working force. Those studied were referred to investigators at the University of California at San

## Occupational health

Francisco via workers' compensation or retirement channels or because they had filed suits alleging wrongful discharge or discrimination; some came as self-referrals because they believed that their psychological discomfort was the result of work stress and needed help to cope with the symptoms and with the work. The study involved comprehensive psychiatric examinations, and most subjects underwent psychological testing. Medical records of health care, often going back into childhood, were reviewed. Many other sources provided relevant data about workers, including personnel records, interviews with relatives and coworkers, reports of medical specialists consulted, and rehabilitation reports.

Though implications of the survey findings are by no means conclusive, some general patterns and useful data were turned up. It was found that there are a number of factors unrelated to the work environment that partially account for long-term occupational stress. Among these are cultural factors. There is a growing sense in our culture that work should be satisfying and should fulfill psychological and spiritual as well as material needs. In recent decades workers have come to expect more from their jobs and to feel cheated when their expectations are unfulfilled. This expectation, however, is in marked contrast to the reality of most workplaces—past and present. In most instances an employer's objective is production and profit rather than the employee's work satisfaction; some employers may even see satisfied workers as unmotivated or underutilized.

The deplorable work environments of the past are well known. They were dirty and dangerous; employment was insecure; pay was very low; and no provisions were made for illness and disability. The steady gains to improve conditions and increase benefits for workers did result in reduced stresses. But an emerging cultural sense that workers should be comfortable on their jobs has oftentimes led to ongoing resentments (and stresses) in workers who are not.

Societal factors also have a key role in long-term work stress. Competition is one of the major organizing forces of our society. Working environments are a variation of the process of natural selection; *i.e.,* of survival of the fittest. On the job "losers" generally do not die, of course, but instead they hold the least satisfying jobs with the fewest rewards. Competition is not limited to the higher status and higher paying jobs such as law, medicine, accounting, and advertising. In fact, it is even more common among those who work in unskilled and semiskilled jobs, where workers often are seen as production units, who in some instances might be replaced by less costly machines. The person who cannot remain "cost effective" for whatever reason—insufficient strength or stamina, temporary illness, etc.—is discharged, often with little notice, and is left without pay or medical benefits.

Based on information from Columbia University Department of Industrial Engineering and Operations Research

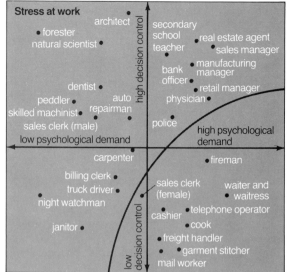

*At right of curve are those jobs considered most stressful in terms of demand and control—factors correlated with increased incidence of heart disease.*

Very few workers in our society are free of this competitive pressure. Some who believe themselves to be secure go into a state of psychological shock when they discover that they have been unexpectedly demoted or fired. To some degree, in a society where competition is encouraged from early in life, stress-reduction efforts run against social trends.

There are also personality factors that contribute to long-term work stress. Individuals who are chronically anxious tend to experience work, as well as home and community interactions, as anxiety provoking. The so-called type A personality lives at a driven, accelerated pace; he is likely to become impatient with colleagues and to experience ongoing occupational frustrations. Paranoid persons who believe that others are talking about them or maligning them or plotting against them are under constant stress at work. The obsessive-compulsive personality finds the workplace stressful because others, including supervisors, are not as careful or as conscientious or as orderly as he is.

There are, in addition, a number of factors specific to the work environment that contribute to long-term occupational stress. Unpredictability and change are often the causes of stress. Workers are uneasy when they do not know how long a job will last or when they fear termination, demotion, or transfer to a less desirable job. Change can make them feel helpless—as if they have no control over their work lives. One who saw himself as a member of a team but suddenly feels like a pawn to be moved about at his superior's will may resign, sabotage equipment, become less productive, incite others, and so forth—actions that may be destructive to himself or provoke reprisals from management and co-workers.

294

Employers sometimes ask workers to produce more than they can, expecting them to be motivated to do as much work as they can. Some workers react to this as a ploy and continue to work at their own pace, while others try to meet unrealistic demands, become frustrated and angry, and feel like failures when they cannot live up to "expectations."

The fear of bodily harm is a common stressor, and many workers are constantly aware of the dangers of their workplaces; e.g., those who work in high places or on poorly supported surfaces are aware of the risk of falling. For others the latent fears are activated when they narrowly avert injury or when they see a fellow worker injured and identify with him. For some, fears of exposure to toxic substances at work and of poisoning make it difficult to spend eight or more hours on the job. Similarly, concern about excessive radiation or noise makes the workplace a stressor.

In some occupations the fear of unprovoked attack is a long-term stressor. Police officers and correctional officers are always aware of the threat of attack, but persons in less obviously dangerous occupations may have the same concerns—bus drivers, persons working alone in stores, and cashiers. There have been many surveys and reports indicating that student assaults on schoolteachers are not uncommon; thus educators, too, may harbor this fear on the job.

There are stressors in the workplace that are unrelated to the job per se—for example, harassment related to race, ethnicity, age, appearance, or sex. The worst forms of teasing, practical joking, focusing on sexuality, etc., would seem to be carried over directly from grammar school locker rooms. Harassers may select a target and be unrelenting in their pursuit, which ends only when the victim leaves or breaks down or finally attacks the persecutor. Then the harasser asserts his innocence, making the victim appear the fool. Some superiors may use their rank to blame their own failures or the failure of the organization on a single worker, and some will bully a worker merely to show who is "boss."

Some workers have identified other stressors. Correctional officers and in some cases schoolteachers work in "buffer" occupations. Their jobs involve handling problem populations that society at large has difficulty coping with, and society then reacts angrily if problems remain unsolved.

There are indeed many other long-term stressors. One that cannot be ignored in the decade of the 1980s is the rapid technological changes that are causing many workers at all levels to live in fear not only that will they lose their jobs but that no one else will want or need them or their skills.

## Reactions to long-term stress

The first sign of long-term stress is a sense of discomfort, usually a sense of uneasiness that persists during most of the time spent at work. Inevitably, this sense invades nonwork time, although some sufferers can be certain that their discomfort is work related because it is absent when they are not working—on weekends or on vacation. For some this sense of unease does not progress to a point where the worker experiences physical symptoms, but almost all describe reduced pleasure from family and social interactions and a tendency to be irritable.

Some complain of insomnia, reduced sexual desires, and fatigue or exhaustion; others become depressed or paranoid or both. Among the physical symptoms commonly reported are numbness, tingling, and breathlessness associated with hyperventilation. Itching is another common symptom; dermatitis produced by scratching may result. Some experience chest tightness and believe they might have heart disease. Other symptoms are headaches, light-headedness, dizziness, visual disturbances, and ringing in the ears and other such noises. Others have gastrointestinal symptoms: pain, burning, difficulty in swallowing, diarrhea, or constipation. Still others complain of body aches and back, shoulder, and neck pain. Family members and others in close contact with the worker report that he or she is irritable, is withdrawn, has lost interest in usual pursuits, shows decline in sexual interest, or is tending to drink more.

## Medical findings

Physicians who examine these workers have found a seemingly high incidence of hypertension, dermatitis, lung disease, heart disease, and ulcers and other gastrointestinal disease. Some physicians conclude that the presence of disease following complaints of stress means that the stress has caused the disease, while others are more cautious about linking the two. Some investigators have noted that hypertension and coronary heart disease in particular seem to be related to risk factors that do not include occupational stress. In some cases an abnormally high blood pressure returns to normal levels when the worker is on vacation or is no longer employed at that workplace, but this result must be interpreted carefully because other variables, such as diet, exercise, and medication, might explain some or all of the difference.

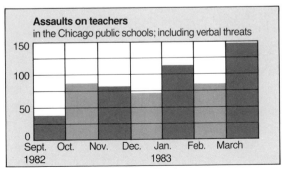

Based on information from Chicago Board of Education

## Changes after leaving a stressful job

Most frequently workers feel relief when they leave a stressful job and experience discomfort when they return to the job. In some instances workers have reported a return of unpleasant feelings and symptoms when passing by the workplace or upon hearing about events there.

For some a determination that they would never return to their former work environment or to one similar accompanies their relief at being removed from the situation. Some workers renounce goals such as status, high pay, and rapid advancement associated with working in their former jobs. Some leave spouses and children because they associate their own former striving with the needs or demands of their families. Some leave the urban areas, hoping to reduce their living costs and find less competitive environments. While some see their salvation as moving down the occupational ladder of status and pay, others are determined to acquire more education and additional skills, believing that a move upward would give them more control over their lives.

Some choose the disability channel and justifiably or unjustifiably complain that they would be unable to do any kind of work available to them or for which they might be trained. Some who have no objective findings of disability sufficient to preclude their participation in the open labor market hold that they have suffered enough and should not be exposed to further suffering and that they should receive money as compensation both for past suffering and also to make future work unnecessary. There are those who experience guilt, anger, helplessness, and depression for years because they continue to dwell on the events that forced them to stop working.

## Consequences of staying on the job

No matter what the stresses, some workers choose to stay on the job because they need the money or are not prepared to search for new employment or remain unemployed or in a disability status. Some are pessimistic about finding employment they consider less stressful. Because they find the job so onerous and at the same time feel that they cannot leave, they have a sense of being trapped or "locked in." The feeling of having no viable alternatives becomes yet another source of discomfort and conflict.

Frequently, however, those who stay on the job are able to resolve their conflicts through negotiation or by superiors' becoming aware of and changing the conditions that are causing worker discomfort. Just as spontaneous changes at work can produce stressful conditions, so too can they relieve them; changes in assignments or managers, moves to new buildings, resignations of peers or subordinates can be either stressors or stress relievers. In some cases even if there are no apparent changes on the job, the workers'

perceptions change with time, sometimes in a way that makes a formerly stressful job seem less so.

## Psychosomatic conditions

No one doubts that body and mind work in harmony. Despite the considerable increases in our knowledge about the electrochemical feedback channels involved in mind-body reactions, we are still unable to relate specific kinds of occupational stresses with persistent bodily changes. While conventional wisdom holds that unpleasant psychological experiences must be physically harmful, the data from research do not yet fully support that tenet.

Most physicians do not doubt that physical or mental stressors can increase heart rate and elevate blood pressure and that the long-term stresses of physically and emotionally demanding work probably bring on heart attacks, strokes, and other diseases. However, evidence that an individual would have remained healthy if he had been transferred or if he had pursued some sort of presumed stress-relieving activity such as exercise is lacking.

## Coping

In light of the lack of hard facts on what produces stress on the job and the great variability of findings among individuals, what conclusions can be drawn about long-term consequences of occupational stress? It should be emphasized that work stress is inevitable; workers should expect it.

In order to minimize stress, people should be prepared for the world of work. Work requires arriving on time and generally conforming to imposed schedules. Workers must be able to tolerate routine and, to some degree, even boredom. Workers should know that there will always be some injustice inside the workplace, just as there are injustices outside.

Work requires skills; in order to progress, one must increase one's work skills. Work becomes stressful when one does not know how to do the job.

Employers must realize that demands for performance beyond workers' physical and psychological abilities or tolerances are counterproductive. Trained persons to whom the workers can turn when they are distressed about their jobs can aid the overwhelmed employee and help him to restructure his thinking and behavior in order to reduce stresses and sometimes to use them to his advantage.

Physicians can help by encouraging their patients to talk about the stresses of their jobs. They can help by recommending stress-reduction techniques, such as meditation, psychotherapy, exercise, and education for other work, all of which serve to relieve the worker's feelings of helplessness. Meantime, medical researchers must carry out carefully controlled studies on the links between occupational stress and disease.

—*Carroll M. Brodsky, M.D., Ph.D.*

# The Ailments of Musicians
## by Fred H. Hochberg, M.D., Robert D. Leffert, M.D., and Lisle A. Merriman

In the past decade considerable attention has been paid to keeping workers physically and mentally healthy and fit to perform their jobs. Distinct diseases and injuries have been linked to distinct working environments and to specific demands on workers. Factory workers, construction workers, truck drivers, athletes, and executives under stress—all suffer well-recognized ills that are related to their jobs. Only recently have the occupational hazards facing a special group—performing musicians—received attention.

Little information is contained in the medical literature on the illnesses and injuries afflicting musicians despite the fact that their work is particularly strenuous, demanding prolonged, often repetitive and intricate movements of the hands and arms as well as highly refined motor control. Take the concert pianist performing Tchaikovsky's Piano Concerto No. 1 in B Flat Minor: He must play loud and fast octaves, simultaneously striking keys with the thumb and fourth or fifth fingers held rigidly apart. These taxing angular movements can produce pain, fatigue, and loss of facility. Overusage symptoms also arise from the forceful rotations required to perform broken octaves (thumb and fifth finger alternating) as in Beethoven's Piano Concerto No. 3 in C Minor; from executing trills (rapid alternation of two adjacent keys) as in Beethoven's Sonata in E Major, Opus 109; and from playing arpeggios (notes struck in succession requiring the passage of the thumb under the hand) such as in the trio of the scherzo movement of Beethoven's Sonata in C Major, Opus 2, No. 3.

The majority of musicians experience careers spanning almost their entire lives. Only a minority develop significant hand or arm disabilities. These musicians—most often pianists or string instrument players—develop difficulties often decades into a previously successful career. The musician who has a well-established, often virtuoso, technique, when faced with the appearance of subtle symptoms affecting the arm or hand, usually does not complain of these difficulties in medical terms. He or she sees them as an impediment to playing and is eager for relief.

The physician is obliged to translate symptoms into syndromes with specific anatomic, physiologic, and neurologic bases. There are four generally recognized categories: (1) inflammatory disorders of tendons, joints, and muscles; (2) degenerative disorders of tendons, joints, and muscles; (3) compression or entrapment of nerves or arteries in the upper extremities; and (4) disorders of motor control affecting discrete hand functions. Each group of disorders represents a unique class of occupational illnesses producing a stereotypical pattern of symptoms in the trained musician.

Recently a multidisciplinary team composed of a neurologist, an orthopedic surgeon, a neurophysiologist, and occupational and physical therapists at the Massachusetts General Hospital in Boston evaluated more than 250 musician-patients. They have also successfully treated many of these sufferers. Physicians are currently trying to determine what factors predispose players to hand and arm problems; among other things they are looking at the musician's musical education, the nature of the repertory, the frequency of practice sessions and concertizing, and the nature of hand, arm, and finger techniques.

## Inflammatory disorders

Inflammatory disorders affecting tendons (the tough bands of connective tissue that join muscles to bones) account for the difficulties in a majority of the musicians who have been examined at Massachusetts General. A number of different sites may be affected. Commonly the area on the outer aspect of the elbow (the lateral epicondyle) becomes painful, particularly with movements involving forceful contraction of the fingers and wrist muscles, such as might occur in playing a very loud chord at the piano. In fact, this condition is quite similar to "tennis elbow" and is of identical origin in pianists and tennis players. It results from misuse or overuse of the wrist extensor muscles and causes inflammation or tendinitis where they attach at the elbow.

Pianists with small hands who habitually perform "large" pieces requiring excessive muscular effort in percussion and octaves may experience inflammation of the tendons that flex the wrist or fingers. Overuse of the thumb as a fulcrum may predispose guitarists, harpists, and occasionally cellists to tendinitis of any of the muscles that move its bones and joints. The finger extensor tendons may become painful and swollen at the back of the wrist where they are contained beneath a ligament and become irritated by repetitive or forceful movements, particularly with the wrist in exaggerated positions. One such position is known as ulnar deviation, in which the wrist turns outward toward the fifth finger. The tendons of the little and ring fingers are particularly vulnerable to this problem and may become swollen and painful.

The musician may experience pain and swelling of the tendons that bend or flex the wrist or fingers on the palmar side of the hand. In many cases there may be little overt evidence of abnormality—*i.e.,* visible on examination—even though the musician may "feel that something is very wrong." Often it is noted that the finger is "slow to respond" or "feels thick" or is "difficult to bend." But this condition can progress to the point where there is sufficient swelling and notable restriction of the range of functional ability.

Often when musicians extend their practice sessions to master a new piece, when they are preparing for a competition or recital, when they are attempting a change in technique, or when they are learning a new instrument, they begin to notice dull but persistent hand pain. Initially, this pain is assumed to be the result of "technical difficulties." The musician soon notices that hand and finger movements are less likely to have the customary "tension" or "force." Movements are "boggy" and hesitant. Upon examination, swelling about the tendons or within their sheaths is apparent. The swelling of the tendons in fingers and the thumb may localize in a nodule on the hand's palmar side that "catches" each time the tendon glides along the edge of its sheath that runs the length of the finger. This "catch" or "trigger" effect can be quite disconcerting to the player; in some cases it is disabling. Harpists frequently experience a painful "snap" when attempting to straighten a finger that has plucked a string—so-called trigger finger.

If tendinitis is allowed to persist untreated, it may result in stiffness that severely restricts motion. In extreme cases actual rupture of the tendon is possible. At the wrist the median nerve, which provides sensation to the thumb and first three fingers, may become compressed owing to the inflammation of synovium (which lines the joints and tendons) and cause carpal tunnel syndrome. This condition results in numbness of the fingers, weakness of the thumb, and nocturnal pain.

Just as tendons may become inflamed by overuse or misuse, joints may be similarly injured with the result that with movement they may ache and be limited in motion. Examination of these inflamed joints will reveal swelling, increased temperature, or painful restriction of the range of motion. In some cases such symptoms may be the result of various other medical conditions such as rheumatoid arthritis or psoriatic arthritis; in musician-patients these rheumatic conditions must be excluded by appropriate specific laboratory tests, X-rays, and clinical evaluation.

298

*At a mirrored keyboard Gary Graffman's severely debilitated right hand, pictured at left, looks normal, while Leon Fleisher's hand displays obvious impairment (right).*

Treatment of the inflammatory conditions of tendons and joints always depends on correct identification of the cause of the problem. Obviously, after underlying rheumatic conditions have been dismissed, a careful investigation of the manner in which the area has been or is being irritated is in order. The physician may be able to evaluate the problem through a careful history taking and physical examination. After this, observation of the musician's playing style is essential. A particularly abnormal, strained, or tense hand or arm position may be quickly identified as a major cause of disability and its existence called to the attention of the musician. Often, videotape is a helpful tool in this regard.

Treatment of a swollen joint or tendon may involve giving the afflicted tissues a rest, requiring cessation of practice for days or weeks. Splinting of the hand and wrist may be indicated, although splints must be used carefully to avoid deconditioning of the muscles or encouraging stiffness.

Medications in the form of anti-inflammatory agents—ranging from aspirin to steroids—can effectively relieve the suffering for many musicians. The so-called nonsteroidal anti-inflammatory agents are the drugs used most often because they generally have fewer unwanted side effects such as stomach irritation or hormonal disturbances. In the most resistant chronic cases or when inflammation is acute before a scheduled performance, injections of anti-inflammatory agents directly into the tendon sheaths or joint may be given. If conservative measures such as local injections or splints do not relieve an inflammatory condition, a surgical procedure may be necessary.

Rehabilitative exercises to regain motion and muscle strength, especially after cessation of playing for a time, are an important part of the therapeutic regimen. Physical and occupational therapists teach and supervise specific exercise programs according to the musician's distinct needs. Particularly when inflammation of tendons and joints has been caused by excessive or misplaced muscular tension, the musician will benefit not only from strengthening exercises but also from learning relaxation techniques. Biofeedback—a self-help regimen that enables the patient to relieve bodily disorders by concentration—may be a useful adjunct to such therapy. The pianist, for example, connected to sensors that measure electrical responses, can simulate basic scales on a biofeedback machine. As messages from his muscles are "fed back" to him on an oscilloscope, he can learn to manipulate his hand movements and gain conscious control of them. A "graded" return to practice, often less than 15 minutes per day, can begin only after inflammation has ceased and strength and range of movement have normalized.

## Degenerative disorders

Like the general population, performing musicians may be heir to a host of degenerative disorders of the upper extremities. In addition, the musician is susceptible to a number of disorders that are specific to his art.

Just as habitual and repetitive use of the shoulders, arms, elbows, wrists, and hands of workers in industry or athletes in professional sports may result in injury or simple "wear and tear" of various anatomic parts such as joints (osteoarthritis), the musician may suffer a similar fate. (Union protection and workmen's compensation, however, are not usually available to protect the artist.) Violinists, for example, may be bothered by neck and shoulder pain resulting from years of supporting their instruments. Conductors and cellists may develop degenerative conditions of the rotator cuff muscles within their shoulders from constant motions with their arms raised. (Welders and housepainters experience quite similar conditions.) Finger joints may respond to chronic pressure on strings by developing osteoarthritis. Appropriate modification of performance techniques or instruments may go a long way toward alleviating the symptoms and preserving the anatomy for extended use; conventional orthopedic management will then have a significantly higher rate of success.

Chronic stress on ligaments in the hand may result in joint instability and the onset of painful arthritis. For example, clarinetists may experience pain in the middle (metacarpophalengeal) joint of the thumb due to a deficiency in firmness, or a laxity of an important ligament of the joint. This condition, "gamekeeper's thumb," was originally described in Scottish gamekeepers, who habitually "clipped" the necks of rabbits with their bare hands—their thumbs greatly outstretched. The condition may be well tolerated if the clarinetist can play

seated (thus supporting the weight of the instrument on the thigh rather than with the hand) or use a neck strap to hold the instrument when playing in a standing position. In some cases surgery will be needed to restore stability to the traumatized joint.

As a consequence of injury to the hand while playing the instrument or, all too commonly, while involved in some everyday activity, the musician may have to accommodate to a chronic abnormality of tendon, bone, or joint that may range from mildly annoying to totally disabling. Sometimes adaptations of style or technique such as refingering will allow continuation of playing for many years. All too often, however, the compensatory mechanisms to cope with a degenerative condition prove to be additionally injurious, and the artist can no longer perform.

In general, therapy for degenerative disorders of the upper extremities rests in understanding the site and extent of damage. Specific treatment must be in response to the musician's particular needs. Secondary inflammations may respond to medication, and muscle atrophy and limitation of movement to rehabilitative techniques, often over a period of weeks to months. Surgical reconstructive efforts are limited to disorders of ligament or joint that are refractory to conservative approaches.

## Nerve compression injuries

Among the musician-patients examined at Massachusetts General, approximately 15% have had strength or sensation difficulties reflecting loss of function of one of the three major nerves controlling the hand. Reference has already been made to the so-called carpal tunnel syndrome, which results from compression of the median nerve at the wrist. Musicians, most often pianists, may complain of tingling or discomfort in the palm or the middle finger of the hand, then a progressive loss of strength and use of the thumb as the sensation spreads and involves all fingers except the fifth. The playing of octaves, arpeggios, and trills involving the first and third fingers may be difficult. Clinical tests may indicate the presence of an afflicted nerve, which becomes symptomatic when the hand is held in a flexed or bent posture (Phalen's maneuver) or produces unique electrical discomfort when the hand is tapped by the examiner over the nerve (Tinel's sign). Electrical studies in which the speed of nerve-impulse transmission is measured may delineate the location and severity of nerve involvement. Although many patients will respond initially to anti-inflammatory medications and conservative regimens, a surgical procedure to release the median nerve, usually resulting in complete restitution of function, represents the most definitive approach to this problem.

The ulnar nerve, which supplies sensation to the little finger and half of the ring finger, also supplies motor power to the flexor tendons that bend the end (distal interphalangeal) joints of these fingers as well as the interosseous muscles (which move the fingers toward or away from each other) within the hand and the adductor muscle of the thumb. If the nerve is impaired at the level of the elbow, not only will numbness of these fingers and inability to press down with them be experienced, but span and dexterity of all fingers will be adversely affected. Less commonly the nerve may be abnormal at the wrist; sensory loss is less likely in such cases, but a clawlike deformity (flexion) may occur in the little and ring fingers. Correct identification of the site of the ulnar nerve abnormality may require not only astute clinical evaluation but confirmation by means of electrodiagnostic tests. Treatment in mildly affected individuals may consist of rest, splinting, and other conservative measures, but more advanced cases may require surgery.

The radial nerve, which is responsible for the ability to raise (extend) the wrist and open fingers, may be compressed by an abnormal band of tissue at the elbow. Sometimes the effects of the nerve compression may become manifest only after repetitive or unaccustomed exercise or injury causes local swelling of the nerve. The nerve then becomes compressed by ligaments. The resultant inability to actively extend the fingers may be subtle, in which case it may be perceived as simply a lack of coordination, or the inability may be quite striking, in which case its true nature is more likely to be correctly identified. Again, whenever possible, conservative therapy is employed, although some patients have required surgery to decompress the radial nerve.

A smaller group of musicians have suffered from a complex of symptoms involving disability of the upper extremities, known as thoracic outlet syndrome. This entity results from positional compression of the major artery extending from the chest into the upper arm (the subclavian artery) and the major nerves, the brachial plexus, between the collarbone (clavicle) and the first rib. In the general population this condition may result from the presence of abnormal or additional ribs, but in musicians the cause is usually weakness or postural abnormality of the muscles supporting the shoulder girdle. The symptoms may be vague feelings of aching or heaviness when the arms are raised to or above the horizontal or numbness along the inner aspect of the elbow extending to the little and ring fingers. A variable amount of muscle weakness may be perceived, and in some cases the instrumentalist may be totally disabled by symptoms.

In addition to clinical examination and X-rays, diagnosis of the thoracic outlet syndrome may be facilitated by electrodiagnostic and noninvasive blood-flow studies with the arm in positions that provoke the symptoms. Treatment is usually in the form of therapeutic exercises, but those patients with severe compression may require surgical treatment to remove the first rib.

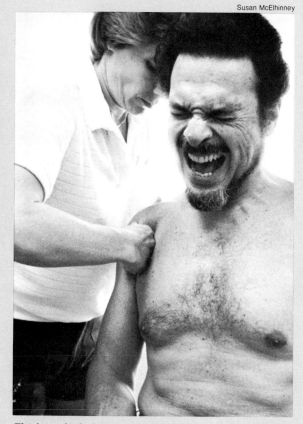

*Fleisher, who had many treatments during his 17-year exile from concertizing, here undergoes a form of physical therapy for the shoulder muscles.*

## Motor control disorders

Disorders of movement that affect hand function—especially particular fingers—account for difficulties in about one-quarter of the musicians who have been examined at Massachusetts General. The renowned 19th-century German composer and pianist Robert Schumann suffered from a loss of function of his right third finger and had to give up his playing career; contemporary pianists Gary Graffman and Leon Fleisher have been afflicted with similar disabilities in the fourth and fifth fingers. When motor control disorders are present in pianists, the right fourth and fifth fingers are the most commonly affected. In part, this may be because melodies in many compositions are written for these weaker fingers of the right hand. Also, the piano's sound is weakest in the upper middle register. Players compensate by exerting more right-hand pressure.

Motor control disorders in guitarists may affect the right third finger; in wind-instrument players the right fourth finger and in harpists the right second and third fingers have been seen as problems. Nonmusicians may also be afflicted; *e.g.*, writers (thumb and wrist), telegraphers (first or index fingers), and typists and legal stenographers (right third and fourth fingers).

Initial symptoms are often ascribed to "tension," "cramping," "stress," or the "battle fatigue" of the concert performer or thought to be of psychosomatic origin. What are at first trivial symptoms soon become sources of great frustration whenever the instrument is approached. The symptoms seldom occur at times other than playing the instrument. Moreover, the right-hand difficulties are never mirrored in the left.

Most often, a performer of professional caliber and regarded for a style emphasizing highly individual forte finger movements experiences a slight involuntary bending, or flexion, of the affected finger. The involuntary curling of the finger continues. The musician then begins to substitute the third finger for the impaired fourth or fifth. The loss of normal rhythmic finger movement during rapid fingering becomes apparent usually over a period of years but in some players has progressed more rapidly—over several weeks.

Since pain, weakness, and altered sensation are not apparent, the performer may initially suspect a problem with "technique." Misdiagnoses are not uncommon; these include Parkinson's disease, multiple sclerosis, and other neuromuscular disorders. The localized and stereotyped nature of the problem, however, makes these processes unlikely. Evaluations of clinical neurological function by a neurologist and by computerized axial tomographic visualization of the brain (CAT scans) and electrical studies of nerves and muscles will serve to exclude these alternative diagnoses. An examination at the piano, using videotaped analyses, often coupled with electrical recordings from the involved muscle groups, usually reveals spontaneous and uncontrolled contraction of flexor muscles with corresponding weakness of extensor muscle groups and sometimes of the supporting muscles of the shoulder girdle. The player is instructed to perform a series of exercises designed to restrengthen weakened muscles. Biofeedback techniques may be used as well to reduce involuntary contractions. These approaches, often combined with medications that help control abnormal movements, have been partially successful in curbing this group of disorders.

## The impaired musician

The introduction of "modern" instruments (the modern piano, harp, guitar, drums) has placed extraordinary demands on performers. Between 1825 and 1900 the piano developed into a versatile instrument that allowed playing at previously impossible levels of speed, force, and virtuosity. Today's Steinways, Bösendorfers, and Baldwins enable smoother sounding, louder, brighter, and faster playing than, for example, the pianoforte of Haydn's time. Not surprisingly, composers began to create more and more intricate and difficult works. Performers often found their execution of compositions was limited by anatomy and physiology. They indulged in hours of repetitive exercises to overcome short span, weakness of the right fourth and fifth fingers, and loss of sound in notes played by the fourth and fifth fingers and to master the intricacies of broken octaves and double stops. By the 1850s a series of popular devices had been created to increase the individual facility of finger movements. Schumann used a homemade gadget to immobilize his third finger while he exercised his fourth and fifth. New "schools" of piano technique emerged, each attempting to ease the demands on the virtuoso player. At the close of the 19th century a surgical procedure, the tenotomy, was offered as a means of freeing the fourth finger from its tendon juncture ties with the third and fifth fingers. (Notable among its failures was Schumann.) Two classic studies of the pianist's problems, by Otto Ortmann (*The Physiological Mechanics of Piano Technique,* 1929) and Arnold Schultz (*The Riddle of the Pianist's Finger and Its Relationship to a Touch-Scheme,* 1936), did little to improve the lot of the performer.

In the coming years, many of our concepts will change as a result of newer physiological information emerging from the study of musicians. For now the vast majority of musicians afflicted with hand and arm difficulties that limit playing ability can be helped. In September 1982 the celebrated pianist Leon Fleisher returned to the concert stage after a 17-year exile, finally having overcome the crippling disability of his right hand. In the intervening years his performing had been limited to small-scale playing with orchestras of compositions written for the left hand (*e.g.,* by Ravel, Prokofiev, Scriabin, and Britten).

Possibly the most common technical error made by musicians is increasing their practice time. At the instrument, most perceive a diminished ability to be the result of a practice schedule that is not rigorous enough. They therefore compensate for this presumed inadequacy by adding hours onto an already taxing schedule (nearly 100% of the musician-patients seen by the physicians at Massachusetts General Hospital practice from five to six hours daily). In most cases they succeed only in doing themselves further injury. By the time they seek medical attention, most are unable to play without some degree of pain.

The disorders presented here do not encompass a full catalog of the ailments of musicians. As knowledge is accumulated, improved treatments will evolve, but ultimately it is hoped that preventive measures, based on solid principles, will protect musicians from occupational hazards.

# Pediatrics

In the past, children first encountered most communicable or transmissible diseases upon entering school. From kindergarten and the first grade on, groups of susceptible children were gathered together in close quarters. Whooping cough (pertussis), measles, chickenpox (varicella), mumps, and a host of infectious agents that cause colds and diarrhea occurred with regularity coincident with the school year. By the age of 15 most children in the United States had experienced each of these diseases.

Two modern phenomena—one positive, one negative—have altered this pattern and changed the face of early childhood. Effective immunizations have vastly reduced or eliminated the risk for many of these previously common infectious diseases at any age. However, the contemporary trend toward clustering children at very early ages in day-care centers and nursery schools has advanced the risk of acquisition of non-vaccine-preventable infectious diseases into infancy and toddlerhood.

## Infectious diseases in day-care centers and nursery schools

Changes in the basic life-style of the average family in the United States have included the emergence of single-parent families and a higher proportion of families in which both parents must or want to work away from the home. This has created the need for a system to care for young children in such families. In 1980, 11 million children in the U.S. received some form of nonparental child care, and at least 1.8 million of these were known to be enrolled in licensed day-care centers. This phenomenon, coupled with other types of groupings of very young children, such as various schools for toddlers, library groups, infant stimulation centers, local social organization groups such as the YMCA infant swimming programs, church groups, etc., has led to new opportunities for transmission of infectious diseases. Whatever the social, educational, economic, and psychological benefits these groupings have, they pose some quite distinct health hazards.

## The day-care-center milieu

Day-care centers serve to exemplify all of the above groupings of very young children. Day-care centers, of course, are not all alike. They vary in size, age range of attendees, activities, socioeconomic makeup of attendees, hours of service, location, and other ways. These characteristics of a given center are critical to the occurrence of infectious diseases. Certain infections will be facilitated if the size and composition of the day-care center are "right" for transmission of their etiologic agent. To better understand the infections encountered in such settings, it is important to explore first some of the specific institutional characteristics.

The size and staffing of day-care centers can influence the degree to which sanitary practices can be maintained in handling food and in tending to the custodial needs of children. Very large centers may serve more meals in one day than many restaurants. They certainly will change more diapers than many nurseries and children's units in hospitals. The staff must also tend to minor illnesses and recognize more serious ones in order to exclude such children. For the staff in large centers to do all of these tasks properly, health and disease-transmission awareness, education regarding sanitary practices, knowledge and application of means to avoid transmission, and almost compulsive personal hygiene practices are required. There are no data that can tell us the extent to which staff is knowledgeable, trained, and diligent in these areas. The size alone of the population attending the center can contribute to chaotic management—especially if the size is disproportionate to the number of staff.

*Today, in an increasing number of families, both parents are working outside the home. As a consequence, more very young children are spending their days in day-care centers and other programs where new opportunities for transmission of infectious diseases are arising.*

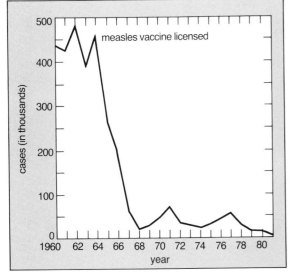

Centers for Disease Control

Centers in which large numbers of children are cared for frequently emphasize the potential for transmission of enteric (gastrointestinal) pathogens. Age is an important factor. Inclusion of infants and toddlers in diapers among the attendees is associated with more frequent outbreaks of infectious agents present in stools. Diapered infants also require more custodial care, which can divert staff from other hygienic efforts and indirectly contribute to the spread of nonstool-transmitted pathogens.

Activity schedules can influence transmissibility. Group play that involves touching, grappling, or other direct physical contact can facilitate spread of some organisms. Outdoor activity may generate exposure to soil that may contain infectious agents.

Socioeconomic factors only indirectly influence the character of the infections one may encounter. If certain infections, such as some forms of diarrhea and tuberculosis, are more prevalent among poor children or attendants, then the possibility of spread is introduced. Since it is recognized that children from lower socioeconomic groups have lower rates of immunization, there is also an enhanced possibility that preventable diseases, such as whooping cough and measles, will occur. Location of the day-care center may also influence infectious risk in the same fashion.

The hours of care that a specific center offers have been correlated with some infections. Apparently the longer a center remains open, the longer the duration of opportunity for transmission of infectious agents. Other factors may also play a role in as yet undefined ways. The transience of the population of attendees or staff may influence rates of infection. The degree of public health regulation and inspection can be a factor in some situations. Whether a physician is available as a consultant can influence the awareness, knowledge, and perceptions of the staff. The ability to contact parents if a child is ill and the ability of the parent to respond promptly can determine the length of exposure for other attendees. Lack of space can result in crowding and enhance communicability.

## Specific infectious hazards

*Hepatitis.* Infants and children tend to remain well or have minimal symptoms, such as diarrhea, when infected by hepatitis A virus. This form of hepatitis is transmitted mostly by person-to-person contact and by the fecal-to-oral route. Food or water and, on rare occasions, objects can become contaminated and become agents of exposure. Adults, on the other hand, become quite sick with hepatitis and will show jaundice, fever, vomiting, and various other symptoms.

In one Arizona county 40% of all cases of hepatitis A infection occurred in persons closely associated with day-care centers. Of interest were the following: (1) adults, including staff and family members, became ill more frequently than children; (2) it was the child attendees at the day-care center who spread the disease; (3) centers whose attendees were diapered children had a high risk; (4) other risk factors included centers with more than 51 attendees, centers remaining open longer than 15 hours per day, and those operated on a private, fee-for-service basis; and (5) transmission could be controlled by widespread administration of gamma globulin to contacts.

*Diarrheal diseases.* Many transmissible infectious agents can cause diarrhea in day-care center attendees. Viruses, bacteria, and parasites have been implicated. In one investigation children had a 25% risk of contracting diarrhea in the first five weeks of attendance and 10% thereafter. If a child was transferred to a new setting, the same 25% risk was encountered. It has been shown that during a specific virus outbreak of diarrhea, the hands of 79% of the attendants yielded the virus. In addition, 20% of the hands of attendants who had no contact with the infected children also yielded the virus.

*Respiratory diseases.* Outbreaks of common viral upper respiratory infections among day-care center attendees are legion. Most involve relatively few serious symptoms and tend to be accepted as "normal." On occasion, however, more serious illness will result in individual children or attendants. Less commonly, a virulent form may occur, such as influenza, measles, or tuberculosis, and spread among the staff and children.

*Serious bacterial disease.* In a few outbreaks much more serious disease, such as meningitis or bloodstream infection, has been traced to contact with infected infants or children in a day-care center. For example, the bacterium *Hemophilus influenzae,* a common inhabitant of the noses and throats of children, will cause meningitis or other systemic infections in children who attend day-care centers. Children less than four years old who also attend such a center have a 500 times greater risk of getting meningitis than do children of the same age not in the day-care setting. Diphtheria, pertussis, and meningococcal infections have also been identified as more common in day-care centers. So-called strep throat infections, more properly termed group A streptococcal tonsillopharyngitis, probably can also be transmitted more commonly in day-care settings.

## Strategies for control

Day-care centers and other large and small groupings of very young children will not disappear. Current socioeconomic conditions and life-styles mandate their existence. Therefore, it is wise that pediatricians and society develop tactics to counteract the high risks of infectious disease acquisition for the growing numbers of susceptible children attending such centers. What can be done?

First, each day-care center should be licensed with local health departments. Sanitation and hygienic standards for personnel should be set, inspections conducted, and infractions identified and corrected if the center is to continue to operate. Second, day-care centers should have an official medical consultant, preferably a pediatrician. The director of the center can then utilize the consultant to set hygienic practices, to train staff, and to assist in solving infectious disease problems if they arise. Further, a system of surveillance for the diseases noted above should be established, and once a disease is detected, parents and personal physicians should be notified with specific recommendations following those of the American Academy of Pediatrics and the U.S. Centers for Disease Control. Specific measures include the following:

1. Any day-care center should have adequate hand-washing facilities readily available to staff. Of all preventive measures, hand washing is the most important and effective.

2. Food preparation should be conducted in a specified area separated from the infant and children's area. Attendees at the center should not have access to the food preparation area, and sanitary and hygienic practices should be rigidly enforced there.

3. If diapered children are among the attendees, a separate area to which other attendees do not have access should be reserved for diaper changing. Provision should be made for secure storage and disposal of soiled diapers. Hand-washing facilities should be in the immediate area.

4. Any sick attendee should be identified on arrival at the center and excluded for the period of illness. Access to parents or guardians should be assured for each attendee in the event of illness occurring during attendance. The staff should be educated to recognize the common signs and symptoms of the illnesses prevalent in day-care center attendees.

5. Immunization records should be reviewed as a condition of acceptance, and attendees whose immunizations are not up-to-date should be excluded until they receive the appropriate vaccines.

6. Upon recognition of a specific infection, the medical consultant or a health department official should be notified and all parents informed. If specific recommendations are applicable (e.g., gamma globulin for hepatitis exposure), the parent should be notified and compliance required for a child's continued attendance.

7. Upon enrollment, parents should be informed of the diseases that should be reported to the director of the center. This recommendation is made in order to ensure that exposure of the remaining attendees is called to the attention of their parents.

## Measles in the 1980s

In recent times measles has killed 900,000 persons per year in less developed countries. As many as 25 of every 100 people infected have died in specific areas of the world. By contrast, in 1982 in the United States, only 1,697 cases were reported, the fewest since 1912, the first year records were kept, and mortality reached an all-time low. Why the discrepancy between the worldwide statistics and those in the U.S. population? What does the change in the frequency of measles mean for the current health milieu in the U.S.?

Measles is a serious infection caused by inhalation of a specific virus that probably exists in nature as a single type (often referred to as "wild" measles virus). Wild virus infects the upper and lower respiratory tract, multiplies there, and spreads to our first line of defense, the lymph nodes that surround the lungs. Within these lymph nodes are collections of certain white blood cells, the lymphocytes, which are organized both to receive infectious agents and to initiate the body's defenses against them. In the initial states of infection the virus multiplies in the lymph nodes until it reaches a level above which it can no longer be contained. Virus erupts into the general blood circulation and is carried to distant parts of the body. New infections are established in multiple organs, and after a period of 11 days or so, sufficient viral growth has occurred to disturb organ function and to produce the typical early symptoms of measles: fever, eye inflammation, a runny nose, and increasing cough. For several days each of these symptoms worsens; the cough becomes a harsh, barking one that frequently persists throughout the day and night. Only then does the characteristic red, pimply rash appear at the hairline, rapidly spreading to the face, trunk, and extremities in the next two to four days. The illness usually lasts 7 to 14 days, with complete resolution if no complications occur.

As the wild virus undergoes its growth cycles, the body girds to protect itself. Lymphocytes become "sensitized," or capable of recognizing the virus components, and begin to produce specific antibody. Eventually the individual's immunologic forces overcome the virus, recovery ensues, and permanent, lifelong immunity results.

Complications are frequent. In the prevaccine era, bacteria infected the respiratory sites of virus proliferation in up to 15% of infected children. Pneumonia, ear and sinus infections, and diarrhea were common. These infections are primarily responsible for the deaths observed in measles victims in less developed countries today. Rarer complications also occur.

In 1963 the pioneering efforts of John Enders and his colleagues culminated in the licensure of an attenuated measles virus that, although live, produced a minimal infection with few or no symptoms but was capable of stimulating the body's defenses in a similar fashion to wild virus infection. Technological refinements led to the current vaccine, which produces even fewer symptoms and an equally adequate immune response. By 1979, 94% of children attending school had received measles vaccine.

In the prevaccine era of 1952 to 1962, measles affected 95% of all children by the time they were 15 years old. With the steadily increasing administration of live measles virus vaccine, measles immunity induced by attenuated virus vaccine without disease has been substituted for wild virus infection. As a result, measles has been virtually eliminated for most U.S. residents. However, pockets of susceptible persons still exist in the population, and measles imported from abroad now threatens to become a major source of infection for these groups.

## A new measles susceptibility

Who are the persons still susceptible to wild virus infection? They can be categorized as shown in the Table on page 304. First, there is a significant percentage of persons among the young adult population who have never received the vaccine or been infected naturally. Among the reasons for lack of vaccine receipt are: (1) religious or other objection to medical care in general or to injections in particular, (2) failure of persons to seek or be provided with medical care, (3) economic hardship, and (4) slippage through the administrative

system. This group is the one in which miniepidemics occur. For example, in 1983 students attending two universities in Indiana experienced an outbreak of measles that involved more than 200 students.

A second group of susceptible persons are those who have received measles vaccine but remain unprotected. Measles vaccine is not perfect; for reasons that are not known, 1 to 3% of the persons injected with the attenuated virus fail to respond with an appropriate defense. This group cannot be spontaneously identified, and only by a costly, not readily available, blood antibody test can it be ascertained that they are still susceptible. A very few adults in this unprotected group are identified, because such tests are used in critical occupations, such as health care work. The vast majority of unprotected people are not identified. Secondary vaccine failure, on the other hand, probably does not occur. That is, once a person is successfully immunized, he remains immune for life.

When measles immunization programs were first begun, a variety of vaccine formulations were used. Some of these, particularly liquid vaccines, were very frail and susceptible to inactivation by physical exposures, such as heat and light. Thus some persons received vaccine that was not "live" and, therefore, remained unimmunized. We do not know who these persons are but believe they are few in number.

*The World Health Organization's immunization program is an important strategy for the prevention of measles on a global scale.*

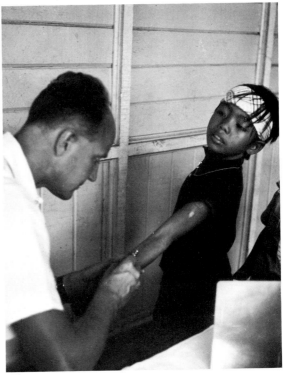

Some children alive today received live measles virus vaccine before they were one year old. Pediatricians and other physicians did not appreciate initially that measles antibody from the mother, transferred during pregnancy, persisted for as long as 11 or 12 months. Hence, a proportion of these children who received their vaccine from 9 to 11 months of age are not protected.

About 600,000 children received a vaccine that no longer is used; i.e., killed measles virus vaccine. This product proved to be ineffective in providing immunity. In fact, some of these individuals will acquire an atypical illness when they are exposed to wild virus.

Finally, a new problem generated by the recent upsurge in immigration from the Far East and the Caribbean accounts for measles susceptibility in the U.S. Among these immigrants are those who have not had measles or received vaccine. Thus they are adding to the pool of susceptible persons.

## Importation of measles

Since global eradication of measles has not been achieved, susceptible persons may acquire the disease abroad and return or immigrate to the U.S. during the disease's incubation period. In fact, such occurrences are now important for the persistence of measles. Both U.S. residents who travel abroad and foreign nationals who visit or permanently immigrate may become the focus of new miniepidemics.

To fully understand this new phenomenon we can examine the occurrence of measles in 1982, when the lowest level of occurrence (1,697 cases, as previously mentioned) of this disease was reported. Twenty-two states had no indigenous cases; that is, no cases in U.S. residents who did not travel or have any known contact with foreign nationals with measles. However, in seven of these states, and in several others, cases of measles were imported from abroad. A total of 119 individual cases were identified from 32 different foreign countries. These 119 persons were responsible for 498 additional cases in eight distinct chains of transmission. Thus a total of 617—36.4% of the total reported cases—were linked to importation from abroad. As long as foreign countries have measles rates that are 10 to 10,000 times that of the U.S., the potential for importation will persist.

A special problem in recent years has been the sudden influx of large numbers of legal and illegal refugees. In emergency situations abroad we may have little control over the entry of persons who are infected but asymptomatic or who have only mild symptoms of early measles. Rapid jet travel facilitates such importations. Slower means of transport may allow sufficient time for definitive diagnosis.

Even in emergencies, staging areas abroad are often established to accomplish three goals: (1) to determine who has measles currently and identify and quarantine those who have had contact, (2) to establish as reliable a history as is possible for natural disease or appropriate immunization, and (3) to administer measles vaccine. Even with such staging procedures, administrative slippage can and does occasionally occur.

A larger and more difficult problem is posed by the illegal entrants into the U.S. Today the greatest numbers come from Mexico, Central and South America, and the Caribbean nations. Not only may measles be imported by these persons, but their illegal status may prevent their seeking medical aid, and thereby the disease may be perpetuated before control measures can be applied.

## Strategies for preventing measles

To ensure reduction in the remaining incidence of indigenous measles and to prevent or eliminate further cases, necessary precautions include:

1. continuing infant immunization programs attempting to reach 100% of children in the U.S.;

2. continuing school immunization regulations that assist in identifying the unimmunized and some of the improperly immunized persons (in the event of a local occurrence of measles, the rigorous exclusion of susceptible children from school and the implementation of an immunization program can stem transmission);

3. attempting to identify those older than high-school age who have escaped both disease and immunization (programs in colleges, in the military, and among any group of young adults can facilitate this effort and are currently a high priority);

4. screening health workers, especially those whose tasks may bring them into contact with cases of measles (if susceptible workers are found, immunization should be urged or mandated);

5. continuing to screen immigrant populations to allow entry only to those who are fully protected (if necessary, administer measles vaccine abroad, apply quarantine measures, and attempt to identify infected persons);

6. educating the public to identify and report measles to health personnel so that transmission can be stopped, susceptible persons can be identified, and immunization can be given (this step is critical in those areas with known aggregations of illegal aliens); and

7. encouraging and assisting the World Health Organization in an effort to eradicate measles globally. Smallpox recently has been eliminated by such an international effort, and it may well be possible to eradicate measles from the face of the Earth as well.

The success of clinical trials of a new aerosol inhalation method of administering measles vaccine was recently reported by Albert B. Sabin (developer of the oral polio vaccine). The ease of application of this experimental new measles immunization could speed world efforts in the battle against the disease.

—Vincent A. Fulginiti, M.D.

# Special Report:
# The Burned Child
## by Norman R. Bernstein, M.D.

Everyone has been burned, usually sustaining minor injuries that give no concept of what a major burn injury entails. A large burn that extends through the skin over a large part of the body is a devastating injury. It never heals without scarring. Each year in the United States some 80,000 people are hospitalized because of serious burns; at least 12,000 die of their injuries; and many thousands are permanently disfigured. We do not know how many end up scarred and live in hiding. About one-third of these patients are children.

Most children are burned in house fires. The United States has more of these than any other country, partly because of the widespread use of wood construction and partly because of the aging of the central cities, where old furnaces and worn electrical wiring are likely to break down. Arson, which is among the most rapidly increasing crimes in the United States, is a notable factor in the causation of thermal injury. Families living near factories and other buildings that may be set on fire for insurance money are also at great risk. Poverty and emotional disturbances in the home can be factors contributing to fires. Disintegrating and angry families are more likely to be careless and cause accidental fires, leaving matches, flammable liquids, and space heaters unattended. Drug abuse, drinking, and falling asleep while smoking all cause countless fires each year. More and more evidence shows that child abuse is another cause of burn injury. Disturbed parents may punish children by burning them with lighted cigarettes, by plunging them into hot water or shoving their hands in stoves, and even by setting them on fire. Tragically, fires commonly strike poor and fragmented families that have little financial or emotional resources to deal with what has happened.

## Medical care of the burned child

A burn injury produces immediate and complex medical consequences. It destroys the skin surface. A major burn goes through all the layers of the skin to the flesh below. Fluids and blood pour out of the body. Shock may follow. The patients must be treated quickly. They must have intravenous fluids to replace body losses. An airway to the lungs must be kept open. Following the resuscitation of the patient, the burn wound itself presents the greatest challenge to care. Infection of the burn wound is one of the biggest threats to the patient's survival.

Blood transfusions are often needed. Body fluids have to be replaced and balanced and the normal composition of salts and protein in the blood sustained. Surgeons attempt to cut off the dead, blackened tissue caused by the original injury. They try to determine the extent of the wound and distinguish the limit of the living tissue. This is difficult in children because of swelling and discoloration of their burns. One reason for rapid removal of charred nonliving tissue is to prevent this tissue from becoming a source of infection and also to cover the burned surface to promote healing. Normal bacteria on the skin of healthy people become highly dangerous in an open burn wound.

Patients are given antibiotics to combat incipient infection, and every attempt is made to cover the wound with bandages, special dressings, chemical antiseptics, and grafted skin—from animals (often pigs), from amniotic tissues, from human skin, or with "artificial" skins. Human skin may be taken from dead bodies (cadavers), from relatives, or from intact parts of the burned child's body surface. The idea is to stop the loss of fluids and enable the body to grow a cell cover over the wound. These initial grafts do not remain as permanent coverings and will drop off within two weeks. However, they can make the difference between life and death in a child with an extensive burn.

Enormous progress has been made in treating burn shock, in rapid resuscitation, and in infection control. The larger the burn area, the greater the danger of death. Today children with burns covering as much as 70 to 85% of their bodies (once fatal) are now surviving thanks to the varieties and uses of grafts, antibiotics, isolation techniques, and anesthetic approaches. Clearer knowledge of nutritional needs has ensured that burned children have all the important nutrients so vital to tissue building and healing.

Today early planning for reconstructive surgery enables the shifting of tissues to cover skin gaps, moving of tendons and eyebrows, remaking of hairlines, replacing lip margins, and reconstructing noses, eyelids, and ears. Steady developments in prosthetics (artificial body parts) provide children with "new" ears, noses, and hair.

In the U.S. more than 150 specialized burn centers have opened in the last 20 years, assuring that children are more likely to be given prompt and appropriate care. At most of these centers there is also an increased awareness of the emotional needs of the burned child and his family. There are intense and important emotional reactions at every stage of burn care. The adjustment of these children depends to a great extent on their inner resources but also on the kind of support and encouragement they receive. Today psychiatrists, psychologists, social workers, play therapists, and teachers are more involved at each stage of burn care, and more attention is given to the return of the child to school and normal life.

## Emotional consequences

The immediate procedures in burn treatment require placing patients in bacterial isolation, separating them from other people who could infect them, and taking many trips to the operating room. During the first weeks after suffering a burn that covers more than 50% of the body, the overwhelming assault of the injury itself as well as the rigorous steps necessary to save the child leaves him dazed. He is likely to be mentally somewhat bewildered but alert and quiet for the first few hours after the injury but then is sure to lapse into a state of confusion and to waver between states of consciousness, dozing, sleeping, and dreaming. Common reactions are delirium, nightmares, hearing voices, seeing imaginary people and animals, and having hallucinations of parents who may have died in the fire. Children may stammer, become incoherent, and lose their ability to speak clearly; they often regress to more babylike states. They may lose control of their bladders and bowels and need to be fed.

Over a period of weeks they become clearer in their thinking, but their terrible plight remains, causing sorrow and dejection when they begin to fully realize what is happening to them; they feel helpless and see no way out.

With a major burn the child is likely to be in the hospital for months and require repeated grafting and dressing changes. After the first few weeks he undergoes regular soaks in a physiotherapy tub, and his wounds are scraped of dead tissue. As the child's condition improves, he will be encouraged to become more active: to move stiff and painful fingers, arms, and legs, and gradually to walk. Usually special pressure masks and body garments that compress scars must be worn for months. The child's image of his own body begins to change from that of a complete and functioning individual into one of a damaged and markedly limited "patient" who needs a lot of help and who suffers continual discomfort.

As the child improves physically, he is given more independence in caring for himself but is still in need of splints and continuing reconstructive surgery. With the cutting away of scars and the covering of some of the injury, efforts are begun to make the child look better. But when he is discharged from the hospital, the burned child may still have to face many more operations; as a child grows, scars contract and often have to be "released," especially around the armpits, so that more normal skin growth can occur. With years of medical care ahead, the child must make the effort to go back to normal school and community life while looking and feeling differently about himself.

No matter how attentive and caring parents and hospital staff may be, the pressures of burn care are impossible to counter completely; the children undergo periods of being downcast, dejected, uninterested in food, getting little joy out of life, and showing no plea-

*In addition to prolonged medical therapy, the badly burned child must adjust to his altered appearance and be prepared for the stares of strangers.*

sure in visitors, other patients, television, flowers, toys, or telephone calls. This phase is to some degree inevitable but usually abates after a month. These children often refuse to participate in their treatment. They are unwilling to move, to get up and go to the tub room. This is all part of the process of coming to grips with what has happened to them.

As the child becomes more active and begins to think of going home and back to school, he is fearful of what he will have to confront in the outside world—especially when facing schoolmates.

A key element to the child's successful recovery is hope: hope that he will survive, hope that the agonizing treatments will end, hope that he will go home, and hope that he will achieve an acceptable role in the world and not be rejected by society because of the scars that make him different. Well-trained mental health workers can be enormously valuable at every stage to minimize the suffering, to enhance cooperation with the medical aspects of treatment, to support the child's acceptance of what has happened, and to help a child master the sadness involved in being permanently scarred and disfigured.

A psychiatrist may prescribe medications for the depression, delirium, or fears that patients show at different stages. He or she also helps the child and the family understand that some pain is unavoidable, even with analgesic medications. The psychiatric counselor helps parents avoid well-intentioned lying to the child about upcoming unpleasant procedures. Children sometimes undergo hypnosis to help alleviate some of the physical pain and emotional anxiety.

Psychiatrists and psychologists also instruct hospital staff members so that they can become more sensitive to the physical and emotional suffering that their patients experience and more helpful in reaching out to them. Consultation is provided to surgeons, internists, pediatricians, and anesthesiologists about handling crises; for example, children who refuse to go to the operating room, refuse to undergo dressing changes, blame or threaten staff for hurting them, or refuse food. A common time for difficulties to arise is in physical therapy, where patients are required to move their burned limbs and may become discouraged because of the physical pain involved.

Children in the hospital for any illness are likely to be cross, tearful, and dependent. The nurses on pediatric wards have to be supportive, friendly, and cheerful and, if possible, give information to the children about what is happening to them, making it clear what the various medical procedures mean. This is also true in the burn center, but the heightened desperation and life-threatening nature of the injuries and prolonged hospitalization that *most* patients face require even more effort from the staff. Mental health workers and other staff must be specially prepared because they are not dealing with a physically normal child who just *feels* ugly, damaged, or less than whole. The burned child is truly handicapped and must face a world that is often aghast and frightened by his appearance and unwilling to have him around. The psychiatrist must work most fundamentally as an explainer of feelings and realities that are not at all pleasant.

The child must make a continuing effort to function with a changed body and to deal with the new way that the world treats him; he has to be ready to face the fears and the revulsion others show, the questions, and the unskilled efforts to sympathize and help that others will make. The younger burned child may adjust very well at first but may be traumatized when he reaches adolescence and has to cope with all of the social problems of psychosexual development, the wishes to be attractive and to participate in the world of dating and sports. These are issues that need to be talked out with parents, with friends, and with professionals. Bitter feelings need to be let out; the burned adolescent needs to build a sense of worth based less on appearance and more on personal character.

Burn centers today tend to have long-term contacts with burn victims and try to help get them the psychological and social care they need as they mature and change over the years.

## The impact on families

Since children are most often burned in home fires, where brothers, sisters, or parents may be injured or killed and homes destroyed, the catastrophe is one for the whole family. At each stage of managing and treating burned children, therefore, the reactions of the family in many ways determine the manner in which care can be implemented.

Burns alter family relationships as well as individual functioning. The cost of burn care runs quickly into the hundreds of thousands of dollars. Unlike many other acute injuries, a burn frequently leads to a permanent change of the person's role in the family. The burn patient requires years of treatment involving multiple operations, physical therapy, special schooling, and special training in how to deal with disfigurement and mobility handicaps.

Parents go through a period of depression. This reaction is an inevitable response to the grief of having lost a "normal" child and all the hopes that were attached to him or her. It may take years for the family to realign itself in its attitudes toward the patient and to work out ways of helping him. It has been found that the most useful way to help such families is to provide them with sustained counseling for years either on an individual basis or in group meetings so that they can work out and express many of the agonies they feel and digest the frightened and depressing emotions they experience in regard to the fate of their burned child. Whether or not they were in any way at fault, parents feel guilty about their part in having allowed the injury to occur. This guilty feeling may pervade the home atmosphere for years. Counseling is helpful in dissipating guilt so that parents can more realistically support the burned child. For families where neglect or abuse is related to the burn, special help is necessary, sometimes requiring the temporary, or even permanent, placement of the child in another home.

One of the basic things a parent needs to do in helping a burned and disfigured child to grow up is to find a balanced approach to parenting, which may mean constantly pushing the child into some activities and helping the patient give up others—such as sports or sunbathing. Parents must learn to be able to scold the child for ordinary misdeeds, slovenliness, poor homework, or failure to do chores. A parent who feels too guilty can get lost in his or her own feelings and may hold the child back from trying to do things that are important in adapting to the world.

Children who have had a severe burn follow a life course different from that of a physically normal child. But the modern approach to burn care is an optimistic one. Technological advances coupled with new psychosocial approaches today are saving the lives of more badly burned children and salvaging a good measure of normal happiness after the tragic scourge of fire.

309

# Skin Disorders

The development of acne during adolescence is so common that it is regarded as a normal part of growing up. An estimated 80% of the population develop acne to some degree. Acne typically begins in early puberty, at around age ten, continues through the teens, and then wanes. However, occasionally it persists or even recurs, and sometimes with greater severity, in the mid-twenties or thirties.

Because acne primarily affects the face, it is perceived as a significant embarrassment, particularly in adolescence, which tends to be a time of emotional turbulence and intense focus on appearance and self-identity. One person in three has acne of such severity that medical treatment would be appropriate, and an estimated 350,000 people in the United States alone have cystic acne, the most serious, scarring form of the disease.

Less than a decade ago dermatologists were basically helpless in treating many severe cases. Fortunately, in recent years new drugs have vastly improved the treatment of all forms of acne, making it possible in most cases to reduce the severity, to prevent permanent physical scars, and hence to reduce the emotional repercussions of having a disfiguring skin disease either temporarily or permanently.

## The onset of acne

The sexual hormones released at puberty, particularly androgens, stimulate activity of the sebaceous, or oil-producing, glands of the skin. These glands are most densely located on the face, upper back, and chest; a square inch of skin on the forehead may contain as many as 2,000 sebaceous glands. They secrete an oily material known as sebum. This substance ordinarily travels through narrow passageways, or ducts, to openings, or pores, on the skin surface, where it forms a thin film that helps to soften and lubricate the skin.

The sudden increase in sex hormones at puberty appears to trigger the production of an excess of sebum, often making the skin look shiny or greasy. For reasons not yet understood, the sebaceous gland ducts may become plugged at this time, impeding the flow of sebum. This development is the first step in the acne process. The plugs in the ducts are referred to as comedones.

The plug often incorporates particles of the skin's dark pigment, melanin; it is this coloring (not trapped dirt, as sometimes is erroneously thought) that makes the plug look dark and accounts for its being called a blackhead. Sometimes a plug lacks pigment and hence is called a whitehead. Whiteheads tend to be deeper and are more likely to lead to inflammation than blackheads.

Behind the obstruction sebum continues to be secreted. The buildup of the oils, along with bacteria that

normally live in the duct and the accumulations of dead skin cells that normally are shed through the duct, may create such pressure that the duct walls leak or rupture. These irritating materials cause an inflammation. The surplus oils, made even more irritating by enzymes in the bacteria, may produce a small papule (a red bump) or a larger pustule (containing yellow-white pus), depending both on whether the rupture occurred close to or farther from the surface and on the degree of irritation of the duct's contents.

If the inflammation is extensive and too deep to drain to the surface, a cyst may result, with swelling above and below the skin surface. As the cyst heals, scar tissue forms and pulls the skin, leaving the characteristic sunken acne pit. Sometimes the contents of the cyst remain impacted or are replaced by tissues produced by the body's immune defense system; the resulting lumps may remain for months or persist indefinitely and are referred to as nodules.

Because the androgenic hormones involved in acne normally are produced in larger quantities in males than females, acne usually is more severe in males. Acne also tends to run in families, although there are many exceptions to this rule.

## Myths and misconceptions

Many notions about acne, though widespread, are not supported by scientific investigations. Acne is not caused by dirt or infrequent bathing, for example. Moreover, it is not caused or worsened by masturbation, constipation, venereal disease, lack of sleep, or intense and angry emotions. Having—or refraining from—sexual intercourse does not affect the course of acne. Oily foods do not increase the production of skin oils. Restrictive diets that eliminate chocolate, french fries, cola drinks, and other foods that are often favored by adolescents are seldom recommended except to the small proportion of people who do note a clear association between ingestion of certain foods and a flare-up of their condition.

## Acne in adults

Not all acne starts in adolescence. A condition known as acne cosmetica appears to be related to the use of cosmetics and moisturizing creams as well as the substitution of cleansing creams for soap and water. It is primarily a problem for women, although men who frequently use moisturizers also may be affected. Presumably the cosmetics block oil ducts; hence, successful treatment requires discontinuance of the offending products and use of a mild soap for cleaning the face.

Not realizing that cosmetics are the culprit, some women attempt to conceal skin eruptions by applying increasingly heavy layers of makeup, which only makes the problem worse. Avoiding makeup for a few days will not bring about noticeable improvement; clearing after makeup is stopped usually takes at least two months. In recent years water-based, oil-free foundations have been formulated, but for some women changing brands of cosmetics will not make a difference; they must avoid makeup and cleansing creams entirely. However, most women with this problem can still wear eye cosmetics, as well as powder blushers and lipsticks.

Another type of acne that may appear in adulthood is occupational acne, which primarily affects workers who come in contact with oils and tars. Although the face usually is affected first, pustules may develop on the forearms and even the body and thighs if the oils soak through clothing.

Several medications may trigger eruptions that mimic acne. These include iodides or bromides in vitamin and mineral preparations, sedatives, asthma and cold remedies, thyroid preparations, and analgesics, as well as certain drugs used for mental illness (*e.g.,* lithium) and anticonvulsants (*e.g.,* phenytoin).

## Treatments that work

Treatment for early noninflammatory acne aims at removing blackheads and whiteheads and preventing the formation of new ones. One standard approach is to promote dryness and mild peeling of the top layer of the skin by using antiacne medications applied directly to the skin.

Many adolescents whose acne is mild can successfully treat themselves with nonprescription lotions, creams, and gels that contain sulfur, benzoyl peroxide, or sulfur combined with resorcinol. Based on the recommendations of a panel of medical experts convened in 1982 by the U.S. Food and Drug Administration (FDA), products containing both benzoyl peroxide and sulfur are available only with a doctor's prescription. Additionally, physicians may prescribe topical preparations of vitamin A acid, also known as retinoic acid.

For inflammatory acne, antibiotics, applied directly to the skin or taken by mouth, often are prescribed. These drugs are thought to work by inhibiting the growth of the bacteria in sebum that trigger inflammation. The most commonly prescribed antibiotic is tetracycline, taken by mouth. While use of the drug usually is halted

| **Nonprescription acne products** | | | | |
|---|---|---|---|---|
| **effective or beneficial** | | | **noneffective or aggravating** | |
| type | products | | type | products |
| benzoyl peroxide medications | Benoxyl 5 Lotion (5%) Benoxyl 10 Lotion (10%) Clear By Design Gel (2.5%) Clearasil Lotion (5%) Clearasil Super-Strength Acne Treatment Cream (10%) Dry and Clear Cream (10%) Dry and Clear Lotion (5%) Fostex BPO Gel (5%) Oxy-5 Lotion (5%) Oxy-10 Lotion (10%) Topex Lotion (10%) | | alcohol cleansers | Noxzema Antiseptic Skin Cleanser Propa P.H. Super Cleanser Sea Breeze Antiseptic for the Skin Seba-Nil Cleanser Ten-O-Six Lotion |
| sulfur medications | Acnomel Acne Cream Fostril Medicated Drying Lotion Postacne Rezamid | | soaps | Betadine Skin Cleanser Clearasil Antibacterial Soap Fostex Medicated Skin Cleanser Fostex Wash Oxy Wash pHisoDerm |
| salicylic acid cleansers | Clearasil Medicated Cleanser Dry and Clear Cleanser Stri-Dex Medicated Pads Therapads Plus | | scrubs | Buf-Puf Cleansing Sponge Epi-Clear Scrub Cleanser Komex Cleanser Listerex Scrub Lotion Loofah Sponges Multiscrub Oxy Scrub Pernox Scrub Cleanser |

Based on information from the FDA

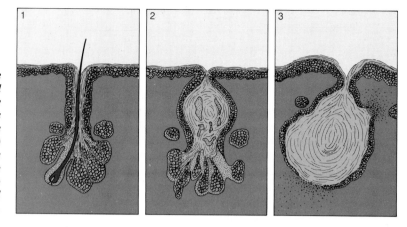

*Recently acne sufferers were given hope by a new drug, 13-cis-retinoic acid (Accutane), which suppresses the activity of the sebaceous glands and reduces sebum. Acne develops in hair follicles when surrounding sebaceous glands (left) oversecrete oily sebum; pressure grows within the follicle (middle); and the follicle wall ruptures, forming a deep lesion filled with sebum, bacteria, and pus (right).*

periodically to see if the acne has slowed down or stopped, tetracycline can be taken safely without interruption for years. It should not be taken by children who have not entered puberty or by women who are planning to become pregnant because it may lead to discoloration and weakness in developing teeth and bones of fetuses. Nontetracycline antibiotics applied directly to the skin are an alternative to oral medications.

In 1982 the FDA approved the drug 13-*cis*-retinoic acid, also known chemically as isotretinoin, marketed under the trade name Accutane. It is taken by mouth for severe cystic acne that has not responded to other forms of treatment. This drug suppresses the activity of the sebaceous glands and reduces the production of sebum. Studies by several researchers show that it provides a dramatic clearing of the skin when it is taken daily for two to four months and that the improvement is sustained for months to years after the treatment is discontinued. However, nearly all patients develop some adverse reactions to the drug, the most common being generalized dryness and itching of the skin. Because more serious reactions, including eye irritation, vague aches and pains, temporary thinning of hair, depression, and gastrointestinal symptoms also may occur, patients who are taking it are closely observed, and it is not recommended for the less severe forms of acne. Because related forms of the drug are known to cause birth defects in animals, the drug also is not recommended for women who are pregnant or intend to become pregnant soon. In July 1983 efforts to warn against the use of the drug in pregnancy were stepped up when it was reported that three pregnant women who had taken the drug had given birth to babies with central nervous system disorders.

While differences in the production of hormones from one person to another have not been implicated as a factor in most cases of the most common form of acne, acne vulgaris, researchers at the Baylor University Medical Center recently reported higher levels of androgens in both men and women with longstanding cystic acne that did not respond to conventional treat-

ment than in control subjects who did not have acne. The Baylor researchers also reported that treatment with a cortisonelike (steroid) drug, dexamethasone, lowered the level of these hormones and provided substantial improvement in most cases. In some women, oral contraceptives were added to further suppress hormone levels. Because it is not yet clear how long the medications must be given or whether the improvement remains after the drugs are stopped, the treatment still is regarded as experimental. Moreover, all steroid-type drugs can produce significant side effects.

## Self-care

While acne cannot be prevented, it can be controlled with medication. The individual with acne also can help minimize eruptions with commonsense skin care. Dermatologists often give their patients the following advice:

Acne sufferers should not overdo washing, and they should not scrub hard; three or four times a day is the maximum most physicians recommend. Since acne is not caused by dirt and since plugs are too deep to be reached by scrubbing, it cannot be washed away. Frequent or harsh washing may, however, prove irritating and may rupture deep pustules or cysts in the skin. Any mild soap is satisfactory; so-called acne soaps have not been proved to be more effective than plain soaps. Cold cream and oily soaps should be avoided since they will leave an oil residue on the skin and further plug ducts.

Acne lesions should not be squeezed, picked, scratched, or popped. Doing so may force their contents into deeper tissue and in the long run may produce more inflammation and scarring.

People with oily hair may need to wash it daily. Hair should be worn away from the face; attempting to hide acne by combing hair forward may bring additional oil onto the face and aggravate the problem.

Sunshine may be a "natural remedy" if used very judiciously—just enough to promote peeling. But sunburned skin is more likely to become irritated when acne medications are applied, and overexposure to the Sun's harmful rays can cause skin cancer. Artificial ultraviolet light for home use is seldom recommended today because of the potential dangers of burning, overexposure, and skin cancer; for the same reasons, physicians urge acne patients to avoid tanning salons.

Women troubled by acne should use soap and water for cleansing rather than cold creams. They should use a minimum of foundation makeup and choose products that are labeled "water-based" and "oil-free."

In selecting recreational activities, people with acne should keep in mind that an acne condition may be worsened by contact sports, where skin is likely to be abraded, or by any activity where heavy clothing, tight-fitting face masks, eye protectors, or chin straps are worn.

If medication has been prescribed, it should be taken as indicated. This may mean continuing it even when skin starts looking better. Worsening of the condition should be brought to the doctor's attention.

### New help for acne scars

While most scars become less noticeable with time, those that remain after acne has run its course may be further reduced in several ways. Some dermatologists and plastic surgeons use dermabrasion; this technique utilizes motor-driven wire brushes or diamond wheels to scrape away the outer skin layers. Another technique involves the use of chemicals such as phenol or trichloroacetic acid to "peel off" the scarred outer layers of skin.

A new technique uses a purified form of animal collagen, a fibrous protein that is a normal component of skin. This substance, which resembles household glue, is injected into the soft, craterlike sunken scars to raise them level with the skin surface. Because the collagen is gradually reabsorbed, implants for acne scars last no more than two to three years. The procedure can be repeated. Some physicians worry that injection of a foreign substance into the body may prove an immunologic time bomb, setting off future allergic reactions or illness. Hence, the treatment is not recommended for people known to have a faulty immune system, including those with such diseases as rheumatoid arthritis or systemic lupus erythematosus.

*—Stanford I. Lamberg, M.D.*
*and Lynne Lamberg*

# Sleep Disorders

An estimated 25 million workers in the United States, or 15 to 30% of the work force, and some 60 million people worldwide are employed in some form of shift work. One in four working men and one in six working women in the United States today frequently change the hours that they work and sleep. They are in occupations that include doctors, nurses, pilots, train engi-

neers, nuclear power plant operators, news media personnel, and diplomats.

Shift work, of course, is not a modern phenomenon. Camp guards and shepherds in ancient times took turns on night watch; sailors have always had to rotate their hours of working and sleeping; and doctors, nurses, and others who care for the sick have always been required to work around the clock. But the 24-hour workday became a practical reality for large numbers of people only about 100 years ago when electric power became basic to modern life and enabled advanced levels of industrialization. In 1882 Thomas Edison opened the first power plant in Manhattan, making it possible to turn night into day on the streets, in factories, and in office buildings and also making it necessary to provide workers' services at all hours. In today's advanced technological world, ever increasing numbers of round-the-clock workers have become essential to a well-functioning society.

Over the years it has become apparent that shift work may have adverse consequences on health. Shift work may disrupt sleep, decrease alertness, trigger gastrointestinal disturbances, and increase the risk of heart disease. It also may strain social and family relations. Further, it may have ominous implications for public health and safety since increased fatigue may play a causal role in air, motor vehicle, industrial, and other accidents. Recently investigators have been able to determine why shift work often causes such problems and to devise effective ways to minimize them. These advances reflect new understanding of inner human clocks that set the pace of daily life.

### Internal clocks

A direct result of living on a planet that rotates on its axis once every 24 hours is that humans, as well as lower animals and plants, have developed "internal clocks." That such events as waking and sleeping are not passive responses to light and dark but, rather, are inborn was first demonstrated in 1729 by Jean-Jacques d'Ortous de Mairan, a French astronomer. He found that a growing plant kept continually in the dark still raised and lowered its leaves at predictable intervals during the day. In addition to influencing patterns of sleep and wakefulness, inner clocks in the brain determine the release of hormones, fluctuations in body temperature, and other aspects of physiology and behavior. These clocks anticipate the customary time of awakening in the morning; they cause body temperature to rise and trigger the release of hormones needed for normal bodily functions.

Because inner clocks follow a rhythm that, while not exactly 24 hours in length, is approximately that long, they are known as "circadian," from the Latin *circa* ("about") and *dies* ("a day"). Humans, if confined to an environment such as a cave or a windowless apartment with no clocks or other indicators of time in the outside world, actually tend to have a natural day that is about 25 hours long. Hence, in time-free environments they drift about an hour later each day as determined by a real-time clock. Squirrel monkeys also spontaneously live on a 25-hour day, while mice tend to function naturally on a 23-hour day.

The typical human "range of entrainment," or day length to which most people can comfortably adjust, is one to two hours more or less than 25 hours. The existence of a 25-hour clock in humans permits relatively easy adaptation to modest changes in the timing of daily activities. Thus, living in a world that is based on a 24-hour day, most people are able to adjust successfully with their inner clocks working in synchrony. However, the inborn preference for 25-hour days explains why most people living on a 24-hour schedule find it easier to stay up later than to go to sleep earlier.

The normal harmonious relationships of the body's internal clocks can be upset by dramatically altering one's daily schedule. Traveling across many time zones, for example, often produces a constellation of symptoms commonly referred to as "jet lag." For a few days after such a trip, people tend to feel sleepy at the time they normally would be sleeping, and if they attempt sleep at a time they normally would be awake, they are likely to sleep poorly. Jet lag symptoms last until the body clock resets itself. While there are individual differences in the amount of time needed to readjust, a standard readjustment time for most people is roughly one day for every time zone crossed.

## Effects on workers

Diminished alertness, fatigue, malaise, and other jet-lag symptoms usually pose little inconvenience to most travelers. "Occupational jet lag," by contrast, may have a significant impact on the performance of shift workers. Work shifts frequently change by eight hours, a difference comparable to flying from Washington, D.C., to Moscow. For travelers, daily events—*e.g.,* rising in the morning, sleeping at night, meal times, and social activities—usually have the same time-of-day relationships that they have when the traveler is at home. Shift workers, however, often follow one schedule on work days and another on days off in order to spend time with family and friends, shop, conduct business transactions, attend school, and engage in numerous other pursuits. Even workers on permanent shifts that differ from the traditional day shift tend to lead less regular lives than day workers. In fact, rotating evening and night shift workers' inner clocks may be chronically out of synchronization.

There have been numerous recent investigations of the lives and health status of shift workers. Among the findings are that these workers seldom are able to sleep as long as they would like, averaging about an hour less sleep in every 24 hours than workers on permanent shifts. Female shift workers are particularly

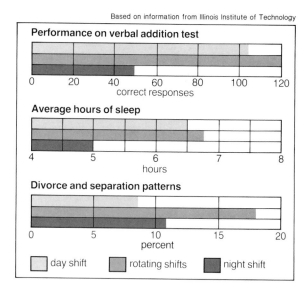

Based on information from Illinois Institute of Technology

Performance on verbal addition test

correct responses

Average hours of sleep

hours

Divorce and separation patterns

percent

day shift    rotating shifts    night shift

prone to accumulate a sleep debt, since typically they continue primary management of household responsibilities along with their outside employment. Shift workers are more likely then other workers to suffer from gastrointestinal disturbances, presumably because frequent changes in meal times, necessitated by changes in work and sleep times, disrupt patterns of digestion and elimination. Female shift workers have higher than normal rates of menstrual irregularities. Shift workers also tend to consume greater amounts of caffeine (to compensate for fatigue while awake) and alcohol (to make it easier to fall asleep).

Many shift workers report that their work schedules interfere with marriage, family life, and friendships and preclude regular participation in religious and community activities. In a study of households in which both parents worked full time, sociologists at the University of Maryland found that in one-third of the couples, at least one spouse worked a shift other than the regular day shift. In one-tenth of the couples, both spouses worked entirely different shifts with no overlap in hours, leaving little time for both spouses or for the entire family to be at home—and awake—together. Such schedules, however, maximize the time that at least one parent can be present in the home to care for children. Moreover, the premium pay that shift work usually brings may be particularly attractive to younger, usually lower paid, workers with family responsibilities.

Questions have been raised about the possible impact of shift work on longevity. In laboratory experiments, when insects and mice have been subjected to weekly shifts of their day-night cycles, their life-spans decreased by 5 to 20%. At present no similar data have emerged from studies of human longevity.

## Shift work and performance

In humans, the lowest levels of certain types of intellectual performance are associated with the lowest point on the body temperature curve. In people who ordinarily sleep from around 11 PM to 7 AM, body temperature is lowest between 4 and 6 AM; hence, fatigue and reduced efficiency, responsible for errors on the job, are most likely to occur around this time in individuals who are accustomed to such a sleep schedule. When work hours are changed abruptly, requiring people to remain awake at times they previously slept, performance rhythms for many tasks take a week or longer to readjust. These findings help explain why workers who rotate shifts have more accidents than those on fixed shifts and why errors are more frequent during the nighttime hours. Scrutinized in various studies were medication dispensing and problem solving by nurses, speed of switchboard operators in answering calls, and accuracy of meter readers. The tendency of long-distance truck drivers to fall asleep behind the wheel and of pilots to make errors in aircraft operation have also been observed. The widely publicized accident at the Three Mile Island nuclear power station in Pennsylvania in 1979 occurred at 4 AM; the operators on duty at the time had been rotating shifts every week. One additional reason for poor performance during night work is that sleep deprivation may cause lapses, or "microsleeps," where people actually fall asleep for a few seconds while they are performing tasks.

In the United States today, a wide variety of shift rotation schedules, known as rotas, are in use and typically have been designed to suit local needs. Eight-hour shifts are the most common, but some jobs involve 12-hour work days. A recent study conducted by the Boston-based Center for Design of Industrial Schedules together with researchers from Harvard and Stanford universities at the Great Salt Lake Minerals and Chemicals Corp. in Ogden, Utah, demonstrated that the application of circadian principles to the design of rotas can minimize some of shift work's adverse consequences. For ten years many workers in this plant had been rotating weekly from a night shift (midnight to 8 AM) to swing shift (4 PM to midnight) to day shift (8 AM to 4 PM).

These workers had more complaints of insomnia than workers on permanent day or swing shifts. Nearly one in three reported having fallen asleep at work at least once in the previous three months. One in four reported never being able to adjust sleep schedules because the rotations took place too often. Their schedules required them to move their sleep and waking activities to an earlier time; i.e., "phase advance." However, the fact that humans have an inborn tendency to function on a day that is longer than 24 hours suggests that rotations that delay the body's natural rhythms, i.e., "phase delay," rather than advancing them, are preferable. Hence, the scientists proposed that the direction of the rotation at the chemical plant be reversed and that shift changes take place three weeks apart to allow more time for inner clocks to realign themselves. On the new routine, workers' complaints that the schedule changed too often dropped from 90 to 20%, and worker satisfaction increased significantly. Production rose 13 to 22% in different areas of the plant during 1981–82; it continues to rise.

## Efforts to optimize work schedules

About half of the shift-work rotations in the United States presently go in what is now generally held to be the "wrong" direction; i.e., they require rotation by phase advance. However, circadian principles are beginning to have an impact on shift-work schedule design. At Exxon Chemical Americas in Houston, Texas, for example, as part of a two-year pilot program begun in 1982, workers meet in small groups to discuss potential problems of eating, sleeping, and social disruption. Additionally, an analysis has been launched of the various types of shift schedules, the specific manufacturing processes, and the timing of critical events in these manufacturing processes, with the goal of developing ways to promote optimal biologic rhythm adaptation. Implementation of rotas that match normal daily rhythms and worker education on "chronohygiene" have been introduced at such large employers as Commonwealth Edison in Chicago, the Argonne (Ill.) National Laboratory, and Ontario Hydro in Toronto.

Work also is in progress to find ways to improve adaptation to shift-work schedule changes. In the United States, scientists at the National Institute of Mental Health are exploring the importance of environmental light in the regulation of human biological clocks. Light has been shown to have a clock-resetting function in animals; preliminary research with human subjects suggests that bright artificial light, such as that used by television crews or in certain industrial settings, may have a similar effect. This work may pave the way for the development of practical guidelines for the regulation of environmental lighting in the work place.

Other studies currently under way are aimed at identifying individual characteristics and social factors that both enhance adjustment to shift work and, conversely, are most likely to impose additional stress. People who feel best and function best later in the day, "night people," appear to adjust more easily than "morning people," for example. Younger workers seem better able to cope with shift changes than their older counterparts. People with digestive disorders or metabolic diseases such as diabetes, who must carefully time their meals and medications, are likely to find frequent shift changes harder to tolerate than people who do not have such problems.

The prevalence of shift work has doubled in the past quarter century, fueling the need for further research on the pertinent health issues. Some manufacturing processes, such as those in chemical and food industries, must be kept going at all times. In petroleum refining, synthetic fiber manufacturing, and some other industries, more than 50% of the workers already rotate shifts. Reduced utility rates that are offered during the evening and night, along with the financial benefits gained from continuous use of costly equipment, are stimulating the expansion of round-the-clock operation. Application of circadian principles to the design of shift-work schedules promises both to minimize adverse health consequences for workers and to maximize productivity for industry.

—*Lynne Lamberg*

# Surgery and Transplantation

For most of recorded history, patients with diseased hearts, livers, kidneys, and other organs were destined to die. In the past 25 years the techniques of organ transplantation have become more and more practical, with a consequent revolution in the medical care of such patients. The problems associated with organ transplantation are manifold: rejection, infection, the psychological trauma of receiving part of another person's body, and the problems of the surgical procedure; however, these problems are closer to being solved than ever before. A recent important development has been the recognition that the drug cyclosporin A, a small polypeptide derived from a fungus, is useful in preventing rejection of a wide range of organs and is improving the results of transplantation compared with the routine immunosuppressive agents used at present. Concurrently, the surgical techniques for heart, lung, liver, and pancreatic transplantation are being perfected.

Unfortunately, while the biological and psychological difficulties associated with organ transplantation are being progressively eliminated, the social and political problems of obtaining sufficient donor organs are immense. To many transplant surgeons a new era has been reached; however, the availability of organs is now the limiting factor in reducing the number of successful transplants. For example, there are tens of thousands of patients worldwide who are on hemodialysis, many of whom are suitable subjects for kidney transplantation. Similarly, there are large numbers of patients who are on waiting lists for heart, liver, pancreas, and lung transplants. In the United States the demand for suitable livers for transplantation is likely to increase with the designation by a National Institutes of Health consensus panel in July 1983 of liver transplantation as a "therapeutic" alternative for some patients with irreversible liver disease. Previously this procedure was designated "research." Procurement and distribution of organs thus is fast becoming a vital part of the art and science of organ transplantation. At the beginning of 1983 an estimated 14,000 Americans were said to be awaiting kidney transplants, while approximately 5,000 Americans in 1983 could benefit from liver transplants.

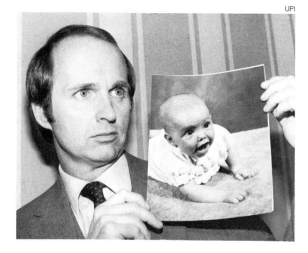
UPI

### The vital need for procurement

There are a number of reasons why procurement of organs is necessary. An organ can be kept outside of the body for only a short time before it is so damaged by a lack of oxygen and nutrients that it can never function again. Kidneys are routinely preserved for up to 72 hours; livers have to be used within 12 hours of removal from a cadaver; and hearts must be used within 3½ to 4 hours of removal. These time spans subsume two distinct periods of ischemia (reduced blood supply): warm ischemia time, which is the period between removal of the organ from the body and the beginning of cooling, and which must be very short; and cold ischemia time, which is the period between the initiation of cooling and the transplantation of the organ, and which can be longer. During the cold ischemia time the organ is preserved either by storage in a cold electrolyte solution or by perfusion on a specially designed machine. In both situations the temperature of the organ is kept at approximately 4° C (39° F), and thus the need for oxygen and nutrients by the organ is markedly diminished owing to its decreased metabolic rate. For this reason cold ischemia time can be much longer than warm ischemia time.

The time constraints imposed by the vulnerability of the organs to damage once outside the body make it necessary for organ procurement groups to work as rapidly and as efficiently as possible. Once brain death has been declared, the organs have to be kept functioning in the body as well as possible while waiting for them to be removed. This is done by providing intravenous fluids, albumin, and certain drugs to maintain a satisfactory flow of blood to the organs. As soon as possible the now brain-dead patient is transferred to the operating room, where the organs are removed and cooled before being distributed expeditiously to the waiting recipients in their various hospitals. Patients who have died outside the hospital are generally not suitable as organ donors except in the case of corneas, which may be taken up to 12 hours after death. The

*Owing to the lack of available transplantable livers and an inadequate system for obtaining them, many parents actively seek organs for their children via the media. Charles Fiske pleaded the case for his daughter Jamie in October 1982 before the American Academy of Pediatrics (opposite page). The grateful father, pictured at left with a healthy Jamie some eight months after her life-saving surgery, is now advising other parents who seek donor livers.*

surgery involved in the harvesting of organs is highly skilled, requiring surgeons who are trained specially for this purpose. The organs are handled as little as possible because excessive handling may cause spasm of the blood vessels. Special care is taken to leave a sufficient length of artery and vein (and ureter in the instance of kidney transplant) so as to facilitate successful interconnection (anastomosis) with the recipient's vessels and organs.

In order to prevent waste when an organ cannot be used in the hospital or local region where it has been harvested, systems of distribution have evolved that allow for the use of organs elsewhere. This is the role of the organ procurement agencies, which began to be initiated in the 1960s and have developed in various parts of the world, often in haphazard fashion, and provide only partial coverage for the demand. Some procurement agencies have been managed by individual transplant programs in hospitals, while others have developed as a result of the formation and subsequent amalgamation of several independent smaller units. For example, in 1969 transplanting institutions geographically distributed between Atlanta and Baltimore organized a kidney-sharing network (the Southeastern Organ Procurement Foundation) within the southeastern United States, which has grown over several years to involve 22 institutions. In this, and in other groups like it, the quality of procurement is assured through continuing education among the various users, including workshops in tissue typing and preservation of organs. Similar procurement agencies have developed in New England, *e.g.,* the New England Organ Bank based in Boston, and in the midwestern, southern, and western regions of the United States. As of 1982 there were 30 regional centers and 155 hospital-based centers in the U.S.

The Eurotransplant Foundation procures organs for transplantation in West Germany, Austria, Belgium, and The Netherlands. Other organizations provide for exchange of organs in the Scandinavian countries,

Australia, Canada, and other countries. Unfortunately, the coverage provided is somewhat uneven owing to lack of overall coordination and to differences in participation. In all parts of the world, patients living in underserved cities may have less opportunity to receive organs, while organs that become available in those cities are less likely to be harvested and made accessible to those who need them.

Owing to these difficulties the growth of national organizations has become essential. In the U.S., for example, the United Network for Organ Sharing (UNOS) represents 65 transplant centers from various sections of the country. This organization, developing out of the Southeastern Organ Procurement Foundation, maintains a data base of about 3,000 patients in more than 25 states, containing important information regarding potential recipients, including demographic details, the patient's hospital, blood group, tissue type, and the results of tests to determine percentage of antibodies against a panel of random donors. Each of these factors is important in matching donor organs with recipients and predicting the success of a transplant. By keeping this information readily available on a computer file, it has become possible to achieve two goals. First is that of preventing patients from receiving organs that are immunologically incompatible with their own defense systems and that would diminish the likelihood of a successful transplantation; second is that of allowing a recipient to be chosen in a geographical area as close as possible to the donor, thus minimizing the transportation time of the organ. This latter aspect has had the favorable consequence of increasing regional donor rates, since an organ harvested in a given region is more likely to be used within that region than outside it. UNOS originally kept a data base only for patients awaiting kidney transplants but since December 1982 has been able to provide information for other organs, including heart, lung, pancreas, liver, and intestines. Since July 1982 a further refinement in the sharing of organs has been established by the Kidney Center in Boston, which was set up to aid in the disposition of organs that cannot be placed under the usual circumstances; *e.g.,* organs that have shown unexpected immunologic reactivity against the planned potential recipients and for which time is fast running out before the organ becomes unusable. This facility places approximately ten kidneys per week, and several have been shared with European centers. Although dealing primarily with kidneys, the center, which utilizes an online widely distributed computer system, is available to assist with the placement of any organ 24 hours a day, seven days a week.

The North American Transplant Coordinators Organization (NATCO) answers the need for the training of professionals who can coordinate the requirements of various organ procurement agencies in the United States. In addition this organization provides professional education through meetings, symposia, a newsletter, and public education to enhance the awareness of the need for cadaver organs and tissues for transplantation. Another important service provided by NATCO is a toll-free 24-hour telephone service to coordinate donation of organs other than kidneys. This is done through a tape-recorded listing of all the hospitals in the U.S. that have patients requiring hearts, livers, lungs, or pancreases. When necessary, specific requirements, such as limitations of donor age and weight or the requirement in some cases for a cross-match test of immunologic compatibility between donor and recipient, are also listed. Typically, if a potential donor is identified anywhere in the U.S. who would fit the requirements outlined in the tape, then that patient's physician would get in touch with the potential recipient's physician. From that point on, the interaction proceeds between the transplantation teams at the two institutions.

At present most teams involved in the transplantation of organs other than kidneys are prepared to fly up to 1,600 km (1,000 mi) in order to harvest these organs. Physicians and medical personnel wishing to make known the availability of human organs for transplantation can use the toll-free telephone number.

The Living Bank in Houston serves the U.S. as a clearinghouse for the registration of people who intend to donate transplantable organs. The information is computerized for instant referral at the time of death. The staff of this nonprofit organization then contacts the organ procurement agency and transplant teams in the state closest to the donor, makes calls to next of kin, and, if needed, counsels the donor's family. Distribution of vitally needed organs is in this way facilitated. The Living Bank contains listings of over 120,000 people in over 60 countries and in all states of the U.S.

Despite these national efforts to aid and optimize organ procurement, most of the actual operational work is performed for hospitals by independent procurement agencies, with a high variance in the range of services provided. For example, with kidneys some agencies only provide placement, while others do virtually everything prior to the actual operation, including tissue-typing, transportation, and necessary follow-up. The costs incurred by the organ procurement agencies are billed to the recipient's hospital and are added to the hospital's kidney acquisition cost. Most hospitals in the U.S. use the Aetna Insurance Co. for this purpose, which reimburses on a cost basis. Figures from 1980 show a variation in costs per kidney ranging approximately from $800 to $11,000. Most of the variation in cost is due to the difference in services provided by the various organ procurement agencies. In the various regions of the country, the cost in 1980 of cadaveric kidney acquisition ranged from $2,579 to $8,784 and averaged $5,788. There are large variations in various other services of procurement agencies. Some export (deliver kidneys to other agencies) more than they import, while others do the reverse. Some represent the collaboration of a few hospitals, while others span large regions. Consequently, in April 1983 congressional hearings were held on the organization of the organ procurement agencies with the goal of improving services.

## Obtaining organs: the problems

A major problem in providing enough organs for transplantation is the wide discrepancy between the number of organs potentially available and the actual number that reach the point of being transplanted into a recipient. It is important to stress that although approximately 60% of all deaths occur in hospitals, the potential donation rate is much lower because of the requirement that the organs (except for corneas) be removed before the patient's heart stops beating and while the body is still functioning physiologically. This necessitates the use of patients who meet the criteria for brain death. Other factors that reduce the donation rate are difficulties identifying potential donors, obtaining consent from the patient's family, and keeping the patient in stable condition long enough to harvest the organ. According to some authorities, corneas, which can be used up to 12 hours after the death of the donor, have a theoretical availability rate of 45 per 100 hospital deaths. Similarly, there should be 26 pancreases available per 100 hospital deaths. The total number of kidneys that should be available is on the order of 2.4 per 100 hospital deaths. The national average, however, is closer to 0.17 per 100. Attempts have been made to increase the actual number of kidneys available to a level closer to the theoretical maximum.

The U.S. Centers for Disease Control in Atlanta carried out a study aimed at increasing the supply of cadaveric kidneys for transplantation. They found that the number of kidneys available could be doubled by a program of education and active surveillance. Such a program must first increase public awareness of the

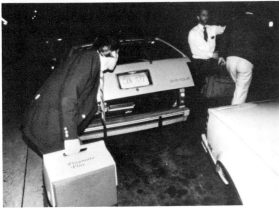

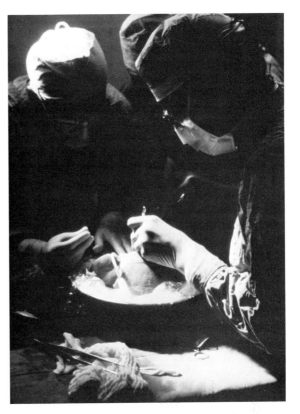

*Organs can be kept outside the body for only a short time. In this photo series a freshly harvested donor liver in New York City is perfused with a solution that will preserve it for less than a day, packed in a cooler, loaded into a waiting car, rushed to an airport, and flown to Pittsburgh, where it is inspected on arrival before emergency liver transplant surgery begins—all within five hours.*

necessity of making organs available; *e.g.,* by making available a document on the back of state driver's licenses that gives consent for the removal of organs after death. Another important part of such a program involves interaction of physicians and nurses with the families of patients with terminal illnesses or who have been in serious accidents; *i.e.,* those who are responsible for deciding the fate of the dying patient's organs. Educational efforts have included commercials on radio and television, pamphlets, lectures, demonstrations, and even the involvement of politicians and other public figures who publicly sign donor cards. However, these methods have not had a great impact, and relatively few kidneys have been transplanted as a result of these maneuvers. A new approach—targeting specific communities—may yield better results. Part of the problem is that there is a huge gap between people's beliefs about organ donation and their actions. About 80% of those surveyed in the U.S. have stated that they are generally willing to become organ donors. But fewer (about 55%) are willing to donate a specific organ, and even fewer (about 35%) would give permis-

sion for use of a dead relative's organs. Even when a donor card is signed, it is often not available to the medical staff, and even when it is, most physicians will still seek the family's permission.

The second step in a program to increase the number of available donors is the involvement of physicians in the identification of potential donors. Many physicians are not enthusiastic about supporting a search for donors; sometimes there is ignorance of the possible benefits, but more frequently there is hesitation to become involved in the seeking of information from families. For adequate supplies of available organs, there must be altruism in a group of people who have no direct benefit from obtaining organs. For example, a typical prospective donor is a young patient who has suffered head trauma or has a malignancy limited to the brain. The neurosurgeon and intensive care unit nurse with responsibility for the patient are committed first and foremost to their living patient and obviously not to an unknown, distant, and as yet unselected patient. The family, to whom the imminent death of the patient is often unexpected and always a tragedy, will

319

have difficulty thinking about organ donation at the painful time of loss.

The passing of the Uniform Anatomical Gift Act in all the United States now allows for two physicians unconnected with the procurement agency or the transplant operation to pronounce the brain death of a patient—a necessity for removal of an organ. Currently the requirements for brain death include unresponsiveness to stimuli of all kinds, lack of spontaneous respiration when taken off a respirator for three minutes, and lack of reflexes, all in the absence of sedative drugs or hypothermia (low body temperature). The electroencephalogram may be confirmatory in diagnosing brain death. At least 27 states have adopted laws that recognize the declaration of death on the basis of loss of brain activity, but in most of the other states the same policy is followed without a literal legal definition.

One legal feature completely absent from the organ donation scene as it currently exists in the U.S. is the practice observed in countries of the Eastern bloc, France, Spain, and other West European nations that allows organs to be taken from deceased patients as long as the family does not object. But such implied consent laws are not as productive of organs as one might expect since objections are common. In the United States there have been a few unfortunate cases of alleged homicide, where it has been claimed that the removal of life-support systems from an otherwise moribund victim by the physician was an independent cause of death. Cooperation with hospital legal departments should preclude such a result and thus should not constitute an obstacle to physician cooperation in seeking donation of organs.

The problems associated with the high ratio of recipients to donors is more apparent with patients requiring kidneys than for other organs, such as heart or liver, because of the possibility of maintenance of life with hemodialysis. For the other types of patient, there often is no artificial means of keeping them alive. Thus the majority waiting for these rarer organs are more likely to die because of a lack of availability. It is paradoxical that the better the medical care of patients with diseased organs, the greater the shortage of transplantable organs will be.

Fortunately, the media are playing a major role in the U.S. in providing the information that transplantation relies on for the availability of donor organs. Unfortunately, increased media coverage can bias the distribution of organs to potential recipients. John Fletcher, assistant director of bioethics at the National Institutes of Health, has said that the trend seems to be that whoever gets the most publicity gets to live. The determination of who should get an organ when there are many waiting is indeed a difficult problem. The American Medical Association's guidelines dictate that organs must be allocated to patients on a medical basis alone and that social worth is not an appropriate criterion. At present the allocation of kidneys is on a very scientific basis. For example, the New England Organ Bank has the following priority list for recipients of kidneys: (1) emergency patients, (2) patients with more than 50% antibodies to a panel of tissues from random donors, (3) patients with 10–50% antibodies to the panel, (4) patients with a full immunologic match, (5) patients with a partial immunologic match, (6) patients at a transplant center that has exported more kidneys than it has imported, and (7) patients in another region (outside of New England). The last standard applies for only one of two kidneys removed. The other kidney is usually offered first to the transplant center that procured both kidneys.

Some believe an organ should go to the recipient who has made the most effort to obtain it. Recently this practice has become the de facto situation for certain children with biliary atresia who require a new liver; their parents have actively sought out the livers. Of course, all these problems concerning who gets an organ would be solved if enough donor organs were available.

## Who can donate?

Most previously healthy children and adults can serve as donors for a wide variety of organs. For example, kidneys can be donated by anyone between 6 months and 85 years, although results may be significantly poorer when the age of the donor is over 55 years. There should be no significant history of high blood pressure or diabetes, no malignancies except perhaps those localized to the brain, no systemic infections at the time of donation, normal kidney function, and, of course, irreversible brain injury as described above. But, as mentioned before, there is a huge difference between a potential donor and an actual donor.

It is expected that as the public becomes familiar with the science and technology of organ donation and witnesses its vast social benefit, the number of recipients of transplanted organs will increase greatly. Similarly, as physicians and other health care workers see how successful transplantations are becoming, they will likely become more willing to take the steps necessary to seek permission from the families of terminally ill patients for removal of organs.

In 1983 at a workshop sponsored by the U.S. surgeon general's office concerning procurement of organs, the need was expressed for more specific donor criteria and additional guidelines for maintaining the donor while harvesting multiple organs. In particular, methods for overcoming barriers in the donation of organs for small children are required. A joint effort by all the groups involved in organized organ procurement is to be initiated by the surgeon general's office in order to move away from the individual character of present-day procurement toward a more unified program.

*—Nathan W. Levin, M.D.*

# Health Education Units

The following articles on important medical topics and health-related concerns are meant to be instructive and practical. It is largely through general health education that individuals can maintain and enhance their physical well-being. While the units emphasize the activation of the layperson's sense of responsibility for his or her own health, their purpose is to inform, not to prescribe.

## Contributors

**Edward L. Applebaum, M.D.**
*Nosebleed; Dizziness*
Professor and Head, Department of Otolaryngology, University of Illinois College of Medicine, Chicago.

**Harvey J. Dworken, M.D.**
*Heartburn; Gallstones and Gallbladder Disease; Constipation*
Professor of Medicine, Division of Gastroenterology, Case Western Reserve University, Cleveland, Ohio.

**Alvin N. Eden, M.D.**
*Eating Well from the Start; Roseola and Fifth Disease; Whooping Cough*
Chairman and Director, Department of Pediatrics, Wyckoff Heights Hospital, Brooklyn, N.Y.;
Associate Clinical Professor of Pediatrics, New York University School of Medicine, New York City.

**Joan Flanagan**
*Support Groups* (in part)
Free-lance writer, Chicago.

**Richard B. Freeman, M.D.**
*Treatment of Kidney Failure* (in part)
President, Renal Physicians Association; Associate Professor of Medicine and Head, Nephrology Unit,
The University of Rochester Medical Center, Rochester, N.Y.

**Jory Graham**
*Support Groups* (in part); *Pain and the Cancer Patient* (in part)
Late syndicated columnist ("A Time for Living," Universal Press Syndicate);
Lecturer; Author *(In the Company of Others),* Chicago.

**Robert S. Hillman, M.D.**
*Preparing for Healthy Travel* (in part); *Traveling with Special Health Problems* (in part);
*Communicating in Foreign Lands* (in part)
Chief of Medicine, Maine Medical Center, Portland;
Professor of Medicine, University of Vermont, Burlington.

**Sheilah M. Hillman**
*Preparing for Healthy Travel* (in part); *Traveling with Special Health Problems* (in part);
*Communicating in Foreign Lands* (in part)
Free-lance medical writer, Cape Elizabeth, Maine.

**Lynne Lamberg**
*Nails*
Free-lance medical writer, Baltimore, Md.

**Nathan W. Levin, M.D.**
*Treatment of Kidney Failure* (in part)
Head, Division of Nephrology and Hypertension, Henry Ford Hospital, Detroit;
Clinical Professor of Internal Medicine, University of Michigan Medical School, Ann Arbor.

**John M. Merrill, M.D.**
*Pain and the Cancer Patient* (in part)
Associate Professor of Clinical Medicine, Medical Oncology Section,
Northwestern University Medical School, Chicago.

**Joann Ellison Rodgers**
*Household Roaches*
National Science Correspondent, Hearst Feature Service, New York City.

**Lionel J. Schewitz, M.D.**
*"Morning Sickness"; After the Baby Is Born*
Chairman, Department of Obstetrics and Gynecology, and Attending Obstetrician and Gynecologist,
Lake Forest Hospital, Lake Forest, Ill.;
Associate Attending Obstetrician and Gynecologist and
Assistant Professor, Rush-Presbyterian-St. Luke's Medical College;
Lecturer, Northwestern University Medical School, Chicago.

**Title cartoons by John Everds**

# Contents

# Nosebleed

The mucous membrane lining the inside of the nose has several important functions, including the warming and humidifying of inhaled air. In order to produce changes in air that is moving rapidly through the nose, the mucous membrane has a rich network of blood vessels, and it is this abundant blood supply that is the source of most nosebleeds.

A nosebleed occurs when one of the blood vessels in the nasal lining breaks. One cause of these broken vessels is the drying out of the membrane. Thus, nosebleeds are common in the months during which central heating is used and indoor humidity is low. A ruptured blood vessel may also result from the congestion that occurs in the nose during respiratory infections or from congestion produced by hormonal changes during pregnancy.

Nosebleeds occur at all ages but are most common in young children and older persons. In children nosebleeds frequently result from abrasion of the inside of the nose by fingers or by foreign objects such as toys and sticks. Also, the colds and other respiratory infections more prevalent in children may produce nasal congestion resulting in nosebleeds. The older adult is prone to nosebleeds because of changes that take place in the nasal blood vessels with aging and as a result of the cumulative effect of nasal irritants, such as cigarette smoke and environmental pollutants.

## Some common misconceptions

Many victims of nosebleed have unfounded fears that the bleeding is a sign of an impending stroke, a brain tumor, or a potentially fatal hemorrhage. Fortunately, most nosebleeds are merely an annoyance and do not signify a serious underlying medical problem. Severe or repeated nosebleeds, however, may be an indication of significant disease in the nose or a generalized disorder of the blood or vascular system. To the victim, a nosebleed is generally a frightening event; often it appears as if a great quantity of blood is being lost, and the bleeding point itself can rarely be seen. The sight of many bloodstained tissues further contributes to these

fears. In fact, the amount of blood lost during most nosebleeds, although difficult to determine exactly, is not enough to be dangerous—unless the individual has preexisting heart disease that would be aggravated by reduction in blood flow to the heart, or unless he or she is anemic. The fear and anxiety that commonly accompany nosebleed are, nonetheless, important complicating factors since they produce temporary elevations in blood pressure that can cause increased bleeding.

Many nosebleeds can be stopped by the simple procedure described below. If the nosebleed does not respond to these measures, prompt medical treatment should, of course, be sought. If one's personal physician or an emergency room doctor cannot control the bleeding, referral to an otolaryngologist (ear, nose, and throat specialist) may be necessary. Although many persistent or recurrent nosebleeds can be controlled by treatment in a doctor's office, hospitalization is sometimes necessary for severe cases.

## Home treatments

Frequently the initial impulse in treating a nosebleed is to have the patient lie down. This measure is counterproductive; if the victim of a nosebleed lies down, the blood tends to run down to the throat, resulting in gagging and choking that only aggravate the bleeding. Furthermore, the supine position raises the blood pressure in the nose, also encouraging the bleeding. The best position is sitting, leaning slightly forward. This posture lowers the blood pressure in the head and allows the blood to flow out of the nose and away from the mouth; a basin or towel held under the nose will catch the blood. To prevent the rise in blood pressure that accompanies panic, the patient should be kept calm.

Because soft blood clots in the nasal passage may interfere with attempts to control the bleeding, they should be evacuated by having the patient gently blow them out. Most bleeding can be controlled by the application of finger pressure, and nosebleeds are no exception. Since most nosebleeds occur from the front of the nose, tight pressure applied to the nasal tip is fre-

*Among children, nosebleeds are more often the result of trauma than of serious underlying disease. Despite special protective equipment, youngsters engaged in contact sports may be unable to avoid an occasional nosebleed.*

quently effective. The tip of the nose should be tightly grasped between the thumb and forefinger and pressure maintained for five to ten minutes. If bleeding resumes after the release of finger pressure, the pressure should be reapplied for another five to ten minutes. Maintaining the patient in a sitting position and tightly pinching the nasal tip will often result in control of the nosebleed. A common error is to pinch the hard upper portion of the nose. This part of the nose is supported by the nasal bones, and they cannot be compressed to control bleeding. Finger pressure must be applied to the lower half of the nose, which is supported by a compressible framework of cartilage and which is the site of most bleeding points.

If the initial effort of finger pressure does not control the bleeding, the next step is to apply a decongestant nasal spray or drops. Most of these readily available products consist of solutions that work by constricting the blood vessels in the nasal mucous membranes. If they can be applied successfully to the bleeding point, these preparations will often produce sufficient vessel constriction to stop the bleeding. Neo-synephrine (phenylephrine hydrochloride), perhaps the most widely available nasal decongestant, is a potent constrictor of blood vessels. After any clots have been blown gently out of the nasal passages, the decongestant solution is sprayed or dropped into the side of the nose that is bleeding. Finger pressure is then reapplied.

If the nosebleed is coming from the most common site of bleeding, just inside the entrance to the nose, blood flow can often be controlled by inserting a small piece of cotton saturated with decongestant into the nostril that is bleeding and pinching the nose tightly over the cotton. Caution must be used not to insert the soaked cotton too far into the nose, or its eventual removal may be difficult.

The application of an ice bag to the nose also induces constriction of the blood vessels and has been advocated for control of nosebleed. It is not as effective as the nasal drops and sprays but should be used if these are not available. The application of ice to the back of the neck has also been recommended, but this measure is probably not as effective as applying the cold pack directly to the nose.

If these simple measures are effective in controlling the nosebleed, precautions must be taken to prevent the bleeding from recurring. The patient should be kept in an upright position and, for several days after the episode, should avoid bending and lifting; pillows should be used at night to keep the head elevated. Because alcohol and hot beverages dilate the nasal blood vessels, they should also be avoided following a nosebleed. Other factors that could cause bleeding to recur are vigorous exercise and straining to have a bowel movement. Further nose blowing, which can dislodge the hard blood clot that has formed over the broken vessel, may also produce a resumption of the bleeding.

## Prevention of simple nosebleeds

To prevent recurrent nosebleeds, the use of humidification is important during seasons when indoor heat is in use. For a small area or single room, floor-model humidifiers and cool-mist vaporizers are effective and relatively inexpensive. If no other means are available, a vaporizer should be placed in the bedroom of the person who gets frequent nosebleeds.

Additionally, the application of petroleum jelly to the nasal mucous membrane twice a day is helpful. A cotton applicator or fingertip can be used to place a small amount of the lubricant just inside both nasal passages; gently massaging the nasal tip will spread the jelly. The petroleum jelly helps to keep the nasal mucous membrane moist and prevents exposure and breakage of the blood vessels in the membrane. Children with recurrent nosebleeds are often helped by this remedy.

## Medical treatments

Persistent or recurrent nosebleeds require medical attention. Effective treatment sometimes consists of cauterization, which seals the broken blood vessel by chemically or electrically burning the tissues surrounding the open vessel. The treatment is usually preceded by the application of a local anesthetic. The physician then touches the bleeding point with a caustic chemical on an applicator stick or uses an electrical cautery device to seal the blood vessel. Cauterization, while very effective, can be used only if the bleeding point is clearly visible and accessible and if the rate of blood flow is not excessively brisk.

Nasal packing may be a more suitable alternative if the bleeding point is not visible or accessible or if bleeding is too rapid for effective cautery. Because it acts by applying sustained pressure to the bleeding point, nasal packing is often indicated if bleeding arises from deep within the back portion of the nose. To alleviate discomfort, the nasal passages are usually anesthetized before the packing is inserted.

The simplest packing material consists of long strips of gauze that are inserted into the nasal passage after being impregnated with a lubricating antibiotic ointment. Generally, the packing is inserted into the nasal passage through the nostril. If the bleeding is from the back portion of the nose, the packing may have to be introduced through the mouth and pulled up behind the palate in order to exert pressure at the most effective point. Additional packing is then inserted through the nostril to completely fill the nasal passage. When a nosebleed is so severe that packing is required in the back of the nose as well as in the nostril, the patient is hospitalized.

Nasal packing is usually left in place for several days, a sufficient time for pressure against the broken blood vessel to cause the vessel to form a clot. If bleeding recurs at the time of pack removal, new packing must be inserted.

Another technique of nasal packing employs a balloonlike device that can be inserted easily into the nasal passage and then inflated so that it compresses the bleeding point. These inflatable devices are preferable to gauze packing in emergency situations and seem to be more comfortably tolerated by the patient. Nasal packing is extremely uncomfortable and may cause gagging or difficulty in breathing. For these reasons, packing of any type is resorted to only if other means of nosebleed control fail.

## Surgery for nosebleeds

Some specialists prefer surgery as the initial treatment for severe or persistent nosebleeds to avoid the discomfort associated with packing. Others prefer to reserve it for those patients whose nosebleeds cannot be controlled by conventional nasal packing methods. Surgery may also be indicated in cases of bleeding following pack removal or for those conditions in which packing is not a feasible alternative.

Surgical treatment for nosebleed blocks the vessels that supply the bleeding point. First the bleeding point is identified, sometimes a difficult process requiring the use of fiber-optic devices for precise visualization. The feeding blood vessel to the affected portion of the nose is then surgically exposed, and the vessel is blocked by applying a metal clip to it or by tying it off. The procedure is performed under either local or general anesthesia and is usually well tolerated, even by older patients.

In recent years an alternative to surgical obstruction of blood vessels feeding nasal bleeding points has yielded encouraging results. Following an X-ray study that identifies the bleeding point and its feeding blood vessel, the blood vessel is injected with tiny synthetic particles that cause it to become occluded. This technique, however, has had limited application and needs further development and refinement before it becomes a standard treatment.

## Complications

If a nosebleed is severe, persistent, or recurrent, complications may develop. The most dangerous complication of a severe nosebleed generally is not the loss of blood itself but the potentially fatal obstruction to breathing that may occur if large amounts of blood or a clot is aspirated (inhaled into the windpipe). Airway obstruction is prevented by having the patient maintain a sitting position and leaning forward.

Persistent or recurrent bleeding may produce enough blood loss to result in shock, a condition characterized by pale, cool skin, weak and rapid pulse, and impaired consciousness. If the victim of severe nosebleed has a preexisting heart or circulatory problem, loss of blood from the nosebleed could contribute to a heart attack or stroke.

The necessarily prolonged maintenance of packing material in the nose is another cause of complications. Precautions must be taken to prevent the packing from becoming dislodged, in which case it could be aspirated and cause airway obstruction. Older persons, especially those with preexisting respiratory problems, have difficulty tolerating the nasal obstruction that results when the nose is packed; supplemental oxygen therapy is usually given to such patients. Nasal packing also may invite an infection of the ears or sinuses, since it blocks the passages connecting these structures to the nose. These infections usually respond promptly to antibiotic therapy.

## Predisposing illnesses

Most nosebleeds do not signify the presence of serious illness, but severe, persistent, or recurrent episodes of nasal bleeding may be due to a significant medical problem. Sometimes nosebleed is the only manifestation of an underlying condition that is diagnosed in the course of managing the bleeding episode. The types of medical problems associated with nosebleed are abnormalities of the blood and its clotting mechanisms, disorders of the blood vessels, high blood pressure, and diseases of the nose and sinuses.

An abnormality of the blood clotting mechanism may have many causes. Various inherited deficiencies of one or more of the blood clotting factors result in abnormal bleeding tendencies; perhaps the best known is hemophilia, although there are others with less obvious and less severe manifestations that may produce only nasal bleeding. Some illnesses require therapy with anticoagulant drugs, medications that intentionally impede blood clotting. Anticoagulants are valuable in the management of certain cardiovascular diseases, but they may, as a side effect, result in nosebleeds.

Even the commonly used drug aspirin interferes with the normal blood clotting process. Patients who take large amounts of aspirin, or those who are very sensitive to the drug's effects, may develop nosebleeds. Leukemia, a cancer of the blood, is characterized by the proliferation of abnormal blood cells and results in impaired blood clotting mechanisms; the disease may become apparent from nosebleeds that manifest the derangements it produces in the blood. Diseases of major organs (such as the liver) responsible for producing the substances necessary for normal blood clotting also cause spontaneous bleeding. Thus patients with severe nosebleeds are commonly tested to determine if an abnormality of the blood cells or blood clotting mechanism is present.

Less often, the small blood vessels in the nose (and elsewhere) may be abnormal and fragile, tending to break easily and bleed either spontaneously or as a result of only slight trauma. This rare condition is usually hereditary. Because of the delicate nature of the blood vessels, nosebleeds in these patients are often difficult to control by ordinary means. In some cases it becomes necessary to remove portions of the nasal mucosa that are frequent sites of bleeding and replace these areas with small skin grafts.

Prolonged, severe nosebleeds may be the initial manifestation of high blood pressure (hypertension). Blood pressure is easily measured by the familiar cuff placed around the arm, and if hypertension is detected, it is treated after the bleeding has been controlled. Rapid lowering of elevated blood pressure may be necessary to stop the bleeding from the nose.

A variety of disorders localized to the nose and its sinuses may result in nosebleeds. Young children have a tendency to put objects in their noses. These foreign objects may go undetected until they elicit an infection that produces discharge or bleeding from the nose. The object is usually detected and removed when the nosebleed is treated. Both benign and malignant tumors in the nose or sinuses may cause nosebleeds. Although bleeding from the nose may be the initial or only manifestation of tumors in these locations, they are usually associated with symptoms of nasal obstruction and facial swelling. Angiofibroma, an uncommon benign tumor that occurs in the blood vessels in the back of the noses of adolescent boys, must be suspected when recurrent nosebleeds appear in these patients.

Generally, however, nosebleeds are common occurrences that are not usually associated with any significant underlying disease. Most are self-limited and will stop spontaneously or can be controlled by simple measures. Many nosebleeds occur because of minor irritations to the nasal mucosa, such as the drying effects of indoor heating in the winter months. When nosebleeds are severe, persistent, or recurrent, however, medical attention must be sought and any underlying serious medical problems ruled out.

*—Edward L. Applebaum, M.D.*

# Health Education Unit 2

# Support Groups

How can you find someone truly understanding to listen to the problems and fears of living with a life-threatening disease such as cancer? Whom can you call at night or on a weekend when you simply need reassurance? Where can you go to learn how to care for an infant with a serious birth defect or an elderly stroke victim? For millions of people today the solution is a support group (also called self-help group, mutual aid society, or simply "network"). Becoming part of a group of people who share your problems and your feelings can give you the security, sense of belonging, and emotional strength that come from knowing you are not alone.

Ironically, the recent proliferation of health-related support groups is a result, simultaneously, of the successes and failures of the medical profession. As advances in science and technology have turned once fatal illnesses into chronic diseases, the human needs of individuals living with chronic conditions have come to the fore. Often such people are well enough to function as part of the mainstream of society, but much of society rejects or ignores them because they are reminders of the precariousness of human health. The medical profession, too, having fulfilled its primary clinical function, often turns its back on the emotional and social consequences of chronic disease or disability.

## The range of groups

A support group may be simple, small, and informal— perhaps only three or four people who share a common problem and meet periodically to talk about their experiences. Members may take turns organizing or hosting meetings or chairing discussions. Small groups usually cover the costs of mailings and meetings through voluntary donations from the participants.

Support groups may also be highly sophisticated, well-organized national or international associations with scores of local chapters. In such organizations the central headquarters coordinates activities on state or provincial, regional, and national levels to influence legislation; raises money for services and research; educates the public; and fights discrimination against its members. Each group tends to develop a structure and style that best meet the needs of its members. One such group, under the auspices of the American Cancer Society, is Reach to Recovery, which deals with the physical, emotional, and social impact of mastectomy.

Another group, Make Today Count, helps patients with cancer and other life-threatening diseases to lead more productive lives.

## Evolution and development

Historically the function of support groups was fulfilled by craft guilds, local parish organizations, and religious communities devoted to long-term care of the sick and the disabled. Later, colonial Americans and pioneers on the frontier relied on one another in times of crisis, simply because there was no other resource. As long as the United States remained a nation of small towns and isolated farms, most people in need derived supportive care from the extended family or local religious institution. In the 19th century, with the growth of large, impersonal urban settlements, Americans began to form mutual aid societies, which were particularly beneficial to city dwellers living and working far from home and family. In the 1830s the French writer-historian Alexis de Tocqueville, traveling in the United States, expressed amazement at that uniquely American institution, the committee, which was the forerunner of the support group as we know it. De Tocqueville was impressed that neighbors could rally to solve community problems simply by delegating responsibility among themselves, on their own initiative and, he noted with some surprise, "without reference to any bureaucrat."

*Alcoholics Anonymous.* The oldest and largest of the 20th-century support groups is Alcoholics Anonymous (AA), founded in 1935 by two confirmed alcoholics who made a mutual pledge to help each other get and stay sober. Having already tried the best professional cures available—without success—they decided to develop a new method to stop drinking. The plan was simple: whenever either of them felt overwhelmed by the desire for alcohol, he would call upon the other for help in resisting the impulse to take a drink. Each man would be available when the other needed someone to talk to. By expanding the support network to other alcohol-

327

ics, the founders not only helped new members sober up but found that they could remain sober themselves. By the end of 1939 almost 100 people had been able to stop drinking with help from this system of mutual support. Their story was published in the book *Alcoholics Anonymous,* the title taken as the name of the new organization. By 1941, AA had 8,000 members in the United States; in 1976 there were one million worldwide.

*The AA model.* The success and growth of AA inspired the founders of other kinds of support groups. Many health-related groups copied aspects of the AA model—small local chapters, frequent meetings, the promise of confidentiality for participants, and round-the-clock availability of help. And, like AA, most groups are open to everyone, regardless of ability to pay. Mended Hearts, for example, is a support group for people undergoing heart surgery. Former heart patients visit preoperative patients to tell them exactly what to expect during and after the surgery. Members report that their own recovery and attitudes are improved by the experience of helping new patients.

## How a support group can help you

Most support groups for people with serious illnesses and permanent disabilities differ from Alcoholics Anonymous in one important respect—people with chronic or life-threatening illnesses cannot change the course of the disease by changing their attitudes or motivation. Instead, the support group concentrates on dealing with the consequences of the disease and helping the patient cope with emotional and practical concerns.

*Emotional benefits.* If you—or a member of your family—are facing a serious illness, a support group can help you to end the feelings of isolation often produced by the physical, emotional, and financial strains of serious illness. Left alone in a sickroom, a patient may imagine that no one else suffers from *his* disease; he is afraid that his case is the *worst* or that being sick is somehow his *fault.* Support groups help both patients and families overcome these anxieties and guilt feelings by sharing them with others who have had the same feelings and experiences. In an effective support group patients change their perceptions of illness. Called upon to be active in helping, to focus on the needs of someone else, they feel less passive toward their own conditions and no longer see themselves as helpless victims. Groups challenge members to emphasize the things they *can* do instead of the things they cannot do.

*Practical help.* Another function of a support group is for the members to share the methods they have developed for coping with day-to-day problems. Whether it is information on making nutritious meals for cancer patients, how to feed a stroke victim, advice on summer camps for children with chronic illnesses, or suggestions about how to get effective help at local social

service agencies, the members of a support group can provide you with tested, useful advice. If they do not have the answers to your questions, they will try to find someone who does—and everyone in the group will probably benefit from the information.

## Limitations of groups

The group approach is not the solution for every patient. Many people are reluctant to discuss intimate problems with strangers, even though every support group has a policy of confidentiality. Nonetheless, some people would rather talk with one person, such as a priest, doctor, or therapist, who represents a tradition of privacy. Also, some people do not feel that help is valid unless it comes from a professional who charges a fee. Furthermore, while support groups supplement professional health care, they cannot replace it. (Some health-related support groups invite professionals to participate; others instead offer members referrals to competent professionals.) Support groups also demand a time commitment, particularly from those who organize and run the group. If you are already under stress because of serious illness or if your work or your family make heavy demands on your time, you may not be able to be an active member.

Unlike churches, clubs, and traditional volunteer organizations that have a stable membership from year to year and a consistent style from place to place, support groups change as their membership changes. This is particularly true of health-related groups, as the participants tend to evolve as they react to the different stages of their disease. Your personal needs will vary as your disease, family, and work change. Thus, a group that was helpful to you last year may now include new members with whom you have less in common.

## Finding a support group

*Your telephone book.* One place to begin looking for a support group is in the white pages of your telephone directory. The official names of most health-related support groups begin with the name of the illness—for example, the Lupus Erythematosus Society of Illinois—thus making it easy to find in the alphabetical listing. Many cities publish Community Pages in a special section of the phone book, and some cities operate an information and referral service. If your community has these services, try them first. The local United Way agency usually operates a free service for referrals to community agencies, as do some of the larger social welfare agencies; *e.g.,* the Salvation Army. These organizations are also listed in the phone book.

*Health professionals.* You may already know professionals—your physician, a nurse, social worker, pharmacist, therapist, or psychiatrist—who can refer you to an appropriate group. If you have been hospitalized, ask the social worker, discharge planner, or the chaplain at your hospital. If your child has been hospitalized at a children's hospital, talk to the public relations director at the hospital or the nurse clinician assigned to your child's hospital floor. Ask other families visiting the same ward. Try mental health centers, which give referrals for a variety of illnesses, not just for mental disorders. Of all the professional sources, the social worker is probably the best equipped to make referrals. Nearly all large hospitals have social service departments, and some of the bigger companies employ a social worker to help employees find special services.

*Newspapers, radio, and television.* The local communications media can be of help. If your daily newspaper carries a trouble-shooting column or an action line, contact the editor of the column. Features editors and health and science editors may also be potential resources. If you get a weekly newspaper, contact the reporter who covers your community or neighborhood. Check classified ads of local papers to see if any support groups are advertising for new members. The more specialized the publication, the more specialized the groups that advertise in it. *GayLife,* for example, lists support groups for gay people with special health and social concerns. Contact your local radio or television station's director of public affairs or the station manager—many stations feature a community bulletin board show, publicizing meetings of support groups and other organizations. Others provide phone referral services much like newspaper action lines.

*Self-help clearinghouses.* More than 20 cities in the United States have special clearinghouses that handle referrals to support or self-help groups. These generally operate through a local university or mental health center. The National Self-Help Clearinghouse at the Graduate School and University Center of the City University of New York has extensive mail and telephone facilities for referrals to local clearinghouses everywhere in the United States. It publishes a newsletter, *The Self-Help Reporter,* runs training programs for professionals and laypersons, publicizes the activities of self-help groups, and works to influence public policy. For a free nationwide list of clearinghouses write to: National Self-Help Clearinghouse, 33 W. 42nd Street, Room 1206-A, New York, N.Y. 10036. (Include a stamped, self-addressed envelope.)

Support groups in Europe may be located through the Information Centre of Research into Self-Help and Health, Eppendorf University Hospital, Pavillon 11, Martinistrasse 52, 2000 Hamburg 20, Federal Republic of Germany. This is a joint project of Self-Help Groups in Health (Hamburg) and the Regional Office for Europe of the World Health Organization (WHO/EURO). They can send you information packets for European groups in English or German.

*The public library.* If you cannot find a particular special-interest support group through local sources, you may have to contact the group's national headquarters. In many cases the local chapter is so small or so new that it operates from the home of one of the officers and has no office address or telephone. The national headquarters will know the local leaders and the newest groups in your area. If there is no existing group in your city or county, the national association can refer you to the nearest group in your state.

The addresses of national organizations are listed in the *Encyclopedia of Associations,* which can be found in most public libraries. In the 1983 edition, under "Health and Medical Organizations," there are more than 1,500 groups, organized into 29 categories. Volume 2 is organized geographically so that you can check on all groups in your area. The *Encyclopedia of Associations* makes no attempt to evaluate the organizations it lists. It merely prints the organization's description of its purpose and activities. Some obviously will not be appropriate to your needs; *e.g.,* professional associations, research foundations, or certain small groups advocating unproved methods of treatment. The larger, patient-oriented organizations probably will be most useful for you. Write the national office for the support groups active in your area and ask for any information about the organization and its purposes. Include a self-addressed, stamped envelope.

If you—or a member of your family—have a rare disease, find out if any of the larger organizations may serve your specific needs. For example, if your child is diagnosed with Werdnig-Hoffmann disease, you can get help from the Muscular Dystrophy Association, which has special programs for victims of 40 different neuromuscular diseases. The library is also a source of directories of support groups for special constituencies, such as handicapped children.

## How to start your own group

If you cannot find an existing support group for patients like yourself, you may want to start one of your own. If there is already a national association, write for its publications on starting a local group. Usually a national headquarters is eager to assist in the formation of new groups—some employ a staff member who helps founders of new groups, and some can supply the names of others in your area who share your concern.

If there is no national group, you will have to find other potential members in your area. Run a classified ad in local newspapers. Post information in the cafeterias and waiting rooms of local hospitals, clinics, mental health centers, medical schools, and pharmacies. Be sure to inform the local news media so they can refer people to the group. Your doctor and other health professionals can be of help. Although it is considered unethical for a physician to tell you the names of other patients with the same diagnosis, it is acceptable for a doctor to inform patients about a support group for their illness. Give your doctor cards with the name of the group, meeting times, and a telephone number where those interested can call for more information.

You can also ask a newspaper advice columnist to help you find members. A few years ago a reader wrote a syndicated advice column inquiring about a support group to help her care for her father, who had Alzheimer's disease; a column researcher discovered the then newly founded Alzheimer's Disease and Related Disorders Association (ADRA), which had just opened a national office in Chicago. The column suggested that the reader contact ADRA and printed its address. Within a month the association received 25,000 inquiries and helped all who responded to form more than 300 family support groups across the United States.

Finally, take every advantage of the human interest value of your effort. Talk to the feature editor of your newspaper and suggest a story on your attempt to find other people with the same illness. Appear on any television or radio talk show—even in the middle of the night. Write a story for the newsletter of your church, union, or neighborhood association. Speak to any local club. And tell everyone you know—word of mouth is still the best form of publicity.

At the present time there is keen interest in support groups for people with serious illnesses. This is only one part of the larger self-help movement, involving everything from home births to jogging. These groups are popular because they meet special individual needs—compassionate listening, worthwhile advice, and an end to isolation. A health-related support group may be the right answer for you, too.

### For further reading

Books about support groups and the needs of people with serious illnesses:

*Alcoholics Anonymous.* 3rd ed. New York: Alcoholics Anonymous World Services, 1976.

Graham, Jory. *In the Company of Others.* New York: Harcourt Brace Jovanovich, 1982.

Kelly, Orville. *Make Today Count.* New York: Delacorte Press, 1975.

Mace, Nancy L., and Rabins, Peter V. *The 36-Hour Day: A Family Guide to Caring for Persons with Alzheimer's Disease, Related Dementing Illnesses, and Memory Loss in Later Life.* Baltimore: Johns Hopkins University Press, 1981.

Wheat, Patte, and Lieber, Leonard L. *Hope for the Children: A Personal History of Parents Anonymous.* Minneapolis: Winston Press, 1979.

Books that can help you start your own support group:

Evans, Glen. "The ABC's of Beginning Your Own Self-Help Group." Chap. 12 in *The Family Circle Guide to Self-Help.* New York: Ballantine Books, 1979.

Flanagan, Joan. *The Successful Volunteer Organization: Getting Started and Getting Results in Nonprofit, Charitable, Grass Roots, and Community Groups.* Chicago: Contemporary Books, 1981.

Humm, Andy. *How to Organize a Self-Help Group.* New York: New York City Self-Help Clearinghouse, 1979.

### Selected support groups

Listed below are the names—and locations of national headquarters—of selected support groups in the field of health care.

Alcoholics Anonymous World Services (AA; New York City)

Living
c/o The Arthritis Foundation (Atlanta, Ga.)

American Cancer Society (New York City)
(includes Reach to Recovery for women who have had mastectomies)

Candlelighters (Washington, D.C.)
(for parents of children with cancer)

Cystic Fibrosis Foundation (Rockville, Md.)

DES ACTION, NATIONAL (New Hyde Park, N.Y.)

American Diabetes Association (New York City)

Epilepsy Concern (West Palm Beach, Fla.)

National Hemophilia Foundation (New York City)

National Hospice Organization (McLean, Va.)

Committee to Combat Huntington's Disease (New York City)

Leukemia Society of America (New York City)

Make Today Count (Burlington, Iowa)
(for people facing a life-threatening illness such as cancer)

Mended Hearts (Dallas, Texas)
(for people undergoing heart surgery)

Muscular Dystrophy Association (New York City)
(concerned with 40 neuromuscular diseases)

National Spinal Cord Injury Association (Newton Upper Falls, Mass.)
(concerned with paraplegia and other paralytic conditions)

Spina Bifida Association of America (Chicago)

*—Jory Graham and Joan Flanagan*

# Dizziness

Dizziness is a symptom, not a disease. It varies greatly in intensity from mild unsteadiness to an incapacitating disorientation. The term dizziness is a vague and general one that means different things to different people. Some use the term to describe unsteadiness when walking. To others, impending faintness or even brief loss of consciousness is described as dizziness. Because the sensations of lightheadedness or giddiness are difficult to describe, people frequently use the term when they experience these symptoms. Dizziness also includes the very disturbing sensation of vertigo. Vertigo is the illusion of motion—perceived either as if the environment were spinning around the individual or as if the individual were spinning within a stationary environment. Vertigo is commonly experienced by young children at play when they stop abruptly after rapidly turning about like tops.

## Normal balance

Ordinarily we are unaware of our normal balance and spatial orientation, which are maintained by several of the body's systems. Sensations from the eyes, inner ears, skin, muscles, and joints are carried by many nerves to the brain; there sensory information is integrated and interpreted in such a way as to provide us with a true picture of our relationship to the ground, space, and solid objects around us. Three basic types of information are sent to the brain: visual (from the eyes), sense of balance (from the inner ears), and orienting sensations of touch and position (from the skin, muscles, and joints).

Visual cues are helpful in perceiving the relationship of the body to familiar objects. Sight becomes less useful to orientation when there are no familiar landmarks in the visual field. A pilot flying through clouds, a diver in murky water, and an astronaut in space lose the contribution to bodily orientation provided by visual input. Persons with loss or distortion of vision (the latter sometimes caused by improper corrective lenses) may complain of dizziness because of the defective orienting information coming from their eyes.

The inner ears are complex structures that contain the principal organs of balance. They are organized into two major divisions—the cochlea, for hearing, and the vestibular system, for balance. The vestibular system is further divided into two parts, the vestibule and the semicircular canals. Three semicircular canals, each positioned in a different spatial plane, contain fluid that moves with every rotation of the head. The movement of this fluid stimulates sensory cells, which in turn send impulses to the brain. The vestibule includes the utricle and the saccule, each of which holds a single sensory structure, the macula, which contains calcium crystals. Gravity, head position, and linear acceleration—forward motion from a full stop; e.g., in a car—influence the position of these crystals, which in turn stimulate sensory cells to send impulses to the brain. Disorders of the inner ear can result in dizziness (as well as in hearing loss). Although the body may eventually adapt to the loss of the balance system in one ear, normally the two inner ears must function together to provide the symmetry needed for proper balance.

In addition to the eyes and inner ears, sensations emanating from the skin, muscles, and joints provide important information. These sites provide the brain with signals that supplement, and in some cases replace, the orienting impulses sent by the eyes and ears. For example, the pressure that is felt on the feet tells the brain that the body is upright. The aviators' expression "flying by the seat of his pants" refers to the pilot's ability to orient himself and his airplane without instruments when flying through clouds and weather that eliminate visual clues. Pilots learn to distinguish up and down and to differentiate a level position from a tilted one by the sensations of pressure exerted against their skin as it comes in contact with the airplane's seat. In a similar manner, nerve impulses from the body's joints provide information about body position and orientation to the brain. Disorders of the nerves and joints may thus cause the complaint of dizziness.

331

*Children at play often invent games and activities that purposely attempt to produce the temporary sensation of dizziness.*

The maintenance of balance and the prevention of dizziness depend on the normal functioning of these various mechanisms. The body can, however, learn to adjust to the complete loss of one of these systems. A blind person, for example, may learn to function quite well by depending on senses other than sight for orientation. If two of the systems are disabled, however, proper balance and orientation become extremely difficult. For instance, a person with loss of inner ear balance function may compensate adequately for this defect until placed in a dark room. The additional loss of visual information will make it difficult for that person to maintain balance and move about.

Two familiar instances of dizziness are associated with a normal reaction to unusual situations affecting the stimulation of the balance system: the view from an extreme height sometimes causes a sensation of dizziness, and the exaggerated movements of a boat or aircraft may result in the unpleasant condition known as motion sickness. Many normal people will also notice a very brief dizzy feeling if they get up too quickly from a

bed or chair. Dizziness not associated with these rather common situations may, however, be a symptom of an underlying disorder and should be evaluated.

## Causes of dizziness

As mentioned above, the sensation of dizziness occurs when there is a disorder of any of the systems that maintain normal balance. Vertigo is often the primary symptom of a disorder of the inner ear. Less commonly, a patient with an inner ear problem will complain of falling toward one side or the other. Because the inner ear contributes to the function of hearing as well as to that of balance, associated symptoms that accompany dizziness originating from this organ commonly include hearing loss, noises in the ear, and the sensation of pressure in the ear.

Various inner ear disorders are associated with the symptom of dizziness. Ménière's disease is a disorder of the inner ear of unknown cause; it produces symptoms of episodic vertigo, hearing loss, and ear noises. It rarely affects children and is uncommon in adults. The diagnosis is sometimes incorrectly applied to any disorder producing vertigo.

The balance system of the inner ear may also be affected by diseases that do not cause associated hearing loss. In one of these conditions, episodes of vertigo sometimes result when an ear that is defective is moved temporarily into a downward position. The patient becomes vertiginous when turning over in bed, for example, or when reaching upward to get something off a shelf. These episodes of vertigo occur only if the involved ear is positioned so as to trigger the disease mechanism in one of the semicircular canals. Fortunately this poorly understood disorder usually runs its course in several months and leaves no permanent sequelae, or aftereffects.

Sudden attacks of severe vertigo sometimes occur and persist for days, resolving without any residual symptoms. Presumably, these uncommon occurrences are due to viral infections of the ear's balance system. Ear infection, trauma, and certain drugs also may damage the inner ear balance system and produce vertigo and imbalance. Occasionally, tumors of the ear and its nerve produce these symptoms. Even ear wax can produce a vague sense of imbalance if it accumulates and blocks the ear canal. Because of the diversity of inner ear disorders that can result in dizziness, consultation with an ear specialist is usually necessary to determine the exact cause and appropriate treatment. It should be noted that the dizziness from inner ear disorders is commonly episodic, with normal periods occurring between the episodes. Faintness and loss of consciousness do not result from inner ear disorders. When these symptoms are present, problems of the inner ear may usually be ruled out as the probable cause of the patient's dizziness.

When impaired circulation to the brain is the cause of

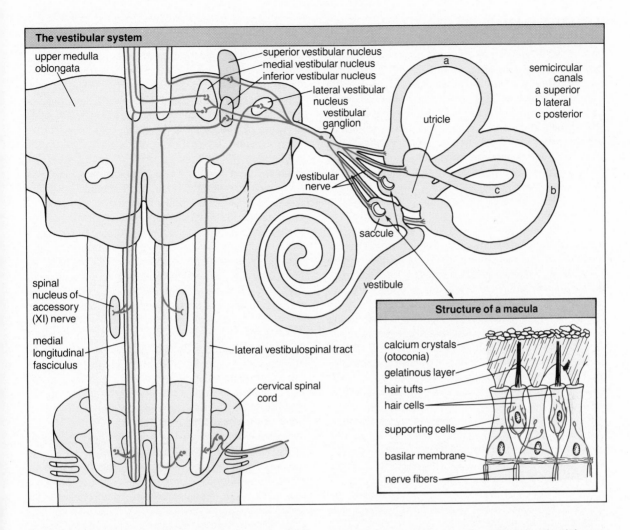

## The vestibular system

upper medulla oblongata

superior vestibular nucleus
medial vestibular nucleus
inferior vestibular nucleus
lateral vestibular nucleus
vestibular ganglion

semicircular canals
a superior
b lateral
c posterior

a

utricle

c

b

vestibular nerve

saccule

vestibule

spinal nucleus of accessory (XI) nerve

medial longitudinal fasciculus

lateral vestibulospinal tract

cervical spinal cord

### Structure of a macula

calcium crystals (otoconia)
gelatinous layer
hair tufts
hair cells
supporting cells
basilar membrane
nerve fibers

dizziness, symptoms of lightheadedness, faintness, vertigo, or loss of consciousness occur. The blood supply to the brain can be impaired as the result of complete obstruction or narrowing of its blood vessels. The vascular obstruction is usually due to atherosclerosis (hardening of the arteries) in older patients. Heart disease that produces an irregular pulse or a weakened cardiac pumping action or other conditions associated with abnormally low blood pressure may also result in diminished blood circulation to the brain and dizziness. The lowered blood pressure that is produced as a side effect of a wide variety of medications has similar manifestations. Dizziness from impaired circulation is often provoked by physical exertion and rapid changes in head position.

Degenerative diseases of or involving the brain (Parkinson's disease, multiple sclerosis, and others) can involve the nerve pathways of the various balance mechanisms. Depending on the site of the brain involved, the symptoms vary greatly from chronic unsteadiness to episodes of vertigo. Brain tumors can have the same effect. The seizures that occur with

epileptic incidents may produce dizziness, but it is usually evident that the accompanying episodic symptoms of impaired consciousness and convulsive body movements are due to the condition causing the seizure.

Disturbing episodes of rapid breathing (hyperventilation), often caused by anxiety, may be another reason for otherwise unexplained dizziness. The patient may be aware only of the lightheadedness and not of the excessively rapid breathing. Tingling sensations in the hands and feet and around the mouth accompany the dizziness of hyperventilation. Serious physical damage does not result from the temporary metabolic changes produced by hyperventilation, but the underlying emotional causes must be sought and treated.

Conditions causing hypoglycemia, or low blood sugar, can produce lightheadedness. When the level of blood sugar, or blood glucose, is low, the brain becomes deprived of this important nutrient, and the patient feels faint or dizzy.

Although all of the causes of dizziness cannot be covered in this discussion, it is evident that they are many and varied. Sometimes several of the causes combine to produce the dizziness commonly seen in the elderly. These patients have difficulty maintaining balance when walking or changing position. They may complain of lightheadedness but do not often have attacks of vertigo. Their symptoms are the result of the combined effects of degenerative diseases of several body systems, including reduced vision, impaired circulation, poor inner ear function, and other disabilities associated with the aging process. The dizziness, while disturbing, is not generally incapacitating, although it can be remedied only to the degree that each component of the process can be treated.

### Evaluation of symptoms

For the physician the first and most important step in the process of evaluating dizziness is a complete description of the symptoms. An accurate description may provide indications typical of a specific disease, or it may suggest intensive evaluation of a particular organ system. If, for example, a patient gives a typical history of Ménière's disease, extensive testing of the eyes, circulatory system, and brain can be avoided. The physician will attempt to characterize the dizziness as gradual or sudden in onset and persistent or episodic in occurrence; the diagnosis will also consider the exact nature of the sensation—vertigo, faintness, lightheadedness, etc.

Because the sensation of dizziness is so variously perceived, obtaining a meaningful medical history may be both time-consuming and difficult. An accurate history, however, can prevent needless tests. The history is followed by a physical examination, in which the physician looks particularly for abnormal eye movements or decreased vision, evidence of ear infection or impaired hearing, and irregular pulse or abnormal blood vessels. The physician also observes the patient's ability to stand erect or to walk without deviation of direction or tendency to fall toward one side.

There is no standard approach to laboratory testing of the dizzy patient, nor should there be; each patient must be evaluated individually. In some cases a diagnosis can be made without any such tests. A history of hyperventilation associated with anxiety and the physical finding of positional vertigo, for example, may be clearly characteristic of the underlying problem. On the other hand, when the cause of dizziness is obscure, extensive testing is needed to determine the precise cause and to rule out the possibility of serious disease.

### Diagnostic tests

If the inner ear is suspected as the cause of dizziness, tests of hearing and balance function may be indicated. Hearing tests not only measure hearing level but also supply information suggesting the site of the hearing loss. The inner ear balance system is tested by recording the patient's eye movements after changes in head position (test for positional vertigo) and through stimulation of the balance mechanism by pumping air or water through the ear canal. These tests detect abnormalities of the balance mechanism and provide some measure of the patient's functional loss.

To evaluate the cardiovascular system, an electrocardiogram (EKG) may be used to detect abnormal heart rhythms. Blood vessel flow studies and arteriograms will be needed if obstruction of blood vessels is suspected. Blood tests are sometimes indicated for dizziness to determine the presence of infections, hormonal abnormalities, or abnormal blood sugar levels.

An electroencephalogram (EEG) is performed if a seizure disorder is suspected. Computerized axial tomography (CAT scanning) of the head provides sophisticated X-ray images useful in the detection of certain neurologic disorders and tumors of the brain and ear.

### Treatment

The symptoms of dizziness should not be treated without accurate diagnosis of their cause. If a cause has been determined—or if the symptoms point to a particular avenue of investigation—referral to an appropriate medical specialist may be indicated for the management of the underlying disorder.

For hyperventilation and other psychological causes of dizziness, management of symptoms is directed at the underlying disturbance, and no other medical therapy may be needed. Some of the inner ear disorders are self-limited (motion sickness, positional vertigo, and viral infection); these require only symptomatic treatment with drugs that suppress the vestibular system. Ear surgery may be required in cases of infection, injury to the balance mechanism, or Ménière's disease. Vascular surgery can sometimes restore blood flow to the brain if the obstructed blood vessels can be repaired or replaced. Dizziness due to degenerative processes, however, is often resistant to medical management.

The symptom of dizziness is an alarming one, and its causes vary in degree of seriousness. Evaluation of dizziness may require sophisticated test procedures and consultation with medical specialists of various disciplines (otolaryngology, neurology, radiology, vascular surgery, ophthalmology, psychiatry, and others). Treatment may be medical or surgical, depending on the cause, although some cases of dizziness are transitory and may simply disappear with time.

*—Edward L. Applebaum, M.D.*

# Pain and the Cancer Patient

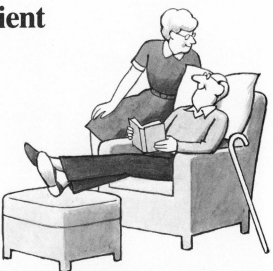

According to a Gallup poll taken in the late 1970s, cancer inspired greater fear in the U.S. population than any other affliction. This remains true today even though Americans survive cancer in greater numbers each year. More than half of the individuals who get cancer this year will live more than five years, and many will be cured of the disease. One reason cancer continues to be viewed with horror, however, is the nearly universal association of cancer and pain. In fact, having cancer should not be inevitably associated with experiencing pain. Likewise, cancer patients should never have to endure intractable pain.

The focus here is on the treatment of cancer pain rather than on treatment of the cause of the pain—the disease itself. The discussion is limited to the medical management of pain and does not consider the more extreme surgical measures, which may provide relief not available from drugs and other therapies.

## New discoveries about pain

*The physiology of pain.* Although few symptoms of illness are as old as pain, the physiology of pain is only beginning to be understood. Many agents for relief of pain (analgesics), from aspirin to narcotics, have long histories, but evidence of their effectiveness has, until recently, been based only upon observation. Their physiologic methods of action remained a mystery.

Real pain, from any site in the body, is ultimately "all in the head," for it is the brain alone that perceives the complex messages transmitted along pain fiber nerves and identifies the unpleasant sensation as pain. The brain localizes the sensation, and the higher centers of the brain interpret the message, registering severity and frequency and eliciting an appropriate response. The end result may be a simple one—*e.g.,* the reflex of withdrawing one's finger from a hot stove—or a complex physiologic adjustment to chronic pain.

Recent studies have revealed not only how the brain perceives pain but also how the brain treats its own pain. Certain drugs, such as lidocaine or procaine, commonly used in dentistry, temporarily block the pain message. Narcotics, however, do not stop the message of pain from being transmitted along the pain fiber nerves; instead, they deal with the direct perception of pain in the brain. Furthermore, research has disclosed that the brain produces its own narcoticlike substances, or natural opiates. These compounds, called endorphins and enkephalins, are synthesized by the brain in minute amounts that are extremely potent—20 to 30 times more powerful than morphine. They are produced as an immediate response to the stimulus of pain, and they continue to be formed even after the stimulus is withdrawn.

The discovery of the brain's capacity to produce pain-relieving chemicals has shed new light on several medical mysteries, including the basis of narcotic action and, possibly, the mechanism by which acupuncture affects pain. A tiny amount of electrical stimulation applied to the skin of a painful area sometimes relieves pain dramatically. This process, called transcutaneous electrical nerve stimulation (TENS), evidently produces endorphin activity deep within the central nervous system; this may well be the basis for a scientific explanation of acupuncture.

*Chronic and acute pain.* The so-called threshold for pain—the level at which an individual first perceives that "it hurts"—is remarkably similar for most people. The tolerance of pain, however, varies enormously. One difference in tolerance depends upon whether the pain is acute or chronic. Acute pain, as from a wound or burn, for example, is often more bearable than chronic pain. Acute pain generally begins to abate almost immediately after the injury. On the other hand, chronic pain may seem to become worse, even when no new injury is involved, or to be more severe than the source appears to warrant. The differences between acute and chronic pain are both physiologic and psychologic and are influenced greatly by therapeutic approach. Physicians are currently less knowledgeable about the physiologic factors but have made considerable progress in understanding the psychology of chronic pain and developing effective treatments.

Psychologically, acute pain has been described as linear; that is, the patient and the physician are well

335

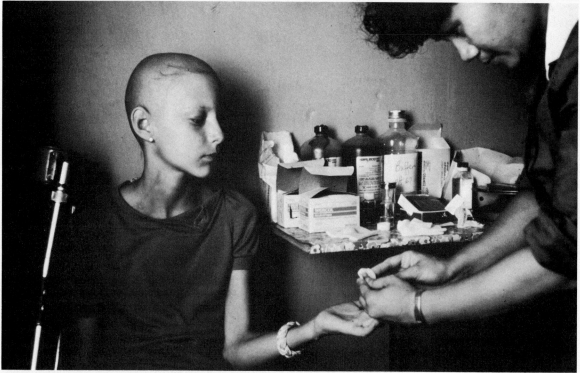

*Cancer patients can be kept free of pain and allowed to carry on normal lives in a nonhospital atmosphere; the child pictured above is attending a special camp for youngsters with cancer.*

aware of its onset and often can predict its cessation. It is comforting to know that the exquisite pain of a paper cut will have vanished by the next day and that even the pain of a fracture begins to ease the moment treatment begins. In contrast, chronic pain has been described as circular; that is, the time of its onset becomes blurred by its continuous, unceasing nature, and the end cannot be foreseen. Each perception of pain carries the reminder of past pain and the prediction of future pain, in a seemingly perpetual cycle. When drugs are withheld or when they are administered only intermittently, the patient's distress understandably increases. Cancer pain can be acute, after chemotherapy, irradiation, or surgery, for example, but if it becomes chronic both patient and doctor are likely to have different—and possibly divergent—views about how the pain should be alleviated.

## The physician's attitude toward pain

Doctors are usually willing to treat acute pain with strong analgesics, often by means of parenteral (injectable) narcotics. They are much less willing either to use oral narcotics or to administer drugs parenterally for the relief of chronic pain. For the cancer patient with chronic pain, the primary question thus becomes "Why does it appear that the doctor allows pain when it might be effectively prevented?"

Cancer patients and their families should be aware of the physician's attitude toward pain and its relief. No physician should resent a cancer patient's inquiry about how his pain will be treated, no matter how early in the course of the therapeutic relationship the question arises. Because of conflicting beliefs and opinions, neither physicians nor hospitals have consistent policies regarding the treatment of severe, chronic pain. It is not surprising that patients wonder why such a routine medical problem is so variously managed.

Physicians' concerns regarding the relief of pain, particularly chronic pain, are twofold: fear of the side effects of analgesics and fear of pharmacologic tolerance—or even true pharmacologic addiction. Side effects are the unintended actions or reactions produced by drugs. They vary from medication to medication and range in consequence from mild to lethal. Even the most common over-the-counter medications, those sold without prescription, carry some risks. Stronger prescription medications have potentially greater side effects. Narcotics such as codeine (available in dozens of oral formulations) or morphinelike drugs (in both oral and injectable forms) normally have broad actions on the body, many outside the realm of pain relief. Even small doses generally have some effect on the gastrointestinal tract—a slowing of muscular activity, for example, which may lead to constipation or nausea. Narcotics also affect the central nervous system, usually producing sedation or, in some cases, a euphoric reaction or a reduction in respiratory drive (the regulation of the normally automatic breathing response). Many doctors are concerned that the side effects themselves may become chronic, or even acute, problems.

The second area of concern is that of pharmacologic tolerance and addiction. Tolerance is the diminished response in any physiologic system to a given dose of a drug over a period of time (usually weeks or months). Addiction is the state in which there is both physical dependence upon the drug (*i.e.,* specific body disturbances follow the withdrawal of the agent) and a behavioral pattern of compulsive drug abuse. Incidence of addiction in patients with no previous history of drug abuse is demonstrably rare, however, and is probably lower among cancer patients than others. In one study of nearly 12,000 patients receiving drug treatment for cancer pain, four cases of addiction were documented.

Tolerance may be a greater problem for the cancer patient and the physician, and knowledge of the phenomenon is essential to both. Tolerance to the sedative properties of narcotics develops early in most patients; thus, although some sedation, or even sleep, may occur when a patient is first getting a sufficient amount of narcotic for pain relief, he or she should be reassured that this reaction will subside. Tolerance to the euphoric effect sometimes produced by narcotics occurs very rapidly; this factor is responsible for the dramatic escalation of dosage required by the drug

abuser or street addict who seeks only this effect. Because gastrointestinal tolerance is slow to develop, cancer patients must take measures to avoid such initial problems as constipation.

Tolerance to the one vital effect of narcotics sought by the cancer patient—pain relief—is variable. Eventually the alleviation of pain requires some increase in dosage for most people with chronic pain. Most studies of cancer patients show that the need for greater analgesic dosage is usually caused by increased activity of the disease, not by drug tolerance. When a patient is no longer obtaining relief from the prescribed dose, he or she must tell the physician so that further diagnostic evaluation of the pain or adjustment of medication, or both, can be made.

### Effective management of pain

The psychologic aspects of pain are perhaps less subtle than the physiologic ones; certainly, they are better understood and are being dealt with more effectively. The methods of chronic pain control used in Britain have been far more advanced than those employed traditionally in the United States. The hospice movement, based on the idea that patients dying of cancer and other diseases can be treated in a nonhospital environment with primary attention to comfort, particularly freedom from pain, has been growing in the United States. One of the more effective pain control regimens developed in British hospices is the so-called Brompton mixture, or the Brompton cocktail, named for

*Transcutaneous electrical nerve stimulation (TENS)—the application of low-voltage electrical current to the skin over a painful area—provides dramatic relief for some kinds of chronic pain.*

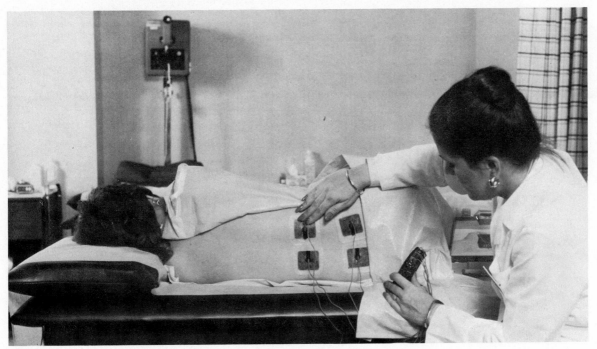

Sidney Tabak

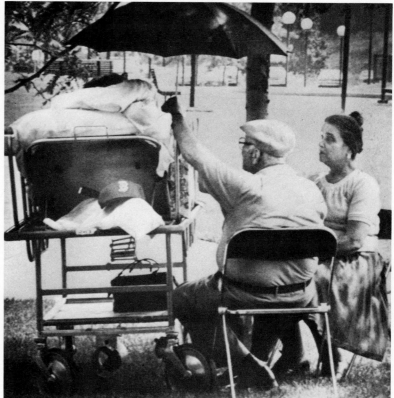

*Increasingly U.S. physicians are expressing the view that the terminally ill deserve to end their lives in comfort, free of pain and in the company of their loved ones. Here a young patient at the University of Massachusetts Hospital, Worcester, enjoys a fresh-air visit with his grandparents.*

the English hospital where it was first used. The original "cocktail" was a mixture of several analgesics, including a potent narcotic, with a palatable syrup and water. Heroin was used in Britain, but because it is not legally available in the United States, other morphinelike substances are usually substituted and have been demonstrated to provide equally effective pain relief. Cocaine has also been tried in such regimens, although subsequent research has shown that the morphinelike substance is the essence of the relief, and morphine-based formulations have fewer side effects and lower abuse potential. It appears, however, that the formula is less important than the pattern of administration.

In the management of acute pain, physicians commonly order analgesics on a "PRN" basis; this, from the Latin *pro re nata* ("according to circumstances"), means that the medication is administered "as needed," with the expectation that the need will gradually decrease as healing progresses. Because of the constant, cyclic nature of chronic pain, however, this is often a poor means of administration and is likely to increase the patient's discomfort rather than reduce it.

Given at regular intervals, *e.g.,* every four hours, rather than PRN, an analgesic can prevent the physiologic effects of increased pain and shatter the vicious cycle of pain–relief of pain–more pain–increased need for

relief. The patient experiences longer intervals of relief, and the memory of acute pain is no longer a constant reminder of the pain itself. The regular use of analgesics actually decreases the risk of drug dependence. Furthermore, the dosage of analgesic needed to alleviate an existing level of pain is larger than the dosage required to prevent recurrent increases in the level of chronic pain. Once pain control is assured, the patient is better able to contend with the other aspects of chronic illness. Likewise, the physician is free to deal with other aspects of the disease. Finally, rational use of analgesics usually helps to prevent adversarial relationships between doctor and patient, doctor and family, and family and patient.

Chronic pain must be treated with whatever medication at whatever dosage provides relief for the patient. Most cancer patients will accept a tolerable degree of pain, particularly if increased dosage of medication or more frequent administration produces undesirable side effects. Clearly, better understanding of the nature of pain—by physicians, patients, and patients' families—is the key to its most effective management and to the maximum comfort of the cancer patient.

*—Jory Graham*
*and John M. Merrill, M.D.*

# Eating Well from the Start

Parents, it seems, have always worried about what their children eat. Now, with evidence that proper childhood nutrition is important for adult health and longevity, parents are even more concerned that their children establish good eating habits. Getting children to eat the right foods can be a difficult, upsetting, and often unsuccessful task. Few things are more frustrating than seeing a child refuse a nutritious meal only to fill up on junk food and snacks. The situation becomes worse as the child grows older, and parents find it increasingly difficult to exercise control over the diet. Despite their best efforts, parents find that outside influences, such as television advertising and the accessibility of school vending machines and fast-food establishments, contribute to eating habits of questionable nutritional value.

### The child's diet: what's right?

The consensus among experts is that proper nutrition starting in infancy can help protect against many dangerous and potentially lethal disorders, among them arteriosclerotic heart disease, hypertension, diabetes, and cancer. Although more and more parents understand the importance of their role in shaping a child's food preferences, they usually do not know how to influence the youngster's tastes. What parents need from professionals are not lectures about encouraging children to eat properly but specific guidelines and suggestions to help them achieve this goal.

Physicians repeatedly hear parents voice the same concerns about children's diets. The following are some of the most commonly asked questions:

1. To what extent should I push my child to eat?

2. Is there anything I can do to help stimulate my child's poor appetite?

3. Why are some children picky eaters, while others eat practically everything on their plates?

4. Is there any relationship between the eating habits of parents and those of their children?

5. Are babies born with natural cravings for sugar or salt?

6. Can a child who makes his or her own food selections be trusted to choose what is healthful?

7. How can adults, who have so much trouble breaking bad eating habits, expect their children to eat more sensibly than they do?

*Sugar and salt.* In 1982, according to figures from the U.S. Department of Agriculture, the average annual per capita consumption of caloric sweeteners (sugar, honey, and corn sweeteners) in the United States was 56 kg (123 lb). It is clear from this statistic that most of us, including our children, eat too much sugar. Getting a youngster to cut down on the daily intake of sweets is not easy. The craving for sweets has a long history. A cave painting found in southern Spain, estimated to be some 20,000 years old, shows a Neolithic man stealing honey from a bees' nest. One theory proposes that early man used sweetness as an indicator in food selection because most sweet-tasting foods were safe to eat. Although it is not known for certain if the taste is genetic or acquired, there is evidence that the human desire for sweets is innate. Studies have shown that taste buds are already present in a four-month-old fetus. At five months fetal swallowing rate increases when a sweet stimulus is injected into the amniotic sac. Further, newborns exhibit positive responses to various sweet solutions but are indifferent to salty solutions. Breast milk, the first food of most infants, is relatively sweet to the taste.

While the taste for sweetness may indeed be genetic, the taste for overly sweetened foods is definitely acquired. Most infants will drink regular, unsweetened water. But a baby who becomes accustomed to sugar water usually will refuse to drink unsweetened water. It is evidently very easy for a baby to develop the taste for oversweetened foods. If parents are taught not to add sugar to water or baby foods, it is much less likely that children will grow up craving and consuming enormous quantities of sugar. Reducing a baby's daily intake of sugar not only will reduce early dental decay but also will reduce those extra calories in the diet that often cause a predisposition to obesity. Another reason to avoid added sugar is the evidence that excessive sugar intake predisposes to elevated levels of fats in the

## Nutritive values of some fast-food favorites

| | serving size | calories | fat | carbohydrates | total sugars | sodium |
|---|---|---|---|---|---|---|
| **hamburgers** | | | | | | |
| Burger King Whopper | 9 oz | 660 | 41 g | 49 g | 9 g | 1,083 mg |
| Jack-in-the-Box Jumbo Jack | 8¼ | 538 | 28 | 44 | 7 | 1,007 |
| McDonald's Big Mac | 7½ | 591 | 33 | 46 | 6 | 963 |
| Wendy's Old Fashioned | 6½ | 413 | 22 | 29 | 5 | 708 |
| **sandwiches** | | | | | | |
| Roy Rogers roast beef | 5½ | 356 | 12 | 34 | 0 | 610 |
| Burger King chopped beef steak | 6¾ | 445 | 13 | 50 | 0.7 | 966 |
| Hardee's roast beef | 4½ | 351 | 17 | 32 | 3 | 765 |
| Arby's roast beef | 5¼ | 370 | 15 | 36 | 1 | 869 |
| **fish** | | | | | | |
| Long John Silver's | 7½ | 483 | 27 | 27 | 0.1 | 1,333 |
| Arthur Treacher's Original | 5¼ | 439 | 27 | 27 | 0.3 | 421 |
| McDonald's Filet-O-Fish | 4½ | 383 | 18 | 38 | 3 | 613 |
| Burger King Whaler | 7 | 584 | 34 | 50 | 5 | 968 |
| **chicken** | | | | | | |
| Kentucky Fried snack box | 6¾ | 405 | 21 | 16 | 0 | 728 |
| Arthur Treacher's Original | 5½ | 409 | 23 | 25 | 0 | 580 |
| **specialty entrees** | | | | | | |
| Wendy's chili | 10 | 266 | 9 | 29 | 9 | 1,190 |
| Pizza Hut Pizza Supreme | 7¾* | 506 | 15 | 64 | 6 | 1,281 |
| Jack-in-the-Box taco | 5½† | 429 | 26 | 34 | 3 | 926 |

* One-half of a 15½-oz, 10-in Pizza Supreme Thin and Crispy.
† Two 2¾-oz tacos.

the common mistake of tasting food before offering it to the baby. If they find it is too bland for the adult palate, they assume that the baby will also find it so. A number of investigations have shown that salt preference often clearly exists in children of preschool age. Once a youngster has acquired a taste for salt, he has a very difficult time losing it. Obviously, then, if the desire is not encouraged during the first few years of life, when most of a child's meals are eaten at home, the intense craving for salt is less likely to develop.

*Fruits and vegetables.* Surveys of the dietary habits of U.S. children also show that many have diets deficient in fruit and vegetable intake. In order to have a balanced, nutritious diet, a child must eat four or more servings daily from the vegetable-fruit group. These foods, in addition to providing vitamins, particularly vitamins A and C, are an important source of natural sugars and starches. Fruits and vegetables, along with whole grains, are also an essential source of dietary fiber, or roughage. Fiber, the indigestible residues found in plant tissues, is not an actual nutrient. It contributes to efficient digestive function and is believed to protect against certain gastrointestinal diseases. Fiber also affects the health of teeth and gums. Authorities on nutrition believe that many diseases, such as diverticulitis and cancer of the colon, are prevalent in Western society because processing removes most of the indigestible fiber from the carbohydrate foods that constitute a major part of the diet in developed countries. Studies of dietary factors and cancer have shown that cancer of the colon and rectum have lower rates of incidence among people whose diets are high in fiber. A possible explanation for this finding is that a high-fiber diet helps food pass more quickly through the digestive tract, thus allowing the food less time to react with certain digestive enzymes in potential cancer-causing ways. Finally, recent evidence suggests that a diet high in fiber is associated with a lowered incidence of cardiovascular disease—possibly because a high-fiber diet generally is lower in saturated fats. At any rate, the evidence is overwhelming that fruits and vegetables are essential for good health and should constitute a significant portion of a child's diet. The development of a taste for fruits and vegetables, especially during the first few years of life when the child eats most meals at home, is the most effective way to establish these foods as part of a lifelong dietary pattern.

*Dietary fats.* The National Academy of Sciences currently recommends that no more than 30% of an individual's total daily caloric intake be obtained from fats. Two major culprits have been implicated as contributing to hardening of the arteries that leads to coronary heart disease: cholesterol, a fat that is produced in the normal human liver, and lipoproteins, fat-protein combinations also formed in the liver. Both also exist in certain foods. Excesses of either cholesterol or lipoproteins can accumulate on the interior walls of blood

blood, which can lead eventually to atherosclerotic heart disease.

The daily consumption of salt in the United States is also much too high and, although there is no proof that excessive salt causes hypertension, it has been shown that blood pressure can be lowered by reducing daily salt intake. As stated earlier, newborn infants are indifferent to salty-tasting solutions; the craving for salty foods is not inherent or genetic but is acquired after birth. Thus, if parents do not add extra salt to baby foods, the infant will not acquire a taste for salt. Baby foods contain enough salt to satisfy all of a child's nutritional needs. Nonetheless, many parents make

*Exposure to a variety of foods at an early age helps children broaden their tastes and preferences. Some youngsters are eager to try new foods, while others need some time and gentle encouragement.*

vessels and can eventually impede or prevent blood flow through affected vessels. This can lead to either a heart attack or a stroke. According to the American Heart Association, reducing total fat intake in the diet is one of the most important steps toward reducing the incidence of coronary artery disease. The association advocates that adults and all children in high-risk categories, such as those who have a family history of early heart disease, be placed on the so-called prudent diet. The prudent diet is low in both cholesterol and lipoproteins. Because egg yolk has the highest cholesterol concentration of any food (250 mg per egg), the diet allows no more than three to four eggs per week. Daily consumption of cholesterol should not exceed 300 mg. A diet low in cholesterol is usually also low in lipoprotein. The prudent diet limits the amount of red meats—such as beef and pork—which are high in saturated animal fats, and encourages their replacement with lean meats—poultry, fish, veal—lower in saturated fats. Other foods that are high in cholesterol—butter, whole milk, and cheese—should be avoided in favor of low-fat or skim milk and low-fat cheeses. Many authorities on childhood nutrition are now begininng to recommend the prudent diet not only for children at high risk for heart disease but for all children, the goal being to prevent atherosclerosis and to establish basic nutritional practices that will carry over into adulthood.

## Food psychology

In addition to establishing good dietary practices and influencing a child's choice of foods, parents can help to instill positive eating habits by their attitudes toward eating problems. Encouraging your child to eat the right foods need not entail a battle of conflicting wills; the association of meals with arguments is certain to result in negative feelings about eating in general.

One fact parents should understand is that appetite varies from child to child. Some children eat voracious-ly; others are very particular about what and how much they eat. The rule for parents, beginning with an infant's first meals, is never to force-feed. Mealtime should be a pleasant experience; coercing or cajoling the child to eat another spoonful of this or that is not only ineffective but probably counterproductive. If a child is given a proper variety of foods, he or she will eat enough to satisfy all the basic nutritional needs. It is also important to remember that appetite increases during periods of rapid growth, in the first year of life, for example, and during adolescence, and decreases when growth slows down. A child is perfectly capable of deciding when a meal is finished and his hunger satiated. In fact, every person—infant, child, teen, or adult—should eat when hungry and stop eating when full. There is little a parent can do to increase a child's appetite. So-called tonics are not effective and should not be used. A child has a much better chance of developing proper adult eating habits if he is not urged to eat when not hungry. This attitude on the part of the parent can also reduce the incidence of childhood obesity, which so often leads to adult obesity.

Since appetites vary so much from child to child and from day to day, there is no point in begging or pleading. There is also no reason to use food as a reward (*e.g.,* "If you finish your spinach, I will give you a piece of cake.") or to equate food with love (*e.g.,* "If you love your mother, you will finish the carrots."). These tactics usually do not work; furthermore, they start a chain of feelings that may eventually lead to more serious problems, including binge eating, overeating as a response to depression, and an overall sense of unpleasantness associated with mealtimes and with food.

On the other hand, keeping a child active is an effective and useful method to stimulate appetite. Activity and exercise also burn up extra calories, thus helping to maintain proper weight. Choice negotiation and compromise are practical forms of inducement. Whenever possible, children should be given a choice of nourishing foods. It is more likely that a child will eat one of two vegetables served rather than one presented with no option. If the child simply refuses to eat a particular dish, the parent may compromise by substituting something that the child will eat. However, it is important not to substitute an unhealthful food for the one that was refused.

A reasonable and gently persuasive approach is likely to be more effective than begging, pleading, or threatening. The child will probably respond positively to statements such as, "This vegetable will make you stronger and help you run faster" or "This fruit will help keep your complexion looking nice," as opposed to authoritarian dictates such as, "You had better eat this; it's good for you."

Like adults, children develop preferences for certain foods and dislikes for others. Their tastes also vary as they mature. Within reason these preferences should be considered in the planning of meals. Again, suitable alternatives may provide an element of choice—a child who refuses to eat cooked cabbage because of its odor may be perfectly happy eating coleslaw.

The habit of between-meal snacking is another area where parents must take a more active and positive role. Studies have shown that 30 to 50% of all the calories consumed by U.S. children are eaten between meals, and a large proportion of these snacks consists of nonnutritious foods, high in empty calories, sugar, and salt. While parents deplore such foods, it is usually a parent who buys them and brings them into the home. There are two ways to discourage a child from eating junk foods: first, limit their availability, and second, provide healthful, ready-to-eat snacks instead. Stock up on nutritious snacks, such as fruits, vegetables, yogurt, cheese, and fruit juices. Since most children like so-called finger foods, it may be helpful to prepare snack foods in an attractive way; *e.g.,* carrot sticks, bite-sized chunks of cheese. As children spend more time outside the home, inevitably they will be exposed to all sorts of junk foods, but parents need not become policemen in this situation. An occasional sweet snack is not harmful as long as it does not take the place of regular, nutritious meals.

School-age children and adolescents eat tremendous amounts of so-called fast foods. The McDonald's restaurant chain recently claimed that they sell about 700 million lb of hamburger and 542 million barrels of french fried potatoes each year. Although there is some nutritive value to the various fast foods, they are comparatively high in calories, fat, and salt and low in fiber content. Again, parents cannot eliminate such foods from their children's diets, but they can provide nutritionally balanced meals at home and instill in children the importance of eating sensibly.

Finally, in terms of their attitudes toward food and eating, parents should be aware of the kind of example they set. The most significant role models in childrens' lives are their parents. This holds true for bad habits as well as good. If children see their parents eating a varied and nutritious diet, they are more likely to do so themselves. If parents are open-minded about food and willing to try new foods, the child will probably develop similar attitudes. Certainly, parents cannot expect a child to develop good eating habits if these are not learned early in life—at home.

Getting your child to eat properly is a difficult undertaking. Nonetheless, mothers and fathers must not abdicate their responsibility in this area of parenting, despite the outside pressures that make the task so frustrating. Your child may not thank you now, or ever, but will appreciate the strength, vigor, and general good health he or she is more likely to enjoy later in life.

*—Alvin N. Eden, M.D.*

# "Morning Sickness"

During the first trimester of pregnancy (*i.e.,* the first three months) more than 50% of women experience some degree of nausea, which sometimes leads to vomiting. These symptoms are often called morning sickness, although they may occur at any time of day—morning, noon, or night—and in some cases persist all day long. Although unpleasant, they are so common that they must be considered a normal, if uncomfortable, accompaniment of early pregnancy. It is intriguing that the human female is the only animal known to be affected by vomiting due to normal pregnancy. Nausea during pregnancy is not a modern affliction; it was clearly described in a papyrus dated about 2000 BC and was referred to by Hippocrates and by the Greek physician Soranus of Ephesus (2nd century AD). Many subsequent authors have described the condition and speculated on its causes and treatment.

Although nausea and vomiting are frequent and normal in pregnancy, it must be remembered that many other disorders may cause these symptoms. Examples of other such conditions are gastritis, appendicitis, dietary indiscretions, hepatitis, gallbladder disease, bowel obstruction, and certain infections. Also, some disorders of pregnancy may cause vomiting; for example, hydatidiform mole, in which no fetus develops, but the placenta becomes enlarged and cystic.

Infrequently, the vomiting in an otherwise normal pregnancy becomes intractable, resulting in dehydration, metabolic disturbances, and, very rarely, coma and death—a condition known as hyperemesis gravidarum. Since the 1940s, the incidence of this condition has decreased markedly, and resultant death has become exceedingly rare—almost certainly because of a better understanding of the condition and the availability of modern fluid and metabolic management.

## Symptoms

Nausea may first appear before the woman is aware that she is pregnant, sometimes even before she misses her first period. Accompanying or preceding the nausea, she may notice an increased sensitivity to or intolerance of certain odors and a change in food tastes and preferences. Sometimes there is a strong desire for unusual foods (pica), and often salivation is increased (ptyalism). The nausea may occur on first awakening but may develop at any time of the day or continue throughout the day. Often the nausea is worst

and most frequent when the stomach is empty, but it may also occur after eating certain foods (usually fatty foods) or when the stomach is full.

Some women will begin to vomit if the nausea increases, but occasionally, episodes of vomiting can be startlingly sudden and without preceding nausea. With correct eating habits and, in some cases, medical therapy, these symptoms usually remain mild and, very frequently, subside with surprising suddenness in about the 12th week of pregnancy. Less fortunate women have symptoms of longer duration or even, rarely, lasting through the entire pregnancy.

Infrequently, the condition worsens steadily in an insidious manner with persistent vomiting. All intake of food and fluid ceases or is vomited soon after ingestion. If untreated, the patient becomes dehydrated, with sunken eyes and dry tongue, and acetone can be found in the blood and urine. The acetone results from the incomplete breakdown of body fat associated with inadequate intake of carbohydrates. As the condition worsens, a number of further metabolic derangements occur, with resultant depletion of body electrolytes and decrease in glucose, glycogen, and other essential energy stores. The pulse rate rises; the urine volume decreases with retention of metabolic waste products; and, finally, drowsiness may precede coma and death.

## Causes

The obvious cause of the nausea is the pregnancy, but the specific causative factors are still unknown. Current theories can be classified as hormonal, allergic, nutritional, and emotional.

*Hormonal.* Some evidence for hormonal causes has been reported, having to do with excess production of or sensitivity to a hormone (chorionic gonadotropin) produced by the placental tissue, but research in this area is not conclusive. Other hormones that are known to cause nausea, such as estrogen, are produced in large amounts during pregnancy and could possibly play a causative role.

*Allergic.* Theories proposing an allergic cause for the nausea are based on very flimsy and peripheral evidence. The strongest evidence supporting such theories is the apparent effectiveness of antihistamine drugs in the treatment of the nausea.

*Nutritional.* There is no substantial evidence to implicate nutritional causes. Vitamin $B_6$ is popular as a treatment, but its effectiveness has not been conclusively proved.

*Emotional.* Most observers agree that emotional factors play some part in severe vomiting associated with pregnancy, but it is most unlikely that they play any significant role in the causation of nausea during pregnancy. Many patients with hyperemesis gravidarum, on the other hand, are emotionally immature, are overly dependent, and have a history of psychosomatic complaints. Their success in interpersonal relationships is often low. Their favorable response to treatment with sedation, emotional support, and limited psychotherapy often confirms the importance of emotional factors.

*Other factors.* Nausea and vomiting appear to be more frequent in multiple pregnancy (twins or more) and also if there has been a previous history of hyperemesis gravidarum or of unsuccessful pregnancies. There is no relationship to race, color, or ethnic background, to the number of previous pregnancies, or to the marital status of the mother.

## Treatment

There are many references to the treatment of vomiting in pregnancy in historical medical writings. One of the earliest such documents, by Soranus, is notable because so much of his advice on diet is sensible by modern standards. Treatment methods in later centuries may have been more dangerous at times, ranging from cupping (the application of warmed cups to the skin, which attached by suction as they cooled) to frequent enemas and periods of starvation. The modern treatment of nausea in pregnancy consists largely in noninterference—based on the sensible principle of doing no harm while treating what is usually a benign, natural, and self-limiting symptom.

The pregnant woman should be made aware of the commonness of the symptom and its benign course. Fears that the pregnancy is abnormal should be allayed after appropriate examination. Emotional support and sympathy from family and physician are important. Sufficient rest should be advised, but participation in normal daily tasks and social activities should also be encouraged.

General principles of good nutrition should be followed, but odors and foods that aggravate the nausea should be avoided. These foods are usually fatty, oily, or heavily spiced. Fluid intake should be high, but many women find that drinking large quantities rapidly may cause nausea; thus, fluid should be taken frequently in small amounts. Most helpful of all is the rule never to allow the stomach to become empty. Some crackers should be eaten immediately after waking up and again just before going to sleep. Frequent small meals or snacks should be eaten throughout the day. If vitamin tablets cause nausea they should not be taken until nausea ceases. Although the woman may feel that emptying the stomach would relieve the nausea, the desire to vomit should be resisted if at all possible because, once started, vomiting becomes more frequent. Also, if salivation is increased, the natural tendency to expectorate (spit out) the extra saliva should be resisted, and the saliva should be swallowed.

These measures will, in the great majority of instances, be found to control the symptoms satisfactorily. However, in about 10 to 20% of those who become nauseated, the symptom is persistent and interferes with daily living. Formerly in such cases, the antinausea (antiemetic) drug Bendectin was prescribed, but in June 1983 Bendectin was removed from the market by the manufacturer as a result of lawsuits alleging instances of fetal malformation. However, no proof of danger to the fetus has been shown. Some physicians believe that the injection of multiple vitamin preparations may alleviate the nausea to some degree.

In those rare instances where vomiting becomes frequent and persistent and little or no nourishment is retained, further medical care is imperative. The physician will usually admit the patient to a hospital and perform tests to rule out other illnesses. Intravenous fluid therapy, balanced to provide necessary calories, electrolytes, and vitamins, is essential. No oral intake will be allowed at first. Counseling and emotional support will be provided. A great majority of patients improve rapidly on such a regimen, and oral intake of food and fluids will be gradually resumed. When the patient is taking nourishment comfortably and has started gaining weight, she can usually return home but should be examined frequently at the physician's office.

## Effects on the mother and infant

The very common nausea and infrequent vomiting of early pregnancy have no significant discernible effect on the mother or fetus, particularly if the mother follows sound nutritional advice. Nausea and vomiting may contribute to slight weight loss or only minimum weight gain in the first 12 weeks of pregnancy.

As described earlier, severe vomiting can lead to quite serious, acute illness in the mother but with successful treatment has not been found to cause any lasting effects on either mother or fetus. The infants born at full term after such an episode in early pregnancy have no detectable abnormalities. In fact, some studies correlate nausea and vomiting in pregnancy with lower miscarriage and newborn disease rates. Thus, despite the discomfort involved, most women find they can tolerate the nausea of pregnancy as a harbinger of the exciting event to come.

*— Lionel J. Schewitz, M.D.*

# Nails

As the discovery of gold-painted nails on Egyptian mummies shows, the decorating of nails is an ancient custom. The Chinese mandarins cultivated such extraordinarily long fingernails that they were virtually unable to use their fingers and hands for any practical activities. Even today, in many cultures, long fingernails connote wealth, ease, and social prominence, suggesting that the wearer need not perform manual labor.

Nails, however, are functional as well as decorative. Forming a solid plate that backs up the soft pads at the ends of fingers and toes, nails help us to pick up and to manipulate small objects. Nails also protect the tips of fingers and toes from injury. Fingernails, moreover, are a well-designed, readily accessible tool for scratching.

Like the skin and hair, nails reflect overall bodily health. Nail growth and appearance may be affected by systemic illness, local infection, and dietary deficiencies. However, nail growth and appearance also are susceptible to environmental and other external factors—including occupational damage and habits such as nail biting—thus sometimes making it difficult to assess all changes in nails.

## How nails grow

Nails appear to grow continuously, unlike hair, which has cyclic periods of active growth and dormancy. Researchers have demonstrated that the rate of nail growth, like that of hair growth, varies from person to person and is different for each nail. As a general rule, fingernails grow roughly 0.1 to 0.12 mm a day, or 0.1 in per month, which is two to four times as fast as toenails and about one-third more slowly than hair. Hence, fingernails take three to six months to completely replace themselves, while toenails may take a year or longer. The longer the finger, the larger the center of nail growth and the more rapid the growth; the nail on the middle finger grows the fastest.

As people age, their nails grow more slowly and become thicker. Nails also grow faster in a warm environment than in a cool one. However, even in climates with marked seasonal changes, heating and air conditioning eliminate any dramatic weather-related changes in the rate of nail growth. Biting, typing, and other minor traumas cause fingernails to grow about 20% faster than usual, most likely because the frequent manipulation of the nail stimulates its growth center. Immobilization, as by paralysis or temporary encasement of the arm, leg, finger, or toe in a cast, slows growth. Viral illnesses such as mumps and influenza may slow or even stop growth temporarily; other illnesses—psoriasis, for example—accelerate it. Pregnancy causes nails to grow as much as a third faster than usual. Furthermore, the nails of one's dominant hand grow faster than those of the other hand.

The folk belief that nails and hair continue to grow after death, although false, is based on an understandable visual illusion. Following death, a decrease in the water content of body tissues causes the skin to contract. When skin pulls away at the margin, the nail appears more prominent and, therefore, longer. Similarly, as the skin shrinks in the beard area of a man's face, whiskers are more visible and seem to grow.

Nails, like hair, are composed primarily of a tightly packed collection of cells composed of the protein keratin. Nails begin to form in about the tenth week of human fetal life. Each nail grows from a nail matrix, which is located at the base of the nail and extends backward beneath the skin about 1 cm ($3/_8$ in), or nearly to the first joint of the finger. Part of the matrix usually is visible on the thumbnail, the nail of the index finger, and sometimes the other nails as well. This area, called the lunula, or half-moon, marks the site at which the nail matrix ends and the nail bed begins. Blood vessels in the nail bed give nails their pinkish coloration. If the matrix is damaged, the surface of the nail will be distorted or deformed. The soft tissue around the sides of the nail is known as the paronychium. The fold of skin at the edges of the nail, which keeps invading microorganisms from the nail matrix, is called the cuticle. At the free edge of the nail, a thin yellow-pink or brown-pink line marks the point at which the nail plate—the visible part of the nail—separates from the nail bed. The nail plate itself is dead tissue, and nothing that is applied to it will affect nail growth.

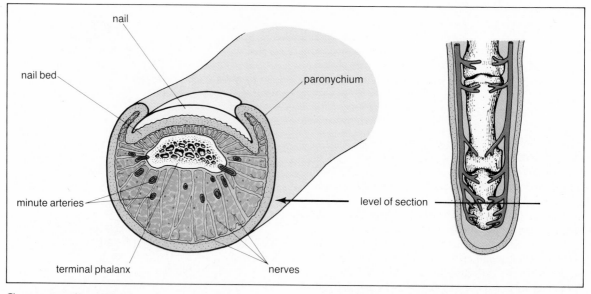

nail

nail bed

paronychium

minute arteries

terminal phalanx

nerves

level of section

## Common nail problems

Many common nail problems are primarily cosmetic in nature and do not require medical treatment. Common-sense nail care, along with the use of appropriate cosmetics, often helps to minimize or camouflage these aesthetic defects.

In addition to being unattractive, nails that break and split easily are a nuisance because they catch on fabrics and other surfaces. Such nails are best kept short; the application of several coats of nail polish may improve their appearance but will not alter their basic character. If polish is used, it should be removed as infrequently as possible; excessive exposure to soap and water also should be avoided to minimize further drying and cracking. Although the daily consumption of gelatin has been suggested as an aid to healthy nails, and some consumers attest to beneficial results, the medical consensus is that such claims are unfounded. Compared with fish, chicken, cheese, beans, and other sources of dietary protein, gelatin is a relatively low-quality protein, and there is simply no evidence that increased gelatin intake causes nails to become stronger or healthier.

A hangnail is a ragged flap of dead skin at the side of the nail, the result of a split in or near the cuticle. As hangnails are both uncomfortable and a potential source of infection, they should be removed with a clean, sharp scissors, taking care not to cut intact portions of the cuticle. To keep the cuticle soft and reduce the likelihood that hangnails will develop, hand creams or lotions should be worked carefully into the cuticle. The cuticle attaches the nails to the surrounding skin and forms a seal that protects the edges of the nails from infection; it should never be cut or trimmed.

Small white spots on nails indicate separations of the nail plate from the skin beneath it; these separations are generally the result of injury, including minor accidents, as well as overaggressive manicuring that involves trimming of the cuticles. A dark spot on a nail most likely is the result of hemorrhage, or bleeding, un-

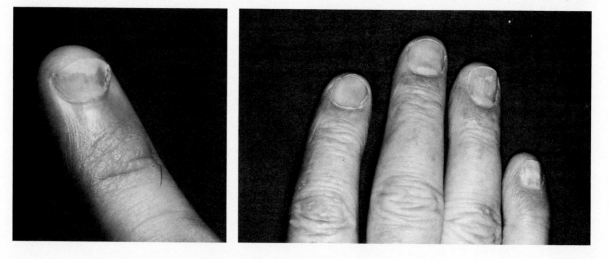

der the nail caused by trauma—such as hitting the nail with a hammer. The formation of a dark stripe running from the base to the tip of the nail may indicate a tumor of the nail matrix and requires medical attention. In the nails of black people, however, such streaks are fairly common and, unless they are newly developed, usually have no medical significance. A minor injury leaves only a local discoloration that grows out with the nail; a severe injury, however, may cause permanent damage. If one injures a nail, applying cold compresses immediately and elevating the affected hand or foot will minimize pain and bleeding. If the pain persists, medical attention should be sought; the doctor may find it necessary to make a small hole in the nail to relieve the pressure of the retained blood. This treatment stops the pain instantly.

Horizontal ridges or lines across a nail indicate some previous damage that occurred while the nail was developing in the matrix. Such a line at the middle of a fingernail, for example, may indicate a transient illness, possibly accompanied by a high fever, approximately six weeks earlier.

Athletic injuries frequently affect the nails. Bowlers, for example, develop worn-down fingernails. In jogging, tennis, racquetball, basketball, and soccer, the toes are persistently rammed into the ends of the shoes; eventually the nail plate may become lifted from the nail bed and bleeding may develop under the toenails. Often the nails appear black. This type of injury tends to be more common in people whose second toe is longer than their big toe (about one in every four persons). Keeping the toenails short and wearing properly fitted, well-padded sports shoes are the best preventive measures. Toe dancers and ice skaters, whose footwear compresses their toes, may suffer permanent damage to their toenails.

Discoloration of nails may occur as a result of contact with photographic or other chemical solutions, cigarettes, hair dyes, furniture stains, and the like. Vitamin deficiencies and certain antibiotic medications also may cause discoloration. Therefore, one may need to consult a dermatologist about such a problem.

Cosmetic products, most commonly synthetic nails and nail builders and extenders, occasionally produce adverse reactions. Since people who pick at or bite their nails are more likely to try to conceal unsightly defects, they are more frequent users of such cosmetics; at the same time, the generally poor condition of their hands, cuticles, and nails makes them more vulnerable to irritation or infection.

There are several products and techniques used to make nails appear longer, smoother, and more symmetrical. "Sculpturing" is one popular technique to conceal nail surfaces that are pitted, cracked, or otherwise irregular. The process involves the application of several coats of an acrylic powder and liquid solvent mixture, which forms a glue that is brushed onto each nail, one layer at a time. In the procedure called nail "wrapping," fiber-containing solutions, papers, or tapes are applied to nails and then coated with polish; this method is used to make nails look longer. Plastic nails may be individually cut and shaped and then glued in place to cover short or defective nails. The chemicals used in these processes in some cases may provoke painful allergic reactions, causing the skin around the nails to swell and crack and creating openings for bacteria and fungi. These allergic reactions and infections can cause permanent nail damage or destruction and require immediate medical attention.

Allergic responses to nail cosmetics are not limited to the area around the nails; they may occur on any part of the body that the nails touch. An employee of a telephone answering service who developed a rash on her cheek, for example, thought she had become allergic to her telephone headset; the real culprit, however, was her nail polish.

Fads in nail decoration may also be health hazards. One such trend currently in vogue is the adornment of the nails with jewels. In order to bolt the stones in place, a hole is drilled through the tip of the nail—this is another process that creates a potential avenue of infection.

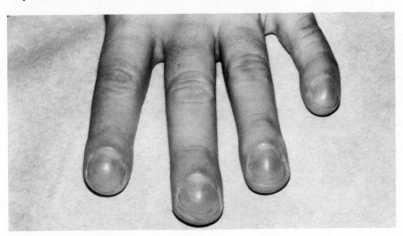

*Onycholysis (opposite page, left), separation of the end of the nail from the nail bed, is characteristic of fungal infection. Discoloration and deformation of the nails can be valuable aids in diagnosing underlying disease. Redness around the nails (opposite page, right) may indicate a connective tissue disorder; clubbing (left) can be a sign of lung or gastrointestinal disease.*

Photographs, Ted Rosen, M.D., Houston

## Medical disorders

Medical problems that involve the fingernails and toenails can be both uncomfortable and potentially dangerous. Such problems often require a visit to a physician, usually a dermatologist (a specialist in disorders of skin, nails, and hair) or a podiatrist (a specialist in disorders of the feet).

*Disorders of the nails.* An ingrown nail is a painful condition that is most common on the big toe. Growth of the upper edge of the nail into the soft tissue surrounding it may produce swelling and redness. If an ingrown nail develops, often it can be gently lifted and a small wad of cotton worked under it. Then the protruding, excess portion of the nail can be cut. The cotton should be left in place for a few days and the toe soaked once or twice a day in a solution of one teaspoon of salt dissolved in a pint of warm water. If the area becomes infected and pus accumulates, the condition should be treated by a physician. The usual procedure is removal of the excess nail and, in some cases, reduction of the nail matrix to prevent recurrences.

Paronychia, inflamed and swollen soft tissue at the side of the nail, often affects people—cooks, housekeepers, doctors, and dentists, among others—whose hands are frequently immersed in water. Splinters under the skin and nail biting may cause the same symptoms. The bacteria or fungi responsible for this problem enter through cracks in the skin and thrive in a moist environment. Medication to eliminate such infections requires a physician's prescription. Keeping the hands as dry as possible and protecting them—for example, by wearing rubber gloves—can prevent future episodes.

Fungal infections, particularly of the toenails, are common among adults. Fungi flourish in the warm, moist environment created by shoes and stockings. Fungal infections often cause the nails to become thick and discolored and to separate from the nail bed. Filing toenails parallel to their flat surface will reduce pressure on the corners of the toe. Oral antifungal drugs, such as griseofulvin and ketoconazole, may be prescribed and taken for three months to a year—or until nails have grown out completely. Such medications are often prescribed more for the hands, where unsightliness may be a prime concern, than for the feet, which tend to be stubbornly resistant to such treatment. Antifungal agents that are applied directly to the nails are of no benefit.

*Underlying disease.* Several systemic diseases are associated with characteristic nail changes. As many as half of all people with psoriasis, a disorder involving abnormally rapid replication of skin cells, have pinpoint-sized pits or furrows in their nails. People with alopecia areata, which causes patchy hair loss, also may develop ridges in their nails. Redness around the nails may be an early indicator of systemic lupus erythematosus, a disorder involving connective tissue. Pale yellow toenails often are seen in patients with diabetes or circulatory disorders; pallor of the nail beds is one indication of anemia. White nails appear in cirrhosis of the liver, and Muercke's lines, pale or white horizontal lines, are characteristic of nephrotic syndrome (deficiency of albumin in blood, often caused by toxic chemicals). Certain typical deformations of the nails are also valuable in the diagnosis of disease. Spooning (koilonychia) is a sign of chronic iron-deficiency anemia. Clubbing—in which the ends of the fingers and toes become knoblike, and the nails curve around them—may be associated with chronic lung disease, lung cancer, digestive disorders, or heart disease.

## Keeping nails healthy

Although "tough as nails" is a common expression, nails often cannot withstand onslaughts from detergents, water, abrasives, chemicals, and rough manual work. Dermatologists offer the following suggestions for the care of the nails:

Nails should not be used as tools to dial the phone, open letters or packages, or turn screws.

The edges of the fingernails should be kept smooth. Toenails should be allowed to grow until the edge reaches the end of the toe; they should be cut straight across, with the corners rounded only slightly to prevent ingrown nails. One who frequently develops ingrown toenails may be wearing shoes that are too tight.

Cuticles should not be trimmed or pushed back; the latter process impairs the connection between cuticles and nails, thus increasing the likelihood of infection. It is helpful, however, to apply cream or lotion to cuticles to keep them soft.

Protect nails, as well as hands, by wearing gloves for dishwashing, cleaning, gardening, and other household chores.

Nail surfaces should not be buffed too hard or vigorously; this makes them thin and may in addition cause damage to the nail bed.

One who has professional manicures should be sure that the instruments used are clean and properly sterilized between clients; otherwise, there is a risk of taking home another person's infection.

*—Lynne Lamberg*

# Roseola and Fifth Disease

Roseola (roseola infantum) and fifth disease (erythema infectiosum) are common, relatively harmless diseases of infants and young children. They are self-limiting and of unknown cause. Both are identified initially by a single symptom—elevated fever in roseola and a typical rash in fifth disease—and a prognosis of complete recovery.

## Roseola

Roseola, which is also known as exanthem subitum, is characterized by three to four days of extremely high fever, which is associated with few, if any, other signs and symptoms of illness. After the period of very high, spiking fever (that is, rising sharply and repeatedly to higher levels), the temperature suddenly drops back to normal; at the same time, a red rash, much like heat rash, appears over the infant's entire body and then gradually fades during the next 24 to 48 hours.

There are two reasons why it is important that parents of infants be familiar with the signs and symptoms of roseola. The first is that roseola is believed to be the most common infectious disease of children under age two that is associated with a rash—it affects about 30% of all children. The second reason is that roseola is the leading cause of simple fever convulsions in infants of this age group.

A simple fever convulsion (or febrile seizure) is a generalized seizure lasting less than 15 minutes (usually less than 5) caused by a high fever and associated with viral or bacterial infection anywhere in the body except the brain or spinal cord. During the convulsion the child's body may twitch or shake violently; loss of consciousness follows, and the eyes roll backward so that the pupils may no longer be visible. Normal, neurologically intact infants and children may experience simple fever convulsions, although the threshold-for-convulsion temperature varies from child to child. Needless to

say, the sight of an infant having a convulsion is terrifying to parents and, to assure a diagnosis of simple fever convulsion, examination of the infant by a physician should not be delayed.

*Causes and transmission.* Although roseola was first described in 1913, its etiology, or specific cause, has yet to be determined. There is, however, a good deal of indirect evidence that the disease is caused by a virus. The relatively long incubation period, low white blood count, failure to respond to any antibiotic therapy, and absence of any bacteria in cultures taken during the disease are typical indications of viral etiology. In laboratory experiments, both blood and throat washings obtained from patients with roseola during the third day of fever and on the first day of appearance of the rash have been shown to be infectious for monkeys and for susceptible infants. These successful experiments in human transmissions of the infection are further evidence for the belief that roseola is caused by a virus, despite the fact that no specific agent has been isolated.

The incubation period of roseola is difficult to determine because contact with the illness usually goes unrecognized. In the experimental human transmission of the disease, the average incubation period was nine days. A number of epidemics of roseola were reported in the 1920s and '30s. In those cases the reported incubation period ranged from 10 to 15 days.

*Incidence.* More than 95% of the cases of roseola occur in infants and children between six months and three years of age. Very occasionally it has been described in older children and in adults. The overwhelming majority of cases, however, occur before age three. There is no sex predilection in roseola, both sexes being equally susceptible. A majority of cases occur during the spring and autumn months, but the disease can occur at any time throughout the year.

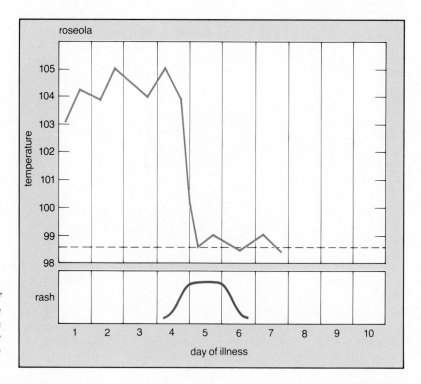

*In the characteristic pattern of roseola, a high, spiking fever is the initial symptom; the rash appears on the fourth or fifth day as the temperature suddenly returns to normal.*

Although roseola is spread by direct contact, it is not as contagious as such other common childhood diseases as measles, German measles (rubella), and chickenpox. Two siblings in the same household are rarely affected, even if both are under three years of age. The occasional epidemics of roseola reported in institutions are the exception rather than the rule.

One attack of roseola usually confers permanent immunity. Reports of children developing roseola more than once are known but may not in fact be accurate. It would be safe to say that if your child has a definite case of roseola, it is highly unlikely that he or she will ever get it again. The fact that roseola is rare in infants under six months of age strongly suggests that the newborn probably acquires some degree of passive protection from the mother (who herself had roseola as a child) during pregnancy. There is no cross-immunity between roseola and either measles or German measles.

*Signs and symptoms.* In a typical case of roseola, an evidently healthy baby six months to three years old suddenly develops a temperature of 104°–105° F. Except for some irritability and decrease in appetite during the time of high fever, the child does not otherwise appear to be ill. Common symptoms such as runny nose; red, tearing eyes; cough; vomiting; or diarrhea are absent. In most cases the high fever continues for three to four or even five days, a very frightening experience for the parents. The administration of antipyretic, or fever-reducing, medications such as aspirin or acetaminophen will lower the temperature for a brief

period of time, after which the fever shoots up to the previous high levels.

After three or four days the fever finally drops rapidly to, and remains, normal. At the time of the drop in the fever a red rash appears all over the body. The rash usually develops first on the trunk and then spreads rapidly to the neck, arms, face, and legs. The roseola rash is similar in appearance to the rashes of German measles or mild, modified regular measles. It consists of discrete rose-pink lesions, about 2 to 3 mm (0.08–0.12 in) in diameter; the lesions are flat and fade with application of pressure. The rash does not itch, and it fades and subsequently disappears after one to two days. The appearance of the rash and the sudden drop in temperature are generally simultaneous, although in occasional cases the rash does not appear until one day after the temperature returns to normal.

Because of the characteristically elevated temperature, the high incidence of fever convulsions in roseola is understandable. In fact, it is not at all uncommon for a fever convulsion to be the first symptom of the disease. Nevertheless, it should be emphasized again that any child who develops a fever convulsion must be examined by a physician as soon as possible in order to determine the cause of the convulsion. Although the diagnosis of roseola may be strongly suspected, it is most important that the child be carefully examined to rule out other illness, particularly because in roseola the fever convulsions occur prior to the characteristic rash that confirms the diagnosis.

*Diagnosis.* The most significant clinical basis for the

diagnosis of roseola is the striking difference between the infant's generally healthy appearance and the high fever. In a few cases the doctor may find some swollen neck glands and a slightly reddened throat and/or tonsils. No specific laboratory test can establish or confirm the diagnosis. White blood counts are of little use, and nose and throat cultures are useful only in ruling out other diseases. Thus, although the physician may strongly suspect roseola based on the clinical picture, the diagnosis cannot be confirmed until the disease has run its course. In cases where fever convulsions are present, therefore, the physician may consider it desirable to perform a spinal tap, a procedure in which a small amount of cerebrospinal fluid is withdrawn from the spinal column by means of a needle. Analysis of the fluid enables the physician to determine the existence of infection in the brain or spinal cord. If a physician is not available to examine the child after the fever convulsion, it is important to take the patient to the emergency room of a nearby hospital for a complete physical examination.

A number of other illnesses besides roseola must be considered in the diagnostic process. German measles has a rash similar to that of roseola, but it appears with the onset of the fever. In regular measles the child is quite obviously ill, with a high fever and a severe cough accompanying the rash. Rashes due to various drug sensitivities also may be difficult to distinguish from the rash typical of roseola.

*Treatment and recovery.* There is no specific treatment for a baby with roseola. An appropriate antipyretic (acetaminophen or aspirin) should be given in the correct dose for age when the baby has a high fever and can be repeated, if necessary, every four hours—but not more often. The baby with high fever should be encouraged to drink as much fluid as possible. If the fever becomes excessively elevated, a tepid bath will help bring it down. Although antibiotics do not in any way alter the course of this infection, the physician may choose to administer antibiotic therapy as long as the diagnosis remains in question. In such cases, however, when the appearance of the rash confirms the diagnosis of roseola, the antibiotic should be immediately discontinued.

Roseola is a benign and self-limited illness. The sole complication is the frequent development of fever convulsions. The prognosis is uniformly excellent, even for those children who do suffer febrile convulsions. It is important to remember that these simple fever convulsions do not result in any permanent brain damage and that all children who contract roseola make rapid and complete recoveries.

### Fifth disease

Fifth disease, or erythema infectiosum, is a mild self-limited contagious disease of childhood characterized by a typical rash and few other signs and symptoms of illness. It is sometimes difficult to differentiate from some of the other infectious childhood illnesses associated with rashes.

First described in 1889, fifth disease was originally believed to be a variant of German measles (rubella); later it was recognized as a separate entity and was given the name erythema infectiosum. In 1905 a French physician assigned numbers to the common pediatric diseases with rashes, designating German measles, measles, scarlet fever, and Dukes' disease (a mild form of scarlet fever) as numbers one through four; erythema infectiosum was fifth on the list, and roseola infantum was assigned the number six. It is not clear why fifth disease continues to be designated by number while the others are now called by name. Per-

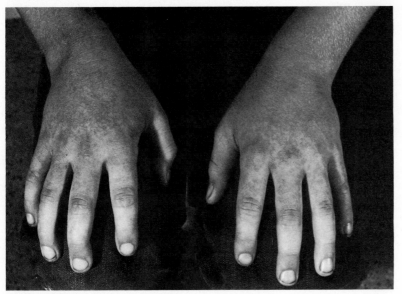

*In the second stage of fifth disease, a typical rash—lacelike in appearance and symmetrically distributed— becomes evident on the youngster's hands, arms, and legs.*

Centers for Disease Control

| Common pediatric diseases | Assigned number |
|---|---|
| rubella | 1 |
| measles | 2 |
| scarlet fever | 3 |
| Dukes' disease | 4 |
| fifth disease (erythema infectiosum) | 5 |
| roseola | 6 |

haps it is simply because erythema infectiosum is difficult to pronounce.

*Cause and transmission.* The exact cause of erythema infectiosum is unknown, although most evidence—*e.g.,* the seasonal and localized nature of small outbreaks—points to a probable viral etiology. But despite several attempts to isolate a specific virus in cultures obtained from patients with clinical evidence of the disease, none has produced conclusive results. The most recent speculation, based on preliminary evidence from a British study, indicates that the human parvovirus may be the specific cause of fifth disease; this theory, however, has yet to be confirmed.

Fifth disease is only mildly contagious, similar in its communicability to roseola; it is not as communicable as measles, German measles, or chickenpox. Many of the outbreaks described were confined to families and institutional populations and did not spread rapidly across large communities and cities. The mode of transmission is unknown, but the disease is assumed to spread by direct contact, from person to person, via droplet spray (as from sneezing and coughing).

*Incidence.* The first cases of fifth disease were reported from Austria and Germany. In the 20th century erythema infectiosum has been recognized and described in countries all over the world. As U.S. physicians are not required to report individual cases to their local health departments, the overall incidence of fifth disease in the United States is unknown.

Erythema infectiosum is primarily a disease of children. Most cases are concentrated in the two- to twelve-year-old age group. It has been reported in young children less than two years of age and, very occasionally, in adults. Incidence is equally divided among males and females.

*Symptoms.* The incubation period of fifth disease has been estimated to be in the range of 6 to 14 days. The most significant feature of the disease is its characteristic rash. In most cases the patient has few or no other symptoms, and only occasionally is the rash accompanied by a low-grade fever.

In most cases of fifth disease the typical rash erupts in three different stages. In the first stage the rash appears on the cheeks as an intensely red eruption—the so-called slapped cheek appearance. The cheek area is fiery red and hot to the touch but not tender. There may, in addition, be other scattered red rashes over the forehead and chin and behind the ears. Within one or two days this first stage rash rapidly fades and disappears.

In the second stage, about one day after the slapped cheek rash appears, another type of rash develops, distributed symmetrically over the arms and legs and, on rare occasions, either the palms of the hands or soles of the feet. This rash is described as lacey in appearance or resembling a pattern of lakes and rivers on a map. The second-stage rash may persist for a week or more before subsiding.

After the second stage of the rash has completely subsided, the third stage occurs in the form of several transient recurrences in the following two weeks or so. The reappearance of the rash during the third stage may be triggered by skin irritants, such as sunlight or extremes of hot and cold.

*Diagnosis and treatment.* Because there are no laboratory tests to identify fifth disease, correct diagnosis must be based entirely on the characteristic appearance of the rash. Since some cases of scarlet fever and German measles may be difficult to differentiate from fifth disease, it is important that a doctor examine the child to rule out these other possibilities. Furthermore, some of these similar diseases require specific treatment—antibiotics, for example, in the case of scarlet fever. Some allergic rashes, especially those due to drugs, may also be similar to the rashes of fifth disease.

There is no treatment for fifth disease; in nearly all cases, however, it is a self-limited and harmless illness. In rare cases complications may develop. The main complication—seen more often in adults than in children—is arthritis (*i.e.,* inflammation and swelling of the joints) or arthralgia (*i.e.,* joint pain). The arthritis is relatively mild and subsides completely after the disease has run its course. It is worth noting that fifth disease—unlike German measles—apparently does not lead to any birth defects if it occurs during pregnancy. The prognosis for a complete and uneventful recovery is uniformly excellent.

—*Alvin N. Eden, M.D.*

# Preparing for Healthy Travel

Today people from the United States are among the most health conscious and health knowledgeable in the world. The past decade has seen an explosion of public information about personal health and health-related topics. Books, newspaper articles, and television and radio spots on fitness and self-help abound; as a result, many people have become extremely sophisticated about health matters, and many consider themselves to be partners with their physicians in the management of their own health care. They expect to be able to ask any questions they please and to receive honest answers. They even expect, in some cases, to participate in the decision-making processes that concern their own care. Thus it is not uncommon today for patients—especially those in the U.S.—to be told of a number of therapeutic alternatives and to be given the opportunity to help choose their own course of treatment, a phenomenon almost unheard of in most parts of the world.

When Americans travel, however, most of them are woefully uninformed and unprepared for even the least alarming health emergency. People take trips for business or pleasure. Accidents and illness do not usually figure in their plans. After all, who plans to be sick or have an accident? As a result, when injuries or illnesses do occur, the traveler is often faced with a crisis in a country where the medical system may be a puzzle and the language more puzzling still.

Another reason so many travelers fail to prepare medically for a trip is that they are able to take so much for granted at home, where, for anyone suffering from a minor ailment, help is just a few feet away. The bathroom medicine cabinet contains most, if not all, of the preparations needed for almost any non-life-threatening emergency. A doctor is as close as the nearest telephone. In cases of really serious illness or injury, most Americans know how to reach their local hospital and, should it be necessary, how to call an ambulance. In addition, most people have health insurance plans to help defray the expenses of costly medical or surgical treatment. In short, Americans are surrounded by a cushion of security that they never stop to think about. When one travels even as few as a hundred miles away from home, many of these comforting assurances disappear.

Yet every traveler can recreate this cushion of security to a reasonable extent before ever leaving home.

Further, it will probably take less time to do it than it does to read about it. Being prepared for health emergencies when you travel is indeed the fabled ounce of prevention worth a pound of cure. Consider the aspirin, so recently unpacked, that you reach for at 2 AM in your Tokyo hotel room. Then consider the alternative: where could you find an aspirin at 2 AM in Tokyo? Or consider the ankle you have twisted on the steps of a London landmark—an injury reported to be one of the most common suffered by U.S. tourists in Great Britain. The most precious elastic bandage you will ever wrap around your ankle is the one you have brought with you for just such an emergency. The most effective and valuable emergency precautions, then, are the ones you take before you leave home.

## Health travel insurance

Perhaps one the earliest preparations you can make prior to a major trip is to call your health insurance company and ask a service representative if your policy covers you when you travel. Be sure to inquire as well about how a claim should be filed. Some companies require meticulously itemized bills or special forms for reimbursement. Should you need to file a claim, you will need to know exactly how to go about doing so. Medicare, incidentally, provides no benefits for travel outside the United States, except in limited circumstances in Mexico and Canada. This information is printed inside the back cover of all regular United States passports (diplomatic passports excluded).

Even if your policy does cover you while you are out of the country, it probably will not pay the doctor or hospital directly. Travelers must usually pay for care when and where it is received and recover the costs later.

If your present policy will not cover you adequately during a trip abroad, it is possible to purchase a short-term policy that will. Special insurance programs for travelers are available from a number of U.S. companies. Travel agents and insurance agencies are good sources of information about these various travel health plans, although individual agencies may offer only one or two plans considered most dependable from their experience. All travelers' health insurance policies are different in the benefits they provide; for this reason, they should be scrutinized carefully by the potential buyer. Some do not reimburse the policyholder for the recurrence of a preexisting condition. Some include emergency air evacuation, while others do not. And so on.

Some package tours offer an optional insurance policy that pays for a return trip home if the traveler is unable to return with the group. Such a policy is worth having, for the tour must, and does, go on without the traveler who has an accident or becomes suddenly ill.

## Practicing preventive medicine

Knowledge is always the traveler's greatest protection. This includes knowledge about first aid, self-treatment of simple illnesses, and, in the special case of a traveler with a chronic or recurrent health problem, a detailed understanding of the management of the illness.

Basic techniques of first aid are easy to learn and can be lifesavers. The treatment of the choking victim, mouth-to-mouth resuscitation, and cardiopulmonary resuscitation (CPR), for example, are skills everyone should know. Courses on more advanced techniques of first aid are generally available in most communities under the auspices of the American Red Cross and local high school and community college systems. Also helpful are any of the various illustrated manuals that deal with the basic techniques for managing massive bleeding, severe lacerations, broken bones, insect bites and stings, thermal burns, choking, drowning, drug overdose, chemical burns of the eye, and similar injuries and traumas. All such accidents are potential problems for the traveler, just as they are at home. In a foreign country, however, where help can be difficult to summon and slow to arrive, your ability to cope with such situations may be valued to an even greater extent. In many cases, first aid—that provided by you or by a traveling companion—can mean the difference between minor and major illness.

While persons suffering from chronic or recurrent illnesses must take special precautions when traveling, even the healthiest traveler should be prepared to deal with unexpected illness. This is particularly important for wilderness trips or vacations to exotic or remote destinations. Much will depend on the preparations you make prior to leaving the country.

A first step might be to visit your dentist and correct any dental problems that could be anticipated to flare up during a trip. Dental services are not as readily available abroad as they are in the United States and can be extremely expensive and time consuming. Furthermore, many of the techniques and materials employed in tooth repair are quite different from those of your own dentist.

Another important precaution is to consult your family physician for advice about special immunizations for travel and for a review of any overdue booster injections. The latter applies primarily to immunizations against tetanus, diphtheria, and polio. While polio no longer appears to be a problem in the United States, it still exists elsewhere, and the traveler who has lost immunity may be at risk. Smallpox vaccinations are no longer required for travel anywhere in the world, and special vaccinations against illnesses such as typhus, typhoid, and yellow fever are required only for specific countries, generally those in the tropics.

For travel to Mexico, Central and South American countries, and those countries bordering on the Mediterranean, prophylaxis against infectious hepatitis is often recommended because of the relatively high incidence of the disease in these areas. A single injection of immune gamma globulin can provide protection for more than one month. Finally, based on your itinerary, the need for malaria prevention or vaccination against cholera should be determined. Information about the relative risk of malaria or typhoid, cholera, and any other diseases requiring special immunization can be obtained from your own personal physician, a local public health office, the World Health Organization, or through the consular services of the countries you intend to visit.

## The medical travel kit

Another important aspect of health care to be considered by any traveler is self-help for minor illnesses. Most of us have developed a number of routines for handling common illnesses. Your home medicine cabinet is probably well stocked with a number of over-the-counter and prescription drugs for problems such as the common cold, sinusitis, athlete's foot, a minor rash, seasonal allergies, or any condition you tend to develop recurrently.

It is important to consider these supplies before taking a major trip. Many of the illnesses contracted abroad are the same as those experienced at home, and they can be managed in the same fashion if you take the necessary medical supplies or drugs with you. And having a familiar medication at hand is far superior than hoping to be able to find the same or a similar product in a foreign country.

Once you have decided on the essentials, it actually takes very little time to assemble a medical travel kit and very little space to store it in your hand luggage, where it will be available at all times and cannot be lost in the confusion of baggage claims at the end of a long journey. The traveler's medical kit is a highly individual item. Just as the contents of no two home medicine cabinets are exactly alike, so no two traveling medical kits will be the same.

The following is a sample list of common prescription and nonprescription items.

*Over-the-Counter (OTC) Drugs and Supplies*
   thermometer
   adhesive tape
   adhesive bandages
   gauze pads
   elastic bandage
   cotton swabs
   antacid
   antimotion sickness preparation
   cold/allergy preparation
   nasal decongestant
   cough medicine/expectorant/cough suppressant
   hemorrhoid preparation
   mild laxative
   painkiller (nonprescription)
   sunscreen
   syrup of ipecac (if traveling with children)

*Prescription (RX) Items*
   extra pair of prescription eyeglasses (or contact lenses and
      any necessary liquid soaking or disinfecting products)
   prescription for eyeglasses
   prescription painkiller
   full supply of any personal prescription drugs in regular use
   starter supply of drugs taken occasionally for recurrent
      chronic illness
   copies of your prescriptions, including generic names
   antidiarrheal drug(s)
   antibiotics

The medical kit should contain at least a starter supply of everything you use at home, including those items you may not use very often. You may suffer, for example, from recurrent urinary tract infections, but have not had one for some time. Should you be ready for one? Yes. Or you have had trouble with arthritis in your knee, but it has not bothered you for quite awhile. Should you bother to pack a supply of an anti-inflammatory drug? By all means. The value of having medical attention within your own reach cannot be overemphasized, for it provides security on a 24-hour basis.

Even the healthiest and best prepared traveler may, however, succumb to the disruption of routine caused by changes in time zones, unusual foods, increased physical exercise, extreme variations in altitude, and exposure to unfamiliar viruses and bacteria. In case your own remedies fail, or if you suffer a serious injury, you should also be prepared for the fact that you may have to seek professional medical help.

## How to find a doctor abroad

In a foreign country, finding a doctor in an emergency is indeed a challenge. The most obvious source is your hotel. Although few but the most luxurious hotels have doctors actually in attendance, many either have a physician on call or know of one to recommend. For the non-life-threatening emergency, the hotel doctor is a good enough choice; in the case of an acute, serious illness, however, there are better options.

The nearest large university hospital or teaching hospital is almost always the best resource for a traveler in search of attention for a serious medical emergen-

cy. At least some members of the resident staff of these hospitals will probably have trained in an English-speaking country. And it is in a teaching hospital that the traveler is most likely to find the broadest range of services and the most up-to-date equipment.

In a few countries, however, these public hospitals are government-operated and do not admit tourists. In Mexico and Spain, for example, only the country's nationals are eligible to be treated in national health service hospitals. Some socialist countries—the Soviet Union and the People's Republic of China, for example—have special hospitals designated for the care of foreign travelers, and admission to any other medical facility simply is not possible. Also closed to American tourists are U.S. military hospitals abroad; these are restricted to military and government personnel and their dependents. It is possible, however, for a seriously ill traveler to be given emergency treatment at a U.S. military hospital and stabilized for transfer to another facility.

Another excellent, dependable source for finding English-speaking doctors throughout the world is the local office of the U.S. consulate. Consular services include providing health information to travelers and helping to arrange emergency transportation for return to the United States in case of a medical emergency. A consul's job, however, is to inform, not to recommend. Travelers are provided with the best information at hand, but they are expected to choose for themselves from the consulate's directory of doctors and hospitals.

Most U.S. consulates abroad keep an alphabetical list of local English-speaking doctors. Not only is this list as dependable as one from any other source; it is free and should be current. In more cosmopolitan parts of the world, lists are lengthy and include identification by subspecialty and educational credentials as well. In smaller towns the lists are commensurately shorter and less detailed. The lists are available in printed form to any traveler who requests them in person at the consulate during regular business hours. After hours there is a duty officer available to provide necessary information.

Unfortunately, there are several pitfalls in this system: there may be no U.S. consulate in the town where the traveler falls ill; some consulates use recorded message devices that do not provide immediate help; in some small cities the U.S. is represented by nationals who work only part-time. If you are planning to visit such small or remote towns, it is advisable to know the telephone number of the nearest metropolitan U.S. consulate or even the U.S. embassy in the capital city, either of which can usually provide information about the nearest local doctors or clinics.

## The cost of medical services

*Physician and hospital charges.* Doctors in foreign countries expect to be paid immediately. So do hospitals. Some foreign hospitals, in fact, demand payment in advance, a sum that may be rather substantial in some countries. Cash deposits in advance are the policy in both France and West Germany, for example. Moreover, bills are presented regularly during the course of hospitalization. Countries where health care is free to travelers, *and then only in certain circumstances,* are few. They include Greece, Great Britain, and Denmark.

The traveler who requires emergency hospitalization, then, must worry not only about choosing a hospital wisely but also about being able to surrender a relatively large amount of cash on short notice. So a truly prepared traveler might wish to consider planning in advance for money to be available in the event of an emergency. There are several alternative arrangements for such cases. A friend or relative can be given temporary power of attorney or a line of credit established at a hometown bank. A U.S. consular officer can also wire home at the traveler's expense to arrange a transfer of funds to cover a health emergency.

*Emergency evacuation.* Emergency evacuation, whether by commercial jet or air ambulance, is unquestionably the most expensive mode of travel. On a commercial carrier more than one seat must always be purchased—depending on the aircraft and special stretcher equipment, as many as four and in first class.

## Quality of care abroad

In the best of circumstances, *i.e.,* having found a highly competent doctor or a full-service teaching hospital, you can expect to receive the best medical care the country has to offer. In a less developed country or in remote areas of a large country, standards of care obviously will not be very sophisticated—but then the same is true of remote areas of the United States.

It should be understood, however, that whatever the quality of care you may receive abroad, it will not exactly match U.S. standards and procedures. Sometimes the care received abroad can seem either more aggressive or more conservative than that one would expect to receive at home. For example, surgical repair of an injured hip might be done in a private clinic in Spain, when a more conservative approach, such as immobilization and emergency evacuation, would be a better course. A ten-day hospitalization in Moscow for treatment of diarrhea may seem overly conservative, but Soviet patients are frequently hospitalized for longer periods than are common in the United States.

## Negligent treatment

The possibility arises, too, that medical care given the tourist may be clearly negligent and result in prolonged illness or even permanent disability. One common tourist complaint concerns the faulty setting of broken

bones that must later be reset. Improperly applied casts can cause nerve damage, and the resetting of broken bones necessarily results in prolonged recovery periods. Whatever the allegations, however, malpractice suits by travelers are always difficult. In some European countries malpractice is almost unheard of; in the Soviet Union and the People's Republic of China, it simply does not exist. The difficulties of retaining experienced counsel and pursuing a case from thousands of miles away pose too great a barrier for most travelers, although there are examples of such cases that have been tried and won.

## Common sense

Finally, the most effective weapon in the battle against accident and illness when traveling may be common sense. It first comes into play as the traveler packs. We are all guilty of taking along far too much when we travel. The burden of excess baggage eventually takes its toll on our backs and nerves alike. Perhaps the most important thing in any traveler's luggage is a pair of sturdy, low-heeled, comfortable shoes. Common sense will dictate, too, the amount of sightseeing that should be attempted in a single day. With so much to see and do, most travelers exhaust themselves early on. Nor is it always their fault. In China one of the standard day tours includes a brisk trip through the Ming Tombs with their many stairs, followed immediately by a lung-bruising climb of the Great Wall. Common sense dictates, then, that a visitor pursue some things vigorously but not everything.

The safety of food and water poses a more complicated problem. Obviously, on the side of common sense, persons with food allergies should make every attempt to find out the contents of an unknown exotic dish. Drinking only bottled water and avoiding fresh, unpeeled fruits and vegetables will help protect you from the scourge known as travelers' diarrhea. As for when it is safe to drink the water, that question is usually best answered by the local people. There are few places where bottled water is drunk just to be fashionable. Therefore, if the nationals drink bottled water, the local water supply is probably unsafe to drink.

FOR ADDITIONAL READING:
Hillman, Sheilah M., and Hillman, Robert S., M.D. *Traveling Healthy: A Complete Guide to Medical Services in 23 Countries.* New York: Penguin Books, 1980.

*Vaccination Certificate Requirements for International Travel and Health Advice to Travellers.* Geneva: World Health Organization, 1983.

—*Robert S. Hillman, M.D.,*
*and Sheilah M. Hillman*

# Traveling with Special Health Problems

Today, travel to most foreign countries need not be limited by a chronic or recurrent health problem. High-quality health care facilities and drugs comparable to those available in the United States can now be found worldwide, and with a little preparation, any traveler can be assured a trouble-free and enjoyable trip. Success largely amounts to anticipating problems before you leave the country and knowing how to secure necessary health services while abroad.

The amount of pretrip planning for health care needs will depend on the length of trip, the countries to be visited, and the nature of the health problem. Within the United States an overnight excursion to a town or major city near home represents little danger to a person with a chronic health problem; health care facilities are fairly standard throughout the country. Nor is there the problem of a language barrier; the services and products available at local drug stores are quite familiar, and the attending pharmacist can be expected to be well trained and to speak English.

For the U.S. citizen who ventures outside the country, such is not necessarily the case. For the traveler abroad a chronic health problem or a major recurrent illness can make it difficult or even impossible to return home at will. Additionally, health care facilities are less familiar, and language difficulties can make access to available health services virtually impossible. Finding even the simplest of medications can become a monumental task when pharmacies are difficult to recognize and unfamiliar in their services and the pharmacist speaks only the language of the host country. Then, even an English-speaking pharmacist may not be able to recognize a traveler's medication or match it with an equivalent drug.

## General considerations

None of these problems is insurmountable, however, if you take the time to research the area to be visited, get advice from health professionals before leaving home,

and organize a survival kit of important documents, medical supplies, and essential drugs. But, most important of all, any traveler with a chronic or recurrent health problem should know as much as possible about his or her medical condition and its appropriate management. The following are a few simple rules for being prepared.

1. Find out about health risks specific to the places you plan to visit and the availability of professional medical services in each. This may take a bit of research. Travel agents and brochures do not generally volunteer information regarding health risks abroad—they are far more knowledgeable about hotels than hospitals. Physicians who have traveled abroad, community immunization clinics, and special clinics for travelers can be good sources for information. In general, it can also be assumed that the quality and sophistication of a country's health services will parallel its level of economic development. Less developed countries often do not have complete health facilities or special technology for illnesses that require complex treatment. Services such as hemodialysis, for example, or coagulation factor therapy for hemophilia patients are not available in every foreign country. These special requirements must be taken into account when planning a trip if your well-being and very survival are dependent on reliable facilities of this nature.

2. Review your travel plans with a physician to assess any risks involved and to get advice concerning special health care needs. While not necessarily expert in all of the potential health risks in every foreign country, a physician can usually provide advice on general principles of health care while traveling. Certainly your doctor can offer valuable, personalized information about the management of a specific chronic illness. For example, in the case of a condition such as diabetes, successful management during a trip abroad depends upon an individualized plan for managing diet, scheduling insulin injections, changing dosage in vari-

*The need for routine dialysis treatments has not prevented this vacationing group of kidney patients from taking a raft trip. The necessary equipment is stowed aboard, and stops are made along the way to maintain the patients' scheduled therapy.*

ous time zones, and, in the case of an expected gastric upset, preventing diabetic ketoacidosis or hypoglycemia. Furthermore, the doctor can probably also identify and refer the traveler to one of the specialized travelers' health clinics now being developed by a number of U.S. universities and hospitals. These clinics can be expected to have detailed information regarding the availability of, for example, refrigeration in more exotic places in the world, as well as the management of both common illnesses and special health risks likely to be encountered while abroad. In addition, many special interest organizations, such as the National Association of Patients on Hemodialysis and Transplantation, publish directories that list both U.S. and foreign treatment centers.

3. Obtain copies of your medical records, including the history of any major health problem, records of laboratory studies or specific tests such as electrocardiograms, and a typed summary of the physician's de-

tailed recommendations about ongoing treatments. These records can be invaluable in surmounting a language barrier. They will also make it possible for a foreign physician to make recommendations that match those of your own physician.

It can also be helpful to have a letter of introduction, particularly if you know in advance that the attention of a medical or surgical specialist will be required during the trip. If your physician knows of a specific practitioner in a foreign country, this letter can be addressed personally. If not, an introductory letter addressed "Dear Doctor" or "To Whom It May Concern" can still be of considerable help in gaining introduction to an overseas hospital or clinic.

4. Learn about the actions, side effects, and appropriate changes in regimens for any drug you take on a regular basis. Such information can be obtained from a physician or from many reference books published for the general public on over-the-counter and prescription

drugs. In addition, you should get from your doctor an extra supply of essential medications and a duplicate prescription for each drug in case a new supply must be purchased abroad. A surprising number of foreign pharmacies will accept a U.S. prescription, eliminating the need to consult a foreign physician simply to replace a lost medication. It is also wise always to take both regular and extra supplies of medications in your carry-on luggage, in case checked baggage should be lost or misplaced.

5. If you plan to be in a foreign country for a long period of time, the recommendation of a specific hospital or individual physician to serve your health care needs can be extremely important. Your own physician can usually identify a suitable hospital or specialist in the major cities of most foreign countries. If not, a travelers' health clinic can generally be of help. Once again, a personal letter of introduction can be quite valuable in smoothing the way.

All of these preparatory measures take time to arrange, so a visit to the physician or travelers' health clinic should be scheduled well in advance of your trip.

## Specific health problems

If one is well versed in managing a health problem at home, travel should not represent a major health threat. Common illnesses such as insulin-dependent diabetes, heart disease requiring daily medication or a pacemaker, thrombotic disease requiring anticoagulant therapy, chronic lung disease requiring medical therapy, or a cancer or blood disorder under active chemotherapy can be treated as well in most foreign countries as they are in the United States. However, the traveler needs to be very knowledgeable about his or her own condition and must be prepared with clear instructions on handling various complications and seeking good health care services while abroad.

*Cancer.* Maintenance cancer chemotherapy, for example, is possible in most foreign countries. However, as with most U.S. treatment centers, various cancer centers abroad follow different routines of therapy, called protocols. For a traveler to receive successful maintenance therapy during a trip, he or she needs to carry the detailed protocol, or set of instructions on the therapy to be given, and, in most cases, the actual drugs to be administered. With this in hand, the patient should have no difficulty in obtaining good care. The network of cancer centers is worldwide, and in most of the major cities in the world, skilled health personnel will be quite happy to assist.

*Blood diseases.* Similarly, a patient with a blood disorder such as hemophilia or an individual requiring anticoagulant therapy for a blood condition can, with a little preparation, manage a trip abroad. As with chemotherapy, it is necessary to determine beforehand the availability of specific services and drugs or blood concentrates in individual countries. If particular supplies or facilities are either unavailable or closed to foreigners, special arrangements must be made in advance. In addition, the traveler usually will need to take an adequate supply of drug or concentrate for use during his stay in the country. For hemophiliacs who travel abroad, the World Federation of Hemophilia publishes a guide to national and international treatment centers. This can be obtained from a local hemophilia center or by contacting the National Hemophilia Foundation in New York City or the World Federation in Montreal.

*Dialysis.* Travel is also quite feasible for dialysis patients if careful preparation is made. The European Dialysis and Transplant Association publishes a list of dialysis centers abroad. There is also *Dialysis Worldwide for the Traveling Patient,* published by the National Association of Patients on Hemodialysis and Transplantation, of Great Neck, N.Y. Information about dialysis for travelers in foreign countries can also be obtained from local dialysis centers. Travel plans should be discussed with the traveler's physician and dialysis center, as restrictions may vary from center to center and may have changed since the latest publication date.

*With a little advance planning—and some occasional mechanical aids—even severely handicapped persons can transcend the evident limits on their mobility.*

M. Kyle McLellan—Picture Group

*Diabetes.* Another common chronic health problem is insulin-dependent diabetes. Diabetics skilled in the management of their disease should be quite confident in their ability to travel abroad. There are issues associated with travel that need to be addressed, however. Travel to Europe or Southeast Asia always involves a sudden change in time zones and, therefore, in scheduling of meals and insulin therapy. These considerations should be discussed in advance with the patient's physician. The diabetic traveler must also be skilled in dealing with changes in dietary content and well prepared to treat common gastrointestinal disorders. In addition, the diabetic should arrange to take adequate supplies of insulin and syringes, preferably enough to last the entire trip. In order to avoid possible confiscation of syringes by customs agents, a letter from a physician or medical records documenting the need for insulin should be in hand.

If the diabetic traveler plans an extended stay, it will be necessary to purchase insulin abroad. In most foreign countries, only U40 and U80 insulins are available; a patient who is normally on U100 insulin must, therefore, be prepared to adjust the dosage appropriately. Again, this should be discussed with the physician prior to leaving home. The American Diabetes Association also provides information and guides for overseas travel. In addition, travel agents may know of special tours where travel routes and hotels are specifically arranged to fit the needs of the severe diabetic.

*Other chronic conditions.* Similar principles of preparation apply to travelers with problems such as colostomy, severe recurrent asthma, chronic obstructive pulmonary disease, and other chronic illnesses. Although the availability of special health care services varies from country to country, these variations generally can be determined ahead of time through the traveler's physician or a specialty association. The overall rule that applies to the adequacy of foreign health care in general is very important to the traveler with a chronic health problem—that is, big cities in economically developed countries will have health care services and supplies similar to those found in the United States. Remote villages and less developed countries cannot be expected to offer the same level of service.

Finally, any traveler with a chronic health problem should wear a neck tag or a bracelet that identifies the condition. Medical identification tags engraved with the words Diabetic, Pacemaker, Allergic to Penicillin, and the like are available from local pharmacies, as well as from special organizations that offer added services along with the identification tags.

The names and addresses of organizations devoted to the concerns of persons with particular chronic disorders can be found in the references listed below. These books are available in most public libraries.

*Encyclopaedia of Associations* (ed. by Denise S. Akey). Detroit: Gale Research Company, 1983.

*Health Services Directory* (ed. by Anthony T. Kruzas). Detroit: Gale Research Company, 1981.

*Yearbook of International Organizations.* Published jointly by the Union of International Associations, Brussels, and the International Chamber of Commerce, Paris, 1981.

FOR ADDITIONAL READING:

Hillman, Sheilah M., and Hillman, Robert S., M.D. *Traveling Healthy: A Complete Guide to Medical Services in 23 Countries.* New York: Penguin Books, 1980.

*—Robert S. Hillman, M.D.,*
*and Sheilah M. Hillman*

# Communicating in Foreign Lands: A Medical Glossary

For the English-speaking traveler it is a comforting notion that English is fast becoming the world's second language. But it is also a fanciful notion, for the truth is that not everybody in the world speaks English or is in the process of learning to do so. The problem of a language barrier, then, and the difficulties it can present are very real for the traveler with a health emergency.

Trying to convey to a Parisian on the Champs Elysée that one is feeling sick and needs medical attention can be challenging and frustrating for both parties, but trying to express your needs to a Turk or a Chinese may be virtually impossible. In the event that one is acutely ill, the problem is further compounded.

Even in Great Britain there are communication barriers of sorts for the U.S. traveler, although the difficulties lie in terminology and usage rather than in the language itself. If you are looking for a pharmacist or druggist, for example, you will find instead a *chemist*—in a *dispensing chemist shop,* not in a drugstore or pharmacy. The hospital emergency room is the *casualty department.*

On a more hopeful note, in most foreign countries there are dependable, English-speaking sources for travelers to use in a medical emergency. Three of the major resources for English-speaking help are the hotel desk clerk or other hotel personnel, the house staff (resident medical/surgical personnel) of a large teaching or university hospital, and the nearest U.S. consulate general.

Sick travelers are well advised to seek help in the hotels where they are registered. Hotel personnel should, however, be relied upon strictly as interpreters and translators, not as experts in recommending medical treatment. It is very important that the traveler receive the help he or she thinks is appropriate to the emergency and that the hotel not be permitted to handle the situation in the way it thinks best. Hotel managers are not in the health care business. Primary in their minds are the comfort, well-being, and peace of mind of their guests. Naturally, they prefer to handle all emergencies as quietly and discreetly as possible. Most, for example, would much rather summon a doctor than an ambulance, even when an ambulance is clearly the better choice.

Even the smallest hotel will have its own way of dealing with health emergencies. If there is no doctor who officially serves hotel guests, the concierge may, for example, have a cousin who knows someone who knows a "good" doctor. And so on. It is far better, then, for the traveler to be in control and to insist on exactly the kind of medical attention required.

The nearest large teaching hospital or university hospital is usually a good choice for the sick traveler seeking English-speaking help. United States consulates throughout the world are another source for the recommendation of English-speaking physicians. In fact, the consulate should always be advised when a U.S. citizen has been hospitalized in a foreign country, and many consuls consider it their duty to visit hospitalized Americans and assist in their release and return home. This is a resource to be used intelligently, though—consular services do not extend to minor problems such as lost luggage or minor ailments such as head colds. Further, the services of U.S. doctors attached to the country's embassies abroad do not extend to tourists.

In the quest for help from English-speakers, travelers are advised to be as resourceful, unembarrassed, and, if necessary, aggressive, as possible. One's own hotel may not employ a single person who knows English, but the closest luxury hotel certainly will. Registered or not, the determined traveler can probably get help there. Nor can any harm come from approaching the nearest passerby or the policeman directing traffic; either may know a few words of English or be able to direct you to someone else who does. Or you may find another U.S. visitor who speaks the language of the country and will act as a translator.

In some cases an English-speaking traveler who speaks a second language may be able to use that language in a country where it is also spoken as a second

361

# Communicating in foreign lands

## Useful words and phrases

| English | French | German |
|---------|--------|--------|
| I am sick. | Je suis malade. (zh'swee ma·lahd) | Ich bin krank. (ikh bin krahnk) |
| I speak only English. | Je parle seulement anglais. (zh'parl sewl·mawn awn·glay) | Ich spreche nur Englisch. (ikh sprekh·uh noor English) |
| help | au secours | Hilfe |
| doctor | médecin | Arzt |
| hospital | hôpital | Krankenhaus |
| accident | accident | Unfall |
| ambulance | ambulance | Krankenwagen |

### Injuries/symptoms

| English | French | German |
|---------|--------|--------|
| animal bite | morsure d'un animal | Tierbiss |
| bloody stools | selles teintées de sang | blutiger Stühl |
| bloody vomit | vomissement teinté de sang | blutiges Ebrechen |
| burn | brûlure | Verbrennung |
| chest pain | douleurs à la poitrine | Brustschmerzen |
| choking | étranglement | Erstickung |
| difficulty breathing | difficultés respiratoires | Atembeschwerden |
| dizzy | le vertige | schwindlig |
| drowned | noyé | ertrunken |
| drug overdose | intoxication médicamenteuse | Arzneimittel-Überdosis |
| fever (with chills) | fièvre (avec des frissons) | Fieber (mit Schüttelfrost) |
| fracture | coupure/fracture | Bruch |
| headache | mal à la tête | Kopfschmerzen |
| heart attack | infarctus du myocarde | Herzanfall |
| internal bleeding | hèmorragie interne | innere Blutung |
| numb | engourdi | empfindungslos |
| pain | douleur | Schmerz |
| poisoning | empoisonnement | Vergiftung |
| shock | choc | Schock |

### Special health problems

| English | French | German |
|---------|--------|--------|
| allergy to: | allergie à: | Allergie Gegen: |
|   bee stings |   piqûres d'abeille/d'insectes |   Bienenstiche |
|   shellfish |   crustacés |   Muscheln |
| blood disease | maladie du sang | Blutkrankheit |
|   hemophilia |   hémophilie |   Hämophilie |
|   leukemia |   leucémie |   Leukämie |
|   sickle cell anemia |   anémie falciforme |   Sichelzellanamie |
| digestive disease | affection digestive | Erkrankung des Verdauungstraktes |
|   colitis |   colite |   Colitis |
|   diabetes |   diabète |   Diabetes |
|   gallstones |   calcus vésicaux |   Gallensteine |
|   liver disease |   maladie hépatique |   Leberkrankung |
|   ulcer |   ulcère |   Geschwür |
| eye/nervous system disease | maladies des yeux et du système nerveux | Augenerkrankung/Erkrankung des Nerven systems |
|   blind |   aveugle |   blind |
|   contact lenses |   verres de contact |   Kontaktlinsen |
|   deaf |   sourd |   taub |
|   epilepsy |   épilepsie |   Epilepsie |
|   glaucoma |   glaucome |   Glaukom, grüner Star |
|   paralysis |   paralysie |   Paralyse |
| heart/blood vessel disease | affection cardio-vasculaire | Herz-Gefässkrankheit |
|   heart failure |   insuffisance cardiac |   Herzfehler |
|   high blood pressure/hypertension |   pression sanguine trop élevée/hypertension |   Hoher Blutdruck/Hypertonie |
|   irregular heart beat/arrhythmia |   palpitations/arythmies |   unregelmässiger Herzschlag/Arrhytmie |
|   phlebitis |   phlébite |   Venenentzündung |
| kidney disease | affection renale | Nierenerkrankung |
|   dialysis patient |   patient dialysé |   Dialyse-Patient |
|   kidney stones |   calculs rénaux |   Nierensteine |
| lung disease | affection pulmonaire | Lungenerkrankung |
|   asthma |   asthme |   Asthma |
|   emphysema |   emphysème |   Emphysem |

| Italian | Spanish | Portuguese |
|---|---|---|
| Io sono malato. | Estoy enfermo. | Estou doente. |
| (e·oh so·no ma·la·toe) | (ess·toy en·fair·mo) | (es·too do·en·tea) |
| Io parlo solo Inglese. | Solo hablo inglés. | Só falo inglês. |
| (e·oh par·lo so·lo een·glay·say) | (so·lo ah·blow een·glaze) | (so fa·lo een·glace) |
| aiuto | socorro | socorro |
| medico | médico | médico |
| ospedale | hospital | hospital |
| incidente | accidente | acidente |
| ambulanza | ambulancia | ambulância |
| | | |
| morso di animale | mordedura de animal | mordedura de animal |
| feci sanguinanti | defecación con sangre | fezes com sangue |
| vomito sanguinante | vómito con sangre | vômito com sangue |
| ustione | quemadura | queimadura |
| dolore al torace | dolor en el pecho | dor no peito |
| soffocamento | asfixia | sufocação |
| difficoltà respiratoria | dificultad para respirar | dificuldade em respirar |
| vertigine | mareos | tontura |
| annegato | ahogado | afogado |
| sovradosaggio di farmaci | sobredosis de drogas | excessiva de medicamento |
| febbre (con brividi) | fiebre (con escalofríos) | febre (com arrepios) |
| frattura | fractura | fractura |
| cefalea, mal di testa | dolor de cabeza | dor de cabeça |
| attacco cardiaco | ataque del corazón | ataque cardíaco |
| emorragia interna | hemorragia interna | hemorragia interna |
| intirizzito | adormecimiento | entorpecido |
| dolore | dolor | dor |
| avvelenamento | envenenamiento | envenenamento |
| shock | choque | estado de choque |
| | | |
| allergia a: | alérgico a: | alérgico a: |
| ape puntura | picadura de abeja | picadas de abelha |
| frutti di mare crostacei | mariscos | mariscos |
| malattia del sangue | enfermedad de la sangre | doenças de sangue |
| emofilia | hemofilia | hemofilia |
| leucemia | leucemia | leuqemia |
| drepanocitosi | anemia drepanocítico | anemia de células falciformes |
| malattia digerente | enfermedad de la digestión | doença do aparelho digestivo |
| colite | colitis | colite |
| diabete | diabetes | diabetes |
| calcoli biliari | calculos biliares | cálculos biliares |
| malattia del fegato | enfermedad del hígado | doenças do fígado |
| ulcera | úlcera | úlcera |
| malattie degli | enfermedad del sistema | doenças dos olhos e |
| occhi/sistema nervoso | ocular/nervioso | sistema nervoso |
| cieco | ceguera | cego |
| lenti a contatto | lentes de contacto | lentes de contacto |
| sordo | sordo | surdo |
| epilessia | epilepsia | epilepsia |
| glaucoma | glaucoma | glaucoma |
| paralisi | parálisis | paralisia |
| malattie del cuore/vasi | enfermedad del corazón/vaso | doenças coração/vasculares |
| insufficienza cardiaca | falla cardiaco | insuficiência cardíaca |
| alta pressione sanguigna/ | alta presión sanguínea | tensão arterial alta/hipertensão |
| ipertensione | | |
| | | |
| battiti cardiaci irregolari/aritmia | latidos irregulares/arritmia | ritmo cardiaco irregular/aritmia |
| | | |
| flebite | flebitis | flebite |
| malattie renali | mal del riñón | doença renaes |
| paziente in dialisi | paciente en diálisis | doente que fàz diálise |
| calcoli renali | cálculos renales | calculos renaes |
| malattie pulmonari | enfermedad del pulmón | doença pulmonar |
| asma | asma | asma |
| enfisema | enfisema pulmonar | enfisema |

## Communicating in foreign lands

language. French, for example, is commonly spoken in Spain and Italy. Spanish is widely understood in Portugal. German is spoken in Greece; Russian is often understood in Yugoslavia and Poland.

Faced with both an emergency and an insurmountable language barrier, travelers may find it extremely frustrating to try to use the telephone without assistance. Although many foreign countries have national or regional telephone numbers to summon emergency help, English is rarely spoken by dispatchers, and the workings of the telephone itself—particularly a pay phone in a public booth—may be totally incomprehensible. Such a telephone call should be made with the help of someone who speaks the country's language and good English as well. Failing that, it is better to strike off on your own in search of the nearest full-service medical facility.

Although the sick or injured traveler can hardly be expected to become an instant linguist, it may be help-ful to know a few words in case of emergency. Often single words prove more effective than whole phrases. To be able to say "sick" in a foreign language and then point to oneself or a companion is surely just as useful (and twice as fast) as being able to say "I am sick," or "She is sick," or "We are sick." Perhaps the most helpful words in any language are "sick," "help," and "please."

FOR ADDITIONAL READING:

Hillman, Sheilah M., and Hillman, Robert S., M.D. *Traveling Healthy: A Complete Guide to Medical Services in 23 Countries.* New York: Penguin Books, 1980.

Jacobson, Helen Saltz. *The Special Diet Foreign Phrasebook.* Emmaus, Pa.: Rodale Press, Inc., 1982.

*—Robert S. Hillman, M.D.,
and Sheilah M. Hillman*

# Heartburn

Heartburn is a relatively common symptom not usually indicative of serious disease. It is generally described by patients as a burning sensation or feeling of oppression starting high in the abdomen or under the lower end of the breastbone (sternum) and rising into the upper chest and neck. Eructation (eruption) of sour fluid into the mouth sometimes accompanies the discomfort. Heartburn may occur transiently in anyone; it is precipitated and aggravated by many factors, among them overeating; smoking; certain foods, such as chocolate and fats; coffee, tea, and alcoholic beverages; some drugs, including aspirin; and obesity. It is often experienced by the person who lies down after a large meal. Heartburn should not be considered to be a symptom of significant disease unless it occurs more often than several times per year or under other circumstances, such as when the stomach is empty or when the patient bends forward.

Although most commonly confused with angina pectoris—chest pain caused by reduced flow of blood to the heart muscle—heartburn differs from angina in several important respects, including the nature of the discomfort, its distribution or radiation, and its time of occurrence. Anginal pain is most often described as a squeezing substernal distress that radiates into the jaw or left shoulder and upper arm; it rarely has a burning character. Anginal pain occurs most commonly during heavy exercise, especially in cold weather, and in the midst of periods of emotional stress, situations that do not usually produce heartburn.

Heartburn may also be confused with the steady substernal pain that is characteristic of diffuse esophageal spasm, usually associated with difficulty in swallowing (dysphagia); it does not have a burning quality but may radiate into the neck and be associated with regurgitation of food or gastric contents. Unlike heartburn, diffuse esophageal spasm is not usually a symptom of esophageal inflammation. Belching, or burping, a common symptom of diffuse esophageal spasm, is less commonly associated with heartburn. In both disorders, however, belching appears to result from the release from the upper esophagus of air unconsciously swallowed in response to the chest discomfort.

## Causes

Most physicians agree that heartburn occurs when normally acidic or bile-containing secretions originating in the stomach come into prolonged contact with an inflamed portion of mucous membrane at the lower end of the esophagus. Under normal conditions a valvelike mechanism, or sphincter, located at the lowermost end of the esophagus prevents gastric contents from flowing upward, or refluxing, into the esophagus. When a swallow of solid or liquid food approaches this area from above, the valve muscle relaxes and permits free passage of the bolus (the mass of chewed food) into the stomach. As soon as the bolus passes, the muscular pressure returns, preventing reflux. A certain amount of harmless reflux occurs in perfectly healthy people without producing heartburn, since the refluxed material is quickly swept back into the stomach by a new wave of muscular activity, or peristalsis, in the esophagus.

Inflammation of the mucous membrane that lines the lower esophagus occurs when this normal "housekeeper" peristalsis ceases—as it may with aging or in certain diseases. Then, stomach acid or bile-containing gastric contents refluxed into the lower esophagus may remain there for prolonged periods, causing the mucous membrane to become inflamed; this condition is called esophagitis. Heartburn is a symptom of esophagitis, and it is believed to occur only when reflux is present and when the normal peristalsis of the lower esophagus is either temporarily or permanently diminished or absent.

## Chronic heartburn and esophagitis

Any disorder associated with reduced resting pressures in the esophageal valve, or lower esophageal sphincter (LES), may lead to esophagitis and chronic heartburn. Primary among these is the spontaneous relaxation of the LES that occurs in many otherwise healthy persons as they age. Gastric reflux into the esophagus is also frequently associated with hiatal hernia, a common condition in which the upper portion of the stomach tends to slide upward into the lower chest because of weakness of the diaphragmatic muscles and ligaments that normally hold the stomach in place. Since many persons with hiatal hernias do not experience reflux or heartburn and because a large number of patients with these complaints do not have hiatal hernias, the frequent association of hiatal hernia and esophagitis may be only coincidental.

In infants LES relaxation is a fairly frequent cause of regurgitative vomiting, a condition called chalasia (relaxation) of the esophagus. However, esophagitis is not usually a complication of chalasia, because gastric contents in infants are usually of low acidity and because LES function generally becomes normal spontaneously within a few weeks or months.

Less common causes of LES relaxation and esophagitis are the prolonged use of a nasogastric tube for decompression of the stomach in certain medical conditions and the disease known as scleroderma, or progressive systemic sclerosis (hardening of tissues). It is not evident why the nasogastric tube reduces pressure in the LES, but it clearly promotes reflux, especially in bedridden patients who must lie flat on their backs. Scleroderma is an uncommon disorder that leads to hardening of the skin and to inflammation and degeneration of muscular tissue in many parts of the body, including the digestive system. Scleroderma in the esophagus reduces peristalsis and relaxes pressure in the LES because of muscular damage, thus promoting both reflux from stomach to esophagus and stasis of refluxed gastric contents in the esophagus, the two primary causes of esophagitis. Patients with scleroderma commonly experience delayed passage of swallowed food through the esophagus and often complain of recurrent episodes of heartburn.

### Complications of esophagitis

The major complications of chronic esophagitis are the formation of esophageal ulcers; stricture, or narrowing, of the opening of the esophagus due to scarring; anemia; aspiration pneumonia; and dysplasia (abnormal cellular changes) of the mucous membrane of the esophagus.

*Esophageal ulcers.* Ulcerations (interruptions or breaks in the mucous membrane) of the esophagus are peptic in nature, similar in all respects to ulcers that occur in the stomach and upper part of the small intestine. Esophageal ulcers are usually round in shape but may also be slitlike. They vary in size from only one millimeter in diameter to more than ten millimeters, and they are usually partially filled with a yellowish white substance exuded by nearby blood vessels. Such ulcers may bleed, or they may perforate the wall of the esophagus; upon healing, they often produce scarring that leads to stricture, or narrowing, of the esophagus.

Esophageal ulcers commonly cause pain in the lower chest under the breastbone and may be suspected when a patient with a history of recurrent heartburn begins to experience a more severe form of distress in the

Courtesy, Dr. John A. LoGiudice, Dr. Walter J. Hogan, and Dr. Joseph E. Geenen

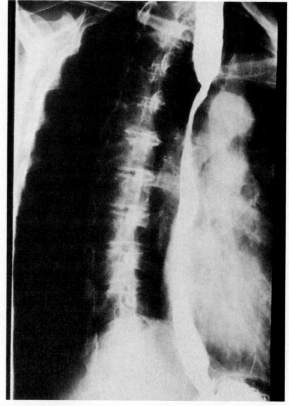

*A stricture, or narrowing, of the esophagus, as seen in this X-ray, may be caused by the growth of abnormal cells in the mucous membrane of the esophageal lining. The abnormal tissue evidently forms as a result of repeated irritation.*

same area. Cigarette smoking and the ingestion of coffee or acidic fruit juices commonly increase the discomfort. The pain is usually aggravated by swallowing, but it may be relieved by the ingestion of milk or antacids.

*Esophageal stricture.* Strictures of the esophagus—i.e., narrowing of the interior opening, or lumen—result from chronic esophagitis or esophageal ulceration, both inflammatory processes that induce a scarring reaction as they heal. The presence of a stricture is first perceived as a painless difficulty in swallowing, epitomized in a recurrent feeling of delayed passage of food through the lower chest area. Ingested food is rarely regurgitated, as patients learn that the discomfort eventually passes and can be relieved by easing the transit of the bolus with the swallowing of liquids. Patients also learn to chew more thoroughly and to avoid tough meat, dry bread, coarse vegetables, and any other foods that are difficult to masticate. Nonetheless, patients with esophageal strictures eventually begin to lose weight in the attempt to cope with the added effort of eating. Paradoxically, the heartburn associated with esophagitis commonly disappears as the symptoms of stricture appear, for the stricture itself actually prevents reflux of gastric contents. The peptic strictures resulting from chronic reflux esophagitis are usually very short in length—generally no more than one to two centimeters (0.4 to 0.8 in)—and are to be distinguished from the much longer and more occlusive strictures that are caused by the ingestion of lye or other corrosive agents.

*Anemia.* The development of anemia is a common complication of prolonged esophagitis and is due to chronic blood loss. Bleeding occurs on the inflamed surface of the lower esophagus; it is usually quite slow, although rarely an esophageal ulcer will erode deep into the submucosal tissue, exposing a fairly large blood vessel and causing a more brisk hemorrhage. Patients are generally unaware of the esophageal bleeding and may be diagnosed as anemic only upon routine physical examination. Blood loss may also be detected by checking stools chemically; grossly black (melenic) stools from bleeding esophagitis are quite uncommon. Patients suffering from anemia may also complain of weakness and shortness of breath on exertion, symptoms that may develop slowly over a period of many weeks.

*Aspiration pneumonia.* A severe but infrequent complication of chronic gastroesophageal reflux, not necessarily associated with esophagitis, is aspiration pneumonia. This disorder results from the unconscious inhalation of refluxed gastric contents, usually while the patient is lying down or sleeping. Aspiration pneumonia generally is not a sudden acute illness but is more likely to be insidious in onset, associated with chronic cough or episodes of wheezing; patients may gradually become progressively short of breath. The illness is often originally considered a form of bronchitis, or even asthma. The true diagnosis usually becomes apparent when patients give an additional history of heartburn or regurgitation and when a chest X-ray shows chronic pneumonic changes in the bases of both lungs.

*Dysplasia.* A recently recognized complication of chronic esophagitis, dysplasia seems to be the result of repeated irritation of the rapidly dividing flat, skinlike cells of the esophageal membrane. For unknown reasons, these so-called squamous cells change into the kind of cells typically seen in the stomach and small intestine. Some may actually secrete mucus or acid, while others appear to adopt the configuration of absorptive cells of the lining of the small bowel. Ulcers and long strictures may develop in dysplastic tissue, and clinical evidence indicates that this tissue may also be associated with an increased risk of cancer of the esophagus. Esophageal dysplasia was first described by N. R. Barrett of England in 1950 and has since been known as Barrett's epithelium.

## Diagnostic measures

Following a complete medical history and physical examination, including blood counts and chemical evaluation of stools for occult (*i.e.,* not readily visible) bleeding, all patients with chronic heartburn should have barium X-ray studies of the esophagus, stomach, and upper small intestine. If these studies show evidence of reflux of barium into the esophagus from the stomach, with no other abnormalities, the diagnosis of gastroesophageal reflux is essentially confirmed. If peristalsis in the esophagus is abnormally slowed, the possibility of scleroderma may be considered. The presence of an ulceration or stricture, however, or the detection of the site of occult bleeding requires direct examination of the esophagus by endoscopy.

Endoscopy consists of the passage of a flexible fiber-optic instrument through the mouth into the esophagus and stomach, a procedure that can be performed quickly and easily under local anesthesia and with mild sedation. Using the endoscope, the physician can look directly at the entire mucous membrane of the esophagus and stomach, photograph areas of abnormality, and distinguish suspicious lesions that may require biopsy. Points of bleeding are easily detected, and ulcerations and strictures can be identified. Endoscopy and X-ray studies establish the causes of nearly all cases of chronic heartburn.

Occasionally a patient with heartburn shows no obvious abnormalities in X-rays or endoscopic examination, in which case further testing may be necessary. Among such procedures are the acid perfusion and pH (acid) monitor tests. The acid perfusion test involves passing a soft tube into the midesophagus and successively running acid and neutral fluids through the tube. In a patient with true acid-reflux heartburn, the symptoms generally will be reproduced when acid is introduced through the tube and will disappear when acid perfusion is stopped and water introduced. Similarly, the pH monitoring test will detect an acid environment in patients with true heartburn but not in those whose symptoms are unrelated to reflux. It may also be desirable to measure the pressure in the lower esophageal sphincter with a special device called an esophageal manometer. Patients with true gastroesophageal reflux have significantly lower than normal pressure in the sphincter.

## Treatment

Treatment of heartburn generally concentrates on the prevention or reduction of the backflow of gastric contents into the esophagus. A secondary but also important consideration is reduction of the acidity of gastric contents to prevent further aggravation of the inflammatory process by those stomach secretions that do reach the esophagus. Nonsurgical treatment is accordingly designed to achieve these goals.

*Measures to relieve reflux.* For reasons that are not clear, weight loss alone often greatly diminishes reflux in patients with weak gastroesophageal sphincters. The goal in this case is merely to reduce the patient's weight to a normal level; further reduction does not seem to be beneficial. Tight undergarments such as girdles and corsets also aggravate reflux and are, therefore, not recommended for persons suffering from heartburn. Patients should be advised to avoid assuming the recumbent position or bending deeply at the waist while working. Bending at the waist can be avoided by the substitution of a stooping posture. Full recumbency at night can be avoided simply by raising the head end of the bed about four to six inches off the floor; *e.g.*, by using wood blocks or bricks. Most patients adjust well to this slight elevation. Extra pillows often are not effective, as they tend to become compressed during the night, and the necessary degree of elevation is lost. Reflux sometimes occurs during the later stages of pregnancy, apparently from increased hormonal secretion that induces weakness in the lower esophageal sphincter; the condition is almost always relieved by delivery, at which time the hormonal levels promptly return to normal.

Avoidance of cigarette smoking and large meals and exclusion of alcohol, chocolate, and caffeine from the diet, plus reduction of fat intake, are measures that can be taken to increase the strength of contraction of the sphincter. Certain drugs, such as propranolol (Inderal) and antispasmodic agents (Bentyl, Pro-Banthine, etc.) are also known to reduce sphincter pressure and should be avoided if possible.

Two drugs, bethanechol chloride (Urecholine) and metoclopramide (Reglan), both generally well tolerated, have been shown in careful studies to increase pressure in the sphincter. Their regular use is often accompanied by marked relief of heartburn.

*Measures to reduce gastric acidity.* Numerous nonprescription liquid antacids reduce the acidity of gastric contents for up to three hours after a single dose, thus temporarily reducing irritation of the esophagus. Of the many liquid antacids available, those consisting of either magnesium or aluminum alkalinizing agents are preferable to antacids containing calcium salts, which have been shown to lead to a secondary increase in gastric acidity. The timing of antacid ingestion is important; they should be taken when gastric acidity is most likely to be increasing, namely, one and three hours after each meal and at bedtime. Although they are more convenient, antacid tablets are not nearly as effective as liquid forms. The usual dose of concentrated antacids is one tablespoon and of regular antacids twice that amount. Since magnesium-containing antacids tend to have a laxative effect if used regularly and aluminum-containing antacids tend to constipate, most patients try to alternate doses of the two types.

Acid secretion itself can be reduced by the use of agents that block the action of histamine on the acid-secreting cells of the stomach. The two such agents currently available, cimetidine (Tagamet) and ranitidine (Zantac), are quite effective and generally well tolerated in full doses for at least two months and for longer periods at reduced dosage. They too have been shown to be very effective in the treatment of reflux esophagitis.

It should be emphasized that very few patients with esophagitis require all of these therapeutic measures for control of symptoms. Most will respond well to a partial regimen.

*Treatment of complications.* Esophageal ulcers and blood loss from esophagitis are generally well managed by use of the measures described above. The patient with anemia should have regular monitoring of stools for occult blood and blood counts for indications of improvement. Iron supplements are frequently necessary for the management of more pronounced cases of anemia. Aspiration pneumonia also responds well to antireflux and acid-lowering measures. Strictures of the esophagus may require enlargement by the passage of rubber dilators through the mouth, a procedure that is not usually difficult or complicated. In combination with antacid and antireflux measures, one or two sessions of dilatation are often sufficient to ease strictures and prevent their recurrence. The abnormal cellular changes of Barrett's epithelium do not disappear after successful medical treatment, however, and bear further watching once they are detected.

*Surgical management.* In about 15% of patients, heartburn and esophagitis or the complications of esophagitis may persist or recur despite adherence to therapeutic measures. Other patients may object to following the course of any prolonged medical therapy. In these cases the best alternative is surgery. The most successful procedure is one in which the upper portion of the stomach is wrapped around and sewn to the lower esophagus. This infolding procedure, or plication, is beneficial both in curing reflux and in preventing further bouts of esophagitis. In a few cases the dysplastic tissues of Barrett's epithelium have actually returned to their normal form after a plication procedure. It is also an effective measure for patients with significant degrees of aspiration pneumonia. The only disadvantages are the trauma, slight risk, and inconvenience of the operation itself. Where hiatal hernia is present, surgical repair of the hernia alone should not be performed for the relief of esophagitis, as the rate of recurrence is extremely high. In any case, surgical treatment of heartburn and chronic esophagitis should always be secondary to attempts at medical management of these conditions.

*—Harvey J. Dworken, M.D.*

# After the Baby Is Born

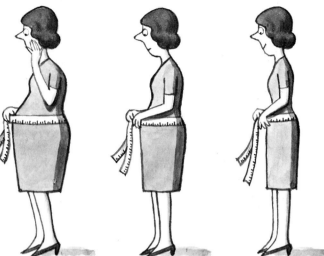

The postpartum period, or puerperium, is that period after birth during which the mother's body returns to the nonpregnant state. Although some changes in pregnancy never disappear completely, adherence to commonsense principles of health care can foster a rapid return to vigor, good muscle tone, and normal weight. During the first few days of the puerperium there is a rapid recovery from fatigue, discomfort, and pain, followed by a more gradual return to the nonpregnant state. It can be of great help to the new mother and her family to know something of the physiologic changes and intense emotional readjustments of this time.

## The immediate postpartum period: normal physical changes

After birth the mother immediately experiences an overwhelming feeling of relief, joy, and sense of achievement and shows great interest in her new infant. Physical fatigue and a desire for sleep usually follow. Later, the mother may experience an episode of shivering and, sometimes, brief nausea and even vomiting. Generally, a feeling of well-being, often accompanied by hunger, soon returns. Slight temporary fever sometimes occurs within the first 24 hours.

*The genital organs.* The uterus shows the most remarkable changes during this period. It weighs about 900 g (2 lb) at the end of labor, losing 450 g (1 lb) during the first week after delivery and 225 g (0.5 lb) in the second week; it then slowly shrinks to about 60 g (2 oz) by the end of six weeks. The length of the uterus gradually decreases by about 1.25 cm (0.5 in) per day; it should no longer be felt in the abdomen by the 12th day. During the puerperium the uterus continues to contract and relax rhythmically; during nursing these contractions increase, often to the point of discomfort, especially in women having delivered their second and subsequent babies. The intensity of these so-called afterpains decreases steadily.

The lining of the uterus (the decidua) is rapidly shed, producing a discharge called lochia, composed of blood and tissue fragments. The bright red lochia gradually become paler but continue to resemble blood for the next seven to ten days. After the tenth day the lochia become yellowish, but when the mother is in an upright position, blood usually appears in the discharge. Although the lochia commonly develop an unpleasant odor, this is not a sign of infection. The discharge stops within three to five weeks after delivery.

If the mother is not breast-feeding, menstruation usually resumes in the sixth to eighth week as the uterine lining, or endometrium, regrows. In nursing mothers the endometrium remains dormant, and menstruation generally ceases temporarily because the hormones that stimulate the ovaries are suppressed. However, many women do menstruate while nursing, in some cases many months before the baby is weaned. A woman's chance of conceiving while nursing and not menstruating is very small but by no means impossible. Once menstruation resumes, this chance becomes higher. The nursing mother who does not wish to conceive must use some form of contraception, whether or not she is menstruating.

The vagina, capacious and smooth-walled after the stretching during birth, shrinks steadily following delivery; the folds in the lining (rugae) reappear in the third week. If the mother breast-feeds, however, the vagina remains thin-skinned and delicate because the dormant ovaries are producing very little estrogen. Thus, when she resumes sexual intercourse, she may notice some soreness and lack of lubrication. If an episiotomy (an incision into the vagina and perineum that enlarges the vaginal opening) was performed during delivery, the sutured tissues may be more tender at first.

*The breasts.* During pregnancy the breasts enlarge, and the nipples and surrounding areolae become more pigmented. For the first two days after birth there is little change, except that a thin, yellowish, watery secretion, called colostrum, is produced. This substance contains some of the mother's antibodies against infection and transfers early immunities to the breast-fed baby. When secretion of milk begins, on the third or fourth day, the breasts become further enlarged, firm, tense, and sometimes tender. This condition, called engorgement, can become quite severe and may even cause a short-lived fever. When severe, the secretion of milk is inhibited; regular suckling relieves the problem, inducing a ready flow of milk that soon adapts to

369

the needs of the infant. After weaning, the breasts are always softer and often smaller than prior to the first pregnancy. Large breasts tend to sag and stretch after pregnancy and nursing.

*The abdominal wall.* The skin and muscles of the abdomen are greatly stretched by pregnancy. Stretched muscles never fully regain their original tone, but some gradual recovery occurs and can be improved by a program of regular exercise. The rectus muscles (a pair of vertical, straplike muscles in the midline of the abdomen) are sometimes widely separated during the pregnancy and do not return fully to the prepregnant position.

*The urinary tract.* The ureters (tubes from the kidneys to the bladder) become dilated by the hormonal effects of pregnancy, which predisposes to urinary infections. Because the bladder is displaced upward and compressed as the uterus enlarges, frequency of urination is common during pregnancy. The bladder is often distended during labor and suffers loss of contractile power for a short time afterward. High fluid intake, during pregnancy and after delivery, helps to prevent infection; following delivery, complete emptying of the bladder by catheterization helps to prevent distension. In predisposed women, stretching of the supporting pelvic tissues may start a process that leads in later life to sagging (prolapse) of the bladder base, rectum, and uterus. Unfortunately, there is no effective preventive measure, although episiotomy, which eases stretching during delivery, may be helpful.

*Bones and joints.* Deficiency of calcium, phosphorus, and vitamin D during pregnancy can lead to softening of the bones. Even with adequate nutrition, however, the supporting ligaments of all the joints are always softened and stretched in pregnancy. This factor, along with increased weight and compensating changes in posture, accounts for a greater incidence of backache among pregnant women. For these reasons many obstetricians advise against very strenuous exercise during pregnancy and the puerperium. On the other hand, regular gentle exercise is advisable (particularly walking and swimming).

*Endocrine system.* Pregnancy is accompanied by extensive endocrine changes, and delivery produces quite sudden variations in these functions. The most extensive variation occurs in estrogen and progesterone levels, which are very high during pregnancy and drop precipitously after birth. After delivery the pituitary gland begins to produce large amounts of prolactin (the hormone that stimulates milk production) and oxytocin (which causes the uterus to contract and milk to eject). Conversely, until lactation ceases, the pituitary produces smaller amounts of gonadotropins (hormones that stimulate the ovaries). These variations play an important role in emotional changes.

*Cardiovascular system.* The work of the heart is increased during pregnancy, largely because of an increase in the volume of circulating blood. In the first few days after delivery, blood volume is reduced through elimination of excess water by the kidneys, and cardiac function returns rapidly to normal. The normal heart adjusts easily to these changes. Many women also have a mild degree of anemia (low red blood cell count) after delivery. It is wise for all women to take an iron supplement during pregnancy and for at least a few weeks after giving birth.

The blood pressure shows minor variations during pregnancy, but even in healthy women a temporary increase is noted by the second week of the puerperium and may take many weeks to return to normal. In women with high blood pressure this additional increase is exaggerated, requiring treatment in some cases.

The veins of the lower limbs are subjected to an increase of pressure during pregnancy, sometimes causing varicose, or dilated, veins. Smaller veins in the lower leg also dilate, often becoming spidery in appearance with blue or red discoloration. These changes are inevitable, but they may be minimized by periodic rest with the legs elevated and regular use of elastic support hose, and they always diminish after delivery. Hemorrhoids—dilated veins within the anus—are another form of varicose veins. Because of pressure from the enlarged uterus, and often aggravated by constipation, hemorrhoids develop to some extent in most pregnant women. During birth they become swollen, more prominent, and sometimes painful. Treatment includes rest, the application of cold packs, and the use of soothing, anesthetic, anti-inflammatory ointments. Later, surgical removal may be advisable.

*The skin.* Early in pregnancy increased pigment appears in the dark areas of the skin, such as that surrounding the nipples and vulva. Occasionally, in white women patchy areas of brownish pigment—the so-called mask of pregnancy—may appear on the face; in black women areas of lighter skin may develop. Other common changes include a vertical, pigmented line on the abdomen, reddish areas on the palms, and small spidery red spots on the upper half of the body. The development of small, soft outgrowths called skin tags is not unusual. Most of these changes disappear after delivery. Likewise, acne that develops during pregnancy generally clears up in the postpartum period. Perspiration is often more profuse during pregnancy and for a short while after delivery.

Stretch marks, caused by stretching and tearing of elastic fibers in the skin, do not completely disappear after pregnancy. These marks are most frequent and extensive on the abdomen but may appear on the breasts or thighs as well. They begin as pink or red lines and usually widen; later they become purplish. After delivery they slowly fade, leaving pale, faintly wrinkled areas. Avoiding excessive weight gain minimizes the extent of stretch marks.

Hair growth on the body and scalp often increases during pregnancy. After delivery some scalp hair is shed, often profusely, for several weeks or months, but regrowth nearly always follows. In rare instances women lose all of their scalp hair after pregnancy; permanent baldness, however, is exceedingly rare.

*Gastrointestinal system.* Stomach and bowel symptoms common in pregnancy include nausea and vomiting, changes in appetite, gassiness, heartburn, and constipation. Most of these disappear after delivery, but constipation tends to persist during lactation and may aggravate hemorrhoids.

*Weight gain and loss.* Normal weight gain during pregnancy should be between 20 and 35 lb. Women who adhere to rules of good nutrition usually are within this range. An average of 14 lb is lost at birth, with a slight additional loss in the following days as the water accumulated during pregnancy is excreted and the uterus shrinks. Loss from accumulated fat stores is slower but usually progresses steadily throughout lactation. Women who do not nurse their infants often lose weight more slowly.

*Recovery from cesarean section.* As almost one in five births today is by cesarean section (delivery through the abdominal wall), a few words about the recovery period are necessary. Some pain, discomfort, and restriction of mobility will occur for a few days after the surgery. However, in modern postoperative care early movement and walking are strongly encouraged. Breast-feeding may be slightly delayed—usually by no more than a few hours. In the absence of complications cesarean section should not adversely affect the patient's recovery and capacity to care for her baby. If possible, however, she should plan to have some help at home for at least one or two weeks after her return. Thereafter, her recovery should be no different from that of a woman who has delivered vaginally.

### Emotional changes and postpartum depression

Pregnancy and motherhood cause significant changes in a woman's life and, as expected, the emotional effects are great. Much emotional energy is invested in preparations for the infant. Anxiety about the pregnancy, the process of labor and delivery, and the health of the baby are common. Any underlying emotional disturbances or tensions in the marriage may be intensified during the pregnancy and postpartum period and sometimes require treatment and counseling.

While happiness and a sense of achievement are predominant in the early postpartum period, it is well recognized that a strong feeling of letdown or even depression is almost universal, usually occurring on about the fourth day after delivery—the "fourth-day blues." This feeling, partly caused by the wide hormonal variations, usually lasts for one day and passes as mysteriously as it began. In some cases it may occur later and last longer; in a few women it develops into a more serious and lasting postpartum depression requiring treatment. Later in the puerperium it is perfectly natural for the new mother to feel temporarily fatigued, exasperated, or anxious, especially during the many minor crises that mark the infant's early life.

### Complications of the puerperium

*Hemorrhage.* Excessive bleeding may occur very early after the birth, before, during, or after the delivery of the placenta (afterbirth). If the placenta remains in the uterus, the physician will remove it. Bleeding after the placental delivery is treated by massage and pressure on the uterus and by administration of oxytocic drugs, which cause contraction of the uterus. Hemorrhage may also occur later, up to several weeks after delivery, sometimes because of retention within the uterus of a portion of the placenta or because of bleeding from the placental bed. Treatment consists of the immediate administration of oxytocic drugs, followed by gentle surgical scraping (curettage) of the uterine cavity. Severe hemorrhage requires the administration of fluids into the veins and, when indicated, blood transfusion. Hemorrhage can also occur from vaginal blood vessels torn during the course of the delivery or from the episiotomy.

*Infection.* Bacterial infection of the uterus, or puerperal sepsis, may manifest itself some days after delivery. Symptoms include fever, pain, and abnormal discharge from the vagina. Before asepsis (*i.e.,* prevention of infection) was practiced and antibiotics were available, this was a greatly feared complication of childbirth that often resulted in maternal death. A variety of bacteria can cause such infection, originating from the mother herself or, less often, from those tending the patient. Identification of the bacterial agents and prompt administration of the appropriate antibiotics usually resolve such infections.

Subinvolution—the slower than normal return of the uterus to nonpregnant size—is probably caused by mild infection within the uterus. Bladder infection also occurs during the postpartum period. The episiotomy may also become infected, and this may result in drainage of pus if not promptly treated.

*Breast complications.* Both nursing and nonnursing mothers almost always experience some degree of breast swelling. In nursing mothers, if swelling is severe when the infant is not suckling strongly, the discomfort can be somewhat relieved by partial emptying of the breasts with a breast pump or expression of milk by hand. In nonnursing mothers the breasts should not be milked; application of cold or warm packs may be helpful. Bromocriptine (Parlodel), a drug that prevents lactation, is effective in such cases.

### Postpartum care

The majority of U.S. births take place in hospitals, but the increasing tendency is to allow patients to return home as soon as possible, sometimes within 24 hours. The current average hospital stay of three to four days is beneficial, however, allowing the mother time to rest and, if she is inexperienced, providing time for instruction about nursing, breast care, and general aspects of infant care.

Most of the rules of postpartum care at home are simple and logical. The mother should follow her own instincts and medical advice and should avoid the often conflicting advice of well-meaning relatives and friends.

*Rest.* Because adequate rest is essential for good health in the postpartum period, the new mother and her family should give careful thought to planning the first weeks at home. The help of a competent adult is invaluable during this period. At a minimum, during the first week at home, the mother should take a one-hour nap both morning and afternoon and should retire early to get the maximum possible rest between the infant's waking times. She should not lift heavy objects or do heavy household tasks for at least two weeks. The frequency and duration of congratulatory visits should be kept to a reasonable minimum. Obviously, no one with a known infectious condition should be permitted into the presence of mother or infant. After the first two weeks at home, the mother's activities can be steadily increased as long as she avoids fatigue.

*Care of the breasts.* The nursing mother should wear a well-fitting, comfortable nursing brassiere with soft absorbent pads over the nipples. These pads should be changed often. Unless there is soreness of the nipples, the modern tendency is simply to keep them clean with a bland soap and water. Cracked, or split, nipples require extra care. The nipple should heal in a few days if it is protected by a nursing shield and treated with a steroid lotion. Breast infection can occur in the lactating mother at any time. Suspected infection, indicated by redness, swelling, pain, and fever, requires prompt consultation with a physician.

*Nutrition.* A sufficient intake of protein foods is foremost in importance. The postpartum diet should also be low in fats and should include adequate amounts of complex carbohydrates. The intake of essential minerals and vitamins should be liberal. For those not allergic to them, milk products are essential for their high calcium content and nutritional qualities. Skimmed milk and skimmed-milk products contain all the essential nutrients without the high caloric content of whole milk. A high fluid intake is also strongly advised but should not consist of carbonated drinks or large amounts of coffee or tea. Water, fruit juices, and milk are best. A high-fiber diet (leafy vegetables and salads, fruit, whole grains) is advisable for both its nutritional value and its effectiveness in preventing constipation. Meals should be eaten at intervals evenly spaced throughout the day, and a wide variety of foods should be included. The advice of a dietitian or nutritionist can be extremely

helpful in developing a well-balanced diet. The guidelines are equally applicable during pregnancy and are especially important for nursing mothers.

Excessive weight gain during pregnancy is unhealthy; it may increase hemorrhoids, back pain, and high blood pressure and can lead to diabetes. Complicated delivery is also commoner in obese women. It is a mistake, however, for the pregnant woman or new mother to try to lose weight rapidly by strenuous dieting, as there is a danger that she will deprive herself and the infant of essential nutrients.

*Exercise.* For the first week after delivery, no extra exercise should be attempted. Thereafter, a slowly increasing routine of exercises should be undertaken to restore muscle strength and tone and to increase cardiovascular fitness.

*Personal hygiene.* Both bathing and showering are permitted, but douches should not be used during the postpartum period. While bleeding and discharge persist, regular cleansing of the vulva and perianal region with soap and water are advisable. Tampons should not be used; only external sanitary pads should be used, and they should be changed frequently. Tenderness in the episiotomy may be relieved by warmth, either from a heating pad (on the lowest setting) or from a warm sitz bath. The latter treatment also relieves tender hemorrhoids. A high fiber diet and liberal fluid intake will help to avoid constipation; other remedies, such as stool softeners and laxatives, should be used only when advised by the physician.

*Medications.* Almost all medications enter the breast milk and are ingested by the suckling infant. Therefore, the nursing mother should not take drugs of any kind except on the advice of a physician.

*Sexual activity and contraception.* Sexual intercourse generally should not be attempted until one week after all bleeding and discharge have ceased completely and, preferably, not until a postpartum examination has been made by the physician. For the discomfort that often accompanies the resumption of sexual relations, a lubricating jelly is often helpful. Although, as noted above, pregnancy is unlikely during lactation, contraception is advisable. At first some form of barrier method—condom, jelly, or foam—is preferable; later, a diaphragm can be fitted or an intrauterine device inserted. Oral contraceptives should not be used by women who are breast-feeding.

*The postpartum examination.* Six weeks after delivery a postpartum examination should be performed by the physician. This is also an opportunity to describe unusual symptoms and to discuss concerns about physical and emotional adjustments. Finally, the new parents and those around them should remember that birth is a miraculous event. Celebration and happiness should not be marred by unnecessary anxieties.

*—Lionel J. Schewitz, M.D.*

# Gallstones and Gallbladder Disease

The gallbladder is a small saclike organ that stores and concentrates bile produced in the liver. In the digestive process, bile helps to break down fats and prepare them for the digestive action of pancreatic enzymes. Concentrated bile accumulates in the gallbladder between meals and, after a meal, is released through a tubular structure, the cystic duct.

Most gallbladder disease results from the formation of gallstones—insoluble masses, usually of cholesterol—within the gallbladder. The presence of stones causes the wall of the gallbladder to become inflamed and, in some cases, secondarily infected by bacteria when stones reduce or obstruct the flow of bile out of the cystic duct. Inflammation may also occur as a complication of sluggish contractions of the gallbladder and incomplete emptying of stored bile. Abdominal pain is the chief symptom of gallbladder disease. The pain is usually steady and of increasing severity; it is commonly accompanied by nausea, vomiting, and abdominal bloating.

Although the functions of the gallbladder are important aids to digestion, they are in no way essential to a healthy life; even after the surgical removal of the gallbladder, digestion continues normally, without discomfort or symptoms of disease. It is believed that the remaining portions of the bile duct system in some measure assume the storage and concentration functions of the absent gallbladder.

## Anatomy and physiology of the gallbladder

*Ducts of the liver and gallbladder.* Bile flows from the liver to the gallbladder through a series of ducts. First it passes from an intricate system of ducts within the liver into a simpler ductal system called the extrahepatic biliary tree. The uppermost elements of the extrahepatic biliary tree are the right and left hepatic ducts, each about 1 or 2 cm (0.4 or 0.8 in) in length and each draining one of the two main lobes of the liver. These ducts converge to form the common hepatic duct, which is about 3 cm (1.2 in) long. This latter structure, in turn, joins the cystic duct and forms the common bile duct, which is about 7.5 cm (3 in) long and empties into the upper small intestine, or duodenum. The cystic duct is almost 4 cm (1.6 in) long; it differs from the other ducts in the biliary tree in that its inner lining, or mucous

membrane, is cast into a series of spiral folds that function as a valve, controlling the emptying of the gallbladder.

At its far end the cystic duct joins the gallbladder, which lies against the undersurface of the liver. The gallbladder is approximately 7 to 10 cm (2.8 to 4 in) long and has a fluid capacity of 30 to 50 ml (1 to 1.6 fl oz). Bile can enter and leave the gallbladder only by way of the cystic duct. Passage of bile from the common bile duct to the upper intestine is controlled by a sphincter, or ring of muscle, at its lowermost point in the wall of the duodenum. Just above this point the bile duct is somewhat widened and, in most people, is joined by the main duct of the pancreas. Thus, both pancreatic secretions and bile enter the small intestine at the same site. This conjunction is important because the main function of bile in digestion is to serve as a detergent, breaking large globules of dietary fat into tiny droplets that are much more readily digested by pancreatic enzymes.

Bile is formed by the liver almost continuously, but its flow into the upper intestine is intermittent and occurs only upon relaxation of the sphincter muscle in the wall of the duodenum. This relaxation generally occurs after meals, stimulated by hormones released from cells in the wall of the duodenum. Between meals bile passes from the liver into the common hepatic duct, up the cystic duct, and into the gallbladder, where it is stored until released by the stimulus of the next meal. At that time the muscular wall of the gallbladder contracts and forces bile toward the intestine. While in the gallbladder, liver bile becomes concentrated as water is absorbed by the mucous membrane, thus changing it from a watery, golden-yellow fluid into a highly viscous, greenish-black solution.

*Composition of bile.* Liver bile derives its golden color from the pigment known as bilirubin, which is primarily a by-product of the destruction of old red blood cells. Bilirubin circulates to the liver and is excreted by that organ into the bile. While bilirubin is chemically altered in the intestinal tract and becomes responsible for the brown color of stool, it has no known physiologic function. More important components of bile are steroids (four-ringed organic compounds), cholesterol, bile acids and their corresponding salts, and lecithin (phosphatidylcholine). By itself cholesterol is insoluble in water; it becomes soluble in bile only in a chemical reaction with the bile salts (formed from the bile acids) and lecithin.

There are four types of bile acid normally present: the primary bile acids, cholic and chenodeoxycholic, synthesized in the liver from cholesterol; and the secondary bile acids, deoxycholic and lithocholic, formed by bacterial action on bile salts after they have entered the lower intestine. Secondary forms appear in the bile after absorption from the lower small intestine and recirculation to the liver. This recirculation process allows the body to conserve vital bile salts—these might otherwise become rapidly depleted, because the daily requirement of bile salts for the digestion of dietary fat is greater than the capacity of the healthy liver to synthesize the necessary amounts. The bile salts are the constituent of bile responsible for its important digestive function as a detergent—that is, a substance capable of breaking down large globules of fat into smaller particles.

In addition to bilirubin, bile acids and salts, lecithin, and cholesterol, the bile also contains water—its main component—and various inorganic salts.

## The formation of gallstones

There are two major types of gallstones, those that are composed purely or mainly of cholesterol (cholesterol gallstones) and those composed purely or mainly of bilirubin and calcium (pigment gallstones). In the Western world about 80% of gallstones are of the cholesterol variety.

*Cholesterol gallstones.* Cholesterol precipitates, or becomes separated, from the bile solution when its concentration exceeds the capacity of the existing concentrations of bile salts and lecithin to render it into soluble molecules. How and why these changes in concentration occur is not clear, but it is known that patients with cholesterol gallstones have lower concentrations of bile acids in their liver bile than do normal individuals. In some cases a tendency for higher cholesterol content is genetic, the occurrence of gallstones being higher in some ethnic populations (as in certain American Indian tribes) than in others. Patients who are obese or diabetic and persons who ingest a diet high in cholesterol also have an increased incidence of cholesterol gallstones. So too do women who have borne children and women who have been treated with female sex hormones for a period of time. Aging also appears to favor the development of cholesterol gallstones in both men and women. The incidence of this disease is very high; it is estimated that one out of every ten persons in the U.S. has gallstones.

*Pigment gallstones.* The formation of pigment stones has nothing to do with concentrations of cholesterol in diet or in the bile. Incidence is roughly equal in the two sexes. Cirrhosis of the liver and certain types of anemia

(sickle-cell anemia, thalassemia) seem to be predisposing factors in the development of pigment gallstones. These disorders are associated with the secretion of increased amounts of bilirubin or of enzymes that decompose bilirubin in the bile.

## Diseases of the gallbladder

Most gallbladder disease is the result of gallstones, which cause the wall of the organ to become inflamed; in some cases secondary infection by intestinal bacteria occurs when stones impede or obstruct the flow of bile out of the gallbladder. The wall of the gallbladder can also become inflamed as a complication of sluggish contractions and incomplete emptying of bile.

The major symptom of gallbladder disease is abdominal pain. The pain, usually steady and of increasing severity, appears most commonly in the upper abdomen, radiating to the right side and occasionally into the back and right shoulder. It may last for a half day or more and is often accompanied by nausea, vomiting, and abdominal bloating. Attacks usually subside spontaneously, leaving the patient weakened for several days. Once the symptoms have disappeared, however, patients may be completely comfortable for days or weeks at a time before the next attack occurs. Attacks often begin late at night following a large meal, but they may appear at any time of the day. Cramping pain, belching, diarrhea, and the passage of flatus (bowel gas) are rarely, if ever, symptoms of gallbladder disease. Attacks are believed to occur when a contraction of the gallbladder, or biliary spasm, forces gallstones against the narrow exit into the cystic duct.

*Cholecystitis.* Fever may occur with biliary spasm if the wall of the gallbladder becomes inflamed, a condition called cholecystitis, or if the bile in the gallbladder becomes infected (acute cholecystitis). Patients with acute cholecystitis may also experience shaking chills, or rigors, in addition to their abdominal pain. High fever and extreme tenderness over the gallbladder in the upper right portion of the abdomen suggest the presence of an abscess, or empyema, in the gallbladder. This complication constitutes an acute emergency and requires prompt treatment with antibiotics, intravenous fluids, and, often, surgery. Occasionally, it may lead to rupture or perforation of the gallbladder with peritonitis (inflammation of the abdominal cavity) and an abscess in or beneath the liver.

*Jaundice.* When gallstones pass out of the gallbladder and into the common bile duct, jaundice appears as a complication of gallbladder disease. Stones lodged in the duct impede, and—on rare occasions—obstruct, the flow of bile from the liver to the small intestine; bilirubin backs up into the bloodstream from the liver, causing yellowing of skin and of the whites of the eyes and darkening of the urine. As is the case with cholecystitis, rigors and fever suggest ascending cholangitis, an infection in the biliary tree that is often accompanied

Photo courtesy, Dr. John A. LoGiudice, Dr. Walter J. Hogan, and Dr. Joseph E. Geenen

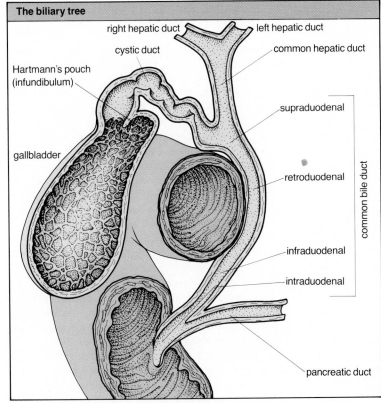

**The biliary tree**

- right hepatic duct
- left hepatic duct
- cystic duct
- common hepatic duct
- Hartmann's pouch (infundibulum)
- supraduodenal
- gallbladder
- retroduodenal
- common bile duct
- infraduodenal
- intraduodenal
- pancreatic duct

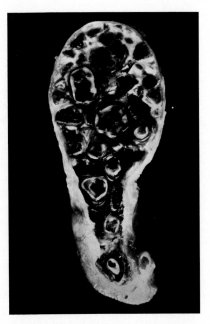

*An extremely severe case of gallstones is revealed in a diagnostic X-ray.*

by deepening jaundice and bacterial growth in the bloodstream.

*Cholecytoses and cancers.* There are also uncommon conditions of the gallbladder wall, called cholecytoses, that are of uncertain cause. They may in some cases cause symptoms similar to biliary spasm. One such condition, the so-called porcelain gallbladder, is considered to be a premalignant disease. Cancer of the gallbladder is extremely rare in the Western world and occurs in an exceedingly small percentage of patients with gallstones. In the Orient bile duct cancer is often related to infection of the liver and bile ducts with a parasitic worm, *Clonorchis sinensis.*

## Diagnosis

The first requisite in the detection of gallstones is that both the patient and the physician be aware of early symptoms. Thus, a single attack of upper right abdominal pain—even if it is fairly mild—should be an indication for prompt studies so that the condition can be treated before serious complications develop.

The diagnostic measures to detect gallstones have improved remarkably in recent years. The technique of ultrasonography, or ultrasound, identifies gallstones simply, safely, and reliably by passing high-frequency, inaudible sound waves through the body. Structures in the path of the waves are delineated by the echoes sent back to the receiver, much as sonar detects a sub-

marine or a school of fish in the sea. Water produces no echo, as sound passes straight through it without deflection. Gallstones, however, create a heavy echo with a dead space beyond, since the substance of stones is completely impenetrable to the sound waves. Tissues such as the liver, pancreas, bile ducts, and blood vessels produce greater or lesser echoes depending on their density. Sonography can indicate the outline of the gallbladder, determine the size of the organ, detect stones contained in it, and provide useful information about the pancreas, bile ducts, and liver. False positive sonograms, *i.e.,* those detecting gallstones where none exists, occur in a small percentage of cases; false negative studies are exceedingly rare. Although fairly expensive, ultrasonographic study of the biliary tract is a highly effective diagnostic tool.

Unlike ultrasonography, oral cholecystography depends on X-rays and may not be the procedure of choice for an acutely ill patient. This test, which has been available for more than half a century, depends on absorption of an iodine-containing substance from the intestine and secretion of it by the liver into the biliary tree. The patient swallows the iodinated tablets the night before the X-rays are taken. This material enters the gallbladder and is concentrated there by absorption of water through the gallbladder wall. As it becomes progressively concentrated, the substance grows dense enough to block the passage of X-rays and thus casts a white shadow—representing the area of the gallbladder—on the exposed film. If the gallbladder contains stones, these register on the film as dark shadows against the white background. They will often be seen to move as the patient changes position. When the wall of the gallbladder is acutely or chronically inflamed, however, or when stones block the entrance into the gallbladder, no shadow will appear. If such nonvisualization occurs on two successive days after two doses of the test material, most physicians feel that a diagnosis of gallbladder disease is indicated. Unlike ultrasonography, oral cholecystography cannot be relied upon to detect gallstones in patients with liver disease, jaundice, or certain intestinal disorders causing malabsorption, as any of these complications can also result in nonvisualization, even if the gallbladder itself is normal.

Oral cholecystography thus is a highly reliable indication of gallbladder disease if it shows gallstones and a good measure of a normal state if it reveals a gallbladder free of stones. It is a less reliable indicator of disease in the gallbladder if nonvisualization occurs. For this reason, and because of the relative ease of ultrasonography and the absence of radiation in the ultrasound procedure, many physicians prefer it to cholecystography. At present, lower cost is the major advantage of cholecystography.

## Treatment

Gallstones are often diagnosed incidentally in the workup for other illnesses or even during routine physical examinations. Stones may be revealed by ordinary X-rays of the abdomen taken for reasons unrelated to the gallbladder. They may also be discovered by abdominal sonograms performed during pregnancy or by oral cholecystograms accompanying barium X-rays of the upper gastrointestinal tract. These stones, detected by chance and usually producing no symptoms, are often referred to as "silent" gallstones. Because most silent gallstones tend to remain silent for many years, most physicians are disinclined to recommend treatment. In fact, clinical evidence suggests that gallstones are silent in a majority of the 15 million people in the U.S. who have them; in a recent study of 125 persons with silent gallstones, fewer than 20% experienced any pain or complications during a follow-up period of 11 to 24 years. Treatment in such cases thus seems unnecessary. The one exception to this dictum is the diabetic patient. Because diabetics are believed to be at increased risk of complications from an attack of cholecystitis, many physicians think that the existence of gallstones in a diabetic patient is a sufficient reason to consider removal of the gallbladder.

When gallstones are diagnosed in patients who have had attacks of biliary spasm or cholecystitis, definitive treatment is usually recommended because the risk of

further, possibly more severe attacks is great. Treatment involves surgical removal of the gallbladder, an operation with a low rate of complications and an almost negligible mortality rate. Patients usually remain in the hospital for five to seven days after surgery and recover at home for three or four weeks. After this period they can return to their normal routines and accustomed diets without difficulty. Of course, if surgery is undertaken to correct severe, acute cholecystitis, empyema (abscess) of the gallbladder, or cholangitis, the postoperative period is likely to be more prolonged and complicated. Antibiotics are usually needed to combat secondary infections, and temporary deviation of the flow of bile by means of tubes in the abdominal incision is often necessary to promote good drainage of the biliary tree. The risk of death in such cases may be as high as 5 to 10%.

It has recently become possible to remove stones in the common bile duct internally by passing an endoscope (a flexible viewing tube) through the patient's mouth and stomach and into the upper small intestine. This instrument enables the surgeon to identify the entrance of the common bile duct into the duodenum. A small knifelike wire passed through the endoscope is used to make an incision widening the duct opening enough to allow retained stones to flow harmlessly into the intestine. This procedure has obviated the need for secondary abdominal surgery to eliminate common bile duct stones in patients who have undergone previous removal of the gallbladder.

Dissolution of gallstones with drugs is also possible in selected cases. (The exceptions are patients with pigment or calcified stones or patients whose gallbladders fail to visualize in oral cholecystography.) This treatment is a direct offshoot of the discovery that cholesterol gallstones form when the concentrations of bile acids fall below a critical level. Patients receive daily oral doses of chenodeoxycholic (chenic) acid for an extended period of time—up to two years—and, gradually, concentrations of chenic acid in bile increase and dissolve the precipitated cholesterol. Stones slowly decrease in size and may even disappear completely. This treatment is fairly well tolerated by patients, although its effectiveness depends on variable factors. Large stones dissolve much more slowly than small ones, for example, and stones may not dissolve completely in stout patients. In one sizable study, complete dissolution of gallstones occurred in about 20% of those treated. It is hoped that the use of another bile acid, ursodeoxycholic acid, may yield even better results. For those patients with symptomatic gallstones who are averse to surgery or in whom the risk of surgery is great, dissolution may provide a preferable alternative.

—Harvey J. Dworken, M.D.

# Household Roaches

Few common household insect pests are more repugnant, abundant, unsanitary, persistent, or resistant to eradication than cockroaches. The more than 2,000 known species are among the most primitive living winged insects. Roaches are supremely successful from an evolutionary viewpoint, having developed an array of ecological and reproductive adaptations to ensure survival and—after more than 345 million years on Earth—exhibiting no sign whatever of extinction. Once used in folk medicine in the treatment of ulcers, cancer, and indigestion (often fried in garlic), today they are at best a nuisance and at worst a health hazard—sometimes a serious one.

## Some facts about roaches

Entomologists identify 55 species of roaches in the United States, of which 7 are considered indoor pests. Scientifically, cockroaches are classified as members of the order Orthoptera and thus are related to grasshoppers, crickets, katydids, and other insects with leathery forewings and membranelike hindwings. All roach species have a characteristic broad, flat, oval body and six long legs; they range in color from reddish-brown to light brown and black. The adult males of most species have wings. Species vary in size from those less than 2.5 mm (0.1 in) long to one South American variety with a wingspan of nearly 190 mm (7 in). The word cockroach is a corruption of the Spanish *cucaracha.*

Cockroaches are virtually universal in distribution, although most thrive in warm, humid, dark environments in tropical or temperate climates. They are found in urban, suburban, and rural areas. Roaches—or their eggs—enter homes, offices, and factories as passengers on food, packages, and clothing. Species have spread northward in the United States concealed within imported foods and food products or household goods of immigrants. A few varieties that live out of doors or shelter within sewers occasionally fly into the home or enter on firewood. Those adapted to indoor environments seek damp cellars and caves, bedrooms, libraries, kitchens, and baths. Once inside, they have numerous strategies to avoid eviction. Although fascinating to entomologists for its ability to survive in diverse habitats, the cockroach is more significant in human terms as a carrier of filth and disease.

A roach's appetite is so prodigious and unselective

that it will not starve under even the most unfavorable conditions. Roaches consume almost any organic material, including food of all kinds, paper, wood, glue, fabric, and dead bugs (especially bedbugs). Moreover, their prolific reproductive abilities ensure that they damage far more material than they can eat as their dirt-laden bodies crawl over any surface they can reach. They also give off an offensive musty-moldy odor that settles on anything they touch, ruining food and appetites. The smell is so distinctive that a professional exterminator recognizes an infestation long before a single roach is spotted.

## Roaches and disease

Scientists who study and test roaches in laboratory settings claim that in nature the insects pose no health threat to humans; they carry no viruses or other pathogens directly responsible for human infection, as, for example, mosquitoes carry the malaria parasite or fleas the germ for plague. But indirectly they are responsible for a variety of illnesses from allergies to food poisoning. There is no estimate of the number of cockroaches in the United States or the number of people made sick by them each year, but certain epidemics of roachborne illness have been well documented.

One of the best known cases involved a two-month epidemic of salmonellosis (food poisoning) among infants and children in a hospital nursery in Brussels more than 30 years ago. Roaches were not suspected as transmitters of the *Salmonella* bacteria because no roaches had ever been spotted in the nursery. Despite isolation of infected patients and enormous care in food preparation, the problem persisted until a night nurse happened to see a few roaches running across the bedclothes of a patient. Analysis of the captured insects revealed that they were indeed carrying the bacteria. The epidemic ended after a thorough extermination program was conducted.

In recent years several studies have also identified cockroaches as an important cause of allergies in susceptible individuals. Many allergy patients show positive skin reactions when tested with extracts made from roach bodies and fluids. Roach allergy is more prevalent in colder environments, where the insects and their victims tend to be housed in close contact for long periods of time, thus increasing exposure and the likelihood of sensitization.

Because of the dirt, odor, and health problems associated with roaches and because they are so resistant to eradication, the general reaction they elicit is one of disgust. It is undeniably upsetting to flip on the kitchen light and find the walls, floors, and cabinets "moving"—alive with bugs. Many people feel that the presence of roaches reflects slovenliness, poor housekeeping, and low economic status. Once established, however, a thriving horde of roaches may persist in even the cleanest and most affluent of households.

## The insect's strategy for survival

The extraordinary ability of roaches to survive is a result of two fundamental characteristics: variety—particularly the ability of different species to exploit different environments—and a complex life cycle that assures propagation.

*Variety.* The U.S. Department of Agriculture (USDA) identifies the following species as particular pests in buildings:

The *American cockroach* is a reddish or dark brown roach, from 30 to 50 mm (1 to 2 in) long. It inhabits damp basements, furnace rooms, and sewers and forages primarily on the first floors of commercial and residential buildings.

*The German cockroach* (Blattella germanica), *common in kitchens and bathrooms, is often mistakenly called the water bug. (Photo shows male at left, female right.)*

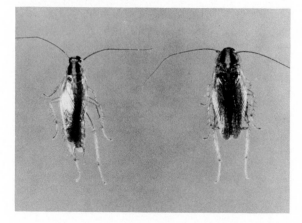

Courtesy, Phillip G. Koehler, University of Florida Institute of Food and Agricultural Sciences; photographs, Ron Stephens

*Male (left) and female of the Oriental cockroach* (Blatta orientalis), *a species that thrives in the damp environment of basements and sewers.*

Smaller, about 25 mm (1 in) long in adulthood, the *Australian roach* has yellow markings on its body and yellow streaks at the base of its wings. These insects develop in warm, damp places in or out of doors and, like the American roach, tend to remain at ground level.

The *brown cockroach,* which may reach a length of 37 mm (1.5 in), can be found in all areas of buildings. Like the brown-banded, or tropical, roach, the brown roach has found a new habitat in colder regions where buildings are centrally heated.

The most common roach pest, found predominantly in kitchens and bathrooms, is the *German cockroach,* often erroneously called the water bug. Light brown in color with two dark stripes running lengthwise along the back, this species is among the smallest, reaching a length of only 12 mm (0.625 in).

One of the filthiest roaches is the shiny black or black-brown *Oriental roach,* also called the black beetle and shad roach. Female adults may be 30 mm (1.25 in) long. A native of Asia, it has been distributed worldwide by commercial ships and planes. These bugs flourish in damp basements and sewers and rarely venture above the first-floor level.

Finally, the *smoky-brown cockroach,* a 37.5-mm (1.5-in)-long black or dark brown insect, prefers warm, very humid areas but will migrate anywhere inside a house or other building.

Because the different species vary in habitat, diet, and other habits, control or eradication strategies that are effective against one may not always work against others. Keeping food tightly covered and the kitchen floor and counters clean may have no impact whatever on roaches that prefer the furnace room or dresser drawers. Likewise, repellents and insecticides may be equally limited in effectiveness.

This variation has also placed unexpected obstacles in the path of research on the use of pheromones—hormones that play a key role in mating—for eradication. Scientists had hoped that by isolating and synthesizing roach pheromones they could develop attractants, substances that draw the insects into traps and poisons. Unfortunately, investigators at the USDA and elsewhere have found that there is no single female roach pheromone that attracts all males of the same species and that only about 70% of a given sex of one species can be expected to respond to its native pheromone. The remainder elude attraction by mechanisms that are still unclear. Further complicating the problem, roaches sometimes cross-react to pheromones—that is, a female Oriental cockroach pheromone may activate the mating instincts of a male American cockroach, while the pheromone from a female American roach will activate a male Oriental. Scientists fear that the extensive use of pheromones as attractants will result in the development of more cross-reactive species.

*Life cycle and survival.* Roaches have a life cycle and reproductive abilities that place additional barriers in the path of control efforts. Unlike other insects, roaches have no pupal, or resting, stage in their life cycle. The roach nymphs emerge from the egg as small adults, lacking only wings and reproductive organs. They undergo a series of 5 to 13 molts, shedding the outside cuticle when it becomes too small, until they reach adult size and reproductive maturity.

In addition, a few species consist solely of females, whose eggs are capable of developing without fertilization, a process known as parthenogenesis. Another few species have adults that are bisexual in the sense that they may reproduce either by parthenogenesis or with fertilization, the females therefore possessing an inherent capability to reproduce without mates when necessary. Under environmentally stressful conditions, this ability adds significantly to the potential for survival of roaches.

Detailed studies on the reproduction of roaches show them to have a complex series of neurologic and glandular functions that control courtship behavior, sexual mating, and egg production. Once again, there is no universal pattern of reproduction. In some cases a male gland secretes a substance that attracts females to mate; in others a virgin female first becomes receptive to male attentions when her eggs reach a particular stage of development.

## Getting rid of roaches

There are two primary strategies in the effort to control cockroaches: prevention—particularly in new buildings and homes—and eradication.

*Methods of prevention.* In the home, especially, it is far easier to prevent a roach problem than to rid the premises of an established infestation. Since roaches may enter a house from outdoors or from adjoining homes or apartments, it is wise to periodically check and fill with plastic wood or putty all cracks in floors,

walls, cabinets, baseboards, and door and window frames. While roaches are adept at foraging, they are certain to be attracted by plentiful meals in the form of crumbs, unrefrigerated leftovers, and accumulations of garbage. Good housekeeping practices at least reduce the likelihood of a heavy infestation.

Food packages, grocery bags, and cardboard boxes of any kind should be thoroughly checked before they are brought into the house. Saving paper bags from supermarkets is not a good idea, as storage areas in such markets are inevitably subject to periodic roach infestations. Similarly, it is wise to remove individual beverage containers from their cartons and dispose of the cartons before bringing the bottles and cans inside.

In the U.S., California was among the first states to require roach proofing in all new public housing. The product used, available commercially, is marketed under the name Drione. Made from silica, it is a pulverized gel that repels water and attracts oils and waxes. When Drione dust is applied to the insides of walls and support structures, it sets up a permanent trap for roaches, since their bodies are covered externally by a waxy cuticle. Trapped in the gel, the roach becomes desiccated and eventually dies. Because Drione is a dust, its safety and acceptability in open living spaces is limited.

*Insecticides.* Extermination by means of insecticides remains the basis of most roach control efforts. The search for more effective roach-killing chemicals and better ways to use existing substances are the major activities of government research projects under way in Maryland and Florida.

Insecticides are applied to problem areas in the form of sprays, dusts, and emulsions. The most effective commonly used insecticides are chlorpyrifos (Dursban), diazinon (Spectracide), malathion (Cythion), propoxur (Baygon), and ronnel (Korlan).

In most areas the development of chemically resistant insect strains has led to the disuse of chlordane, which has been prohibited for indoor use by the Environmental Protection Agency. Most pest control companies prefer diazinon and chlorpyrifos. Resistance is a continuing problem, and one that is widely misunderstood by the public. Entomologists in the government's roach control projects have found that some, but not all, pesticides regain their effectiveness if discontinued for a while. In the case of chlordane, for example, resistance is known to persist for at least eight or ten years once it has been established. In the case of malathion, staggered use will maintain its usefulness.

The pesticide industry is currently developing new types of compounds designed to be safer and more effective than any of the traditional antiroach products now available. One such compound recently registered with the Environmental Protection Agency, amidinohydrazone, is a stomach poison that is toxic only when the roach ingests it. It is longer lasting and safer, activated only when inside the pest, and of proven low toxicity to humans and other animals. Registration is also expected soon on the first of a new class of insecticides called synthetic pyrethroids, which are similar to a natural product extracted from chrysanthemums. This class of compounds is also low in toxicity, long lasting, and, according to laboratory tests, highly effective.

Whether applied by professionals or amateurs, insecticides must be used properly to be effective. To locate roach hiding places, experts advise entering a dark room quietly, turning on the lights, and observing as the pests retreat. Likely places are cabinets, pantries, water pipes, motor compartments of refrigerators, storage compartments of stoves, spaces beneath bathroom and kitchen sinks, under dish drainers, under kitchen furniture and appliances, behind mirrors, and in closets and bookcases.

Because most current pesticides are toxic to humans, food and utensils should be removed from cabinets before any spray or dust is applied. Treated areas should be covered with paper before household articles are replaced.

*Biological controls.* Scientists are focusing increasing attention on the potential of repellents, both natural and synthetic, that keep roaches away but do not destroy them. After years of discounting reports by chefs and housewives about the roach-repelling properties of bay leaves and cucumber skins, chemists have, in fact, isolated the offensive substances (nonenal and cineole) and produced analogs. Laboratory tests show them to be highly effective. At the USDA's Biologically Active Natural Products Laboratory, scientists are testing a variety of natural chemicals, including an extract from the bark of a tree native to India. Both the bark and leaves have been used traditionally in India to keep roaches away.

Powdered boric acid and borax also act as mild insecticides. In some available commercial preparations, they are mixed with dog food or other ingredients and compressed into bait tablets. These preparations are most effective in places such as office buildings where food is not abundant.

In recent years a group of insect control compounds has been developed. Known as insect growth regulators, or IGR's, these compounds mimic natural roach sex hormones. They prevent individual insects from reaching sexual maturity, thus making reproduction impossible. The first, methoprene, was developed for flea control. None of these products is yet available commercially, however.

Scientists are also studying roach behavior as a clue to control. An understanding of mating habits, food preferences, and other aspects of natural history may well reveal effective methods of interfering with the overwhelmingly successful ecological adaptation of most roaches. For example, this research has already demonstrated that sanitation—in addition to reducing available sources of food—lures roaches to forage farther away from their habitual hiding places, thus making them more visible and easier to exterminate.

At the USDA's Agricultural Research Service laboratories in Gainesville, Fla., computers have been used to plot and predict roach population growth. Using mathematical simulations of life cycles, taking into account the many variables (such as availability of food, water, and beneficial climate), scientists are able to design insecticide programs that coordinate maximum kill and minimum repopulation. Computer programs are also being adapted to work with the IGR's for the most effective use of both.

*Failure of eradication efforts.* For a number of reasons, including the insect's extraordinary tenacity, efforts to eradicate cockroaches are not always successful. One reason is improper application of insecticides—either the use of inadequate concentrations of effective ingredients or infrequent applications that actually build resistance. Experts estimate that 99% of all so-called insecticide failures are due to improper application of the chemicals or inadequate strength of the compound.

In some cases roaches persist because of failure to identify the correct origins of the infestation. In other cases homeowners fail to do a thorough cleaning before beginning a maintenance program, so that some of the initial infestation remains and inevitably reproduces.

Some of these problems are the result of general ignorance about the chemical contents and properties of insecticides. For example, a given pesticide may or may not provide residual benefits. Most chemicals sold to consumers act rapidly and appear to be efficient. Unfortunately, the effects of these products last only briefly and kill only those roaches that happen along shortly after application. In other words, they have no residual benefits. Unfortunately, the consumer generally learns how such products work only by the expensive and lengthy trial-and-error process.

Some entomologists allege that the pesticide industry purposely generates public confusion by altering the generic, or common, names of active ingredients and by frequently changing ingredients and their ratios. While most people can remember a brand, or trade, name, they tend to forget long chemical names—and the USDA is not allowed to recommend products by brand name. Until the industry agrees to provide generic names that consumers can remember and check against generic lists provided by government agencies, product selection will remain difficult at best. However, it is possible that new classes of roach-controlling compounds will soon make the job of eradication both easier and safer.

*—Joann Ellison Rodgers*

# Constipation

There are two elements that are integral to constipation: the frequency of bowel movements and the character of stools (the contents of the movement itself). A person may be considered constipated if either or both of these elements is abnormal for a sustained period of time. In a normal individual subsisting on a Western diet, the number of bowel movements ranges from 3 to 21 per week, and stools tend to be moist, soft, and formed. Where diets are high in undigestible fiber, as in rural portions of underdeveloped nations, healthy persons may pass as many as four or five bulky stools per day, and constipation is almost nonexistent. Constipation should thus be diagnosed when movements consistently occur less than thrice weekly, when stools are consistently hard, dry, small, and difficult to pass, or when an individual feels that evacuations are consistently incomplete. It is important to keep the term *consistently* clearly in mind, because transient reductions in frequency of movements or alterations in the character of stools are not unusual and are not clinically significant unless they recur often.

## Normal function of the colon

It is generally agreed by physicians that constipation results from slowed movement of digestive residues through the colon, or lower bowel. The colon is a tubular segment of intestine about 1.5 to 1.8 m (5 to 6 ft) in length. It is a continuation of the considerably longer small intestine, or upper bowel, and has a different physiologic function. The small intestine serves to digest and absorb food from the stomach and, in the process, receives a great deal of water and salts from its own secretions and from those of the liver and pancreas. Fluids and food fibers that are not absorbed in the small intestine pass into the colon. The prime functions of the colon are to conserve fluid and salts by reabsorption and to store the relatively dehydrated residues until the next convenient time for a bowel movement.

The movement of colonic contents is controlled by contraction and relaxation of muscular tissue that lines the wall of the lower bowel. In the right side of the colon this muscular activity tends to be largely back and forth, producing "mixing motions" that facilitate the absorption of water and salts. Occasional propulsive waves occur in this part of the bowel, pushing colonic contents farther along. On the left side of the colon muscular action does not have this mixing motion but tends most of the time to produce steady contractions that temporarily hold back the passage of stool. Once or twice a day a sweeping propulsive (peristaltic) wave passes through the left colon and forces stool into the lower (sigmoid) colon and rectum. Distention of the rectum by stool causes the upper portion of the anal canal to relax by reflex action and produces the urge for a bowel movement. At this point defecation is under voluntary control, through relaxation of the lower portion of the anal sphincter and contraction of accessory muscles that surround the rectum and suspend it from the bony pelvis. If voluntary defecation does not occur, the urge subsides but reappears within an hour or two.

## Mechanisms of constipation

The normal action of the colon suggests a number of possible neuromuscular mechanisms for what is known as functional constipation. The term *functional* is employed here to indicate constipation brought about by abnormalities in colonic and anorectal (*i.e.,* of the anus and rectum) muscular actions or by dietary habits, rather than by colonic obstructions resulting from bowel tumors, kinks, or twists. One such mechanism is an increase in the spastic contractions of the descending and sigmoid portions of the colon, which results in slowed passage of bowel contents; this condition is called the irritable bowel syndrome. Another form of functional constipation results from reduced muscular tone and decreased peristalsis in the left colon; this type of constipation is considered idiopathic (of unknown cause). Thus, both increased and decreased muscular activity in the left colon may lead to constipation. In irritable bowel syndrome stools are typically hard, small, and scanty; in idiopathic constipation stools tend to be soft, dry, and equally scant.

Defective relaxation of the upper anal musculature in response to rectal distention may also cause constipation. This so-called habit constipation occurs in patients who regularly suppress their urges to defecate. Constipation among children and young adults is usually of the habit variety. Normal defecatory urges tend to be suppressed while the patient is at school or at play. Repeated suppression of the urge results in the accumulation of large amounts of densely packed stool in the rectum and lower colon, often without symptoms of any sort. The size and dryness of these fecal impactions often make it extremely difficult for such patients to move their bowels when they finally attempt to do so. Their stools may be so large and bulky that they can actually clog a toilet.

Patients who are weak and bedridden often have constipation because of reduced food intake, reduced peristalsis, and decreased ability to exert voluntary control over the anal and accessory rectal muscles. Persons who eat irregularly or whose diets are extremely low in nondigestible food fiber become constipated because of reduction in the force of the intestinal reflex that stimulates peristalsis in the colon.

Some younger patients may suffer constipation from an uncommon anorectal disorder in which there is a congenital absence of nerve cells in a short or long segment of lower bowel; this condition is called Hirschsprung's disease, after the Danish pediatrician who first identified it. Because of the absence of nerve cells, patients with Hirschsprung's disease display continuous spasm in the affected areas of bowel, including the upper anal muscle. The spastic anal segment does not relax normally in response to rectal distention and acts as an obstruction to the passage of stool, resulting in severe constipation. Other patients with lower spinal cord disease or injury, such as paraplegics, may suffer from constipation because they lack the voluntary control needed to relax the anal muscle and to contract the accessory muscles of defecation.

Certain drugs that affect colonic muscular activity may also cause constipation. Notable among these are codeine, morphine, and a number of antidiarrheal agents derived from them, including paregoric, diphenoxylate (Lomotil), and loperamide (Imodium). These agents act by increasing the absorption of salts and water in the lower small intestine, leading to thicker and drier stool; they also increase spastic contractions in the lower colon. Drugs containing aluminum, calcium, or iron (including many common antacids and even vitamin mixtures) reduce colonic activity and thus may also cause constipation. There are, furthermore, a number of therapeutic agents used in the treatment of various cardiac disorders and hypertension (high blood pressure) that depend for their effects on reducing the activity of the autonomic (involuntary) nervous system. Thus, constipation due to reduced colonic muscular activity is a common side effect of their use; among these are propranalol (Inderal) and other beta-blocking agents and prazosin (Minipress). Finally, it should be

noted that several other categories of drugs—including tranquilizers, antidepressants, antihistamines, and muscle relaxants—contain agents that may cause constipation by their effects on colonic motility.

## Complications

While usually innocuous, constipation may result in a number of potentially serious complications. Among these are disorders in the anorectal area, including hemorrhoids, anal fissures, and perianal abscesses; fecal impactions; rectal prolapse; and, possibly, diverticulosis of the colon.

*Hemorrhoids* are swollen veins in the anal canal. External hemorrhoids are those covered by skin; internal hemorrhoids are those covered by anal mucous membrane. They are believed to result from prolonged periods of straining at stool and are probably aggravated by the use of the Western-style toilet seat, which—as opposed to simple squatting—offers no support to perianal structures during defecation. Hemorrhoids tend to occur earlier in women who have borne children than they do in men or in women who have never been pregnant.

*External hemorrhoids* usually appear as swellings under the skin around the anus. They are often accompanied by increased secretions from the glands in the overlying skin; these secretions cause the moist skin to become soft and tender. Because this tenderness is commonly perceived by patients as an itching sensation, the resulting abrasion from scratching can lead to further damage to the skin, often with bleeding. The best treatment is to avoid scratching and to keep the skin as dry as possible with applications of talc or cornstarch. The itching may be relieved by the application of witch hazel or, occasionally, creams containing hydrocortisone or other glucocorticoids.

Clotting of blood inside an external hemorrhoidal vein is a common complication that occurs as a result of slowed blood flow and inflammation of the hemorrhoid. While these thrombosed external hemorrhoids may and often do become extremely painful, a physician can relieve the discomfort fairly quickly by making a simple incision into the distended vein and removing the clotted blood inside it.

*Internal hemorrhoids* rarely cause pain and commonly produce no symptoms. Bleeding is one possible complication. Bleeding from an internal hemorrhoid may be profuse; it usually occurs during defecation and results from rupture of a thin-walled hemorrhoidal vein. The blood is fresh in appearance and may be visible on the surface of the stool or spurt freely into the toilet bowl as the patient strains to defecate. Such bleeding is usually alarming to patients when it first appears—as well it might be, since it raises the specter of bowel cancer. The condition should be evaluated promptly by a physician. A definitive diagnosis can usually be accomplished by a few simple tests, beginning with a digital examination of the rectum. The rectum and the proximal 25 to 60 cm (10 to 24 in) of the colon are inspected by means of a sigmoidoscope, a tubular, lighted instrument specially designed for this purpose. The anal canal should be carefully examined with an anoscope. A sample of stool taken from above the anus will also be examined for visible evidence of blood and for traces of microscopic, or occult, blood. If the site of the bleeding is not clearly visible during these examinations, an X-ray examination of the entire colon (using a barium enema for visualization) is indicated to exclude other possible causes of bleeding.

The treatment of bleeding internal hemorrhoids is generally fairly simple. Relief of constipation by means of stool-softening and bulking agents is a cardinal feature of therapy. A further regimen of daily hemorrhoidal suppositories (cocoa butter, aluminum paste) and warm tub baths for two weeks or so is also useful.

Prolapse of internal hemorrhoids is a second complication, in which there is a tendency of enlarged hemorrhoidal veins to push through the anal muscle and to appear between the buttocks as a swollen, often slightly tender mass. Prolapse occurs most commonly with defecation but may occasionally happen spontaneously while the patient is walking or lifting a heavy object. Bleeding frequently accompanies the prolapse. Treatment is the same as for bleeding hemorrhoids, with the added suggestion that patients should learn to exert gentle finger pressure against prolapsed hemorrhoids in order to push them back into place.

*Anal fissures*—slits, or clefts, appearing in the mucous membrane of the anal canal—may develop as a complication of hemorrhoids in patients with constipation, or they may appear when no hemorrhoid is present. Fissures usually become secondarily infected with intestinal or cutaneous bacteria; infection is likely to cause inflammation, which may produce great pain and spasm in the anal area. Since the pain is aggravated by defecation, an existing constipation condition is usually worsened by anal fissures. They may also be associated with fresh anal bleeding. Treatment usually consists of agents to soften stool along with measures to heal the fissure, such as suppositories and creams containing anti-inflammatory agents, and frequent warm tub baths. Deep, unresponsive fissures, however, may require freezing or excisional surgery.

*Perianal abscesses* result when infection from a fissure or a pitlike crypt penetrates deeply into the tissues around the anus. The body responds to this bacterial infestation with a heavy outpouring of pus, a fluid containing the white blood cells whose function is to engulf and digest such foreign organisms. If the pus cannot drain freely to the exterior, it accumulates in tissues, forming an abscess. Patients with perianal abscesses note both local pain and swelling and occasionally become feverish. Treatment consists of surgical incision and drainage of the abscess, a simple process if the accumulation of pus is superficial. If the abscess is deep, however, surgical relief may require general anesthesia and a fairly large incision. Drainage usually continues for a few days after incision, then gradually subsides as the abscess cavity closes from within. Occasionally the drainage does not abate completely, and an infected sinus tract, or fistula, develops between the anus and the outside skin. This fistula usually also requires surgical excision.

*Fecal impactions* are large, firm masses of stool in the rectum that patients are unable to pass without medical intervention. The appearance of an impaction generally is heralded by increasingly scanty bowel movements for several days followed by complete constipation for a day or two. Patients commonly experience frequent urges to defecate but are unable to move their bowels fully, even after using enemas or glycerin suppositories. They often complain of a bearing-down discomfort in the rectal area and are aware of the mass that they are powerless to move.

Impactions occur chiefly among patients who are confined to bed or capable of only limited physical activity. They may also appear after barium X-rays of the digestive tract (as a consequence of the constipating action of the barium), during long automobile trips, following anorectal surgery, and after starting a new medication that reduces bowel motility. Fecal impactions are best avoided by paying close attention to bowel regularity in patients at greatest risk, by encouraging physical activity—especially during periods where increased immobility is common—and by recommending simple laxatives when constipating agents such as barium have been ingested. The definitive treatment is forcible disruption of the stool mass. The physician inserts a gloved finger into the rectum, breaks up the impaction, and instills mineral oil rectally to lubricate the passage of the stool fragments.

*Rectal prolapse* is the downward slippage of the rectum through the anal ring to the point where a short or even fairly long segment of the bowel is everted, or turned outward, so that it protrudes outside of the body. Variable degrees of prolapse may result from chronic constipation and resultant straining at stool, although many cases occur in elderly patients, probably from weakening of rectal supporting structures and accessory muscles of defecation.

Prolapsed rectal tissue can often be returned to its normal position by gentle manipulation of the everted bowel. If anal muscle strength is good and straining at stool is avoided by the use of mild laxatives, the prolapse may not recur. The best treatment for recurrent rectal prolapse, however, is a surgical procedure in which the upper rectum and sigmoid colon are tacked to the rear wall of the pelvic cavity.

*Diverticulosis of the colon* has, by inference if not by direct observation, been attributed in many cases to chronic constipation. Thus, it has been noted that in

Constipation

geographic areas where constipation is rare, diverticulosis is also rare; the reverse is also true. A diverticulum is a single outpouching, or protrusion, of colonic mucous membrane through a space between adjoining fibers in the muscular layer of the colon. The term diverticulosis refers to a condition of the colon in which many diverticula are present, predominantly in the descending and sigmoid regions. While uncomplicated diverticula generally cause no symptoms, they may at times be obstructed with stool or mucus and become inflamed, a condition called diverticulitis. Inflammation is associated with steady or cramping pain, fever, and, at times, diarrhea. Occasionally an area of diverticulitis may perforate, just as an inflamed appendix might, and lead to localized peritonitis (inflammation of the lining of the abdominal cavity). In other cases, uninflamed diverticula may become sites of hemorrhage.

Uncomplicated diverticulitis frequently responds to simple medical treatment—a course of antibiotics and maintenance on a liquid diet until the inflammation subsides. Afterward, prevention may be accomplished by a diet high in fiber and by bulking agents. A single episode of hemorrhage may be treated successfully in the same fashion. Complications—perforation of a diverticulum, recurrent hemorrhage, or recurrent attacks of diverticulitis—invariably require surgical correction.

## Management of constipation

Once a pattern of constipation becomes established, patients should seek medical advice for its management rather than continuing with self-treatment. Since constipation may be a harbinger of something more than a simple disorder of colonic function, certain diagnostic studies should be undertaken to exclude the presence of potentially serious problems such as cancer of the colon or diverticulitis. These tests ought to be performed even though the constipation appears to be relieved by simple laxatives.

Studies useful in the evaluation of constipation include: a complete medical and dietary history; physical exam, including digital examination of the rectum; appraisal of several specimens of stool for the presence of occult (not visible) bleeding; examination of the rectum and lower colon with a sigmoidoscope; and X-ray examinations of the colon with barium and air. A diagnosis of functional constipation may be made with certainty if these relatively inexpensive and extremely reliable tests prove to be normal. The medical history may be particularly important in identifying patients who are not really constipated but have misconceptions about the normal frequency of bowel movements.

The goal in treatment of constipation is not to purge the colon daily but rather to establish a pattern of regular, easily passed bowel movements every day or two. In many cases this pattern can be developed by setting up a dietary program of three meals a day, emphasizing foods high in fiber content. By remaining in the intestine, fiber residues contribute to the weight and moisture of stool and thus ease its passage through the bowel. Foods high in fiber content are primarily fruits, vegetables, and cereals, especially bran and whole wheat. Of these, peas, beans, broccoli, potatoes with skin, apples, strawberries, popcorn, and peanuts are excellent sources of fiber. Bran (about 22–28 g [0.8–1 oz] per day) is probably the best agent of all because a large part of its fiber consists of indigestible lignin, and it has a considerable capacity to retain water. It is also advisable for patients to exercise briskly 20 to 30 minutes daily and to learn not to suppress physiologic urges for defecation.

Laxatives may be needed at times to establish the desired bowel pattern, especially at the start of treatment. For this purpose bulking agents, particularly various preparations of psyllium mucilloid (Metamucil, Effersyllium, L. A. Formula), are often beneficial. These products help to increase stool bulk and moisture and are especially welcome to patients who are unable to ingest bran. Mineral oil is a lubricating agent that is occasionally effective as a laxative, but it should not be used regularly since it may cause anal irritation, interfere with the absorption of certain vitamins, and lead to an oil-induced type of pneumonia. Another stool lubricant, docusate (Surfak, Colace), is often useful but not as effective as the bulking preparations.

The laxatives classified as osmotic agents consist of salts that are poorly absorbed in the small intestine and thus tend to reduce fluid absorption as well. The fluids that are not absorbed remain in the stools, keeping them soft and moist. Milk of magnesia, Epsom salts, and lactulose are examples of osmotic laxatives. Small doses of osmotic agents tend to be effective laxatives and may be used every two or three days for patients who are in the process of adapting to a high-fiber diet. Large doses, however, are cathartic and may lead to severe dehydration and depletion of body salts.

Stimulant laxatives, or cathartics, such as cascara, castor oil, phenolphthalein (Ex-Lax, Correctol), bisacodyl (Dulcolax), and senna (Perdiem), act by directly increasing muscular contractions in the bowel. While they are effective in managing occasional bouts of constipation, their regular use should be discouraged because they may induce a form of dependence in which normal stimuli to colonic motility are no longer effective. If overused, these drugs may also cause spastic, painful contractions of the bowel. Similar dependence may also be induced by the regular use of enemas.

The management of constipation is most successfully achieved by a program consisting of a diet high in fiber, regular eating habits, daily exercise, and the occasional use of bulking laxatives. Osmotic laxatives may be helpful at times, but the routine use of stimulant laxatives should be avoided.

—*Harvey J. Dworken, M.D.*

# Whooping Cough

Whooping cough, or pertussis, is an acute, highly contagious bacterial infection of infants and children. Before a program of routine immunization against whooping cough was begun in the 1940s, this illness was one of the leading causes of infant death in the U.S. Whooping cough is a much more dangerous disease than is usually believed. Because of its severe complications and the high mortality rate in infants and small babies, U.S. physicians and health authorities feel it essential that all infants be immunized against this disease during the first few months of life.

In 1906 two French bacteriologists, Jules Bordet and Octave Gengou, first described the bacterium *Bordetella pertussis* (*Hemophilus pertussis*) that causes whooping cough. The course of the disease is characterized by an initial period of nonspecific respiratory symptoms that progresses to a spasmodic cough, which is accompanied by a typical inspiratory (*i.e.,* upon inspiration, or inhalation) whooping sound.

Whooping cough is highly contagious; it is transmitted by direct contact with an infected person. The usual mode of transmission is via droplet spray, such as from sneezing or coughing. Contagion rates of up to 90% have been reported in contacts within unimmunized households. In its communicability whooping cough is comparable to both chickenpox and measles. A patient is most likely to spread the infection during the first, or catarrhal, period of the illness, before the typical spasmodic cough has made the diagnosis obvious. The incubation period of whooping cough is about one week; most cases will develop within ten days of exposure. An infant or child who is free of symptoms two weeks after being exposed to the disease usually will escape infection.

## Stages

Whooping cough can be divided into three distinct clinical stages—the catarrhal stage, the paroxysmal stage, and the convalescent stage.

The catarrhal stage begins with the symptoms typical of an upper respiratory infection or common cold: sneezing, tearing of the eyes, a runny nose, and, usually, a low-grade fever. If there is no definite history of exposure to whooping cough, it is often assumed that the symptoms are those of an ordinary cold. The catarrhal stage lasts for about seven days. At this point, however, the cough, rather than improving—as would

be the case in the usual upper respiratory infection—gradually becomes more severe and is likely to be most troublesome at night.

This increase in the severity of the cough marks the start of the second and more dangerous stage of pertussis, the paroxysmal stage. In this stage the cough typically occurs in explosive bursts. The patient develops a series of short, loud, rapid coughs, all of which occur during a single expiration of breath, followed by a sudden, deep inspiration of breath producing a crowing sound, or whoop. In many cases a number of these paroxysms, or coughing spasms, follow one after another until the child finally dislodges and coughs up the thick plug of mucus that caused the paroxysm. Typically, the child vomits at the end of the attack. During an attack the victim has great difficulty breathing and, naturally, becomes extremely frightened. The face characteristically turns red or even, on occasion, blue (a sign of cyanosis, or decreased oxygen in the blood); the eyes bulge and the tongue protrudes. Following such an episode, the patient is exhausted, dazed, and often covered with perspiration as a result of the tremendous amount of energy that has been expended in trying to breathe. Obstruction of the airway may be so severe as to cause sudden death from asphyxia during one of these paroxysms of coughing.

In a mild case of whooping cough there are only a few paroxysmal attacks each day. In the more severe cases as many as 40 or more paroxysms can occur daily. Paroxysmal attacks are more likely to develop during the night and can be triggered by eating, drinking, or physical exertion. An attack can also be stimulated by suggestion, merely from the sound of another's coughing. Before immunization against whooping cough became routine, large numbers of infants and small children were hospitalized each year with the disease. During epidemic times entire pediatric wards were commonly filled with small babies suffering from pertussis. At night one infant might have a paroxysmal attack while all the other patients were asleep. Within minutes most or all of the others on the ward also would be seized with paroxysms of coughing and whooping. The paroxysmal stage of the disease lasts anywhere from four to six weeks. During the first two weeks the paroxysmal attacks tend to increase in both severity and frequency, after which they decline and gradually subside.

The third, or convalescent, stage begins after the paroxysmal episodes have ceased entirely. During this period the patient continues to cough, but the cough is no longer associated with the whooping and is not followed by vomiting. The character of the cough is similar to that of ordinary bronchitis. The convalescent period usually lasts between two and three weeks; the cough gradually decreases in severity and finally stops.

## Diagnosis and incidence

The diagnosis of whooping cough can be made easily during the paroxysmal stage, when the most typical symptoms—bursts of rapid coughs on expiration and the inspiratory crow or whoop—are present. However, infants less than six months old may not develop the typical whoop. In such cases the clinical diagnosis of whooping cough is suggested by the paroxysmal nature of the coughing, the red or blue appearance of the face during an attack, and the vomiting that follows. It is during the first stage of pertussis that diagnosis is most difficult. Whooping cough is, of course, suspected if the patient is known to have been exposed to the disease, and the diagnosis can be confirmed by means of a few simple laboratory tests, including nose and throat cultures and a complete white blood count.

Because spasmodic coughing is not unique to whooping cough, a number of other respiratory illnesses must be considered in the differential diagnosis. Severe paroxysmal coughing may indicate acute bronchiolitis, bronchopneumonia, or interstitial pneumonia. Another disease that can mimic the spasmodic cough of pertussis is cystic fibrosis of the pancreas. Furthermore, a foreign body of any kind stuck in the air passages may cause a cough that can be confused with the typical cough of pertussis. In some cases a chest X-ray, in addition to appropriate cultures and blood tests, is necessary for a definitive diagnosis.

Whooping cough is worldwide in distribution. It affects individuals of all races and nationalities and can strike at any time during the year. Although usually seen only in infants and small children, it has been reported in adults as well. The rare cases of occurrence in elderly people are generally quite severe. Little or no immunity to pertussis is transferred from the mother to the newborn; infants, therefore, are at extremely high risk of developing the disease. Forty percent of all deaths from whooping cough occur in infants less than five months old, and 70% occur during the

Ken Spencer

*The symptoms of the first, or catarrhal, stage of whooping cough are easily mistaken for the symptoms of an ordinary cold or upper respiratory infection.*

first year of life. Statistics indicate that more than two-thirds of all cases are seen in children who are under seven years of age.

One of the unusual features of whooping cough is its distribution according to sex. Many studies have shown that both incidence and death rate are significantly higher in females than in males. The sex ratio in pertussis has been known for many years and is consistent in all population groups. What makes this statistic of particular interest is that all other common infectious diseases of childhood characteristically occur with greater frequency and severity among males. The reason for the reverse sex ratio in whooping cough is not known.

## Complications

The most common and usually the most severe complication of whooping cough is pneumonia. It accounts for 90% of the deaths of pertussis victims under three years of age and is especially dangerous in infants under one year. Pneumonia usually develops during the most severe period of the paroxysmal stage and should be suspected if at that time the patient's inspiratory rate increases and the breathing becomes progressively more labored. The patient, already exhausted from the paroxysmal coughing, becomes even weaker from the effort needed to get enough air into the congested lungs. With the development of pneumonia there are fewer paroxysms of coughing; this can be a sign of impending respiratory failure and even death. The pneumonia must be treated with an appropriate antibiotic and, in some cases, with oxygen.

Convulsions and brain damage are other serious complications of whooping cough. During a severe paroxysmal attack, the child cannot catch his breath and may become unconscious from lack of oxygen in the blood or develop a convulsion because of insufficient supply of oxygen to the brain. Decreased oxygen supply can also cause bleeding within the brain and even atrophy of the brain tissue, in some cases resulting in permanent brain damage.

Other less severe complications of whooping cough include hernias and prolapsed rectum, both caused by muscle strain associated with the severe explosive coughing. Nosebleeds and hemorrhage within the eye have also been reported as side effects of whooping cough. The onset of asthma has been observed in a number of children after recovery from the disease.

## Treatment

Once a child has contracted whooping cough, there is no specific treatment. The patient must be separated from all susceptible persons, staying home from school and out of public places during the period of communicability. Because of the extreme contagiousness of pertussis it is recommended that an infant under one year of age not be brought into a house in which there is a case of whooping cough. Although antibiotics cannot cure the disease, some have been found to lessen both the duration and the severity of the illness. Therefore, most authorities recommend the use of appropriate antibiotics. An immune serum globulin has been available for pertussis since the 1940s, although its effectiveness as a treatment for the disease is currently under question.

Supportive measures constitute the most important treatment. The patient should be confined to bed and kept as quiet as possible. The room should be well ventilated. Factors that initiate coughing, such as overactivity, excitement, smoke in the air, and sudden changes in temperature, must be avoided. Any patient who develops severe complications such as pneumonia or convulsions must immediately be hospitalized. Infants less than a year old with severe paroxysms of coughing should also be hospitalized because of the possibility of choking during an attack. Close nursing supervision is of vital importance in such cases. These choking episodes can quickly and easily be relieved by means of gentle aspiration, or suction, through a soft catheter (tube) in the infant's throat. This relatively simple maneuver can make the difference between death from choking and complete recovery. The family's physician or pediatrician is the person most qualified to decide the best course of treatment.

## Immunization

Immunization with pertussis vaccine (administered in combination with diphtheria and tetanus vaccines) is the only preventive method currently available. In the past decade, however, because of publicity about adverse side effects of the pertussis vaccine, including the possibility of brain damage, there has been widespread controversy about the routine use of the vaccine. As a result, many U.S. parents have been asking their physicians if it is really necessary for an infant to be vaccinated against whooping cough. The answer—according to the U.S. Public Health Service, the American Academy of Pediatrics, and an overwhelming majority of U.S. physicians—is an emphatic "yes."

According to these authorities, except in a few rare cases the advantages of immunization far outweigh the disadvantages. An exception should be made in the case of any otherwise normal infant who developed a severe reaction, such as a convulsion or collapse, following a previous diphtheria-pertussis-tetanus (DPT) immunization. In such cases the pertussis element of the vaccine should be eliminated from the next injection, and the child should receive diphtheria-tetanus (DT) vaccine instead. Also to be excepted are infants already diagnosed as having any neurologic impairment or known history of seizures or convulsions. Obviously, then, every infant should have a complete physical exam, including a detailed medical history, prior to immunization.

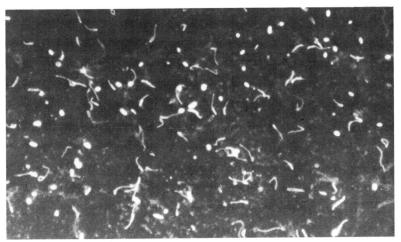

Bordetella pertussis, *the causative agent of whooping cough, was first isolated in 1906 by two French bacteriologists.*

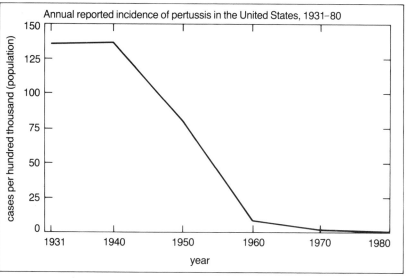

Annual reported incidence of pertussis in the United States, 1931–80

*This graph provides ample evidence of the dramatic decline in the incidence of whooping cough since the 1940s, when the program of routine mass immunization was initiated.*

Notwithstanding these specific exceptions, all other normal infants and children should be vaccinated against the disease. Unfortunately, there is no existing technique for predicting severe reactions to pertussis vaccine; current research in genetics, however, indicates that a reliable method for identifying those at risk from the vaccine may soon be developed.

While public debate about the pertussis vaccine is of relatively recent origin, physicians have been aware of the risks involved ever since the vaccine became available for general use. Severe reactions are extremely rare, however, occurring only in about one of every 300,000 instances of injection of the vaccine. It should be emphasized that severe neurologic complications, including brain damage, are also caused by the disease itself—and with greater frequency. One study showed the rate of serious neurologic damage among recovered pertussis patients to be as high as 14%.

Historical evidence supports these conclusions. During the era before the U.S. began a program of routine immunization, an average of about 200,000 cases of whooping cough were reported each year, with an average annual mortality of about 7,000. In New York City alone it was estimated that the disease caused an average of about 40 deaths per year. With the advent of routine immunization, however, both the number of cases of whooping cough and the deaths attributed to it began to decline dramatically. Statistics from the U.S.

Centers for Disease Control show that during the decade of the 1970s the average number of deaths in the United States due to whooping cough was about ten per year.

Furthermore, experience in both Great Britain and Japan illustrates what can happen if immunization is discontinued. In the 1970s, because of growing concern about neurologic complications attributed to the pertussis vaccine, both countries decided to end their programs of immunization of infants and children; the results—recurrence of whooping cough epidemics and an increase in the death rate of victims of the disease—are clear evidence that the benefits of the vaccine far outweigh its rare complications. In fact, British physicians are currently reevaluating the clinical evidence; at least one recent study has indicated that the complications formerly attributed to immunization are not caused by the pertussis vaccine but are precipitated by it in children with an existing predisposition to neurologic disorders.

U.S. health authorities fully recognize that the pertussis vaccine currently in use is not perfect; nonetheless, it is highly effective. Until a better vaccine is developed, it seems essential that every child—with the exceptions previously cited—should be immunized against this dangerous disease.

—*Alvin N. Eden, M.D.*

Health Education Unit 18

# Treatment of Kidney Failure

The kidneys are paired organs located in the small of the back under the lower rib cage. Each kidney contains about 1.3 million nephrons, which are the functional units of the kidney. The arterial blood is carried to each nephron and enters the glomerulus, a tuft of capillaries, where it is filtered. About 20% of the total amount of blood ejected in each heartbeat is filtered through the kidneys. The resulting product is a fluid free of blood cells and protein. The fluid then passes into the renal tubule, where vital substances are removed from the fluid and toxic materials are secreted. The tubule is divided into four major sections: the proximal convoluted tubule, the loop of Henle, the distal convoluted tubule, and the collecting duct. The fluid, now called urine, is collected from the tubules in the renal pelvis and carried down two paired tubes, the ureters, into the urinary bladder. Approximately 150 liters (39.6 gal) of fluid are filtered by a single glomerulus each day, 99% of which is reabsorbed during its passage down the tubule. Thus the normal individual produces an average of 1.5 liters (1.6 qt) of urine per day.

The functions of the kidney can be divided into three categories: (1) excretory—the majority of waste products produced in the body pass through the glomeruli and are discarded through the tubules; (2) regulatory—the kidney responds to the needs of the body to conserve or excrete water and to maintain a balance in the chemical composition of body fluids by retaining ions and substances vital to normal function of all organs; and (3) endocrine—the kidney produces substances that regulate blood pressure, bone structure, and production and growth of red blood cells by the bone marrow. Thus the normal kidney allows the body to adjust to deprivation of fluids and vital chemicals through its conservation functions and to compensate for excess ingestion of water, salt, and other materials by its excretory mechanisms. The excretory, regulatory, and endocrine functions operate continuously, on a minute-to-minute basis, in response to signals received from a complex detection system in the kidney itself, and in the brain, heart, blood vessels, and other organs of the body.

## Diseases of the kidney

The disorders that markedly impair kidney function are divided into two categories: acute renal failure and chronic renal failure. Acute renal failure, a sudden cessation of all functions of the kidney, can be due to a variety of conditions. One such condition is shock, in which an inadequate blood supply to the kidneys prevents them from performing their usual functions. If the interference in blood flow is severe, kidney cells die from lack of oxygen, glucose, and other materials necessary to maintain cell life. The duration of kidney failure may be as long as four weeks. Usually, however, the cells will regenerate if normal blood supply to the tissues is restored. Other causes of sudden loss of function include exposure to toxic substances and certain drugs, abrupt onset of primary diseases of the kidney such as glomerulonephritis (inflammation of glomerular cells), or obstruction of urine flow through the ureters or out of the bladder. Correction of these conditions also usually leads to complete recovery.

Chronic renal failure occurs when a disease affecting the kidney results in progressive, irreversible loss of functional kidney tissue. The kidney, like many other organs, has considerable reserve capacity. Thus the disease process may go on for months or even years before the patient develops uremia (literally, urine in the blood), the characteristic sign or symptom of kidney disease. The three basic functions of the kidneys are progressively compromised. Waste products that are normally filtered from the blood are retained in the body, causing irritation or direct toxicity to virtually every organ system. The regulatory processes become less efficient, resulting in either fluid overload or dehydration, and the balance of body fluids becomes deranged. Finally, the subsequent failure of endocrine functions may lead to hypertension, bone disease, and anemia. When the percentage of functional nephrons is reduced to less than 10%, multiple potentially lethal conditions develop. If uncorrected, chronic renal failure is fatal.

Most of the diseases that cause progressive renal failure have no known cause or curative treatment. Major exceptions include hypertension (high blood

389

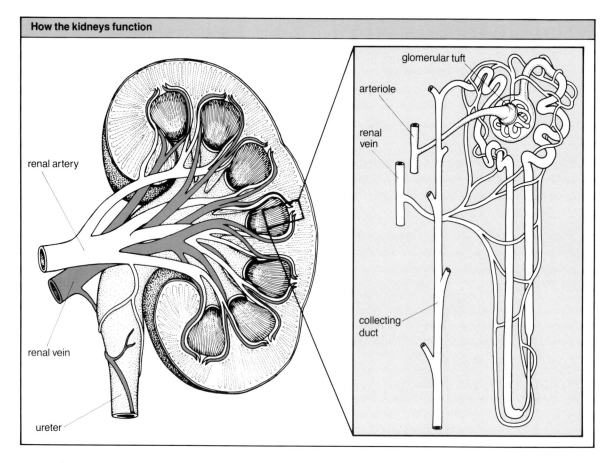

renal artery

renal vein

ureter

glomerular tuft

arteriole

renal vein

collecting duct

pressure), some forms of glomerulonephritis, and obstruction of urine flow. For the remainder, the course of the disease may be delayed—often for many years—by a conservative regimen consisting of rather simple measures, such as dietary regulations and treatment to control blood pressure.

Transplantation of human kidneys is becoming more common; about 4,500 such procedures were performed in the United States in 1982. Donor kidneys may be obtained from living relatives of the patient or from cadavers. The prediction of success is based on a number of variables, including the successful matching of donor and recipient tissues, the prevention of infections, and the administration of precise doses of immunosuppressive drugs, which impair the body's normal ability to reject foreign proteins. The survival rate of well-matched kidneys from relatives is more than 90% at one year and more than 60% for cadaver kidneys. While almost all transplant recipients receive dialysis for some time prior to the transplantation, all patients with kidney failure are not candidates for transplants. The most significant constraints limiting the feasibility of transplantation are the patient's age, presence of recurrent kidney diseases, severe systemic disease (*e.g.,* heart disease), and anatomic abnormalities that preclude satisfactory placement of the kidney. The recent development of cyclosporin, a drug for suppressing rejection, appears to be of great promise for improving the survival of transplant recipients.

## Dialysis—treatment with the artificial kidney

At the present time most patients who have lost kidney function are treated with artificial devices that remove toxins and restore body fluids to normal, or at least tolerable, levels. The process is known as dialysis and can be performed by one of two modes, hemodialysis or peritoneal dialysis.

*How dialysis works.* Hemodialysis is a process in which blood is passed through a tube or chamber within a semipermeable membrane. The exterior of the membrane is bathed in a special solution called the dialysate. Waste products and other materials in the blood pass through the membrane into the dialysate and are discarded. Excess water can be removed from the blood by increasing pressure inside or by producing negative pressure outside the dialysate compartment, causing ultrafiltration of fluid through the membrane and into the dialysate.

In peritoneal dialysis a catheter is used to infuse fluid into the abdominal (peritoneal) cavity. One of the principal techniques of peritoneal dialysis consists of repeated filling and draining of the abdomen with fluid consisting of electrolytes and glucose solutions that are equal to the ideal body fluid composition. The glucose concentration may be increased to draw water from the body fluids in situations where the patient has excess fluid that cannot be excreted by the impaired kidneys. The fluid flows into the abdominal cavity, is allowed to remain—or dwell—in the peritoneal cavity for a period of 60 minutes, and then is drained and discarded. During the "dwell time," toxins from the body fluid flow across the peritoneal membrane into the dialysate. The repeated exchanges of fluid may continue for 24 to 36 hours, depending on the patient's blood chemistries and overall physical condition. This entire procedure is repeated two or three times a week. In the method known as chronic ambulatory peritoneal dialysis (CAPD), dialysate is kept within the peritoneal cavity at all times; draining and refilling are performed at four- to eight-hour intervals.

Each dialysis method has special advantages and disadvantages. For hemodialysis, permanent access to the bloodstream must be made available by means of a surgically created shunt or fistula to which tubing can be attached during the process and removed between treatments. Hemodialysis treatment also requires an elaborate array of devices to deliver dialysate of an exact chemical composition and at a precise temperature and flow rate. The safety of the procedure is monitored by devices that measure pressure and detect blood and air leaks and malfunctions of mixing pumps. For peritoneal dialysis, a catheter must be inserted into the abdominal cavity. The major complications of this method are recurrent infections and eventual scarring of the lining of the abdominal cavity.

For optimum rehabilitation hemodialysis must be performed three times a week; each treatment takes from three to six hours. Patients may be treated in full-care or self-care centers or trained to conduct the entire procedure at home. Thus involvement of the patient covers a spectrum ranging from no participation in the treatment to total responsibility. Cost and advantages vary, but self-, or home, dialysis is less expensive—between $12,000 and $18,000 per patient per year. Full-care is the most expensive form of treatment and may cost as much as $30,000 per patient annually. In the United States most patients with chronic kidney failure are treated by means of hemodialysis. Fewer than 20% receive peritoneal dialysis, although CAPD is being used more frequently. For patients on home dialysis, intensive training is necessary. Patients usually communicate on a regular basis with hospital or dialysis center staff. Home visits by members of renal care teams ensure that the environment is satisfactory and that procedures are followed properly.

No form of dialysis entirely replaces the complex functions of the human kidney. The normal kidney is an exquisitely controlled organ that adjusts fluid volume and composition on a continuous basis, depending on need. Dialysis treatments cause sudden shifts in fluid balance, which often result in distressing symptoms such as leg cramps, headaches, and fatigue. Furthermore, the endocrine functions of the normal kidney are not performed by these artificial devices, and hormone deficiencies inevitably cause complications over an extended period of time. Bone disease occurs because of improper regulation of calcium and vitamin D. High blood pressure commonly results from excess body water. Anemia may require frequent transfusions. Most of these problems can be controlled by medication or adjustments in the treatment regimen, but constant monitoring is necessary to detect early evidence of any developing disorder.

*Living with dialysis.* Because kidney disease often fails to cause troublesome symptoms until it has progressed to a critical stage, many patients do not seek medical attention until the need for dialysis or transplantation is imminent. The impact of chronic illness itself and the psychological and social adjustments to prolonged treatment cannot be underestimated. Imagine the shock of being told that you must begin treatment with the artificial kidney in the next few days or weeks; that you must immediately consult a urologist, other physicians, a social worker, and a dietitian; that you must undergo surgery in order to be connected to a mechanical device; that you must travel to a hospital or treatment center three times a week and stay for four hours each visit; and that you must make radical changes in your diet and life-style. Furthermore, if transplantation is not a likely alternative, you may be dependent on dialysis for the remainder of your life. You have been granted an indefinite extension of your life but only under the most stringent conditions. Fortunately, there are experienced professionals who function as a team to relieve some of the burdens of the adaptation process. Thousands of kidney patients have made this difficult adjustment and have done it well. If necessary, you too can learn to live with dialysis.

## The renal care team

The physician acts as the captain of the renal care team, coordinating the activities of the nurses, technicians, social workers, dietitians, and others whose professional expertise is vital to the care of dialysis patients. Initially the physician performs a thorough physical examination and obtains the radiologic and laboratory tests necessary for assessment of the patient's current status. In conjunction with the patient and his family and with other professionals, the physician choses an appropriate form of treatment. The details of treatment are prescribed: the kind of dialyzer, the duration and frequency of therapy, and the determination of blood-flow and fluid-removal rates. The purpose of any necessary drugs is explained to the patient—*e.g.,* agents for the control of high blood pressure and maintenance of sound bone structure and appropriate nutritional supplements. The physician also reviews periodic tests on a monthly or weekly basis and directs the course of therapy accordingly. Therapy may change under various circumstances, including the development of illnesses unrelated to the kidney disorder.

For in-center treatment and for the training of patients for home dialysis, the nurse provides most of the "hands on" care. The nurse is most capable of promoting continuity of care and usually knows the patient best, having spent much time—often more than 15 hours a week—with the patient. An understanding of the individual's social and professional life helps the nurse to schedule treatment with minimum disruption to the patient's personal needs.

The dietitian functions as an integral part of the renal care team by establishing consistent, high-quality standards of nutritional care. In addition the dietitian provides accurate nutritional information to the patient and his family and educates other members of the staff on this subject.

The hemodialysis technician has primary responsibility for the mechanical aspects of dialysis. The duties involve a certain amount of direct patient care: assessing the patient pre- and posttreatment, initiating and discontinuing each treatment, and monitoring therapeutic parameters during treatment. In addition to these clinical functions, the technician is responsible for routine maintenance of all dialysis equipment to ensure proper and safe operation. In the event of equipment malfunction, the technician analyzes the problem and makes necessary adjustments or repairs.

The administrative manager provides administrative direction, supervision, and support to the dialysis unit. The manager monitors both the financial and operational aspects of the unit in order to maximize productivity and financial reimbursement, minimize expenses, and ensure quality care.

The very important function of the social worker is to help both patient and family adjust to the alterations in their day-to-day lives. As an active member of the renal care team, the social worker participates in the development and implementation of patient care plans and evaluates the impact of treatment on the patient's social and emotional well-being.

## Economic and social considerations

More than 20 years have passed since it was first demonstrated that the lives of critically ill patients could be maintained by means of routine dialysis treatments. Although many people were restored to a state of health that allowed them to conduct most of their normal activities, there was debate regarding the quality of life of dialysis patients and the wisdom of spending the vast amount of money needed to treat all acceptable candidates. In 1967 a study by the U.S. government pronounced dialysis and transplantation to be accept-

able modes of therapy. Accordingly, a national program, supported by government funds, was recommended to cover the high costs of lifesaving treatments for patients with kidney failure. Legislation passed in 1972 included a mandate for Medicare to pay virtually all costs of treatment by dialysis or transplantation for eligible Americans with kidney failure. The medical community responded promptly to make such treatment available to all those in need. The program, designated the End-Stage Renal Disease (ESRD) Program, which is presently administered by the Department of Health and Human Services (HHS), covers most of the costs for about 70,000 patients receiving dialysis treatment.

In the decade since the initiation of the program, Congress and the executive branch have promulgated an enormous body of rules and regulations providing incentives to institutions, physicians, and patients to ensure freedom of choice of the modality of therapy. As a consequence the bureaucracy and paperwork associated with the program have steadily expanded. The projected cost of the ESRD program had been grossly underestimated—the initial legislation predicted first-year costs of approximately $250 million, rising to a maximum of about $1 billion. Yet for fiscal year 1983 the estimated cost of the program was $1.5 billion, and the federal government was predicting the need for a further increase to support the entire program with Medicare funds.

In 1981, because of growing concern over the magnitude of federal expenditure, HHS proposed radical changes in payment procedures. The new regulations, which became effective in June 1983, reduced reimbursements to hospitals, centers, and health care professionals for institution-based treatment of dialysis patients. At the same time, the legislation contained financial incentives to encourage the less expensive process of home dialysis. Thus both patients and physicians lost some degree of freedom of choice.

The message of the 1983 legislation is clear: in times of shrinking resources costs must be cut if the program is to remain viable and equitable. For the first time in U.S. history, the rationing of medical care has become a distinct reality. The dilemma of "tragic choices," now focused on the ESRD program, is likely to affect all therapies requiring expensive technological equipment. Nonetheless, the history of the health profession is replete with examples of difficult issues solved despite seemingly overwhelming difficulties. If allowed to pursue new avenues of knowledge, the medical and scientific communities will continue to make progress in the prevention and treatment of kidney disease and will undoubtedly achieve greater success in the long-term solution of transplantation.

—*Richard B. Freeman, M.D.,*
*and Nathan W. Levin, M.D.*

# FIRST AID HANDBOOK

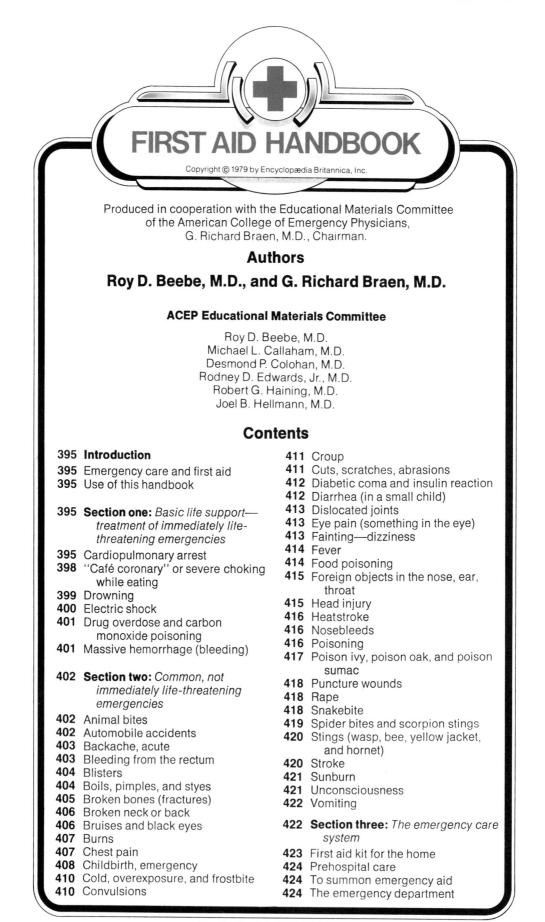

# FIRST AID HANDBOOK

Produced in cooperation with the Educational Materials Committee
of the American College of Emergency Physicians,
G. Richard Braen, M.D., Chairman.

## Authors

## Roy D. Beebe, M.D., and G. Richard Braen, M.D.

### ACEP Educational Materials Committee

Roy D. Beebe, M.D.
Michael L. Callaham, M.D.
Desmond P. Colohan, M.D.
Rodney D. Edwards, Jr., M.D.
Robert G. Haining, M.D.
Joel B. Hellmann, M.D.

## Contents

**Illustrations by John Youssi**

## Emergency Care and First Aid

Properly administered first aid can make the difference between life and death, between temporary and permanent disability, or between rapid recovery and long hospitalization. First aid is most frequently employed to help a family member, a close friend, or an associate, and everyone should be familiar with first aid techniques and should know how best to use the emergency care system.

Public education and public awareness of potential roles in first aid have lagged behind the development of the emergency care system, which includes emergency medicine as a special area of medicine, better equipped and better staffed emergency facilities, paramedical care, communications, and transportation. The concept of first aid as simply the immediate care of the injured person is obsolete. Today a person administering first aid must be able to establish priorities in care and must understand and implement *basic life support* in an attempt to maintain vital functions. Education will reduce the chances of error and the possibly harmful results of well-meant but misdirected efforts.

Accidents are the leading cause of death among persons one to 38 years of age. In addition, over 800,000 Americans die annually of heart attacks, and a great majority of these die before they reach a hospital. The annual cost of medical attention and loss of earning ability amounts to billions of dollars, not to mention the toll in pain, suffering, disability, and personal tragedy. Thus, the delivery of quality emergency care and public education in basic life support and first aid must be accorded a high priority.

## Use of This Handbook

The purpose of this handbook is both to educate and to serve as resource material for commonly encountered emergencies. It is arranged in three sections. The first deals with basic life support and the treatment of immediately life-threatening emergencies. One must understand these concepts *before* an emergency arises, since the necessary techniques must be employed immediately, almost by reflex, if the victim is to be saved.

The second section deals with emergencies that are not immediately life-threatening. It covers the common emergencies in alphabetical order.

The final section covers prevention, preparation, and use of the emergency care system. Prevention is still the least expensive medicine, and several of its most important principles will be discussed. Each home should be prepared for an emergency by having a readily accessible first aid kit, appropriate telephone numbers, etc. This section also discusses what to do and what to expect at the emergency department.

# Section One:
## Basic Life Support—Treatment of Immediately Life-Threatening Emergencies
### Cardiopulmonary Arrest (Heart and Respiratory Failure)

Cardiac arrest is the most life-threatening of all emergencies. If circulation and breathing are not reestablished within minutes, the brain will suffer irreparable damage. Cardiopulmonary resuscitation (CPR), or basic life support, if begun early enough, can be lifesaving. This very simple procedure requires no special equipment and can be begun by *any person* who has taken the time to receive appropriate instruction. Before attempting to utilize this procedure, one would be well advised, in addition to reading the description of basic life support that follows, to undertake formal certification in CPR. Such instruction is readily available through the American Heart Association or the Red Cross.

### What Is Cardiopulmonary Arrest?

There are two absolutely vital systems in the body that must function if life is to continue: the *respiratory* system (lungs and respiratory tree) and the *circulatory* system (heart and blood vessels). The overall function of these two systems is to get oxygen into the blood and then to all parts of the body.

| 0-4 MIN. | CLINICAL DEATH | BRAIN DAMAGE not likely |
| 4-6 MIN. | | BRAIN DAMAGE probable |
| 6-10 MIN. | BIOLOGICAL DEATH | BRAIN DAMAGE probable |
| OVER 10 MIN. | | BRAIN DAMAGE almost certain |

*Phases of brain damage and death following cardiac arrest.*

If either of these systems fails, or "arrests," death occurs very quickly unless the function is restored by CPR.

Respiratory or breathing failure has two basic causes: 1) obstruction of the intake of air or exchange of oxygen into the blood, and 2) impairment of the part of the brain (respiratory center) that controls the rate and depth of breathing. Obstruction can result from several factors, including the presence of large pieces of foreign material (such as food) in the upper airway, swelling and closure of the airway (as in severe acute allergic reactions), and damage to the oxygen-exchanging membranes in the lung (from drowning and smoke inhalation). By far the most common cause of upper airway obstruction that occurs in the patient who has been rendered unconscious is the flaccid tongue that falls backward against the back of the throat and obstructs the airway. The respiratory center may be suppressed by drugs (narcotics, sedatives, alcohol), and carbon monoxide, electric shock, and an interrupted supply of oxygen to the brain, as when the heart has stopped.

If the heart stops pumping, or arrests, the tissues of the body do not receive the blood and oxygen they need. When this happens to the brain, there is an almost immediate loss of consciousness and breathing stops.

### What To Look For

If a cardiopulmonary arrest has occurred, the victim *always:* is unconscious; has no pulse in the neck (carotid pulse); is not breathing. The carotid pulse can be checked by feeling with the thumb and middle finger on either side of the windpipe (trachea). If a pulse is present, it will be felt here.

### What To Consider

Any person who suddenly collapses (becomes unconscious), has no detectable pulse in the neck, and is not breathing has suffered a cardiopulmonary arrest. (A person who collapses while eating and is unable to breathe may well have a large piece of food caught in his windpipe. This is not literally a cardiac arrest,

*Lifting the jaw forward will help to open the airway. This is the preferred technique if there is suspected neck injury.*

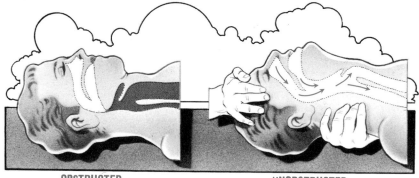

**OBSTRUCTED**              **UNOBSTRUCTED**

*The back of the tongue may obstruct the airway. Lifting the victim's neck and tilting the head backward will open the airway. This method should not be used if there is any suspicion of neck injury.*

but has been called a "café coronary" and will be discussed below.)

### What To Do: The ABC's of CPR

If a person suddenly collapses and loses consciousness, it must be decided immediately whether a cardiopulmonary arrest has occurred. Any delay can result in permanent brain damage or death. Try to awaken the victim. If he cannot be awakened and if there are no palpable pulses (carotid) in the neck, begin the ABC's of cardiopulmonary resuscitation.

**(A) Airway. The first requirement is to assure a clear, unobstructed airway.**
  1. Place the victim on his back.
  2. Hyperextend the neck (lift the victim's neck and tilt his head backward as shown in the illustrations) and then lift the victim's chin forward; this lifts the tongue away from the back of the throat and helps to enlarge the airway. (Hyperextending the neck should not be done if there is any suspicion of neck injury.)

3. Listen for breathing by placing your ear near the victim's mouth, and watch the victim's chest for signs of breathing.
4. If there is no evidence of breathing, open the victim's mouth and remove any obvious foreign materials—false teeth, food, vomitus.

**(B) Breathing (Mouth-to-Mouth Resuscitation).** **If opening and clearing the airway do not produce spontaneous breathing, it will be necessary to breathe for the victim.**

1. With the victim's head in the hyperextended position, pinch his nostrils closed, take a deep breath, and place your mouth tightly over his mouth.
2. Exhale quickly and deeply, four times in rapid succession, each time removing your mouth and letting air escape passively from the victim's mouth.
3. If there is great resistance to your breath, no rise in the victim's chest, and no escape of air from his mouth, the airway may still be obstructed.
   a) Further hyperextend the victim's neck and lift his jaw.
   b) Look again for foreign objects in the mouth and throat.
   c) If none are found, you will have to try a different approach. Roll the victim on his side toward you and deliver four firm slaps between the shoulder blades. With the victim on his back, place your fist just above his navel and forcefully push once. Combined, these may force air out of his lungs and dislodge any foreign body that is trapped deeper in the airway; if so, the material should be removed from the victim's mouth.
4. If the mouth cannot be opened or is severely damaged, mouth-to-nose resuscitation may be used.

**(C) Chest Compression.** **After assuring an open airway and delivering four breaths, check for carotid pulse in the neck, on either side of the windpipe. If there is no pulse, perform chest compression, or external cardiac massage.**

1. Kneel beside the victim.
2. Place the heel of your hand just below the middle of the victim's breastbone and your other hand on top of the first. Do not let your fingers touch the victim's ribs or you may compress the wrong part of the chest.
3. Leaning directly over the patient, give a firm thrust straight downward. Let the weight of your shoulders do the work.
4. The breastbone should be pushed downward about two inches in the adult, and the compressions should be repeated 60 to 80 times each minute. (Note: Use of this procedure may crack some of the victim's ribs; proceed carefully, but do not stop CPR, since the alternative is death.)
5. CHEST COMPRESSION (EXTERNAL CARDIAC MASSAGE) SHOULD ALWAYS BE ACCOMPANIED BY ARTIFICIAL RESPIRATION!
   a) If there are *two rescuers:* one ventilation should be interposed between every five compressions at a compression rate of 60 per minute.
   b) If there is only *one rescuer:* two ventilations should be interposed between every 15 compressions at a compression rate of 80 per minute.

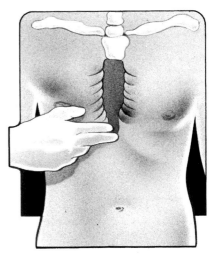

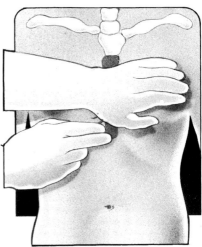

*Find the tip of the sternum. The correct hand position for cardiac compression is two finger breadths above the tip of the sternum.*

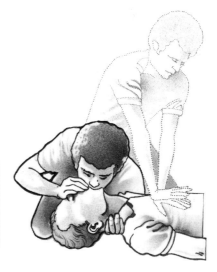

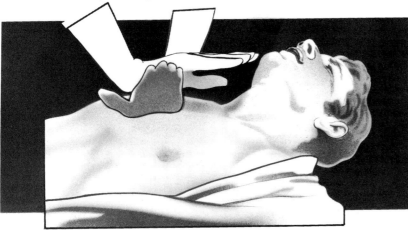

*Place the heel of one hand on the sternum, and the heel of the other hand on the back of the first. Compressions of the chest should be done without placing the fingers on the chest wall.*

*In "one-man" resuscitation, give two breaths between compressions at the rate of two breaths for every fifteen compressions.*

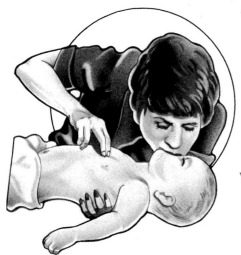

One person can resuscitate an infant by giving quick breaths while compressing the chest with the fingers of one hand.

6. If the victim is a child, the ABC's of CPR are the same except:
   a) Foreign bodies are more common in the airway.
   b) The person administering CPR puts his mouth over both the mouth and the nose of the victim.
   c) If an infant's head is flexed back too much, further obstruction of the airway can occur.
   d) Shallower breaths (puffs) should be used at 25 to 30 per minute.
   e) Exert pressure over the center of the breastbone, as the heart chambers (ventricles) to be compressed are higher in a child's body.
   f) Using only your fingertips, compress the chest ¾ to 1½ inches at a rate of 100 to 125 compressions each minute.

### What Not To Do

1. Do not try to use CPR on any person who is alert and awake, or on any person who is unconscious but is breathing and has pulses.
2. Never compress the upper or lower ends of the breastbone; CPR is effective only when the flexible part of the breastbone that lies directly over the heart is compressed.
3. Do not interrupt CPR for more than 15 seconds, even to transport the victim.
4. Unless you are completely exhausted, do not stop CPR either until the victim is breathing adequately on his own and has a pulse, or until the care of the victim is taken over by more experienced medical personnel.
5. If the victim is revived, do not leave him unattended, because he may arrest again and require further CPR.

## "Café Coronary" or Severe Choking While Eating

Anyone who collapses while eating may well have had a heart attack, but he may be choking on a large piece of food (usually meat). This most frequently occurs in older people, usually those who have poor teeth or false teeth, and frequently it is associated with some alcohol intake.

### What To Look For

1. Before collapsing and losing consciousness, a victim who has been eating, possibly while also talking or laughing, may suddenly stand up and walk from the table, clutch his throat, or exhibit violent motions.
2. *He will not be able to talk.*
3. He may become blue.

### What To Consider

The victim may be having a heart attack, but heart attack victims usually are able to talk prior to collapsing; they usually do not display quick violent motions, but collapse suddenly.

### What To Do

The person will soon become unconscious and die if the obstructed airway is not cleared.

If the person is still standing:
1. Ask the victim to nod if he has food stuck in his throat.
2. Stand behind him and place one clenched fist in the middle, upper abdomen just below the ribs. Place your other hand on top of the first hand.
3. Give a very forceful pull of the clenched fist directly backward and upward under the rib cage (a bear hug from behind).
4. This will, ideally, act like a plunger and force the diaphragm upward, pushing any air left in the lungs out the windpipe and expelling or loosening the trapped object. The procedure may be repeated several times.
5. Once loosened, the foreign object can be pulled out.

If the victim has already collapsed:
1. Place him on his back, open his mouth and look for and remove any visible foreign material.
2. If none is seen, place the heel of your hand on the victim's mid-upper abdomen and give a forceful push.
3. This should dislodge the foreign material into the mouth, from which it can be removed. Repeat the procedure as often as necessary.

Food obstructing the airway in a "café coronary" may be loosened or expelled by an upper abdominal thrust or hug; using the fist of one hand placed in the abdomen just below the rib cage, give a forceful jerk upward.

398

4. If, after the object has been cleared, the victim still is not breathing, is unconscious, and is without a pulse, begin CPR.

### What Not To Do
Do not stop CPR efforts until the victim revives or more experienced personnel arrive.

### What To Expect
If the problem is noted early and foreign material is removed, the chances for the victim's survival are excellent.

## Drowning
Fatal drowning and near drowning are common occurrences. Like cardiac arrest and "café coronary," drowning requires immediate action and basic life support.

### What Is It?
Near or reversible drowning is much more common than fatal drowning. The near drowning victim may have no symptoms or he may need help because of severe respiratory distress and confusion. The drowned victim will be unconscious, will have no pulse, and will not be breathing.

### What To Consider
1. The water may damage the lining of the lungs, resulting in a decreased ability to exchange oxygen from the air into the blood. Following a near

*If there is a chance that a drowning victim has also injured his neck, particular care should be taken to protect the neck from further injury. The victim may be floated onto a board for removal from the water (see following page).*

drowning the victim may suffer a cardiac arrest.
2. Always consider the possibility of an associated injury—for example, a broken neck, which is likely if the victim has dived into the water.

### What To Do

1. Begin mouth-to-mouth resuscitation if the victim is unconscious and is not breathing, even while he is still in the water.
2. Give four quick breaths, followed by one breath every five seconds.
3. Remove the victim from the water without interrupting artificial respiration except for a few seconds (one minute at most). Once he is out of the water begin CPR.
4. If the victim has a suspected spinal injury, he should be placed on his back on a flat board for removal.
5. The victim of near drowning should be taken to the hospital *immediately*. If oxygen is available it should be used, and the victim should be watched closely for the possibility of cardiac arrest.
6. The distressed victim who has difficulty breathing, has blue color, and is semiconscious may require only artificial respiration, but be sure.

### What Not To Do

1. Do not use the manual (arm lift) method of artificial respiration; it doesn't work.
2. Do not try to drain water from the victim's lungs.
3. Do not fail to take near drowning victims to the hospital immediately; such victims may quickly develop respiratory difficulty.
4. Do not stop CPR until more experienced medical personnel take over, or until you are completely exhausted.

## Electric Shock

### What Is It?

Even the relatively low voltages of electrical appliances that are used around the home can cause fatal electrocution. Death results from paralysis of the breathing center in the brain, from paralysis of the heart, or from uncontrolled, extremely rapid twitching (fibrillation) of the heart muscle.

### What To Look For

1. The possibility of electrocution should be considered whenever an unconscious victim is found near an electric wire, a socket, or an appliance.
2. Electrical burns may or may not be apparent.

### What To Consider

1. There are other possible reasons for unconsciousness, such as a head injury, seizure, or drug or alcohol ingestion.
2. Think of possible associated injuries (head injury, neck injury) before moving the victim.

## What To Do

1. Disconnect the victim from the electrical source as quickly and safely as possible. This can be done by disconnecting the plug or appliance or by shutting off the main switch in the fuse box.
2. Alternately, use a dry, nonconductive, nonmetallic stick or pole to move the wire or victim. Do Not Touch The Victim Until He Is Disconnected Or You May Become Another Victim.
3. If the victim remains unconscious and shows no pulse or respiration, begin CPR immediately. Continue until the victim revives or until more experienced medical personnel take over.
4. If there is an associated head, neck, or back injury, let trained medical personnel transport the victim.
5. Upon awakening, victims of electric shock often are confused and agitated, and, for a short time, they may need protection from falls and additional injuries.

## What Not To Do

1. Do Not Touch The Victim Until He Is Disconnected.
2. Do Not Move The Victim If There Is A Head, Neck, Or Back Injury, Except To Remove Him From Danger.

## What To Expect

Even with adequate CPR the victim may need more advanced life support such as electric heart shock. However, he generally can be managed with basic CPR until more advanced life support becomes available.

## Drug Overdose and Carbon Monoxide Poisoning

### What Is It?

Although deaths from drug overdose and carbon monoxide poisoning may be associated with suicide attempts, such deaths do occur in other settings. An unsuspecting heroin addict may inject an exceptionally pure cut of the narcotic. A child may explore the medicine cabinet and ingest some sleeping pills, pain pills, or even antidiarrheal pills. Carbon monoxide poisoning occurs frequently in automobiles with faulty exhaust systems, in industry, and in burning buildings. These poisons all suppress the breathing center in the brain.

### What To Do

1. If the person who has ingested pills is unconscious and without pulse or breathing, begin CPR.
2. If the victim is unconscious and is not breathing, but *has* pulses, perform mouth-to-mouth resuscitation only. Respiratory arrest is common in drug overdoses.
3. When transferring the victim to the hospital, take along any bottles and pills that may be associated with the poisoning.
4. Remove the victim from the carbon monoxide exposure and begin CPR.

### What To Expect

Following a large drug overdose, even with adequate CPR the victim may not begin to breathe on his own or may not wake up for many hours, and he may need extended life support at the hospital in an intensive care unit.

## Massive Hemorrhage (Bleeding)

Following the control of a victim's cardiorespiratory function, the next most urgent priority for the person giving first aid is to control hemorrhaging.

### What Is It?

If major bleeding occurs, a large vessel (artery or vein) may be involved. Lacerated arteries tend to produce a pulsating stream of blood, signifying an injury that needs immediate first aid.

### What To Consider

If the victim is bleeding massively, shock or inadequate blood circulation may develop and the victim may become unconscious or may have a cardiopulmonary arrest.

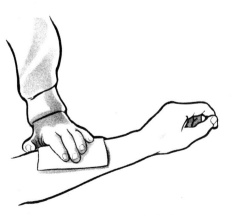

*Direct, firm pressure is frequently the best way to stop bleeding.*

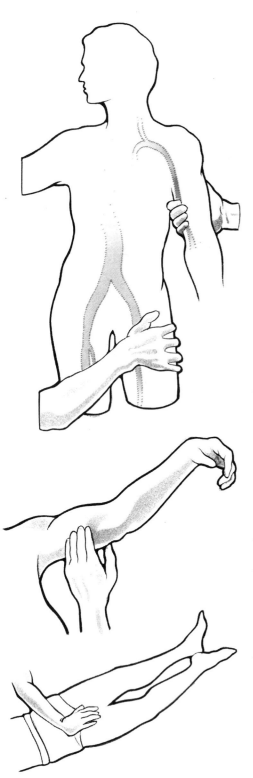

*If bleeding is too extensive to stop with direct pressure, locate the brachial or femoral arteries and apply pressure to stop bleeding distal to those points.*

## What To Do

1. Have the victim lie down to prevent fainting.
2. If he already has fainted, raise his feet higher than his head.
3. If the victim is unconscious, and there are no pulses or breathing, begin CPR.
4. With a clean cloth or sterile dressing, apply *direct pressure* over the wound to halt the bleeding. Most major bleeding (even arterial) will stop in a few minutes if this method is used.
5. Maintain the pressure until better trained medical personnel take over.
6. If severe bleeding of an arm or leg does not stop after several minutes of direct pressure, try to stop the circulation in the artery supplying the blood by pressing firmly against it with your hand or fingers. There are points (shown in the illustrations) on each side of the body where arterial pressure can be used to stop bleeding. (There are also pressure points in the head and neck, but they should *not* be used because of the danger of interrupting the supply of blood to the brain or the intake of air.)
7. When the bleeding stops, tie the dressing firmly in place.

## What Not To Do

1. DO NOT TRY TO USE ARTERIAL PRESSURE POINTS IN THE HEAD OR NECK.
2. THE USE OF TOURNIQUETS SHOULD BE DISCOURAGED because they are often ineffective and do more harm than good.
3. If the injury has been caused by a large foreign object that is protruding from the victim's body, do not remove it, or you may further aggravate the injury.

## What To Expect

1. Most bleeding can be controlled by direct pressure.
2. Lacerations of the scalp bleed profusely but are rarely associated with massive blood loss.
3. Lacerations of the torso may have penetrated into the chest or abdomen and must be evaluated by a physician.

# Section Two:
## Common, Not Immediately Life-Threatening Emergencies

### Animal Bites

All animal bites (dog, cat, and wild animal, as well as human) are dangerous and need medical attention. In addition to the injury itself, there is a chance of infection, including tetanus and rabies.

Bites from wild animals, particularly skunks, foxes, raccoons, and bats, always should be evaluated by a physician.

### What To Do

1. Thoroughly scrub the wound with soap and water to flush out the animal saliva. This should be done for at least ten minutes.
2. Cover the wound with a dry, clean cloth or dressing.
3. Consult a physician immediately for further cleansing, infection control, repair, and possibly for tetanus and rabies prevention.
4. If possible the animal should be caught or identified and reported to the local authorities for observation.

### What Not To Do

Do not mutilate the animal, particularly its head. (If it is a wild animal and is killed, tests can be run by the local authorities to determine if it was rabid.)

### Automobile Accidents

Even with the slower, safer speeds on U.S. highways, automobile accidents still account for the largest number of the nation's accidental deaths, as well as for numerous fatalities elsewhere. Automobile accidents may cause complex or multiple injuries, and priorities must be considered for the care of the injured.

## What To Do

1. Turn the car's engine off if it is still running.
2. Do as much first aid as possible *in* the car.
3. Move the victim only under the following circumstances.
   a) The car is on fire.
   b) Gasoline has spilled and there is a *danger* of fire.
   c) The area is congested, unsafe, and presents the danger of a second accident.
4. Check the patient for breathing and pulses.
5. Control any hemorrhaging.
6. If there is a head and neck injury or fracture of an extremity, wait for medical help before moving the victim, except to insure breathing or to stop significant bleeding.
7. If the victim must be moved to a medical facility, splint any fractures and support his head, neck, and spine on a backboard.
8. As soon as possible the accident should be reported to the appropriate authorities.

## What Not To Do

Do not move unnecessarily a victim who is unconscious or who has a head or neck injury. It may be necessary to move a victim who has no pulse and is not breathing, or who is bleeding severely.

## Backache, Acute

Most frequently, back pain is of recent onset and follows some type of acute exertion or unusual activity, such as lifting a heavy object. The pain usually results from muscular strain and may not become bothersome until hours after the exertion. Back pain that is associated with acute injury or with pain radiating down the legs may indicate a serious problem and demands immediate medical evaluation. In addition backache accompanied by blood in the urine might indicate injury to the kidney or the presence of a kidney stone, while backache with fever or urinary pain might signify the presence of a urinary tract infection.

## What To Do

1. If a backache is nagging, mild, of recent onset, and is associated with recent activity, and if there is no pain radiating into the hip or leg, and if there is no bowel or urinary problem, it may be treated with:
   a) Absolute bed rest for 24–72 hours.
   b) A firm, nonsagging bed—a bed board might be used.
   c) Local heat or warm tub baths.
   d) Aspirin or an aspirin substitute might be helpful.
2. If the back pain is severe, with pain radiating into the hip or legs, or if it is associated with bowel or urinary problems, the victim should see a physician as soon as possible.
3. If the back pain follows an accident, it should be evaluated by a physician.
4. Back pain that does not improve within 48 hours should be evaluated by a physician.

## Bleeding from the Rectum

The acute onset of bright red bleeding from the rectum may be caused by bleeding *hemorrhoidal* veins. The usual history includes constipation and straining to defecate, leading to bright red blood dripping into the toilet bowl and onto the toilet paper, frequently with associated rectal pain. The problem is common among pregnant women.

Rectal bleeding requires medical evaluation. If the stools are black and tarry, it is imperative to get a medical evaluation as soon as possible. The possibility that the bleeding originates higher in the intestinal tract must be considered, since bleeding within the rectum may be a sign of an ulcer, tumor, or inflammation.

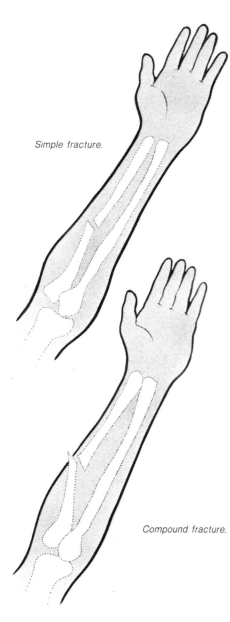

*Simple fracture.*

*Compound fracture.*

## What To Do

1. If the bleeding is due to hemorrhoids:
   a) Warm tub baths three or four times daily may promote healing.
   b) Lubricating ointment such as petrolatum may decrease irritation to the hemorrhoids during bowel movements.
   c) Drinking plenty of fluids will soften the stool, as will bran cereals or stool softeners available from drug stores.
2. If bleeding persists, see a physician.
3. Get a physician's evaluation for black, tarry stools or for bright red rectal bleeding that is not known to be from hemorrhoids.

## Blisters

Blisters are generally caused either by burns or by friction on the skin. Burn-related blisters can result from contact with flame or hot objects or with certain chemicals, and from severe sunburn or scalds. Blisters represent injuries to only a partial thickness of the skin. When a blister breaks, there is a loss of the natural protective insulation of the skin. Open, broken blisters are vulnerable to infection and tend to promote the loss of body fluids by evaporation. If blisters are very large, evaporation may be severe and may result in dehydration.

### What To Do

1. Small blisters should not be opened. They should be protected with dry, soft dressings to prevent rupture.
2. Blisters resulting from contact with chemicals should be immediately and copiously washed with tap water to dilute the offending agent.
3. If a blister ruptures, the area should be washed gently but thoroughly with mild soap and water. The skin that covered the blister should be carefully removed, and the wound should be covered with a dry, sterile dressing.
4. Blisters of large areas of the body should be treated by a physician.

### What To Expect

1. The pain from blisters usually subsides after one to two days.
2. Almost all blisters break and slough after four or five days, and the wound heals in about two weeks.
3. Ruptured blisters often become infected. Note any increased redness, pain, swelling, or heat about the wound, and be particularly aware of any red streaking up the extremity, pus from the wound, or fever.

## Boils, Pimples, and Styes

When sweat glands of the skin become plugged, there may be bacterial growth and an accumulation of infected material (pus) inside the gland. Frequently, the accumulation of pus is absorbed by the body's natural defense processes. Occasionally, the area of infection expands, forming an abscess or boil (called a stye when on the eyelid). These are painful swellings that are red, warm, and can vary from less than a half inch to several inches in size. When these infections have reached this stage, the only way that the body can heal itself is to let the pus out through the skin.

### What To Do

1. Apply warm, moist compresses as often as possible throughout the day (for 15 minutes every four hours).
2. When the boil or stye "points" and then ruptures, wipe the pus away gently with a dry, sterile cloth and cover it with a dressing. Continue to use warm, moist compresses.
3. If there are multiple boils or if the infection seems to be large, contact a physician.

### What Not To Do

Do not attempt to squeeze or puncture boils, pimples, or styes. If hot compresses are used, early boils and styes may resolve. Most will "point" and rupture in two or three days and will then rapidly heal.

404

# Broken Bones (Fractures)

A broken bone should be suspected whenever a person complains of pain with the loss of the normal use of an extremity. Fractures are seldom in and of themselves life-threatening emergencies, and one must make sure that the victim is safe from further harm and has good respiration and pulses before making any attempt to immobilize or move an injured person. Any victim suspected of having a broken neck or broken back should be handled in a special manner. (*See* Broken Neck or Back, below.)

There are two types of fractures that are important to recognize. Most fractures are "simple" or "closed," and the broken bone does not protrude through the skin. There are times, however, when the broken bone does pierce the skin; such breaks are known as "compound" or "open" fractures.

A word about sprains is in order here. Sprains may be managed at home if they are very mild. Aspirin, rest, elevation of the affected extremity, and local ice packs are the best treatment. If a sprain is severe, however, it should be treated like a fracture, and medical attention should be sought.

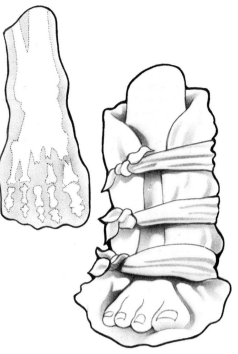

*A simple splint for a broken ankle or foot may be made with a pillow or folded blanket or jacket and secured with roller bandages, tape, and so forth.*

*A broken forearm should be splinted and a sling should be applied. If a splint is not available, the sling itself will reduce the pain.*

*A broken bone in the lower leg should be splinted before transporting the victim.*

## What To Do

1. Make certain that the victim is breathing adequately and has pulses before even considering first aid for the fracture.
2. When there is reason to suspect multiple broken bones, or when the neck, back, pelvis, or thigh might be broken, it would be best to let trained emergency personnel transport the victim to the hospital.
3. If the broken bone protrudes through the skin, cover it with a dry sterile dressing, but do not try to push it back in. If there is excessive bleeding, use direct pressure to stop it. (*See* Massive Hemorrhage, above.)
4. If the victim must be moved, the fracture should be immobilized with splints to prevent further damage and to make the victim more comfortable (the pain of a fracture is caused by the two ends of the broken bone rubbing together). The basic principle of splinting is to immobilize the broken bone by securing the affected limb to some firm object (a piece of wood, broom handle, ski pole, several newspapers or magazines, or even an injured leg to the uninjured leg). Both ends of the splint must extend beyond the area of suspected fracture; the splint may be secured with bandages, belts, sheets, or neckties. Most injuries of the arm, wrist, or hand can be stabilized simply with a sling.

## What Not To Do

1. Do not try to transport any accident victim who has an obviously unstable

*A broken collarbone can be splinted by first applying a sling to the arm, and then applying a wrap around the arm and chest, to reduce movement of the arm.*

405

(floppy) extremity without stabilizing or splinting it first. Even though fractures can be disturbingly displaced, deformed, and very painful in themselves, they rarely represent life-threatening emergencies. If fractures are immobilized adequately, there frequently is a marked reduction in pain.

2. Do not attempt to move a victim with a suspected broken neck or back without trained medical personnel, unless it is absolutely necessary to do so.

## Broken Neck or Back

The possibility of injury to the spine (neck and back) must be considered whenever a person is:

1. Involved in an accident of any type and subsequently complains of back or neck pain, has any degree of paralysis or weakness of an extremity, or has numbness or tingling of an extremity or part of his body.
2. Injured about the face or head in an accident, or is rendered unconscious.

### What To Do

1. Make certain the victim is breathing and has pulses.
2. Unless it is absolutely necessary, do not move the victim, but let trained medical personnel do it.
3. Unless he is unconscious, the victim is safest on his back; avoid attempts to pick up his head or to move his neck.
4. If the victim is unconscious, convulsive, or vomiting, he should be rolled—carefully, and preferably by two people—onto his side, and his head should be supported very carefully on a pillow or coat.
5. If it is absolutely necessary to move the victim, he should be placed on a firm board. This should be done cautiously, with several people supporting the whole spine and the head. The neck or back should not be flexed (chin moved toward the chest or head dropped back).

### What Not To Do

1. Do not allow any accident victim who complains of neck or back pain to sit or stand.
2. Do not give the victim anything to eat or drink.

## Bruises and Black Eyes

Any direct trauma to the soft tissues (skin, muscles, etc.) of the body may injure the blood vessels as well. The damaged blood vessels then leak blood which, when it accumulates under the skin, at first looks black, in a few days looks yellow-brown, and then is reabsorbed. Also, direct trauma may cause swelling or fluid collection under the skin. The area about the eye, because of the loose tissue present, is particularly prone to this swelling, and when blood collects the result is a "black eye."

Bruises are frequent problems and are usually benign in that they represent minimal injury and get better by themselves. However, if the force is adequate, associated injuries can occur, including fractures, ruptured abdominal organs, collapsed lungs, and injuries to the eyeball. If there is an obvious deformity, severe pain, or impaired motion of an extremity, or if there is impaired vision, blindness, severe pain in the eye itself, or double vision, a physician should evaluate the injury.

### What To Do

1. As soon as possible, place a cold compress or an ice bag (a towel soaked in ice water or a towel-covered plastic bag of ice) on the bruise. This will reduce the pain and swelling and should be continued for several hours.
2. Restrict any movement of the injured part, because the less it is used during the first few hours, the less it will swell. Elevation of the bruised part above the level of the heart also decreases swelling.

If the injury is only a bruise, the victim should be able to use the extremity. Most bruises and black eyes will enlarge and worsen in appearance for up to 48 hours after the injury, after which they will gradually shrink. The blue-black color becomes yellow-brown and then disappears in 10–14 days. If multiple bruises that are not associated with trauma appear over the body, a physician should be contacted, because this may indicate a blood clotting disorder.

# Burns

The skin can be burned by flames, hot objects, hot liquids (scalds), excessive sun exposure, chemicals, and contact with electricity. There are three degrees or depths of burns:

First degree—reddened, hot, very painful, no blisters. Heals spontaneously.

Second degree—painful, red, blistered. Usually heals spontaneously.

Third degree—deep burns can be white or black and are always painless. These may require skin grafts.

Many burns that appear to be first degree may later develop blisters and may actually be second degree. Second-degree and third-degree burns frequently become infected and need more attention and care than do first-degree burns. Electrical burns frequently look small but may be much deeper than suspected. Burns in children and older people are more serious.

## What To Do

1. For sunburn see below.
2. For flash burns, scalds, and small burns, towels or sheets soaked in cool water should be applied immediately for comfort.
3. If it is a chemical burn, the area should be washed copiously and continuously (under a running faucet if possible) for 15–30 minutes.
4. The burn should be dressed with sterile, dry, soft dressings.
5. If burns involve large areas of the hands or face, they should be examined by a physician.
6. Electrical burns should be treated by a physician.
7. Burns, like cuts, require tetanus prevention.

## What Not To Do

1. Do not apply ointments, sprays, or greases to large wounds.
2. Never use butter on any burn.
3. Do not break blisters.
4. Do not pull off any clothing that adheres to the burn.

If a small burn becomes encrusted, has pus, or shows red streaking, it may be infected and should be seen by a physician. If large areas of the body have second- or third-degree burns, there may be an excessive water loss from the body with consequent shock. People with extensive burns, especially young children and old people, are very likely to go into shock, and they should be transported to a hospital emergency department as soon as possible. "Shock," in this case, refers to a low level of circulating bodily fluids, not to a psychological state.

# Chest Pain

It is well established now that most heart attack deaths result from *treatable* disturbances of the heartbeat. The overall emphasis must be to get the person with a heart attack into an intensive care unit as soon as possible. To accomplish this there must be:

1. Equipped and staffed emergency departments.
2. Better prehospital care and transportation.
3. Public education on the signs and symptoms of a heart attack.
4. Public education on the techniques of basic life support—CPR. (*See* Cardiopulmonary Arrest, above.)

Denial of the pain and its significance, ascribing it to other causes (heartburn, gas, or pulled muscles), and trying different remedies (antacids or antiflatulence medications) often lead to fatal delays in proper medical treatment. Everyone must be aware of the significance of chest pain and heart attack.

Severe chest pain must always be considered a medical emergency. A correct diagnosis can only be made by a *physician*, using an appropriate medical history, an examination, and sometimes several laboratory tests—an electrocardiogram, chest X-ray, and blood tests.

There are several aspects of chest pain that are important. Heart attack pain is often described as a *dull* ache, tightness, squeezing, or as a heavy feeling that is usually diffusely located over the front of the chest. It is often associated with aching in the shoulders, neck, arms, or jaw. Many people become short of breath, sweaty, nauseated, and may vomit. If any of these symptoms occurs in an adult, he must be transported immediately to the nearest physician or emergency department.

### What To Do

1. Chest pain, especially with the symptoms listed above, demands *immediate* medical attention. An ambulance should be called immediately.
2. While waiting, make the person comfortable and reassure him.
3. Do not give him anything by mouth except what a physician has prescribed.
4. Do not make him lie down if he is more comfortable sitting.
5. Do not leave him unattended. He may suffer a cardiac arrest and may require basic life support (CPR).

There are many other causes of chest pain that may need medical attention. Chest pain associated with fever and cough could be a symptom of pneumonia. Chest pain associated with coughing up blood or associated with thrombophlebitis (pain in the calf or thigh) might represent a blood clot in the lungs. A collapsed lung might cause chest pain and sudden shortness of breath.

There are numerous causes of chest pain, such as severe heartburn, viral pneumonia, inflammation of the cartilages of the ribs, and pulled muscles, that are not life-threatening, but a physician must make these diagnoses.

## Childbirth, Emergency

*Childbirth is a natural and normal phenomenon, and it rarely requires advanced medical training to carry out a safe delivery.* For a variety of reasons (inadequate transportation, very short labor, etc.) many babies are born unexpectedly, outside of the hospital.

*Labor* is the cyclical contraction of the uterus (womb) which helps to open up the end of the uterus (cervix) to allow passage of the baby. These contractions usually are painful and occur with increasing frequency and duration until the delivery. The duration of labor is different for every woman. Frequently labor lasts for 12 or more hours for a first baby, but the time may be reduced to a few hours or less for the woman who has borne several children.

*Delivery* is the passage of the baby through the birth canal and the vagina. The mother will usually experience *rectal* pressure and will know that the child is being born. The reflex action is to push or "bear down." The child's head and hair will be visible at the opening of the vagina. If the woman is "pushing" and the infant is visible, the birth is imminent. If a foot, an arm, the buttocks, or the umbilical cord is first to appear, take the mother to a hospital immediately.

### What To Do

1. Let nature take its course. Do not try to hurry the birth or interfere with it.
2. Wash your hands and keep the surroundings (sheets, etc.) as clean as possible. (Fresh newspaper is often sterile, if sheets or blankets are unavailable.)
3. Support the emerging baby and let it slide out.
4. Once the baby is delivered, support him with both hands, keeping his head lower than the rest of his body to allow the fluid to drain from his mouth.
5. Place the infant on a dry towel or sheet and cover him immediately. Heat loss is a problem for newborn babies.
6. Aluminum foil wrapped around the baby's body will retard heat loss.
7. If the baby is not breathing begin mouth-to-mouth resuscitation, very gently, using puffs of air from your cheeks.
8. It is not necessary to cut the umbilical cord, and one may choose to have this done at the hospital. If medical care will be significantly delayed, however, use the following procedure to cut the cord: using a clean (boiled) ribbon, cord, or string, tie the cord tightly at two points, one that is four inches from the baby and the other at least eight inches from the baby. Cut the cord with clean, boiled scissors between the two ties.
9. Do not wash the white material from the baby (this is protective).
10. Warmly wrap the infant and transport it to the hospital.
11. After the child has been delivered, knead the womb by applying firm pres-

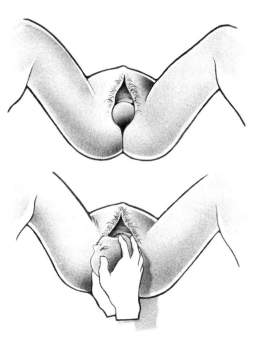

If childbirth is imminent, the top of the baby's head will begin to bulge through the mother's labia. Support the head with one hand on each side (not over the baby's face), and ease the shoulders out. The baby will be quite slippery, so be careful not to drop it.

sure to the lower abdomen.

12. The mother should remain lying down until the bleeding stops and the placenta (afterbirth) has been expelled.

13. When the placenta is expelled, minutes after the birth of the child, it should be retained and taken to the hospital for examination.

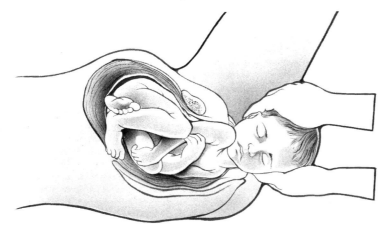

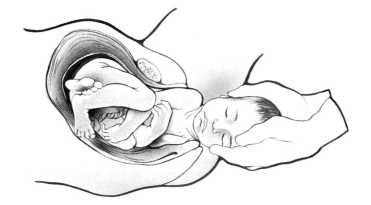

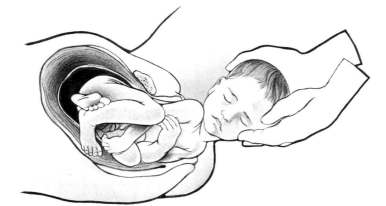

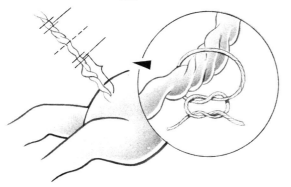

*After delivery, the umbilical cord may be tied using a sterilized cord. Tie the cords at four and eight inches from the baby.*

| CORE TEMPERATURE | SYMPTOMS |
|:---:|:---:|
| 94° | CONFUSION |
| 90° | HEARTBEAT BECOMES IRREGULAR |
| 86° | LOSS OF MUSCLE STRENGTH — DROWSINESS AND UNCONSCIOUSNESS |
| 77° | CARDIAC ARREST AND DEATH |

*As the body's core (central) temperature drops, the victim becomes confused and ultimately may die.*

## Cold, Overexposure, and Frostbite

**Overexposure.** Each year many people die from cold exposure resulting in *hypothermia*. The people who are particularly at risk include elderly persons with poor circulation, individuals who unpreparedly become exposed to low temperatures and high winds, and people who are intoxicated with alcohol. Poor circulation, poor protection from the elements, and alcohol dilate blood vessels in the skin and allow heat loss that lowers the body core (central) temperature. Malfunction of the brain, heart, and lungs may then occur.

### What To Do

1. Remove the person from cold exposure and place him in the warmest place possible.
2. Cover the patient to prevent further loss of body heat.
3. If the victim is awake and able to swallow, give him *warm, nonalcoholic* drinks.
4. Watch for a cardiac arrest and be prepared to carry out CPR.

### What Not To Do

1. Do not give alcoholic beverages.
2. Do not leave the person unattended.
3. Do not risk burning the person by the use of hot water bottles.

**Frostbite.** Frostbite is a common injury in winter weather, particularly when low temperatures are combined with wind. Exposed, small parts of the body are the most susceptible (nose, ears, fingers, toes, and face). Again, the elderly and the intoxicated are the most susceptible. Initially, the involved part begins to tingle and then becomes numb. Frozen tissue usually is dead white in color.

### What To Do

1. Remove the person from the cold as soon as possible.
2. Every effort should be made to protect the frozen part. If there is a chance that the part might refreeze before reaching medical care, it may be more harmful to thaw it and let it refreeze than to await arrival at the treatment area for thawing.
3. Rapid rewarming is essential. Use lukewarm (not hot) water between 100° and 110° F (37– 43° C) or use warmed blankets. Within about 30 minutes, sensation may return to the part, which may become red and swollen. At first the rewarmed part will tingle, but it will begin to be painful and tender to the touch.
4. When the part is warm, keep it *dry* and clean. If blisters appear, use sterile dressings.
5. See a physician as soon as possible.

### What Not To Do

1. Do not give alcoholic beverages.
2. Take care not to burn the person by using water that is too hot.
3. Do not let the part refreeze.
4. Do not rub the injured part; friction may cause further damage.

## Convulsions

Convulsions and epileptic attacks are frightening to watch. The victim's lips may become blue, he may make a crying noise, his eyes may roll back, and his body may be jerked by uncontrollable spasms. Many seizures occur in people with known seizure disorders who have forgotten their medications, in alcohol abusers who have recently stopped drinking, and in children with an acute febrile illness (febrile seizures or seizures associated with fever in children). *Febrile convulsions* are quite common among children aged six months to three years. They result from an abrupt rise in the child's temperature and are generally of short duration (usually ending by the time the victim arrives at the emergency department). The victim usually awakens soon after the seizure.

### What To Do

1. Turn the victim onto his side so that saliva is able to drain out without being inhaled into the victim's lungs.

2. If it can be done safely, place a rolled handkerchief in the victim's mouth between his teeth to prevent him from biting his tongue. Do not force a spoon or other object into the victim's mouth.
3. Most people who have had a seizure need prompt medical attention at the nearest emergency department.
4. The child with febrile convulsions is treated by reducing the fever. Cool towels or sponge baths may help to lower the child's temperature.
5. If the victim has fallen or shows evidence of head trauma, he should be assumed to have a broken neck and should be treated accordingly. (*See* Broken Neck or Back, above.)

### What Not To Do

1. Do not force objects into the mouth of the convulsing person.
2. Do not get bitten by the convulsing person.
3. Do not try to restrain the convulsive movements. Protect the victim from further injury.

Following the seizure (most last less than ten minutes) the person will usually fall asleep or will be confused.

Do not assume that the seizure is "just a seizure" in either a child or an adult, since seizures may be signs of other problems such as head injury, meningitis, or tumor.

## Croup

### What Is It?

In the fall and winter months, when houses are dry and warm, young children (usually younger than three years) may develop a "croupy," barking cough. This condition usually is caused by a viral inflammation of the trachea (windpipe) and of the larger airways, and the infection may cause severe respiratory distress.

### What To Do

1. For mild cases (most cases), lowering the temperature in the room and using a humidifier will quickly help the croupy breathing. A bathroom filled with steam from a running shower may be helpful.
2. Aspirin and liquids may be used to combat low-grade fever.
3. If there is a high fever, difficulty in swallowing or talking, or respiratory distress, the child should be seen by a physician as soon as possible.

Most cases of croup are mild, and they will usually clear up after two or three days if corrective measures are taken.

## Cuts, Scratches, Abrasions

Small cuts, abrasions, and scratches are common occurrences and generally require only thorough cleansing and bandaging for protection. Some cuts are larger and may require stitches for closure to minimize scarring, to reduce the chance of infection, and to restore function. Deeper cuts may involve blood vessels, and they may cause extensive bleeding or may damage muscles, tendons, or nerves.

### What To Do

1. All minor wounds and abrasions should be *thoroughly* washed. There should be no dirt, glass, or foreign material left in the wound. Mild soap and water are all that are necessary.
2. Bleeding can be stopped by direct pressure that is applied over the wound with a sterile, dry dressing, and by elevating the injured part.
3. Most wounds should be covered with a dressing to protect them from further harm and contamination.
4. All bites (human or animal) should be treated by a physician because of the likelihood of infection. (*See* Animal Bites, above.)
5. If there is any question about the need for sutures, the wound should be examined by a physician.
6. If the wound is dirty or extensive, or if the victim's tetanus immunization is not up to date, there may be the need for a booster immunization.

7. Watch carefully for signs of infection (usually they do not appear for several days). The signs are:
    a) a reddened, hot, painful area surrounding the wound,
    b) red streaks radiating from the wound,
    c) swelling around the wound, with fever and chills.
  If an infection appears, see a doctor at once.

## Diabetic Coma and Insulin Reaction

Diabetics have difficulty using the sugar in their blood. *Insulin* lowers the blood sugar level. As would be expected, it may be difficult to adjust the daily insulin requirement to the intake of sugar-containing foods and to the individual's activity level. Because of this, some diabetics occasionally suffer either from *insulin reaction* (which is a blood sugar level that is too low) or from *diabetic coma* (which can be thought of as a blood sugar level that is too high).

Insulin reaction, or acute hypoglycemia, may cause the person to become acutely confused, incoherent, sweaty, or shaky. Eventually, the person may lose consciousness.

### What To Do

1. Determine if the victim is a diabetic.
2. If he is *conscious*, give him some form of sugar (a lump of sugar, candy, sweets, or soft drinks that are not artificially sweetened).
3. Even if recovery is prompt, all victims should be evaluated by a physician.

### What Not To Do

Do not try to give sugar to someone who is unconscious.

Diabetic coma with hyperglycemia (a high blood sugar level) is quite different. The onset is more gradual, taking several hours or longer. The victim may have warm, flushed skin, with a very dry mouth and tongue. He frequently may be drowsy but rarely is unconscious. His breath may smell fruity (like nail polish remover), and he may be dehydrated.

### What To Do

A person in a diabetic coma needs prompt treatment by a physician.

## Diarrhea (in a small child)

Diarrhea may be caused by many factors, ranging from simple nondigestion of eaten foods to such conditions as bacterial or viral infections of the intestinal tract. In a small child, acute prolonged diarrhea may rapidly cause dehydration and death. The younger the child and the more prolonged the diarrhea, the more dangerous is the threat to health. Maintenance of adequate hydration is the main goal of therapy.

The signs of dehydration are: lethargy, dryness of the mouth and armpits, sunken eyes, weight loss, and the absence of urination. A child who continues regularly to wet his diapers generally is not dehydrated.

### What To Do

1. Small children with acute diarrhea should be given water, liquid Jell-O, or pediatric salt solutions. Milk and whole foods should be withheld for the first 24 – 48 hours of the diarrhea. In acute diarrhea, the bowel is unable to digest and absorb some of the sugars in milk, which worsens the diarrhea.
2. If the diarrhea persists for more than 48 hours, a physician should be contacted.
3. If the diarrhea causes signs of dehydration, or if the child stops taking in fluids, a physician should be contacted immediately.
4. Almost all diarrheal states in children are well on the road to recovery within 48 hours. For the bottle-fed child, half-strength formula can be substituted for regular formula for one or two days before resuming full-strength formula. If the diarrhea persists, a physician should be consulted.

### What Not To Do

1. Do not continue milk and whole food during an acute diarrheal state.
2. Do not use adult antidiarrheal medications for children.

412

## Dislocated Joints

It is frequently impossible to tell the difference between dislocated joints and broken bones until X-rays have been taken.

### What To Do

1. Probable dislocations in the hand, arm, shoulder, or jaw usually do not require an ambulance for transportation to the hospital. Victims should, however, be transported safely and comfortably.
2. If there is a dislocation of the hip or knee, ambulance transportation will be needed.
3. Slings or splints may be helpful. (*See* Broken Bones, above.)

### What Not To Do

Do not attempt to move or manipulate the joint, or to set a dislocation yourself; the bone may be broken if these procedures are done improperly.

## Eye Pain (something in the eye)

Even a small speck of dirt in the eye can cause intense pain. The covering of the eye is quite sensitive and, even after the foreign material is removed, there may be a feeling of irritation. Redness and tears are frequently present.

### What To Do

1. Examine the eye by pulling the lower lid down while lifting the upper lid off the eyeball. Most specks will be visible.
2. Gently splash water from a faucet to attempt to remove the foreign material.
3. Gently attempt to wipe the speck off with a moistened corner of a clean cloth, handkerchief, or cotton swab.
4. If the speck does not come off *easily*, or if there is persistent discomfort, a physician should be seen as soon as possible.
5. If irritating liquids are splashed into the eye, irrigate the eye with cool tap water for 30 minutes and then seek medical attention.

## Fainting — Dizziness

Fainting is a sudden but momentary loss of consciousness. There are a variety of causes for it, including fatigue, hunger, sudden emotional upset, poor ventilation, etc. The person who has fainted looks pale and limp but is breathing and has a normal pulse. Simple fainting is not associated with chest pain or seizures, and the unconsciousness does not last for more than one or two minutes.

*If a person faints, place him on his back or side and elevate the legs above the head.*

### What To Do

1. Place the victim on his back or side, with his legs higher than his head.
2. Check his airway, breathing, and pulses.
3. Apply cold compresses to the victim's forehead, and have him inhale aromatic spirits of ammonia.

4. If fainting is associated with chest pains, seizures, or severe headache, or if it lasts more than one or two minutes, the victim should be transported by ambulance to a physician.
5. If a person reports that he feels faint, have him sit with his face in his lap or stretch out on his back until he feels better.

Fainting is a relatively common problem and almost always quickly resolves in one or two minutes. Nevertheless, other causes should be considered—heart attack, stroke, internal bleeding, and insulin reaction.

## Fever

Fever is an elevated oral temperature above 98.6° Fahrenheit or above 37° Celsius. Fever is a manifestation of the body's response to infection (viral or bacterial) or to foreign substances that the body is attempting to reject. People with fever frequently report muscle and bone pains, headaches, chills, and a hot feeling. Viral infections (colds, influenza, and even viral gastroenteritis) almost invariably are associated with low-grade fevers and are the most common causes of such fevers.

In susceptible children younger than three years of age, a *rapidly* rising fever may induce febrile seizures. (*See* Convulsions, above.)

### What To Do—Adults

1. Aspirin and acetaminophen (aspirin substitute) are the two most effective antifever medicines available. If used appropriately, they not only effectively lower the temperature but also will provide some relief for the bone and muscle aches.
2. The person with fever should take a lot of fluids, as higher temperatures increase evaporation of water and thus accelerate dehydration.
3. Bed rest helps.
4. If the fever is very high (102° or more) and persistent (most fevers last less than 24 hours), a physician should be consulted.
5. Fever associated with chest pains, shortness of breath, cough, or with the production of sputum, or with confusion, headache, a stiff neck, abdominal pain, or earache should be evaluated by a physician as soon as possible.

### What To Do—Children

1. Fever of 100° or more in an infant (less than 30 days old) is always an emergency, and the child should be seen immediately by a physician. Every household should have a thermometer for taking children's temperatures.
2. In addition to fluids and bed rest, children with temperatures over 100° may be given aspirin or acetaminophen (aspirin substitute) every four hours in doses of not more than 60 mg for each year of life.
3. The child *should not be* overly dressed but should be dressed lightly (T-shirt and diapers are enough).
4. If a child develops a temperature of 103° or more, and the fever does not respond to aspirin or acetaminophen, the child should be placed in a tub of lukewarm water (not cold) and should be sponged for at least 30 minutes.
5. If the fever still does not respond, a physician should be contacted.
6. Any child with a febrile seizure, lethargy, signs of dehydration, or excess irritability should be seen by a physician.

### What Not To Do

Do not sponge a child with alcohol; it is potentially toxic and is flammable. The sudden cold is often frightening to a child.

## Food Poisoning

Food poisoning is a term applied to the combination of nausea, vomiting, or diarrhea that is attributed to contaminated food. The symptoms may be identical to those of viral gastroenteritis (stomach flu), but with the lack of an associated fever. Some other causes of the same symptoms include emotional stress, viral infections, inorganic or organic poisons, or food intolerance. Food poisoning itself is caused by toxins produced by bacteria growing in the food. The most common organism causing food poisoning is the *Staphylococcus*. In

*Staphylococcus* food poisoning, vomiting and diarrhea generally develop within one to 18 hours following ingestion of the contaminated food.

### What To Do

1. Generally, food poisoning resolves spontaneously within a few hours. Clear liquids should be offered as tolerated.
2. If vomiting or diarrhea is prolonged, dehydration may develop. In some cases, medical attention should be sought.

### What Not To Do

1. Do not take antibiotics. They are useless in this type of poisoning.
2. Do not force the victim of food poisoning to drink fluids if he has any respiratory difficulty. Victims who develop respiratory difficulty should be seen immediately by a physician.

## Foreign Objects in the Nose, Ear, Throat

### Nose

1. If the object cannot be withdrawn or teased out easily, consult a physician at once.
2. Do not allow violent nose-blowing.
3. Do not deeply probe the nose yourself. You may push the object deeper into the nostril or you may cause harm to the nasal tissues.

### Ear

1. If the object cannot be withdrawn easily, consult a physician.
2. The tissues of the ear are very delicate and can easily be damaged. Pushing the object in further may even rupture the eardrum.

### Throat

1. Large objects caught in the throat can cause severe difficulty in breathing (*see* Café Coronary, above). This requires immediate care.
2. Small objects can be swallowed—coins, fishbones, etc. Such smaller objects that get caught or that irritate the throat and that cause no difficulty in swallowing or breathing should be given a chance to pass. Drinks of water followed by eating soft foods—such as bread—may help. If the object remains caught or if irritation persists for more than two or three hours a physician should be notified.
3. Someone who has an irregular object—such as a pull tab from a beverage can, a piece of wire, or glass—caught in his throat needs immediate medical attention.

## Head Injury

Injuries to the head may include lacerations and contusions of the scalp, fractures of the skull, or brain injuries. Whenever someone has suffered a serious injury to his head, one must always consider whether there might have been an associated injury to the neck. If there is a possibility of an associated neck injury, the victim should not be moved except by skilled personnel unless there is a chance that he might inhale secretions or vomitus. In that case, the victim may be very carefully rolled onto his side.

### What To Do

1. Severe, deep lacerations should not be cleansed or irrigated. Instead, sterile dressings should be placed over the wound and should be secured snugly with a roller bandage. Heavy pressure should not be applied to severe lacerations because there may be an associated fracture of the skull and too much pressure may drive a fragment of bone into the brain.
2. Note any loss of consciousness or altered mental status. An examining physician will need this information.
3. Make sure that the victim's pulse and respiration are normal. If the victim might inhale his secretions or stomach contents, very carefully turn him onto his side. Note the size of the victim's pupils. If the victim is unconscious or confused and one of his pupils becomes larger than the other, this is a medical emergency and he should be seen immediately by a physician.

*If there is an open head injury, apply a sterile dressing and secure it with a roller bandage. If there is significant bleeding, apply the roller bandage firmly.*

4. Keep the victim lying down, but do not place a pillow under his head since doing so may cause further damage to the neck if it also has been injured.
5. Make sure that the victim's airway remains open. At times, CPR or artificial respiration (see above) may be needed.

Any head injury accompanied by a loss of consciousness should be evaluated by a physician as soon as possible. Even though the victim may regain consciousness, further brain damage may develop.

## Heatstroke (sunstroke), Heat Exhaustion (heat prostration), and Heat Cramps

Heatstroke is a failure of the body's ability to keep itself cool and maintain a normal temperature. The first symptom is usually confusion, irrational behavior, passing out, or seizures. The patient has a fever, and the pulse is usually rapid and weak. Heatstroke generally affects the elderly, young infants, persons with heart disease, athletes or others doing hard work under hot conditions, and persons who have been drinking alcohol. This is a very serious condition, and immediate treatment is necessary.

### What To Do

1. For heat exhaustion, move the victim to a cool place and elevate his legs. If he can take fluids by mouth, give him small amounts of water.
2. Heat cramps may also be treated with salt solutions taken orally (½ teaspoon of salt in a glass of water).
3. Heatstroke, manifested primarily by a very high temperature, should be treated by placing the patient in a cool place, by removing his clothing, and by applying cool water or ice packs to his body. The victim's extremities should be massaged vigorously to aid circulation, and immediate cooling is crucial.
4. If the victim has suffered from heatstroke, heat exhaustion, or prolonged heat cramps, medical attention should be sought.

### What Not To Do

1. Avoid giving water without added salt, because this may further deplete the body's salt concentration.
2. Avoid the immediate reexposure of the victim to the heat, because he may be very sensitive to high temperatures for a time.

## Nosebleeds

Nosebleeds are generally caused by trauma to the nose, which can result from nose-picking, from colds when there is hard nose-blowing, or from drying of the nasal mucosa. Most commonly, nosebleeds originate from the area of the nasal septum. Nosebleeds may also be associated with hypertension, bleeding disorders, or nasal tumors.

### What To Do

1. To prevent the inhalation or swallowing of blood, have the person sit up and lean forward.
2. Gently squeeze the nose closed for 10 to 15 minutes by the clock.
3. If the bleeding stops have the victim rest quietly for a few hours. During this time there should be no stooping, lifting, or vigorous nose blowing. Seek medical attention if the nosebleed is profuse or prolonged. The blood loss from a nosebleed can be considerable, and some people even go into hemorrhagic shock following a nosebleed.

### What Not To Do

Do not allow the victim to resume normal activities for a few hours after the nosebleed has subsided.

## Poisoning

Poisoning is a common occurrence, particularly in households in which there are children. For the most part poisoning is accidental, but occasionally someone will ingest a poison during a suicide attempt. Households should be equipped to handle poisoning, and syrup of ipecac should be available.

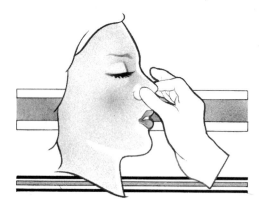

*A nosebleed frequently can be stopped by firmly pinching the nose closed.*

Generally there are five kinds of poisons that might be ingested: a) pesticides, b) drugs, c) strong alkalies and acids, d) petroleum products, e) poisonous plants.

Two of these, petroleum products and strong alkalies and acids, are worthy of special note, because vomiting should *never* be induced if they have been ingested. Examples of petroleum products include turpentine, paint thinner, furniture polish, gasoline, and liquid shoe polish. Examples of strong alkalies include drain cleaner, lye, and some bleaches. In the case of strong alkalies or other strong substances that may cause chemical burns, the mouth and esophagus are burned when the poison is swallowed. If the person is made to vomit, he will be burned a second time as the chemical is passed up the esophagus and out the mouth again. In the case of petroleum products,. vomiting may lead to inhalation of the poison, with a resulting chemical pneumonia.

The best way to handle poisons is to take precautions against their ingestion, particularly when small children are present. Medicines, detergents, and cleaning products should all be placed on a high shelf, not under the sink where children can easily find them. In addition, poisons should be kept in appropriate containers. It is dangerous to keep gasoline or furniture polish in a soft drink bottle because a child may drink from that bottle, thinking that it contains a soft drink.

### What To Do

1. Initially, give ½ glass of water or milk to anyone who has ingested a poison, unless the victim is *unconscious* or is having convulsions.
2. Decide whether or not to induce vomiting. Look in the victim's mouth for burns that might indicate the ingestion of an acid or alkali. Also, smell the victim's breath to see if it smells like a petroleum product. If either sign is present, do not induce vomiting. If the poisoning has been caused by pesticides, drugs, or poisonous plants, vomiting may be induced by putting one's fingers into the back of the victim's throat to induce gagging and vomiting, or by using syrup of ipecac. Children should be given approximately one teaspoon to one tablespoon of syrup of ipecac, and adults should be given two tablespoons. Vomiting should occur within 20 to 30 minutes.
3. Contact your local physician or emergency department for further instructions. A Poison Control Center may recommend specific antidotes. Antidotes that are listed on the packaging of poisonous products may not be correct or the procedure for their administration may be faulty. It may be better to contact a Poison Control Center for specific instructions.
4. If respiratory difficulty or shock develop, they should be treated appropriately.

### What Not To Do

1. Do not allow poisons to be within the reach of children.
2. Do not induce vomiting if alkalies, acids, or petroleum products have been ingested.
3. If the victim is unconscious or is having convulsions, do not give him water, and do not induce vomiting.
4. Do not store poisonous materials in food bottles or jars.

## Poison Ivy, Poison Oak, and Poison Sumac

Contact with poisonous plants such as poison ivy, oak, or sumac frequently produces local itching and redness in allergic individuals. In some people the rash that develops is characterized by vesicles (small blisters). More severe reactions include headache, fever, and malaise.

### What To Do

1. Contaminated clothing should be removed and all exposed areas of the body should be washed with soap and water.
2. Once the rash has developed, soothing lotions may be applied to the skin. Many of these lotions are available without prescription at a pharmacy. Cool, moist compresses also are valuable for relieving itching.
3. If blisters appear and begin to ooze, they may be treated with wet dressings —sterile gauze pads saturated with a solution of baking soda and water

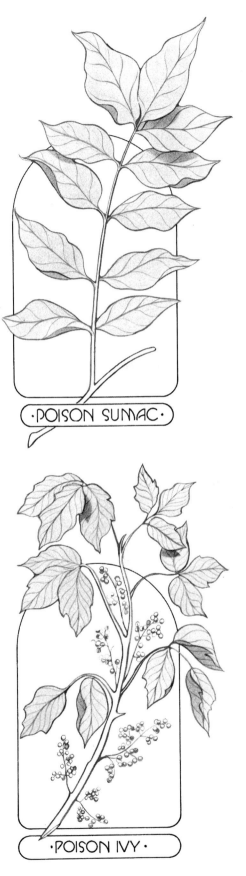

·POISON SUMAC·

·POISON IVY·

417

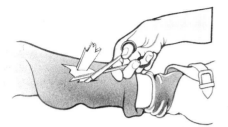

Objects stuck deep through the skin (or into the eye) should not be removed. If the object is too large to be secured in place by simply using a dressing, a paper cup taped over it may reduce further injury.

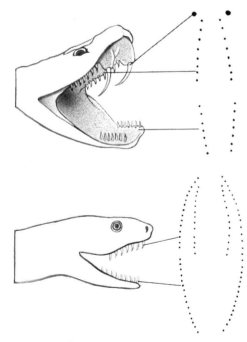

Pit vipers generally produce conspicuous fang marks. Nonpoisonous snakes and coral snakes will not leave fang marks.

(one tablespoon of baking soda to one pint of water).

4. If a severe reaction occurs, if there is a fever, or if a large area of the body is involved, seek medical advice.

## Puncture Wounds

Puncture wounds are created by penetrating objects such as nails, knives, sticks, and needles. Puncture wounds do not bleed as readily as lacerations and thus there is less natural cleansing of the wound and a higher rate of infection.

### What To Do

1. The site of the puncture wound should be cleansed with soap and water, after which a clean dressing should be applied.
2. For severe puncture wounds, seek medical attention to guard against tetanus infection and for consideration of antibiotic therapy.

### What Not To Do

Do not remove any foreign object that is protruding from the wound. As moving the object may cause further damage, the physician should attend to such wounds.

## Rape

Rape is the unlawful carnal knowledge of a woman by a man, forcibly and against the woman's will. In the United States, rape is common, and friends or relatives are frequently called on to render assistance to rape victims.

### What To Do

1. The rape victim should be protected from further harm and should be assured that she is safe.
2. If she is injured and is bleeding, direct pressure should be applied to the bleeding points. Never, however, apply hard pressure to the rectal or vaginal areas.
3. If she has a broken extremity, it should be treated appropriately.
4. Always remember that a rape victim has an absolute right to refuse medical, legal, or psychological help; however, she should be encouraged to see a physician as soon as possible.

### What Not To Do

1. Even though the victim may feel unclean, she should be advised not to bathe, douche, or urinate, because doing so may destroy some evidence needed by the medical examiner.
2. The scene of the crime should not be touched, because this may invalidate existing evidence that would lead to the conviction of the attacker.
3. The victim should be advised not to change her clothing until she has been examined medically, because some evidence may be lost.

The trauma of the rape victim does not end with the rape itself. She may develop psychological problems or have marital difficulties for days or even years following the incident. In many communities, counseling services have been established specifically for the benefit of these victims.

## Snakebite

In the United States there are two groups of poisonous snakes: the coral snakes and the pit vipers. The coral snake is found from North Carolina to Florida, through Louisiana to central Texas. The Sonoran coral snake is found in Arizona and southwestern New Mexico. The pit vipers include the copperhead, water moccasin, and rattlesnake. Rattlesnakes and other pit vipers account for the greatest number of the venomous snakebites in the United States, while coral snakes account for a very small number. Coral snakes produce relatively inconspicuous fang marks. Pit vipers produce a more conspicuous injury, with fang marks surrounded by swelling and blood-filled blisters.

The effect of a poisonous snake's bite depends on the size of the victim, the location of the bite, the amount of venom injected, the speed of absorption of the venom into the victim's circulation, and the amount of time between the bite and the application of specific antivenom therapy.

418

copperhead

water moccasin

coral snake

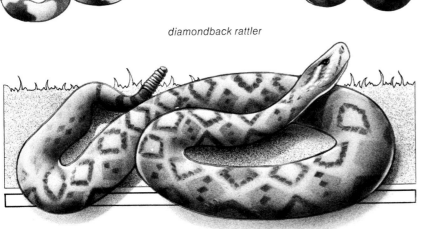
diamondback rattler

## What To Do

1. First aid begins with reassuring and calming the victim.
2. The victim should be transferred to a physician as soon as possible. Even if the bite was inflicted by a nonpoisonous snake, a physician may want to give tetanus prophylaxis and antibiotic therapy.
3. Immobilization of the bitten extremity will help retard absorption of the toxin.
4. A tourniquet applied above the bite may retard systemic absorption of the venom and may be useful when there is a delay in reaching an emergency department. The tourniquet should not be so tight as to cause disappearance of peripheral pulses in the foot or the hand.

## What Not To Do

1. Incisions over the fang marks are not recommended.
2. Do not give the victim alcohol in any form because it may increase absorption from the skin.

## Spider Bites and Scorpion Stings

The reaction to the toxins of spiders and scorpions varies from mild, with resulting local pain, redness, and swelling, to severe, with convulsion, nausea, vomiting, muscular pain, and even shock. In the United States the two spiders that are generally the most harmful are the black widow spider (*Latrodectus mactans*) and the brown recluse (*Loxosceles reclusa*).

## What To Do

1. Wash the wound with soap and water and apply a clean dressing.
2. A medication like aspirin may help relieve the pain.
3. For spider bites, scorpion bites, and any insect bite associated with intense pain, severe swelling, and discoloration, a physician's evaluation should be sought.
4. If the spider or scorpion has been killed, don't discard it. A physician may be able to further identify the species if he sees it.

brown recluse

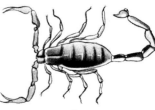
scorpion

black widow

*The brown recluse spider is about one inch in length overall, including the legs; it has a dark, violin-shaped marking on its lighter back. Scorpions range from one-half to seven inches in length. The body of the female black widow spider is about one inch long, and there usually is a reddish, hourglass-shaped marking on the underside of the abdomen.*

419

## Stings (Wasp, Bee, Yellow Jacket, and Hornet)

The stings from these insects are relatively common, and they rarely cause death except in highly sensitive individuals. The sting may be painful, but the symptoms are usually mild and are of short duration.

Some people are highly sensitive to insect stings and may develop an allergic reaction, possibly with anaphylaxis (a massive allergic reaction) and subsequent death.

### What To Do

1. Most people have no problem from an insect sting, and relief from the local discomfort can be obtained from various home remedies—local cool compresses or a solution of cool water and baking soda.
2. Aspirin or an aspirin substitute sometimes helps.
3. If the person is highly sensitive to insect bites and has developed allergic reactions in the past, seek *immediate* medical attention. If medical attention will be delayed more than a few minutes, attempt to remove and discard the stinger and attached venom sac (in the case of the honeybee) by carefully scooping it out with a fingernail. Ice should be applied to the area of the bite.

*wasp*   *yellow jacket*

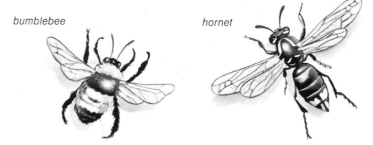

*honeybee*   *bumblebee*   *hornet*

## Stroke

Strokes are often referred to as cerebral vascular accidents. "Cerebral vascular" refers to the blood vessels in the brain, which are affected either by a clot or by rupture with subsequent hemorrhage. Major strokes may be accompanied by facial weakness, an inability to talk, the slurring of speech, loss of bladder and bowel control, unconsciousness, paralysis or weakness (particularly on one side of the body), or difficulty in breathing and swallowing. Sometimes strokes are associated with vomiting, convulsions, or headaches.

The most important things to watch are breathing and vomiting. Recovery from strokes is quite variable.

### What To Do

1. If the victim is having difficulty breathing, his airway should be opened. (*See* Cardiopulmonary Arrest, above.)
2. The victim should be positioned on his side so that his secretions will drain out of his mouth and not into his airway.

420

3. If vomiting occurs, the victim should be kept on his side and his mouth should be wiped clean of vomitus.
4. Get prompt medical attention for all stroke victims.

### What Not To Do

1. Fluids should never be administered by mouth unless the victim is fully conscious.
2. The victim should not be left alone for any length of time because of the chance of his vomiting and then inhaling the vomitus.

## Sunburn

Ordinary sunburn is caused by overexposure to the sun's ultraviolet rays. The initial symptoms may begin as early as one hour after exposure and are manifested in painful redness and swelling of the area, and, in more severe cases, in the formation of blisters over the sun-exposed areas. When very large areas of skin are involved, fever, gastrointestinal upset, and weakness may occur.

Fair-skinned people and people taking certain medications should avoid exposure to the sun. Even dark-skinned people should initially avoid being in the bright midday sun for longer than 30 minutes. For added protection there are many good sun-screening ointments, creams, and lotions available. The most common and most effective ingredient in these is para-aminobenzoic acid (PABA), which screens out the ultraviolet rays that cause sunburn.

### What To Do

1. Mild sunburn can be treated at home with cool compresses.
2. If there is an accompanying fever, aspirin may help.
3. Commercially available lotions often have a soothing effect on the skin.
4. For more severe cases, it may be necessary to consult a physician.

### What Not To Do

1. Avoid further exposure to the sun until the acute reactions have subsided.
2. Avoid greasy preparations.

Sunburns usually resolve themselves, but occasionally the blisters become infected. If much of the skin has peeled off, the underlying skin will be quite sensitive to reexposure to the sun for several days or weeks.

## Unconsciousness

Unconsciousness is a sleeplike state from which one may or may not be arousable. A person in "stupor" may be aroused with stimulation and only then with difficulty, while a person in coma cannot be aroused even by the most powerful stimuli.

The most common causes of unconsciousness are fainting, intoxication with alcohol, head trauma, strokes, poisoning or drug overdoses, seizures, diabetic acidosis, hypoglycemia, various types of shock, and hypoxia. Elderly, poorly nourished, or otherwise debilitated people are more prone to unconsciousness regardless of the nature of their illness.

The cause of unconsciousness is often difficult for even a physician to diagnose, and laymen should be careful not to ascribe a patient's unconscious state to something like intoxication. Alcoholics are of course not immune to other more serious causes of unconsciousness.

### What To Do

1. Any unconscious person should be checked for an open airway and for palpable carotid pulses (*see* Cardiopulmonary Arrest, above).
2. If the person is not arousable but is breathing well and has good carotid pulses, he should be placed on his side so that he will not inhale any stomach contents if he vomits.
3. Anyone who is comatose should be evaluated by a physician. If drug ingestion or poison is suspected, the containers from the suspected toxin should be brought to the emergency department. Observations made about the person before his lapse into unconsciousness also will be of great help to the examining physician.

### What Not To Do

1. Unconscious persons should not be left alone for any length of time, except for summoning help.
2. Fluids should never be administered by mouth and vomiting should never be induced.
3. Do not unnecessarily move an unconscious person unless you are certain he does not have a neck injury.

If unconsciousness resulted from a fainting attack, the victim may awaken within a few minutes. If unconsciousness recurs or if the person remains unconscious for several minutes, an evaluation by a physician should be sought.

## Vomiting

Vomiting is the action by which the stomach rids itself of its contents. Vomiting can be caused by disturbances in either the abdomen or the head.

Causes of vomiting arising in the abdomen include: irritation or mechanical obstruction at any level of the intestinal tract, or irritation of abdominal organs like the gallbladder.

Causes of vomiting that originates in the vomiting centers in the head include: emetics (drugs), various toxins (poisons), increased pressure inside the head, decreased oxygen content of the blood in the head, disturbances of the semicircular canals of the ear (as occurs with seasickness), and, occasionally, psychological factors.

Severe or prolonged vomiting may lead to dehydration. When vomiting is associated with respiratory difficulty it may indicate that some of the vomitus was inhaled, and this is a medical emergency.

Simple acute vomiting may be caused by the effects of alcohol on the stomach lining, by dietary indiscretions, by viral gastroenteritis, or by the morning sickness of pregnancy. Severe or prolonged vomiting may reflect more severe gastrointestinal or systemic disease.

### What To Do

1. Care should be taken to turn bedridden people onto their sides, so that they do not inhale any vomited stomach contents.
2. If a comatose person vomits, he should be turned onto his side and the vomitus should be cleared from his mouth.
3. After the initial episode of vomiting, solid food should be withheld temporarily and clear liquids should be given. (A clear liquid is one through which it is possible to read a newspaper.)
4. If the person goes twelve hours without vomiting, solid foods may be resumed, beginning with dry foods such as crackers.
5. If vomiting is prolonged or associated with severe abdominal pain, seek medical attention.

### What Not To Do

1. Milk or formula should not be given to infants until the vomiting has subsided.
2. Solid foods should not be given to adults and children until the vomiting has subsided.

# Section Three:

## The Emergency Care System

To be most effective, emergency care must begin as soon as possible at the scene of an accident. In the home—one of the most common accident sites—there are two important steps that should be taken *before* an accident occurs: prevention and preparation.

The cheapest and most effective medicine is prevention. Every attempt to make the home as safe as possible is mandatory. Accidents in the home may be prevented by keeping stairways well lit and entryways unobstructed, by the careful placement of loose rugs, by proper care and maintenance of electrical appliances and cords, and by the proper shielding and use of power tools.

# First Aid Kit for the Home

Every home should have a separate box (not just the medicine cabinet)
containing at least the following supplies

### First Aid Tools
Thermometer, oral
Thermometer, rectal
Flashlight
Hot water bag
Pair of scissors
Pair of tweezers
Packet of needles
Safety matches
Ice bag

### First Aid Material
Aspirin, adult
Aspirin, children's, or aspirin substitute
Bottle of ipecac syrup (2 to 3 oz)
Bottle of aromatic spirits of ammonia
Antiseptic cream for burns
Sunscreen medication (para-aminobenzoic acid)

### First Aid Dressings
Sterile 4″ × 4″ dressings
Gauze (2″ wide) for bandaging
Box of assorted adhesive dressings
1″ adhesive tape

### Appropriate List of Telephone Numbers
911 (the universal emergency call number in some communities)
Local hospital emergency department
Ambulance or rescue squad
Police department
Family physician
Poison Control Center (if one is available in the area)
Fire department

Particular care should be taken in the home to prevent poisoning. All prescription and over-the-counter drugs (including aspirin, cold remedies, and vitamins) should be stored in "child-proof" containers. In addition, old medications should be flushed down the toilet. The passage of time may cause drugs either to lose their potency or, through evaporation, to increase in potency. All medicine should be stored out of the sight and reach of children.

All cleaning solutions, drain and oven cleaners, solvents, and petroleum products (kerosene, gasoline, turpentine, charcoal lighter), insect spray, roach tablets and roach powder should be stored on high or locked shelves where children can't get at them. Never put any of these substances in a beverage or food container. Beverage bottles look particularly inviting to toddlers.

## Prehospital Care

Whenever there is *anything but* the most simple injury or medical problem, it is best to call an experienced ambulance or rescue squad. It is always better to err on the side of calling EMS people rather than procrastinating at the victim's expense. Many services are upgrading their capabilities with better equipment and training. Most ambulance drivers and attendants are at least basic Emergency Medical Technicians (EMT's). The EMT's have received 81 hours of intensive first aid training, have passed a minimal proficiency test, and are certified by a state health agency. Many communities also have advanced EMT's (paramedics) available for emergency care. These individuals are basic EMT's but have had an additional 500 to 1,000 hours of intensive training in advanced life support (defibrillation, use of intravenous medications, advanced airway management, etc.). They generally function through radiocommunications with a hospital-based physician.

## To Summon Emergency Aid

Have the telephone numbers of an ambulance service or, if none is available, the local police or fire department readily accessible. When you call, be as calm as possible. *Do not* hang up until all of the following information has been given: a) your name; b) your location (how to get there); c) your telephone number; d) the type of emergency (number of people involved, etc.).

## The Emergency Department

The emergency department of the local hospital is the best facility to evaluate and treat true emergencies. Because many people may be seeking emergency care at the same time for different degrees of emergencies, the emergency department might seem to be a very confusing place. Most emergency departments, however, are organized to quickly establish priorities for care, and to provide appropriate treatment for each individual as soon as possible within the limits of those priorities.

The system starts with the nurse, who usually sees the victim first and, by means of a few basic medical questions or tests (temperature, blood pressure, pulse, etc.), attempts to determine the nature of the victim's problem. This nurse is trained to recognize life-threatening problems and to assure that they are seen and evaluated first. In an emergency department patients are not seen on a first-come, first-served basis. For example, a person with a sprained ankle would have to wait to be seen until a man with severe chest pains had been treated.

Better hospital emergency departments have physicians present around the clock to see and treat emergencies. These physicians are specialists in the treatment of emergency problems. Their availability in the hospital and their special training make them the physicians best suited to initially evaluate and stabilize any true emergency. The emergency physician's practice frequently is confined to the emergency department, and he should not be assumed to be in competition with one's regular physician.

# ndex

This is a three-year cumulative index. Index entries to *World of Medicine* articles in this and previous editions of the *Medical and Health Annual* are set in boldface type, *e.g.,* **Eye Diseases and Visual Disorders.** Entries to other subjects are set in lightface type, *e.g.,* hemodialysis. Additional information on any of these subjects is identified with a subheading and indented under the entry heading. The numbers following headings and subheadings indicate the year (boldface) of the edition and the page number (lightface) on which the information appears.

### Eye Diseases and Visual Disorders
**84**–232; **82**–261
acute mountain sickness complications **82**–261
cancer **81**–226
diabetes complications **83**–251
first aid **83**–413; **82**–413; **81**–413
headache symptoms and effects **81**–27
infectious diseases and interferon's use **81**–259
microsurgery and treatment use **82**–312

All entry headings, whether consisting of a single word or more, are treated for the purpose of alphabetization as single complete headings and are alphabetized letter by letter up to the punctuation. The abbreviation "il." indicates an illustration.

# f

N

ow there's a way to identify all your fine books with flair and style. As part of our continuing service to you, Britannica Home Library Service, Inc. is proud to be able to offer you the fine quality item shown on the next page.

B

ooklovers will love the heavy-duty personalized **Ex Libris** embosser. Now you can personalize all your fine books with the mark of distinction, just the way all the fine libraries of the world do.

T

o order this item, please type or print your name, address and zip code on a plain sheet of paper. (Note special instructions for ordering the embosser). Please send a check or money order only (your money will be refunded in full if you are not delighted) for the full amount of purchase, including postage and handling, to:

---

**Britannica Home Library Service, Inc.**
**Attn: Yearbook Department**
**Post Office Box 6137**
**Chicago, Illinois 60680**

**17 68**

---

(Please make remittance payable to: Britannica Home Library Service, Inc.)

# IN THE BRITANNICA TRADITION OF QUALITY...

## EX LIBRIS
## PERSONAL EMBOSSER

A mark of distinction for your fine books. A book embosser just like the ones used in libraries. The 1½" seal imprints "Library of _____" (with the name of your choice) and up to three centered initials. Please type or print clearly BOTH full name (up to 26 letters including spaces between names) and up to three initials.
Please allow six weeks for delivery.

Just **$20.00**

plus $2.00 shipping and handling

This offer available only in the United States.
Illinois residents please add sales tax

## Britannica Home Library Service, Inc.